Portrait of America

Portrait of America

Volume II   from Reconstruction to the Present

Second Edition

Stephen B. Oates
University of Massachusetts, Amherst

Houghton Mifflin Company
Boston
Dallas
Geneva, Illinois
Hopewell, New Jersey
Palo Alto
London

For Greg and Stephanie With my Love

*Cover: Needlepoint by Lois K. Williams
Courtesy of Hope Hanley*

Selection 36 is reprinted by permission of the author, Gerda Lerner. It originally appeared under the title "The Feminists: A Second Look."

Copyright © 1978, 1973 by Houghton Mifflin Company. The selections reprinted in this book are used by permission of and special arrangement with the proprietors of their respective copyrights. All rights reserved. No part of this work may be reproduced or transmitted in any form or by any means, electronic or mechanical, including photocopying or recording, or by any information storage or retrieval system, without permission in writing from the publisher.

Printed in the U.S.A.
Library of Congress Catalog Card Number: 77-77432
ISBN: 0-395-25373-X

Contents

Preface to the Second Edition ... ix

I Reunion and Reaction

1. Why They Impeached Andrew Johnson
   David Donald ... 2

2. Radical Rule in the South
   Kenneth M. Stampp ... 11

3. Mississippi: The Past That Would Not Die
   Walter Lord ... 27

II Thunder in the West

4. Bury My Heart at Wounded Knee
   D. Alexander Brown ... 42

5. Day of the Cattleman
   Ray Allen Billington ... 50

6. The Wild, Wild West
   Peter Lyon ... 63

III Gilded Age Kaleidoscope

7. The New Industrial Order
   Bernard A. Weisberger ... 84

8. The Road to Populism
   Eric Goldman ... 97

9. New Worlds, New Visions
   Oscar Handlin ... 112

10. "Remember the *Maine!* To Hell with Spain!"
    William E. Leuchtenburg ... 124

IV
For a
Better World

11 A Cross of Gold
John A. Garraty — 134

12 Here Come the Wobblies!
Bernard A. Weisberger — 148

13 Theodore Roosevelt: The Conservative as Progressive
Richard Hofstadter — 162

14 The End of A Dream
E. David Cronon — 182

V
This Side of
Paradise

15 The Return to Normalcy
Arthur M. Schlesinger, Jr. — 200

16 Revolution in Manners and Morals
Frederick Lewis Allen — 220

17 Henry Ford: Symbol of an Age
Roderick Nash — 236

18 The Klan Rides
John Higham — 243

VI
"You Have
Nothing to Fear
but Fear Itself"

19 The Contagion of Fear
Arthur M. Schlesinger, Jr. — 254

20 Franklin D. Roosevelt: The Patrician as Opportunist
Richard Hofstadter — 268

21 The Grapes of Wrath
John Steinbeck — 286

22 Hard Times: Personal Recollections of the Depression
Studs Terkel — 301

VII
The World in
Flames

23 Day of Infamy
James McGregor Burns — 318

24 This Mighty Endeavor
Charles B. MacDonald — 336

VIII Balance of Terror

25 The Falling Sun
Fletcher Knebel and Charles W. Bailey II — 352

26 Truman's Cold War Crusade
James Paul Warburg — 368

27 Eisenhower, Dulles, and the Irreconcilable Conflict
Stephen E. Ambrose — 377

28 Years of Shock
Eric Goldman — 393

IX The Fire Next Time

29 The Mobilization of Black Strength — 412

30 Uncle Tom's Children
Richard Wright — 422

31 Letter from Birmingham Jail
Martin Luther King, Jr. — 430

X The Ordeal of Modern America

32 "They've Killed the President!"
Robert Sam Anson — 444

33 Vietnam—Time of Illusion
Jonathan Schell — 460

34 Presidential Sin from Jefferson to Nixon
Fawn M. Brodie — 480

35 The Counter-Culture
William L. O'Neill — 494

36 The New Feminists
Gerda Lerner — 524

Preface to the Second Edition

The second edition of this anthology, like the first, is dedicated to the proposition that historical writing can be literature. In compiling selections for it, I chose writings distinguished as much for their literary merit—for the human drama they chronicle, the enigmas they capture, and the truths they imply—as for their analytical explanations. I deliberately sought biographical portraits, dramatic narratives, and artful essays by some of our best literary craftsmen. These writings portray the American past as a story of real people who actually lived, who struggled, enjoyed triumphs, and suffered failures and heartbreaks just like people in our own time. Thus *Portrait of America* is an attempt to capture the living past. It is, in the words of Aldous Huxley, an effort "to render, in literary terms, the quality of immediate experience."

The anthology is intended for use largely in college survey courses. It could be utilized as a supplement to a textbook or to a list of paperback readings. Or, for instructors who provide their classes with detailed, comprehensive lectures and who find a textbook redundant and a paperback list too expensive, *Portrait of America* could serve as the basic reading. There is much in the way of thought-provoking material gathered here: essays replete with ideas, narratives and biographies that capture real-life situations, and personal accounts of such subjects as life during the Great Depression. Furthermore, as I chose secondary materials, I tried not to compromise new historical interpretations just to get a provocative selection. For example, I chose the works of David Donald and Kenneth M. Stampp because their accounts of Reconstruction are both imaginatively presented *and* modern in their approach.

Generally, this is the guideline I followed in compiling and revising the entire volume, although my first criterion was always that selections must be artfully composed and suffused with human interest and human insight. My feeling is that, since college survey audiences are not professional ones, they might enjoy reading history if it were presented in exciting and palatable form. I hope *Portrait of America* presents history that way. The introductions to the selections are an effort to tie them all together so that they might stand more or less as connected episodes.

As I set about revising the anthology, I made substantial changes in the period since World War II, updating and improving the selections on the Cold War and Vietnam, on the recent presidents, and on the blacks and the feminist movement. In all, I strove to offer as balanced a coverage as possible, alternating essays with biographical portraits and dramatic narratives, within the traditional "periods" that historians have used to order the American past since the Civil War. Still, as in the first edition, the unifying element in the present volume is its emphasis on artful and humanistic historical writing.

Many people helped me in the preparation of this volume—too many, in fact, to mention them all by name. All I can do is offer them my warmest thanks. Several people, though, were especially generous with their time and their professional counsel—Professor Charles C. Alexander of Ohio University and Professors Robert W. Griffith, Stephen E. Pelz, Gerald W. McFarland, Richard Minear, and Jack Tager, all of the University of Massachusetts, Amherst. Very useful reviews were provided by Professors Gerald S. Henig, California State

University at Hayward; James B. Lane, Indiana University; and James F. Cook, Floyd Junior College. All three have been extremely helpful and I wish to thank them for their advice and encouragement. I am also indebted to Mr. Mark Gerstein for his inspired advice and to Mr. Douglas E. Herman and his fellow Teaching Assistants at Ohio University who furnished me with a rigorous and illuminating critique.

S.B.O.

I Reunion and Reaction

1
Why They Impeached Andrew Johnson

David Donald

Until the 1930s, most historical writers viewed Reconstruction as "a tragic era" when fanatical Radicals like Old Thad Stevens and Charles Sumner attempted to create a Congressional dictatorship in Washington, to "put the colored people on top" in the South, and to turn that maligned region over to hordes of beady-eyed Carpetbaggers and roguish Scalawags who "stole the South blind." According to this view, still popular among many Americans today, Reconstruction was a "blackout of honest government," a time when the "Southern people were literally put to the torch," a period so rife with "political rancor, and social violence and disorder," that nothing good came out of it. Possibly the only good that happened was the triumph of white supremacy, when Southern redeemers took their states away from "the niggers and Carpetbaggers" and put an end to the corruption. From about 1900 to the 1930s, a whole procession of books appeared which advanced this view of Reconstruction, but it found its most popular expression in D. W. Griffith's epochal motion picture, *Birth of a Nation*, a blatantly racist film which eulogized the Ku Klux Klan. Produced in 1915, *Birth of a Nation* played to millions of white Americans over the ensuing decades.

The underlying assumption of the old view of Reconstruction was that Negroes were inherently inferior—they were "lazy, dishonest, and extravagant"—and so any attempt to grant them equal political rights with white people was misguided. But in the 1930s and 1940s some historical writers began to question the conventional wisdom about Reconstruction, including the anti-Negro prejudice that underlay it. Once science and psychology had dispelled the myth that Negroes were inferior to whites, most historical writers abandoned the old interpretation with its racist underpinnings and tried to approach Reconstruction with more critical detachment and with more insight into the complexities of that troubled period. Since then at least two parallel reinterpretations have been under way. One has sought to re-evaluate the role of Andrew Johnson in the rise of Congressional or "Radical" Reconstruction. Another has offered a more benign view of Radical Reconstruction itself, contending that it was neither harsh nor even very radical.

The essay by David Donald reflects the re-evaluation of Andrew Johnson in the Reconstruction story. Examining how Congressional Reconstruction emerged from the political struggles of 1865–1867, Donald concludes that Johnson invited much of that program—and the impeachment proceedings which followed—because of his own intransigence.

Reconstruction after the Civil War posed some of the most discouraging problems ever faced by American statesmen. The South was prostrate. Its defeated armies straggled homeward through a countryside desolated by war. Southern soil was untilled and exhausted; southern factories and railroads were worn out. The four billion dollars of southern capital invested

---

From "Why They Impeached Andrew Johnson" by David Donald. Copyright © 1956 by American Heritage Publishing Co., Inc. Reprinted by permission from *American Heritage*, December 1956, pp. 21–25, 102–103.

in Negro slaves was wiped out by advancing Union armies, "the most stupendous act of sequestration in the history of Anglo-American jurisprudence." The white inhabitants of eleven states had somehow to be reclaimed from rebellion and restored to a firm loyalty to the United States. Their four million former slaves had simultaneously to be guided into a proper use of their new-found freedom.

For the victorious Union government there was no time for reflection. Immediate decisions had to be made. Thousands of destitute whites and Negroes had to be fed before long-range plans of rebuilding the southern economy could be drafted. Some kind of government had to be established in these former Confederate states, to preserve order and to direct the work of restoration.

A score of intricate questions must be answered: Should the defeated southerners be punished or pardoned? How should genuinely loyal southern Unionists be rewarded? What was to be the social, economic, and political status of the now free Negroes? What civil rights did they have? Ought they to have the ballot? Should they be given a freehold of property? Was Reconstruction to be controlled by the national government, or should the southern states work out their own salvation? If the federal government supervised the process, should the President or the Congress be in control?

Intricate as were the problems, in early April, 1865, they did not seem insuperable. President Abraham Lincoln was winning the peace as he had already won the war. He was careful to keep every detail of Reconstruction in his own hands; unwilling to be committed to any "exclusive, and inflexible plan," he was working out a pragmatic program of restoration not, perhaps, entirely satisfactory to any group, but reasonably acceptable to all sections. With his enormous prestige as commander of the victorious North and as victor in the 1864 election, he was able to promise freedom to the Negro, charity to the southern white, security to the North.

The blighting of these auspicious beginnings is one of the saddest stories in American history. The reconciliation of the sections, which seemed so imminent in 1865, was delayed for more than ten years. Northern magnanimity toward a fallen foe curdled into bitter distrust. Southern whites rejected moderate leaders, and inveterate racists spoke for the new South. The Negro, after serving as a political pawn for a decade, was relegated to a second-class citizenship, from which he is yet struggling to emerge. Rarely has democratic government so completely failed as during the Reconstruction decade.

The responsibility for this collapse of American statesmanship is, of course, complex. History is not a tale of deep-dyed villains or pure-as-snow heroes. Part of the blame must fall upon ex-Confederates who refused to recognize that the war was over; part upon freedmen who confused liberty with license and the ballot box with the lunch pail; part upon northern antislavery extremists who identified patriotism with loyalty to the Republican party; part upon the land speculators, treasury grafters, and railroad promoters who were unwilling to have a genuine peace lest it end their looting of the public till.

Yet these divisive forces were not bound to triumph. Their success was due to the failure of constructive statesmanship that could channel the magnanimous feelings shared by most Americans into a positive program of reconstruction. President Andrew Johnson was called upon for positive leadership, and he did not meet the challenge.

Andrew Johnson's greatest weakness was his insensitivity to public opinion. In contrast to Lincoln, who said, "Public opinion in this country is everything," Johnson made a career of battling the popular will. A poor white, a runaway tailor's apprentice, a self-educated Tennessee politician, Johnson was a living defiance to the dominant southern belief that leadership belonged to the plantation aristocracy.

As senator from Tennessee, he defied the sentiment of his section in 1861 and refused to join the secessionist movement. When Lincoln later appointed him military governor of occupied Tennessee, Johnson found Nashville "a furnace of treason," but he braved social ostracism and threats of assassination and discharged his duties with boldness and efficiency.

Such a man was temperamentally unable to understand the northern mood in 1865, much less to yield to it. For four years the northern people had been whipped into wartime frenzy by propaganda tales of Confederate atrocities. The assassination of Lincoln by a southern sympathizer confirmed their belief in southern brutality and heartlessness. Few northerners felt vindictive toward the South, but most felt that the rebellion they had crushed must never rise again. Johnson ignored this postwar psychosis gripping the North and plunged ahead with his program of rapidly restoring the southern states to the Union. In May, 1865, without any previous preparation of public opinion, he issued a proclamation of amnesty, granting forgiveness to nearly all the millions of former rebels and welcoming them back into peaceful fraternity. Some few Confederate leaders were excluded from his general amnesty, but even they could secure pardon by special petition. For weeks the White House corridors were thronged with ex-Confederate statesmen and former southern generals who daily received presidential forgiveness.

Ignoring public opinion by pardoning the former Confederates, Johnson actually entrusted the formation of new governments in the South to them. The provisional governments established by the President proceeded, with a good deal of reluctance, to rescind their secession ordinances, to abolish slavery, and to repudiate the Confederate debt. Then, with far more enthusiasm, they turned to electing governors, representatives, and senators. By December, 1865, the southern states had their delegations in Washington waiting for admission by Congress. Alexander H. Stephens, once vice president of the Confederacy, was chosen senator from Georgia: not one of the North Carolina delegation could take a loyalty oath; and all of South Carolina's congressmen had "either held office under the Confederate States, or been in the army, or countenanced in some way the Rebellion."

Johnson himself was appalled. "There seems in many of the elections something like defiance, which is all out of place at this time," he protested. Yet on December 5 he strongly urged the Congress to seat these southern representatives "and thereby complete the work of reconstruction." But the southern states were omitted from the roll call.

Such open defiance of northern opinion was dangerous under the best of circumstances but in Johnson's case it was little more than suicidal. The President seemed not to realize the weakness of his position. He was the representative of no major interest and had no genuine political following. He had been considered for the vice presidency in 1864 because, as a southerner and a former slaveholder, he could lend plausibility to the Republican pretension that the old parties were dead and that Lincoln was the nominee of a new, nonsectional National Union party.

A political accident, the new Vice President did little to endear himself to his countrymen. At Lincoln's second inauguration Johnson appeared before the Senate in an obviously inebriated state and made a long, intemperate harangue about his plebeian origins and his hard-won success. President, Cabinet, and senators were humiliated by the shameful display, and Charles Sumner felt that "the Senate should call upon him to resign." Historians now know that Andrew Johnson was not a heavy drinker. At the time of his inaugural display, he was just recovering from a severe attack of typhoid fever. Feeling ill just before he entered the Senate chamber, he asked for some liquor to steady his nerves, and either his weakened condition or abnormal sensitivity to alcohol betrayed him.

Lincoln reassured Republicans who were worried over the affair: "I have known Andy for many years; he made a bad slip the other day, but you need not be scared. Andy ain't a drunkard." Never again was Andrew Johnson seen under the influence of alcohol, but his reformation came too late. His performance on March 4, 1865, seriously undermined his political usefulness and permitted his opponents to discredit him as a pothouse politician. Johnson was catapulted into the presidency by John Wilkes Booth's bullet. From the outset his position was weak, but it was not necessarily untenable. The President's chronic lack of discretion made it so. Where common sense dictated that a chief executive in so disadvantageous a position should act with great caution, Johnson proceeded to imitate Old Hickory, Andrew Jackson, his political idol. If Congress crossed his will, he did not hesitate to defy it. Was he not "the Tribune of the People"?

Sure of his rectitude, Johnson was indifferent to prudence. He never learned that the President of the United States cannot afford to be a quarreler. Apprenticed in the rough-and-tumble politics of frontier Tennessee, where orators exchanged violent personalities, crude humor, and bitter denunciations, Johnson continued to make stump speeches from the White House. All too often he spoke extemporaneously, and he permitted hecklers in his audience to draw from him angry charges against his critics.

On Washington's birthday in 1866, against the advice of his more sober advisers, the President made an impromptu address to justify his Reconstruction policy. "I fought traitors and treason in the South," he told the crowd; "now when I turn around, and at the other end of the line find men—I care not by what name you call them—who will stand opposed to the restoration of the Union of these States, I am free to say to you that I am still in the field."

During the "great applause" which followed, a nameless voice shouted, "Give us the names at the other end. . . . Who are they?"

"You ask me who they are," Johnson retorted. "I say Thaddeus Stevens of Pennsylvania is one; I say Mr. Sumner is another; and Wendell Phillips is another." Increasing applause urged him to continue. "Are those who want to destroy our institutions . . . not satisfied with the blood that has been shed? . . . Does not the blood of Lincoln appease the vengeance and wrath of the opponents of this government?"

The President's remarks were as untrue as they were impolitic. Not only was it manifestly false to assert that the leading Republican in the House and the most conspicuous Republican in the Senate were opposed to "the fundamental principles of this government" or that they had been responsible for Lincoln's assassination; it was incredible political folly to impute such actions to men with whom the President had to work daily. But Andrew Johnson never learned that the President of the United States must function as a party leader.

There was a temperamental coldness about this plain-featured, grave man that kept him from easy, intimate relations with even his political supporters. His massive head, dark, luxuriant hair, deep-set and piercing eyes, and cleft square chin seemed to Charles Dickens to indicate "courage, watchfulness, and certainly strength of purpose," but his was a grim face, with "no genial sunlight in it." The coldness and reserve that marked Johnson's public associations doubtless stemmed from a deep-seated feeling of insecurity; this self-educated tailor whose wife had taught him how to write could never expose himself by letting down his guard and relaxing.

Johnson knew none of the arts of managing men, and he seemed unaware that face-saving is important for a politician. When he became President, Johnson was besieged by advisers of all political complexions. To each he listened gravely and non-committally, raising no questions and by his silence seeming to give consent. With Radical Senator Sumner, already intent upon giving the freedmen both homesteads and the ballot, he had repeated interviews during the first month of his presidency. "His manner has been excellent, & even sympathetic," Sumner reported triumphantly. With Chief Justice Salmon P. Chase, Sumner urged Johnson to support immediate Negro suffrage and found the President was "well-disposed, & sees the rights & necessities of the case." In the middle of May, 1865, Sumner reassured a Republican caucus that the President was a true Radical; he had listened repeatedly to the Senator and had told him "there is no difference between us." Before the end of the month the rug was pulled from under Sumner's feet. Johnson issued his proclamation for the reconstruction of North Carolina, making no provisions for Negro suffrage. Sumner first learned about it through the newspapers.

While he was making up his mind, Johnson appeared silently receptive to all ideas; when he had made a decision, his mind was immovably closed, and he defended his course with all the obstinacy of a weak man. In December, alarmed by Johnson's Reconstruction proclamations, Sumner again sought an interview with the President. "No longer sympathetic, or even kindly," Sumner found, "he was harsh, petulant, and unreasonable." The Senator was depressed by Johnson's "prejudice, ignorance, and perversity" on the Negro suffrage issue. Far from listening amiably to Sumner's argument that the South was still torn by violence and not yet ready for readmission, Johnson attacked him with cheap analogies. "Are there no murders in Massachusetts?" the President asked.

"Unhappily yes," Sumner replied, "sometimes."

"Are there no assaults in Boston? Do not men there sometimes knock each other down, so that the police is obliged to interfere?"

"Unhappily yes."

"Would you consent that Massachusetts, on this account, should be excluded from Congress?" Johnson triumphantly queried. In the excitement of the argument, the President unconsciously used Sumner's hat, which the Senator had placed on the floor beside his chair, as a spittoon!

Had Johnson been as resolute in action as he was in argument, he might conceivably have carried much of his party with him on his Reconstruction program. Promptness, publicity, and persuasion could have created a presidential following. Instead Johnson boggled. Though he talked boastfully of "kicking out" officers who failed to support his plan, he was slow to act. His own Cabinet, from the very beginning, contained members who disagreed with him, and his secretary of war, Edwin M. Stanton, was openly in league with the Republican elements most hostile to the President. For more than two years he impotently hoped that Stanton would resign; then in 1867, after Congress had passed the Tenure of Office Act, he tried to oust the Secretary. This belated firmness, against the letter of the law, led directly to Johnson's impeachment trial.

Instead of working with his party leaders and building up political support among Republicans, Johnson in 1866 undertook to organize his friends into a new party. In August a convention of white southerners, northern Democrats, moderate Republicans, and presidential appointees assembled in Philadelphia to endorse Johnson's policy. Union General Darius Couch of Massachusetts marched arm in arm down the convention aisle with Governor James L. Orr of South Carolina, to symbolize the states reunited under Johnson's rule. The convention produced fervid oratory, a dignified

Republican congressmen who managed the impeachment of Andrew Johnson in 1868. Back row (left to right): James F. Wilson, George S. Boutwell, and John A. Logan. Front row (left to right): Benjamin F. Butler, Thaddeus Stevens, Thomas Williams, and John A. Bingham. Photograph by Mathew Brady. (U.S. Signal Corps Photo No. 111–B–4371 [Brady Collection] in the National Archives.)

statement of principles—but not much else. Like most third-party reformist movements it lacked support and grass-roots organization.

Johnson himself was unable to breathe life into his stillborn third party. Deciding to take his case to the people, he accepted an invitation to speak at a great Chicago memorial honoring Stephen A. Douglas. When his special train left Washington on August 28 for a "swing around the circle," the President was accompanied by a few Cabinet members who shared his views and by the war heroes Grant and Farragut.

At first all went well. There were some calculated political snubs to the President, but he managed at Philadelphia, New York, and Albany to present his ideas soberly and cogently to the people. But Johnson's friends were worried lest his tongue again get out of control. "In all frankness," a senator wrote him, do not "allow the excitement of the moment to draw from you any *extemporaneous speeches*."

At St. Louis, when a Radical voice shouted that Johnson was a "Judas," the President flamed up in rage. "There was a Judas and he was one of the twelve apostles," he retorted. ". . . The twelve apostles had a Christ. . . . If I have played the Judas, who has been my Christ that I have played the Judas with? Was it Thad Stevens? Was it Wendell Phillips? Was it Charles Sumner?" Over mingled hisses and applause, he shouted, "These are the men that stop and compare themselves with the Saviour; and everybody that differs with them . . . is to be denounced as a Judas."

Johnson had played into his enemies' hands. His Radical foes denounced him as a "trickster," a "culprit," a man "touched with insanity, corrupted with lust, stimulated with drink." More serious in consequence was the reaction of northern moderates, such as James Russell Lowell, who wrote, "What an anti-Johnson lecturer we have in Johnson! Sumner has been right about the *cuss* from the first. . . ." The fall elections were an overwhelming repudiation of the President and his Reconstruction policy.

Johnson's want of political sagacity strengthened the very elements in the Republican party which he most feared. In 1865 the Republicans had no clearly defined attitude toward Reconstruction. Moderates like Gideon Welles and Orville Browning wanted to see the southern states restored with a minimum of restrictions; Radicals like Sumner and Stevens demanded that the entire southern social system be revolutionized. Some Republicans were passionately concerned with the plight of the freedmen; others were more interested in maintaining the high tariff and land grant legislation enacted during the war. Many thought mostly of keeping themselves in office, and many genuinely believed, with Sumner, that "the Republican party, in its objects, is identical with country and with mankind." These diverse elements came slowly to adopt the idea of harsh Reconstruction, but Johnson's stubborn persistency in his policy left them no alternative. Every step the President took seemed to provide "a new encouragement to (1) the rebels at the South, (2) the Democrats at the North and (3) the discontented elements everywhere." Not many Republicans would agree with Sumner that Johnson's program was "a defiance to God and Truth," but there was genuine concern that the victory won by the war was being frittered away.

The provisional governments established by the President in the South seemed to be dubiously loyal. They were reluctant to rescind their secession ordinances and to repudiate the Confederate debt, and they chose high-ranking ex-Confederates to represent them in Congress. Northerners were even more alarmed when these southern governments began to legislate upon the Negro's civil rights. Some laws were necessary—in order to give former slaves the right to marry, to hold property, to sue and be sued, and the like—but the Johnson legislatures went far beyond these immediate needs. South Carolina, for example, enacted that no Negro could pursue the trade "of an artisan, mechanic, or shopkeeper, or any other trade or employment besides that of husbandry" without a special license. Alabama provided that "any stubborn or refractory servants" or "servants who loiter away their time" should be fined $50 and, if they could not pay, be hired out for six months' labor. Mississippi ordered that every Negro under eighteen years of age who was an orphan or not supported by his parents must be apprenticed to some white person, preferably the former owner of the slave. Such southern laws indicated a determination to keep the Negro in a state of peonage.

It was impossible to expect a newly emancipated race to be content with such a limping freedom. The thousands of Negroes who had served in the Union armies and had helped conquer their former Confederate masters were not willing to abandon their newfound liberty. In rural areas southern whites kept these Negroes under control through the Ku Klux Klan. But in southern cities white hegemony was less secure, and racial friction erupted in mob violence. In May, 1866, a quarrel between a Memphis Negro and a white teamster led to a riot in which the city police and the poor whites raided the Negro quarters and burned and killed promiscuously. Far more serious was the disturbance in New Orleans two months later. The Republican party in Louisiana was split into pro-Johnson conservatives and Negro suffrage advocates. The latter group determined to hold a constitutional convention, of dubious legality, in New Orleans, in order to secure the ballot for the freedmen and the offices for themselves. Through imbecility in the War Department, the Federal troops occupying the city were left without orders, and the mayor of New Orleans, strongly opposed to Negro equality, had the responsibility for preserving order. There were acts of provocation on both sides, and finally, on July 30, a procession of Negroes marching toward the convention hall was attacked.

"A shot was fired . . . by a policeman, or some colored man in the procession," General Philip Sheridan reported. "This led to other shots, and a rush after the procession. On arrival at the front of the Institute [where the convention met], there was some throwing of brick-bats by both sides. The police . . . were vigorously marched to the scene of disorder. The procession entered the Institute with the flag, about six or eight remaining outside. A row occurred between a policeman and one of these colored men, and a shot was again fired by one of the parties, which led to an indiscriminate firing on the building, through the windows, by the policemen.

"This had been going on for a short time, when a white flag was displayed from the windows of the Institute, whereupon the firing ceased and the police rushed into the building. . . . The policemen opened an indiscriminate fire upon the audience until they had emptied their revolvers, when they retired, and those inside barricaded the doors. The door was broken in, and the firing again commenced when many of the colored and white people either escaped out of the door, or were passed out by the policemen inside, but as they came out, the policemen who formed the circle nearest the building fired upon them, and they were again fired upon by the citizens that formed the outer circle."

Thirty-seven Negroes and three of their white friends were killed; 119 Negroes and seventeen of their white sympathizers were wounded. Of their assailants, ten were wounded and but one killed. President Johnson was, of course, horrified by these outbreaks, but the Memphis and New Orleans riots, together with the Black Codes, afforded a devastating illustration of how the President's policy actually operated. The southern states, it was clear, were not going to protect the Negroes' basic rights. They were only grudgingly going to accept the results of the war. Yet, with Johnson's blessing, these same states were expecting a stronger voice in Congress than ever. Before 1860, southern representation in Congress had been based upon the white population plus three fifths of the slaves; now the Negroes, though not permitted to vote, were to be counted like all other citizens, and southern states would be entitled to at least nine additional congressmen. Joining with the northern Copperheads, the southerners could easily regain at the next presidential election all that had been lost on the Civil War battlefield.

It was this political exigency, not misguided sentimentality nor vindictiveness, which united Republicans in opposition to the President.

Johnson's defenders have pictured Radical

Reconstruction as the work of a fanatical minority, led by Sumner and Stevens, who drove their reluctant colleagues into adopting coercive measures against the South. In fact, every major piece of Radical legislation was adopted by the nearly unanimous vote of the entire Republican membership of Congress. Andrew Johnson had left them no other choice. Because he insisted upon rushing Confederate-dominated states back into the Union, Republicans moved to disqualify Confederate leaders under the Fourteenth Amendment. When, through Johnson's urging, the southern states rejected that amendment, the Republicans in Congress unwillingly came to see Negro suffrage as the only counterweight against Democratic majorities in the South. With the Reconstruction Acts of 1867 the way was open for a true Radical program toward the South, harsh and thorough.

Andrew Johnson became a cipher in the White House, futilely disapproving bills which were promptly passed over his veto. Through his failure to reckon with public opinion, his unwillingness to recognize his weak position, his inability to function as a party leader, he had sacrificed all influence with the party which had elected him and had turned over its control to Radicals vindictively opposed to his policies. In March, 1868, Andrew Johnson was summoned before the Senate of the United States to be tried on eleven accusations of high crimes and misdemeanors. By a narrow margin the Senate failed to convict him, and historians have dismissed the charges as flimsy and false. Yet perhaps before the bar of history itself Andrew Johnson must be impeached with an even graver charge—that through political ineptitude he threw away a magnificent opportunity.

2
Radical Rule in the South

Kenneth M. Stampp

In *The Era of Reconstruction*, Kenneth Stampp offers a thoroughgoing "revisionist" critique of the entire Reconstruction period. He agrees with David Donald that Johnson's intransigence—along with the black codes adopted by Southern ex-Confederates—helped bring on Radical Reconstruction. But Stampp goes on to argue that the so-called Radical Republicans were not really vindictive (given the nature of the Civil War) and that their program was neither harsh nor very thorough. In his chapter on Republican rule in the South, excerpted here, Stampp eschews the black-and-white stereotypes of the old interpretation and attempts to portray what the much-maligned Carpetbaggers, Scalawags, and Negro politicians were really like. And he asks, and tries to answer as fairly as he can, some crucial questions: Was corruption in the South widespread or isolated during Radical rule? Did the Republican regimes do anything constructive? How did they treat the ex-Confederates? And what, finally, is the legacy of Radical Reconstruction for our time?

When Lord Bryce, in the 1880's, wrote *The American Commonwealth*, he commented at length on the southern state governments created under the radical plan of reconstruction. What he had to say about them was not remarkable for its originality, but a few passages are worth quoting to give the flavor of the approaching historical consensus. "Such a Saturnalia of robbery and jobbery has seldom been seen in any civilized country. . . . The position of these [radical] adventurers was like that of a Roman provincial governor in the latter days of the Republic. . . . [All] voting power lay with those who were wholly unfit for citizenship, and had no interest as taxpayers, in good government. . . . [Since] the legislatures were reckless and corrupt, the judges for the most part subservient, the Federal military officers bound to support what purported to be the constitutional authorities of the State, Congress distant and little inclined to listen to the complaints of those whom it distrusted as rebels, greed was unchecked and roguery unabashed."[1] In drawing this unpleasant picture Lord Bryce anticipated the generalizations of the Dunningites, as did many others.

Each of the eleven states of the former Confederacy, during all or part of the decade between 1867 and 1877, fell under the control of the radical Republicans. Tennessee was the first to be captured by them—indeed, it never had a Johnson government—but it was also the first to be lost. Tennessee was "redeemed," as southern white Democrats liked to call their return to power, as early as 1869. The last three states to be redeemed were South Carolina, Florida, and Louisiana, where the radical regimes lasted until the spring of 1877.

What, according to the conservatives, were

From pp. 155–185 in *The Era of Reconstruction* by Kenneth M. Stampp. Copyright © 1965 by Kenneth M. Stampp. Reprinted by permission of Alfred A. Knopf.

[1] James Bryce: *The American Commonwealth*, 3 vols. (New York, 1888), Vol. II, pp. 476–8.

the sins of the radical governments? The new governments, they said, expelled from power the South's experienced statesmen and natural leaders and replaced them with untrained men who were almost uniformly incompetent and corrupt. Among the radical leaders, the Yankee carpetbaggers, crafty adventurers who invaded the postwar South for political and economic plunder, were the most notorious. The scalawags, who assisted the carpetbaggers, were mostly degraded and depraved poor whites, betrayers of their race and section who sought a share of the radical spoils. The Negroes, ignorant and illiterate, played an essentially passive political role, casting their votes as radical agents of the Union League and Freedmen's Bureau told them to. Since the members of the radical coalition owned little or no property themselves, they increased state and local taxes until they came near to ruining the whole class of white property holders. Their extravagant appropriations, their waste, fraud, and corruption, caused shocking increases in southern state debts and brought some states to the edge of bankruptcy. Finally, said the conservatives, the radical governments threatened to destroy the white civilization of the South and to reduce it to African barbarism.

We must first consider the charge that the radicals expelled from power the South's natural leaders. One of the characters in Margaret Mitchell's popular novel, *Gone With the Wind*, complains that everybody who was anybody in the good old days was nobody in the radical regimes. A conservative Tennesseean reported that the radicals in his state were "the party paying no taxes, riding poor horses, wearing dirty shirts, and having no use for soap." According to a Nashville newspaper, most of the so-called loyal men of the South were "the merest trash that could be collected in a civilized community, of no personal credit or social responsibility." Thus, concludes a historian of reconstruction in Tennessee, "the power, wealth, culture, and natural leadership" of the state had been evicted from political control.[2] An upper-class Virginian sent Thad Stevens a bitter protest against being subjected to "our former slaves and the mean white surfs [sic] of the earth. . . . We are the children of the Lees, Clays, Henrys, Jeffersons and Jacksons. Tell me if we are to be ruled by these people." This would seem to suggest that to some extent and in some places southern class divisions were sharpened during the era of reconstruction. But southern conservatives exaggerated the degree to which the division between them and the radicals was along class lines.

In any case, those who have referred to the South's ante-bellum political rulers as its natural leaders are seldom explicit about what they mean. Remembering what had happened to the South under the guidance of her prewar politicians, it would be hard to argue that they had won the right to lead because they had governed so wisely or so well. If it is valid to judge statesmen by their understanding of the problems of their age, and by their efforts to find constructive solutions, the old southern leaders would have to be pronounced failures on both counts; and many of them were, moreover, singularly irresponsible. Their strength was rooted in their economic power derived from large property holdings, and in their experience in the techniques of political manipulation. The conservatives' repeated complaint that the radicals paid no taxes and owned little property is highly suggestive, for their whole conception of natural political leadership ultimately boils down to this. When the radicals won control in the South, they did not displace a responsible political élite which had traditionally taken a large view of things; nor did they discharge a trained body of civil servants. This being the case, the change in leadership was far less disastrous than it has often been made to appear.

But the customary charges against the new southern leadership are extremely severe and

[2] E. Merton Coulter: *William G. Brownlow* (Chapel Hill, 1937), pp. 282–3, 337.

need to be weighed carefully. It is essential, therefore, to examine in some detail each of the three elements in the radical coalition—the carpetbaggers, scalawags, and Negroes—to test the validity of the generalizations conservatives used to characterize them. The term "carpetbagger" was applied to recent northern settlers in the South who actively supported the radical Republicans.[3] Since the term has an invidious connotation, it is used here only for lack of another that is equally familiar but morally neutral. The so-called carpetbaggers were not all poor men who carried their meager possessions with them in carpetbags; they were not all ignorant; they were not all corrupt. Rather, they were a heterogeneous lot who moved to the South for a variety of reasons.

Among the carpetbaggers were some who fitted the stereotype: disreputable opportunists and corruptionists who went south in search of political plunder or public office. Because these carpetbaggers were so conspicuous and gained such notoriety, conservative southern Democrats succeeded in portraying them as typical, though actually they constituted a small minority.

Few of the carpetbaggers came to the South originally for the purpose of entering politics; many of them arrived before 1867 when political careers were not even open to them. They migrated to the South in the same manner and for the same reasons that other Americans migrated to the West. They hoped to buy cotton lands or to enter legitimate business enterprises: to develop natural resources, build factories, promote railroads, represent insurance companies, or engage in trade. A large proportion of the carpetbaggers were veterans of the Union Army who were pleased with the southern climate and believed that they had discovered a land of opportunity. Others came as teachers, clergymen, officers of the Freedmen's Bureau, or agents of the various northern benevolent societies organized to give aid to the Negroes. These people went south to set up schools for Negroes and poor whites, to establish churches, and to distribute clothing and medical supplies. They were of all types—some well trained for their jobs, others not. Seldom, however, can they be dismissed as meddlesome fools, or can the genuineness of their humanitarian impulses be doubted. But whether honest or dishonest, northern settlers who became active in radical politics incurred the wrath of most white southern conservatives. For their supreme offense was not corruption but attempting to organize the Negroes for political action.

A scalawag is by definition a scamp, and white Southerners who collaborated with the radicals were thus stigmatized by the pejorative term that identified them. In southern society, according to one critic, scalawags constituted the "tory and deserter element, with a few from the obstructionists of the war time and malcontents of the present who wanted office."[4] But here, as in the case of the carpetbaggers, the facts were more complex than this. All scalawags were not degraded poor whites, depraved corruptionists, or cynical opportunists who betrayed the South for the spoils of office.

The cases of three distinguished scalawags will illustrate the inadequacy of any simple generalization about the character or origin of this class of radicals. The first is that of Lieutenant General James A. Longstreet of the Confederate Army, a graduate of West Point and one of Lee's ablest corps commanders. After the war Longstreet moved to New Orleans and became a partner in a cotton factorage business and head of an insurance firm. In 1867, argu-

---

[3] "From contemporary usage . . . we derive the following as a nonvaluational definition: the men called carpetbaggers were *white Northerners who went south after the beginning of the Civil War and, sooner or later, became active in politics as Republicans.*" Richard N. Current: "Carpetbaggers Reconsidered," in *A Festschrift for Frederick B. Artz* (Durham, 1964), p. 144.

[4] Walter L. Fleming: *Civil War and Reconstruction in Alabama* (New York, 1905), p. 402.

ing that the vanquished must accept the terms of the victors, he joined the Republican party and endorsed radical reconstruction. In 1868 he supported Grant for President, and in subsequent years Republican administrations gave him a variety of offices in the federal civil service. The second case is that of James L. Orr of South Carolina, a secessionist who had sat in the Confederate Senate. After serving as the Johnsonian governor of his state, Orr switched to the radicals and in 1868 was rewarded with a circuit judgeship. In a private letter he explained why he now supported the Republicans: It is "important for our prominent men to identify themselves with the radicals for the purpose of controlling their action and preventing mischief to the state." The third case is that of R. W. Flournoy, a large slaveholder in antebellum Mississippi. Flournoy joined the radicals not for personal gain but because of a humanitarian interest in the welfare of the freedmen. In a letter to Stevens he once explained that he supported the Republicans as the party to whom the Negro "can alone look . . . for protection." Flournoy's support of racial equality made him one of the most hated scalawags in the state. None of these men fitted the scalawag stereotype.

Others unfortunately did. Among those who gave the scalawags their reputation for corruption was Franklin J. Moses, Jr., of South Carolina. The son of a distinguished father, Moses entered politics before the war and was known as an ardent secessionist. In 1867, after a brief period as a Johnsonian, he joined the radicals. Both as a legislator and, from 1872 to 1874, as governor he looted the public treasury and repeatedly accepted bribes for using his influence to secure the passage of legislation. Other scalawags appeared to be pure opportunists who simply joined the winning side. Joseph E. Brown, Georgia's Civil War governor, provides a classic example. After the war, claiming that he had sense enough to know when he was defeated, Brown quit the Democrats and urged Southerners to accept the radicals' terms. During the years of reconstruction, in addition to his political activities, he found the time (and the opportunity) to become a wealthy capitalist: president of a railroad, a steamship company, a coal company, and an iron company. When the radicals were overthrown in Georgia, Brown, as always, landed on his feet and returned to the Democratic party. Now he helped to organize a powerful Democratic machine that dominated the state for many years and eventually sent him to the United States Senate.

Always a minority of the southern white population, more numerous in some states than in others,[5] the scalawags usually belonged to one or more of four distinct groups. The first and largest of these groups was the Unionists. Having been exposed to severe persecution from their Confederate neighbors during the war, southern Unionists were often the most vindictive of the radicals; they were quite willing to support those who would now retaliate against the secessionists, and they hoped that congressional reconstruction would give them political control in their states. Early in 1866 a North Carolinian wrote Stevens that Union men were disillusioned with Johnson but still hoped "that traitors will be punished for the treatment that union men received at their hands."

However, a very large proportion of this Unionist-scalawag element had little enthusiasm for one aspect of the radical program: the granting of equal civil and political rights to the Negroes. They favored the disenfranchisement of the Confederates to enable them to dominate the new state governments, but they were reluctant to accept Negro suffrage.

---

[5] In the presidential election of 1872, according to a recent estimate, approximately 150,000 white Southerners voted Republican; they constituted about 20 per cent of the white voters. These scalawags were most numerous in Tennessee, North Carolina, Arkansas, Texas, and Virginia. Allen W. Trelease: "Who Were the Scalawags?" *Journal of Southern History*, XXIX (1963), p. 458.

"There is some small amount of squirming about the privileges extended to the recent slaves," a Virginia Unionist informed Stevens, "but time will overcome all this as there is no union man who does not infinitely more fear and dread the domination of the recent Rebels than that of the recent slaves." In 1866, General Clinton B. Fisk, an officer of the Freedmen's Bureau, told the congressional Committee on Reconstruction that in Tennessee "among the bitterest opponents of the negro . . . are the intensely radical loyalists of the [eastern] mountain districts. . . . The great opposition to the measure in the Tennessee legislature, giving the negro the right to testify and an equality before the law, has come from that section, chiefly. In Middle Tennessee and in West Tennessee the largest and the wealthiest planters . . . have more cordially cooperated with me in my duties than the people of East Tennessee." The planters believed that they could control the Negro vote, and the scalawags feared that they would.

Insofar as there was any relationship between scalawags and the class structure of the South, it resulted from the fact that a minority of the poor whites and yeoman farmers were attracted to the radical cause.[6] There had always been, as we have seen, an undercurrent of tension between them and the planter class, and some of them deserted President Johnson when it appeared that his program would return the planters to power. Lower-class whites who joined the radicals sometimes hoped for a seizure of the planters' lands. In South Carolina, according to a Union officer, the idea of confiscation "was received with more favor by this caste than by the Negroes." He recalled numerous occasions when "dirty, ragged, stupid creatures slyly inquired of me, 'When is our folks a-gwine to git the lan'?'" But it was never easy for the yeomen or poor whites to become scalawags, for support of the radicals meant collaboration with Negroes, or at least acquiescence in Negro suffrage. As a result, this class of scalawags was most numerous in areas with a small Negro population. Elsewhere a few lower-class whites managed to submerge their race prejudice, but the great majority preferred the old conservative leadership to a party that seemed to preach equality of the races.

A third source of scalawag strength came from Southerners engaged in business enterprise and from those living in regions, such as East Tennessee, western Virginia and North Carolina, and northern Alabama, which were rich in natural resources and had an industrial potential. Among such men there was considerable support for the economic policies of the Republican party—for the national banking system, the protective tariff, and federal appropriations for internal improvements. In general, the radical governments invited northern capitalists to invest in the South, granted loans or subsidies to the railroads, and gave charters and franchises to new corporations. Some of the scalawags were thus identified with the concept of a New South whose economy would be more diversified than that of the Old.

Finally, the radicals drew a little of their scalawag support and some of their leaders from upper-class Southerners who had been affiliated with the Whig party before the Civil War. The Whig party had been particularly attractive to the more affluent and socially secure members of southern society, and after the war many Whigs were reluctant to join their old foes, the Democrats. A few of them now looked upon the Republican party as the heir to the Whig tradition and wondered whether it might be possible not only to join but also to control its organization in the South. Upper-class Whig scalawags found it relatively easy to accept equal civil and political rights for Negroes, first, because among them race hatred was less often the prime motivating

---

[6] Most of the lower-class whites who became scalawags had been Unionists, but some had supported the Confederacy.

force of political action and, second, because they were optimistic about their chances of controlling the Negro vote. In Mississippi, for example, James L. Alcorn, elected governor on the Republican ticket in 1869, had been a prominent Whig planter before the war, as had been numerous other leading scalawags. Thus it would appear that the scalawags were in part an absurd coalition of class-conscious poor whites and yeoman farmers who hated the planters, and class-conscious Whig planters and businessmen who disliked the egalitarian Democrats. But politics has a logic of its own, and the history of American political parties is full of contradictions such as this.

Joining the carpetbaggers and scalawags in the radical coalition was the mass of southern Negroes, most of them illiterate, many easily intimidated. Because of their political inexperience and economic helplessness, they were sometimes misled and victimized not only by Republicans but also by southern white Democrats. But it would be far from the truth to say that their political behavior during reconstruction was altogether passive or irresponsible. This was untrue, if for no other reason, because the issues of reconstruction, so far as the Negroes were concerned, were relatively simple and clear-cut. Given their condition and the limited political choices open to them, most Negroes responded to the appeals of rival politicians in a manner that had an obvious logic to it.

To begin with, suffrage was not something thrust upon an indifferent mass of Negroes. Their leaders had demanded it from the start; and when the Johnson governments limited the ballot to the whites, many meetings of southern Negroes sent protests to Congress. In Tennessee, for example, Negroes first petitioned the legislature for the ballot, then asked Congress not to seat Tennesseeans until their petition was granted. On May 7, 1866, a meeting of freedmen in New Bern, North Carolina, resolved "That so long as the Federal Government refuses to grant us the right to protect ourselves by means of the ballot . . . we will hold it responsible before God for our protection."

Moreover, most Negroes fully appreciated the importance of achieving literacy, and they took advantage of the limited educational opportunities offered them with almost pathetic eagerness. They also understood that in the rural South land was the key to economic independence and that they needed government aid to get it. In 1865 they heard rumors that Congress would provide each of them with forty acres and a mule at Christmas time; the next year they heard the same rumors again; once more in 1867 they hoped to get land when the radicals formulated their reconstruction program. But each time the Negroes were disappointed, and by 1868 they knew that the Republicans in Congress were not going to assist them.

Nevertheless, an overwhelming majority of Negro voters continued to support the Republican party, and in 1868 they helped to elevate General Grant to the presidency. In the political campaigns of the reconstruction era, Democratic candidates occasionally tried to bid for the Negro vote, but the record of the Johnson governments and the commitment of the Democratic party to white supremacy caused the mass of Negroes to remain loyal Republicans. "The blacks know that many conservatives hope to reduce them again to some form of peonage," a Tennessee carpetbagger wrote Stevens. "Under the impulse of this fear they will roll up their whole strength . . . and will go entirely for the Republican candidate whoever he may be." As long as southern Democrats opposed Negro suffrage and insisted that white supremacy was the central political issue, this condition could hardly have changed. It was this that made it easy for the agents of the Republican Union League to mobilize and "control" the Negro vote. Yet white Democrats often cited this solid Negro support of the Republicans to illustrate the political irresponsibility of the freedmen. It was a curious argument, however, for the practical choice offered the Negro voters was between a party that gave them civil and political rights and a party whose stock-in-trade was racist demagoguery.

Perhaps the most important generalizations to be made about the role of the Negroes in reconstruction are the following. First, while they had influence in all of the southern radical governments—more in some than in others—they did not control any of them. They served in all of the state legislatures, but only in South Carolina, one of the two southern states in which they outnumbered the whites, were they in the majority.[7] In Mississippi, the other state in which the Negroes had a numerical majority, the carpetbaggers controlled politics; while in Tennessee, where the scalawags dominated the radical government, there were practically no Negro officeholders at all. Few Negroes were elected to higher offices; none became the governor of a state. At various times South Carolina had a Negro lieutenant governor, secretary of state, treasurer, speaker of the house, and associate justice of the state supreme court; Mississippi had a Negro lieutenant governor, secretary of state, superintendent of education, and speaker of the house; Louisiana had a Negro lieutenant governor, secretary of state, treasurer, and superintendent of public education; Florida had a Negro secretary of state, and superintendent of public instruction. Nearly all of them were men of ability and integrity. Fourteen Negroes were elected to the United States House of Representatives, six of them from South Carolina. Two Mississippi Negroes served in the United States Senate: Hiram R. Revels for a one-year unexpired term, and Blanche K. Bruce for a full term. (Revels and Bruce, incidentally, are the only Negroes who have ever been elected to the Senate from any state, North or South.)* In general, however, white men dominated the higher offices of the southern radical governments. The Negroes, though filling many city and county offices, ordinarily were unable to advance beyond the state legislatures.

Second, the Negroes soon developed their own leadership and were not always the mere tools of white Republicans. In 1868 a Florida carpetbagger reported to Stevens that white radicals were having trouble getting the Negroes to support ratification of the new state constitution. "The colored preachers," he wrote, "are *the great power* in controlling and uniting the colored vote, and they are looked to, as political leaders, with more confidence ... than to any other source of instruction and control." Some of the Negro leaders were corruptible, some incorruptible; some had great ability, some little. Most of them were conservatives on all issues except civil and political rights.

Finally, the Negroes were seldom vindictive in their use of political power or in their attitude toward native whites. To be sure, there were plenty of cases of friction between Negroes and whites, and Negro militiamen were sometimes inordinately aggressive. But in no southern state did any responsible Negro leader, or any substantial Negro group, attempt to get complete political control into the hands of the freedmen.[8] All they asked for was equal political rights and equality before the law. Thus, in 1866, a group of North Carolina Negroes in thanking Congress for the Civil Rights Act promised that "whenever the Elective Franchise is also guaranteed to us we will ask no further special protection from the Federal

---

[7] South Carolina's first radical legislature contained 87 Negroes and 69 whites. The Negroes, however, had a majority only in the lower house. The upper house contained twice as many whites as Negroes.

* In 1966, after this was written, Edward Brooke was elected U.S. Senator in Massachusetts—Ed.

[8] However, Negro leaders did protest when they thought that white radicals were trying to monopolize the offices.

South Carolina legislature during Radical Reconstruction. Of the 146 members of that legislature, 90 were blacks. Like the Negroes in other Republican legislatures in the South, "nearly all of them were men of ability and integrity." While the South Carolina legislature was hardly a model of efficiency or honesty, as Stampp points out, it did try to restore the state's war-ravaged economy and to establish a good public school system. It also passed a law which made it a crime to call a man "yankee" or "nigger." (Courtesy of The Library of Congress.)

Government, for then united with our white friends in the South we will be able to secure for ourselves every desired or desirable means of prosperity." Negroes did not desire to have political parties divided along racial lines; rather, unlike most white Democrats, they were eager to drop the race issue and work with the whites within the existing party framework.

Many Negroes at this time were even willing to postpone action on social segregation, especially in the schools, preferring to avoid conflict over this issue while they concentrated on civil and political rights. A South Carolina Negro legislator declared: "I venture to say to my white fellow-citizens that we, the colored people, are not in quest of social equality. I for one do not ask to be introduced in your family circle if you are not disposed to receive me there." And yet a northern white conservative affirmed that in South Carolina radical reconstruction "is barbarism overwhelming civilization by physical force. It is the slave rioting in the halls of his master, and putting that master under his feet." Such a description should be taken for what it was: the hyperbole of partisan politics.

The first step in the organization of new southern state governments, as required by the reconstruction acts, was the election of delegates to conventions to frame new state constitutions. Since these conventions were controlled by the radicals, since they were the first political bodies in the South to contain Negroes,[9] white conservatives subjected them to violent denunciation. They contemptuously called them "black and tan conventions"; they described the delegates as "baboons, monkeys, mules," or "ragamuffins and jailbirds." The South Carolina convention, according to a local newspaper, was the "maddest, most infamous revolution in history."

Yet, the invectives notwithstanding, there was nothing mad and little revolutionary about the work of these conventions.[10] In fact, one of the most significant observations to be made about them is that the delegates showed little interest in experimentation. For the most part the radicals wrote orthodox state constitutions, borrowing heavily from the previous constitutions and from those of other states. To find fault with the way these southern constitutions were drawn is to find fault with the way most new state constitutions have been drawn; to criticize their basic political structure is to criticize the basic political structure of all the states. They were neither original nor unique. There was no inclination to test, say, the unicameral legislature, or novel executive or judicial systems.

Nor did the conventions attempt radical experiments in the field of social or economic policy. Since land reform had been defeated in Congress, a few delegates tried to achieve it through state action. The South Carolina convention provided for the creation of a commission to purchase land for sale to Negroes. In Louisiana, some Negro delegates proposed that when planters sold their estates purchases of more than 150 acres be prohibited. One white scalawag suggested a double tax on uncultivated land. A few delegates in other states advocated various policies designed to force the breakup of large estates. But these and all other attacks upon landed property were easily defeated.

As for the freedmen, the new constitutions proclaimed the equality of all men by quoting

---

[9] The number of Negroes and whites in the various conventions was as follows:

	Negro	White		Negro	White
Alabama	18	90	Mississippi	16	84
Arkansas	8	58	North Carolina	15	118
Florida	18	27	South Carolina	76	48
Georgia	33	137	Virginia	25	80
Louisiana	49	49	Texas	9	81

[10] The Democrats accused the Republican delegates of wasting time and of extravagance. The printing bills of some of these conventions were unnecessarily high, but in general these accusations have relatively little evidence to support them.

or paraphrasing the Declaration of Independence. Negroes were given the same civil and political rights as white men. "The equality of all persons before the law," proclaimed the Arkansas constitution, "is recognized and shall ever remain inviolate; nor shall any citizen ever be deprived of any right, privilege, or immunity, nor exempted from any burden or duty, or account of race, color, or previous condition." But on the subject of the social relations of Negroes and whites, most of the radical constitutions were evasive. South Carolina provided that its public schools were to be open to all "without regard to race or color," but only the state university actually made an attempt at integration. The Louisiana constitution declared: "There shall be no separate schools or institutions of learning established exclusively for any race by the State of Louisiana." In New Orleans from 1871 to 1877 about one third of the public schools were integrated, and white resistance was remarkably mild; but elsewhere in Louisiana segregation was the rule. Outside of South Carolina and Louisiana the radicals made no explicit constitutional provision for social integration. The Mississippi convention first defeated a proposal that segregated schools be required, then defeated a proposal that they be prohibited; the result was that the new constitution ignored the issue altogether. The only reference to segregation in it was a vague statement that "the rights of all citizens to travel upon public conveyances shall not be infringed upon, nor in any manner abridged in this state." But whether or not this clause prohibited segregation in public transportation is far from clear.

Yet, though the new constitutions were essentially conservative documents, they did accomplish some modest reforms, most of which were long overdue. In general, they eliminated certain undemocratic features of the old constitutions, for example, the inequitable systems of legislative apportionment that had discriminated against the interior regions of Virginia, North Carolina, and South Carolina. In the states of the Southeast, many offices that had previously been appointive were now made elective, and county government was taken out of the hands of local oligarchies. The rights of women were enlarged, tax systems were made more equitable, penal codes were reformed, and the number of crimes punishable by death was reduced. Most of the constitutions provided for substantial improvements in the state systems of public education and in the facilities for the care of the physically and mentally handicapped and of the poor.[11]

In South Carolina, according to the historians of reconstruction in that state, the radical convention was an orderly body which accomplished its work with reasonable dispatch. It produced a constitution "as good as any other constitution that state has ever had" —good enough to remain in force for nearly two decades after the white Democrats regained control. This was, in fact, the state's first really democratic constitution; for, in addition to removing distinctions based on race, it provided for manhood suffrage, abolished property qualifications for officeholding, gave the voters the power for the first time to select the governor and other state officers, and transferred the election of presidential electors from the legislature to the voters. Another important provision related to public education: unlike the previous constitution, "the fundamental law of the state carried the obligation of universal education" and aimed at "the creation of a school system like that of Northern states." Other reforms included an extension of women's rights, adoption of the state's first divorce law, strengthening of the state's fiscal power,

[11] Attempts to accomplish a sweeping disenfranchisement of Confederate sympathizers were defeated either in the conventions or, as in Virginia and Mississippi, by popular vote. The disenfranchisement accomplished by these constitutions seldom went beyond those disqualified for holding office by the Fourteenth Amendment, and all made provision for the eventual restoration of the franchise even to them.

revision of the tax system, and modernization of the judiciary and of county government.[12]

The responsible behavior of South Carolina's radical constitutional convention was in striking contrast to the angry and irresponsible criticism of the Democrats. Chiefly because of its provisions for racial equality, they ridiculed the new constitution as "the work of sixty-odd negroes, many of them ignorant and depraved, together with fifty white men, outcasts of Northern society, and Southern renegades, betrayers of their race and country." Specifically, the Democrats charged that manhood suffrage was designed to further the ambitions of "mean whites"; that Negro suffrage would bring ruin to the state; that the judicial reforms were "repugnant to our customs and habits of thought"; and that the public school requirements were "a fruitful source of peculant corruption." In spite of this fanciful criticism by a party whose chief appeal was to racial bigotry, the work of the radical convention was ratified by a majority of nearly three to one.

At the time that the new constitutions were ratified, elections were held for state officers and legislators. After the elections, when Congress approved of the constitutions, political power was transferred from the military to the new civil governments. Thus began the era of radical government in the South—an era which, according to tradition, produced some of the worst state administrations in American history. Some of the southern radical regimes earned their evil reputations, others did not; but viewed collectively, there was much in the record they made to justify severe criticism. To say that they were not always models of efficiency and integrity would be something of an understatement. "The great impediment of the Republican party in this state," wrote a Tennessee radical, "is the incompetence of its leaders. . . . After the war the loyal people in many counties had no competent men to be judges, lawyers or political leaders." Indeed, all of the radical governments suffered more or less from the incompetence of some, the dishonesty of a few, and above all the inexperience of most of the officeholders. Unquestionably the poorest records were made in South Carolina during the administrations of the carpetbagger Robert K. Scott and the scalawag Franklin J. Moses, Jr., and in Louisiana during the administrations of the carpetbaggers Henry C. Warmoth and William P. Kellogg.

The sins of various radical governments included fraudulent bond issues; graft in land sales or purchases and in the letting of contracts for public works; and waste and extravagance in the use of state funds. Governor Warmoth was reputed to have pocketed $100,000 during his first year in office, though his salary was $8,000; another governor was accused of stealing and selling the supplies of the Freedmen's Bureau. A scalawag governor admitted taking bribes of more than $40,000; another fraudulently endorsed state bonds over to a group of railroad promoters. In Louisiana under both Warmoth and Kellogg there was corruption in the granting of charters and franchises, in the negotiation of construction contracts, in the use of school funds, in the collection of state taxes, and in the awarding of printing contracts. Some of the radical legislators, especially in South Carolina, apparently made bribery an integral part of the process of transacting legislative business. One South Carolina legislature issued bonds valued at $1,590,000 to redeem bank notes valued at $500,000; it voted a bonus of $1,000 to the speaker when he lost that amount in a bet on a horse race. For a time the legislators of this state enjoyed the services of a free restaurant and bar established for their private use; they billed the state for such "legislative supplies" as hams, ladies' bonnets, perfumes, champagne, and (for one unfortunate member) a coffin. The cost of state printing in South Carolina between 1868 and

---

[12] Francis B. Simkins and Robert H. Woody: *South Carolina during Reconstruction* (Chapel Hill, 1932), pp. 90–111.

1876 was greater than the cost had been from 1789 to 1868. On one occasion, as the legislature was about to adjourn, a Democratic newspaper in Charleston wrote the following epitaph: "In life it has been unlovely, and in death it has not belied its record. As it lived, it has died—an uncouth, malformed and abortive monstrosity, its birth a blunder, its life a crime, and its death a blessing."

Meanwhile, the credit of some of the southern states was impaired as public debts mounted. In Florida the state debt increased from $524,000 in 1868 to $5,621,000 in 1874. In South Carolina a legislative committee reported that between 1868 and 1871 the state debt had increased from $5,403,000 to $15,768,000, but another committee insisted that it had increased to $29,159,000. By 1872 the debts of the eleven states of the former Confederacy had increased by approximately $132,000,000. The burden on taxpayers grew apace. Between 1860 and 1870 South Carolina's tax rate more than doubled, while property values declined by more than fifty per cent. In Tennessee a radical reported that during the first three years after the war taxes had increased sevenfold, though property had declined in value by one third. Throughout the South the tax burden was four times as great in 1870 as it had been in 1860. Such rates, complained many southern landholders, were confiscatory; and, indeed, taxes and other adversities of the postwar years forced some of them to sell all or part of their lands. Sympathy for South Carolina's planter aristocracy caused a northern conservative to ask: "When before did mankind behold the spectacle of a rich, high-spirited, cultivated, self-governed people suddenly cast down, bereft of their possessions, and put under the feet of the slaves they had held in bondage for centuries?"

High taxes, mounting debts, corruption, extravagance, and waste, however, do not constitute the complete record of the radical regimes. Moreover, to stop with a mere description of their misdeeds would be to leave all the crucial questions unanswered—to distort the picture and to view it without perspective. For example, if some of these governments contained an uncommonly large number of inexperienced or incompetent officeholders, if much of their support came from an untutored electorate, there was an obvious reason for this. Howard K. Beale, in a critique of various reconstruction legends, observed that the political rulers of the ante-bellum South "had fastened ignorance or inexperience on millions of whites as well as Negroes and that it was this ignorance and inexperience that caused trouble when Radicals were in power. . . . Wealthy Southerners . . . seldom recognized the need for general education of even the *white* masses."[13] Even in 1865 the men who won control of the Johnson governments showed little disposition to adopt the needed reforms. In South Carolina the Johnsonians did almost nothing to establish a system of public education, and at the time that the radicals came to power only one eighth of the white children of school age were attending school. The Negroes, of course, had been ignored entirely. It was probably no coincidence that the radicals made their poorest record in South Carolina, the state which had done the least for education and whose prewar government had been the least democratic.

As for the corruption of the radical governments, this phenomenon can be understood only when it is related to the times and to conditions throughout the country. One must remember that the administrations of President Grant set the moral tone for American government at all levels, national, state, and local. The best-remembered episodes of the Grant era are its numerous scandals—the Crédit Mobilier and the Whiskey Ring being the most spectacular of them—involving members of Congress as well as men in high administration circles.

[13] Howard K. Beale: "On Rewriting Reconstruction History," *American Historical Review*, XLV (1940), pp. 807–27.

There were, moreover, singularly corrupt Republican machines in control of various northern states, including Massachusetts, New York, and Pennsylvania. But corruption was not a phenomenon peculiar to Republicans of the Gilded Age, as the incredible operations of the so-called Tweed Ring in New York City will testify. Indeed, the thefts of public funds by this organization of white Tammany Democrats surpassed the total thefts in all the southern states combined.

Clearly the presence of carpetbaggers, scalawags, and Negroes in the radical governments was not in itself a sufficient explanation for the appearance of corruption. The South was being affected by the same forces that were affecting the rest of the country. No doubt the most important of these forces were, first, the social disorganization that accompanied the Civil War and hit the defeated and demoralized South with particular severity; and, second, the frantic economic expansion of the postwar period, when the American economy was dominated by a group of extraordinarily talented but irresponsible and undisciplined business leaders. These entrepreneurs' rather flexible standards of public morality provided an unfortunate model for the politicians.

Whether southern Democrats would have been able to resist the corrupting forces of the postwar decade had they remained in power is by no means certain. Perhaps the old ruling class would have been somewhat less vulnerable to the temptations of the Gilded Age, but the record of the Johnson governments was spotty at best. In Louisiana the conservative government created by Lincoln and Johnson wasted a great deal of public money. In Mississippi the state treasurer of the Johnson government embezzled $62,000. (This, by the way, far surpassed the record of the only thief in the radical government, who embezzled $7,000.) E. Merton Coulter discovered that during the era of reconstruction some Democratic officeholders "partook of the same financial characteristics as Radicals" and "took advantage of openings" when they found them. He quotes a Georgia editor who claimed that the extravagance and corruption "benefitted about as many Democrats as Republicans"; and he notes that a Democratic administration in Alabama "in lack of honesty differed little from the administrations of the Radicals between whom it was sandwiched."[14]

In the 1870's, when the South's so-called "natural leaders" returned to power, that troubled section did not always find itself governed by politicians distinguished for their selfless devotion to public service. In Mississippi the treasurer of the Democratic regime that overthrew the radicals in 1875 immediately embezzled $316,000, which broke all previous records! Elsewhere in the next decade eight other state treasurers were guilty of defalcations or embezzlements, including one in Louisiana who defrauded the state of more than a million dollars. Georgia was now ruled by a Democratic machine that was both ruthless and corrupt, a machine whose record was so offensive that by the end of the 1880's the white masses—some even willing to accept Negro support—rose in political rebellion against it. Reports about the Mississippi Democratic regime of the late nineteenth century are particularly colorful. One white editor charged that an "infamous ring" of "corrupt office-seekers . . . [had] debauched the ballot boxes . . . incurred useless and extravagant expenditures, raised the taxes, [and] plunged the State into debt." At the Mississippi constitutional convention of 1890, a white Democratic delegate gave the following description of politics in his state during the previous fifteen years: "Sir, it is no secret that there has not been a full vote and a fair count in Mississippi since 1875. . . . In other words we have been stuffing ballot boxes, committing perjury, and here and there in the state carrying the elections by fraud and violence.

[14] Coulter, *The South during Reconstruction*, pp. 152–3.

... No man can be in favor of perpetuating the election methods which have prevailed in Mississippi since 1875 who is not a moral idiot." Twelve years later an editor claimed that it would tax "the range and scope of the most fertile and versatile imagination to picture a condition of greater political rottenness" than existed in Mississippi at that time.

In the final analysis the crucial question about the extravagance and peculations of the radical governments is who the chief beneficiaries were. Only a few of the Negro and white radical leaders profited personally. The funds they stole, the money that prodigal legislators used for their own benefit, accounted for only a small fraction of the increased debts of the southern states. Nor did the total sums involved in bribery rise to a very impressive figure. And why was the tar brush applied exclusively to those who accepted the bribes and not to those who offered them? Under these circumstances is it really more blessed to give than to receive? For when the bribe-givers are identified we have located those who profited most from radical misdeeds. These men were the construction contractors, business speculators, and railroad promoters, or their agents, who hoped to persuade legislators to give them contracts, franchises, charters, subsidies, financial grants, or guarantees. They were the men who were also corrupting Congressmen and northern legislatures.

In Virginia much of the history of reconstruction concerns the rivalry of the Baltimore and Ohio Railroad and the Southside line for control of the Virginia and Tennessee Railroad. Both lines fought to control elections and legislators and backed whichever party promised to serve them, until, in 1870, the legislature ended the dispute by approving the consolidation plans of the Southside. Louisiana's reconstruction politics was enlivened by the attempt of a railroad and steamship corporation, headed by Charles Morgan of New York, to prevent the state from subsidizing a rival line between New Orleans and Houston, until Morgan forced the new line to take him in. In Alabama the North and South Railroad and the Alabama and Chattanooga Railroad battled for access to the ore deposits around Birmingham. In the process the competing groups corrupted both Johnson and radical legislatures, and in the latter both Republicans and Democrats.

Most of the debt increases in the southern states resulted not from the thefts and extravagance of radical legislators but from the grants and guarantees they gave to railroad promoters, among whom were always some native white Democrats. In Florida more than sixty per cent of the debt incurred by the radical regime was in the form of railroad guarantee bonds. In North Carolina the radical government, prodded by the carpetbagger Milton S. Littlefield, a skilled lobbyist, issued millions of dollars of railroad bonds. Among those who benefited were many of the state's "best citizens," including George W. Swepson, a local business promoter and Democrat. Most of Alabama's reconstruction debt—$18,000,000 out of $20,500,000—was in the form of state bonds issued to subsidize railroad construction, for which the state obtained liens upon railroad property. When one measure for state aid was before the Alabama legislature, many Democrats were among the lobbyists working for its passage. Yet, complained a radical, the Democrats who expect to profit from the bill "will use the argument that the Republican party had a majority in the Legislature, and will falsely, but hopefully, charge it upon Republicans as a partisan crime against the state."

Indeed, all of the southern states, except Mississippi, used state credit to finance the rebuilding and expansion of their railroads, for private sources of credit were inadequate. This policy had been developed before the war; it was continued under the Johnsonians; and in some cases when the Democrats overthrew the radicals there was no decline in the state's generosity to the railroads. While the radicals controlled the southern legislatures, not only they but many members of the Democratic minority as well voted for railroad bond issues. According to an historian of reconstruction in Louisiana, "Such measures were supported by members of both parties, often introduced by Democrats, in every case supported by a large majority of Democrats in both houses."[15] The subservience of many postwar southern legislatures to the demands of railroad and other business promoters is in some respects less shocking than pathetic. For it expressed a kind of blind faith shared by many Southerners of both parties that railroad building and industrialization would swiftly solve all of their section's problems. No price seemed too high for such a miracle.

In several states, for obviously partisan reasons, the actual increase in the size of the public debt was grossly exaggerated. In Mississippi, for example, there was a durable legend among white Democrats that the radicals had added $20,000,000 to the state debt, when, in fact, they added only $500,000. Mississippi radicals had guarded against extravagance by inserting a clause in the constitution of 1868 prohibiting the pledging of state funds to aid private corporations—a clause which the conservatives, incidentally, had opposed. In Alabama, apart from railroad bonds secured by railroad property, the radicals added only $2,500,000 to the state debt. They did not leave a debt of $30,000,000 as conservatives claimed. In most other states, when loans to the railroads are subtracted, the increases in state debts for which the radicals were responsible appear far less staggering.

As for taxes, one of the positive achievements of many of the radical governments was the adoption of more equitable tax systems which put a heavier burden upon the planters. Before the war the southern state governments had performed few public services and the tax burden on the landed class had been negligible; hence the vehement protests of the landholders were sometimes as much against radical tax policies as against the alleged waste of taxpayers' money. The restoration governments often brought with them a return to the old inequitable fiscal systems. In Mississippi the subsequent claim of the conservatives that they had reduced the tax burden the radicals had placed upon property holders was quite misleading. The conservatives did lower the state property tax, but, as a consequence, they found it necessary to shift various services and administrative burdens from the state to the counties. This led to an increase in the cost of county government, an increase in the rate of county taxes, and a net increase in total taxes, state and county, that Mississippi property holders had to pay.

As a matter of fact, taxes, government expenditures, and public debts were bound to increase in the southern states during the postwar years no matter who controlled them. For there was no way to escape the staggering job of physical reconstruction—the repair of public buildings, bridges, and roads—and costs had started to go up under the Johnson governments before the radicals came to power. So far from the expenditures of the reconstruction era being totally lost in waste and fraud, much of this physical reconstruction was accomplished while the radicals were in office. They expanded the state railroad systems, increased public services, and provided public school systems—in some states for the first time. Since schools and other public services were now provided for Negroes as well as for whites, a considerable increase in the cost of state government could hardly have been avoided. In Florida between 1869 and 1873 the number of children enrolled in the public schools trebled; in South Carolina between 1868 and 1876 the number increased from 30,000 to 123,000. The economies achieved by some of the restoration governments came at the expense of the schools

---

[15] Ella Lonn: *Reconstruction in Louisiana after 1868* (New York, 1918), pp. 36–7.

and various state institutions such as hospitals for the insane. The southern propertied classes had always been reluctant to tax themselves to support education or state hospitals, and in many cases the budget-cutting of the conservatives simply strangled them.

Thus radical rule, in spite of its shortcomings, was by no means synonymous with incompetence and corruption; far too many carpetbagger, scalawag, and Negro politicians made creditable records to warrant such a generalization. Moreover, conditions were improving in the final years of reconstruction. In South Carolina the last radical administration, that of the carpetbagger Governor Daniel H. Chamberlain, was dedicated to reform; in Florida "the financial steadiness of the state government increased toward the end of Republican rule."[16] In Mississippi the radicals made a remarkably good record. The first radical governor, James L. Alcorn, a scalawag, was a man of complete integrity; the second, Adelbert Ames, a carpetbagger, was honest, able, and sincerely devoted to protecting the rights of the Negroes. Mississippi radicals, according to Vernon L. Wharton, established a system of public education far better than any the state had known before; reorganized the state judiciary and adopted a new code of laws; renovated public buildings and constructed new ones, including state hospitals at Natchez and Vicksburg; and provided better state asylums for the blind, deaf, and dumb. The radicals, Wharton concludes, gave Mississippi "a government of greatly expanded functions at a cost that was low in comparison with that of almost any other state."[17] No major political scandal occurred in Mississippi during the years of radical rule—indeed, it was the best governed state in the postwar South. Yet white conservatives attacked the radical regime in Mississippi as violently as they did in South Carolina, which suggests that their basic grievance was not corruption but race policy.

Finally, granting all their mistakes, the radical governments were by far the most democratic the South had ever known. They were the only governments in southern history to extend to Negroes complete civil and political equality, and to try to protect them in the enjoyment of the rights they were granted. The overthrow of these governments was hardly a victory for political democracy, for the conservatives who "redeemed" the South tried to relegate poor men, Negro and white, once more to political obscurity. Near the end of the nineteenth century another battle for political democracy would have to be waged; but this time it would be, for the most part, a more limited version—for whites only. As for the Negroes, they would have to struggle for another century to regain what they had won—and then lost—in the years of radical reconstruction.

[16] William W. Davis: *The Civil War and Reconstruction in Florida* (New York, 1913), pp. 672–3.
[17] Wharton, *The Negro in Mississippi*, pp. 179–80.

3

Mississippi: The Past That Would Not Die

Walter Lord

Southern ex-Confederates opposed Radical rule in the South for several reasons. For one thing, the Republicans not only enfranchised the freedman, which for most ex-Confederates was bad enough, but then used the black vote to help keep the Republicans in power. For another, Southerners were convinced that the Republicans really were stealing everything in sight and really did want to "put the colored people on top." While this was simply not true, Southerners believed what they wanted to believe. For a few years Southern ex-Confederates tolerated Radical rule, then they began to move: in 1869 and 1870 they "redeemed" Tennessee and Virginia at the polls, voting out the Republican administrations there. Then, after Congress pardoned all ex-Confederates in 1872, the redeemers launched the restoration movement in earnest: they escorted Republicans—black and white alike—out of their towns and states, threatened to kill Negroes who tried to vote, and turned out by the thousands to elect redemption candidates in local and state elections. Contrary to Southern myth, there were not enough Federal troops stationed in the South to police the redemption movement and prevent violence. Moreover, most of the old Congressional Radicals were gone now (some had died, others had been voted out of office), and the new Republican leaders were tired of Reconstruction and simply looked the other way while Republican governments all over the South disintegrated. By 1876, all ex-Confederate states except Louisiana, South Carolina, and Florida had been restored to "home rule." When the presidential election of that year ended in a dispute between Republican candidate Rutherford Hayes and Democrat Samuel Tilden, Southern leaders agreed to a compromise: Hayes would become president and the Republicans, in exchange, would include a Southerner in Hayes' cabinet, provide the South with generous internal improvements, give Southerners control of Federal patronage in their section, and withdraw all Federal troops, thus leaving the Negro question in the hands of local white authorities. The conservatives who ran the redeemed South were happy indeed with the Compromise: they were chiefly interested in industrializing their section and believed that the Republican concessions would help them. Moreover, with the South again in control of its race relations, the redeemers intended to use the black vote to support their own economic programs. So, ironically enough, Reconstruction ended and the era of the New South began.

Walter Lord describes how the redemption movement worked in ex-Confederate Mississippi. He presents a fair if somewhat critical account of the Republican regime the redeemers overthrew, and goes on to examine the fate of blacks and whites alike in the grim, difficult years that followed.

Northern fury grew as one Southern state after another followed Mississippi's lead with Black Codes of their own. Finally, in 1867 Congress threw out President Johnson's Reconstruction program, launched a far harsher one of its own. The Confederate-dominated state governments

---

From pp. 13–35 in *The Past That Would Not Die* by Walter Lord. Copyright © 1965 by Walter Lord. By permission of Harper & Row, Publishers, Inc.

were scrapped and the South divided into five military districts, each under martial law. Negroes were given the vote, new constitutional conventions held. No state could get back in the Union until Congress approved its new government . . . until it granted Negro suffrage . . . until it passed the Fourteenth Amendment, guaranteeing (among other things) "equal protection of the laws" to all persons in a State.

Mississippi eventually knuckled under, but only after three more years of rear-guard defiance. By 1870, however, the state was "reconstructed," and by 1873 the local Radical Republicans were riding high. The electorate was 57% Negro—mostly illiterate and easily controlled. The legislature boasted 64 Negroes and 24 carpetbaggers. The Speaker of the House, the Lieutenant Governor, the Superintendent of Education were all Negroes. The new Reconstruction Governor himself was an ex-Union officer—General Adelbert Ames, a remote, tactless New Englander who seemed to stay away from Mississippi as much as he could.

It would later be argued that this state government turned in an impressive performance, and indeed there were many bright spots. The Negro legislators included at least 15 well-educated, conscientious clergymen. The carpetbaggers were often solid Middle Westerners who had come not to loot but to farm. The Negro troops had all been withdrawn, and only a token force of Federals remained—for instance, 59 at Natchez, 129 at Vicksburg, about 700 men altogether. The state debt never got out of hand. There was little stealing—the only major case involved the carpetbag treasurer of the state hospital in Natchez who took $7,251.81. And all the while important things were being accomplished—war-damaged bridges repaired, Northern innovations like free hospitals established, courts expanded to take care of the freedmen, and a whole public school system launched.

All this was done, but it would take the perspective of a century to appreciate it. At the time the white people of Mississippi felt only bitterness. They didn't care if most of the troops were gone; one blue uniform was too many. They didn't know about worthy projects; they only knew taxes were soaring—up 1300% in five years. They didn't notice that most key officials were honest; in their frayed poverty, they only saw any sign of waste: why, the state contingency fund even paid for Governor Ames' bedpan. And perhaps most important, they knew little about the conscientious work of many Negroes in top-level positions; they only knew their own county, where they were in daily contact, and that was often appalling.

Negro sheriffs, clerks and magistrates thrashed about in confusion and ignorance. In Warren County the sheriff couldn't write a simple return. In Issaquena County not one member of the Board of Supervisors—responsible for handling the county's business—could read a contract. There wasn't a justice of the peace in Madison County who could write a summons.

Petty corruption spread everywhere, often induced by light-fingered whites. Hinds County ran up a bigger printing bill in nine months than the whole state paid in 1866–67. The Wilkinson County Board of Supervisors shelled out $1,500 for three bridges—containing 4, 8 and 20 planks apiece. Vicksburg's Republican candidate for mayor staggered under 23 indictments. Nor were the dethroned Democrats entirely innocent. An officer in Vicksburg's clean government group was caught charging the city $500 to move a safe from the river to the courthouse.

Little matter—it was all the same to most of white Mississippi. Reconstruction was to blame, and that meant the Negroes. Free voting and the shadow of federal bayonets might make them invulnerable to ordinary political tactics, but there were other ways. . . .

The shifting seasons merged into one long blur of desperate violence. There was the sunny

October morning when Thomas Dabney's daughters heard a hail of shots and watched a Negro's riderless horse race across the Burleigh lawn . . . the starlit winter night in Monroe County when carpetbagger A. P. Huggins knelt on a lonely road as the KKK delivered 75 lashes with a stirrup strap . . . the bright March day when the Meridian courthouse erupted in rifle fire and the Radical judge fell dead on his bench . . . the lazy summer afternoons near Yazoo City when small boys drilled with real guns, wearing the sacred Confederate gray. An intercepted letter had told of 1,600 rifles buried at Satartia by Negroes "all prepared for Bussness."

Violence and more violence. Partly it was a case of bitterness and frustration, but it also went deeper than that. To Northern visitors it seemed that Mississippians were just made that way. Perhaps it was the lingering spirit of the frontier, or perhaps the lush, richly scented countryside itself: it so invited languor—and sudden storms.

"Life is not sacred as it is in the North," wrote correspondent Charles Nordhoff:

> Everybody goes armed, and every trifling dispute is ended with the pistol. The respectable people of the State do not discourage the practice of carrying arms as they should, they are astonishingly tolerant of acts which would arouse a Northern community to the utmost, and I believe that to this may be ascribed all that is bad in Mississippi—to an almost total lack of a right opinion; a willingness to see men take the law into their own hands; and, what is still worse, to let them openly defy the laws, without losing, apparently, the respect of the community.

In this atmosphere there was no hope for a man with the "wrong" attitude, whatever his credentials. At Aberdeen the town teacher, Dr. Ebart, had an impeccable Southern background, but he favored Negro schools, and that was the end of his job. On the other hand, if a man thought "right," anything could be forgiven. General C. E. Furlong was an ex-Union officer on the hated Sherman's staff, but he helped rout the Negroes at the Vicksburg riots —and became an instant hero.

The pressure was too much. The white Republicans soon melted away. Many crossed over to the Democratic fold; others fled North; only a few stood by the helpless mass of Negroes. The moderates, who might have been a third force, seemed mesmerized by the fury of the blast. "The quiet, sensible and orderly people," mused a puzzled Charles Nordhoff, "seem to have almost entirely resigned the power and supremacy which belong to them."

This was the picture by 1875, when the Democrats decided that the time had come formally to recapture the state. A skillfully conceived strategy—to be known as the Mississippi Plan and later copied throughout the South—took care of the two chief obstacles: the Negro majority and federal bayonets.

"We are determined to have an honest election if we have to stuff the ballot box to get it," shouted one Democratic leader, and this was only a small part of the plan. Newspaper notices warned Negroes that they would be thrown off their land if they voted the Republican ticket. Democratic "rifle clubs," usually sporting conspicuous red shirts, drilled endlessly near Negro sections. In Hinds, Lowndes and other counties, cannon appeared and fired "salutes" near Republican rallies.

The Negro voters got the message, but the Democrats still faced the danger of federal intervention. The trick here was not to let things go too far, and the Democratic campaign chairman, General J. Z. George, proved a past master at the art of intimidation by indirection. Still, it was a delicate tightrope. The embattled Governor Ames was calling Washington for help, and the slightest slip might bring in the federals. . . .

A crash of rifle fire scattered the 1,200 Negroes swarming around the Republican bar-

"EVERY THING POINTS TO A DEMOCRATIC VICTORY THIS FALL."—SOUTHERN PAPERS.

White redeemers keeping Negroes from voting. In 1875, native whites moved to "redeem" Mississippi from Republican rule. To accomplish it, they had to eliminate the Republicans' Negro vote, which they did through intimidation at the polls (as shown here) or through outright violence. (Courtesy of The New York Public Library, Astor, Lenox and Tilden Foundations.)

becue at the little town of Clinton on September 4. Here and there men fell—not all of them black. Two young white hecklers were cut down by return fire as they scurried from the scene. It seemed that Negroes too could feel strongly about elections.

Wholesale shooting began, and for days undeclared war raged around Clinton. On September 8 Governor Ames appealed to General Grant for troops to restore peace and supervise the coming elections. The whole future of Mississippi hung in the balance. A nod from the President, and all of General George's intricate strategy would fall apart.

Grant looked the other way. "The whole public are tired out with these annual autumnal outbreaks in the South," the President sighed, "and the great majority are ready now to condemn any interference on the part of the government." Word was passed to Governor Ames through Attorney General Pierrepont to try harder, exhaust his own resources before calling on Washington for aid.

It was really not Grant's fault. The country was indeed tired of Reconstruction, and the President was but echoing the national mood. Most people had never been for Negro civil rights in the first place. Freedom, yes; but that didn't necessarily mean all the privileges of citizenship. At the end of the war only six Northern states let Negroes vote, and in 1867 the District of Columbia rejected Negro suffrage 7,337 to 36. Nor did anyone feel the Fourteenth Amendment had much to do with education. In fact, stalwart Union states like New York, Pennsylvania and Ohio all had segregated schools. Congress itself set up a segregated school system in Washington only weeks after approving the Fourteenth Amendment.

These feelings were rising to the surface, now that the initial exhilaration of winning the war was over. Other forces were at work too: the implacable Thaddeus Stevens had died . . . anti-Grant Liberals were happy to attack everything about the Administration, including Reconstruction . . . Northern investors were anxious to resume "normal" relations with the South . . . the nation's eyes were turning to fresh, exciting visions in the Far West.

The new mood showed itself in various ways. Congress had indeed passed the Civil Rights Act of 1875 (protecting the Negro in public places like trains and restaurants), but it was the dying gasp of a lameduck session. Besides, it was a shaky victory. A school integration provision had been defeated; also a force bill giving the measure teeth. Even more significant, the Supreme Court was now nibbling away at the earlier Reconstruction Acts. And in the background came a steady chorus from the press, "Let the South solve its own problems." The President understood and gave the nation its way.

The Silver Cornet Band led the Jackson victory parade to General George's house on Election Night, November 2. The returns were rolling in, and huge Democratic majorities were piling up: Morton, 233 to 17 . . . Deasonville, 181 to 0 . . . Yazoo City, 4,052 to 7. In the end the Democrats carried 62 of the state's 74 counties. In the time-honored fashion of all political leaders everywhere, General George gave full credit to the rank and file "for the redemption of our common mother, Mississippi."

Governor Ames was a practical man. Exactly 146 days later, in exchange for the Democrats' withdrawing a set of impeachment charges, he resigned his office, packed his bags and left the state forever. In the word of the times, Mississippi had been "redeemed."

To Mississippi's Negroes redemption meant a loss of power but not the trappings. The men now running the state came from the old cotton-planting gentry, who got along well with their former slaves. Some of these leaders, like L. Q. C. Lamar, were far more interested in corporation law than 8-cent cotton, but they still had a tradition of *noblesse oblige* and gave the Negroes considerable leeway—as long as they were "good."

This arrangement was further cemented by a sort of gentlemen's agreement with Washington after the election of 1876. The South accepted Hayes' dubious claims to the Presidency, and in return the grateful Republicans adopted Grant's hands-off attitude as the new Administration line. The last troops were withdrawn and the old Confederacy left free to work out its own problems. But at the same time it was always understood that the Negroes would retain at least their surface gains. The redemption leaders happily agreed. In fact, the Jackson *Clarion* accepted the obligation on the very morning after the great 1875 victory. Observing that Negroes helped make the triumph possible, the paper declared that the state must now "carry out in good faith the pledges of equal and even justice to them and theirs in which they placed their confidence."

So the Negroes continued to vote and often held minor offices. Nor were they barred from most public places. The two races drank at the same bars and ate at the same restaurants, though at separate tables. In Jackson, Angelo's Hall echoed with Negro laughter one week, white the next. And when life was done, both races could rest together in Greenwood Cemetery.

With the Negro's role settled, Mississippi's redemption government launched a massive economy wave. The conservative land-owning leaders had been hit hardest by the staggering taxes of Reconstruction, and now they were determined to end all that. State expenditures were slashed from $1,430,000 in 1875 to $518,000 in 1876. Teachers' salaries alone fell from $55.47 a month in 1875 to $29.19 the following year.

In a way it was all justifiable. Mississippi remained wretchedly poor. In 1877 the state's per capita wealth was only $286, compared to $1,086 in the Northern states. Even as late as 1890 there were only 46 banks in the state with combined cash assets of but $635,000. The war had wiped out Mississippi, and there just seemed no way to get going again. In these days the idea of federal recovery aid was unknown—between 1865 and 1875 Washington spent $21 million on public works in Massachusetts and New York, but only $185,000 in Mississippi and Arkansas.

Still, whatever the justification, Mississippi paid a high price for her sweeping economies. Letting roads disintegrate meant even more stagnant communities. Appropriating merely $5,392 a year for health meant the end of nearly all services. Spending only $2 a head on schoolchildren (against $20 in Massachusetts) meant mounting illiteracy and a new generation utterly untrained to advance in life.

Nor was cost-cutting the answer. Despite all the economies, conditions continued to slide. From the mid-'70s to the early '90s cotton sagged from 11 cents to 5.8 cents a pound. Field hand pay fell from $15 to $12 a month . . . when there was any cash at all. More often there was the sharecropping system, which saw little money ever change hands. Yet the plantation owners themselves were certainly not getting rich. Under a vicious system of liens, they mortgaged their future crops for months or even years ahead to get the tools and supplies needed for tomorrow.

Everything seemed to conspire against Mississippi. While crop prices fell, the farmer's costs soared. Freight rates rigged in the East increased his shipping charges. Combinations like the jute-bagging trust raised the cost of his supplies. Ever higher tariffs added more to his burden. Creditors insisted that he plant only cotton; and shackled to a one-crop system, his land quickly eroded. Even nature joined the conspiracy—a flood, freeze or drought usually came along to spoil the all-too-few good years. Whether holding out in some paint-peeled mansion or hanging on in the squalor of a dog-trot cabin, most Mississippians knew only the bitterest poverty.

The state's landed leaders proved utterly unable to cope with the situation. They came from the lowlands—the cotton belt that ran everything in prewar days. They owed their authority to an odd combination of ante bellum nostalgia and redemption heroics—certainly not new ideas. They easily took to the laissez-faire views of Eastern business—tax concessions, hard money, railroad grabs like the Texas-Pacific. They shied away from new panaceas like government regulation and flexible currency. Their most lustrous figure, L. Q. C. Lamar, shuddered at the Greenback movement's "boundless, bottomless, and brainless schemes."

Such men neither understood nor even liked the upcountry farmers who scratched away at the red clay hills to the east. Desperately these red-necks—along with a growing number of poor white tenants all over the state—turned to new and more radical sources of hope, like the Farmers' Alliance and later the Populists.

And all the while they smoldered with growing hate—hatred for the Yankee banks and railroads that squeezed them so tightly . . . hatred for the Black Belt leaders who seemed to care so little . . . and, above all, hatred for the Negroes to whose level they were sinking so fast.

Jim Crow laws began to sprout . . . the first in twenty years. In 1888 Mississippi became the first state to have segregated waiting rooms. In 1890 Jackson extended the racial barrier beyond death by establishing a separate cemetery for Negroes. The rules grew even more strict as the margin narrowed between white and colored living standards. If race was all the whites might have left, then all the more reason to guard this sacred heritage. Woe to the Negro who flirted with crossing the line.

Lynchings multiplied at a fearful rate—nobody knows how many, for the press handled the incidents as casually as the weather. "Four Negroes were lynched at Grenada last week," remarked the Raymond *Times* on July 18, 1885, "also one at Oxford." That was the whole item.

With Mississippi in this mood, it certainly didn't help matters when the big landowners met the red-neck challenge with thousands of Negro votes from the black counties they controlled. A weird political duel developed as the '80s wore on, utterly lacking in logic or principle. The old conservative leaders represented traditional white supremacy, yet relied on Negro votes to hold their power. The mass of poor whites had much in common with the Negro, yet fought him as a mortal enemy. The remaining Republicans in the state stood for the Negro's freedom, yet deserted him as a hopeless handicap. No wonder the Negro himself soon lost interest. Untrained in politics anyhow, he found Mississippi's brand far too confusing. Usually he just sold his vote to the highest bidder or was thrust aside while someone else cast it for him.

The situation proved too sordid to last. In 1890 a special convention assembled in Jackson to draw up a new state constitution. "Let us have the questionable and shameful methods of controlling the ballot box stopped," urged Delegate Miller of Leake County. "These methods are demoralizing to our young men and there is general outcry that they must cease."

The solution, most people felt, was to take away the Negro's vote. Even the Black Belt leaders now agreed—the advantage it gave them was outweighed by the cost (usually a dollar a vote) and the ever-haunting possibility that the Negroes might some day decide to go back into politics for themselves. It was, of course, a little odd to keep Negroes from casting votes in order to stop white people from stealing them, but nobody worried too much about that. A far greater problem was how to do it. The Fifteenth Amendment specifically guaranteed the Negroes the right to vote.

Clearly, the trick was to frame a set of qualifications that would technically apply to everybody but actually eliminate the Negro without touching the white. A poll tax alone was not enough—it might discourage more whites than

Negroes. Nor would a literacy test do—there were thousands of good white voters who couldn't even write their names. In the end the convention came up with a series of devices which were, in the words of one delegate, "a monument to the resourcefulness of the human mind."

Most important were the new qualifications: all voters had to be able to read any section of the state constitution, or understand it when read to him, or give it a reasonable interpretation. This, of course, dumped the final decision into the lap of the examining registrar . . . who would know exactly what to do.

Reregistration began immediately. In 1885 over 1,600 Negroes had qualified in Panola County; by 1896 the figure stood at 114. The same thing happened everywhere: in Coahoma County only 4% of its once-eligible Negroes now could vote; in De Soto only 5%; in Tunica only 2%. Loyal Mississippians held their breath—how would the nation react to this giant wink at the Fifteenth Amendment?

They need not have worried. The White House was in friendly hands—first under the conservative Grover Cleveland, later under the benign William McKinley. Congress was no threat either—in 1894 it repealed most of the remaining civil rights laws. The Western Populists were bitter at the Negroes for sticking by their old masters. The Southern progressives felt that white solidarity would weld all classes more closely together. Eastern liberals recalled the reactionary leaders who engineered Reconstruction—and found it easy to sympathize with Mississippi. And above all, there was the American mood—a moment of bursting national pride and pious imperialism. As the liberal *Atlantic Monthly* noted with a touch of gentle irony: "If the stronger and cleverer race is free to impose its will upon the 'new-caught sullen peoples' on the other side of the globe, why not in South Carolina and Mississippi?"

The Supreme Court added its blessing in 1898. In *Williams* v. *Mississippi* the justices solemnly declared there was no reason to suppose that the state's new voting qualifications were aimed especially at Negroes. It was a predictable decision, for the Court had already shown its hand. In 1883 it had greatly diluted the civil rights laws by ruling that the Fourteenth Amendment only protected a Negro against discrimination by a state, not by private parties like stores and restaurants. In 1896 the Court went a step further: it said that a Louisiana Negro named Homer Plessy had no right to ride in a railroad car reserved by state law for whites as long as there were also "separate but equal" accommodations for Negroes. This time a state was clearly involved, but the Court maintained there was no discrimination. The Fourteenth Amendment required equality, Justice Brown conceded, but "in the nature of things it could not have been intended to abolish distinctions based on color. . . ."

"Our Constitution is color-blind," countered Justice John Marshall Harlan in a lone dissent, "and neither knows nor tolerates classes among citizens." He went on for two pages but caused little stir. The majority opinion in *Plessy* v. *Ferguson* prevailed. "Separate but equal" was good enough for most Americans.

As the new century dawned, it was clear that the Negro—stripped of his gains, abandoned by the courts and rejected by the country—was in a highly vulnerable position. And for the Negro in Mississippi—the state which had invented the Black Codes in 1865, pioneered the "Mississippi Plan" in 1875 and led the way to disenfranchisement in 1890—the future looked bleak indeed. If it needed any underlining, that came from Massachusetts where Adelbert Ames, Mississippi's ex-Reconstruction governor, pondered in retirement. For championing Negro rights, he had been forced out and nearly impeached; but by 1900 even he had finally come around. "I did not know then," he reflected, "that a superior race will not submit to the government of an inferior one."

The "superior race" was taking no chances. When Mississippi fell under the progressive spell and adopted direct primaries in 1902, the Democratic leaders made sure they were open to whites only. It seemed the progressive movement had nothing to do with the Negro. In fact, it actually worked against him, for the red-necks and poor whites who supported the trend most strongly were still the very people who feared and hated the Negro most bitterly.

This was fully appreciated by the eloquent man with the flowing locks who ran for governor in 1903. James K. Vardaman lived in Greenwood in the cotton-planting Delta, but his appeal lay with the people of the hills. He campaigned in a great lumber wagon drawn by eight white oxen, adding drama and excitement where before there was none. He pulled coarse, vulgar jokes to the delight of an electorate weary of proper aristocrats. And above all, he struck the right chord. "The Negro, like the mule," he cracked, "has neither pride of ancestry nor hope of posterity."

Vardaman's appeal proved irresistible. He was swept into office in an election that saw the triumph of the hills over the lowland conservatives who had so long ruled the state. And out with the aristocrats went their sometimes apparent sense of *noblesse oblige* toward the Negroes.

"The way to control the nigger is to whip him when he does not obey without it," thundered Vardaman, "and another is never to pay him more wages than is actually necessary to buy food and clothing." It soon turned out there were other ways too. The Holly Springs Normal School—the state's only institution for training Negro teachers—had an annual budget of only $2,500 and hadn't been painted for 17 years. But even that was too much. Vardaman swiftly vetoed the 1904 appropriation: "I killed the bill and I killed the school!"

Tighter Jim Crow laws cemented the Negro in his place. One new measure segregated streetcars for the first time; another drew the color line in hospitals; another required Negro nurses for Negro patients.

Nor could the Negro look to his old white friends for any real help. The conservative leaders, seeing how the wind was blowing, vied for red-neck support with ever more incendiary speeches. Campaigning against Vardaman for the Senate in 1907, John Sharp Williams—a patrician to his fingertips—reassured crowds that he matched his opponent on racial matters. All men running for office, declared Williams, "are paying no more attention to Negroes in Mississippi than they are to the mules tied up by those Negroes."

For the next thirty years Mississippi's white leadership never relaxed its pressure. In 1922 a new Jim Crow law kept up with the times by segregating taxis. In 1930 another new law prohibited "publishing, printing or circulating any literature in favor of or urging inter-racial marriage or social equality." And if anybody stepped out of line, there were always stronger measures. Lynching happily declined all through the '20s (thanks mainly to the efforts of the very Southern women it was supposed to protect), but the figure was still high—and Mississippi led the union.

These were the days of the revived KKK, fundamentalism and the Scopes trial, and it followed that there was less patience than ever with Negro education. In 1930 there were about 3,700 colored schools in the state, but 3,243 of them were one- and two-teacher affairs, often housed in old churches, sheds and cabins. Half had no desks, and the blackboard was usually a strip of oilcloth tacked to a wall. Perhaps it made little difference, for 2,719 of the teachers had never finished high school—half of those in Sunflower County tested around the fourth-grade level.

On those rare occasions when public money filtered down, it was quickly siphoned off for white use. For 1928–29 Bolivar County received $99,368.24 from the state school fund, earmarked for the county's Negro children. A hungry Board of Education quickly diverted $50,562.60 of this amount to white schools instead, then added all the available local tax money. In the end Bolivar spent $45.55 per white child, $1.08 per Negro. At that, neither got much of an education—during the same period California's rate was $115 per child.

The depression only made matters worse. New Deal pump-priming rarely touched the Mississippi Negro. Through 1935, for instance, there was only one PWA Negro school project in the state. Mississippi itself was already reeling from floods and the crop-killing boll weevil of the '20s. Now with cotton sinking to 5 cents a pound, nobody could spare any money for "niggers." Negro wages fell to 10 cents an hour.

World War II saw better jobs and pay, but no change in status. And with peace, Mississippians were no different from many others—they only wanted to get back to the way things used to be. An official committee examining Alcorn, the state Negro college in Claiborne County, was horrified to detect strong traces of a liberal arts program. "There has been too much of a nonrealistic feeling that the purpose of a college education has been to prepare youth for white collar jobs," scolded the committee. It urged that Alcorn return to the program established in 1878 and concentrate again on things like sanitation and domestic arts—"skills which actually prepare people to make a living."

Negro voting also called for attention. The Supreme Court had outlawed the white primary in 1944, and now the returning Negro veterans were showing signs of interest. Running in the Democratic primary for the Senate in 1946, Theodore Bilbo—the spiritual heir of James K. Vardaman—called on "every red-blooded American to get out and see that no nigger votes."

When Negro clergyman T. C. Carter tried to cast his ballot at Louisville that July, four white men twice blocked his way. When Mr. and Mrs. V. R. Collier attempted to vote at Pass Christian, a crowd of men threw Collier down and threatened to kill him if he tried to vote that day. It happened all over the state.

"A certain patience," suggested the gentle Mississippi poet, William Alexander Percy, "might well be extended to the South; if not in justice, in courtesy." Nor was Percy the only moderate to ask for more time as the turbulent '40s unfolded.

The trouble was, "more time" all too often meant that the Negro simply drifted farther back. When Mississippi tightened its voting qualifications in 1890, it was argued that the Negroes were not yet ready, since 60% were illiterate. By 1950 the figure had fallen to less than 9%, but fewer Negroes than ever were allowed to register.

In Panola County, where the number of Negro voters had dropped from 1,600 to 385 in the 1890s, the number was now down to 2. During the same period the figure in Holmes County fell from 434 to 8; in Tallahatchie County from 245 to 1.

Nor did "more time" mean more money for Negro education. In 1886 Negro teachers averaged $27.40 a month; in 1939 the figure was $28—a gain of 60 cents. During the '40s take-home pay increased, but so did the gap between Negro and white teachers. The ratio stood at three to two in 1890, but 2.5 to one in 1950. In 1900 the state spent three times as much on a white student as it did on a Negro; in 1950 the margin was the same.

Moreover, the quality of Negro education fell steadily behind. In 1945 half the teachers still hadn't been through high school. There were only seven regionally accredited Negro schools in the whole state. A Negro boy had less than one chance in 20 of going to a school where he could learn a foreign language.

"More time" was equally meaningless on jobs. In 1902 a Negro church in Jackson listed members in a wide range of interesting occupations—a bakery owner, a fashionable dress designer, a representative of tailoring firms, numerous painters and craftsmen. Negro William H. Smallwood was Jackson's leading expert on leases and deeds in the '80s. In 1905 Greenville listed numerous Negro doctors, lawyers, bookstore owners, cotton samplers. By 1950 all this was over. White workers had crowded out Negroes and monopolized the field. After World War II Greenville experimented with an imaginative plan for training Negro auto mechanics, but the results were disappointing. It proved impossible to place them.

In social life "more time" also found the Negro drifting back. In the 1890s prominent Negroes like J. R. Lynch had lived on Capitol Street, not far from General George himself. By 1950 this was unheard of. All the time, an elaborate system of social taboos continued to multiply, putting the Negro ever more firmly in his place—don't shake hands with one . . . don't let one in the front door . . . and never, never call one "Mr." or "Mrs."

Oddly enough, many Mississipians remained very fond of the Negro. "It is an historic fact," declared Senator James Eastland, "that the Southern white people are the best friends he has ever had." An overstatement, but still it was true that countless white people took care of Negroes when they were sick, fed them when they were hungry and lent them money when they were broke. To a sensitive person like Will Percy, life seemed an endless stream of good deeds: one day he would offer legal help to Nick, a field hand arrested for a shooting scrape . . . the next, he would have to forgive Lege, the gardener, for wrecking the Percy car . . . then he would be intervening for Jim, a houseboy in trouble with the sheriff.

The picture wasn't all that rosy. Even those whites who felt most deeply the spirit of *noblesse oblige* had to trim their sails during hard times. And more and more whites didn't have the spirit at all, as lumbering and other industries crowded out the plantation tradition.

In any case, the Negro had to be "good" and "know his place." Still, it was often a happy relationship, and to most visitors the mystery was how so many white people could be so devoted to the Negro and at the same time so firmly hold him down.

A Clarksdale housewife inadvertently supplied an "answer," while trying to set a newcomer straight. "People up North," she explained, "just don't realize all the things we do for Negroes. We don't hate them at all. We're always untangling their problems—which is anything but easy, for after all they're animals, simply animals." A farmer from Calhoun County put it a little more bluntly: "The best way to understand how people here feel is to put it the way my daddy put it: the nigger has no soul. He is like a duck, a chicken or a mule. He just hasn't got a soul." Certainly not all people in Mississippi felt this way, but a surprisingly large number—probably a majority—unconsciously agreed with the red-neck logger who summed it all up: "Let's face it; the nigger is a high-class beast."

Once this curious premise was accepted—that the Negro was something less than a real person—everything fell into place. It explained why the people of Marks were so proud of the paved streets in the Negro section—something that might elsewhere be taken for granted. It explained why a Delta housewife felt she was making a major concession when she said she was willing to let her cook use her bomb shelter in the event of nuclear war. It explained why a different standard of justice was meted out to Negroes—lenience when the matter was between Negroes, harsh treatment when a white was involved. And, of course, it explained the whole strange mixture of kindness and meanness. A man might feel kindly toward a "duck, a chicken or a mule," but he certainly wouldn't want to vote with one, or especially send his child to school with one.

Above all, it explained white Mississippi's deepest fear and obsession: "the mongrelization of the race." If a man really believed a Negro was "like a duck, a chicken or a mule," he understandably didn't want his daughter to marry one. And, paradoxically enough, he seemed sure she might. The inevitable progression was still at work: incidental contact at school must lead to social contact outside, which in turn must lead to mixed marriages and inferior offspring.

It did no good to point out that, even assuming any basis for such weird racial theories, all the experience of integrated schools elsewhere indicated that there would be no significant trend to intermarriage. The standard answer: why take any chances? "We just don't want any of those black babies with blue eyes," declared a plantation manager near Perthshire.

Nor did it do any good to suggest that Negroes might want to go to integrated schools simply to get a better education. The average Mississippian was convinced that sex was all "they" thought about. Social equality still meant what Thomas Nelson Page said in 1904: "To the ignorant and brutal young Negro, it signifies but one thing: the opportunity to enjoy, equally with the white man, the privilege of cohabiting with white women."

And the feeling was compounded by a constant, ceaseless fear of Negro rape. Visitors couldn't hope to understand how deeply this gnawed, for it stemmed from a combination of unique, mysterious forces: the dread of being overwhelmed, the sanctity of Southern Womanhood, whispered superstitions of Negro sexual prowess. Actually, there was little danger. As that astute observer William J. Cash remarked, a Southern white woman had less chance of being raped by a Negro than of being struck by lightning. Yet there were occasional cases, and the barest hint was enough to send most Mississippians racing to man the barriers of total segregation.

Statistics seemed to back up the white state of mind. The Negroes did indeed have a far higher crime rate. Although they were only 45% of the population by 1950, they committed 75% of the state's crime. But was this a basic quality or a symptom of something else? There was almost an invitation to lawlessness in a legal system that saw a Negro in Sunflower County fire five shots at another and get off with a $10 fine.

White Mississippians also had reason to worry about Negro sexual customs. Some 25% of colored births were illegitimate; the rate of venereal disease among Negroes was 15 times that among whites. Yet here too the question arose, was this inherent or more likely a matter of living conditions? After all, as State Judge Tom Brady explained matters, "We have not and do not punish the Negro—except in rare instances—for desertion, illegitimacy or bigamy." With the brakes off, no wonder the girls' basketball coach at a Calhoun County Negro high school once saw his season ruined because the team was pregnant.

The whites also pointed out that Negro children did far worse at school. In 1949, for instance, when a group of colored pupils took the Metropolitan Achievement Test in Sunflower County, they scored two full grades behind the white norms. But it happens that most of the Negro children had no desks; many sat on the floor; some had teachers who couldn't do fractions; and all belonged to a school system that the University of Mississippi's Bureau of Educational Research labeled "a dreary spectacle."

Mississippi, of course, was not alone in this pattern of white and Negro relationships. There were similarities in all the Southern states, and, for that matter, the rest of the country too. Still, there were also differences—differences that by 1950 made Mississippi a special case.

One obvious difference lay in population. In 1950 Mississippi was 45% Negro—the highest percentage in the country. True, the figure was slipping—some 87,187 Negroes had left the state since 1940—but the percentage was still high compared to other states. Besides, in some parts of Mississippi the whites were far outnumbered. Tunica County, for instance, had

17,700 Negroes, only 3,900 whites. And there was always the past—those fearful days when a defeated, shattered, white minority lived in constant dread of an untrained but politically powerful Negro majority. Mississippians had long memories, and the specter of those times lingered on.

A more subtle but more important difference was the state's special brand of poverty. In 1950 Mississippi was easily the poorest in the Union. Her citizens had only half the per capita income enjoyed by the rest of the country. Both races suffered—in Issaquena County even the whites averaged only $967 a year. The state's Agricultural and Industrial Board worked hard to bring in new business, but its very sales pitch hinged on conditions remaining depressed. One brochure boasted, "There are available at least two applicants for each new job offered." The fight for jobs—the battle to hold the few advantages left—made the white people all the more determined to hold the line against any sign of Negro advance.

Still another distinction was the state's low level of education. Poor people can't afford the best schools, and Mississippi was no exception. In 1950 the state paid the lowest faculty salaries in the Southeast, and the ablest teachers naturally drifted elsewhere. Poverty also meant that many people couldn't afford to go to school at all—half the state's adults had only eight years' exposure. Nor was low Negro attendance by any means the whole explanation: the whites alone averaged less than ten years. The significance of all this emerged in many ways. Mississippi had the fewest number of patents for its population of any state in the Union . . . the fewest doctors and nurses . . . the next to smallest number of dentists . . . the poorest trained teachers. There was, in short, a striking lack of educated leadership.

Life in Mississippi also had a stagnant quality that made the state a special case. Jackson, Greenville, the Gulf Coast might be thriving, but their shiny motels were deceptive. Far more meaningful were the scores of sleepy little towns quietly withering away. In 1950 county seats like Mayersville, Carrollton and Pittsboro had fewer people than any time since 1900. Whole counties were fading away. Carroll, Jefferson, Claiborne, all had less population than in 1840. The downward trend had been going on for some time, but the new mechanical cotton picker gave it an extra shove. The machine was a godsend to the big plantations, but it doomed thousands of field hands, dirt farmers and the whole network of stores and suppliers that kept them going. Some ten people were leaving Mississippi for every one person coming in, and, still worse, those departing included 75% of the state's college graduates.

The strange emptiness of Mississippi gave the place an air of isolation that was another of its special qualities. Even Alaska had a greater percentage of its population in urban areas. There were no really large cities—in 1950 the capital, Jackson, was still under 100,000. Nor was there any of the culture that serves as a link with the outside world. Jackson's only bookstore was run by the Baptist Church and limited largely to religious topics. Elsewhere there wasn't even that—Oxford, the state's center of learning, had no regular bookstores at all. Nor were there adequate libraries to fill the gap. Twenty-seven of the state's counties had no library that met any standards whatsoever. Even the newsstands had little to offer; they rarely displayed the better-known national magazines, featured instead a host of titles devoted to lust and horror.

As a result, Mississippi inevitably took little interest in the rest of America, and by 1950 the rest of America took little interest in her. Poverty and isolation had done their work. In fact, the last major Presidential candidate who had bothered to visit the state was Henry Clay.

All this led to an enormously self-contained existence; and that, in turn, became one more difference that set Mississippi apart from the rest of the Union. In the words of a native, "Mississippi is not a state but a club." Everybody seemed to know everybody else. Doors always seemed open—all a visitor needed was a name that clicked. Personal relationships were the key to everything.

This small world gave Mississippians certain virtues fast disappearing from the rest of the world. People were immensely courteous to one another and never seemed particularly hurried. A man would go ten miles out of his way to show a stranger the right road. The smallest purchase wound up with a friendly clerk's "Come back and see us some time."

But by the same token, everybody knew exactly what everybody else was doing. A 70-mile drive through the Delta elicited the most minute details about the homes along the way: this man had a new brown dog . . . that man sold a field last week . . . the family over there was fighting with the insurance adjuster. It was impossible to take a step—or a stand—in Mississippi without the rest of the state instantly knowing about it.

The tendency to conform was enormous. Far more than elsewhere, men wore the same necktie (dark), drove the same cars (cream-colored), lived for the same football games (Ole Miss—LSU), and above all belonged to the same party (Democratic). The state's allegiance was never better expressed than in 1890, when Chancellor Edward Mayer of the University of Mississippi declared, "I have never failed to vote Democratic, I have never scratched a ticket, and I would not, no matter whom the party might nominate for its candidate."

The New Deal did indeed strain the allegiance, but characteristically Mississippi still conformed at the moment of truth—election day. When the state finally strayed from the fold in 1948, the rationalization developed that Mississippi was still holding to the true faith; it was the rest of the Democrats who had bolted away.

The more postwar America changed, the more Mississippi retreated into its own self-contained little world. Bypassed by the march of events, the state saw little connection between itself and all the strange new things going on—the UN, Marshall Plan, NATO, welfare measures at home. All this meant only more centralized government, and the people were in no mood for that—states' rights were the very heart of the South's solution to the race problem. Mississippi became increasingly suspicious of "outside interference" and increasingly proud of its own way of life. Once again thoughts turned to the glorious past. . . .

"For any Southern boy fourteen years old," wrote Mississippi's own William Faulkner, "not once but whenever he wants it, there is the instant when it's still not two o'clock on that July afternoon in 1863, the brigades are in position behind the rail fence, the guns are laid and ready in the woods . . . and it's all in the balance, it hasn't happened yet."

It might only be added that in the Mississippi of 1950 the daydream was not limited to 14-year-old boys. Every age lived with the fantasy. The state officially observed Confederate Memorial Day, Lee's and Jefferson Davis' birthday . . . while studiously ignoring Lincoln and the national Memorial Day. Jackson boasted its Rebel Concrete Company, Rebel Garment Company, Rebel Roofing & Metal Company. Hattiesburg had its Rebel Theatre, Oxford its Rebel Cosmetology College. Schoolboys loved to dress up in Confederate uniforms . . . older men wistfully told how it all might have been different if only Pemberton had held at Champion Hill. ("It still breaks my heart when I think of it," one confessed.) Confederate flags hung from porches all over the state; and in case anyone ever needed reminding, there was always the reproachful gaze of the noble stone soldier who stood atop the Confederate monument in every courthouse square. . . .

Lord God of hosts,
Be with us yet,
Lest we forget,
Lest we forget.

II Thunder in the West

4

Bury My Heart at Wounded Knee

D. Alexander Brown

In the forty years after the Civil War, American pioneers conquered and exploited an immense inner frontier that lay between California and the Mississippi River. It was an area as diverse as it was expansive, a region of windy prairies, towering mountains, painted deserts, and awesome canyons. Heading east out of California or west from the Mississippi, Americans by the thousands poured into this great heartland, laying off cattle ranches and farms, building towns and mining camps, and creating a variety of local and state governments. People moved to the frontier for several reasons: to start a new life, seek glory and adventure, strike it rich in a single, fabulous windfall, and prevail over the West's challenging environment.

Still, the winning of the West was not all romance. For whites who went there cheerfully infiltrated Indian lands and hunting grounds, and white and Indian conflicts broke out all across the frontier line, thus opening a gruesome chapter in the westward movement after the Civil War. The fact was that most white Americans regarded Indians as pagans who deserved Christian violence. If they stood in the way of people who knew how to use the soil (most Western Indians, after all, were nomads who were abysmally ignorant about agriculture), they should be exterminated. And so, terrible wars broke out whenever whites and Indians came into contact. Trying to reduce the violence, the federal government in 1867 decided to confine the Indians to small, remote reservations in areas of the West spurned by white men. As several writers have pointed out, the white man's treatment of the Indians in the late 1860s contrasted sharply with the way he treated the Negroes of the South. The Congress that approved the small reservation policy, with its philosophy of strict segregation and inequality for Western Indians, was the same Congress that attempted to give Southern blacks equal political rights with white people.

But many tribes refused to surrender their ancient hunting grounds, refused to be herded onto reservations and made to "walk the white man's road," and they fought back savagely. Between 1869 and 1876, over two hundred pitched battles took place between the Indians and the United States Army. Perhaps the most famous was the fight at the Little Bighorn, where an army of Sioux and their Indian allies massacred George Armstrong Custer and 265 men from the United States 7th Cavalry. But the Indian victory was short-lived. In the fall of 1876, the United States Army trapped the Sioux and compelled them to surrender. They ended up in out-of-the-way reservations in the Dakota Territory.

Extermination of the buffalo, not military conquest, finally ended Indian resistance. For centuries Plains Indians had relied on the buffalo for the very sustenance of life: they ate buffalo meat and used the hides for clothing and shelter. But in the 1870s white hunters started killing the animals by the millions. Some did it to protect overland trains from stampedes; others shot the bison for the sport of it. Between 1872 and 1876, white marksmen mowed down 3,000,000 buffalo a year. By 1878 the animal was virtually extinct.

Faced with starvation, the Indians had no choice but to abandon their way of life and submit to segregation on small reservations in the Dakotas, in Oklahoma, New Mexico, Oregon, Idaho, and Montana. By 1890, thanks to decades of bloodletting with white Americans, scarcely 200,000 Indians remained in the United States.

Defeated and broken in spirit, many reservation Indians turned to religion for comfort in a hostile world. The Sioux took up the Ghost Dance, a sacred ritual that reaffirmed tribal unity and prophesied the return of the buffalo. Intimidated by such a "frightful conglomeration of rituals and customs," the United States government outlawed the Ghost Dance. But the Sioux went on dancing anyway. D. Alexander Brown describes the tragic consequences.

You may bury my body in Sussex grass,
You may bury my tongue at Champmédy.
I shall not be there. I shall rise and pass.
Bury my heart at Wounded Knee.
STEPHEN VINCENT BENÉT

During the decade following Custer's defeat on the Little Bighorn, the warring tribes of Indians in the American West were gradually shorn of their power and locked within reservations. Many of the great chiefs and mighty warriors were dead. The buffalo and antelope had almost vanished; the old ceremonies of the tribes were becoming rituals without meaning.

For the survivors it was a time without spirit, a time of despair. One might swap a few skins for the trader's crazy-water and dream of the old days, the days of the splendid hunts and fighting. One might make big talk for a little while but that was all.

In such times, defeated peoples search for redeemers, and soon on many reservations there were dreamers and swooning men to tell of approaching redemption. Most of them were great fakers, but some were sincere in their vagaries and their visions.

As early as 1870 the defeated Paiutes of Nevada had found a redeemer in Tavibo, a petty chief, who claimed to have talked with divine spirits in the mountains. All the people of the earth were to be swallowed up, the spirits told him, but at the end of three days the Indians would be resurrected in the flesh to live forever. They would enjoy the earth which was rightfully theirs. Once again there would be plenty of game, fish, and piñon nuts. Best of all, the white invaders would be destroyed forever.

When Tavibo first told his vision to the Paiutes, he attracted very few believers. But gradually he added other features to his story, and he went up into the mountains again for further revelations. It was necessary for the Indians to dance, everywhere; to keep on dancing. This would please the Great Spirit, who would come and destroy the white men and bring back the buffalo.

Tavibo died shortly after he told of these things, but his son, Wovoka, was considered the natural inheritor of his powers by those Paiutes who believed in the new religion of the dance. Wovoka, who was only 14 when his father died, was taken into the family of a white farmer, David Wilson, and was given the name of Jack Wilson. In his new home the boy's imagination was fired by Bible stories told to him; he was fascinated by the white man's God.

On New Year's Day of 1889, a vision came to Jack Wilson (Wovoka) while he lay ill with fever; he dreamed that he died and went to heaven. God spoke to him, commanding him to take a message back to earth. Wovoka was to tell the Indians that if they would follow God's commandment and perform a "ghost dance" at regular intervals their old days of happiness and prosperity would be returned to them.

From pp. 5–9, 11–13, 16 in "The Ghost Dance and Battle of Wounded Knee" by D. Alexander Brown. Copyrighted 1966—AMERICAN HISTORY *Illustrated*, published 10 times annually by The National Historical Society, Gettysburg, Pennsylvania.

In January 1889 on the Walker Lake Reservation, the first Ghost Dance was performed on a dancing ground selected by Wovoka. The ceremony was simple, the Paiutes forming into a large circle, dancing and chanting as they constricted the circle, the circle widening and constricting again and again. The dancing continued for a day and a night, Wovoka sitting in the middle of the circle before a large fire with his head bowed. He wore a white striped coat, a pair of trousers, and moccasins. On the second day he stopped the dancing and described the visions that God had sent to him. Then the dancing commenced again and lasted for three more days.

When a second dance was held soon afterward, several Utes visited the ceremony out of curiosity. Returning to their reservations, the Utes told the neighboring Bannocks about what they had seen. The Bannocks sent emissaries to the next dance, and within a few weeks the Shoshones at Fort Hall Reservation saw a ritual staged by the Bannocks. They were so impressed they sent a delegation to Nevada to learn the new religion from Wovoka himself.

Perhaps more than any other of the tribes, the Cheyenne and Sioux felt the need for a messiah who could lead them back to their days of glory. After the story of Wovoka was carried swiftly to their reservations, several medicine men decided to make pilgrimages. It was a mark of prestige for them to travel by railroad, and as soon as they could raise enough money, they purchased tickets to Nevada. In the autumn of 1889, a Cheyenne named Porcupine made the journey, and a short time later Short Bull, Kicking Bear, and other Sioux leaders traveled all the way from Dakota.

The Sioux accepted the Ghost Dance religion with more fervor than any of the other tribes. On their return to the Dakota reservations, each delegate tried to outdo the others in describing the wonders of the messiah. Wovoka came down from heaven in a cloud, they said. He showed them a vision of all the nations of Indians coming home. The earth would be covered with dust and then a new earth would come upon the old. They must use the sacred red and white paint and the sacred grass to make the vanished buffalo return in great herds.

In the spring of 1890 the Sioux began dancing the Ghost Dance at Pine Ridge Reservation, adding new symbols to Wovoka's origanal ceremony. By June they were wearing ghost shirts made of cotton cloth painted blue around the necks, with bright-colored thunderbirds, bows and arrows, suns, moons, and stars emblazoned upon them.

To accompany the dancing they made ghost songs:

The whole world is coming,
A nation is coming, a nation is coming.
The Eagle has brought the message to the tribe.
The father says so, the father says so.
Over the whole earth they are coming,
The buffalo are coming, the buffalo are coming.

Mainly because they misunderstood the meaning of the Ghost Dance religion, the Government's policy makers who ran the reservations from Washington decided to stamp it out. If they had taken the trouble to examine its basic tenets, they would have found that in its original form the religion was opposed to all forms of violence, self-mutilation, theft, and falsehood. As one Army officer observed: "Wovoka has given these people a better religion than they ever had before."

The Ghost Dance might have died away under official pressure had not the greatest maker of medicine among the Sioux, Sitting Bull, chosen to come forth from his "retirement" near Standing Rock agency and join the new religion of the dance. Sitting Bull was the last of the great unreconciled chiefs. Since his return from Canada, where he had gone after the Custer battle, he had been carrying on a feud with the military as well as with civilian reservation agents.

When Kicking Bear, one of the early emissaries to Wovoka, visited Sitting Bull in late 1890 to teach him the Ghost Dance, Agent James McLaughlin ordered Kicking Bear escorted off the reservation. Sitting Bull may or may not have believed in the messiah, but he was always searching for opportunities to bedevil the authorities. Kicking Bear was hardly off the reservation before Sitting Bull set up a dance camp and started instructing his followers in the new religion. In a short time the peaceful ghost songs became warlike chants.

Efforts of authorities to put a stop to ghost dancing now led to resentment and increased belligerency from the Indians. Inevitably the Army was drawn into the controversy, and in the late autumn of 1890 General Nelson Miles ordered more troops into the plains area.

Suspecting that Sitting Bull was the leading trouble-maker, Miles arranged informally with Buffalo Bill Cody to act as intermediary. Cody had scouted with Miles in former years and had also employed Sitting Bull as a feature attraction with his Wild West show. "Sitting Bull might listen to you," Miles told Cody, "when under the same conditions he'd take a shot at one of my soldiers."

Buffalo Bill went at once to Fort Yates on the Standing Rock Reservation, but authorities there were dismayed when they read Miles's written instructions to Cody: "Secure the person of Sitting Bull and deliver him to the nearest commanding officer of U.S. troops." James McLaughlin, the reservation agent, and Lieutenant Colonel William Drum, the military commander, both feared that Cody's actions might precipitate a general outbreak throughout the area. The military authorities immediately took it upon themselves to get Buffalo Bill drunk, send a wire to Washington, and have his orders rescinded.

"All the officers were requested to assist in drinking Buffalo Bill under the table," Captain A. R. Chapin later recorded. "But his capacity was such that it took practically all of us in details of two or three at a time to keep him interested and busy throughout the day." Although the rugged Cody managed to keep a clear head through all this maneuvering, he had scarcely started out to Sitting Bull's encampment before a telegram came from Washington canceling his orders.

Meanwhile Agent McLaughlin had decided to take Sitting Bull into custody himself, hoping to prevent a dangerous disturbance which he felt would result if the military authorities forced the issue and tried to make an arrest. McLaughlin gave the necessary orders to his Indian police, instructing them not to permit the chief to escape under any circumstances.

Just before daybreak on December 15, 1890, forty-three Indian police surrounded Sitting Bull's log cabin. Lieutenant Bull Head, the Indian policeman in charge of the party, found Sitting Bull asleep on the floor. When he was awakened, the old war leader stared incredulously at Bull Head. "What do you want here?" he asked.

"You are my prisoner," said Bull Head calmly. "You must go to the agency."

Sitting Bull yawned and sat up. "All right," he said, "let me put on my clothes and I'll go with you." He called one of his wives and sent her to an adjoining cabin for his best clothing, and then asked the policeman to saddle his horse for him.

While these things were being done, his ardent followers who had been dancing the Ghost Dance every night for weeks, were gathering around the cabin. They outnumbered the police four to one, and soon had them pressed against the walls. As soon as Lieutenant Bull Head emerged with Sitting Bull, he must have sensed the explosive nature of the situation.

While they waited for Sitting Bull's horse, a

fanatical ghost dancer named Catch-the-Bear appeared out of the mob. "You think you are going to take him," Catch-the-Bear shouted at the policemen. "You shall not do it!"

"Come now," Bull Head said quietly to his prisoner, "do not listen to anyone." But Sitting Bull held back, forcing Bull Head and Sergeant Red Tomahawk to pull him toward his horse.

Without warning, Catch-the-Bear suddenly threw off his blanket and brought up a rifle, firing point-blank at Bull Head, wounding him in the side. As Bull Head fell, he tried to shoot his assailant, but the bullet struck Sitting Bull instead. Almost simultaneously Red Tomahawk shot Sitting Bull through the head. A wild fight developed immediately, and only the timely arrival of a cavalry detachment saved the police from extinction.

News of Sitting Bull's death swept across the reservations, startling the Indians and the watchful military forces in the Dakotas. Most of the frightened followers of the great chief immediately came into Standing Rock agency and surrendered. Others fled toward the southwest.

Those who were fleeing knew exactly where they were going. They were seeking to join forces with a Ghost Dance believer, an aging chief named Big Foot. For some time, Big Foot had been gathering followers at a small village near the mouth of Deep Creek on Cheyenne River. As the Ghost Dance craze had increased, so had Big Foot's forces, and even before the fatal shooting of Sitting Bull, a small party of cavalrymen under Lieutenant Colonel Edwin V. Sumner, Jr. had been assigned to watch his movements.

As soon as news of Sitting Bull's death reached Big Foot, he began preparations to break camp. Lieutenant Colonel Sumner accepted the chief's explanation that the Indians were preparing to proceed eastward to the Cheyenne River agency where they would spend the winter. Big Foot was unusually friendly, and declared that the only reason he had permitted the fugitives from Sitting Bull's camp to join his people was that he felt sorry for them and wanted them to return to the reservation with him. Sumner was so convinced of Big Foot's sincerity that he permitted the band to keep their arms—a decision that was to precipitate the tragedy of Wounded Knee.

Before dawn the next day, December 23, Big Foot and his ever-increasing band were in rapid flight, moving in the opposite direction from the Cheyenne River agency. The question has never been settled as to whether they were heading for Pine Ridge agency, as Big Foot's followers later claimed, or for the Sioux recalcitrants' stronghold in the Badlands. Perhaps Big Foot did not know that Kicking Bear and Short Bull had withdrawn to the stronghold in the Badlands. But it is a fact that a few days earlier those two leaders, who had once visited the messiah in Nevada, were in the Badlands. And they had with them several hundred fanatical followers, keyed up to a high frenzy as a result of their continual dancing and chanting.

Learning of Big Foot's escape from Sumner's cavalry, General Miles ordered Major Samuel M. Whitside of the 7th Cavalry to intercept the Indians, disarm them, and return them to a reservation. On December 28, Whitside's scouts found the fugitives on Porcupine Creek and when the major sighted a white flag fluttering from a wagon, he rode out to meet it. He was surprised to find Big Foot lying in the bed of the wagon, swathed in blankets, suffering severely from pneumonia.

Whitside shook hands with the ailing chief, and told him that he must bring his people to the cavalry camp on Wounded Knee Creek. In a hoarse voice that was almost a whisper, Big Foot agreed to the order. Whitside, on the advice of one of his scouts, decided to wait until the band was assembled beside the cavalry camp before disarming them.

During the ensuing march, none of the cavalrymen suspected that anything was amiss. The Indians seemed to be in good humor; they talked and laughed with the soldiers, and smoked their cigarettes. Not one of the cavalrymen seemed to have been aware that almost all of these Indians were wearing sacred ghost shirts which they believed would protect them from the soldiers' weapons. And the soldiers seemed to be completely ignorant of the fact that their prisoners were obsessed with the belief that the day of the Indians' return to power was close at hand. One of the most fanatical members of the band was a medicine man, Yellow Bird, who all during the march was moving stealthily up and down the line, occasionally blowing on an eagle-bone whistle and muttering Ghost Dance chants.

When the column reached Wounded Knee, the Indians were assigned an area near the cavalry camp. They were carefully counted; 120 men and 230 women and children were present. Rations were issued, and they set up their shelters for the night. For additional cover, Major Whitside gave them several army tents. The troop surgeon, John van R. Hoff, went to attend the ailing Big Foot, and a stove was set up in the chief's tent. Whitside, however, did not entirely trust Big Foot's band. He posted a battery of four Hotchkiss guns, training them directly on the Indians' camp.

It was a cold night. Ice was already an inch thick on the tree-bordered creek, and there was a hint of snow in the air. During the night, Colonel James W. Forsyth of the 7th Cavalry rode in and took command. Significantly there were now at Wounded Knee five troop commanders—Moylan, Varnum, Wallace, Godfrey, and Edgerly—who had been with Reno and Custer at the Little Bighorn. With Big Foot were warriors who had fought in the same battle. Much would be made of that in days to come.

In Forsyth's command was a young lieutenant, James D. Mann, who was to witness the opening shots of the approaching fight. "The next morning," Mann said afterwards, "we started to disarm them, the bucks being formed in a semi-circle in front of the tents. We went through the tents looking for arms, and while this was going on, everyone seemed to be good-natured, and we had no thought of trouble. The squaws were sitting on bundles concealing guns and other arms. We lifted them as tenderly and treated them as nicely as possible.

"While this was going on, the medicine man [Yellow Bird] who was in the center of the semi-circle of bucks, had been going through the Ghost Dance, and making a speech, the substance of which was, as told me by an interpreter afterwards, 'I have made medicine of the white man's ammunition. It is good medicine, and his bullets can not harm you, as they will not go through your ghost shirts, while your bullets will kill.'

"It was then that I had a peculiar feeling come over me which I can not describe—some presentiment of trouble—and I told the men to 'be ready: there is going to be trouble.' We were only six or eight feet from the Indians and I ordered my men to fall back.

"In front of me were four bucks—three armed with rifles and one with bow and arrows. I drew my revolver and stepped through the line to my place with my detachment. The Indians raised their weapons over their heads to heaven as if in votive offering, then brought them down to bear on us, the one with the bow and arrow aiming directly at me. Then they seemed to wait an instant.

"The medicine man threw a handful of dust in the air, put on his war bonnet, and an instant later a gun was fired. This seemed to be the signal they had been waiting for, and the firing immediately began. I ordered my men to fire, and the reports were almost simultaneous."

Mass burial of Indians killed at Wounded Knee. That tragedy brought an end to the long, bitter years of Indian resistance in the West. (Courtesy of the Montana Historical Society, Helena.)

Things happened fast after that first volley. The Hotchkiss guns opened fire and began pouring shells into the Indians at the rate of nearly fifty per minute. What survivors there were began a fierce hand-to-hand struggle, using revolvers, knives, and war clubs. The lack of rifles among the Indians made the fight more bloody because it brought the combatants to closer quarters. In a few minutes, 200 Indian men, women, and children and sixty soldiers were lying dead and wounded on the ground, the ripped tents blazing and smoking around them. Some of the surviving Indians fled to a nearby ravine, hiding among the rocks and scrub cedars. Others continued their flight up the slopes to the south.

Yellow Bird, the medicine man, concealed himself in a tent, and through a slit in the canvas began shooting at the soldiers. When one of the 7th Cavalry troopers ran forward to slash open the tent, Yellow Bird killed him by pumping bullets into his stomach. Angry cavalrymen responded with heavy fire, then piled hay around the tent and set it to blazing.

Big Foot died early in the fighting from a bullet through his head. Captain Edward Godfrey, who had survived the Little Bighorn (he was with Benteen), was shocked when he discovered he had ordered his men to fire on women and children hidden in a brush thicket. Captain George Wallace, who also had survived the Custer fight (with Reno's battalion), was shouting his first order to fire when a bullet carried away the top of his head.

On the bloody campground, Surgeon Hoff did what he could for the wounded. He disarmed a wounded Indian who was still trying to fire his rifle. The warrior staggered to his feet and looked down fixedly at the burned body of Yellow Bird. "If I could be taken to you," the wounded Indian muttered to the dead medicine man, "I would kill you again."

Disillusionment over the failure of the ghost shirts had already affected most of the other survivors. With blood flowing from her wounds, one of the squaws tore off her brilliantly colored shirt and stamped upon it.

As it was apparent by the end of the day that a blizzard was approaching, the medical staff hastily gathered the wounded together to carry them to a field hospital at Pine Ridge. In the affair 146 Indians and 25 soldiers had been killed, but the full totals would not be known until several days afterward because of the snowstorm that blanketed the battlefield.

After the blizzard, when a burial party went out to Wounded Knee, they found many of the bodies frozen grotesquely where they had fallen. They buried all the Indians together in a large pit. A few days later, relatives of the slain came and put up a wire fence around the mass grave; then they smeared the posts with sacred red medicine paint.

By this time the nation's press was having a field day with the new "Indian war." Some journalists pictured the Wounded Knee tragedy as a triumph of brave soldiers over treacherous Indians; others declared it was a slaughter of helpless Indians by a regiment searching for revenge since the Little Bighorn. The truth undoubtedly lay somewhere between these opposite points of view. Certainly it was a tragic accident of war.

At Wounded Knee, the vision of the peaceful Paiute dreamer, Wovoka, had come to an end. And so had all the long and bitter years of Indian resistance on the western plains.

5
Day of the Cattleman

Ray Allen Billington

With the Indians out of the way, Americans were free at last to conquer the vast Great Plains—the country's last frontier. Westering farmers had stopped at the edge of this enormous grassland, whose arid climate and shallow topsoil seemed unsuited to agricultural techniques devised in the East. But if the farmers had to await new methods and machinery to invade the Great Plains, another group of Westerners—the irrepressible cattlemen—found the windy prairies almost ideal for open-range cattle raising. For twenty years the cattle kings ruled the grasslands from Texas to the Dakotas and left an indelible mark on both the history and character of the West. Ray Allen Billington, author of many books about the frontier, sketches the story of the cattle kingdom with a vivid brush, describing the long drives, the rise and fall of the cow towns, and the howling blizzards of 1886 and 1887 that ended the open-range period of the cattle industry.

... In the two decades after the Civil War great herds of bellowing longhorns, guarded by colorfully garbed cowboys on spirited ponies, spread over the [Great Plains], bringing fortunes to their owners and romance to the annals of the frontier. That was the day of the cattleman, the day when the longhorn steer was King of the West.

The giant industry had its beginnings in southern Texas. Cattle introduced there by Spaniards in the eighteenth century—scrawny, tough beasts bred by Moorish herdsmen—multiplied rapidly, especially in the triangle formed by the junction of the Rio Grande and the Gulf of Mexico. Conditions were ideal in that spot; the climate warm, the grass green all year, water plentiful from tributaries of the Nueces, the range so open that cattle drifted from feeding ground to feeding ground without encountering trees. Moreover few Indian raiders ventured south of San Antonio. In that ideal setting Mexican ranchers learned how to care for cattle on the open range. They learned to herd on horseback, to identify their own beasts by brands, to use a "roundup" to mark new-born calves. By the time Americans invaded Texas the Nueces Valley was a great cattle range, where thousands of steers roamed freely over the unfenced grassland under the watchful eye of mounted cowboys.

The intruders from the United States were farmers rather than ranchers, but they contributed to the growth of the infant Texan cattle industry nevertheless. Their eastern milch cows, breeding with the Mexican herds, produced a variety of strains more suitable to the American market than the original Moorish type. One clearly distinguished breed was the "Texas-Mexican," tall and gaunt, splashed with patches of white, and with enormous horns twisting

---

Reprinted with permission of Macmillan Publishing Co., Inc., from *Westward Expansion* by Ray Allen Billington. Copyright © 1967 by Macmillan Publishing Co., Inc.

back toward the body. Another was the "Spanish," which resembled the crossbreed but was somewhat smaller with shorter horns and gentler spirit. A third, the "Long-haired Texans," were round, well-formed beasts with long legs, heavy body, medium horns, and a heavy coat of brownish color. The "Wild Cattle" of western Texas were thin, blue-horned, mealy-nosed, and brown in color. All were tough and wiry, able to care for themselves on parched summer prairies or during winter blizzards.

The Americans who controlled Texas after its independence paid little attention to the increasing herds, largely because no market for beef was near enough to make sales profitable. A few were driven to Austin or Galveston, a few more to New Orleans, some even to the Ohio Valley where an adventurous herdsman sold a thousand head in 1846. Others were marketed in the gold fields of Colorado, Arizona, and California during the late 1850's, but in each case the expenses of the drive and the difficulties of overland herding discouraged any large-scale attempts. For the most part the cattle were allowed to roam wild over the lush grasslands, drifting northward in search of new feeding grounds as they increased in numbers until they blanketed western Texas between the Rio Grande and the upper Panhandle. They multiplied especially during the Civil War years when drives to market were stopped by Union control of the Mississippi, until by the close of the war some 5,000,000 longhorns roamed Texas. Most were "mavericks" that could be claimed by anyone bothering to affix a brand, although a few were held on ranches in the belt of open country east of the Cross Timbers.

By 1865 a few astute Texans recognized that the millions of cattle might be turned into tidy profits. They knew good steers could be had for the asking in their own state, or could be purchased for $3 or $4 a head from ranchers. They learned that the upper Mississippi Valley, its livestock supplies depleted by war, was willing to pay up to $40 a head for marketable beasts.

Only a little arithmetic was required to demonstrate the fortunes to be made from that price differential. If a cattleman could get a herd of 3,000 longhorns to the northern markets his profits would amount to $100,000; if all 5,000,000 Texas cattle could be driven north the state would be enriched to the extent of $180,000,000! Nor was this simply a fantastic dream. Texans were aware that the hardy animals could be driven overland without difficulty so long as the journey lay through open prairie. They knew, too, that railroads were jutting westward into the northern Plains; the Missouri Pacific Railroad reached Sedalia, Missouri, in 1865 and could be used as a shipping point to eastern markets. Why not capitalize upon the happy combination of circumstances to amass King Midas' own wealth for themselves?

The "Long Drive" was the result. During the winter of 1865–66 a number of Texans and a few business men from Iowa and Kansas quietly rounded up herds, laid in camp equipment, and hired cowboys. In late March, when the grass on the northern Plains began to green, they started. Each band of a thousand or more cattle was driven by half a dozen cowboys, all adept in the use of the lasso and six-shooter, and paid $25 to $40 a month. A chuck wagon carrying food and equipment, with the cook at the reins, broke trail, followed by the horse wrangler and his horses; then came the longhorns, strung out over a mile of prairie. At the "point" or head of the column two riders kept the cattle on their course, others guarded the flank, and two more rode at "drag" in the rear to spur on halting beasts. The whole "outfit" was commanded by a trail boss who received a salary of $125 a month.

Experience soon taught the bosses to drive the cattle slowly at first and to watch them carefully at night, but within a week the steers were "road broken" enough to move ahead more rapidly. After that the larger herds were guarded by only two hands at night, then drifted slowly away from the bedding ground at

Plains cowboys at their chuck wagon during roundup. (Photograph by A. A. Forbes, courtesy of the Western History Collections, University of Oklahoma Library.)

daybreak, grazing as they went. After an hour or so the pace was speeded up until noon when a halt was made at some stream where the cook, who had galloped ahead in the chuck wagon, had dinner waiting. The cattle grazed for a few hours while the men ate, then were driven rapidly on until nightfall. That was the pattern followed by the dozens of herds that left Texas in the spring of 1866; in all some 260,000 head started for the Missouri Pacific railhead at Sedalia.

Nevertheless the Long Drive was far from successful. Bad luck plagued drovers from the beginning. Heavy rains in Texas muddied trails, swelled streams, and made life so unpleasant that many cowboys deserted their jobs. Beyond the Red River where the Sedalia Trail crossed a corner of the Indian Territory herds were frequently stampeded by red men who then demanded a reward for returning the beasts to their owners. Still farther north the wooded hills of the Ozark Plateau terrified the cattle; longhorns accustomed to the open range bolted rather than enter forested regions. When that obstacle was passed another was encountered in the irate farmers of Missouri, who were out in force to repel herds which might infect their own cows with the dread Texas Fever. At every county line armed bands of backwoodsmen halted drovers, shot cattle, or fought it out with cowboys. The successive barriers kept all but a few steers from reaching Sedalia, but the $35 a head received for those convinced Texan cattlemen the Long Drive would be successful if they could find a less hazardous route to market.

The honor of laying out a better trail went not to a drover but to Joseph M. McCoy, an Illinois meat dealer, who realized a fortune awaited anyone controlling the spot where southern sellers and northern buyers could meet most advantageously. That point, he reasoned, must lie on the Kansas Pacific Railroad, then building westward from Kansas City; this would allow herders to avoid wooded areas and settlements while driving cattle northward. Officials of the line proved so enthusiastic McCoy was able to exact promises of low freight rates from them, but the president of the road connecting Kansas City with St. Louis and the markets of the East, the Missouri Pacific Railroad, thought the plan fantastic and refused to co-operate. Undaunted, McCoy turned to a second railroad having eastern connections from Kansas City, the Hannibal and St. Joe Railroad. Before the winter of 1866–67 was over he signed a contract assuring him favorable shipping terms for cattle between the Plains and Chicago.

McCoy's next task was to select the point on the Kansas Pacific tracks where the Long Drive would end. After careful study he chose the little hamlet of Abilene, Kansas, because, as he wrote, "the country was entirely unsettled, well-watered, excellent grass, and nearly the entire area of country was adapted to holding cattle." Abilene—a drowsy little village with a handful of settlers and so little business the one saloon keeper spent part of his time raising prairie dogs for tourists—was transformed overnight by his decision. During the spring of 1867 McCoy imported lumber for stockyards, pens, loading chutes, barns, a livery stable, and a hotel to house the cowhands. All was bustle and confusion as the building program was rushed to completion; by July McCoy was able to send riders southward to intercept Sedalia-bound herds with welcome news of a new market at Abilene. Unfortunately most of the drovers had gone too far to be turned back, but 35,000 Texas steers passed through McCoy's loading chutes that fall. The banquet held on September 5, 1867, to celebrate the first shipment of cattle east was a gala affair, where southern drovers and northern dealers toasted the wedding of their sections and talked joyfully of the profits that would be theirs in the future.

Abilene assured success for the Long Drive. Cattlemen who reached there in 1868 with 75,000 head were enthusiastic over the trail northward—the Chisholm Trail, they called it —and carried word to Texas of the ease with which steers could be driven where there were no settlements, hills, or wooded areas. Their advertising started the tide rolling; between 1868 and 1871 nearly 1,500,000 Texan beeves were loaded in the Abilene yards. By that time the advance of settlement in eastern Kansas and the march of railroads across the Plains conspired to shift the cattle trail farther westward. Ellsworth, lying sixty miles west of Abilene on the Kansas Pacific Railroad, and Newton on the newly built Atchison, Topeka and Santa Fe Railroad, were the terminal points for the Long Drive between 1872 and 1875, receiving about 1,500,000 head. After 1875 the center was Dodge City, Kansas, which shipped 1,000,000 Texas beeves eastward in the next four years. In all 4,000,000 cattle reached the Kansas railroads during the years when the Long Drive was a feature of the cattlemen's frontier.

That was the time when the "cow towns"— Abilene, Newton, Ellsworth, Dodge City—were catapulted into the national limelight as models of unbridled corruption. They were drab hamlets most of the time, their dusty streets lined with ramshackle saloons, gaudy dance halls, gambling dens, hurdy-gurdy palaces, and red-light houses, but when each new band of cowboys "hit town" at the end of the Long Drive they blossomed into tinseled paradises where the most discriminating tastes in debauchery could be satisfied. Mobs of mounted cowboys "took over" by day, their six-shooters roaring while respectable citizens cowered behind locked doors. Faro dealers and dance hall girls reigned at night, reaping a financial harvest that justified the dreary months of waiting between drives. Seldom did a group of drovers leave without contributing to the population of "boot hill"—the cemetery reserved for those who died with their boots on—for barroom brawls, drunken duels, and chance shootings were so common that no one bothered to punish the murderers. In the "cow towns," as in the mining camps, the combination of easy money, rugged life, and inadequate restraints created an atmosphere which to easterners typified the whole "Wild West."

Romantic as it was, the Long Drive was economically unsound. The difficulties which beset drovers were many. Their cattle lost so much weight in the 1,500 mile journey northward that few could be sold to eastern stockyards at good prices; most went as "feeders" to some Nebraska or Iowa farmer for fattening on corn. Their expenses increased steadily, especially after 1867 when natives in the Indian Territory discovered that an ancient congressional statute forbade traffic across their lands without special permission. First the Cherokee, then the tribes farther west, capitalized on the situation by charging ten cents a head for all steers driven through their reservations. Far worse, from the cattlemen's point of view, was the hostility of Kansans. Irate farmers, knowing Texas Fever was carried by disease-transmitting ticks which infected Texas cattle, were always out in force to repel northward-bound herds. At first they resorted to shooting, but that was outmoded when their control of state legislatures allowed them to erect legal barriers. Both Missouri and Kansas passed quarantine laws in 1867, forbidding the entrance of cattle during the summer and fall when ticks were most active, and Kansas in 1884 ruled that no Texas steers could be driven into the state except in December, January, and February. Drovers evaded the laws at first, but as the growing agricultural population demanded and secured enforcement, the Long Drive came to an end. Congress, after listlessly debating a "National Cattle Trail" immune to state interference, refused to aid the Texans. The only solution was to grow cattle near the railroads. That would not only allow cattlemen to evade barriers erected by farmers and Indians, but place them in a better position to bargain with buyers who dictated prices in the Kansas "cow towns."

In Texas railroads came to the cattle country. During the 1870's the Missouri, Kansas and Texas Railroad, the Texas and Pacific Railroad, and numerous other lines opened communication with St. Louis, New Orleans, and Memphis. The possibility of direct marketing encouraged dozens of ranchers to stake out claims on the grassland between the Cross Timbers and the Pecos Valley where nutritive bunch grass, mesquite, and grama grass provided adequate fodder. Within a decade the whole Panhandle was carved into enormous ranches, some of them so large that cowboys rode a hundred miles from their homes to reach their front gates.

The problem of growing cattle near the northern railroads was just as easily solved. The climate was harsh, with roaring winter gales and occasional ice storms, but cattle could weather the worst blizzards so long as they drifted before the wind with their rumps to the tempest. Only when ice blanketed the ground was there any real danger, and that happened infrequently. During most of the year steers could feast on short prairie grass or scrape away snow to munch winter-cured fodder. The longhorns' ability to thrive on the northern Plains was demonstrated long before the close of the Civil War by traders who bartered sleek oxen for worn-out livestock along the immigrant trails, and by small ranchers who supplied the Montana gold fields with fresh beef. By 1868 herds dotted the High Plains country from the Rio Grande Valley to the Big Horn Basin, amply demonstrating that cattle could be grown anywhere. Only two things were needed to transform the local industry into a mammoth enterprise: adequate markets and improved steers to satisfy the discriminating taste of eastern consumers.

Both were provided during the 1870's. Railroads pushed steadily across the northern Plains during the decade: the Union Pacific, the Kansas Pacific, the Santa Fe, the Northern Pacific, the Burlington, and other smaller lines. At the same time mechanical improvements in meat handling and slaughtering—modern killing methods, refrigerator cars, and cold storage—widened the market for western beef. From the open range to the kitchen range was an easy step, and the demand for American meat mounted until all the East and much of Europe was fed by Plains ranchers. The quality of western beef was improved at the same time. As tough Texas cows were brought north, they were bred with heavier Hereford and Angus bulls to produce round-bellied, white-faced cattle which combined the stamina of longhorns with the weight and tenderness of eastern breeds. Able to survive cold winters and fetch an excellent price at the Chicago stockyards, the hybrids proved an ideal stock for the northern range.

The distinctive breed was developed in Kansas, for there Texas longhorns and eastern cattle first met. From the beginning of the Long Drive enterprising ranchers were on hand to purchase cows that were too scrawny or sickly to be sold; they were then fattened on prairie grass, bred with Hereford bulls, and used to build up herds of healthy cattle that showed little trace of their rangy Texas ancestors. As the ventures proved profitable, more and more cattle were diverted from the "cow towns" to stock the northern range, while the brisk demand for Hereford bulls drove their price up to $1,000. By the end of the 1860's ranches covered most of Kansas and Nebraska as well as portions of the Indian Territory where land was leased from the natives. Many drovers from Texas, finding they must compete with sleek steers from the nearby range when selling their herds, moved to Kansas themselves or laid out ranches there where they could fatten and hybridize their stock before sale.

From Kansas ranching spread into Colorado as soon as the Kansas Pacific and Union Pacific railroads joined that area to the outside world. Most of the cows needed to stock the range came from Texas, driven northward over the Goodnight-Loving Trail after that route was laid out in 1866. By 1869 1,000,000 longhorns grazed within the borders of Colorado Territory, and the herds were improving so rapidly that stockmen clamored for laws against further Texas importations lest stray bulls corrupt their Hereford-crossed strains. Statutes authorizing ranchers to shoot any loose Texan bull on sight testified to the regard with which they held their herds.

The advance of the cattle frontier into Wyoming began in 1868 when a Colorado rancher, J. W. Iliff, drove one of his herds to the plains near Cheyenne. His exorbitant profits from sales of beef to construction crews on the Union Pacific Railroad and miners prospecting the South Pass country, called attention to the richness of the range; others followed until by 1871 100,000 cattle pastured there, most of them under the watchful eye of small cowmen who owned only a few hundred head. The number increased rapidly after 1873 when the panic hurried the stocking of the northern range by lowering the price of Texan cattle. The center of the industry in Wyoming was the Laramie Valley, a region of rolling bench lands where grass and water abounded, and in the plateau country just west of the Laramie Mountains. After those regions filled ranchers spread their herds over most of the territory.

Extensive cattle raising in Montana began in 1871 when eight hundred Texas longhorns were driven into the Beaverhead River Valley by an enterprising herder with an eye on the lush market in nearby mining camps. Plentiful grass in that mountainous upland and the failure of

Montana's mining population to increase as rapidly as expected allowed the herds to multiply rapidly; by 1874 the surplus above local needs reached 17,000 head and good beef steers sold for as low as $10. Those depressed prices transformed Montana ranching from a local to a national enterprise; eastern buyers, hearing sleek beeves could be purchased for a low sum, flocked in during the autumn, ready to pay up to $18 a head. The herds were driven south to the Union Pacific tracks at Granger, Wyoming —a difficult route through sparsely grassed country—but profits were great enough to convince Montana ranchers they must look to the East rather than to mining camps for future markets.

With plentiful sales promised, the cattle frontier could move out of the mountain valleys into the broad plains of eastern Montana where rich grass, plentiful streams, and protecting hills offered ideal pasturage. For a few years the advance was slow; Sitting Bull was on the warpath and neither man nor beast was safe until after 1878 when the last band of Sioux was driven onto a reservation. Then great herds were driven north from Colorado or Wyoming to stock the promising grassland. "Eastern Montana has suddenly awakened," wrote an editor. "... Stock is pouring in from every hand." Marketing remained difficult—cattle must be driven south to the Union Pacific Railroad or east to the Northern Pacific tracks at Bismarck —but no amount of isolation could discourage a stock raiser in that day of expansion. Ranches filled Montana, then spilled over into Dakota territory during the 1870's.

By 1880 the cattle industry was firmly planted throughout the Great Plains. A traveler riding northward from lower Texas would seldom be out of sight of herds of white-faced longhorns, grazing under the watchful eye of bronzed cowboys; he would find them in the Panhandle country, along the Pecos Valley of New Mexico, on the sun-baked plains of the Indian Territory, among the rolling prairies of western Kansas and Nebraska, scattered through the high grasslands of eastern Colorado and Wyoming, and dotting the wind-swept plains of Montana and Dakota.

. . .

Texas longhorns, Kansas Herefords, and adventurous cattlemen from all the West had created a new empire—the Cattle Kingdom. "Cotton was once crowned king," wrote an exuberant editor, "but grass is now."

Underlying the breath-taking expansion which engulfed an area half the size of Europe within a span of fifteen years was the age-old hope for sudden wealth. Conditions on the Great Plains seemed to promise cattlemen fabulous profits. The land was free—millions of acres of it—all carpeted with rich grass and safe from meddlesome government agents. Cattle to stock the range were cheap; longhorns could be purchased in Texas at $7 or $8 a head, driven north to a likely spot, crossed with an imported eastern bull, and allowed to multiply as nature dictated. The rancher had only to sit back and watch his wealth increase, knowing every healthy steer would fetch from $50 to $60 at the nearest railroad. A few years of frugal living, while profits were turned back into the herd, would allow any pioneer to pyramid a modest investment into a handsome fortune.

There was no lack of adventurers to people the cattlemen's frontier. Most were young men who had scraped necessary capital together, bought their herds, and started out alone in search of a likely grazing spot. Because grass and water were necessary, a site was always selected on the bank of a stream. There the prospective rancher either homesteaded 160 acres or simply appropriated the land he needed. If a few straggly trees grew nearby he built a log cabin; if not he scooped a dugout from the bank of the river or threw together a tent of buffalo skins. With that simple equipment, a supply of beans, bacon, and coffee, and a horse or two, he was ready to watch his cattle graze, watch them fatten, watch them multiply. When beef animals were cut away to be sold he used the proceeds to buy more stock, build a ranch house, and erect corrals for his horses. Three or four good years were enough to put the business on a paying basis, with herds so large cowboys were hired to watch them.

By that time other ranchers were moving in nearby, along the same stream or across the divide on the banks of the next waterway. They were not near neighbors in the eastern sense of the words—they might be fifteen or twenty miles away—but they were close enough to cause trouble unless a system of frontier law was devised. How could each rancher keep his cattle separate from those of his neighbor? How could he sustain his claim to a portion of the public domain? How could he keep newcomers from overcrowding the range? Distant legislatures could not solve those problems; like frontiersmen throughout America's history cattlemen must make their own laws. The body of custom and rule they worked out allowed expansion to go on with a minimum of disorder.

Basic to the system was the sensible concept that control of a stream included control of adjacent lands. Thus a rancher staking out a claim to one bank of a creek secured a "range right" to as much of the river as he pre-empted and all the land running back to the "divide," or highland separating his stream from the one lying beyond. This was his land, even though he did not own a foot of it legally; public opinion, backed by the effective argument contained in six-shooters, gave him a right to use it without fear of intrusion. The usual ranches in the Great Plains contained thirty or forty square miles.

The imaginary "range lines" between holdings were respected by humans, but cattle drifted from ranch to ranch in their search for better pasturage until herds of several owners were frequently hopelessly intermingled. Ranchers' attempts to keep their steers separate from those of their neighbors gave prominence to two customs—"line-riding" and the "roundup." In line-riding, cowboys were stationed along the borders of each ranch, usually in groups of twos, ten or twenty miles apart, with a dugout to protect them in winter and the open sky as their canopy in summer. Each morning they set out from their lonely posts, riding in opposite directions until they met the cowboy from the nearest camp on either side. Herds belonging to their employer were driven back from the border; those of neighbors were "drifted" in the direction of their own ranch.

Vigilant as line-riders might be, animals did intermingle. Twice each year, in the spring and fall, "roundups" were held to separate mixed herds and identify new-born calves. At the time agreed upon, each rancher sent a chuck-wagon and "outfit" to a designated spot. Then the cowboys fanned out over the range, driving all cattle in the vicinity toward camp, until a herd of several thousand was assembled. While the milling mass of animals was held together, riders of the ranch where the roundup was held made the first "cut," riding skillfully through the herd to single out animals bearing their employer's brand. Those brands—distinctive marks burned into the flanks with red-hot branding irons—were registered to avoid confusion; some symbols of better-known ranches became as famous as baronial symbols of feudal days. As calves always followed the mothers, they could now be lassoed, thrown, and marked with the iron.

After the first division, cowboys from other ranches cut out their own cattle; a process repeated until the last cow was branded. Then the owner of the ranch where the roundup took place held back his herd while the rest were driven to the next ranch, where the procedure was duplicated. That went on until the last range was visited and the cattle of the whole region branded and returned to their owners. The work was hard—cowboys spent eighteen or twenty hours a day in the saddle for weeks at a time—but the roundup was one of the most colorful institutions in the history of the frontier. The thousands of bellowing cattle, blazing branding fires, scores of mounted cowboys, and scattered chuck wagons, all hazy with dust and drenched by a brilliant sun, caught the imagination of easterners as did nothing else in the Far West.

Eastern imagination, in turn, has given the nation one of its most enduring legends: the myth of the glamorous cowboy. Actually the clean-cut heroes of Hollywood and the television screen bear little resemblance to the hard-working men who tended cattle in the heyday of the open range. Cowboys, as one of them put it, were simply hired hands on horseback, doomed to a life of dull routine as they "rode line" separating the unfenced ranches, doctored sick animals, or drifted herds from pasturage to pasturage. Little wonder that when they "hit town" on rare occasions they indulged in the riotous conduct that has come to typify them for cinema addicts the world over. There was little romance in their lonely lives; even the widely publicized "ten-gallon" hats, chaps, knotted handkerchiefs, and colorful shirts that they sometimes wore to charm strangers were often displaced by a working garb of overalls, a cast-off army overcoat that had seen service in the Civil War, and a derby hat. Even their individualism has been exaggerated; many joined a labor union, the Knights of Labor, and a group struck one ranch during the 1884 roundup. The true heroes of the Cattle Kingdom were not the cowboys, but the ranchers whose shrewd management allowed the conquest of a new frontier.

Even they could not forestall the inevitable, and by 1880 the days of the open range were numbered. Overstocking was responsible. During the early 1880's the whole western world awakened to the possibilities of the Cattle Kingdom. Markets were expanding as railroads pushed into the Great Plains and steamships brought European consumers closer to the United States. Soon the entire world would be willing to pay handsomely for western beef! Any doubting scoffer could be convinced by the steady price rise at the Chicago stockyards, an advance that carried choice steers to a high of eight or nine cents a pound. Anyone could reap a fortune by doing nothing more than watch his animals multiply on free government land.

Even the unvarnished truth would have started a rush to the Plains, but that was not the literary diet fed Americans by magazines and newspapers. Western editors, never notable for understatement, filled their columns with statistics proving that anyone investing $25,000 in cattle could run his fortune to $80,000 in five years, or stated authoritatively that profits of 40 and 50 per cent annually were the rule rather than the exception. Those tall tales were spread wholesale through the eastern farm journals. Typical was an item in the *Breeder's Gazette:*

> A good sized steer when it is fit for the butcher market will bring from $45.00 to $60.00. The same animal at its birth was worth but $5.00. He has run on the plains and cropped the grass from the public domain for four or five years, and now, with scarcely any expense to its owner, is worth forty dollars more than when he started on his pilgrimage. A thousand of these animals are kept nearly as cheaply as a single one, so with a thousand as a starter and an investment of but $5,000 in the start, in four years the stock raiser has made from $40,000 to $45,000. Allow $5,000 for his current expenses which he has been going on and he still has $35,000 and even $45,000 for a net profit. That is all there is to the problem and that is why our cattlemen grow rich.

Struggling farmers in the East, reading those statements, developed such a feverish state of mind that many accepted as true the sly tale given wide circulation by Bill Nye, the Laramie *Boomerang* humorist: "Three years ago a guileless tenderfoot came into Wyoming, leading a single Texas steer and carrying a branding iron; now he is the opulent possessor of six hundred head of fine cattle—the ostensible progeny of that one steer."

Propaganda such as that could have only one effect; by the summer of 1880 the rush to the new El Dorado was on. Trains were jam-packed with youngsters from eastern farms and factories, some with savings strapped about their waists, others ready to borrow at interest rates which varied from 2 per cent a month to 1 per cent a day. What did those fantastic charges matter when beef sold at the Chicago yards for $9.35 a hundred! Their frantic bidding on cattle to stock the range sent prices skyrocketing; ordinary stock that sold for $8 a head in 1879 brought $35 in Texas by 1882 and were resold in Wyoming at $60. So great was the demand that between 1882 and 1884 the eastern cattle shipped westward as range stock balanced the number sent east to market! While the boom lasted between 1880 and 1885, the whole Plains country was inundated with thousands of ranchers and millions of cattle without stamina or experience to survive there.

More disastrous than the rush of men was the flow of capital from the East and Europe. Investors caught the fever in 1882 when they read in financial journals of the Prairie Cattle Company's 42 per cent dividend or the 40 per cent profits of Montana ranchers. Before the year was out business men, bankers, lawyers, and politicians were forming companies to share in those fortunes. Their recipe for prosperity was simple; they put up capital, a few ranchers were taken in to furnish experience, and the government provided land. During 1883 twenty stock-raising corporations, capitalized at $12,000,000, were formed in Wyoming alone. Some staked out range rights, but more consolidated smaller ranches already in existence; typical was the Swan Land and Cattle Company which used $3,750,000 raised by stock sales in the East to combine three eastern Wyoming ranches into a hundred-mile estate containing 100,000 head of cattle. All over the West grizzled cow hands who had "ridden the line" for years found themselves seated about directors' tables where eastern bankers listened respectfully to their opinions.

From the East the mania spread to Europe. English capitalists became interested when a parliamentary committee soberly reported in 1880 that profits of 33⅓ per cent could be expected in American ranching; an estimate which appeared less fantastic after an Edinburgh corporation, the Prairie Cattle Company, declared a dividend of 28 per cent in 1881. For the next four years English and Scottish investors, with the vision of 40 per cent profits before them, poured their money into corporations to compete with American companies for range rights and cattle. All over London "drawing rooms buzzed with stories of this last of bonanzas; staid old gentlemen, who scarcely knew the difference between a steer and a heifer, discussed it over their port and nuts." The flow of wealth from across the Atlantic hurried overstocking and brought the day of reckoning nearer.

Experienced cattlemen were thoroughly alarmed by 1885. They knew the arid plains could support the thousands of steers pastured there only when weather conditions were exceptionally favorable. They realized pasturage was wearing thinner each year, and that herds could no longer be driven to green feeding grounds when grass gave out, for all the Plains were pre-empted. In their panic they sought to insure themselves against the hard times ahead. Some fenced the range to protect their own pastures from intruding cattle; by the end of 1885 the Plains country was entangled in a barbed-wire network of its own making. One Colorado company had 1,000,000 acres enclosed, while a group of Texas Panhandle ranchers stretched a steel barrier from the Indian Territory to the Rio Grande to keep Kansas cattle from their feeding grounds. Few bothered to purchase the land they fenced; most simply enclosed part of the public domain, then stood ready to protect their holdings by "gun law."

Equally indicative of the fears besetting experienced ranchers during the cattle boom was the way in which they rushed into stockbreeders associations. Those co-operative enterprises offered many advantages; they kept intruders out of full-stocked ranges, supervised roundups, ran down "rustlers," fought prairie fires, offered bounties for wolves, and protected the brands of members. Usually they began as local groups, formed when stockmen of one region met, drew up articles of agreement to protect the range, and in typical frontier fashion agreed to abide by the will of the majority. As they multiplied several combined to form territorial associations which prescribed the roundup districts for a whole territory, formulated rules for branding and drives, restricted the number of cattle allowed on the range, and even set up courts to settle disputes between members. Live-Stock Associations blanketed the Great Plains by 1885, typifying both the frontiersmen's tendency toward self-government and the cattlemen's fear of range overstocking.

More than fencing and organization were needed to keep the cattle boom alive. By the summer of 1885 hundreds of ranchers felt the squeeze of mounting costs and falling prices. Each year more profits went into fencing, dues to Live-Stock Associations, and increasingly expensive cattle; each year after 1882 sums paid them at the Chicago stockyards diminished as overproduction drove beef prices downward. The experienced among them realized the downward spiral had begun; some sold their herds rather than risk wintering cattle insufficiently fattened on the overcrowded range, further depressing prices. To make matters worse a presidential order in August, 1885, forced stockmen who had leased lands in the Indian Territory to leave that region. Some 200,000 beeves were driven into the crowded ranges of Colorado, Kansas, and Texas that fall. Only a cycle of bad years was needed to prick the inflationary bubble and send the whole Cattle Kingdom toppling.

That began during the winter of 1885–86, a cold blustery winter which took a frightful toll on the northern Plains. The summer of 1886 was hot and dry, withering grass and drying up streams. Stockmen, noting the weakened condition of their herds, became panicky as fall approached. Some cattle were driven into Canada or onto leased lands on the Crow Reservation in Montana; others were sent east to be boarded by farmers along the agricultural frontier. Still more were dumped on the market. Prices tumbled amidst the selling spree, until steers worth $30 a year before went begging at $8 or $10 each. "Beef is low, very low, and prices are tending downward, while the market continues to grow weaker every day," complained the *Rocky Mountain Husbandmen*. "But for all that, it would be better to sell at a low figure, than to endanger the whole herd by having the range overstocked."

Those who sold, even at low prices, were wise. The winter of 1886–87 was long famous in western annals. Snow blanketed the northern Plains in November, so deep that starving animals could not paw down to grass. In early January a warm "chinook" wind brought some relief, but late in the month the worst blizzard ever experienced by ranchers howled across the West from Dakota to Texas. In the past cattle had withstood tempests by drifting before them; now they piled up against fences to die by the thousands. On the heels of the storm came a numbing cold which drove temperatures to sixty-eight degrees below zero. Ranchers, huddled about their stoves, did not dare think of what was happening on the range—of helpless cattle pawing at frozen snow in search of a little food or fighting to strip bark from willows and aspens along streams, "dogies" and unseasoned eastern cattle floundering in drifts, whole herds jammed together in ravines to escape the frosty blast and dying by the thousands. When spring finally came cattlemen saw a sight they spent the rest of their lives trying to forget. Carcass piled upon carcass in every ravine, gaunt skeletons staggering about on frozen feet, heaps of dead bodies along the fences, trees stripped bare of their bark—those were left as monuments to the thoughtless greed of ranchers.

The cold winter of 1886–87 ended the "open range" phase of the cattle industry. A few small ranchers struggled on, encouraged by excellent grazing conditions during the summer of 1887, but the great livestock corporations were unable to stand the strain. With creditors clamoring at their doorsteps they dumped steers on the market so rapidly the Chicago price for grass-fed beef tumbled from $2.40 a hundred in the spring of 1887 to $1.90 in the fall. Nor did conditions improve during the next half-dozen years as Texas growers unloaded stock no longer needed on the northern Plains, and farmers depressed the market by selling heavily during a cycle of dry years which depleted supplies of feed corn. Under those conditions company after company slid over the line into bankruptcy; the giant Swan Land and Cattle Company of Wyoming succumbed in May, 1887, and the Niobrara Cattle Company of Nebraska soon followed. The few that persisted faced constant criticism from those who remembered the suffering of 1886–87. "A man who turns out a lot of cattle on a barren plain without making provision for feeding them," wrote one western editor, "will not only suffer a financial loss but also the loss of the respect of the community in which he lives." In Wyoming alone the number of cattle declined from 9,000,000 head in 1886 to 3,000,000 nine years later.

Hostile public opinion and financial necessity both dictated that in the future cattle and grass be kept in even balance. That could not be done on the open range; the only solution was for each rancher to fence his lands, restrict his herds to a reasonable size, and insure adequate winter food by growing hay. Fencing went on rapidly in the High Plains country through the later 1880's—with cattlemen buying some land, leasing more, and enclosing all they dared in addition—until mowing machines and hay rakes were as common a sight in the West as chuck wagons in former days. And the cowboy, that romantic knight of the saddle, spent his days digging post holes, jacking up wagon wheels as fence tighteners, and haying. "I remember," reminisced one sadly, "when we sat around the fire the winter through and didn't do a lick of work for five or six months of the year, except to chop a little wood to build a fire to keep warm by. Now we go on the general roundup, then the calf roundup, then comes haying—something that the old-time cowboy never dreamed of—then the beef roundup and the fall calf roundup and gathering bulls and weak cows, and after all this a winter of feeding hay. I tell you times have changed." The day of the open range was gone; the West was becoming a land of big pastures, stocked with carefully bred, carefully sheltered beeves.

Oldtimers who sorrowed at those changes had another cause for alarm, for during the 1880's two dangerous invaders pressed upon the borders of the Cattle Kingdom. From the west came the sheepherders. Those unromantic individuals moved into the trans-Mississippi country during the 1870's, driven from their Ohio Valley pasturages by low prices for wool and high prices for feed. Seeking new grazing grounds where fodder was less expensive, they went first to California, New Mexico, and the mountain parks of the southern Rocky Mountains, then during the 1880's invaded the Plains country. Ranchers scoffed at first, but when they learned sheep could be raised with half the effort and twice the profit of steers, many made the transition. Others fought back. They claimed sheep ruined the grass by close cropping, and were ready to back their argument with "shooting irons." Open warfare between drovers and cowboys raged along the western border of the cow country for years, accounting for twenty deaths, a hundred injuries, and 600,000 sheep destroyed (most of them driven over cliffs) on the

Wyoming-Colorado range alone. Yet no force could hold back such a profitable enterprise, and herds of bleating "woolies" encroached steadily on the cattlemen's domain.

More dangerous were the invaders pressing upon the eastern fringes of the Cattle Kingdom —the pioneer farmers. Their advance onto the Great Plains began just as ranchers staked out their empire, and for the next years they pressed westward, despite the bitter hostility of cowmen. The stubborn advance of homesteaders against gun-toting cowboys, sullen sheepherders, and the terrifying obstacles of nature wrote the last epic chapter in the history of the American frontier.

6
The Wild, Wild West

Peter Lyon

Surely no chapter in the American saga has been more romanticized than that of the West. Sensational magazines, dime novels, Grade B Westerns, and television horse operas have all enshrined the West as a fabled land where Right confronted Wrong in dramatic showdowns—where Good always triumphed over Evil, Cowboys over Indians, iron-fisted sheriffs over sissified outlaws, straight-shooting Robin Hoods over the Corrupt Establishment. The very mention of men like Wild Bill Hickok and Bat Masterson, Wyatt Earp and Doc Holliday, Billy the Kid and Jesse James, calls to mind glorified Western heroes who provide enduring masculine examples for worship and emulation.

The fact is that the real Billy the Kid, the real Jesse James, Wild Bill Hickok, Bat Masterson, and Wyatt Earp were anything but the glamorized he-men of Western mythology. Peter Lyon, pulling back the curtains of legend, describes what these characters were like in real life and suggests how they were inflated into fabled American supermen, widely admired for their two-fisted individualism and celebration of violence.

The world of the Wild West is an odd world, internally consistent in its own cockeyed way, and complete with a history, an ethic, a language, wars, a geography, a code, and a costume. The history is compounded of lies, the ethic was based on evil, the language was composed largely of argot and cant, the wars were fought by gangs of greedy gunmen, the geography was elastic, and the code and costume were both designed to accommodate violence. Yet this sinful world is, by any test, the most popular ever to be described to an American audience.

Thousands of books have been written about it, many of them purporting to be history or biography; all but a very few are fiction, and rubbish to boot. It has, of course, afforded wondrously rich pickings for the journeymen of the mass entertainments; scores of writers for pulp magazines, motion pictures, comic strips, radio, and television have hacked their way over its trails. Even artists of the first rank have drawn upon it. Mark Twain reported as fact some grisly rumors about one of its heroes; Aaron Copland composed the music for a ballet that glorified one of its most celebrated killers; Puccini wrote an opera about it; George Bernard Shaw confected an exceedingly silly play about it.

And it has not disappeared. It is still around, over thataway just a piece, bounded on three sides by credulity and on the fourth by the television screen. It will never disappear.

Any discussion of the conquest of the West may be likened to an animated gabble down the length of a long dinner table. At the head of it, where historians have gathered, the talk is thoughtful and focuses on events of weighty consequence. One man mentions the discovery of precious metals, which inspired adventurers by the scores of thousands. Another man tells

---

Reprinted by permission of International Creative Management. Copyright © 1960, 1969 by Peter Lyon. Originally appeared in *American Heritage*, August 1960.

of the Homestead Act of May, 1862, under the terms of which, within a generation, 350,000 hardy souls each carved a 160-acre farm out of raw prairie. A third speaks of the railroads that were a-building, four of them by 1884, to link the Mississippi Valley to the Pacific Coast. When it comes to the Indians, the historians all wag their heads dolefully, for they agree that the westward expansion came about only by virtue of treaties cynically violated and territory shamelessly seized.

The picture that emerges from their talk is one of grueling hard work; of explorers and trappers and bearded prospectors; of Chinese coolies toiling east and Irish immigrants toiling west, laying track across wilderness; of farmers with hands as hard as horn, sheltered from the blizzards and the northers only by sod huts; of ranchers and longhorn cattle and cowboys weary in the saddle. The quality evoked by their talk is of enduring courage, the greater because it is largely anonymous. The smell that hangs over their talk is of sweat.

But at the foot of the table, below the salt, where sit the chroniclers of the Wild West, the talk is shrill and excited, and the smell that hangs overhead is of gunpowder. For here the concern is with men of dash and derring-do, and the picture that emerges from the talk is of gaudy cowtowns and slambang mining camps: curious settlements in which the only structures are saloons, gambling halls, dance palaces, brothels, burlesque theaters, and jails; in which there are no people, but only heroes and villains, all made of pasteboard and buckram, all wearing six-guns, and all (except for the banker) with hearts of 22-carat gold.

In this never-never land, the superhero is the gun slinger, the man who can draw fastest and shoot straightest; in brief, the killer. Sometimes he swaggered along the wooden sidewalks with a silver star pinned to his shirt, a sheriff or a United States marshal, but whether he was outlaw or officer of the law, if he applied himself diligently to the smashing of the Ten Commandments, with special attention to the Sixth —that is, if he was a sufficiently ugly, evil, and murderous killer—he was in a way to become a storied American hero.

We propose to trundle five of these paragons— Billy the Kid and Jesse James, Wild Bill Hickok, Bat Masterson, and Wyatt Earp—up for inspection at close range. Nor will the ladies be ignored: we will ask Calamity Jane and Belle Starr, the Bandit Queen, to curtsy briefly. But before entering this gallery of Papier-Mâché Horribles, we may find it instructive to reflect upon the technique by which an uproariously bad man can acquire a reputation at once inflated, grisly, and prettified. This will require some small knowledge of the economics of the Wild West and a brief peek at the sources available to the chroniclers of this hazy world, this world so clouded by the black gunsmoke of all those Navy Colt .45's.

There were, broadly speaking, two ways of making money in the Wild West. One, as has been suggested, demanded hard, hard work of farmer, cowhand, railroader, or miner. But as always seems to be the case in this bad old world, there were some few men who did not care for hard work. Either they had tried it personally, for a day or two, and found it repugnant, or they had conceived a distaste for it by watching others try it, or perhaps they had simply heard about others who had tried it and so come to a bad end. In any case, these men determined never to work but to rely, rather, on their wits.

Now how could a quick-witted man get rich out on the bare, bleak plains? Clearly the first step was to head for those outposts of civilization, however malodorous to a discriminating rogue, where a little heap of wealth had been piled up through the labor of others. This meant the cowtowns, the mining camps, and the slowly shifting railroad settlements. Here he could gamble with the chumps: few professional gamblers starve. Here he could trade on women of easy virtue, or no virtue whatever, who were in even greater demand west of the Mississippi than east of it. Here he could buy a share of a dance hall or saloon: either enterprise was gilt-edged. Before long he would have found, as others have before and since, that these careers lead straight into politics. He might have concluded that it was cheaper to stand for office himself than to pay tribute to some stupider, lazier politician. So were marshals and sheriffs born.

But what of the dull-witted man who didn't choose to work? He had behind him a life of violence bred by the Civil War; often his thick skull held no learning whatever save how to ride, shoot, kill, burn, rob, rape, and run. With the end of the war he doffed his blue blouse—or, more often, his gray—and headed west toward a short, gory life of bank heists and train robberies. So were outlaws born.

For the man who was preternaturally active and had no objection to a day in the outdoors, there was a third, coarsening, semi-legal path to quick dollars: he could slaughter bison. Only the Indians would object, and who cared a hoot for the Indians? A treaty of 1867 guaranteed that no white man would hunt buffalo south of the Arkansas River; by 1870, when the army officer commanding at Fort Dodge was asked what he would do if this promise were broken, he laughed and said, "Boys, if I were hunting buffalo I would go where buffalo are"; in 1871 the massacre began in earnest. One hunter bagged 5,855 in two months. It has been estimated that 4,373,730 bison were killed in the three years 1872–74. To shoot the placid beasts was no easier than shooting fish in a barrel, but it was certainly no more difficult. And splendid practice, as safe as on a target range, for the marksman who might later choose to pot riskier game—a stagecoach driver or the leader of a posse. So were killers trained.

For the purposes of American myth, it remained only to make over all these sheriffs, outlaws, killers, and assorted villains into heroes. Considering the material on hand to work with, this transfiguration is on the order of a major miracle. It was brought about in two ways. First, whilst the assorted plug-uglies were still alive, hosannas were raised in their honor (a) by the "National Police Gazette," a lively weekly edited from 1877 to 1922 by Richard K. Fox and commanding a circulation that reached into every self-respecting barbershop, billiard parlor, barroom, and bagnio throughout the Republic; and (b) by each impressionable journalist, from the more genteel eastern magazines, who had wangled enough expense money out of his publisher to waft him west of Wichita. Fox required no authentication and desired none; his staff writers simply pitched their stuff out by the forkful, to be engorged by yokels from Fifth Avenue to Horner's Corners. The aforesaid round-eyed journalists, on the other hand, got their stuff straight from the gun fighters themselves, so naturally it was deemed wholly reliable.

Second, after the assorted plug-uglies had been gathered to their everlasting sleep, the latter-day chroniclers crept eagerly in. They (or at least a few of them) would be careful and scholarly; they would write nothing that was not verified either by a contemporary newspaper account or by an oldtimer who knew whereof he spoke from personal knowledge. Thus, whatever they printed would be the truth, the whole truth, &c.

One flaw in this admirable approach was that the contemporary newspaper accounts are not reliable. How could they be, when the newspapers themselves were flaring examples of the sort of personal journalism in which bias as to local politics and personalities customarily displaced respect for facts? Any halfway independent and intelligent reporter for the newspapers of the Wild West knew that, when he wrote about the gunmen of his community, he was describing an interconnected underworld, a brotherhood that embraced outlaw, politician, and sheriff quite as amicably as does the brotherhood of gangster and corrupt official in the cities of our own time. Such an insight normally flavored his copy.

The other flaw was that the stories of oldtimers came not from personal knowledge of what happened so much as from the files of the imaginative "National Police Gazette." Venerable nesters could be found all over the Southwest, fifty years after the timely deaths of Billy the Kid or Jesse James or Belle Starr, clamoring to testify to the boyish charm of the one, the selfless nobility of the other, and the amorous exploits of the third. Their memories were all faithful transcripts of the "Gazette's" nonsense. Its editor's classic formula for manufacturing heroes had so effectively retted the minds of his readers that they could never thereafter disentangle fiction from fact.

Analysis of this Fox formula for heroes reveals that it has ten ingredients, like a Chinese soup:

(1) The hero's accuracy with any weapon is prodigious.

(2) He is a nonpareil of bravery and courage.

(3) He is courteous to all women, regardless of rank, station, age, or physical charm.

(4) He is gentle, modest, and unassuming.

(5) He is handsome, sometimes even pretty, so that he seems even feminine in appearance; but withal he is of course very masculine, and exceedingly attractive to women.

(6) He is blue-eyed. His piercing blue eyes turn gray as steel when he is aroused; his associates would have been well advised to keep a color chart handy, so that they might have dived for a storm cellar when the blue turned to tattletale gray.

(7) He was driven to a life of outlawry and crime by having quite properly defended a loved one from an intolerable affront—with lethal consequences. Thereafter, however,

(8) He shields the widow and orphan, robbing only the banker or railroad monopolist.

(9) His death comes about by means of betrayal or treachery, but

(10) It is rarely a conclusive death, since he keeps on bobbing up later on, in other places, for many years. It is, indeed, arguable whether he is dead yet.

With these attributes in mind let us gather around the first exhibit—a man narrow-waisted and wide-hipped, with small hands and feet, whose long curly hair tumbles to his shoulders —in sum, a man who looks like a male impersonator. His label reads

Wild Bill Hickok

James Butler (Wild Bill) Hickok was born on a farm in La Salle County, Illinois, on May 27, 1837. He died on the afternoon of August 2, 1876, in Saloon No. 10, on the main street of Deadwood, in the Dakota Territory, when a bullet fired by Jack McCall plowed through the back of his head, coming out through his cheek and smashing a bone in the left forearm of a Captain Massey, a river-boat pilot with whom Hickok had been playing poker. During his lifetime Hickok did some remarkable deeds, and they were even more remarkably embroidered by himself and by a corps of admiring tagtails and tuft-hunters. When he died, he held two pair—aces and eights—a legendary combination known ever since as "the dead man's hand." It is the least of the legends that has encrusted his reputation, like barnacles on an old hulk.

Was he brave? His most critical biographer, William E. Connelley, has said that fear "was simply a quality he lacked."

Was he handsome? He was "the handsomest man west of the Mississippi. His eyes were blue —but could freeze to a cruel steel-gray at threat of evil or danger."

Was he gallant? His morals were "much the same as those of Achilles, King David, Lancelot, and Chevalier Bayard, though his amours

The real-life Wild Bill Hickok, shown here with his satin lapels and slicked-down ringlets, told "fabulous fibs" about himself and left a checkered career as an army scout, a sometime lawman, a professional gambler, a rake, and a killer. (Courtesy of Culver Pictures.)

were hardly as frequent as David's or as inexcusable as Lancelot's."

Had he no minor vices? Very few: "Wild Bill found relaxation and enjoyment in cards but he seldom drank."

Could he shoot? Once in Solomon, Kansas, a pair of murderers fled from him. "One was running up the street and the other down the street in the opposite direction. Bill fired at both men simultaneously and killed them both." Presumably with his eyes closed. Again, in Topeka, in 1870, Buffalo Bill Cody threw his hat into the air as a target. "Wild Bill shot an evenly spaced row of holes along the outside of the rim as it was falling, and before it touched the ground." To appreciate fully this miracle of marksmanship, one must remember that Hickok was shooting black-powder cartridges. (Smokeless powder did not come into general use until about 1893.) Each time he fired, therefore, he put a puff of black smoke between himself and his target. After his first shot, he could not have seen his target. But then, nothing is impossible to the gun slinger of the Wild West.

But surely he was modest? Yes, indeed. "Faced with admirers, he blushed and stammered and fled."

Was he a sure-enough killer? Once he was asked how many white men he had killed, to his certain knowledge (Indians didn't count). Wild Bill reflected. "I suppose," he said at last, "I have killed considerably over a hundred." But this was in 1866: he would have another ten years to improve his record. To another reporter, he remarked: "As to killing men, I never think much about it.... The killing of a bad man shouldn't trouble one any more than killing a rat or an ugly cat or a vicious dog." Of course, it helps if one is as good a judge as Hickok of the badness of a man, or the ugliness of a cat.

But was a good man not obliged to kill a bad man, to tame the Wild West? And, after all, was Wild Bill not a pillar of righteousness in those sinful times? What about his lustrous reputation as marshal of the Kansas cowtowns?

Hickok was, perhaps, a United States deputy marshal operating out of Fort Riley in February, 1866, and charged with rounding up deserters and horse thieves; but the record of his tenure is fuzzy.

In mid-August, 1869, he was elected sheriff of Ellis County—of which Hays was the biggest town—to fill an unexpired term. He failed of re-election in November. A brief time in which to tame a tough town—nor does the record show any notable success. He may have killed a man named Jack (or Sam) Strawhorn (or Strawhan) who tried to get the drop on him; he may have killed two soldiers who talked tough at him; he may have thrashed Tom Custer, a brother of General George Custer; he may have killed three soldiers whom Custer had vengefully sicked on him—all the evidence bearing on these matters is likewise fuzzy. What is certain is that Hickok left Hays in a hurry one winter night, lest he be further beset by the Seventh Cavalry.

In April, 1871, Hickok was appointed marshal of Abilene, and now the picture grows sharper. It was an auspicious conjunction of man and town: each was at the height of notoriety. As for the town, which was all of five years old, 1871 would be its peak year as a cowtown; 600,000 cattle would pass through its yards on the way to eastern markets; and all summer, cowboys by the hundreds would jam its saloons and dance halls—the Alamo, the Bull's Head, the Mint, and the Gold Room—to squander a year's wages. As for the man, "Harper's Monthly" had published not long before a lurid account of Hickok's fatal skill in battle, as told to George Ward Nichols by Wild Bill himself. There was, for instance, Hickok's version of the McCanles affair. In truth, Hickok had shot down Dave McCanles from behind a curtain, shot a second man from behind a door, and mortally wounded a third man who was running for his life. But as Wild Bill told the tale to the bug-eyed Nichols, he had been attacked by McCanles and a gang of nine "desperadoes, horsethieves, murderers, regular cut-throats," but had slain six men with six shots and dispatched the other four "blood-thirsty devils" with his knife.

A man whose fame rested on such fabulous fibs was just the sort needed to quell the frequent riots of a wicked cowtown. At least, so thought Joseph McCoy, the founder of Abilene and, in 1871, also the town's mayor. Moreover, McCoy knew where to find his man, for Hickok was right in town, gambling for a living at the Alamo. Wild Bill took the job. He slung two six-guns at his hips; he thrust a knife in the red sash he affected. In this fashion, he occasionally patrolled the streets.

But only occasionally. Most hours of most evenings he could be found at the Alamo, gambling with the cowboys. Most hours of most nights he had business in Abilene's red-light district. Meantime the taxpayers of Abilene chafed. Nor were the cowboys happy; for they were persuaded that Hickok wore the star only to protect the extortions of the professional gamblers, madames, and saloonkeepers.

Matters came to a head on the night of October 5. A bunch of cowboys had been hurrahing the town in their traditional and tiresome fashion—forcing merchants of clothing to outfit poorly clad strangers, obliging passers-by to stand drinks for all hands—and Hickok reportedly warned them to quiet down. Back in the Alamo at his poker table, Wild Bill heard someone fire a shot. He plunged out into the darkness to confront a Texan named Phil Coe. Some say that Coe's gun was already back in its holster, some that it was dangling in his hand. Whichever the case, Hickok fired, felling Coe, and then, when he heard someone running toward him, at once wheeled and plugged his own deputy, one Mike Williams, in a typical exhibition of coolness, calm, and nerve. He was relieved of his official duties six weeks later.

After that there was nothing left but to exploit his celebrity in show business. He joined Buffalo Bill Cody's stock company, an ignoble enterprise, but quit before long. In June, 1876, a Kansas newspaper reported, from Fort Laramie, that Wild Bill "was arrested on several occasions as a vagrant, having no visible means of support."

Later that month he galloped into Deadwood with a retinue that included, of all people, Calamity Jane. He settled down to gambling, as was his wont; she to drinking, as was hers. A little more than a month later Jack McCall shot him from behind, for no particular reason.

Hickok had been a brave army scout and an able Indian scout; he had also been a liar, a frequenter of bawdy houses, a professional gambler, and a killer. His score, according to a conservative chronicler of his deeds, was thirty-six men killed, apart from his service in the Army and against the Indians. What more fitting, for such a man, than to enshrine him on television, during the children's hour?

There is a tale that tells of how Calamity Jane, furious when she hears of Wild Bill's death, pursues his killer and corners him in a butcher shop, where she has to be restrained from splitting his brisket with a cleaver. Alas! not true. There is another tale that tells of how Calamity, on her deathbed years later, whispers, "What's the date?" When she is told it is August 2, she smiles and murmurs, "It's the twenty-seventh anniversary of Bill's death." Then, while the violins sob a little in the background, she adds, "Bury me next to Bill." This is likewise horsefeathers. (She died on August 1, 1903.) Yet the legends persist in linking the two together.

Were they lovers? Wild Bill's adherents flatly deny it, claiming that their man was far too fastidious. What their denial lacks in gallantry, it makes up in logic. Calamity was the most celebrated female of the Wild West, but she was no rose.

She may have been born in 1852, in Missouri (or Illinois); her name may have been Mary Jane Canary (or Conarray). Her mother may have been a prostitute, and later a madame in Blackfoot, Montana, around 1866, managing a house that may have been called the Bird Cage. Notable citizens of the Wild West share an irritating nebulosity when it comes to recorded data.

There are seven different theories as to how she came by her name, none of them plausible enough to concern us here. This much is certain: Calamity Jane loved the company of men and, as time went on, she craved booze more and more.

Assuming that she was born in 1852, she was thirteen when she bobbed up in Montana, conjecturally an orphan; seventeen when, wearing men's clothes, she was consorting with the railroad section gangs in Piedmont and Cheyenne, Wyoming; twenty when, in Dodge City, she made a cowboy crooner called Darling Bob Mackay dance tenderfoot (i.e., obliged him to scamper about by firing bullets at his feet) because he had said something indelicate about her underwear; twenty-three, and the only female member, when she joined a geological expedition into the Black Hills; and twenty-four when, the only woman amongst 1,500 men, she left Fort Laramie with a bull train hauling supplies for General Crook's expedition against the Sioux.

Not long after, a scandalized colonel caught her swimming naked with some of her buddies in Hat Creek, near Sheridan, and promptly banished her. Undaunted, she got Grouard, Crook's chief of scouts, to appoint her an Indian scout under his command—or so it was said, but never proved.

By then the unfortunate woman was a seriously sick alcoholic, ready for any man's exploitation if only she could get a drink. Greedy showmen hired her for appearances in dime museums; her ghostwritten memoirs appeared, published in a cheap pamphlet, and Calamity took to hawking copies for whatever she could get.

And then, long after Calamity was dead, a woman appeared who produced a paper certifying the marriage on September 1, 1870, of Martha Jane Cannary and James Butler Hickok; she claimed to be the daughter of Wild Bill and Calamity Jane. She claimed it right out loud, to an audience of several million persons, over a network of radio stations. But presently the document was characterized as a forgery by experts, and the chroniclers of the Wild West could return to their speculations.

And here let us leave Calamity and Bill.

For we have come to our second Horrible—a slope-shouldered man whose blue eyes blink incessantly (he has granulated eyelids), and whose short whiskers grow dark on his chin and lower lip. We are now in the presence of the bandit-hero. He is

Jesse James

Any study of Jesse Woodson James (September 5, 1847–April 3, 1882)—the celebrated Missouri ruffian, murderer, bank robber, train robber, and American demigod—is best prefaced by a quick glimpse at his mother, Zerelda E. Cole James Simms Samuel. She was, by all accounts, a notable woman.

After attending a Roman Catholic convent school in Lexington, Kentucky, she married a Baptist seminarian, Robert James. He left her to seek gold in California, where he died. Her second husband, Simms, having died as she was about to divorce him, she married a third, "a meek man." "She was, all her life, a religious woman," says one of Jesse's admiring biographers. "Love became her religion," says another. "She was a woman thoroughly good and noble," the first biographer insists. Most certainly, the second agrees; and then informs us that, after her notorious son had been killed, she "boldly" showed tourists around Jesse's old farm, "extracting every dime she could from them." "This woman who had always been so upright," he adds, sold the tourists stones allegedly from Jesse's grave but actually from the creek. She also sold tourists enough shoes from the horses her two bandit sons had ridden "to fill a wagonbed."

But hear her cry out at Jesse's funeral, while two ministers lead the mourners in singing "We Will Wait Till Jesus Comes."* "Oh, my generous, noble-hearted Jesse," she moans, clearly enough to be heard by the reporters attending.

*Or, as it may have been, "What a Friend We Have in Jesus." As seems always to be the case in these histories of Wild West personages, the authorities cannot agree on anything, no matter how grave of import.

"Oh, why did they kill my poor boy who never wronged anybody, but helped them and fed them with the bread that should go to his orphans?"

Her poor, generous, noble-hearted boy, who never wronged anybody, was the leader of a gang of comparably generous, noble-hearted thugs who, in fifteen years, held up eleven banks, seven trains, three stages, one county fair, and one payroll messenger, in the process looting some $200,000 and killing at least sixteen men. What the mothers of these sixteen said at their graves has unfortunately not been recorded.

Jesse's deification proceeded along the routine lines laid down by the "Police Gazette"—his prankish charm, his courteous behavior to women involved in his stick-ups, his protection of fictitious widows from villainous bankers seeking to foreclose fictitious mortgages, and all the rest—but in his case a unique attribute was added, one guaranteed to inflame the partisan passion bred of the Civil War. For Jesse symbolized the gallant Rebel, ground down beneath the boot of the victorious Yankee oppressor, and such was the potency of this bogus magic that his death kept the sovereign state of Missouri in an uproar for an entire decade.

Jesse grew up in an atmosphere of hate. Missouri men rode across the line into Kansas to cast fraudulent votes they hoped would make Kansas a slave state; Kansas men resisted; Missouri men rode again to raid and kill; Kansas men rode back in vengeance. When the Civil War erupted, there was a whole generation of teen-age toughs living in the tier of Missouri counties that border on Kansas, all of them handy with guns and knives, all of them committed on the political issues of the day, all of them itching to start a rumble. To name just a handful of these hellions: there were Frank James, eighteen, and his brother Jesse, fourteen; Cole Younger, seventeen, Jim Younger, thirteen, and two other brothers, Bob and John, who were still just children; Jim Reed, sixteen; Ed Shirley, about eighteen, and his sister, Myra Belle, thirteen.

All these younsters (except Myra Belle) became bushwhackers—i.e., Confederate irregulars—most of them serving under the infamous William C. Quantrill, the psychopathic turncoat and killer who is justifiably remembered as "the bloodiest man known to the annals of America." Frank James and Cole Younger were with Quantrill when, in August 1863, the town of Lawrence, Kansas, was sacked and 182 of its citizens murdered. Jesse James and Jim Younger were with Quantrill's lieutenant, Bloody Bill Anderson, at the Centralia massacre a year later, when more than two hundred Federal soldiers were shot down, many of them being prisoners. Jesse is credited with killing the commander, Major H. J. Johnson. Jesse was then seventeen.

With the end of the war, most of the bushwhackers laid down their guns and went to work as decent citizens. Not, however, this handful.

The James and Younger brothers (and probably Jim Reed) hitched together a gang of like-minded hooligans that went right on robbing and killing. Their first score, at Liberty, Missouri, on February 14, 1866, was against the Clay County Savings Association Bank, an institution where, it may be presumed, many of their friends and neighbors kept their money. Frank and Jesse missed this caper, but their henchmen stole a sum estimated at from $62,000 to $75,000; they killed one man. Why should they turn back after such a success?

In between robberies and murders, they occupied themselves variously. When Cole Younger, for example, hid out in Texas in 1868, who should he find down there near Dallas but li'l ole Myra Belle Shirley! Why, the last time he saw Myra Belle, back in Jasper County, she was just a scrawny kid in pigtails! But before long she was the mother of his illegitimate daughter, a girl she named Pearl Younger. And when Jim Reed came south in 1870, also on the lam, Myra Belle took him also into her house,

Raised in an atmosphere of hate, Jesse James (shown above) was an incorrigible killer outlaw who blinked his eyes constantly. (Courtesy of Culver Pictures.)

and she cleaved unto him and presented him also with an illegitimate child, a boy she named Ed Reed. For his part, Jim Younger whiled away the time between robberies by serving as deputy sheriff in Dallas.

But the acknowledged leader of "The Boys," as they were fondly called, had no use for such tomfoolery because, we are told, he was too pious. Jesse James was baptized and added to the strength of the Kearney Baptist Church near his home in 1868 (soon after he had killed a man in a bank robbery at Richmond, Missouri). He sang in church choirs; he even organized a group of the faithful and taught hymn-singing (a few months after murdering the cashier of a bank in Gallatin, Missouri). His Bible, we are assured, was well-thumbed; but apparently he skipped the chapters in Exodus where are listed the Ten Commandments, for he continued to kill and to steal, and at least twice he did not remember the Sabbath day, to keep it holy, but rather used it as the occasion for a train robbery.

By 1874 Jesse's crimes were a chief issue in Missouri's gubernatorial campaign: whether or not to suppress outlawry so that "capital and immigration can once again enter our state." But nothing was done; his raids continued.

By 1881 the baying was so close at Jesse's heels that pious or no, he likewise took off for Myra Belle's recherché resort for the criminally inclined. She had removed to a country place on the Canadian River in Oklahoma, which for nostalgic reasons she called Younger's Bend. Belle, having by now given the boot to such sometime outlaw-lovers as Jack Spaniard, Jim French, Jim July, John Middleton, and an Indian known as Blue Duck, had actually gotten married to a Cherokee named Sam Starr. She was in consequence now known as Belle Starr, and could Jesse have known that she would one day be celebrated all over the country as the Bandit Queen, or the Female Jesse James, he might have cursed a tiny curse, pious man that he may have been notwithstanding. But he was dead before then, shot in the back of the head by "the dirty little coward," Bob Ford.

Myra Belle Shirley, horse thief, cattle thief, suspected robber of stagecoaches, constant concubine and protector of desperate criminals, was shot in the back and killed near Eufaula, Oklahoma, on February 3, 1889. A neighbor, Edgar Watson, was accused of her murder, but the charges against him were dismissed. It was rumored that she was slain by her son, Ed Reed, with whom she had had incestuous relations. He was angry with his mother, for she had whipped him after he rode her favorite horse without her permission. So it went, out in the glamorous, romantic Wild West. Scarcely a day passed without some gay and gallant gun slinger shooting his way into the affections of future generations.

Her old neighbor Jesse James lies under a small stone near the site of the Kearney Baptist Church. The stone is all that has been left by souvenir hunters of what was once a pretentious monument, on which had been carved this inscription:

In Loving Remembrance of My Beloved Son
JESSE JAMES
Died April 3, 1882
Aged 34 Years, 6 Months, 28 Days
Murdered by a Traitor and Coward Whose
Name Is Not Worthy to Appear Here.

His mother and stepfather lie in graves on either side of his. On her stone is carved MOTHER, and on his is carved PAPPY.

But had Jesse really been killed in 1882? There were folk in Clay County—and elsewhere, too—who whispered that the murder had been staged, that Jesse still lived and would ride again. He "couldn't" have died. The flood of dime novels about him, the plays, the six motion pictures contrived by Hollywood, this was not enough: the gullible still swore that Jesse lived. Naturally, this being the case, men claiming to be Jesse began to appear one after another. But at length time ran out on them. The last claimant bobbed up in 1948, which meant that he had to act 101 years old, an irksome role. This scalawag at least had the wit to take an appropriate alias. He asserted that he had lived through the years as Frank Dalton, a name which, since it recalled the Dalton gang of the 1890's, fitly closed the circle of Wild West outlawry.

It is time to turn to our next exhibit. Here we have two men mounted on the same pedestal, standing shoulder to shoulder; pals, pards till hell freezes. Each is expressionless, poker-faced; each is clad in black broadcloth and white linen; each affects a handlebar moustache; each has hard blue-gray eyes; each wears a star; at each hip hangs a six-gun. Clearly we are now confronting the men who tamed the Wild West. Sure enough, for their labels read

Wyatt Earp and Bat Masterson

Here are two of the regnant superheroes of the televised Wild West. Once upon a time they faced the same foes in the same filmed fables, but times have changed; they have gone their separate sponsored ways. This is a pity, for in real life the two were thick as thieves.

Each week we are shown—in bland, bright little slices of televised entertainment—just how they scrubbed the Wild West clean, including the back of its neck and behind its ears. Clean-cut and clean-shaven, Wyatt romances Nellie Cashman, the "miners' angel," or he avenges the murder of some Indian friends, or he traps some mining executives who would thieve silver bullion. Elegant and clean-shaven, Bat foils a horse-race swindler, or he gallantly assists some ladies in their struggle for woman's rights, or by examining the brushwork he perceives that some oil paintings are spurious. All this is only so much ingenious fretwork on the Earp-Masterson legend, contrived by worthy successors to the staff writers of the "National Police Gazette." But the legend is itself such an imposing structure as to require no further embellishment.

The legend tells us that Marshal Earp cleaned up two Kansas cowtowns, Ellsworth and Wichita, singlehanded. He then joined forces with Bat Masterson to clean up Dodge City, "the wickedest little city in America." So much accomplished, Marshal Earp turned his attention to the featherweight task of pacifying Tombstone, Arizona, a hotbed of outlaws unparalleled in history, whilst Sheriff Masterson proceeded to stamp out sin in the mining camps of Colorado. Thereafter both men retired, breathing easily, having made the Wild West safe for the effete tenderfeet of the East.

Both men, the legend adds, were courteous to women, modest, handsome, and blue-eyed. We are also told that Earp was the Wild West's speediest and deadliest gun fighter. For his part, Masterson disdained to pull a gun, preferring to clout an adversary senseless with his cane, whence his nickname. But he was quite willing to testify to his pal's prowess and so contribute to the legend. Earp, so Masterson has assured us, could kill a coyote with his Colt .45 at four hundred yards.*

Masterson himself, who was in truth a poor shot, killed at most four men throughout his career (not counting Indians). Indeed, these two differ sharply from other Wild West heroes in that they rarely fired their six-guns in anger. They were both sly, cunning, cautious men, who early learned that shooting might reap a bloody harvest. In consequence, they walked warily, carrying a big bluff. In their time, the Wild West killer and outlaw was dying out, to be replaced by the confidence man. Confidence men rarely kill; they are too artful. Both Earp and Masterson were, among other things, eager students of the technique of early confidence games.

They first met in 1872, when both were hunting buffalo on the Salt Fork of the Arkansas, in direct violation of the Indian treaty. Earp was twenty-four; Masterson was nineteen. They seem to have recognized that they were kindred souls, but they parted, not to come together again until the summer of 1876, in Dodge City. During those four years Bat was, so to say, preparing himself to be a peace officer. He stole

---

*Such skill calls for some respectful analysis. At four hundred yards a coyote cannot be seen against his natural background, so we shall assume the animal is silhouetted against the sky. Even so, an expert using a rifle with a globe sight would congratulate himself if he hit such a target with any regularity, much more if he killed it. A pistol, of course, will not carry so far directly; the marksman must use Kentucky windage—i.e., he must aim appreciably above his target so that his bullet will carry. Masterson admitted that "luck figures largely in such shooting." If, instead of "largely," he had said "completely," he would have come closer to that coyote.

forty ponies from some Indians and sold them for $1,200, he killed other Indians both as a free-lance buffalo hunter and as an army scout, and he got into a brawl with an army sergeant at Sweetwater, Texas, over a dance-hall girl. The girl was killed while trying to shield Masterson; Bat was wounded, but he killed the soldier.

Meantime Earp, by his own account, had engaged in even more impressive heroics. First there was his mettlesome exploit at Ellsworth in 1873. To hear him tell it, Earp stepped out of a crowd, unknown and unheralded, and stalked alone across that familiar sun-baked plaza to disarm an able and truculent gun fighter, the Texas gambler Ben Thompson. Not only that, but Thompson was backed up at the time by a hundred pugnacious cowboy friends. How could Earp ever have dared to do it? He would seem to have been cloaked in invisibility, for others who were present never saw him—not the reporter for the Ellsworth newspaper; not Thompson himself; not Deputy Sheriff Hogue, to whom Thompson voluntarily turned over his gun; and not Mayor James Miller, to whom Thompson gave bond for his appearance when he might be wanted later.

Is it possible Earp was not there at all?

In May, 1874, Earp arrived in Wichita, another rowdy cowtown, where, he said later, Mayor Jim Hope promptly made him the marshal. Let Earp speak: "In two years at Wichita my deputies and I arrested more than eight hundred men. In all that time I had to shoot but one man—and that only to disarm him. All he got was a flesh wound."

And now a look at the minutes of the Wichita city commission. They show that Earp was elected on April 21, 1875, as one of two policemen to serve under the marshal and assistant marshal. They show further that on April 19, 1876, the commission voted against rehiring him. A month later it was recommended that the vagrancy act be enforced against Earp and his brother Jim.

Judging from the Wichita newspapers, Earp seems not to have won much of a reputation during his one year as a policeman. They keep referring to him as "Policeman Erp," which makes him sound like a walking advertisement for Dr. Brown's Celery Tonic. Now and then he arrested a suspected horse thief; but the longest newspaper story about him describes how he was arrested, fined, and fired from the police force for violating the peace on April 5, 1876. All this resulted from an election-eve fracas in which Earp slugged an opposition candidate for city marshal. And so he turned up in Dodge City, another cowtown.

Dodge was run by a small clique of saloonkeepers who, as the years went on, took turns at being mayor. Most saloons were routinely outfitted with gambling layouts. In 1878 the town council enacted an ordinance against gambling. Had its members gone out of their minds? No: they were moved by sound common sense. For, with a law on the books prohibiting gambling, any chump who complained that he had been cheated could be forthwith walked Spanish to the hoosegow on the grounds that he had been breaking the law.

A town run along these lines clearly required something special in the way of a peace officer: a man who would know how and when to enforce the freakish laws, who would know how to wink at the artful ways in which cowpokes from Texas were mulcted. We are told that the saloonkeeper who was mayor in 1876 sent for Wyatt Earp.

Earp told his skillful biographer, Stuart Lake, that he appointed Bat Masterson as one of his deputies. Earp also asserted that he was paid $250 a month, plus a fee of $2.50 for each arrest; he and his deputies, he said, arrested some three hundred persons a month, or enough to bring in about $750 a month. (One month in 1877, he recalled, the fees reached almost $1,000 from nearly four hundred arrests; that was the peak.) Earp's share would have brought his income to more than $400 a month, nice money for the time and place.

And now to the town records. Earp was never marshal of Dodge. He served two terms as assistant marshal: from May, 1876, to September, 1876, and from May, 1878, to September, 1879. (During that month of 1877 when, by his own account, he and his deputies arrested nearly four hundred rowdy cowboys, Earp was not a peace officer at all. In fact, he was himself arrested that month for brawling with a dance-hall girl.) His salary as assistant marshal was $75 a month. The fee paid for an arrest (and conviction) was only $2. The docket of the police court shows that during 1878 there were only sixty-four arrests; during 1879 there were only twenty-nine arrests.

One interpretation of this remarkable decline in arrests—from three hundred or four hundred a month in 1876–77 to just four a month in 1878–79—is that lion-hearted Wyatt Earp had tamed the town. There is another interpretation.

At all events, it is clear that Earp's income in 1878 could not have been much more than $80 a month—not much money for the time and place. Bat Masterson's income was about the same. Both had to add to it. Both did: as professional gamblers.

It has been argued that professional gambling in the Wild West was honest. This is to impose on credulity. Obviously it was no more honest than professional gambling whenever and wherever—which is to say, no more honest than it had to be.

Earp was a professional gambler long before he got to Dodge; his reputation around Hays City, according to Dr. Floyd Streeter, a Kansas historian, was that of a card player who was "up to some dishonest trick every time he played."

Masterson, who left Dodge in July, 1876, to follow the gold rush to Deadwood, got no further than Cheyenne, Wyoming, where he did so well as a faro banker that he stuck. But he was back in Dodge for the cattle season of 1877. On June 6 he was arrested, jugged, and fined $25 and costs for an act of hooliganism. Then he returned to his faro bank.

However, he badly wanted a star. Every professional gambler needed a star; the badge of office permitted its wearer to carry a gun, which in turn provided just the psychological advantage necessary in a game of chance played for high stakes. (Only peace officers were permitted to carry guns in Dodge City; all others were obliged to check their weapons in racks provided for the purpose.) And so Bat decided to run for sheriff of Ford County.

His electioneering technique was simplicity itself: he bought an interest in the Lone Star Dance Hall. Only thus could a candidate convince the bizarre electorate of Dodge City that he was a sound citizen and a responsible taxpayer. In November, 1877, Bat was elected by a three-vote margin. He took office in January, and what is more, he started off in high gear by catching some would-be train robbers. But as the months wore on, like Earp, and like Hickok before them both, he whiled away his evening hours as a professional gambler along with cronies like Doc Holliday, an alcoholic ex-dentist, and Luke Short, a dandiprat. Earp banked faro at the Long Branch Saloon for a percentage of the house's gross. He and Bat and the others spent so many nights in Dodge's brothels that they were nicknamed "the Fighting Pimps."

There was justification for the slur. Earp lived with a girl called Mattie Blaylock; since no record of any marriage has ever been found, she is presumed to have been his common-law wife. And Nyle Miller, director of the Kansas State Historical Society, and an authority on the dossiers of Earp and Masterson, has established that, according to the census of 1880, Bat Masterson was living with Annie Ladue, nineteen, described as his "concubine," whilst his younger brother, Jim Masterson, by then Dodge's marshal in his turn, was living with Minnie Roberts, sixteen, also a concubine. As Mr. Miller has commented acidly, "Maybe that was the way some of the officers in those days kept watch over juvenile delinquents. They just lived with them."

By that time Bat was no longer sheriff, having been walloped in his bid for re-election by George Hinkle, a bartender. Earp had also turned in his star. Dodge was not appreciably tamer, but the silver strike in the Arizona hills meant that there might be more money lying around loose in Tombstone; he followed his brother Virgil there in December, 1879. With him came Mattie; with him too were other Earps, his brothers Jim and Morgan and their wives; and presently, tagging along after him, came Doc Holliday with his common-law wife, Big Nose Kate Fisher, a Dodge prostitute.

Tombstone, they soon found, was strangely unlike Dodge City. Four churches were going up. (Groton's future headmaster, Endicott Peabody, was the young Episcopalian clergyman.) There were carpets in the saloons, forsooth, and French phrases on the menus in restaurants. No doubt about it, the Wild West was running out of steam.

Dogged traditionalists, Wyatt Earp got a job as a shotgun messenger for Wells Fargo and his brother Jim caught on as a faro banker.

Wyatt was not, as the legend has it, a United States marshal at this time. His brother Virgil was appointed a deputy marshal for southern Arizona in November, 1879, and was appointed an assistant town marshal of Tombstone in October, 1880; but Wyatt, after a brief term as civil deputy sheriff of Pima County, went back to gambling at the Oriental Saloon.

A word about Doc Holliday. He was, from every account but Wyatt's, a mean and vicious man. He was Georgia-born, tubercular, and fond of killing. After killing two Negroes in Georgia, he fled; after killing a man in Dallas, he fled; after killing a soldier near Fort Richardson, he fled; after wounding a man in Denver, he fled. It was the pattern of his life. Then he met Earp. "Doc idolized him," Masterson said later. And Earp, for his part, found much to admire in Holliday.

"With all of Doc's shortcomings and his undeniably poor disposition," Earp told Stuart Lake, "I found him a loyal friend and good company...."

Earp's trouble began on the night of March 15, 1881, when a stagecoach left Tombstone carrying eight passengers, and, we are told, $80,000 worth of bullion.* Bandits attempted to halt this miracle of transportation. They failed, but in the process they killed the driver and one passenger. The killer was, according to a statement by his wife, Doc Holliday; and the talk around town was that the brain behind the bungled holdup was Wyatt Earp's. Moving fast, the Earps persuaded Big Nose Kate to retract her statement and bundled her out of town lest she contradict the retraction. There remained the task of silencing forever Holliday's accomplices.

Wyatt went to one of their friends, Ike Clanton, and offered a deal. If Clanton would arrange to have those accomplices hold up another stage so that Earp and Holliday could ambush them, he, Earp, would guarantee that Clanton would be paid the reward for their capture. Clanton seems to have considered this offer seriously, but at length he refused. The rebuff was serious, for Ike was a blabbermouth who could not be trusted to keep the offer quiet.

Nor did he. Scared stiff that he would be shot for a stool pigeon, Clanton denied everything, so loudly and publicly that Doc Holliday overheard him and reported to Wyatt. That was in mid-October. Something would have to be done.

On October 26, Ike Clanton was back in Tombstone with his younger brother, Billy. With them were Frank and Tom McLowry and another youngster, Billy Claiborne. All these men were cattle rustlers or, at the very least, hard cases. That morning Virgil Earp, as town

---

*It is always instructive to examine Wild Western estimates. At $1 per fine ounce, $80,000 worth of bullion would weigh two and a half tons, a load sure to snap the axles of any coach.

marshal, deputized his brothers Wyatt and Morgan, and thereafter the three prowled the streets, seeking to pick a quarrel with the Clantons or the McLowrys. Virgil Earp clubbed Ike Clanton with the barrel of his revolver. Wyatt Earp deliberately jostled Tom McLowry and then struck him. But despite the provocations, there was no fight.

That afternoon the Clanton brothers, the McLowry brothers, and Claiborne went to the O. K. Corral to pick up their horses and ride out of town. Wyatt, Virgil, and Morgan Earp, together with Doc Holliday, went after them. Sheriff John Behan tried to interfere, but he was brushed aside.

The Earps and Holliday marched into the corral. Somebody spoke; somebody started shooting. After a couple of minutes, Billy Clanton was dead, Frank and Tom McLowry were dead, and Ike Clanton and Billy Claiborne, having run for their lives, were safe. Morgan Earp was hit in the left shoulder; Virgil in the leg; Holliday in the left hip.

The Earp apologists have described these slayings as a triumph of law and order. In Tombstone the reaction was somewhat different. A sign over the caskets of the dead proclaimed: MURDERED IN THE STREETS OF TOMBSTONE. A mining engineer named Lewis, who had witnessed what he called cold-blooded murder, was one of three men appointed by the Citizens' Safety Committee to tell the Earps that there should be no more killing inside the town's limits, and that, if there were, the committee would act without regard to law; finally, Virgil Earp was fired as town marshal on October 29.

In any case, friends of those slain took matters into their own hands. Virgil Earp was ambushed and wounded on December 29. In March, 1882, Morgan Earp was picked off in the middle of a billiard game, by a sharpshooter who fired through a window from an alley in back. By this time Wyatt Earp had apparently at long last managed to be deputized by a federal marshal. (No records exist in either the Department of Justice or the National Archives to show that he ever held a regular commission as U.S. marshal or deputy.) He in turn deputized such gunmen as Doc Holliday, Turkey Creek Jack Johnson, and Texas Jack Vermillion, and took off in pursuit of his brother's killers.

He rode and he rode, but he never came back. He rode north and east to Colorado where, he hoped, he would be safe. Behind him he left Mattie, his common-law wife, who had taken in sewing at a penny a yard when money was scarce. Behind him, too, he left a town so far from being tamed that President Chester Arthur was obliged, a few months later, to threaten martial law. It was left to a short-spoken, sawed-off, former Texas Ranger named John H. Slaughter to restore order to Cochise County.

And meanwhile, what of Bat Masterson? He had hustled back to Dodge City from Tombstone in April, 1881, in response to a hurry-up plea for help from his younger brother Jim. This worthy, still Dodge's marshal and also co-owner of a dance hall, had got into a scrape with his partner, A. J. Peacock, and the man they employed as bartender, Al Updegraff, but Jim Masterson was apparently too timid to do his own fighting. His big brother stepped off the train at noon on April 16. Peacock and Updegraff were there waiting, and once again the tiresome shooting commenced. It was laughable. They all fired their guns empty, without effect. Some unknown hero, using a rifle, wounded Updegraff from behind. Masterson was fined $8 for shooting his pistol on the street. The Ford County "Globe" commented, "The citizens are thoroughly aroused and will not stand any more foolishness," while the Jetmore "Republican" referred caustically to "the old gang." Bat and his brother were ordered out of town.

Like a cat, Bat landed on his feet in Trinidad, Colorado, where in addition to running a gambling concession he appears to have been appointed a peace officer. Certainly he had some political influence. For, when an Arizona sheriff came to Denver with a request for the extradition of Wyatt Earp and Doc Holliday, Masterson helped protect them. He got out a warrant for Holliday's arrest on the charge of running a confidence game. This superseded the request for extradition, after which the charges against Holliday were of course dropped. "I know him well," Bat told a reporter for the Denver "Republican," speaking of Holliday. "He was with me in Dodge, where he was known as an enemy of the lawless element."

But the trail led down from glory. In the 1890's Masterson ran a faro layout at the Arcade in Denver, then notoriously the crookedest town in the country. (Earp was dealing nearby, at the Central.) But around the turn of the century Bat was ordered to leave even Denver—it was like being told he was too low for the sewer. In 1902 he went to New York where he was at once arrested. On the train from Chicago he had, it seems, fleeced a Mormon elder of $16,000 by using marked cards in a faro game. No matter: New York was then also corrupt; Bat was bailed by John Considine, a partner of Big Tim Sullivan, who bossed the town. The elder was persuaded to mumble that he must have been mistaken when he identified Masterson. When Bat was again arrested, this time for illegally carrying a gun, his friends pulled on strings that led all the way to the White House; and such was the magic of the Wild West legend that President Theodore Roosevelt appointed Masterson a deputy U.S. marshal for the southern district of New York. The term of the appointment was brief. Then Bat was put out to pasture as a sports writer for the "Morning Telegraph." He died at his desk in 1921.

Meantime Earp had married a San Francisco woman named Josephine Marcus. As late as 1911 he was accused of complicity in a confidence game, but in the main he had retired to live off his investments. He died in Los Angeles in 1930. The ugliest bit of his past has been dug up, with some disgust, by Frank Waters. It concerns Mattie, the girl Earp deserted in Tombstone. Alone and friendless, Mattie drifted first to Globe and then to a mining camp near Willcox, Arizona. She was reduced to prostitution for a living. In July, 1888, she died of an overdose of laudanum, a suicide. The coroner who sent her few belongings back to her family in Iowa tucked into the package a letter in which he wrote that Mattie had been deserted by "a gambler, blackleg, and coward." Among her effects was a Bible that had been presented to Earp when he was in Dodge. The inscription read: "To Wyatt S. Earp as a slight recognition of his many Christian virtues and steady following in the footsteps of the meek and lowly Jesus."

Amen.

We have come at last to our fifth Horrible, a slight, short, buck-toothed, narrow-shouldered youth whose slouch adds to his unwholesome appearance. He looks like a cretin, but this may be deceptive. As we crane cautiously forward, we can see that his label reads

Billy the Kid

This young outlaw is less interesting as a human being than as a sort of Rorschach ink blot by which one may elicit fantasies and so study their inventors. It is safe to say that at least a thousand writers have used Billy the Kid as a vessel into which to pour their passions, prejudices, and opinions; but it is likely that no two portraits of him jibe. He has been endowed with every imaginable personality; from the way he has been described one could conclude that he was the original Man With a Thousand Faces; his alleged backgrounds are as various; so even are his names.

The best guess is that he was born November 23, 1859, in New York City, and called Henry McCarty. There was a younger brother, Joe. Around 1863 the family went west to Kansas. The father may have died here; at all events

Mrs. Catherine McCarty was married on March 1, 1873, with her two sons as witnesses, to William H. Antrim, in Santa Fé, New Mexico. The newlyweds settled in Silver City, near the Arizona border, and here Mrs. Antrim died on September 16, 1874. Henry McCarty was not yet fifteen.

He killed for the first time three years later: a blacksmith called Windy Cahill, in a saloon near Camp Grant, Arizona. There followed some gambling and some horse stealing. He was next a principal figure in the celebrated Lincoln County War, an affair which, including skirmishes and at least one pitched battle, went on for more than a year. The villains of this "war" were politicians, involved in their customary muttonheaded struggle for power, and guilty of their customary nonfeasance, misfeasance, and malfeasance. The Kid seems to have been caught up in it chiefly because he wasn't old enough to know any better. Several persons were killed in the course of this "war," and the Kid may have killed one or more of them; none can say for sure. In any case, his side lost, and for the rest of his brief life he was an outlaw, a hunted man.

He stole some more livestock. He killed a man named Joe Grant, who had thought to shoot first. He rode with some exceedingly case-hardened characters, including Hendry Brown, John Middleton, and Dave Rudabaugh. Sheriff Pat Garrett and a posse first caught the Kid near Stinking Springs. He stood trial for murder, was found guilty, and was sentenced to be hanged. There were two men guarding him in the jail at Lincoln, but the Kid managed to get hold of a gun, killed them both, and fled again, again a free man.

Garrett, implacable, continued his pursuit. One brightly moonlit night he shot and killed the Kid in Fort Sumner, New Mexico. It was July 14, 1881. Henry McCarty, alias William Bonney, alias The Kid, was not yet twenty-two.

And now the fun began.

The first book to follow the Kid's death appeared a month later and was subtitled, "The

Short, slight, slouchy, narrow-shouldered, and buck-toothed, Billy the Kid was a moronic gun slinger who rode the outlaw trail in the Arizona and New Mexico territories. (Courtesy of Sy Seidman.)

history of an outlaw who killed a man for every year in his life," a fiction which was seized upon and inflated by nine out of every ten writers who followed. The author of this book was a man named Fable, appropriately enough, and he described the Kid as wearing "a blue dragoon jacket of the finest broadcloth, heavily loaded down with gold embroidery, buckskin pants, dyed a jet black, with small tinkling bells sewed down the sides . . . drawers of fine scarlet broadcloth . . . and a hat covered with gold and jewels. . . ."

The "Police Gazette" published a biography too, as did Pat Garrett. Both poured gore liberally over the Kid. Garrett added a nice touch: he said that Billy, to show his skill, once shot the heads off several snowbirds, one after another. (J. Frank Dobie has remarked tartly, of this story, that it didn't happen because it couldn't happen.)

By 1889 a Frenchman, the Baron de Mandat-Grancey, had written a wondrous book called "La Brèche aux Buffles"—this was his way of saying Buffalo Gap—in which he reported how Billy the Kid killed his prison guard, a man named William Bonny. Other accounts appeared: the Kid had been a dishwasher in his youth; no, he had been a bootblack in New York City's Fourth Ward; no, he had gone to college in the East and was really an Ivy League type.

The number of his killings mounted steadily. Soon he had killed twenty-three men, one for each of his now twenty-three years, not counting seven Mexicans whom he shot "just to see them kick." A play about him opened in 1906 and ran for years. By 1918 its producers claimed it had been seen by ten million people. It was in 1906, too, that a dime novel appeared in which the Kid was described as an Apache who had been killed by Buffalo Bill, assisted by Wild Bill Hickok.

Then, oddly, the Kid dropped out of sight for a generation. When he reappeared, he had been twenty-four years old, and killed twenty-four men. Walter Noble Burns sentimentalized him so successfully that Hollywood brought out the first of some twenty movies about him. (Of these, the two best-known, perhaps, are those that starred Robert Taylor and Jane Russell.) Somebody made up the wonderful story that the gun Garrett had used to kill the Kid was the same gun worn by Wild Bill Hickok when he was shot in Deadwood. Somebody else wrote that the judge who sentenced the Kid ordered him to be hanged by the neck until "you are dead, dead, dead," to which Billy retorted, "You go to hell, hell, hell!"

The further away the mythmakers got from him, the more precisely they described him. He was "a boy of talent and exceptional intelligence," "good natured and of a happy, carefree disposition," with "an unusually attractive personality." He was also "an adenoidal moron, both constitutionally and emotionally inadequate to a high degree." He killed forty-five men. He never killed anybody.

He was driven to a life of crime because, at the age of twelve, he killed a man who made a slurring remark to his mother. "His blue-gray eyes at times could turn cold and deadly." Pat Garrett never shot him at all, that night at Fort Sumner, for he was still alive in 1920, when he was known as Walk-Along Smith.

In one sense, it is, of course, perfectly true that Billy the Kid did not die. He is the most imperishable of our folk heroes. Under his name there will always appear, whenever appropriate, a figure freshly refurbished so as to embody the hero who appropriately symbolizes the need of the hour: brutal killer, avenging angel, mama's boy, slayer of capitalist dragons, bewildered cat's paw, or gay, gallant, carefree cowpoke. The face is blank, but it comes complete with a handy do-it-yourself kit so that the features may be easily filled in.

What, in summary, of the world of the Wild West? Manifestly, it was an underworld, corrupt and rotten. Its heroes, vaunted for their courage, in fact showed only the rashness of the alcoholic or the desperation of the cornered rat. They were popularly supposed to have honored the Wild West's so-called code, which forbade the shooting of an unarmed man and likewise the shooting of an armed man until he had been faced and warned of the peril in which he stood. But look at our five—the most celebrated heroes of all:

Hickok made his reputation by killing, from his hiding place, two unarmed men and then mortally wounding a third unarmed man who was running for his life.

Jesse James murdered at least two unarmed bank tellers, not because they had offered resistance, but when they were cowering at the bandit's feet.

Wyatt Earp and his brothers, shielded by police badges, provoked a fight, shot first, and killed men who, according to three eyewitnesses, were holding up their hands.

Bat Masterson is saved from any similar charge chiefly because he was such a poor shot.

Billy the Kid shot and killed from ambush, not once, but several times. Indeed, only the first of his authenticated killings seems to have come about in a man-to-man fight, and even on that occasion his opponent was unarmed.

What heroes, to be exalted by the Republic!

As outlaws, they were first adored because, it was argued, they robbed only the railroad monopolist and the banker, the men most heartily hated west of the Mississippi. As law officers, they were first adored because, it was argued, they enforced the peace in perilous circumstances, against overwhelming odds. Both propositions are cockeyed. Outlaw or law officer, it made little difference, they were one brutal brotherhood. The so-called law officers more often caused than quelled crime. Hendry Brown, an outlaw in New Mexico, could ride to Kansas and pin on a sheriff's star; Jim Younger, an outlaw in Missouri, could ride to Texas and pin on a deputy sheriff's star; even Billy the Kid rode for a time as a member of a bailiff's posse and, had his side won the Lincoln County War, might well have come down to us in folklore as a force for law and order. The whole boodle of them careened through lives of unredeemed violence and vulgarity, to fetch up—where else? In the Valhalla of the comics, the movies, and television.

But surely the producers of the popular entertainments do not pretend that they are purveying history? Surely they concede that their Wild West peep shows, especially on television, are at most so much embroidery basted onto the national folklore? Yet these entrepreneurs persist in using names of real people and real places. They cite dates of real occurrences—usually, to be sure, absurdly wrong. They lard their diversions with such sly phrases as "based on actual events" or "a colorful look at our American heritage." Speaking of Wyatt Earp, they describe him as "one of the real-life heroes of yesterday . . . one of the greatest marshals in the annals of history . . . this famous straight-shootin', fast-ridin', fair-playin', clean-livin' lawman. . . ." They transform vicious, alcoholic gun fighters like Johnny Ringo and Clay Allison into sheriffs, symbols of justice and peace. They portray Jesse James as an innocent youth unfairly forced into a career of crime, and Belle Starr as a winsome, dewy-eyed ingénue who looks for all the world like Miss Cream Puff of 1960.

And even granting the assumption that the purveyors of this sludge are concerned not with history but with legend, what a shameful and ghastly legend it is! to be despised, if not on the sufficient grounds of its ugly violence, then on the grounds of its even uglier vulgarity.

The moral, of course, is that crime, when commercially exploited, does pay, and the more sadistic the better. The Wild West—portrayed by irresponsible men who care not a hang for the truth of history so long as they can count their audiences in the scores of millions—has become a permanent industry and has created for the world an enduring image of America.

III Gilded Age Kaleidoscope

7
The New Industrial Order

Bernard A. Weisberger

of problems that were to plague America for years to come. In a fast-moving narrative that catches the spirit of the postwar boom, Bernard Weisberger traces the rise of America's new industrial order, describes both the merits and drawbacks of consolidation itself, and portrays the controversial "robber barons" as a complex gallery of individuals who ranged from "gay and gaudy vulgarians" to literate, self-made men. Then, with his narrative as a backdrop, we go on to examine other features of the Gilded Age: the turbulent political struggles which the boom produced, the plight of the immigrant in industrial America, and the Spanish-American War of 1898.

Technology in Triumph

Traditional accounts of American industrial growth begin with the ending of the Civil War, but it is a mistake to trace economic growth by essentially political milestones. By economic measure, the industrialization of American life began long before 1865. Railroad construction, bank loans, the value added to raw materials by manufacture, immigration, the size of investments in agricultural and other machinery, and production of certain key commodities such as pig iron and bituminous coal had increased by as much as two hundred per cent between 1840 and 1860. An important current economic theorist, Walt W. Rostow, has even asserted that the American "takeoff" into sustained, modern, dominating economic growth was completed by 1860, and what took place thereafter was a flight to maturity. In fact, the 1860s show an uneven pattern of growth in the production of goods considered essential to "industrialism," which is understandable in the light of the war. Naturally cotton produc-

From the 1820s on, the United States industrialized at an impressive rate of growth. While the Civil War itself may have impeded some areas of economic enterprise, the federal government emerged from that conflict more than ready to encourage and to subsidize industrial activities; and the postwar growth was swift and awesome. One Republican Administration after another not only maintained a protective tariff to minimize foreign competition, but gave away millions of dollars worth of public land to railroad companies, allowed Western cattle barons—those examples of supreme "rugged individualism"—a gigantic Federal subsidy in the form of free range on public territory, adopted a hard-money policy which pleased big businessmen, and—except for the Interstate Commerce and Sherman Anti-Trust acts, both enacted because of popular unrest—cheerfully refused to regulate or restrict the consolidation of America's industrial order.

It was the Gilded Age, Mark Twain called it, an era between Appomattox and the turn of the century when American capitalism, growing for decades now, produced mighty combinations that controlled most of the nation's wealth. While the industrial revolution did make the United States a powerful country, it also created a multitude

From Bernard A. Weisberger, *The New Industrial Society, 1848–1900.* Copyright © 1969 by John Wiley & Sons, Inc. Reprinted by permission.

tion decreased. The annual mileage of newly built railroad line dropped quite sharply from over 3400 in 1854 to only 574 in 1863, and did not exceed the 1854 level until 1869. There was no spectacular increase in the rate of growth of sales of agricultural implements. Production of iron and coal trended upward, but with no sharp wartime spurt. One distinguished economic historian has even argued that the war retarded industrialization by concentrating productive efforts on short-run military needs. This view has been challenged, however, and the argument seems to turn on *which* indices of production are evidences of "industrialization," and on the length of the periods over which growth or decline should be measured. Whoever is right, the unqualified assertion that the Civil War "hastened" industrialism can no longer be made safely.

Nevertheless, there is no doubt that the postwar rate of climb was swift. Railroad mileage, for example, which stood at approximately 35,000 in 1865, doubled in the next eight years, passed the hundred thousand mark in 1881, and by 1900 had very nearly doubled even this figure, reaching a total of 193,000 miles at the end of the century. The national rail net mileage reached its maximum with 254,000 miles of track in 1916. Construction of new line reached a yearly high of nearly 13,000 miles in 1887. Although the most spectacular building feats were in the Far West, where five transcontinental lines were stretched across desert and mountain, there was more economic meaning in the growth of the feeder lines in older sections. Industrial growth thrived on a truly national market, which saw Chicago harvesters, Texas beef, Minneapolis flour, Waterbury clocks, and Toledo glass rushed to almost any populated place on the map at thirty or more miles an hour. Railroad growth also stoked the fires of the steel mills, the second great element in modern industrial power. As the builders cried out for the tough new metal after 1865 (to replace older, cast-iron rails in addition to laying new track, much as modern airlines converted to jet operation), there was an escalation of demand that spurred investment, modernization, and prodigies of production in a steel industry which had scarcely existed until the discovery of the Bessemer process just before the Civil War began. Steel was also wanted for bridges, machinery, wire, armorplate, and construction work, and it was not unnatural that the total of American-produced steel ingots and castings should rise from less than 20,000 long tons in 1867 to a world-leading ten million long tons in 1900.

The consumption of energy other than that provided by human and animal muscle rose steadily. Bituminous coal production increased from about 13 million short tons in 1867 to 212,316,000 short tons in 1900. In 1860 there was no such thing as an American petroleum products industry; by 1899 more than 1 billion gallons of kerosene, 300 million gallons of fuel oils, and 170 million gallons of lubricating oils were manufactured. This took place before the gasoline engine created its own revolution in demand. Electricity as a source of both light and power became a practical reality in the 1880s but, by 1912, industry alone was using more than 11 million kilowatt hours in a single year. Central generating plants, to provide illumination and street railway transportation for entire cities, were commonplace. The total horsepower for doing basic industrial work produced from all sources—steam, electricity, wind, water, and work animals—was approximately 2,535,000 in 1860 and 46,215,000 in 1900. This was nearly an 18-fold increase in energy applicable to production in one lifetime. Small wonder that Henry Adams declared in 1904 in a prophetic image: "Power leaped from every atom. . . . Man could no longer hold it off. Forces grasped his wrists and flung him about as though he had hold of a live wire."

Year after year the nation's factories poured out capital goods such as agricultural, mining and construction machinery, locomotives, generators, chemicals, and such consumer items as flour, fabrics, canned foods, clothing, boots and shoes, furniture, lamps, cutlery, stoves, wagons, hardware, paints, lacquers, paper and printing presses, cigars, and sewing machines. In a generation the country moved from a homemade to a store-bought society. And this revolutionary transformation was achieved by technical change that enabled mass production to bring an infinite variety of goods within the reach of every man's purse. Andrew Carnegie wrote exultantly that with steel billets selling at $15 a gross ton, the consumer got 1 pound of steel for two thirds of 1 cent. Into this pound went 2 pounds of iron ore, mined and transported 1000 miles, 1⅓ pounds of coal mined, roasted into coke, and carried 50 miles, and ⅓ pound of limestone quarried and transported 140 miles. Carnegie gave primary credit for this incredible cheapening of cost to automatic machinery.

Actually there were few industries in which mechanization did not work magic. The publicized inventions that come readily to mind—the telephone, the typewriter, the electric light, all dating from the 1870s—were but the peak of the iceberg. There were also innumerable significant but little-known industrial innovations. Consider two examples. In glassmaking, during the years between 1880 and 1916, machines were developed that automatically blew and shaped bulbs, tumblers, lamp chimneys, and bottles. Machines were developed that automatically produced glass tubing and rods of uniform thickness for any purpose. Other machines automatically rolled out continuous sheets of window glass between rollers as rapidly as five feet (of seven-foot wide glass) per minute. Moreover, there were improvements in furnaces, fuels, and additives to molten glass, which improved quality as well as quantity. Between 1880 and 1919, the number of firms making glass jumped from 169 to 317. The number of workers involved increased from 24,000 to 83,600. But the physical volume of the glass produced increased 10-fold, and the value of the glass produced increased more than 12-fold—from approximately $21 million in 1880 to $261,884,080 in 1919. Or consider the daily newspaper. In 1840, a good-sized "big-city" newspaper consisted of 4 or 6 pages, was sold to perhaps 4000 subscribers daily, and cost between 5 and 10 cents. In the ensuing 50 years, machines were developed that printed both sides of a continuous sheet of paper and automatically cut and folded finished pages, while other machines set type mechanically. By 1890, as a result of work such as that of the Hoe Company in press technology or Ottmar Mergenthaler, developer of the linotype, a major New York newspaper such as the *New York World* reached perhaps 300,000 people daily with an edition of 16 or more pages, for 2 cents. By the end of the century, the newspapers were even larger—and Sunday editions contained colored supplements, photographs, and other attractions in as many as 64 pages of wood-pulp paper (itself a post-Civil War development).

It was in lowly personifications such as the throw-away beer bottle and the colored comics that the miracle of productivity revealed itself to many Americans who never saw a blast furnace or a dynamo. But whatever shape technological triumph took, it was the dominating cultural, social, intellectual, and political fact of the age.

The Organization of Abundance

Changes such as these brought on sweeping reorganizations of the system by which business in the United States was managed. The paradox of mass production was that it produced items for pennies through the use of machines and a transportation network costing hundreds of millions of dollars. These monster complexes demanded strong centralized control. The wasteful duplication inherent in free competition became a heavy burden on persons who produced on a large scale. In the "game of business," it was necessary each year for a player to put up higher and higher stakes to stay at the table, and this led to a further paradox. Small players had to drop out, and the nation could not afford to lose many really big players, since they took too many investors and employees down with them. Hence, to some extent, the game had to be rigged.

A revealing sign of the trend toward bigness and combination was the rise of the corporation. The partnership, which was the favored form of combining capital in colonial times, had serious drawbacks for large-scale enterprise. It was vulnerable to deaths, arguments among partners, and individual failures, and could not amass the really great sums of capital demanded by modernized industry.

In the corporation, by contrast, shares of stock could be sold in enormous quantities. Shareholders were able to sell or transfer their holdings freely and to elect directors who, through appointed professional managers, could conduct the business. An individual shareholder could only lose the value of his own shares in case of trouble. Thus, directors might come and go, shareholders might die and sell out, but the corporation went on undisturbed, raising and spending millions. These qualities of durability and bigness explain the growing popularity of corporate organization, especially in fields such as banking, canal building, and railroading, during the early phases of economic growth, when the need for large outlays over long periods became apparent. New York's Erie Railroad, for example, was begun in 1833 with an estimated construction cost of three million dollars. By the time it was completed from Lake Erie to the mouth of the Hudson, in 1851, its actual expense had exceeded fifty million dollars.

Corporation charters originally had been granted only by special acts of the state legislature to individual applicants but, during the 1840's, Jacksonian Democrats in industrial states succeeded in replacing this system with general incorporation laws, which allowed any group, on payment of a fee, to create a company and sell stock. The path was thus open for widespread use of this organizational device, which was so well suited to the new age of big business. Data for early corporations are not available, but the triumph of the system is revealed by figures which show that, in 1904, almost seventy per cent of all manufacturing employees were in corporation-owned establishments.

But there was a price for this growth. The corporations themselves, grown to monstrous size, became "privileged members of society." The Southern Pacific Railroad, for instance, with a virtual monopoly of rail transport in California and limitless funds to hire lawyers, lobbyists, and editors, dominated the life of that state for two decades after 1880. To the bigness of the corporations there was joined an impersonality summed up in the popular phrase that a corporate entity had neither a soul to be damned nor a body to be kicked. Moreover, there was another problem connected with the system—a problem that arose because shares of stock could be bought, sold, and swapped on the open market, for profit, by men who had no interest in the fate of the businesses represented by the stock certificates.

A kind of elegant gambling took place, involving two types of transactions known as "buying long" and "selling short." A contract was made to buy or sell stocks for a set price on some future date. If the price had risen at the appointed time, the buyer profited: he got stocks at less than the going rate. If the price had fallen, the seller got more than the market figure for the shares he unloaded. The trouble with this simple wager was that the speculative buyers (or "bulls") and sellers (known as "bears") did not leave the price to chance. Bulls often made heavy secret purchases in order to bid up prices temporarily and artifi-

1885 cartoon depicting the railroad as robber baron. Perhaps the cartoonist had in mind railroad tycoon Cornelius Vanderbilt, who once remarked, "Law? What do I care about the law. Hain't I got the power?" (Courtesy of The New-York Historical Society.)

cially. Bears were not above buying control of a company and then issuing shares of stock far in excess of the value of its properties (a process known as "watering the stock"), finally dumping the shares on the market to drive prices down. Other forms of knavery were possible through manipulation of the securities market. Unethical majority stockholders (and the directors whom they controlled) could use a company's assets to support loans, expansion, or construction that was economically unsound but that promised immediate profits to persons on the inside. A master of this kind of manipulation was Jay Gould. He was once a store clerk and tannery operator who, in the 1880s, became a multimillionaire owner of half the rail lines in the Southwest. He also owned a newspaper, the New York City elevated railway system, and the Western Union telegraph company without any evident knowledge of (or interest in) journalism or transportation.

Rascality, on a grand scale, was not typical of the American business system, but it had painful consequences. Companies—railroads, in particular—were left with enormous debts, based not on the companies' actual earning power but on the false paper value of their watered stocks. Even worse, the wild fluctuations in stock prices involved the banks, which lived by investing other people's money in securities. When a sudden fall in the market wiped out a bank or banks, business loans were called in, factory doors closed, goods could find no buyers at any price, and the whole nation lurched into a sickening depression. In 1873, the failure of a major banking house triggered a paralyzing four-year slump. It was a national lesson in the complexity and the interdependence of the new economic system. It was also evidence of the dangers in a pattern of corporate financing which often divorced the ownership of an enterprise from responsibility for its management.

Yet the corporations, socially troublesome as they were, checked each others' power through competition, where it existed. The genuine problems of the age of big business emerged more starkly when individual firms, bled by price wars and the costs of modernization, forsook competition and combined. Once again certain railroads—pioneers of American industrial development—took a pace-setting role in the 1870s by setting up "pools." These pools were arrangements whereby allegedly competing lines divided traffic among themselves, and then shared earnings periodically on a prorated basis. An example was the so-called "Iowa Pool" of 1870, in which three lines running between Chicago and Omaha shared equally the heavy grain and livestock shipments of the route. Another example was the South Improvement Company. It was an organization of oil refiners and directors of the New York Central, the Erie, and the Pennsylvania railroads that aimed at dividing the oil-carriage business between Cleveland and the Atlantic Coast. The Pennsylvania railroad was to get 45 per cent of the traffic, and the other two lines were to divide the balance evenly. In order to encourage the shippers to go along with this practice of "evening" the shipments, they were given rebates on the published rates—and, as an added advantage, rebates on the shipments of their competitors! In theory, these were merely rewards for allowing the railroads to save money by efficient planning but, in fact, the rebates allowed the "eveners" to ruin their competitors. The railroads, therefore, by giving up competition themselves, were enabling certain shippers to dominate their own industries. Public outcry against this abuse of the railroads' role as "common carriers" soon forced an end to the South Improvement Company. Yet pools not only continued to exist among railroads but also were organized in the coal, iron, and other industries. Production quotas were allotted, and prices were set. The consumer lost the benefit of prices lowered by competition, although it has been argued that he also got the benefit of an industry that could improve itself by planning ahead with certainty. The thorny question remained, however: How could some public control be exerted over the policies of the "planners"?

The pool, as a device for combination, had a drawback. It enjoyed no legal standing, and therefore its ground rules could not be enforced in court. In 1882, a new instrument was invented that added an unforgettable word to American history—the "trust." The first modern industrial trust was created by one of the refining firms involved in the South Improvement Company: Standard Oil of Ohio. The stockholders in Standard Oil turned over their properties to the management of a board of "trustees," chosen from among themselves. The trustees could also hold the stocks of other oil-producing, marketing, and refining corporations under the same agreement. Thus a large number of companies in the same business, while retaining their individual identity under various state laws and appearing to be freely competing firms, could actually be operated as a single business.

Standard Oil was so extraordinarily successful—by 1898 it refined 83.7 per cent of the oil in the United States—that it became the symbol for concentration, and "trust" became a synonym for any dominating concern or group of concerns in an industry (even where the formal device of trusteeship was not used). The Standard Oil corporation was the creation of a mild-looking, pious, Cleveland businessman named John D. Rockefeller, who entered the oil industry on a full-time basis in 1865. By a brilliant combination of long-range planning, exacting cost accountancy, occasional gambles, and unhesitating use of economic power, he brought stability to the business of drilling, pumping, processing, and selling oil—a venture so risky at first that its symbol was the wildcat.

The story of Standard Oil's rise to the top defies compression into a few paragraphs, but the significant thing about it was how well it showed the two sides of the coin of concentration. At the time of Rockefeller's greatest power, the nation enjoyed the modern marvel of an oil business capable of supplying plentiful, regular, and cheap quantities of lubricants and illuminants to any spot on the globe that was civilized enough to use them. Yet Standard's dominance of every aspect of oil transactions (from hole-in-the-ground to customer) made a joke out of the cherished myth that American economic life offered opportunity to all through free competition. When critics of the new social order looked for horrible examples, Standard Oil's name led all the rest.

But it was only one of many. The advantages of combination were irresistible and, by the late 1890s, combinations of producers were achieving productive prodigies but were squeezing the life out of competition in many diverse fields—iron and steel, whiskey, cordage, biscuits, matches, lead, sugar, and cottonseed oil. The formal "trust" device itself was replaced by another legal entity—the holding company—a single firm that held controlling blocks of the stock of other firms. As one historian notes, this "signalized the final triumph of the corporation, for now corporations could be made to combine corporations." After 1890, holding companies, or outright mergers, became even more conspicuous on the industrial scene. A landmark in size was reached in 1901, when United States Steel was formed, merging 158 companies involved in steelmaking into a single organization capitalized at nearly one and one-half billion dollars. The number of major combinations rose from 12 to 305 between 1897 and 1903, despite clamors of alarm (to be discussed later) concerning the political and social effects of such monstrous aggregations of wealth. "You might as well endeavor to stay the formation of clouds, the falling of the rains, or the flowing of the streams, as to attempt . . . to prevent organization of industry," observed Rockefeller's counsel, S. T. C. Dodd, with considerable satisfaction. Fifty years after the end of the Civil War, names such as Standard Oil, U.S. Steel, General Electric, American Telephone and Telegraph, and American Tobacco were already symbols of a new strength that controlled the lion's share of manufacturing in the United States.

New Patterns of Leadership

A portentous side effect of the new gigantism in industrial organization was the emergence of the "big businessman" as a social model and hero. Wealth had always bred social and political power. A William Byrd of colonial Virginia, a John Hancock of Revolutionary Massachusetts, a John Jacob Astor of the republic's early days, all bestrode their local communities self-confidently, knowing that their lands, ships, storehouses, and trading posts made them men of might. The thrust of "Jacksonian democracy," in fact, had been toward reducing the frankly asserted privileges of the already rich, and toward opening the avenues of affluence to new blood.

But the post-Civil war corporation heads were something new. They were no longer simply rich men, enjoying the fruits of traffic in goods and lands. They controlled the indispensable tools of the new economy. As railroad owners they dominated the arteries of the nation. As manufacturers they set the prices of things absolutely indispensable to modern existence—power and the coal to produce it; bread for the industrial worker; farm machinery to harvest the wheat for the bread; and steel to make the farm machinery. As bankers they dealt in millions and hundreds of millions of dollars, and when they made a mistake, every business establishment in the country was likely to rock because of it. It was no wonder that their generation thought of them as towering figures, whether denouncing them as "monopolists" or hailing them as "captains of industry." Their actual power might be limited by innumerable circumstances, but they seemed as titanic as their own creations.

Yet they also seemed to be of common clay, and thus to vindicate triumphantly the Jacksonian claim that any American, given a chance, might prove himself to be the stuff of kings. Although studies show that a significant percentage of business leaders in this period came from successful families, there were enough conspicuously self-made millionaires to sustain the belief that success in America was open to all who were capable. The new nabobs symbolized what the national energies could achieve under liberty and with the help of God and progress. They played their part well, imprinting themselves on the public consciousness by conspicuous expenditure, opulent charities, and open manipulation of allies and rivals in politics and business.

The real history of American business leadership in this era must eventually rest on the study of thousands of unsung managers and owners in a variety of trades and industries. Yet no view of the so-called "Gilded Age" is complete without a brief glance at a few of the tycoons who were interviewed, courted, quoted, sought as patrons, given honorary degrees, immortalized in the christening of ships, streets, schools, buildings, and babies, and not infrequently were elected to legislatures as august as the United States Senate.

Some were gay and gaudy vulgarians, a type especially common among the Pacific Coast miners who struck it rich. Such a man was Colorado's H. A. W. Tabor, who built an opera house for Denver, discovered a portrait of Shakespeare in the lobby, and demanded that it be replaced with his own, crying: "What the hell has Shakespeare done for Denver?" Another ostentatious financier was the corpulent prince of Erie, Jim Fisk, a one-time peddler who bought himself steamboat lines so that he might wear an "admiral's" uniform to work. He also bought an opera house so that he might be, in Vernon L. Parrington's unforgettable phrase, "a patron of the arts—and especially of the artists, if they were of the right sex."

Other tycoons were candidly interested in power rather than the high life, although they lived well enough. Two self-made railroad barons illuminate that pattern. Collis P. Huntington was one of the "Big Four" who "built" the Central Pacific—the western portion of the first transcontinental railroad, completed in 1869. That is, he was one of four Sacramento hardware and grocery merchants—the others were Mark Hopkins, Charles Crocker, and Leland Stanford—who invested in a short line to the gold camps of the Sierras which, eventually, with government loans and subsidies, grew into a line connecting with the Union Pacific in Utah and completing the link across the country. After 1869 the Central's owners used their profits and position to create a new rail system in California, the Southern Pacific, which soon achieved an almost complete monopoly of transport in California, and had ranchers, shippers, courts, and legislatures either battling its influence or dancing to its tune until the end of the century. Huntington outlived the other partners and was, it is generally agreed, the chief planner and decision maker. While Crocker and Hopkins remained engrossed in operational details, and Stanford sought the political footlights (becoming Governor and Senator), Huntington remained backstage and unabashedly fought to control from his office the railroad traffic of the entire Southwest. Like Cornelius Vanderbilt, he enjoyed being a railroad mogul and nothing else. Vanderbilt, whose eighty millions worth of corporate properties included the New York Central in 1877, began life as a ferryboatman from Staten Island. He graduated to ownership of riverboats (whence he derived the title "Commodore") and then railroads. He came to live in a splendid brownstone mansion on New York's Fifth Avenue, and to give his name and a large sum of money to a university in Nashville, but essentially he never changed his roughneck manners or his delight in winning fights by fair means or foul. "Law?" he is alleged to have once said. "What do I care about the law. Hain't I got the power?"

Of quite another stripe was John D. Rockefeller. He was a man of quiet demeanor who had a bookkeeper's love for saving fractions of a cent and could apply it to enterprises of imperial grandeur and thus make millions. His Standard Oil Company was the yardstick by which other monopolies were measured in 1890. Rockefeller, actually, was not interested in money for money's sake. He began a career of donations to good causes with weekly gifts of change to the collection plate. At his death he had bestowed hundreds of millions of dollars on higher education, medical research, and religion through institutes and foundations bearing his name. What he liked about a giant business organization was not its power to produce profit but its visible proof of the virtues of order, organization, and planning. When Standard Oil was at its peak, every refiner, every retailer, every engineer, every driller, every railroad president was part of a superb mechanism designed to produce oil and oil products cheaply and copiously. Planless competition, in Rockefeller's view, could not do that. He lived an orderly, comfortable life—almost personifying the rational qualities of his supercorporation as he imposed orderliness on the untidiness of mortality.

One cannot speak of America in the late nineteenth century without mentioning Andrew Carnegie. Born when Andrew Jackson was President, he came to America as a Scottish immigrant, aged thirteen, and first worked in a textile mill. He became successively a telegraph messenger, an operator, a railroad dispatcher and minor official, then a young businessman in the iron and steel trade. At fifty he headed the country's largest steel corporation. In 1901 he sold out his holdings for a quarter of a billion dollars and retired to travel and philanthropy. His talents were literary and persuasive. He got orders for steel by the millions of tons, bought factories, hired experts, stimulated them to incredible feats of production, made his deliveries, and acted as if he were having the time of his life. He wrote books to prove that evolution produced millionaires (ignoring the assistance of the tariff on steel and the inventions of other men in making his own fortune), and to command millionaires to give their winnings to society and die poor. He praised democracy, capitalism, and the Anglo-Saxon people, hobnobbed with friends ranging from Mark Twain to the Emperor of Germany, and was not in evidence when his associates ruined competitors or broke strikes. He did not simply create or use industrial power, he celebrated it and was its advocate.

If Rockefeller was industry's superorganizer and Carnegie was its supersalesman, Junius Pierpont Morgan was its superfinancier. He was not at all self-made. His father was a banker, and he was born to security and securities in 1837. Between 1880 and 1910 he became a specialist in financing industrial reorganizations and combinations through massive loans —and his price always included a share of control of the new corporations, so that he could wage war on wasteful competition (and competitors), which he disliked no less than Rockefeller. In other respects he was quite different from the abstemious Standard Oil magnate, since Morgan frankly lived like a Renaissance prince, spending his money freely on yachts, jewelry, paintings, rare manuscripts, and other aids to good living. Although a devout Episcopalian, he never pretended that the Lord had simply lent him his wealth to be used as modestly and frugally as possible.

All the figures in any gallery of rich men of the 1870s, 1880s, or 1890s radiated a sense of the power inherent in the new forms of production of wealth. Whatever they did or did not do, they seemed to say by their very existence: "Two generations ago, this was a country of a few million souls, most of them farmers. Look on us and see what it has become!" This was their meaning for their contemporaries, who did, indeed, look on them wide-eyed.

The Benevolently Neutral State

The victories of big-scale industrial organization were not exclusively the result of machine production and venturesome capitalists. Behind the boom of the postwar years there stood a national government which, at times, actively assisted in the nation's economic modernization and, at other times, was willing to assist business growth by a "hands-off" policy of avoiding taxes and regulations that might hinder the pursuit of maximum profit and thus discourage investment. One long-standing interpretation of the entire Civil War era, in fact, maintains that this linkage between the objectives of businessmen and congressmen was the most significant outcome of the conflict. With Southern planters out of power for a decade and a half—1861 to 1876—Republican leaders, in particular, were able to procure the passage of high protective tariffs, loans and land grants to the railroads, contract-labor legislation allowing the recruitment of low-paid foreign workers, and banking laws weakening the power of agrarian sections to set up their own sources of credit. This was the argument for looking at the war as a "second American Revolution" which confirmed the dominance of "industrial capitalism" over "planter capitalism."

However, like the case for the Civil War as a "cause" of industrial progress, this version of events requires some modification in the light of recent study. The national government in the 1850s had launched exploring expeditions in the polar seas, as well as in the Atlantic and Pacific, whose purpose was not only to gather scientific data but also commercial information. Army surveyors had compiled massive volumes of evidence on the merits of several proposed routes for a transcontinental railroad. An aggressive diplomacy in the Caribbean had shown that the United States was not at all indifferent to the possible future needs of American traders and investors in areas south of the border. The voting on measures to support these operations had not lined up businessmen versus farmers but, instead, had shown many varieties of economic activity, interest groups, and demands. "Agrarian" representatives did not vote as a bloc, but cast their ballots on economic issues according to whether they spoke for large farmers or small, slaveholding or nonslaveholding planters, well-developed sections where industry and agriculture were striking a balance (as in the Ohio Valley) or newer sections still tied to a single-crop economy (as with the states west of the Mississippi). And spokesmen for "business" included bankers, merchants, manufacturers, and transportation executives, who differed widely on the effects of particular governmental acts and policies. The trend toward greater government assistance to economic development was under way well before 1861. Moreover, the wartime Congress of 1862, in which "agriculture" was supposedly a hapless minority, passed the Homestead Act, offering a free 160-acre farm from the public domain to any actual settler. It passed the Morrill Land Grant Act, giving to the states large donations of public land in order to endow agricultural studies in colleges and universities. And it passed the bill creating the Department of Agriculture, although that office did not reach Cabinet rank until 1889. It would seem more accurate to say that the major difference between the Congresses that sat in 1860 and 1862 was that the 1862 Congress had no substantial bloc in its ranks dedicated to fighting for the interests of slavery.

The record shows a pattern of aid to business enterprise which, like certain kinds of embroidery, is boldly visible but not simple in design. The tariff is an example. In 1862 and 1864, Congress passed measures that raised the general level of duties on almost every article imported into the country to approximately 37 per cent at first, and then to 47 per cent. The 1864 measure was passed with only five days of debate in both houses of Congress. Everyone agreed that the need to raise revenue was critical. What was a wartime emergency policy, however, remained in force uninterruptedly through year after postwar year, but the pressure for retention was drawn from many sources and from both parties. A general ten per cent reduction in the level of duties in 1872 concealed the fact that on many individual items the duty exceeded 80 per cent of the foreign manufacturer's price—and since domestic prices only needed to match the foreign price plus the duty to be competitive, then as soon as American costs of production dropped to a par with the foreign costs, the duty was almost a gift to the American manufacturer. From 1870 onward, for example, the duty on steel rails was $28 a ton. By 1880, English factories could produce rails at $36 a ton, but the American price was $67, even though American steel was then almost as cheap to make as English. Eventually a number of factors reduced the cost to the consumer of American-made rails but, for a time, the steelmakers had profited very handsomely by their government's barrier to foreign rivals. However, in spite of the demonstrated effect of the duties in raising prices, no massive antitariff protest moved Congress to action before the middle 1880s. Perhaps this was because too many diverse groups shared in the advantages of protection.

Again, it is an oversimplification to say that railroad land grants, like the tariff, were concessions to business need wrung from a reluctant public. The most publicized grant was a donation of twenty "sections" (square miles) of public land per mile of construction, made to the Union Pacific and Central Pacific railroads by acts of 1862 and 1864 to help in the completion of the first transcontinental line. In addition, the lines received loans (not gifts) ranging between sixteen thousand and forty-eight thousand dollars for each mile of finished track. These loans were to be repaid to the government with interest, and the government enforced this provision. In addition, the United States paid only half fare on the subsidized line for moving troops and supplies. This policy of endowing railroad construction was not new, but had commenced by 1850. Long before the Civil War began, nearly twenty million acres of federal land had been dispensed in aid of railroad construction, mainly in the Mississippi Valley. Wartime and postwar grants to three other transcontinental lines, among others, helped to swell the final total of the grants to approximately 130,000,000 acres, but no more grants on this scale were made after 1871. Moreover, they involved less than 7 per cent of the national domain in area, although somewhat more in value, and the mileage built with this aid was only one-fifth of the national total as of 1880, when most grants had been finally claimed. The percentages were much higher in the Far Western states most affected by land-grant railroad building, but it should be noted that almost every American in this period believed firmly that the whole nation would be served by bringing western lands, in William H. Seward's words, "into cultivation and settlement in the shortest space of time and under the most favorable auspices." It seemed to make sense to give away a small portion of the nation's landed heritage in order to improve the value of the rest. Only in the hurly-burly of politics twenty years after the Civil War did the cry of "giveaway" to "land monopolists" rise loud in the land.

A similar observation is valid for the Contract Labor Law in 1864, denounced by unions until its repeal twenty-one years later. It did not, as charged, involve the government in the recruitment of cheap industrial labor. The act simply authorized foreign workers to sign contracts binding them to employment in the United States for fixed periods, and made these agreements valid in the courts. The number of these contracts registered with the United States Commissioner of Immigration was small, and while a few skilled workers—particularly in the glass trade—were "imported" by employers, the bulk of the immigrant labor force in factories, railroad work gangs, and mines, was hired from among those who had come to this country without either government or private assistance.

The National Banking Acts of 1863 and 1864 also have been cited as a sign of the government's benevolence toward business. These acts created a system of "national banks," which were to receive charters upon the purchase of certain quantities of United States government bonds. The banks were to deposit these bonds with the Treasury and were to receive, in return, circulating notes. They profited handsomely by lending out these notes at interest and simultaneously collecting interest on the bonds that backed them. More significantly, a prohibitive tax imposed on the notes of state banks reduced the competition of those banks in furnishing currency. Yet one clear purpose of this legislation was to sell bonds for the war, and far from giving favored bankers a monopoly on the issuance of notes, the Treasury put four hundred million dollars of its own paper currency—the famous "greenbacks"—into circulation. Postwar efforts to retire these greenbacks met repeated opposition. A long struggle, lasting until 1896, was opened. Its main issue was whether the government should control and inflate the money supply, and for whose benefit. Its various episodes were triggered by proposed acts for regulating the supply and value of gold, silver, and other forms of money. But the core of the matter is that in this contest battle lines were never neatly drawn between parties, sections, or classes.

In short, it cannot be denied that the tariff, banking, labor, and railroad legislation of the Civil War and Reconstruction years was designed to encourage and assist private enterprise in railroad construction, manufacturing, and the financing of these and kindred undertakings. But such aid was never unlimited, never without some restrictions, and never without support from a broad sampling of the population.

This public approval was entirely natural in view of the country's dominant social outlook. There was almost universal agreement among the men of the 1870s and 1880s that the production of tangible wealth was the chief end of man, that he glorified himself in the acquisition of property, and that the government acted most laudably when it helped him to realize his material ambitions on the widest possible scale. Almost every man in public life was infatuated with the country's material progress, regardless of party or section. In 1884 the Republican Presidential candidate, James G. Blaine, published *Twenty Years of Congress,* a partisan history of national legislation from 1861 to 1881. Blaine concluded with a loving glance at national economic statistics, and declared that rising population and production figures made the era "incomparable," and that "such progress was not only unprecedented but phenomenal. . . . It could not have been made except under an industrial system which stimulated enterprise, quickened capital, assured to labor its just reward." The next year there appeared *Three Decades of Federal Legislation* by Samuel Sullivan ("Sunset") Cox, a lifelong Democrat, a work that covered the same span of Congressional history. It, too, concluded with a chest-thumping review of the growth figures in the 1880 census and a declaration that "Our country, with its institutions of benevolence and learning, its wealth, splendor, commerce, and liberties, has become the cynosure of all eyes and the refuge of all lands." Pride in the size of the gross national product went beyond party labels.

Despite these praises, there were numerous Americans who, by the 1880s, expressed strong reservations about the compatibility of the new industrial order with the American theory and practice of liberty and equality. . . . Moreover, the economic boom brought about realignment of sectional patterns, producing conflicts that could not be solved by the admission of new states as formerly had been done to balance the interests of slavery and free labor in the Senate. It also was the basis of a shift of power among classes, which could not be reversed by the simple exercise of the ballot. Industrial growth sent men westward and overseas, changed the very shape of their thinking about the society they lived in and its meaning, pitted opposing spokesmen against each other in state and national legislatures and in the courts, and virtually turned the entire history of modern America into the story of a reaction to dynamic economic forces. But . . . we must remember that the men who first saw the light of modern industrialism in America believed that they were included in the dawning of a day not of struggle but of infinite promise.

8

The Road to Populism

Eric Goldman

In the Gilded Age, politics became a big business, too, as money flowed into government circles at an unprecedented rate. Men now entered politics for the same reason that men went into business: to make their fortunes. And the new politics also derived much of its vocabulary from the world of industry. "A political party," William H. Seward contended, "is in one sense a joint stock company in which those who contribute the most direct the action and management of the concern." The United States Senate became known as the Millionaires' Club because only the rich and powerful seemed able to get in. And a sizable portion of both major parties not only vigorously defended the industrial barons but were as eager to accept their campaign contributions as the barons were ready to give them. A number of politicians shamelessly took bribes as well.

Arrayed against the Captains of Industry and their political allies were a number of dissident interest groups, incipient in the 1870s but growing. These groups represented people who were hurt by industrial consolidation—workers, farmers, and small or aspiring businessmen who wanted their share of American wealth. As these people organized and sought redress of their grievances, grim political battles ensued, culminating in the Populist revolt of 1892.

Early on a September afternoon, 1873, a newsboy yelled an extra about the failure of Jay Cooke's bank, and a policeman promptly arrested the boy. Jay Cooke was one of the most successful of all the new successes, the renowned financier of the war against Rebellion, a man who could sit in his seventy-two room mansion and casually discuss with "Ulysses" the way to raise children; businesses run by Jay Cookes simply did not close their doors. With the confirmation of the news and the rapid spread of bank failures, people still consoled one another that this was only a panic. Bustling America, guided by tough-minded businessmen, was much too strong to be laid low very long. A few stupefying weeks, banks and businesses going down like dominoes, and the word "panic" lost its power to console. The United States had to face the depression of 1873.

The country had known hard times before, but only when it was overwhelmingly agricultural. Now it learned how much more serious depression could be in a rapidly industrializing society. The years of economic distress from 1873 to 1879 threw a garish light on the whole structure of opportunity. Military control was removed from the South during the depression, but the former Confederacy returned to a nation almost as frustrated by hard times as the South had been by defeat. Millions of industrial workers, confident of a golden future a short while ago, were unemployed or desperately worried about holding their jobs. Many a small investor, once so sure of a brownstone and a carriage, found his life's savings wiped out over-

---

From pp. 24–49 of *Rendezvous with Destiny* by Eric Goldman. Copyright 1952, 1956 by Alfred A. Knopf, Inc. Reprinted by permission of Alfred A. Knopf, Inc.

night. Farmers' gilt-edged mortgage certificates turned from bright symbols of hope to nagging reminders of overconfidence. If the hard times boomed migration westward, the new pioneers passed covered wagons dragging east like whipped animals, their covers chalked with "Going back to our wife's folks" or "In God we trusted, in Kansas we busted."

No less disturbing were the large-scale corporations that rose above the shambles of hard times. The industrialization of the United States had been marked by the steady combination of businesses, and the depression rendered small entrepreneurs still less able to resist the consolidators.

. . .

Still more disturbing, the depression of 1873 gave the United States its first taste of widespread violence caused by economic hardship. At the blackest period of the depression the country was swarming with "tramps," who were usually factory or farm hands looking vainly for a livelihood and drifted into gang life. Here and there bands of these men allied with professional criminals, drinking, stealing, raping, and murdering.

No large city entirely escaped bitter strikes, and in the summer of 1877 the first nationwide strike produced the first labor rioting that reached into many states. The trouble started when the principal railroads, refusing to decrease high dividends on watered stocks, decreed a ten per cent cut in wages. First on the Baltimore & Ohio lines in West Virginia, then north and west all the way to Canada and California, the workers hit back. Their violent strikes provoked the use of troops by business-minded governments, and the use of troops provoked more violence.

The turbulence reached a climax in Pittsburgh. Twenty-five people were killed and many more wounded when soldiers came into collision with a mob of strikers and strike sympathizers. Disorder ricocheted across the city. Barrels of liquor were tapped and drunk on the spot; stores were broken into for food, clothing, and furniture; long lines of freight cars were looted and set on fire. The incendiarism spread until the four-story Union Depot, two thousand cars, the railroad machine shops, a grain elevator, and two roundhouses with 125 locomotives had been destroyed. Two days later the city awoke to its hangover of ashes and caskets. Railroad executives and storekeepers wrathfully estimated their losses at five to ten millions; railroad workers sullenly went back to work with the wage cut intact. The nation, uneasy and irritated, wondered what America was coming to.

In San Francisco a pale, tense young man wrote some more bitter words on his yellow foolscap. For Henry George, the depression was the last straw. As a boy he had listened to Uncle Thomas proclaim that any lad who worked hard was sure to get ahead swiftly in America. From his thirteenth year George had worked hard, as a delivery-boy, seaman, typesetter, gold prospector, clerk, salesman, and editor, only to find himself still an impoverished nobody. In the late Sixties he managed to acquire some standing as a newspaperman and was sent to New York to arrange telegraphic news for a struggling San Francisco paper; the near-monopolistic Associated Press saw to it that he went home once more a failure. A few years later the depression of 1873 engulfed San Francisco, and Henry George had enough. Far into the night, in his rugless, ill-heated room, he piled up the sheets of foolscap, pounding into them the angry eloquence of *Progress and Poverty*.

"The present century," the book began, "has been marked by a prodigious increase in wealth-producing power.... It was natural to expect, and it was expected, that ... the enormous increase in the power of producing wealth would make real poverty a thing of the past." But "disappointment has followed disappointment. ... We plow new fields, we open new mines, we found new cities; we drive back the Indian and exterminate the buffalo; we girdle the land with iron roads and lace the air with telegraph wires; we add knowledge to knowledge, and utilize invention after invention.... Yet it becomes no easier for the masses of our people to make a living. On the contrary, it is becoming harder. ... The gulf between the employed and the employer is growing wider; social contrasts are becoming sharper; as liveried carriages appear, so do barefooted children."

This situation was made worse by depression, George went on, but hard times were not the basic explanation. The United States had been a wondrous land of opportunity only because of its vast area of public lands. "The child of the people, as he grows to manhood in Europe, finds all the best seats at the banquet of life marked 'taken,' and must struggle with his fellows for the crumbs that fall.... In America, whatever his condition, there has always been the consciousness that the public domain lay behind him.... The general intelligence, the general comfort, the active invention, the power of adaptation and assimilation, the free, independent spirit, the energy and hopefulness that have marked our people, are not causes, but results—they have sprung from unfenced land. This public domain has given a consciousness of freedom even to the dweller in crowded cities, and has been a wellspring of hope even to those who have never thought of taking refuge upon it." But now the United States had used up much of its public domain. With industrialization helping to speed up the concentration of wealth and power, the New World was beginning to repeat the Old World's dismal story. It was re-enacting the European experience not only, as Samuel Tilden had said, by creating a corrupt ruling class; it was headed toward rigid economic and social stratification and a consequent narrowing of opportunity for the masses.

Progress and Poverty, published in 1879, was not out a year before its author was a national figure. Across the country, farmers squinted over the book's fine print. "Tens of thousands of industrial laborers," the economist Richard Ely noted, "have read *Progress and Poverty* who never before looked between the covers of an economics book." Troubled Americans who were neither factory hands nor farmers helped make *Progress and Poverty* one of the ten or so most widely selling non-fiction works in the history of the United States. The young man who had wanted to get ahead so fervently and had been stopped so often, with his moving arraignment of his times, his warning that America was moving down the weary road of Europe, his summons to recreate opportunity, had caught the mood with which thousands of Americans felt the depression of 1873.

The Eighties lumbered ahead, now prosperous, now dragging through months of economic upset. In good years and in bad, sometimes even more so during the stretches of general prosperity, the sense of frustrated opportunity continued to gnaw at large numbers of Americans.

During the Eighties huge corporations kept rising like so many portents of a Europeanized future. In the decade after the depression more than five thousand firms were wrought into giant combines, virtually all of which were pushing toward monopolies in their fields. At the end of the decade United States Senator John Sherman, whose basic friendliness to business could not be questioned, spoke the worry of a good many of his countrymen. "If we are unable or unwilling [to take action against the trusts]," Sherman told the Senate, "there will soon be a trust for every production and a master to fix the price for every necessity of life."

For most industrial workers of the Eighties, real wages were rising with aggravating slowness, and each year extremes of wealth jutted out more irritatingly. A titan like Marshall Field made five hundred to seven hundred dollars an hour; his nonexecutive employees were paid twelve dollars a week or less for a fifty-nine-hour week. Quickly made fortunes were lavished

Keppler's 1889 caricature accurately reflects the influence of the trusts on the U.S. Senate. The presiding officer was a Wall Street banker, and the leading senators represented manufacturing, oil, railroad, utility, gold, and silver interests. "If we are unable or unwilling [to take action against the trusts]," one senator told his colleagues, "there will soon be a trust for every production and a master to fix the price for every necessity of life." (Courtesy of Culver Pictures.)

with infuriating conspicuousness—on a mansion in red, yellow, and black bricks, the purchase of a titled husband for the daughter, banquets where the cigarettes were wrapped in hundred-dollar bills, or a poodle was draped with a fifteen-thousand-dollar collar. Just around the corner, slums were sprawling out, filthy, heatless, so dark their corners could not be photographed until flashlight photography was invented in 1887.

Along with extremes of wealth came walls of impersonality. By the Eighties a large percentage of factory hands worked in big plants, where the owner was as remote as any feudal lord had ever been from his serfs. The dry-goods shop was becoming the department store, and in department stores the clerk did not first-name the boss or presume to take his daughter to church. Without the familiar relations, callousness was easy, almost inevitable. An inventor remarked that he could sell a time-saving device in twenty places and a lifesaving invention scarcely at all. Doctors thought nothing of charging two dollars a visit to workingmen whose wages were a dollar-and-a-half a day. The first move to protect children from the vice and disease of the slums came from the president of New York's Society for the Prevention of

Cruelty to Animals, who, as a kind of afterthought, founded the Society for the Prevention of Cruelty to Children. "Land of opportunity, you say," a Chicago worker snarled at a spread-eagle speaker. "You know damn well my children will be where I am—that is, if I can keep them out of the gutter."

The newest immigrants, the millions pouring into the United States from southern and eastern Europe, were finding that America was no longer in a come-one, come-all mood. Many of the older settlers, feeling crowded and cornered, had little welcome for any newcomer, and every prejudice in the American collection was roused by immigrants who were predominantly impoverished and unskilled, short and dark in appearance, Catholic or Jewish in religion. Rapidly the national speech was acquiring phrases that carried as much sneer and hiss as any in the language—"wop" and "dago" for the Italian, "bohunk" for the Hungarian, "greaseball" for the Greek, and "kike" for the Jew.

A member of a Congressional committee, questioning a railroad-construction boss in 1890, asked: "You don't call ... an Italian a white man?"

The construction boss was surprised that a United States Congressman should ask so silly a question. "No, Sir," the construction boss said. "An Italian is a Dago."

Organized anti-Catholicism, dormant since the Know-Nothing movement of the 1850's, flared up again in the form of the American Protective Association; anti-Semitism, which had scarcely appeared previously, spread widely. Lincoln Steffens never forgot his introduction to what opportunity could mean in the new immigrant slums. A Russian-Jewish woman pulled him up the tenement stairs to point out how her three little girls were watching a prostitute across the airway serve a customer. *"Da se'en Sie,* there they are watching, always they watch. They count the men who come of a night.... My oldest girl says she will go into that business when she grows up; she says it's a good business ... and you can dress and eat and live."

For all the discontented of the cities, the frontier was losing much of its ability to keep hopes high. It was not simply that most of the best acres had passed into private hands; Americans were beginning to realize that the land might be cheap or even free, but transporting yourself and the family to the homestead, buying essential tools, and sustaining a wife and children during a season or two of sodbusting cost a sum beyond the resources of the usual urban employee. One Fall River worker, asked why he did not go west, expressed the new attitude toward homesteading with savage simplicity. "Well," he said, "I never saw over a $20 bill.... If some one would give me $1,500 I will go."

Out among those who had managed to go, in all agricultural areas of the nation, times were hard and growing harder. For the farmer, the Eighties differed from the unbroken depression years of the Seventies only in leaving him worse off economically. The price of manufactured articles the farmer had to buy and the cost of shipping his crop were sky-high; the amount he received for his products was plummeting down; and the policies of a creditor-minded Washington made it more and more difficult for him to escape his mortgage. Often the farmer lost money by shipping and selling, and for want of a profitable market, apples lay under the trees, milk was fed to the hogs, corn or cotton was used as fuel. "Many a time," Vernon Parrington remembered from his boyhood near Pumpkin Ridge, Kansas, "have I warmed myself by the kitchen stove in which ears were burning briskly, popping and crackling in the jolliest fashion. And if while we sat around such a fire watching the year's crop go up the chimney, the talk sometimes became bitter ... who will wonder?"

In both the South and the Midwest, special circumstances increased the difficulties of the farmer. By clinging to the one-crop system, Southerners were making themselves prisoners of the price of cotton. Midwesterners were discovering that methods of agriculture learned in the East were unsuited to the Great Plains. Worse yet, the reckless destruction of the forests brought a succession of droughts and floods, and periodically the Midwest was ravaged by chinchbugs, corn borers, or, most destructive of all, plagues of grasshoppers. The bugs swirled down in pelting hordes, ruining the heads of grain, chirping and flaring around the helpless farmers, covering everything with brown disaster.

Noneconomic facts thickened the pall over rural America. As urbanization accelerated and the farm regions sank more deeply in debt, the whole prestige of agricultural life skidded down. Once the tiller of the soil, his head raised high in prickly independence, had been the very symbol of the American way. Now the sneer word "hayseed" was coming into common usage and farmers had to watch their own sons and daughters maneuvering to be off to the city.

Life in the less settled regions of the West brought additional aggravations. Many a pioneer had sung his way to a homestead only to settle into an existence of dreary grubbing. Log-cabin living, a long buckboard ride from the nearest town, meant a nagging loneliness and lack of comforts. Not one farmer in three hundred could get a daily newspaper, and families that lived five miles from the village post office were lucky to receive mail once a week. Women especially paid the price of isolation; for want of the simplest medical care, thousands died in childbirth or lost their babies in infancy. Hamlin Garland, a product of the North Dakota frontier, set out to describe the life of backcountry women but confessed, when his book was done, that he had stopped far short of the truth. "Even my youthful zeal," Garland wrote, "faltered in the midst of a revelation of the lives led by the women.... Before the tragic futility of their suffering, my pen refused to shed its ink."

In Kansas, a handsome Irish woman, grown sad-eyed watching the blighting of dreams, caught the mounting national restlessness in five volcanic words. What was needed, said Mrs. Mary Ellen Lease, was to raise "less corn and more HELL."

The hell was raised. The immediate result of the discontent was an enormous increase in the support for liberalism. Reformers of the 1872 type, coming up out of their storm cellars after the Greeley debacle, found a far more receptive audience for their assaults on Grantism. By the Eighties, liberal triumphs were becoming common on the municipal, state, and federal levels. In 1885 and again in 1893, the White House itself was taken over by Grover Cleveland, a liberal's liberal complete with an abhorrence of corruption and a zeal for local rule, decreased tariffs, governmental economy, and economic liberty.

Yet all the while that lower-income discontent was strengthening liberalism against Grantism, more and more of the discontented were thinking along non-liberal lines. Theoretically, liberalism of that day offered an honest, efficient government, holding its activities to a policing minimum, which would leave all citizens free and equal in their drive to get ahead. But liberal politicians had to function amid endless pressures, agrarian, laborite, and capitalist, and the pressure from large-scale business interests was easily the most potent. The liberals, moreover, were predisposed by the very origins of their doctrine toward the more successful groups. Increasingly liberalism became a pro-corporation credo.

Liberal-minded jurists might applaud local rule and uphold it rigidly when the federal regulation of business was proposed; they reacted differently when a state legislature passed a law controlling the activities of corporations. President Cleveland might be all for keeping the government out of economic life and he did keep it out so far as most legislation benefiting low-income groups was concerned. He also heartily approved maintaining a gold standard, which favored creditors over debtors, he assumed a tax system that kept the burden off corporations, and he used federal troops to help the Pullman Company defeat a strike of its pitifully squeezed workers. It was all honest enough; no one would have thought of offering Grover Cleveland a bribe. The more important point was that a good many Americans were wondering whether honesty was enough. "Cleveland might be honest," the agrarian leader William Jennings Bryan snapped, "but so were the mothers who threw their children in the Ganges."

Even if liberalism had been able to preserve an exact governmental impartiality toward all groups, it could hardly have satisfied the new discontent. A twelve-dollar-a-week worker dependent on a twelve-million-dollar corporation for his livelihood, or a small farmer desperate about a mortgage owed to a J. P. Morgan bank, was hardly interested in having an impartial government. He wanted a government that would be on his side, helping him fight what seemed to him unfair and overwhelming odds. In 1887 Congress appropriated ten thousand dollars to aid drought sufferers in buying new grain seed, and Cleveland vetoed the item with a declaration that "though the people support the Government the Government should not support the people." It was a perfect statement of liberal doctrine, and a perfect illustration why liberalism seemed irrelevant or downright evil to thousands who were quite sure that, even if the government should not support them, it should certainly help them support themselves.

With a curse for Grover Cleveland, farmers and workingmen were hurrying into organizations that spoke neither the tone nor the program of liberalism. Three "Farmers' Alliances"—a Western and a Southern organization and a separate Negro Alliance in the South—were growing at a phenomenal rate, and taking on an emotional intensity that recalled the days of the crusade against slavery. The agrarian bitterness came closest to a call for armed revolution in the South, where the farmers' poverty was deepest and where rule by manufacturers and bankers smacked of another Yankee invasion. The official history of the Southern Alliance had the title, *The Impending Revolution,* and the Arkansas author of the book explained: "Thousands of men who had already lost all hope of a peaceable solution of the great question of human rights are calmly waiting the issue."

A wide variety of non-liberal movements churned the lower-income districts of the cities. The Eighties had scarcely begun when Terence Powderly, a deaconish machinist who turned to labor organizing only after he was blacklisted during the depression of 1873, found himself the head of a half a million belligerent "Knights of Labor." By 1885 the railroad workers in the Knights were powerful enough to force representatives of the mighty Jay Gould to sit down at the same table and discuss a strike settlement, the first such demonstration of union power in American history. When the Knights won something that could be called a victory, their membership leaped another hundred thousand and encouraged union activity throughout the country.

Urban agitations that had been present even in the halcyon late Sixties took on added impetus—especially the drive for an eight-hour day and the "Greenback–Labor" demand to break the control of banks over the currency. A new agitation, the single-tax movement, was having a pervasive effect. To remedy the curse of poverty amid progress, Henry George's book had called for a "single tax" on the increase in the value of land as communities grew up around it. This increase, George argued, was totally unearned; taxing it one hundred per cent would smash concentrated wealth and spread the national wealth around in a way that would reopen opportunity. Few farmers could be attracted by a program of heavy land taxes, but for the urban discontented here was a plan of alluring simplicity. "No man," the official Knights of Labor organ testified in 1887, "has exercised so great an influence upon the labor movement of to-day as Henry George."

The immigrant slums were finding their single-taxism in the old-country doctrines of anarchism and socialism. Anarchism looked as if it might rival the European success of the "Black International" until a bomb went off during an eight-hour demonstration in 1886 and killed the movement by associating it with black-bearded horror. Socialism showed no such signs of demise. Led by Daniel De Leon, a fiery if highly dialectical immigrant, it was gaining a wide and tenacious hold in the sweatshops of the big cities. Before the Eighties were done, socialism, in a Utopian form, was even trickling through to the middle classes. A raft of novels advocating some variety of Utopian socialism appeared, and in 1888 one of these novels, Edward Bellamy's *Looking Backward*, swept together the collectivist yearnings into a far from negligible movement. Soon *Looking Backward* was selling at the rate of ten thousand copies a week and ardent Bellamy clubs were gathering in professors, ministers, and tradesmen as well as farmers and industrial workers.

With dissidence permeating both the urban and rural regions, reformers naturally dreamed of a national union of the discontented. There were certainly plenty of encouraging facts. Whatever their doctrinal differences, the Farmers' Alliances, Knights of Labor, socialists, single-taxers, even the anarchists, were united by a fear of big business and by an impatience with liberalism's refusal to sanction governmental action in behalf of the poor. Two local elections of the Eighties sent a special thrill of hope through the coalitionists. In 1886, single-taxers, socialists, union members, and thousands of citizens who were just plain irritated supported Henry George with such fervor that he barely missed winning the mayorship of New York; a rising young liberal named Theodore Roosevelt ran third. Then, in the state and national elections of 1890, candidates backed by the Alliances scored a series of striking victories in the South and West. Five United States Senators, six Governors, and forty-six Congressmen championing bold new economic legislation, a single-taxer almost mayor of the nation's metropolis—weren't these facts sure harbingers of a new national party of urban and rural discontent, which would take power as the coalition Republican Party had triumphed in 1860? With the approach of the Presidential election of 1892, more than thirteen hundred delegates converged on Omaha to get under way just such a coalition, the "People's" or "Populist" Party.

Hour after hour anger swept through the cavernous old Coliseum Building. July 1892 brought as wilting a heat as Omaha had ever known, the city frolicked in a Fourth-of-July mood, near-by saloons had laid in an extra supply of liquor. But nothing could distract the delegates from their rounds of furious speeches, wild applause, and fierce resolutions. From all parts of the United States, some bumping along hundreds of miles in buckboards, others using their last folding money for train fare, the Populists had gathered to launch an all-out assault on the political and economic masters of America. They did it with the dedicated wrath of a camp meeting warring on the Devil himself.

Any delegate who strayed from the mood of the convention was promptly hurled back on a wave of emotion. Midway in the proceedings a member of the Resolutions Committee, pointing out that the Union Pacific had not provided the reduced rates usually granted for convention delegates, proposed that the railroad be asked to rectify this "oversight." Instantly Marion Cannon, of California, was on his feet, his face livid. An oversight? Ask a corporation to be fair? Cannon shouted. The "customary courtesy was denied deliberately and with insolence. I do not want this Convention . . . to go back to the railroad company, hat in hand, and ask for any privileges whatever. The Democrats and Republicans secured half-fare, but we—not connected with railroads, but producers of the earth—have been refused equal terms." The delegates thundered approval as Cannon concluded: "We can stand the refusal."

On the afternoon of July 4, a plump, genial Irishman with a reputation for quips and politicking mounted the rostrum and this day he sounded like a prophet out of the Old Testament. "We meet in the midst of a nation brought to the verge of moral, political, and material ruin," Ignatius Donnelly cried. ". . . Corruption dominates the ballot-box, the Legislatures, the Congress, and touches even the ermine of the bench. . . . Our homes [are] covered with mortgages. . . . The urban workmen are denied the rights of organization for self protection; imported, pauperized labor beats down their wages; a hireling standing army, unrecognized by our laws, is established to shoot them down, and they are rapidy degenerating into European conditions. A vast conspiracy against mankind has been organized. . . . If not met and overthrown at once it forebodes terrible social convulsions . . . or the establishment of an absolute despotism."

This was the kind of language the delegates wanted to hear. When the specific proposals of the platform continued in the same tone, the convention exploded into a demonstration unprecedented in all the turbulent history of American political gatherings. With the last thrust at "tyranny and oppression," the delegates rose in a cheering, stomping, marching mass. Hats, coats, papers, fans, umbrellas went up in the air, leaders were bounced from shoulder to shoulder, every state tried to outdo the next in noise and movement. Texans whooped and beat on coffee cans. Nebraskans chanted: "What is home without a mortgage? Don't all speak at once." New Yorkers hoisted a beaming old man to the platform, thrust a baton in his hand, yelled wildly while he pretended to lead the musicians in hymns and marching songs. "Good-Bye, My Party, Good-Bye," the delegates sang. Then, to the tune of "Save a Poor Sinner, Like Me," they shouted how "the railroads and old party bosses together did sweetly agree" to deceive and exploit "a hayseed like me." And, breaking through the bedlam time and again, came the "People's Hymn," sung to the consecrated music of the "Battle Hymn of the Republic":

> They have stolen our money, have ravished our homes;
> With the plunder erected to Mammon a throne;
> They have fashioned a god, like the Hebrews of old,
> Then bid us bow down to their image of gold.

Edwin Godkin read the reports from Omaha and erupted in an editorial that was all anger and foreboding. Carl Schurz, proclaimed the Republic near "the precipice," poured out a thirty-four-page letter pleading for Cleveland's re-election. In free-trade clubs, in universities, at soirées, wherever liberals gathered, the news from Omaha left men furious and frightened. Here was a drastically, alarmingly different reformism, bursting up from the bottom.

The leaders at Omaha made it emphatically plain that they intended to base their movement on the groups which the Best People were sure represented the worst people. Populism, almost the first words of the Omaha platform declared, was to be a "permanent and perpetual . . . union of the labor forces of the United States. . . . The interests of rural and civic [urban] labor are the same; their enemies are identical." Since the convention was predominantly agrarian, Populist leaders were careful to emphasize their interest in labor's problems, and resolutions adopted by the convention supported the most important labor demands of the day. The delegates warmly backed a shorter work week and roundly condemned both the use of Pinkerton men in strikes and unlimited immigration, which "crowds out our wage earners."

Another resolution provoked a debate which showed that these pro-labor statements were no mere contrivances on the part of leaders, slipped by an indifferent rank and file. A Knights of Labor union was engaged in a hard-fought strike against Rochester clothing manufacturers, and the resolution not only expressed support of the strikers but called on "all who hate tyranny and oppression" to boycott the goods of the manufacturers. Sympathy for strikers was one thing; a secondary boycott was going far (so far that its legality was decidedly in question). A secondary boycott was going much too far for a Texas delegate, who wanted to table the resolution, and for a New Yorker, who proposed dividing it so that he could vote for the sympathy and against the boycott.

Promptly, two of the most unmistakably agrarian delegates were on their feet in defense of the boycott. "There is no such thing as a boycott," roared "Cyclone" Davis, of Texas. "It only consists in letting your enemies alone and staying with your friends."

Then Ignatius Donnelly, from agricultural Minnesota, took up the fight. "This resolution," Donnelly declared, "is a declaration that free men will not clothe their limbs in the goods of manufacturers of this slave-making oligarchy. [Loud cheers.] It is war to the knife and the knife to the hilt. [Loud cheers.] I trust that those who have staggered away from this resolution because of the opprobrium that a hireling press has applied to the word boycott, will withdraw their opposition, and that the resolution may be adopted by a rising vote. [Tremendous applause.]" A motion to strike out the boycott clause was overwhelmingly defeated, and the whole resolution was adopted by acclamation.

Among the delegates conspicuous in the uproar was a coal-black Negro, marching about the Coliseum Building with an American flag fluttering from a cane and apparently feeling gaily at home. A number of important Populist leaders not only aimed to unite the discontented of the cities and the countryside. They sought something that no American party has achieved before or since: a political coalition of the poor whites and the poor blacks of the South. The Southern Farmers' Alliance was conspicuously friendly to the Colored Farmers' Alliance. Committees of white Southern Populists ceremoniously met with black colleagues, joint platforms were adopted, and Negro delegates were named to local and national Populist conventions. The most important Southern Populist leader, Tom Watson of Georgia, regularly held mixed meetings, despite violent attempts to prevent them. When Georgians threatened to lynch a Negro Populist leader, the state witnessed an unprecedented sight. At Watson's call, two thousand white Populists assembled to protect the Negro. For two days and nights, their arms stacked on Watson's veranda, the white men grimly carried out the Populist doctrine that the issue was poverty, not color.

The groups on which Populism was depending for support, so different from the most ardent followers of liberalism, were offered an appropriately different program. The Populists took over the liberal demand for honest, efficient political leaders, but the reformed government was to be no reflection of upper-income, better-educated America. Civil-service reform was not emphasized at Omaha; it smacked too much of establishing a permanent ruling group and contradicted the Jacksonian faith that any well-intentioned American was good enough to carry on government for his fellows. Populist government was to be by and for "the people," or, to use a more revealing phrase that the Populists borrowed from pre-Civil War reformers, by and for "the producers." The Populist reversion to the practice of dividing the population into producers and nonproducers was the surest indication of their view of America. It indicated their belief that "producers"—those who worked with their hands—were the men who really created the wealth of the nation. In the Populist view, the producers should run the country and should receive a value from their labor which gave little or no return to men whose chief function was providing capital.

In their eagerness to increase the political power of the producers, the Populists urged the secret ballot and endorsed three adventurous techniques for direct democracy: the popular election of United States senators; the initiative, giving the voters the right to legislate over the heads of their representatives; and the referendum, providing the voters with a veto over the actions of the legislature. The initiative and referendum proposals seemed so radical in 1892 that their chief advocate at Omaha, a representative of a New Jersey workingmen's organization, had to argue vigorously for including them in the platform, but he was ultimately successful. Populists could not resist any idea that promised to end the political control of corporations. In fact, so intense was the Populist hatred of politics as it was being practiced that the Omaha gathering whooped through a resolution unique in the history of American conventions, conservative or radical. No one who held a federal, state, or municipal office, the delegates decreed, could sit in a future Populist convention.

And all politics or political machinery was but a means; the end was economic and social reform. The Populists swept together the discontent with both Grantism and liberalism into a bold doctrine of continuous state intervention in behalf of the producers. Governments were to stop aiding the corporations, directly or indirectly, and were to start passing legislation beneficial to Americans who had little or no capital. The issue that excited liberals and old-style Republicans so much—the tariff—was just a "sham battle" to the Populists. "We believe," the Omaha platform emphasized, "that the powers of government should be expanded ... as rapidly and as far as the good sense of an intelligent people and the teachings of experience shall justify, to the end that oppression, injustice and poverty shall eventually cease in the land."

The Populist eye was on the Interstate Commerce Act of 1887, which put controls over railroads, and the Sherman Anti-Trust Act of 1890, which declared combinations in restraint of trade illegal. These the Populists wanted to strengthen and, in strengthened form, to make the models for state and federal interferences in economic life that would regulate all corporations and would splinter into small units those which had reached the monopoly stage. For years the Populists had watched extremes of wealth piling up, unchecked by legislation; the Omaha platform proposed to reverse, or at least halt, the trend by a graduated federal income tax. In the minds of most Populists, one of the chief enemies of the farmer was a rigid currency system, and the delegates demanded "a national currency, safe, sound and flexible, issued by the general government only." Government-operated postal savings banks were to take the savings business out of the hands of private bankers. Federal subtreasuries, "or some other systems," should be established to lend money to farmers at no more than two per cent interest and to see to it that the supply of currency fluctuated with the demand for agricultural credits. "All land now held by railroads and other corporations in excess of their actual needs," the Omaha convention added, "... should be reclaimed by the government and held for actual settlers only." On the general subject of the railroads, those prime ogres of the farmers, the Populists were ready for the most drastic kind of governmental power. The United States was to own and operate the railroads. It was, moreover, to own and operate the telegraph and telephone systems, which were approaching the monopoly stage and which the Populists felt were being run with an arrogant disregard of the consumer's interest.

The obvious socialism of these last proposals brought the most anguished of all cries from liberals. They were startled and outraged that free men could seriously propose handing over such great powers to the state, and their vehemence underlined the fundamental difference in the liberal and Populist approaches. The liberal, however much his practices might deviate from his doctrine under the pressure of the corporations, kept his principal emphasis on liberty, the freedom of the individual in political, economic, and social relations. The Populist did not forget liberty, but in the troubled Nineties the essence of liberty to a large number of Americans was the freedom to escape poverty and to rise in economic and social status. The Populists stressed opportunity rather than sheer liberty.

Most of the Populists, like so many of the liberals, found their hero in Thomas Jefferson. This may have been a tribute to the many-sided Jefferson, but it was also an example of the confusion that results from applying a man's thought in a different age. Liberals looked to the Jefferson who feared centralized power; Populists, to the Jefferson who considered capitalist power the chief enemy of the aspiring masses. Tom Watson, ardent Jeffersonian and bitter opponent of liberalism, caught the heart of Populism when he spoke of the movement's "yearning, upward tendency." Populism's central target, Watson continued, was "monopoly —not monopoly in the narrow sense of the word—but monopoly of power, of place, of privilege, of wealth, of progress." Its battle cry was: "Keep the avenues of honor free. Close no entrance to the poorest, the weakest, the humblest." Re-create an America that said to ambition: "The field is clear, the contest fair; come, and win your share if you can!"

In the elections of 1892 the Populists became the first third party to carry a state since the GOP started on its way in 1856. The contingent of Populist-minded United States Senators rose to five; the number of Representatives to ten. Populist governors were elected in Kansas, North Dakota, and Colorado, while the number of sympathetic state legislators and county officials mounted to fifteen hundred. In the important Illinois election the Democrats swept the state, but the result was more a defeat for the Populist Party than for reform. At the head of the victorious state ticket as John P. Altgeld, who agreed substantially with every important plank in the Omaha platform.

The next year the dissenters acquired a powerful ally. Hard times settled over the country again, bringing all the jolting effect of a second severe depression in one generation. The twelve months that began in the middle of 1894 have been called the *"année terrible"* of the post–Civil War period and the phrase is not overly dramatic for the record of savage strikes and brutal labor repression, deepening agricultural distress, and a national atmosphere of foreboding at the top and bitterness at the bottom.

1894 made labor history, with nearly 750,000 workingmen out in miltant strikes. The leader of the Pullman strikers, sent to jail by Cleveland's liberalism, sat mulling over the situation and came out a full-blown socialist. "We have been cursed with the reign of gold long enough," Eugene Debs told wildly cheering crowds. ". . . We are on the eve of a universal change." In the clay hills of the South, across the scorched prairies, the farmer's agitation was rapidly becoming, as one supporter described it, "a religious revival, a crusade, a pentecost of politics, in which a tongue of flame sat upon every man." It was "a fanaticism like the crusades," a Kansas observer added. "At night, from ten thousand little white schoolhouse windows, lights twinkled back hope to the stars. . . . They sang . . . with something of the same mad faith that inspired the martyr going to the stake. Far into the night the voices rose, women's voices, children's voices, the voices of old men, of youths and of maidens rose on the ebbing prairie breezes, as the crusaders of the revolution rode home, praising the people's will as though it were God's will and cursing wealth for its iniquity." Hamlin Garland, watching the Populists flail away in Congress, was sure that the country was approaching "a great periodic upheaval similar to that of '61. Everywhere as I went through the aisles of the House, I saw it and heard it. . . . The House is a smoldering volcano."

In Indianapolis, a ruche-collared lady measured the political situation and went off to see the cathedrals of Europe. "I am going to spend my money," she said, "before those crazy people take it."

The ruche-collared lady, had she been a bit more discerning, might well have been a good deal less precipitate. The structure of Populism was as rickety as the worst of the sharecropper homes.

The attempt of Southern Populists to form a poor-white, poor-Negro coalition proved politically disastrous. As a group, low-income Southern whites were harsh enemies of the Negro, and the Southern conservatives seriously injured Populism by calling it the "nigger's party." Impoverished but anti-Negro farmers clung to the "white man's party," the Democratic, and turned toward the leadership of demagogues like South Carolina's Ben Tillman and Mississippi's James Vardaman, who combined reform and racist attitudes in a formula similar to the one Adolf Hitler was to perfect. Quite typically, Vardaman denounced "the concentration of riches in the hands of the few" in the same speeches that lashed out at any proposal to give the vote to a "veneered savage," no matter what his "advertised mental and moral qualifications may be. I am just as much opposed to Booker T. Washington as a voter ... as I am to the cocoanut-headed, chocolate-colored, typical little coon, Andy Dotson, who blacks my shoes every morning."

South or North, the Populist Party was failing to achieve the shape of a genuine urban-rural movement. Under the whiplash of their debts, farmers were increasingly concentrating on demands for inflation, particularly for inflation by the alluringly simple method of free silver, and this emphasis was decidedly counter to the urban trend. Most industrial workers were coming to believe that they would be more hurt than helped by any type of inflation, and they generally shared the businessman's feeling that inflation by free silver was something out of a cracked pot.

Again and again Populists with a broad urban-rural approach, like the Chicago intellectual Henry Demarest Lloyd, warned that concentrating on free silver would wreck Populism. Many Southern leaders, sure that a sweepingly radical approach was needed, joined in the warning. But the Midwestern farmers, the most powerful faction in the Populist Party, were not to be swayed. As the elections of 1896 approached, the Iowa leader James Weaver spoke for much of Midwestern Populism when he said: "I shall favor going before the people ... with the money question alone, unencumbered with any other contention whatsoever."

On its part, labor was hurrying in a direction that made coalition difficult. By the Nineties the Knights of Labor, which included farmers and tradesmen and stood for a wide variety of reforms, was giving way to the American Federation of Labor, an organization devoted to labor with belligerent exclusiveness. Samuel Gompers, master architect of the federation, was determined to keep the AFL tightly reined to the purpose of larger wages, better working conditions, and shorter hours for industrial labor. At times Populism seemed to offer so much to labor that Gompers wavered, but he was soon back to his original position. Complete co-operation between the unions and the Populist Party, Gompers wrote, was "unnatural." The Populist Party consisted mainly of *"employing* farmers," whose "purposes, methods, and interests" diverged from those of the *"employed* farmers of the country districts or the mechanics and laborers of the industrial centres." The AFL would be more friendly to the Populists than it had been to any previous third party—and there Gompers drew the line.

• • •

Equally disruptive was the rising strength of socialism in the cities. The principal socialist leader, Daniel De Leon, filled his journal with denunciations of Populism as "conservative" and "retrograde." De Leon insisted upon running socialists against Populists; in the five states that had both tickets in 1892, the two parties polled approximately equal votes, with complete futility for both. The Populists returned the antipathy in full degree. The typical Populist shared the general American prejudice in favor of men and ideas that could be called old-stock American or, next best, could be associated with western Europe. Socialism was, beyond all argument, an imported doctrine. Most of the socialists were conspicuously European in origin, and a considerable percentage of them were immigrants from eastern Europe. Socialists usually felt no more comfortable at Populist meetings than they would have been among the D.A.R.

The anti-foreign feeling among reformers was so widespread that it split the socialists themselves. One of the few old-stock socialist leaders, Algie Simons, continually and publicly assailed any European orientation of the movement. There were, Simons maintained, two distinct wings in the party. The Western one, he wrote with obvious approval, "is quite largely agrarian in its origin, comes almost wholly from economic development, and is peculiarly American in its make-up." The Eastern one was primarily "urban, arrived at its conclusions quite largely through direct ideological propaganda, and is still (though rapidly losing this phase) formed mainly among those born in other countries." Privately, Simons complained: "In the East, the Socialist Party is run by Jews." Attitudes that were so divisive among socialists were doubly divisive in the relations between socialists and Populists.

Apart from this involved psychological factor, Populists and socialists found it difficult to work together for the simple and sufficient reason that the Populists were not socialists. The Populist Party might call for extending the powers of government as far as "good sense" dictated, and it might advocate the socialization of the railroads and the telegraph and telephone systems. But most Populists, sons of the agrarian tradition, emphatically did not want a society in which the principal means of production would be owned by the state. They believed in the system of free enterprise, even cherished it as the heart of the American way of life. They considered their program anything but a demand for a new economic system. Populists thought of themselves as engaged in a work of restoration, a restoration of the good old days, when, as they liked to believe, there was open competition and plenty of opportunity for everyone.

However sharp the conflict between rural Populists and urban radicals, the differences were mild compared with the clash between rural Populists and the "middle classes" of the cities. Regardless of occupation or income, the populations of the cities were becoming increasingly middle-class in outlook, and Populism offended a whole congeries of middle-class attitudes. The Populists made politics urgently important; the middle-class approach made politics the resort of the shifty-eyed and the incompetent, who found it easier to be accommodating than to go to work. The Populists were, inescapably, the party of the failures; the middle-class view, more or less consciously, considered associating oneself with movements speaking for the successful a prerequisite to one's own success. The Populists lambasted the successful industrialist and banker; urban people of middle-class attitudes, including slum-dwellers and clerks grubbing to support their families, looked up to the magnate as the man who had made the most of American opportunity, the "captain of industry," the glamour figure to be excused his frailties as a later generation was to excuse movie stars their divorces.

With special emphasis, the middle-class attitude esteemed respectability and modernity, and the most prominent Populist leaders easily left the impression of a howl from the backwoods. The Omaha convention master, Ignatius Donnelly, had a reputation for the kind of theories that too many lonely nights on the prairie can produce. He had founded a community in which everybody was to love everybody else, insisted, through 478 pages of *Atlantis*, that Plato's "lost isle" had really existed, and produced *The Great Cryptogram* to prove that Francis Bacon had written all of Shakespeare's plays, most of Marlowe's works, Montaigne's essays, and Burton's *Anatomy of Melancholy*. The 1892 Presidential candidate of the Populist Party was that ancient warhorse of agrarian agitation, James Weaver. Its other leaders included the cadaverous Tom Watson, with a windmill oratory straight out of the hills of Georgia; "Sockless" Jerry Simpson, the only American to achieve immortality by being accused of going without stockings; the hulking, red-whiskered Norwegian, Kittel Halvorson, always giving off the air of a man in troubled communion with the Infinite; and a band of female orators led by the bony-handed Mary Ellen Lease, speaking with unladylike ferocity about unladylike topics.

In the official history of the Omaha convention the Populist author went far out of his way to write of Candidate Weaver's friends among "the very best circles" of Des Moines, his "neat and tasty" home, the "chic" daughter and the wife who stayed away from public platforms. The Populist author of the history, a Kansas City reporter who knew his middle classes, was trying.

Although Populism ultimately failed as a third-party movement (as a later selection will show), the Populists nevertheless had a powerful impact on American politics. Theirs was the first significant political movement in the United States to discard laissez-faire as the solution to industrial woes, and to insist that the federal government also had responsibility for social welfare. Most importantly, the Populist revolt ushered in a new era of reform in the United States, an era in which many Populist demands became politically respectable and were eventually enacted into law.

9

New Worlds, New Visions

Oscar Handlin

ica often posed a stunning contrast with the peasants' dream of the New World as a land of boundless opportunity and universal equality. Oscar Handlin, a Pulitzer Prize winning historian, shows what it was like to be an immigrant in those years, telling the story of "the uprooted" from the viewpoint of the peasants themselves. Although some critics have challenged Handlin's technique, his narrative is nevertheless a vivid re-creation of the immigrant experience in the United States.

The Gilded Age witnessed a tremendous surge of immigration from Europe, as peasants there seemed more drawn to the romantic lure of America than ever before. They came over by the millions, crowding into American cities at the same time that native-born farmers were moving there, too. Between 1850 and 1900, some sixteen and a half million immigrants arrived in the United States, more than half of them coming in the 1880s and 1890s. There was also a significant shift in the source of immigration. The "old" immigrants came largely from northern and western Europe—from Britain, Ireland, Germany, and the Scandinavian countries. But in the 1890s most immigrants were from eastern and southern Europe—from Russia, Serbia, Austria-Hungary, and Italy—and most were Catholic or Jewish in religion. When they arrived in America's northeastern cities, they invariably antagonized native-born Protestants, who blamed them, quite unfairly, for America's growing urban problems.

Since most immigrants were peasants, they were ill prepared for life in the crowded cities and factory towns. Conditions there left them shocked and bewildered, with an overwhelming sense of rootlessness. Indeed, the reality of industrial Amer-

Often, they would try to understand. They would think about it in the pauses of their work, speculate sometimes as their minds wandered, tired, at the close of a long day.

What had cut short the continuous past, severed it from the unrelated present? Immigration had transformed the entire economic world within which the peasants had formerly lived. From surface forms to inmost functionings, the change was complete. A new setting, new activities, and new meanings forced the newcomers into radically new roles as producers and consumers of goods. In the process, they became, in their own eyes, less worthy as men. They felt a sense of degradation that raised a most insistent question: Why had this happened?

More troubling, the change was not confined to economic matters. The whole American universe was different. Strangers, the immigrants could not locate themselves; they had lost the polestar that gave them their bearings. They would not regain an awareness of direction until they could visualize themselves in their new context, see a picture of the world as it appeared from this perspective. At home, in the wide frame of the village, their eyes had taken

---

From *The Uprooted*, Second Edition Enlarged, by Oscar Handlin. Copyright 1951, © 1973 by Oscar Handlin, by permission of Little, Brown and Co. in association with the Atlantic Monthly Press.

112

in the whole of life, had brought to their perceptions a clearly defined view of the universe. Here the frame narrowed down, seemed to reveal only fragmentary distorted glimpses that were hardly reminiscent of the old outlines.

The peasants brought with them from their life on the soil the preconceptions and basic assumptions that had controlled their attitudes and influenced their actions. Before emigration they had lived in intimate contact with nature, never much removed from the presence of the objects of the physical universe. All around were things not made by men's hands, things that coexisted with men. Between these things and men there were differences. But they were also held together by the most powerful ligatures, for the universe was not made up of entirely disparate, disconnected objects but of elements which varied only imperceptibly from each other. Men and things were alike subject to natural processes, alike responsive to the same moving forces.

Everything the peasant saw about him was, like himself, a being. All the objects of nature, of whatever shape or form or substance, were literally animated, perhaps to greater or lesser degrees, but all were essentially capable of life and growth. All were God's creatures, man and the beasts too, and also the trees, the meadows, the stars, the sun, fire and water, the days of the week and the seasons of the year. Yes, even clods and stones had being.

In all these entities, the characteristics of animation were the same as those among men. All had individuality. So, the animals of the barnyard had each his own name, and those of field and forest—not so intimately known— were represented by imaginary titled heads of their species. Trees, rocks, springs, had also each its appellation, and every day of the year its own designation from the saint or festival that gave it its quality.

With the name went the ascription of personality: each being had character, had the capacity for action, had some degree of volition. All the objects of nature, being animate, had understanding enough to react meaningfully to conditions about them. They had a kind of intelligence which, while different from man's, was not necessarily inferior. In fact, other beings knew things humans did not know: birds and beasts could foretell changes in the weather; at the approach of danger, geese would fall a-clamoring in the enclosures, dogs run nervously about. Animals even had a sense to judge bad action; for instance, bees, it was said, would not stay with a thief.

It was incumbent upon men, dealing with these beings, to be careful, to stay on good terms with them, to give them their due lest they retaliate. Each day thus had its own character and, if not respected, would return after a year to exact vengeance. A violated tree, or one not properly bound with straw, would bear no fruit; neglected land would yield no grain; the mistreated cow would give no milk; an unclean fire would go out. Accidental injuries to these beings, when they occurred, had to be explained and the victims appeased if possible. The utmost caution was worth while, for those who won them over could use the foresight of animals to good advantage. So, the friendly birds, if only rightly understood, could with certainty give the sign for the best time for sowing.

Among all natural beings there existed also the relationship of solidarity. All were so connected with each other that what happened to any one affected every other. If the birds flew away to the woods, then the snow would soon decide to fall. If the sparrows were permitted to eat cherries in the summer that would help the grain to thrive. Such attributes as richness and the capacity for growth were therefore transferable and fecundity could be bestowed by one object on another. The peasant rubbed fertile soil onto his cow to be sure she would bear often.

There were also special kinds of solidarity within species of things. All animals were particularly related and, when danger threatened, warned each other, at times indeed could speak among themselves. There was a more intimate relationship within each class of animals; the cows lowing softly to one another had their own secrets. This was the identical solidarity that men felt for other men. Did not the peasants' lives revolve about their membership in a natural community that cared for them?

To whatever degree it was general, solidarity among all beings sprang from the common situation in which they found themselves. All the objects of nature were engaged in growth. They participated thereby in the same struggle against decay. The solidarity among them was the inner recognition that man and beast, plant and living soil, in some measure fought the same battle. A breach of solidarity was treachery in the face of the enemy of all and merited the severest punishment. To cut down a fruit tree, to kill a stork, to waste, was a hideous disruption of the order of nature, an invitation to calamitous retaliation.

A sacrifice was justified only when it involved a lesser retreat before decay in the interests of greater growth. Thus it was proper to clear trees in order to bring new lands under cultivation; increased production would expiate the destruction. So, also, animals gave up their lives, willingly as it were, to the end that men might eat. But even in such legitimate instances, it was best to be cautious, to act according to appropriate forms. Special rites to ward off unfavorable consequences accompanied the slaughter or any other measure that might involve some hidden breach of solidarity.

If man had to proceed warily in encounters with the world of natural objects, he was compelled to be doubly careful when it came to the mysterious realm of unnatural beings that also existed about him. This realm was not continuous with his own world. It was a dread level of being, inhabited by spirits of many kinds that took many shapes. Fairies, elves, leprechauns might perhaps be visualized, though not reliably; but no mind could conceive of the variety of forms that might be assumed by vampires, specters, souls adrift on earth or released for some special end from hell or purgatory. These beings could enter the natural world, but there was no solidarity between them and the objects of nature.

The affairs of the spirits were ever a source of concern to the peasant. They had powers beyond those of the poor human and could interfere when they liked with his own affairs —sometimes beneficently assisting him, sometimes through malice or mischief bringing utter ruin down upon the unfortunate victim who had offended them. Their imminent presence called for constant caution. They might do no more than make trouble with their pranks; or they might possess the bodies of people and animals; or they might betray men into disastrous temptations. They added an awesome dimension to a universe already terrifyingly vast. Among so many hazardous forces, the peasant had to walk carefully, be constantly alert to the presence of all the elements about him.

The safest way was to know the hidden causal connections among objects and events. Such knowledge gave some persons a measure of control over the activities of the beings about them. Command of magic—that is, of the certain ways, of the certain words, of the certain rites—would appease or neutralize hostile forces, enlist the support of friendly ones. That would give the peasant security.

Only, where was that knowledge found? The wily ones who had it would not share for nothing. In the stress of great need there was no choice but to seek out the witch or wizard who could converse with their familiar spirits. Yet everyone knew what frightful bargains were exacted for such assistance.

It was much safer, when each decision could have incalculable consequences, to follow the traditional time-proven patterns. One could seek guidance from the special vision of pilgrims, seers, and idiots. But the most certain advice came from the wise old ones who knew from the experience of the past what ways were the most reliable. Safety lay in adherence to routines that had been effective before; new actions were doomed to dangerous failure. When all was said and done, all things had their given course, and would follow that course.

Yes, all things follow their course. *We sow to reap, and reap to sow again. And grow to die.* Childhood, youth, maturity, old age, death, come each like the seasons in their destined order. In this endless rotation is the meaning of growth.

Ponder the matter as the face of the earth changes, as the signs of living life give way to the dead emptiness of winter. This season, in its occurrence and recurrence, marks the end and start of the peasant year. This is the time of death and the period antecedent to new births.

A dulling chill creeps across the poorly protected countryside; frequent blasts rip the frozen branches from the trees. In northern places, the still snow hides the land. Everywhere, shortening days give notice of the change in all time. Briefly the peasants hurry out while the sun still shines to perform the necessary tasks, then back to the cold interior.

Within, the precious light is brief. Long dusks sink over the silent village. The open fire or ever-burning gleaming stove throws strange shadows over rooms suddenly become unfamiliar. Later, little islands of brightness around the sputtering pine knot, the candle, or lamp, give the place a new appearance. Outside is the unknown silence broken by mysterious creakings, by the rustle of beasts, by sounds whose meaning no man knows.

The few indoor tasks are done and it is not yet the time when sleep will come. The old ones retell the stories that all their listeners know; and reverie sinks down over men's minds. Questions come.

Of what did the peasants think day after day in the winter? Not in those exceptional hours when sudden storms shook the hut and drove the icy cold through its creviced walls; not in the desperate last weeks when stored-up stocks ran low, and hunger waited at the door, but day after day—what did they think in the long cold stillness?

As all living things receded before the winter, their minds turned to the mystery of life which was death. Indeed what was that daily round of deeds of theirs, so dull, so squalid? Like the beasts of burden beneath the yoke they were, caring only for the present task, cut off always by the tedious darkness from the sight of the marvels, of the hidden prodigies beyond their range of vision. Then indeed there was a yearning towards a life uniting all things— fancy and reality, a dream existence for which, under the miserable conditions of their earthly days, their weary hearts insatiably longed.

Strange things happened in the long dead night of winter as men reviewed their lives, remembered. On All Souls' Day there welled up in every heart a pervasive sense of desolation, a distressed silent recollection of those gone to lie beneath the drooping trees and looming crosses of the churchyard, the home of the dead. From place to place, the rites that marked the day were different. But everywhere men felt renewed the consciousness of utter helplessness. Were they more than little twigs, blown about they knew not where in the vastness of the great universe?

Winter confronted the peasants with death in all its hated, feared, despised features. It was as if all the emotions brought forth at a funeral were stretched out, attenuated, prolonged for the season—the sense of irreparable loss, the desolate thoughts of their own inevitable fate. All hopes and joys were vain. They were themselves like stray clouds, drifted from the unknown, destined for the unknown, and moved by unknown impulses.

To what purpose then did men live?

To those who awaited its coming in eagerness and expectation, spring brought back the signs of life. The sun resumed its blessed mastery over the land. The warmth returned and the light played again on walls whitened, or at least cleaned, for the Easter.

In the fields the grain rises again. Again the leaves break forth. These are not the grain and leaves of last year. The new is not the old. Yet the new and the old are related. They are related by the death of the old which was necessary for the birth of the new.

Is it not so with men who live to die, and die so that those who come will later live? In dying they do not end, any more than does the cut grain or fallen leaf. All live on, regenerated —in generation after generation.

What is the religion of the men who live through winter and spring? It is the affirmation that life is victorious over death. Though the trees stand bare in winter, yet will they be clothed in spring with green leaves and sweet-scented blossoms. Though a man's life be sown with labor, with hardship, with blood, a crop will come of it, a harvest be reaped.

That affirmation was the peasant's faith, his own explanation of his place in the universe. But overlaid on this natural religion was one taught by the priests, a religion that stemmed from outside the village, from the monasteries, the towns, the nobility. By now Christianity was well-established, in some regions for more than a thousand years. Yet it had by no means destroyed the older order of beliefs. The magical practices and the ideas they embodied held on even in places where the Church made an effort to fight them. And more often than not, the priest was himself rooted in the village and was content to allow the peasants to identify their own notions with elements of Christian doctrine, to effect a practical if not a dogmatic reconciliation.

Christianity did add to the earlier peasant ideas a conception of sin and the faith in a supernatural redemption. The distinction between good and evil he heard reiterated from the pulpit the peasant identified with his own distinction between helpful and harmful forces. In the galaxy of spirits, the peasant found a place for the devil and his imps, operating for their own hellish purposes. To resist their designs he learned to call upon an army of saints, each with its own province and potency. In these terms, he came to think of the world as the field of battle between two spiritual communities, the divine and the demoniacal, which struggled for the soul of man.

The burden of choice, already heavy, thus became heavier. Any act now might be wrong not only in the sense that it could bring on hostile consequences, but also in the sense that it might partake of evil. A bad decision was induced by spirits who were unfriendly and also devilish, was damaging and also sinful. Man bore the weight not simply of his mistakes but of his guilt also. His lot was to suffer and, as well, to expiate.

Yet to him, in his troubled state, Christianity brought also the miracle of redemption. Poor thing that he was, his soul was yet a matter of consequence. For him the whole drama of salvation had been enacted: God had come to earth, had suffered as a man to make for all men a place in a life everlasting. Through that sacrifice had been created a community of all those who had faith, a kind of solidarity that would redress all grievances and right all wrongs, if not now, then in the far more important aftermath to life.

Therefore it is well to look not to the present but to the eternal future, not to this world in which there is nothing but trouble and woe but to the next in which will come ease and consolation. Here evil increases and multiplies like the thistles in the woods. Here all things are vain and to no purpose like the bubbles which the wind tosses up on the surface of the waters. Yet let our souls but fly to Jesus as the birds fly south in winter and they will find comfort and joy and an end to all sorrow.

And in those moments of meditation when the comfort comes, we know this hope is not merely a delusion personal to us. The evidence is in the visible community which together participates in the mystery of salvation. Within the divine universe is this village, and within this village we men. This is our reassurance; thus we know where we are in the world.

These were the contents with which the hearts and minds of the peasants were laden as they came to the New World. This was the stock of ideas on which they drew when they came to account for their situation in America, once they had arrived and were at work and the work they did seemed not fit work for a man. Now there would be new questions. Would the old answers do when these people tried to explain what had happened to them?

They found it difficult, of course, to reconstruct a coherent record out of the excess of their experience since they had left the village. Many impressions remained fragmentary, unrelated to any whole adjustment.

This they knew, though, and could not mistake it: they were lonely. In the midst of teeming cities, in the crowded tenements and the factories full of bustling men, they were lonely.

Their loneliness had more than one dimension. It had the breadth of unfamiliarity. Strange people walked about them; strange sounds assailed their inattentive ears. Hard pavements cut them off from nature in all its accustomed manifestations. Look how far they could, at the end of no street was a familiar horizon. Hemmed in by the tall buildings, they were fenced off from the realm of growing things. They had lost the world they knew of beasts and birds, of blades of grass, of sprays of idle flowers. They had acquired instead surroundings of a most outlandish aspect. That unfamiliarity was one aspect of their loneliness.

Loneliness had also the painful depth of isolation. The man who once had been surrounded with individual beings was here cast adrift in a life empty of all but impersonal things. In the Old Country, this house in this village, these fields by these trees, had had a character and identity of their own. They had testified to the peasant's *I*, had fixed his place in the visible universe. The church, the shrine, the graveyard and the generations that inhabited it had also had their personality, had also testified to the peasant's *I*, and had fixed his place in a larger invisible universe.

In the new country, all these were gone; that was hard enough. Harder still was the fact that nothing replaced them. In America, the peasant was a transient without meaningful connections in time and space. He lived now with inanimate objects, cut off from his surroundings. His dwelling and his place of work had no relationship to him as a man. The scores of established routines that went with a life of the soil had disappeared and with them the sense of being one of a company. Therefore the peasant felt isolated and isolation added to his loneliness.

Strangeness and isolation oppressed even those who returned to the soil. They too were lonely. Everywhere, great wastes of empty land dissevered the single farm from the rest of the world. Wrapped up in the unfamiliar landscapes of prairie distance or forest solitude, the peasants found nowhere an equivalent of the village, nowhere the basis for re-establishing the solidarity of the old communal life. Therefore they were each alone, in city and in country, for that of which they had been a part was no longer about them.

The shattering loneliness disrupted the communion of persons and places and events. This was difficult enough for those who found agri-

Newly arrived Italian immigrants. "This they knew, though, and could not mistake it: they were lonely. In the midst of teeming cities, in the crowded tenements and the factories full of bustling men, they were lonely...." (Courtesy of George Eastman House Collection.)

culture their calling; the change of scene upset the traditional calendar, falsified the traditional signs of nature that paced the year's activities. But that destroyed communion was more difficult still in the urban places. In the cities, the seasons lost entirely their relevance. For the worker, winter and spring were very much alike; whether he worked and how he worked had nothing to do, as it had at home, with the passing cycle of the year.

If the outward aspects were the same—the falling snow or warm summer wind—that only made more poignant the sense of lost significance. And they never were long the same;

tinged with soot, the virgin snow at once acquired the pavement's gray, or the dull wind dragged the smell of city heat through confining streets. So it was with the noteworthy days. Formal observances persisted for a time; the villagers longingly went through the motions, celebrated saints' days, mourned at the time of memories. But snatched out of context these occasions had not the old flavor. Self-conscious under the gaze of strangers, the peasants could no longer find the old meanings. For all peasants, and particularly for those dominated by the mechanical monotony of factory or construction labor, their loneliness entailed also the desolating loss of the precious sense of solidarity. Without that, was there any purpose left to life?

Was it not true, did not your whole experience teach you the futility of striving? *What needs must be no man can flee!* How helpless were humans before the forces arrayed against them! Of what value were calculations? In the Old Country, at least, you could take care, do what was necessary in the proper way at the proper time, follow experience and use the knowledge of generations. Even so, your very emigration is evidence of the slight value of all precautions. Search back over your lifetime. Think: have you reason to believe that wiser decisions on your part could have stayed the famines, put off the displacements? And how much deeper is your helplessness now than then; now you cannot even recognize the proper ways.

Every element of the immigrants' experience since the day they had left home added to this awareness of their utter helplessness. All the incidents of the journey were bound up with chance. What was the road to follow, what the ship to board, what port to make? These were serious questions. But who knew which were the right answers? Whether they survived the hazards of the voyage, and in what condition, these too were decisions beyond the control of the men who participated in it. The capricious world of the crossing pointed its own conclusion as to the role of chance in the larger universe into which the immigrants plunged.

It was the same with their lives after landing. To find a job or not, to hold it or to be fired, in these matters laborers' wills were of slight importance. Inscrutable, distant persons determined matters on the basis of remote, unknown conditions. The most fortunate of immigrants, the farmers, knew well what little power they had to influence the state of the climate, the yield of the earth, or the fluctuations of the market, all the elements that determined their lot. Success or failure, incomprehensible in terms of peasant values, seemed altogether fortuitous. Time and again, the analogy occurred to them: man was helpless like the driven cog in a great machine.

Loneliness, separation from the community of the village, and despair at the insignificance of their own human abilities, these were the elements that, in America, colored the peasants' view of their world. From the depths of a dark pessimism, they looked up at a frustrating universe ruled by haphazard, capricious forces. Without the capacity to control or influence these forces men could but rarely gratify their hopes or wills. Their most passionate desires were doomed to failure; their lives were those of the feeble little birds which hawks attack, which lose strength from want of food, and which, at last surrendering to the savage blasts of the careless elements, flutter unnoticed to the waiting earth.

Sadness was the tone of life, and death and disaster no strangers. Outsiders would not understand the familiarity with death who had not daily met it in the close quarters of the steerage; nor would they comprehend the riotous Paddy funerals who had no insight of the release death brought. The end of life was an end to hopeless striving, to ceaseless pain, and to the endless succession of disappointments. There was a leaden grief for the ones who went; yet the tomb was only the final parting in a long series of separations that had started back at the village crossroads.

In this world man can only be resigned. Illness takes a child away; from the shaft they bring a father's crippled body; sudden fire eats up a block of flimsy shanties, leaves half of each family living. There is no energy for prolonged mourning. Things are as they are and must remain so. Resist not but submit to fortune and seek safety by holding on.

In this world the notion of improvement is delusive. The best hope is that matters grow not worse. Therefore it is desirable to stand against change, to keep things as they are; the risks involved in change are incomparably more formidable than those involved in stability. There is not now less poverty, less misery, less torture, less pain than formerly. Indeed, today's evils, by their nearness, are far more oppressive than yesterday's which, after all, were somehow survived. Yesterday, by its distance, acquires a happy glow. The peasants look back (they remember they lived through yesterday; who knows if they will live through today?) and their fancy rejoices in the better days that have passed, when they were on the land and the land was fertile, and they were young and strong, and virtues were fresh. And it was better yet in their fathers' days, who were wiser and stronger than they. And it was best of all in the golden past of their distant progenitors who were every one a king and did great deeds. Alas, those days are gone, that they believed existed, and now there is only the bitter present.

In this world then, as in the Old Country, the safest way was to look back to tradition as a guide. Lacking confidence in the individual's capacity for independent inquiry, the peasants preferred to rely upon the tested knowledge of the past. It was difficult of course to apply village experience to life in America, to stretch the ancient aphorisms so they would fit new conditions. Yet that strain led not to a rejection of tradition but rather to an eager quest for a reliable interpreter. Significantly, the peasants sought to acknowledge an authority that would make that interpretation for them.

Their view of the American world led these immigrants to conservatism, and to the acceptance of tradition and authority. Those traits in turn shaped the immigrants' view of society, encouraged them to retain the peasants' regard for status and the divisions of rank. In these matters too striving was futile; it was wiser to keep each to his own station in the social order, to respect the rights of others and to exact the obligations due. For most of these people that course involved the acceptance of an inferior position. But was that not altogether realistic? The wind always blew in the face of the poor; and it was in the nature of society that some should have an abundance of possessions and others only the air they breathed.

The whole configuration of the peasant's ideas in the United States strengthened the place in his life of the established religion he brought with him. It was not only an institutional reluctance to change that held him to his faith, but also the greater need that faith satisfied in the New World.

Emigration had broken the ties with nature. The old stories still evoked emotional responses in their hearers; and the housewives still uttered imprecations and blessings and magic words to guard against the evil eye. But it was hard to believe that the whole world of spirits and demons had abandoned their familiar homes and come also across the Atlantic. It was hard too to continue to think in terms of the natural cycle of growth, of birth, death, and regeneration, away from the setting in which it was every day illustrated in peasant life.

Instead these immigrants found their Christianity ever more meaningful. Here they discovered the significance of their suffering. It was true, what the priest said, that evil was everywhere present in the world; they had themselves experienced the evidence of it. It was true they were imperfect and full of sin, not worthy of a better lot. What they tried bore no results. What they touched turned to dust.

Still all this toil and trouble was not without purpose. What seemed on the surface like the rule of chance in the world was not really so, but part of a plan. The whole of it was not yet revealed, man could not see the end, only the start, because this was not an earthly plan. Rather it extended far beyond this immediate existence and would reach its culmination in an altogether different life that came after the release of death.

Fixing his vision on that life eternal which would follow this, the peasant perceived that caprice in mundane things was an element in an ordered design. If injustice now seemed to triumph, then it was only that retribution should come after. Did the evil flourish, then would they be punished. Were the good oppressed and humiliated, it was to make their rewards the richer. This he knew was the mystery and the reason for his being in the universe.

As he participated in that other mystery of the divine sacrifice that assured him salvation, all the scattered elements of his existence became whole. Let him but have faith enough in the God Who had gone to the cross, for him; Who had come over the water, with him; and he would be repaid for the loss of his home, for the miseries of the way, and for the harshness of his present life. Not indeed in this world, but in an everlasting future. For the lonely and isolated, for the meek and humble, for the strangers, there was hope of a sort, and consolation.

. . .

The migration to America had destroyed the context of the peasants' natural religion. Yet the resigned passivity with which they once had faced the endless round of births, deaths, and regenerations had lived on into the New World. The circumstances of their coming, alone and among foreigners, had perpetuated that sense of helplessness, had driven into the texture of their Christianity an otherworldly fatalism.

Never would they understand how this had happened or even that it had happened. They were never capable of contrasting their own situation with that of those other uprooted ones who remained in the Old World. Not all who left the village had gone to America; and the ideological development of those whose remove was to some other place in their own country took a distinctive turn of its own.

In England, for instance, the peasants displaced by the eighteenth-century revolutions in agriculture had drifted often into the growing industrial cities where they encountered circumstances as trying as those that met the transatlantic immigrants. In England too the migrants became an exploited proletariat; and their intellectual adjustment, in some respects, was analogous to that of the peasants in the United States. In England too could be seen the pessimistic reflections of a miserable life, the conservatism that grew out of resistance to inexorable changes, and the continued willingness to accept authority and to recognize status.

But there was also a significant difference. The peasants who came to America brought with them their established churches to be re-established in new communities in the New World. They transferred their faith intact and rarely were tempted to deviate from it; their foreignness alone sufficed to keep them out of the native American denominations. The peasants who migrated within England, however, did not bring their own churches with them. In London and in the rising manufacturing towns there were some churches of the established religion, of course. But they were not peasant churches; were the poor newcomers to crowd in among the pews of the well-dressed city folk, they would hardly feel at home. Those who did not remain entirely unchurched were more likely to resort to the humble chapels of the dissenters, where all benches were alike. They would be less strangers there than in the elegant edifices of the urban parishes.

A like development occurred in parts of Germany where a number of pietistic sects in the disturbed areas of the southwest weaned away some of the peasants at the end of the eighteenth century and early in the nineteenth. In Scandinavia there were similar inroads, by Methodists in Sweden, by Haugeans in Norway.

His situation made the dissenter a protester. Standing outside the established church he had to account for his difference. Incapable of justifying his affiliation by the universality of his group, he could only justify it by its particularity. This was a small group, but a select one, a group into which members were not born but into which they came. These were chosen people, people who bore a mission that demanded they be different.

Redemption for the dissenter was not the simple reward of faith; it was the product of achievement of a mission. Not resignation but a striving toward improvement was the way; and life on earth was not merely an entry into the afterlife but an opportunity by which man could demonstrate what he could make of himself. This world was therefore a place of intrinsic significance and humans had power by their wills to control their fates within it.

These people had not found their adjustment to the disruption of the old village life complicated by the transfer to a New World, a transfer so frightening that those involved in it could not venture to think outside the terms of their peasant heritage.

Sometimes the dissenting peasants, already displaced, made a second move; or more often their children did. Their American experience would then be not like that of the peasants who had come directly, but more like that of other dissenters who had never been peasants. Among the artisans and traders gathered up in the general stream of migration were several groups that had never been members of an established church, never shared fully the village views.

In that sense, the extreme of dissent, because they were altogether outside the Christian community, were the Jews. Although they had lived in close contact with the peasants for hundreds of years, they had remained apart, strangers in the society. Although the contact between the village and the Jewry was always close, often intimate, the separateness of the two persisted. Among the Jews too the role of dissenter in the midst of a solidary community evoked the consciousness that they were a chosen people, that they had a unique destiny and mission, and that the world was a field in which they could profitably labor toward improvement.

The difference that already marked the dissenters off from the peasants in advance of emigration was deepened by the experience of settlement in the United States. The dissenters had always occupied an abnormal place in peasant society; they had been the outsiders who did not belong. In America they found their position the only normal one; here, there was no established church, no solidary community; everyone to some degree was an outsider. Since the dissenters had often larger resources of capital and skill than the peasants and were more fortunate in their economic adjustment, the impact of immigration was often stimulating. They could come to identify America with their New Canaan and interpret their mission in terms of an American success.

Yet even these people were immigrants and bore with the peasant the marks of their migration. No matter how fortunate their lot, they had lost an old home and had suffered the pains of fitting themselves to a new environment. There was no danger any immigrants would grow complacent about their settlement or forget their strangeness. They had only, any of them, to think of what ideas were held by Americans longer in the land to know what a cleavage there yet was between the old and new comers. Confronted with the prevalent notions of the inevitability of progress, of the essential goodness of man and his capacity to rule his own life, of the optimistic desirability of change, peasants and dissenters alike felt a chill distrust, a determination to resist, a threat to their own ideas.

That determination was expressed in their criticism of the deficiencies of life in the United States. To the immigrants America seemed unstable; it lacked the orderly elements of existence. Without security of status or the recognition of rank, no man, no family, had a proper place in the social order. Only money talked, for Americans measured all things in terms of gold and invariably preferred the superficial and immediate to the permanent and substantial.

These reactions reflected the urge to strengthen old values and to reaffirm old ideals. Precisely because migration had subjected those to attack, it was necessary aggressively to defend them, to tolerate no change because any change might have the most threatening consequences. In that sense all immigrants were conservatives, dissenters and peasants alike. All would seek to set their ideas within a fortification of religious and cultural institutions that would keep them sound against the strange New World.

10

"Remember the *Maine!* To Hell with Spain!"

William E. Leuchtenburg

The last quarter of the nineteenth century marked the Second Age of Imperialism, a time when the industrial nations of Europe—Britain, Germany, France, Holland, and Russia—claimed colonies in Africa and spheres of influence in distant China. The United States, flexing its imperial muscles in the 1890s, was alive with "aggressive, expansionistic, and jingoistic" feelings as well. And these feelings, together with a genuine desire to help Cuba win its independence, drove the United States into a needless war with Spain, now a second-rate power whose old American empire had all but disintegrated.

The Spanish-American War did not make the United States a world power. The country was already a world power when the conflict began. But the war did leave America with colonial possessions in both the Caribbean and the Pacific, and it convinced Americans themselves that they had an imperial destiny in the world theater. Out of this awareness came American demands for equal commercial rights in China (called the Open Door Policy), the moralistic, gunboat diplomacies of Theodore Roosevelt and Woodrow Wilson, and American involvement in World War I.

The United States in the 1890's became more aggressive, expansionistic, and jingoistic than it had been since the 1850's. In less than five years, we came to the brink of war with Italy, Chile, and Great Britain over three minor incidents in which no American national interest of major importance was involved. In each of these incidents, our secretary of state was highly aggressive, and the American people applauded. During these years, we completely overhauled our decrepit Navy, building fine new warships like the *Maine*. The martial virtues of Napoleon, the imperial doctrines of Rudyard Kipling, and the naval theories of Captain Alfred T. Mahan all enjoyed a considerable vogue.

There was an apparently insatiable hunger for foreign conquest. Senator Shelby M. Cullom declared in 1895: "It is time that some one woke up and realized the necessity of annexing some property. We want all this northern hemisphere, and when we begin to reach out to secure these advantages we will begin to have a nation and our lawmakers will rise above the grade of politicians and become true statesmen." When, in 1895, the United States almost became involved in a war with Great Britain over the Venezuelan boundary, Theodore Roosevelt noted: "The antics of the bankers, brokers and anglo-maniacs generally are humiliating to a degree. . . . Personally I rather hope the fight will come soon. The clamor of the peace faction has convinced me that this country needs a war." The Washington *Post* concluded: "The taste of Empire is in the mouth of the people. . . ."

In the early nineteenth century, under the leadership of men like Simón Bolívar, Spain's colonies in the New World had launched a series of successful revolutions; of the great

---

"The Needless War With Spain": © Copyright 1957 by American Heritage Publishing Co., Inc. Reprinted by permission from *American Heritage* Magazine, February 1957.

Spanish empire that Cortes and Pizarro had built, the island of Cuba, "the Ever Faithful Isle," was the only important Spanish possession to stay loyal to the Crown. Spain exploited the economy of the island mercilessly, forcing Cubans to buy Spanish goods at prices far above the world market, and Madrid sent to Cuba as colonial officials younger sons who had no interest in the island other than making a quick killing and returning to Spain. High taxes to support Spanish officialdom crippled the island; arbitrary arrests and arbitrary trials made a mockery of justice; and every attempt at public education was stifled.

The island of Cuba had been in a state of political turbulence for years when in 1894 the American Wilson-Gorman Tariff placed duties on Cuban sugar which, coupled with a worldwide depression, brought ruin to the economy of the island. The terrible hardship of the winter was the signal for revolution; on February 24, 1895, under the leadership of a junta in New York City headed by José Martí, rebels once more took the field against Spain. At first, the American people were too absorbed with the Venezuelan crisis to pay much attention to another revolt in Cuba. Then, in September, 1895, came the event which changed the course of the Cuban rebellion: William Randolph Hearst, a young man of 32 who had been operating the San Francisco *Examiner* in a sensational fashion, purchased the New York *Morning Journal*, and immediately locked horns with Joseph Pulitzer and the *World* in a circulation war that was to make newspaper history.

Hearst capitalized on the fact that the American people had only the most romantic notions of the nature of the Cuban conflict. The rebels under General Máximo Gómez, a tough Santo Domingan guerrilla fighter, embarked on a program of burning the cane fields in the hope not only of depriving the government of revenue but also of so disrupting the life of the island that the government would be forced to submit. Although there were some noble spirits in the group, much of the rebellion had an unsavory odor; one of the main financial supports for the uprising came from American property owners who feared that their sugar fields would be burned unless protection money was paid.

While Gómez was putting Cuba to the torch, American newsmen were filing reports describing the war in terms of nonexistent pitched battles between the liberty-loving Cubans and the cruel Spaniards. The war was presented, in short, as a Byronic conflict between the forces of freedom and the forces of tyranny, and the American people ate it up. When Hearst bought the *Journal* in late 1895, it had a circulation of 30,000; by 1897 it had bounded to over 400,000 daily, and during the Spanish-American War it was to go well over a million.

The sensational newspapers had influence, yet they represented no more than a minority of the press of the country; and in the South and the Middle West, where anti-Spanish feeling became most intense, the representative newspaper was much more conservative. Certainly the yellow press played a tremendous part in whipping up sentiment for intervention in Cuba, but these feelings could not be carried into action unless American political leaders of both parties were willing to assume the terrible responsibility of war.

By the beginning of 1896 the rebels had achieved such success in their guerrilla tactics that Madrid decided on firmer steps and sent General Don Valeriano Weyler y Nicolau to Cuba. When Weyler arrived in February, he found the sugar industry severely disrupted and the military at a loss to meet the rebel tactic of setting fire to the cane fields. Weyler declared martial law and announced that men guilty of incendiarism would be dealt with summarily; he was promptly dubbed "The Butcher" by American newspapermen.

By late 1896 Weyler still had not succeeded in crushing the insurrection, and his measures became more severe. On October 21 he issued his famous *reconcentrado* order, directing the "reconcentration" of the people of Pinar del Río in the garrison towns, and forbidding the export of supplies from the towns to the countryside. Reasoning that he could never suppress the rebellion so long as the rebels could draw secret assistance from people in the fields, Weyler moved the people from the estates into the towns and stripped the countryside of supplies to starve out the rebellion. Since many of the people had already fled to the towns, the *reconcentrado* policy was not as drastic as it appeared; yet the suffering produced by the policy was undeniable. Lacking proper hygienic care, thousands of Cubans, especially women and children, died like flies.

When William McKinley entered the White House in 1897, he had no intention of joining the War Hawks. "If I can only go out of office . . . with the knowledge that I have done what lay in my power to avert this terrible calamity," McKinley told Grover Cleveland on the eve of his inauguration, "I shall be the happiest man in the world." McKinley came to power as the "advance agent of prosperity," and business interests were almost unanimous in opposing any agitation of the Cuban question that might lead to war. Contrary to the assumptions of Leninist historians, it was Wall Street which, first and last, resisted a war which was to bring America its overseas empire.

The country had been gripped since 1893 by the deepest industrial depression in its history, a depression that was to persist until the beginning of 1897. Each time it appeared recovery might be on its way, a national crisis had cut it off: first the Venezuelan boundary war scare of December, 1895, then the bitter free silver campaign of 1896. What business groups feared more than anything else was a new crisis. As Julius Pratt writes: "To this fair prospect of a great business revival the threat of war was like a specter at the feast."

McKinley was not a strong President, and he had no intention of being one. Of all the political figures of his day, he was the man most responsive to the popular will. It was his great virtue and, his critics declared, his great weakness. Uncle Joe Cannon once remarked: "McKinley keeps his ear to the ground so close that he gets it full of grasshoppers much of the time." If McKinley was not one of our greatest Presidents, he was certainly the most representative and the most responsive. Anyone who knew the man knew that, although he was strongly opposed to war, he would not hold out against war if the popular demand for war became unmistakable. "Let the voice of the people rule"—this was McKinley's credo, and he meant it.

The threat to peace came from a new quarter, from the South and West, the strongholds of Democracy and free silver. Many Bryanite leaders were convinced that a war would create such a strain on the currency system that the opposition to free silver would collapse. Moreover, with the opposition to war strongest in Wall Street, they found it easy to believe that Administration policy was the product of a conspiracy of bankers who would deny silver to the American people, who would deny liberty to the people of Cuba, who were concerned only with the morality of the counting-house. Moreover, Bryan was the spokesman for rural Protestantism, which was already speaking in terms of a righteous war against Spain to free the Cubans from bondage. These were forces too powerful for McKinley to ignore. McKinley desired peace, but he was, above all, a Republican partisan, and he had no intention of handing the Democrats in 1900 the campaign cry of Free Cuba and Free Silver.

While McKinley attempted to search out a policy that would preserve peace without bringing disaster to the Republican party, the yellow press made his job all the more difficult by whipping up popular anger against Spain. On February 12 the *Journal* published a dispatch from Richard Harding Davis, reporting that as the American steamship *Olivette* was about to leave Havana Harbor for the United

States, it was boarded by Spanish police officers who searched three young Cuban women, one of whom was suspected of carrying messages from the rebels. The *Journal* ran the story under the headline, "Does Our Flag Protect Women?" with a vivid drawing by Frederic Remington across one half a page showing Spanish plainclothes men searching a wholly nude woman. War, declared the *Journal*, "is a dreadful thing, but there are things more dreadful than even war, and one of them is dishonor." It shocked the country, and Congressman Amos Cummings immediately resolved to launch a congressional inquiry into the *Olivette* outrage. Before any steps could be taken, the true story was revealed. The *World* produced one of the young women who indignantly protested the *Journal*'s version of the incident. Pressured by the *World,* the *Journal* was forced to print a letter from Davis explaining that his article had not said that male policemen had searched the women and that, in fact, the search had been conducted quite properly by a police matron with no men present.

The *Olivette* incident was manufactured by Hearst, but by the spring of 1897 the American press had a new horror to report which was all too true. Famine was stalking the island. Cuba had been in a serious economic state when the rebellion broke out in 1895; two years of war would, under any circumstances, have been disastrous, but the deliberate policies pursued both by the insurgents and by the government forces made the situation desperate. It was a simple matter for Hearst and Pulitzer reporters to pin the full responsibility on Weyler.

By the middle of July, McKinley had formulated a policy which he set down in a letter of instructions to our new American minister to Spain, General Stewart L. Woodford. The letter emphasized the need of bringing the Cuban war to an end and said that this could be done to the mutual advantage of both Spain and the Cubans by granting some kind of autonomy to Cuba. If Spain did not make an offer to the rebels and if the "measures of unparalleled severity" were not ended, the United States threatened to intervene.

On August 8 an Italian anarchist assassinated the Spanish premier; and when Woodford reached Madrid in September, a new government was about to take over headed by Señor Sagasta and the Liberals, who had repeatedly denounced the "barbarity" of the previous government's policy in Cuba. Sagasta immediately removed General Weyler, and the prospects for an agreement between the United States and Spain took a decided turn for the better.

While Woodford was carrying on skillful diplomatic negotiations for peace in Madrid, the Hearst press was creating a new sensation in this country with the Cisneros affair. Evangelina Cisneros was a young Cuban woman who had been arrested and imprisoned in the Rocojidas in Havana, guilty, according to the American press, of no other crime than protecting her virtue from an unscrupulous Spanish colonel, an aide to Butcher Weyler. The Rocojidas, Hearst's reporter told American readers, was a cage where the innocent beauty was herded with women criminals of every type, subject to the taunts and vile invitations of men who gathered outside.

When it was reported that Señorita Cisneros, whose father was a rebel leader, was to be sent for a long term to a Spanish penal colony in Africa or in the Canaries, the *Journal* launched one of the most fabulous campaigns in newspaper history. "Enlist the women of America!" was the Hearst war cry, and the women of America proved willing recruits. Mrs. Julia Ward Howe signed an appeal to Pope Leo XIII, and Mrs. Jefferson Davis, the widow of the president of the Confederacy, appealed to the queen regent of Spain to "give Evangelina Cisneros to the women of America to save her from a fate worse than death." When the *Journal* prepared a petition on behalf of Señorita Cisneros, it obtained the names of

Mrs. Nancy McKinley, the mother of the President, and Mrs. John Sherman, the wife of the secretary of state, as well as such other prominent ladies as Julia Dent Grant and Mrs. Mark Hanna.

It was a startling coup for Mr. Hearst, but he had not yet even begun to display his ingenuity. On October 10, 1897, the *Journal* erupted across its front page with the banner headline: "An American Newspaper Accomplishes at a Single Stroke What the Best Efforts of Diplomacy Failed Utterly to Bring About in Many Months." Hearst had sent Karl Decker, one of his most reliable correspondents, to Havana in late August with orders to rescue the Cuban Girl Martyr "at any hazard"; and Decker had climbed to the roof of a house near the prison, broken the bar of a window of the jail, lifted Evangelina out, and, after hiding her for a few days in Havana, smuggled her onto an American steamer. Decker, signing his dispatch to the *Journal* "Charles Duval," wrote: "I have broken the bars of Rocojidas and have set free the beautiful captive of monster Weyler. Weyler could blind the Queen to the real character of Evangelina, but he could not build a jail that would hold against *Journal* enterprise when properly set to work." The Cuban Girl Martyr was met at the pier by a great throng, led up Broadway in a triumphal procession, taken to a reception at Delmonico's where 120,000 people milled about the streets surrounding the restaurant, and hailed at a monster reception in Madison Square Garden. The Bishop of London cabled his congratulations to the *Journal*, while Governor Stephens of Missouri proposed that the *Journal* send down 500 of its reporters to free the entire island.

On October 23 Sagasta announced a "total change of immense scope" in Spanish policy in Cuba. He promised to grant local autonomy to the Cubans immediately, reserving justice, the armed forces, and foreign relations to Spain. On November 13 Weyler's successor, Captain-General Blanco, issued a decree modifying considerably the *reconcentrado* policy, and on November 25 the queen regent signed the edicts creating an autonomous government for the island. In essence, Madrid had acceded to the American demands.

While Woodford was conducting negotiations with a conciliatory Liberal government in Madrid and while there was still hope for peace, the fatal incident occurred which made war virtually inevitable. On January 12, 1898, a riot broke out in Havana, and Spanish officers attacked newspaper offices. The nature of the riot is still not clear; it was over in an hour, and it had no anti-American aspects. If the United States now sent a naval vessel to Havana, it might be buying trouble with Spain. Yet if a riot did break out and Americans were killed, the Administration would be stoned for not having a ship there to protect them. For several days McKinley wavered; then he ordered the *Maine* to Havana, but with the explanation that this was a courtesy visit demonstrating that so nonsensical were the rumors of danger to American citizens that our ships could again resume their visits to the island.

As the *Maine* lay at anchor in Havana Harbor, the rebels, with a perfect sense of timing, released a new propaganda bombshell. In December, 1897, in a private letter, Señor Enrique Dupuy de Lôme, the Spanish minister at Washington, had set down his opinions of President McKinley's annual message to Congress: "Besides the ingrained and inevitable bluntness (*grosería*) with which it repeated all that the press and public opinion in Spain have said about Weyler," De Lôme wrote, "it once more shows what McKinley is, weak and a bidder for the admiration of the crowd, besides being a would-be politician (*politicastro*) who tries to leave a door open behind himself while keeping on good terms with the jingoes of his party." De Lôme added: "It would be very advantageous to take up, even if only for effect, the question of commercial relations, and to have a man of some prominence sent here in order that I may make use of him to carry on a propaganda among the Senators and others in opposition to the junta."

De Lôme had, to be sure, written all this in a private letter (which was stolen by an insurgent spy in the Havana post office), not in his official capacity, and his characterization of McKinley was not wholly without merit, but it was a blunder of the highest magnitude. Not only had De Lôme attacked the President, but he had gone on to suggest that the negotiations then going on over a commercial treaty were not being conducted in good faith. Throughout the letter ran precisely the tone which Hearst had been arguing expressed the Spanish temper —a cold, arrogant contempt for democratic institutions. The State Department immediately cabled Woodford to demand the recall of the Spanish minister, but Madrid had the good fortune of being able to tell Woodford that De Lôme, informed of the disaster the night before, had already resigned.

A week after the publication of the De Lôme indiscretion, at 9:40 on the night of February 15, 1898, came the terrible blow which ended all real hope for peace. In the harbor of Havana, the *Maine* was blown up by an explosion of unknown origin. In an instant, the ship was filled with the sounds of shrieking men and rushing water. The blast occurred in the forward part of the ship where, a half hour before, most of the men had turned in for the night; they were killed in their hammocks. Of the 350 officers and men on board, 260 were killed. By morning the proud *Maine* had sunk into the mud of Havana Harbor.

"Public opinion should be suspended until further report," Captain Sigsbee cabled to Washington, but even Sigsbee could not down his suspicions. The *Maine* had gone to a Spanish possession on a courtesy call, and the *Maine* now lay at the bottom of Havana Harbor. What could it mean but war? "I would give anything if President McKinley would order the fleet to Havana tomorrow," wrote Theodore Roosevelt. "The *Maine* was sunk by an act of dirty treachery on the part of the Spaniards." Volunteers lined up for war service, even though there was no one to enlist them; in New York 500 sharpshooting Westchester businessmen volunteered as a unit for the colors. The *Journal* reported: "The Whole Country Thrills With War Fever."

The cause of the explosion of the *Maine* has never been finally established. That Spain deliberately decided to blow up the *Maine* is inconceivable, although it is possible that it might have been the work of unauthorized Spanish extremists. The one group which had everything to gain from such an episode was the rebels; yet it seems unlikely that either they or Spanish hotheads could have carried out such an act and remained undetected. The most likely explanation is that it was caused by an explosion of internal origin; yet the evidence for this is not conclusive. In any event, this was the explanation that the Navy in 1898 was least willing to consider since it would reflect seriously on the care with which the Navy was operating the *Maine*.

The move toward war seemed relentless. On March 9 Congress unanimously voted $50,000,000 for war preparations. Yet the days went by and there was no war, in part because important sectors of American opinion viewed Hearst's stories of the atrocious conditions on the island with profound skepticism. Senator Redfield Proctor of Vermont decided to launch his own investigation into conditions on the island. On March 17, after a tour of Cuba, Proctor made one of the most influential speeches in the history of the United States Senate.

Proctor, who Roosevelt reported was "very ardent for the war," had not generally been regarded as a jingo, and no man in the Senate commanded greater respect for personal integrity. Proctor declared that he had gone to Cuba skeptical of reports of suffering there, and he had come back convinced. "Torn from their

The sinking of the Maine, *Havana Harbor, February 15, 1898. Who or what caused the explosion was never established, but the yellow press blamed it on the Spanish and demanded war. This lithograph, by Kurz & Allison, not only shows the explosion, but contains before-and-after cameos and portraits of one of the survivors (Captain Charles Sigsbee, right) and the commander of the North Atlantic Squadron (Admiral Montgomery Sicard, left). (Courtesy Chicago Historical Society.)*

homes, with foul earth, foul air, foul water, and foul food or none, what wonder that one-half have died and that one-quarter of the living are so diseased that they can not be saved?" Proctor asked. "Little children are still walking about with arms and chest terribly emaciated, eyes swollen, and abdomen bloated to three times the natural size. . . . I was told by one of our consuls that they have been found dead about the markets in the morning, where they had crawled, hoping to get some stray bits of food from the early hucksters."

The question of peace or war now lay with McKinley. The Spaniards, Woodford had conceded, had gone about as far as they could go; but with the *Maine* in the mud of Havana Harbor, with the country, following Proctor's speech, crying for war, how much longer could McKinley hold out? The jingoes were treating his attempt to preserve peace with outright contempt; McKinley, Roosevelt told his friends, "has no more backbone than a chocolate éclair."

"We will have this war for the freedom of Cuba," Roosevelt shouted at a Gridiron Dinner on March 26, shaking his fist at Senator Hanna, "in spite of the timidity of the commercial interests." Nor was McKinley permitted to forget the political consequences. The Chicago *Times-Herald* warned: "Intervention in Cuba, peacefully if we can, forcibly if we must, is immediately inevitable. Our own internal political conditions will not permit its postponement. . . . Let President McKinley hesitate to rise to the just expectations of the American people, and who can doubt that war for Cuban liberty' will be the crown of thorns the free silver Democrats and Populists will adopt at the elections this fall?"

On March 28 the President released the report of the naval court of inquiry on the *Maine* disaster. "In the opinion of the court the *Maine* was destroyed by the explosion of a submarine mine, which caused the partial explosion of two or more of the forward magazines," the report concluded. Although no one was singled out for blame, the conclusion was inescapable that if Spain had not willfully done it, Spain had failed to provide proper protection to a friendly vessel on a courtesy visit in its waters. Overnight a slogan with the ring of a child's street chant caught the fancy of the country:

Remember the Maine!
To hell with Spain!

"I have no more doubt than that I am now standing in the Senate of the United States," declared Henry Cabot Lodge, "that that ship was blown up by a government mine, fired by, or with the connivance of, Spanish officials."

Desiring peace yet afraid of its consequences, McKinley embarked on a policy of attempting to gain the fruits of war without fighting. On March 29 Woodford demanded that Spain agree to an immediate armistice, revoke the reconcentration order, and co-operate with the United States to provide relief; Spain was given 48 hours to reply. On March 31 Spain replied that it had finally revoked the reconcentration orders in the western provinces; that it had made available a credit of three million pesetas to resettle the natives; that it was willing to submit the *Maine* controversy to arbitration; and that it would grant a truce if the insurgents would ask for it. In short, Spain would yield everything we demanded, except that it would not concede defeat; the appeal for a truce would have to come from the rebels. Since the rebels would not make such an appeal, since they were confident of ultimate American intervention, the situation was hopeless; yet Spain had come a long way. Woodford cabled to Washington: "The ministry have gone as far as they dare go to-day. . . . No Spanish ministry would have dared to do one month ago what this ministry has proposed to-day."

For a week the Spaniards attempted to cling to their last shreds of dignity. On Saturday, April 9, Madrid surrendered. Driven to the wall by the American demands, the Spanish foreign minister informed Woodford that the government had decided to grant an armistice in Cuba immediately. Gratified at achieving the final concession, Woodford cabled McKinley: "I hope that nothing will now be done to humiliate Spain, as I am satisfied that the present Government is going, and is loyally ready to go, as fast and as far as it can."

It was too late. McKinley had decided on war. Spain had conceded everything, but Spain had waited too long. Up until the very last moment, Spanish officials had feared that if they yielded to American demands in Cuba, it might mean the overturn of the dynasty, and they preferred even a disastrous war to that. Proud but helpless in the face of American might, many Spanish officials appeared to prefer the dignity of being driven from the island in a heroic defensive war to meek surrender to an American ultimatum. In the end they surrendered and promised reforms. But they had promised reforms before—after the Ten Years' War which ended in 1878—and they had not kept these promises. Throughout the nineteenth century, constitutions had been made and remade, but nothing had changed. Even in the last hours of negotiations with the American minister, they had told Woodford that the President had asked the Pope to intervene, when the President had done nothing of the sort. Even if their intentions were of the best, could they carry them out? Spain had had three full years to end the war in Cuba and, with vastly superior numbers of troops, had not been able to do it. And the insurgents would accept nothing from Madrid, not even peace.

On Monday, April 11, McKinley sent his message to Congress, declaring that "the forcible intervention of the United States as a neutral to stop the war, according to the large dictates of humanity and following many historical precedents" was "justifiable on rational grounds." The fact that Spain had met everything we had asked was buried in two paragraphs of a long plea for war. It took Congress a full week to act. On Monday night, April 18, while the resolution shuttled back and forth between the two chambers and the conference room, congressmen sang "The Battle Hymn of the Republic" and "Dixie" and shook the chamber with the refrain of "Hang General Weyler to a Sour Apple Tree." At three o'clock the next morning the two houses reached an agreement—the United States recognized the independence of Cuba, asserted that we would not acquire Cuba for ourselves, and issued an ultimatum to Spain to withdraw within three days. On April 20 President McKinley signed the resolution. War had come at last. But not quite. Although hostilities had begun, not until four days later did Congress declare war. When it did declare war, it dated it from McKinley's action in establishing a blockade four days before. To the very end, we protested our peaceful intentions as we stumbled headlong into war.

We entered a war in which no vital American interest was involved, and without any concept of its consequences. Although McKinley declared that to enter such a war for high purposes, and then annex territory, would be "criminal aggression," we acquired as a result of the war the Philippines and other parts of an overseas empire we had not intended to get and had no idea how to defend. Although we roundly attacked Spain for not recognizing the rebel government, we, in our turn, refused to recognize the rebels. Although we were shocked by Weyler's policies in Cuba, we were soon in the unhappy position of using savage methods to put down a rebel uprising in the Philippines, employing violence in a measure that easily matched what Weyler had done.

It would be easy to condemn McKinley for not holding out against war, but McKinley showed considerable courage in bucking the tide. McKinley's personal sympathy for the Cubans was sincere; only after his death was it revealed that he had contributed $5,000 anonymously for Cuban relief. It would be even easier to blame it all on Hearst; yet no newspaper can arouse a people that is not willing to be aroused. At root lay the American gullibility about foreign affairs, with the penchant for viewing politics in terms of a simple morality play; equally important were the contempt of the American people for Spain as a cruel but weak Latin nation and the desire for war and expansion which permeated the decade. The American people were not led into war; they got the war they wanted. "I think," observed Senator J. C. Spooner, "possibly the President could have worked out the business without war, but the current was too strong, the demagogues too numerous, the fall elections too near."

IV   For a Better World

11
A Cross of Gold

John A. Garraty

Despite violent labor conflicts and a long, enervating depression, American industry continued to expand and consolidate throughout the 1890s; and the rate of climb was even faster in the first decade of the twentieth century. By then, economic concentration had resulted in a handful of giant combinations dominating each area of industrial activity. In 1909, one per cent of American business enterprises produced forty-four per cent of the nation's manufactured goods. Money and property were so maldistributed that one per cent of the United States population—the corporate magnates and their families—owned seven-eighths of the country's wealth. Middle-class families were getting by, though precariously. And the rest—industrial workers in America's teeming, dilapidated cities and debtor farmers in the South and West—lived in poverty.

The Grange and Populist movements, as Ray Ginger observed, were the first serious challenges to the new industrial order and the corporate bosses who controlled it. While Populism failed as a third-party movement, it made thousands aware of the need for reform—the need to correct the abuses of monopolistic capitalism and to protect the mass of the nation's little people. The Democrats, in absorbing Populism and running William Jennings Bryan for president, trumpeted for reform. So did liberal intellectuals and crusading journalists—the celebrated Muckrakers—who exposed glaring malpractices both in business and in municipal government. Thanks to these men and women, thanks to tensions caused by rapid and unmanaged industrial growth, and thanks to a genuine desire to revive humanitarian democracy, there emerged the complex Progressive movement, which lasted from the late 1890s through World War I.

In reality, Progressivism consisted of independent and often contradictory movements. In rural areas, Progressives sounded like the old Populists, with their ringing demands for regulation of banks and railroads. In the cities, Progressives generally came from the middle-class; they were professional men, white-collar employees, and small businessmen who had been profoundly shaken by the unrest of the 1890s. Now, entering local and state politics, they intended to remove the wrongs that had produced the troubles of that decade and to maintain a truce between industrial bosses on the one hand and angry railroad and factory workers on the other. Also, some urban Progressives felt that big business, big-city machines, and organized labor were egregious threats to their prestige and well-being, and so they strove to protect themselves by curtailing the power of these agencies. Not all Progressives, though, were from the middle-class. Some workers, for example, joined the reform movement and demanded legislation that would protect them from the worst evils of industrial capitalism. At the same time, some corporation managers became Progressives, too, hoping that reform might actually help them by restricting their small, aggressive competitors. But for the most part the Progressives were victims of monopolies and were anxious indeed to dismantle the biggest of them and control the rest.

Progressivism transcended party labels, as Republicans and Democrats alike took up the banners of reform. In the Democratic Party there were Woodrow Wilson and William Jennings Bryan, the latter reflecting the Populist sentiments of rural Progressivism. In the Republican Party there was fighting Bob La Follette, governor of

Wisconsin, who made his state a model of Progressivism. And there was tough-talking Theodore Roosevelt, the first Progressive President.

Part IV seeks to illuminate the Progressive era through biographical portraits of Bryan, Roosevelt, and Wilson. But the Progressives were not the only reformers in those tumultuous early years of the new century. A revolutionary labor movement also got under way in the United States—the Industrial Workers of the World—which attacked the iniquities of unbridled capitalism, too, and offered a radical antidote for American society that earned them infamy and imprisonment. Thus *Portrait of America* contains an account of the Wobblies as well as biographies of the Progressive leaders themselves.

We begin with John A. Garraty's portrait of Bryan, the Great Commoner, whose career spanned a half century of challenge and conflict.

"The President of the United States may be an ass," wrote H. L. Mencken during the reign of Calvin Coolidge, "but he at least doesn't believe that the earth is square, and that witches should be put to death, and that Jonah swallowed the whale." The man to whom the vitriolic Mencken was comparing President Coolidge was William Jennings Bryan of Nebraska, one of the dominant figures in the Progressive movement. According to Mencken, Bryan was a "peasant," a "zany without sense or dignity," a "poor clod," and, in addition, an utter fraud. "If the fellow was sincere, then so was P. T. Barnum," he sneered.

It was certainly easy enough, and tempting, for sophisticates to come to the conclusion that Bryan was a buffoon and a fake. His undignified association in his declining years with the promotion of Florida real estate and his naïve and bigoted religious views, so pitilessly exposed by Clarence Darrow during the famous "Monkey Trial" in Dayton, Tennessee, lent substance to the Mencken view of his character. So did Bryan's smug refusal, while Secretary of State under Woodrow Wilson, to serve alcoholic beverages at Department receptions and dinners because of his personal disapproval of drinking, and his objection to the appointment of ex-President Charles W. Eliot of Harvard as Ambassador to China on the ground that Eliot was a Unitarian, and therefore not a real Christian. "The new Chinese civilization," said Bryan, "was founded upon the Christian movement." Eliot's appointment might undermine the work of generations of pious missionaries, he implied. Bryan's unabashed partisanship—he talked frankly after Wilson's election of filling government positions with "deserving Democrats"—did not seem to jibe with his pretensions as a reformer. And his oratorical style, magnificent but generally more emotional than logical, was disappointing to thinking people. John Hay called him a "Baby Demosthenes" and David Houston, one of his colleagues in Wilson's Cabinet, stated that "one could drive a prairie schooner through any part of his argument and never scrape against a fact." Being largely a creature of impulse, Bryan was, Houston added, "constantly on the alert to get something which has been represented to him as a fact to support or sustain his impulses."

But these flaws and blind spots were not fundamental weaknesses: they should never be allowed to overshadow Bryan's long years of devoted service to the cause of reform. If there were large areas about which he knew almost nothing, there were others where he was alert, sensible, and well-informed; certainly he was not a stupid man, nor was he easily duped or misled. Although a professional politician, as his remark about "deserving Democrats" makes clear, he was utterly honest personally and devoted to the cause of the people, as he understood it.

"Bryan": Copyright 1961 by American Heritage Publishing Co., Inc. Reprinted by permission from *American Heritage* Magazine, December 1961.

He was perfectly attuned to the needs and aspirations of rural America. In the early nineties he was in the forefront of the fight against high tariffs on manufactured goods. Later in the decade he battled for currency reform. At the turn of the century he was leading the assault against imperialism. During Theodore Roosevelt's primacy he was often far ahead of the intrepid Teddy, advocating a federal income tax, the eight-hour day, the control of monopoly and the strict regulation of public utilities, woman suffrage, and a large number of other startling innovations. Under Wilson he played a major part in marshaling support in Congress for the Federal Reserve Act and other New Freedom measures. Whatever his limitations, his faults, or his motives, few public men of his era left records as consistently "progressive" as Bryan's.

For years he led the Democratic party without the advantage of holding office. Three times he was a presidential candidate; although never elected, he commanded the unswerving loyalty of millions of his fellow citizens for nearly thirty years. He depended more on his intuition than on careful analysis in forming his opinions, but his intuition was usually sound; he was more a man of heart than of brain, but his heart was great.

Bryan was known as the Great Commoner, and the title was apt. He was a man of the people in origin and by instinct. He was typical of his age in rendering great respect to public opinion, whether it was informed or not. To Bryan the voice of the people was truly the voice of God. "I don't know anything about free silver," he announced while running for Congress early in the nineties. "The people of Nebraska are for free silver and I am for free silver. I will look up the arguments later." (It should be added that he did indeed "look up the arguments later." Less than a year after making this promise he arose in the House to deliver without notes a brilliant three-hour speech on the money question, a speech of great emotional power, but also fact-laden, sensible, and full of shrewd political arguments. When he sat down, the cheers rang out from both sides of the aisle.)

Bryan was born in Salem, Illinois, in 1860, a child of the great Middle West. Growing up in the heart of the valley of democracy, he absorbed its spirit and its sense of protest from his earliest years. After being graduated from Illinois College in 1881, he studied law in Chicago and for a time practiced his profession in Jacksonville, Illinois. But in 1887, stimulated by a talk with a law-school classmate from that city, he moved west to Lincoln, Nebraska. He quickly made his way in this new locale. Within a year he was active in the local Democratic organization, and in 1890, a month before his thirtieth birthday, he won his party's nomination for congressman.

Nebraska was traditionally a Republican state, its loyalty to the party of Lincoln forged in the heat of the Civil War. But by 1890 tradition was rapidly losing its hold on voters all over the Middle West. For the farmers of the American heartland were in deep trouble, and the Republican party seemed unwilling to do much to help them.

Tumultuous social and economic changes shaped the nation in the years after Appomattox. Within a single generation the United States was transformed from what was essentially a land of farmers into a modern industrial society, and in the process the Middle West was caught in a relentless economic vise. During the flush times of the sixties, when the Union Army was buying enormous amounts of food and fodder, and foreign demand was unusually high, the farmers of the region had gone into debt in order to buy more land and machinery. In the seventies and eighties, however, agricultural prices, especially those of such major staple crops as wheat and cotton, fell steeply. Wheat, which had sold as high as

$2.50 a bushel in wartime, was down to fifty cents by the early nineties.

The impact of this economic decline was intensified by the changing social status of the farmer. Agriculture was losing its predominant place in American life. In the days of the Founding Fathers, about ninety per cent of the population was engaged in working the soil, and the farmer was everywhere portrayed as the symbol of American self-reliance and civic virtue. "Those who labor in the earth," Jefferson said, "are the chosen people of God." But as the factory began to outstrip the farm, the farmer lost much of his standing. While the old symbol remained—it was especially in evidence around election time—a new and disturbing image of the farmer as a hick, a rube, a hayseed—a comic mixture of cocky ignorance, shrewd self-interest, and monumental provincialism—began to challenge it.

Naturally the farmers resented their loss of both income and prestige, but there was little they could do about either. Price declines were largely a response to worldwide overproduction, resulting from improvements in transportation and the opening up of new farmlands in Australia, Argentina, Canada, Russia, and elsewhere. Nor did the farmers, who desired manufactured goods as much as everyone else, really want to reverse the trend that was making them a minority group in a great industrial nation. But as they cast about for some way out of their plight, they were profoundly disturbed by certain results of the new development which did seem amenable to reform.

Industrial growth meant the mushrooming of great cities. These gave birth to noxious slums where every kind of vice flourished, where corrupt political organizations like the venal Tweed Ring in New York were forged, and where radical political concepts like socialism and anarchism sought to undermine "the American way of life." In the words of Jefferson, the farmers' hero, cities were "ulcers on the body politic."

Giant industries also attracted hordes of immigrants; these seemed to threaten the Middle West both by their mere numbers and by their "un-American" customs and points of view. Could the American melting pot absorb such strange ingredients without losing much of its own character?

Furthermore, to the citizens of Nebraska and other agricultural states, the new industrial barons appeared bent on making vassals of every farmer in America. The evidence seemed overwhelming: Huge impersonal corporations had neither souls nor consciences; profit was their god, materialism their only creed. The "interests," a tiny group of powerful tycoons in great eastern centers like Boston, New York, and Philadelphia, were out to enslave the rest of the country. Farmers worked and sweated only to see the "interests" make off with most of the fruit of their toil. Too many useless middlemen grew fat off the mere "handling" of wheat and cotton. Monopolistic railroads overcharged for carrying crops to market, unscrupulous operators of grain elevators falsely downgraded prime crops and charged exorbitant fees. Cynical speculators drove the price of staples up and down, sometimes making and losing millions in a matter of minutes, without the slightest regard for the effect of their operations on the producers whose sweat made their deadly game possible.

Conspiring with bankers and mortgage holders, all these groups combined to dictate the federal government's money policy. Population and production were surging forward; more money was needed simply to keep up with economic growth. Yet the government was deliberately cutting down on the amount of money in circulation by retiring Civil War greenbacks. On debt-ridden farmers plagued by overproduction, the effect of this deflation was catastrophic. Or so it seemed from the perspective of rural America.

While undoubtedly exaggerated, this indictment of the "interests" was taken as gospel throughout large sectors of the South and West. As a result, demands for "reform" quickly arose. The leading reformers were for the most part sincere, but few of them were entirely altruistic and many were decidedly eccentric. Participating in the movement for a variety of motives but without coming to grips with the main problem of American agriculture—overproduction—were coarse demagogues like Senator "Pitchfork Ben" Tillman of South Carolina, and unwashed characters like the wisecracking congressman from Kansas, "Sockless Jerry" Simpson. There were professional orators like the angry Mary Ellen Lease (her detractors called her "Mary Yellin' "), and homespun economic theorists like "Coin" Harvey and "General" Jacob Coxey, who believed so strongly in paper money that he named his son Legal Tender. The excesses of such people frightened off many Americans who might otherwise have lent a sympathetic ear to the farmers' complaints; others who might have been friendly observed the antics of the reformers with contempt and wrote off the whole movement as a joke.

Since neither of the major parties espoused the farmers' cause wholeheartedly, much of the protest found its way into various third-party organizations. At first, discontented elements concentrated on opposing the government's policy of retiring the paper money put in circulation during the Civil War. To save these greenbacks from extinction a Greenback (later Greenback-Labor) party sprang up. In 1878 its candidates polled a million votes, but decline followed as currency reformers turned to other methods of inflation.

Meanwhile the Patrons of Husbandry, better known as the Grange, originally a social organization for farm families, had begun to agitate in local politics against the middlemen who were draining off such a large percentage of the farmers' profits. In the seventies the Grangers became a power in the Middle West; in state after state they obtained the passage of laws setting maximum rates for railroads and prohibiting various forms of discrimination. The operations of grain elevators were also subjected to state regulation by "Granger Laws" in states such as Illinois, Iowa, Wisconsin, and Minnesota. The Grange abandoned political activity in the eighties, but other farm organizations quickly took its place. These coalesced first into the Northern Alliance and the Southern Alliance, and around 1890 the two Alliances joined with one another to become the Populist party.

Although William Jennings Bryan was a Democrat, he had grown up amid the agitations of the Granger movement. His father had even run for Congress in the seventies with Greenback party support. The aspirations and the general point of view of the midwestern farmers were young Bryan's own. Public men, he admitted late in life to the journalist Mark Sullivan, are "the creatures of their age. . . . I lived in the very center of the country out of which the reforms grew, and was quite naturally drawn to the people's side."

And they to his, one must add. Discontented farmers in his district were on the lookout for men who understood them and their problems. In 1888 the Republicans had carried the seat by 3,000 votes; now, in 1890, Bryan swept in with a lead of 6,713.

Bryan made an excellent record in his first Congress. He was a hardworking member, studying the technicalities of the tariff question for months before making his first important speech. But he saw that the tariff was rapidly being replaced by the money question as the crucial issue of the day. When he yielded the floor after completing his tariff speech, he collared a young Texas congressman named Joseph W. Bailey, who posed as a financial expert. Sitting on a sofa in the rear of the House chamber, he quizzed Bailey about the problem of falling prices. Bailey told him the tariff had little or no effect on the plight of the farmer; the whole difficulty arose from "an appreciation in value of gold." Interested, Bryan demanded a list of books on the subject and was soon deep in a study of the money question.

To a man like Bryan, studying the money question meant searching for some means of checking the deflationary trend that was so injurious to his farmer constituents. He quickly discovered that most farm-belt financial authorities felt this could best be done by providing for the free coinage of silver. In 1873 the United States had gone on the gold standard, which meant that only gold was accepted for coinage at the mint. By going back to bimetallism, the amount of bullion being coined would be increased, and if the favorable ratio of sixteen to one between silver and gold were established, the production of silver for coinage would be greatly stimulated.

To press for the free coinage of silver at a ratio of sixteen to one with gold seemed less radical or dangerous than to demand direct inflation of the currency through the printing of greenbacks. Silver, after all, was a precious metal; coining it could not possibly lead to the sort of "runaway" inflation that had helped ruin the South during the Civil War. Debtors and other friends of inflation could also count on the powerful support of silver-mine interests. The free-coinage issue thus had a powerful political appeal. Despite the opposition of most conservative businessmen, the silverites were able, in 1878 and again in 1890, to obtain legislation providing for the coinage of *some* silver, although not enough to check the downward trend of prices.

Within a month after his tariff speech Bryan was calling for free coinage, and he stressed the issue in his successful campaign for reelection in 1892. But the new President, Democrat Grover Cleveland, was an ardent gold-standard man, and when a severe depression struck the country early in 1893, he demanded that the Silver Purchase Act of 1890, which had raised the specter of inflation in the minds of many businessmen, be repealed by Congress at once. In this way he committed his party to the resumption of the single gold standard.

Bryan refused to go along with this policy. Threatening to "serve my country and my God under some other name" than "Democrat" unless the Administration changed its mind, he resisted the repeal of the silver act in a brilliant extemporaneous speech. Cleveland carried the day for repeal, but Bryan emerged as a potential leader of the silver wing of the Democrats.

In 1894 he sought a wider influence by running for the United States Senate. In those days senators were still chosen by the state legislatures; to be elected Bryan would need the support of Nebraska's Populists as well as of his own party. He worked hard for fusion, but Populist support was not forthcoming. Though the Democrats backed Populist candidate Silas A. Holcomb for the governorship, the Populists refused to reciprocate and ran their own man for the Senate seat. The Republican candidate therefore won easily.

At this stage the Populists were trying hard to become a truly national party. Their program, besides demanding the free coinage of silver and various land reforms desired by farmers, called for government ownership of railroads, a graduated income tax, the direct election of U.S. senators, the eight-hour day, and a number of additional reforms designed to appeal to eastern workingmen and other dissatisfied groups. As early as 1892 their presidential candidate, James B. Weaver, had polled over a million votes; in 1894 the party won six seats in the Senate and seven in the House of Representatives. At least in Nebraska, the Populists were not yet ready to merge with the "conservative" Democratic organization.

Defeat for the Senate did not harm Bryan politically. He was still in his early thirties; to one so young, merely having run for the Senate brought considerable prestige. Also, he had conducted an intelligent and forceful campaign. Even so it was a defeat, certainly not calculated to lead him to the remarkable decision that he made after the Nebraska legislature had turned him down. This decision was to seek nomination for the Presidency of the United States itself!

The young man's "superlative self-assurance" (one might call it effrontery but for the fact that his daring plan succeeded) staggers the imagination. Many men within his party were far better known than he, and his state, Nebraska, was without major influence in Democratic affairs. With Cleveland and the national organization dead-set against free coinage and other inflationary schemes, Bryan's chances of capturing the nomination seemed infinitesimal. But if bold, his action was by no means foolish. Democratic voters were becoming more and more restive under Cleveland's conservative leadership. At least in Bryan's part of the nation, many thoughtful members of the party were beginning to feel that they must look in new directions and find new leaders if they were not to be replaced by the Populists as the country's second major party. Recognizing this situation before most politicians did, Bryan proceeded to act upon his insight with determination and dispatch.

First of all, he set out to make himself known beyond his own locality. Accepting the editorship of the Omaha *World-Herald* at a tiny salary in order to obtain a forum, he turned out a stream of editorials on the silver question, which he sent to influential politicians all over the country. He toured the South and West with his message, speaking everywhere and under all sorts of conditions: to close-packed, cheering throngs and to tiny groups of quiet listeners. His argument was simple but forceful, his oratory magnetic and compelling. Always he made sure to meet local leaders and to subject them to his genial smile, his youthful vigor, his charm, his sincerity. He did not push himself forward; indeed, he claimed to be ready to support any honest man whose program was sound. But he lost no chance to point out to all concerned his own availability. "I don't suppose your delegation is committed to any candidate," he wrote to a prominent Colorado Democrat in April of 1896. "Our delegation may present my name." When the Democratic convention finally met in Chicago, Bryan believed that he was known personally to more of the delegates than any other candidate.

Few delegates took his campaign seriously, however. At the convention, one senator asked Bryan who he thought would win out. Bryan replied characteristically that he believed he himself "had as good a chance to be nominated as anyone," and proceeded to tick off the sources of his strength: Nebraska, "half of the Indian Territory, . . ." but before Bryan could mention his other backers the senator lost interest and walked off with some of his cronies. The candidate, amiable and serene, took no offense. A majority of the delegates favored his position on silver. No one had a clear lead in the race. All he needed was a chance to plead his case.

The opportunity—Bryan called it an "unexpected stroke of luck," although he planned for it brilliantly—came when he was asked to close the debate on the platform's silver plank. When he came forward to address the jam-packed mob in the Chicago auditorium he was tense, but there was a smile on his face, and to observers he seemed the picture of calm self-confidence. He began quietly, but his voice resounded in the farthest corners of the great hall and commanded the attention of every delegate. He was conscious of his own humble position, he told the throng, but he was "clad in the armor of a righteous cause" and this entitled him to speak. As he went on, his tension evaporated and his voice rose. When he recounted the recent history of the struggle between the forces of gold and silver, the audience responded eagerly. "At the close of a sentence," he wrote later, "it would rise and

William Jennings Bryan on the campaign trail. Willa Cather recalled that Bryan's moving eloquence made "rugged men of the soil weep like children." His voice was so powerful that, without straining, he could make himself heard at rallies of tens of thousands. In the election of 1896, Bryan traveled an unprecedented 18,000 miles, gave over 600 speeches, and spoke directly to some 5,000,000 Americans. (Courtesy of Brown Brothers.)

shout, and when I began upon another sentence, the room was still as a church."

He spoke for silver as against gold, for the West over the East, for "the hardy pioneers who have braved all the dangers of the wilderness" as against "the few financial magnates who, in a back room, corner the money of the world."

We have petitioned, and our petitions have been scorned; we have entreated, and our entreaties have been disregarded; we have begged, and they have mocked when our calamity came. We beg no longer; we entreat no more; we petition no more. *We defy them!*

The crowd thundered its agreement. Bryan proceeded. One after another he met the arguments of the party's Cleveland wing head on. Free silver would disturb the business interests? "Gold bugs" were defining the term too narrowly. Remember that wage earners, crossroads merchants, and farmers were also businessmen. The cities favored the gold standard? Their prosperity really depended upon the prosperity of the great agricultural regions of the land, which favored bimetallism. "Burn down your cities and leave our farms," he said, "and your cities will spring up again as if by magic; but destroy our farms and the grass will grow in the streets of every city in the country."

Now Bryan was absolute master of the delegates. "I thought of a choir," he recalled afterward, "as I noted how instantaneously and in unison they responded to each point made." The crowd cheered because he was reflecting its sentiments, but also because it recognized, suddenly, its leader—handsome, confident, righteously indignant, yet also calm, restrained, and ready for responsibility. His mission accomplished, it was time to close, and Bryan had saved a marvelous figure of speech, tested in many an earlier oration, for his climax. "You shall not press down upon the brow of labor this crown of thorns," he warned, bringing his hands down suggestively to his temples; "you shall not crucify mankind upon a cross of gold." Dramatically he extended his arms to the side, the very figure of the crucified Christ.

Amid the hysterical demonstration that followed, it was clear that Bryan had accomplished his miracle. The next day, July 9, he was nominated for the Presidency on the fifth ballot.

The issue was clear-cut, for the Republicans had already declared for the gold standard and nominated the handsome, genial, and thoroughly conservative William McKinley. As a result, the Populists were under great pressure to go along with Bryan. While the Democrats had not adopted all the radical Populist demands, their platform contained a number of liberal planks in addition to that on free silver, including one calling for a federal income tax and another for stiffer controls of the railroad network. For the Populists to insist on nominating a third candidate would simply insure the election of the "gold bug" McKinley. Not every important Populist favored fusion; some were ready to concede defeat in 1896 and build their party for the future on broadly radical lines. "The Democratic idea of fusion," said Tom Watson of Georgia angrily, is "that we play Jonah while they play whale." But the rich scent of victory in the air was too much for the majority to resist. "I care not for party names," said "Sockless Jerry" Simpson bluntly; "it is the substance we are after, and we have it in William J. Bryan." Indeed, Bryan's friendly association with the Populists in earlier campaigns and his essentially Populistic views on most questions made it difficult for the party to oppose him. "We put him to school," one anti-Bryan Populist later remarked, "and he wound up by stealing the school-books." In any case, the Populist convention endorsed him; thus the silver forces united to do battle with the Republicans.

Both Bryan and McKinley men realized at once that this was to be a close and crucial contest. Seldom have the two great parties divided so clearly on fundamental issues; a showdown was inevitable; a major turning point in American history had been reached. Silver against gold was but the surface manifestation of the struggle. City against countryside, industry against agriculture, East against South and West, the nineteenth century against the twentieth—these were the real contestants in 1896.

After Bryan's nomination McKinley's manager, Mark Hanna, abandoned plans for a vacation cruise in New England waters and plunged into the work of the campaign. The situation was "alarming," he told McKinley. A "communistic spirit" was abroad, business was "all going to pieces." A mighty effort was called for. Hanna raised huge sums by "assessing" the great bankers, oil refiners, insurance men, and meat packers, using the threat of impending business chaos and wild inflation to loosen the purse strings of the tycoons. While McKinley, "the advance agent of prosperity," conducted a dignified and carefully organized campaign from his front porch in Canton, Ohio, . . . 1,400 paid speakers beat the bushes for votes in every doubtful district. The Republican campaign committee distributed more than 120,000,000 pieces of literature printed in ten languages to carry its message to the voters. Boiler-plate editorials and other releases were sent free to hundreds of small-town newspapers. Hanna, Theodore Roosevelt said, "has advertised McKinley as if he were a patent medicine!" The Republican organization reached a peak of efficiency and thoroughness never before approached in a political contest; the campaign marked a methodological revolution that has profoundly affected every presidential contest since.

Bryan had little money, and no organizational genius like Hanna to direct his drive. But he too effected a revolution that has left its mark on modern campaigning. McKinley's front porch technique was novel only in the huge number of visiting delegations that Hanna paraded across his man's lawn and the exaggerated care that the candidate took to avoid saying anything impolitic. It had always been considered undignified for a presidential nominee to go out and hunt for votes on his own. Bryan cast off this essentially hypocritical tradition at the very start. He realized that the concerted power of business and the press were aligned against him, and that his own greatest assets were his magnificent ability as a political orator and his personal sincerity and charm. His opponent could afford to sit tight; *he* must seek out the people everywhere if they were to receive his message. Between summer and November he traveled a precedent-shattering 18,000 miles, making more than 600 speeches and addressing directly an estimated 5,000,000 Americans. His secretary estimated that he uttered between 60,000 and 100,000 words every day during the campaign.

On the stump he was superb. Without straining his voice he could make himself heard to a restless open-air throng numbered in the tens of thousands. He was equally effective at the whistle stops, outlining his case from the rear platform of his train while a handful of country people gazed earnestly upward from the roadbed. He was unfailingly pleasant and unpretentious. At one stop, while he was shaving in his compartment, a small group outside the train began clamoring for a glimpse of him. Flinging open the window and beaming through the lather, he cheerfully shook hands with each of these admirers. Neither he nor they, according to the recorder of this incident, saw anything unusual or undignified in the performance. Thousands of well-wishers sent him good luck charms and messages of encouragement. "If the people who have given me rabbits' feet in this campaign will vote for me, there is no possible doubt of my election," he said in one speech. It was because of this simple friendliness that he became known as "the Great Commoner."

Bryan was also unfailingly interesting. Even his most unsympathetic biographer admits that he spoke so well that at every stop the baggagemen from the campaign train would run back to listen to his talk—and this despite a schedule that called for as many as thirty speeches a day.

Such a campaign is an effective means of projecting an image of a candidate and his general point of view. It is not well suited for the making of complicated arguments and finely drawn distinctions; for that the McKinley approach was far superior. Wisely, for it was clearly the issue uppermost in the minds of most voters, Bryan hammered repeatedly at the currency question. He did not avoid talking about other matters: he attacked the railroads and the great business monopolists and the "tyranny" of the eastern bankers. He deplored the use of militia in labor disputes and of the injunction as a means of breaking strikes. He spoke in favor of income taxes, higher wages, and relief for hard-pressed mortgagees. But the silver issue was symbolic, and the Democratic position sound. There *was* a currency shortage; deflation *was* injuring millions of debtors and pouring a rich unearned increment into the pockets of bondholders. To say, as Henry Demarest Lloyd did at the time and as many liberal historians have since, that Bryan made free silver the "cowbird" of the reform movement, pushing out all other issues from the reform nest and thus destroying them, is an exaggeration and a distortion. All effective politicians stick to a small number of simple issues while on the stump; otherwise, in the hectic conflict of a hot campaign, they project no message at all. There is no reason to suspect that, if elected, Bryan would have forgotten about other reform measures and concentrated only on the currency.

For a time Bryan's gallant, singlehanded battle seemed to be having an effect on public opinion, and Republican leaders became thoroughly frightened. In addition to money, threats and imprecations now became weapons in the campaign. A rumor was circulated that Bryan was insane. The *New York Times* devoted columns to the possibility, and printed a letter from a supposed psychologist charging that he was suffering from "paranoia querulenta," "graphomania," and "oratorical monomania." "Men," one manufacturer told his workers, "vote as you please, but if Bryan is elected . . . the whistle will not blow Wednesday morning." According to the *Nation,* which was supporting McKinley, many companies placed orders with their suppliers "to be executed in case Mr. Bryan is defeated, and not otherwise." A Chicago company that held thousands of farm mortgages politely asked all its "customers" to indicate their presidential preferences—a not very subtle form of coercion but probably an effective one. In some cases men were actually fired because of their political opinions.

By the time election day arrived the McKinley managers were so confident of victory that Hanna began returning new contributions as no longer necessary. Nevertheless, a final monumental effort was made to get out the vote. Free transportation was provided to carry citizens to and from the polls, men were paid for time lost in voting, and in doubtful districts floaters and other disreputables were rounded up and paraded to the ballot boxes. Everywhere in the crucial North Central states the Hanna machine expended enormous efforts, and in these states the decision was made. McKinley carried them all and with them the nation. In the electoral college McKinley won by 271 to 176, but the popular vote was close—7,036,000 to 6,468,000. The change of a relative handful of votes in half a dozen key states would have swung the election to Bryan.

The victory, however, was McKinley's, and conservatives all over America—and the world —echoed the sentiment of Hanna's happy telegram to the President-elect: GOD'S IN HIS HEAVEN, ALL'S RIGHT WITH THE WORLD! A watershed in the economic and social history of the United States had been crossed. The rural America of the nineteenth century was making way for the industrial America of the twentieth. Soon business conditions began to improve, agricultural prices inched upward, new discoveries of gold relieved the pressure on the money supply. While McKinley and Hanna (now senator from Ohio) ruled in Washington, the era of complacent materialism and easy political virtue that had entered American politics on the coattails of General Grant seemed destined to continue indefinitely. Reform, it appeared, was dead.

That these appearances were deceiving was due in considerable measure to William Jennings Bryan. Unchastened by defeat and always cheerful ("It is better to have run and lost than never to have run at all," he said), he maintained the leadership of his party. Consistently he took the liberal position on important issues. Despite his strong pacifism he approved of fighting Spain in 1898 in order to free Cuba. "Humanity demands that we should act," he said simply. He enlisted in the Army and rose to be a colonel, although he saw no action during the brief conflict. The sincerity of his motives was proved when the war ended, for he then fought against the plan to annex former

Spanish colonies. Running for President a second time in 1900, he made resistance to imperialism an issue in the campaign along with free silver. If both of these were poorly calculated to win votes in 1900, they were nonetheless solidly in the liberal tradition. Bryan lost to McKinley again, this time by 861,459 votes, and leadership of the reform movement passed, after McKinley's assassination, to Theodore Roosevelt. But Bryan continued the fight. In 1904, battling almost alone against conservatives in his own party, he forced the adoption of a fairly liberal platform (including strong antitrust, pro-labor, and antitariff planks), and when the conservative Judge Alton B. Parker was nonetheless nominated for President, Bryan kept up his outspoken criticism. While remaining loyal to the Democratic party he announced boldly: "The fight on economic questions ... is not abandoned. As soon as the election is over I shall ... organize for the campaign of 1908."

In that campaign Bryan, once more the Democratic nominee, was once more defeated in his personal quest of the Presidency, this time by Roosevelt's handpicked successor, William Howard Taft. Immediately he announced that he would not seek the office again, thus throwing the field open to other liberals.

Although he thus abandoned formal leadership of the Democrats, Bryan continued to advocate reform. Throughout the Taft administration he campaigned up and down the country to bolster the liberal wing of his party. When the 1912 nominating convention met in Baltimore, he introduced and won approval of a highly controversial resolution denouncing Wall Street influence, and he stated repeatedly that he would not support any candidate who was under the slightest obligation to Tammany Hall. The platform, as one historian says, "was a progressive document, in the best Bryan tradition." In the end Bryan threw his support to Woodrow Wilson. While this alone did not account for Wilson's nomination, it was very important in his election, for it assured him the enthusiastic backing of millions of loyal Bryanites.

Nothing reveals Bryan's fine personal qualities better than his support of Wilson, for the former Princeton professor had opposed the Great Commoner since 1896, when he had called the Cross of Gold speech "ridiculous." In 1904 he had publicly demanded that the Bryan wing be "utterly and once and for all driven from Democratic counsels." As late as 1908 he had refused to appear on the same platform with Bryan. Mr. Bryan, he said, "is the most charming and lovable of men personally, but foolish and dangerous in his theoretical beliefs." During the campaign of that year he refused to allow Bryan to deliver a campaign speech on the Princeton campus.

By 1912 Wilson had become far more liberal and no longer opposed most of Bryan's policies; even so, had Bryan been a lesser man he would not have forgiven these repeated criticisms. But he was more concerned with Wilson's 1912 liberalism than with personal matters, despite the publication of an old letter in which Wilson had expressed the wish to "knock Mr. Bryan once and for all into a cocked hat!" He shrugged off the "cocked hat" letter, and when Wilson paid him a handsome public tribute they became good friends. Furthermore, during the 1912 campaign, Bryan campaigned vigorously for Wilson, making well over four hundred speeches within a period of seven weeks. When Wilson won an easy victory in November, Bryan reacted without a trace of envy or bitterness. "It is a great triumph," he declared. "Let every Democratic heart rejoice." A few months later he said in a speech in Chicago:

> Sometimes I have had over-sanguine friends express regret that I did not reach the presidency.... But I have an answer ready for them. I have told them that they need not weep for me.... I have been so much more

interested in the securing of the things for which we have been fighting than I have been in the name of the man who held the office, that I am happy in the thought that this government, through these reforms, will be made so good that a citizen will not miss a little thing like the presidency.

Wilson made Bryan Secretary of State. He was needed in the administration to help manage his many friends in Congress. The strategy worked well, for Bryan used his influence effectively. His role was particularly crucial in the hard fight over the Federal Reserve bill, but his loyal aid was also important in passing income tax legislation and a new antitrust law and in other matters as well.

In managing foreign affairs Bryan was less successful, for in this field he was ill-prepared. Because of his frank belief in the spoils system, he dismissed dozens of key professional diplomats, replacing them with untrained political hacks. Naturally the Foreign Service was badly injured. His policy of not serving alcoholic beverages at official functions because of his personal convictions caused much criticism at home and abroad. "W. J. Bryan not only suffers for his principles and mortifies his flesh, as he has every right to do," the London *Daily Express* complained, "but he insists that others should suffer and be mortified." The Secretary's continuing Chautauqua lectures, at which he sometimes appeared on the same platform with vaudeville entertainers and freaks, were attacked by many as undignified for one who occupied such a high official position.

Bryan had answers to all these criticisms: the State Department had been overly snobbish and undemocratic; Wilson had agreed to his "grape juice" policy before appointing him; no one should be ashamed of speaking to the American people. He could also point to his "cooling-off treaties" with some twenty nations, which provided machinery for avoiding blow-ups over minor diplomatic imbroglios.

Unfortunately Bryan had but a dim understanding of Latin American problems and unwittingly fostered American imperialism on many occasions. His narrow-minded belief that he knew better than local leaders what was "good" for these small countries showed that he had no comprehension of cultural and nationalistic elements in other lands. Although well intended, his policies produced much bad feeling in South and Central America. Bryan did suggest lending Latin American nations money "for education, sanitation and internal development," a policy that anticipated our modern Point Four approach to underdeveloped areas. Wilson, however, dismissed the idea because he thought it "would strike the whole country . . . as a novel and radical proposal."

When the World War broke out in 1914, Bryan, like his chief, adopted a policy of strict neutrality. America, he said, should attempt to mediate between the belligerents by suggesting "a more rational basis of peace." Bryan believed in real neutrality far more deeply than Wilson, who was not ready to face the possibility of a German victory. "We cannot have in mind the wishes of one side more than the wishes of the other side," Bryan warned the President after the latter had prepared a stiff note of protest against German submarine warfare. And when, after the sinking of the *Lusitania*, Wilson sent a series of threatening messages to Germany, Bryan resigned as Secretary of State. He never again held public office.

It would have been better for Bryan's reputation if he had died in 1915; instead he lived on for another decade, as amiable and well-intentioned as ever but increasingly out of touch with the rapidly changing times. He made no effort to keep up with the abrupt intellectual developments of the twentieth century, yet he was accustomed to speak his mind on current issues and continued to do so. There had always been those who had considered his uncomplicated faith in time-tested moral principles and in popular rule rather naïve; in the cynical, scientific, and amoral twenties only a relative handful of rural oldtimers saw much virtue in his homilies on the people's unfailing instinct to do always what was "right" and "good." In the world of Calvin Coolidge the old Populist fires no longer burned very brightly, and Bryan's anti-business bias seemed terribly old-fashioned. Many had considered him an anachronism even in Wilson's day; by Harding's he had simply ceased to count in politics. More and more he confined himself to religious questions. His ardent piety was heartwarming, but he was a smug and intolerant Fundamentalist whose ignorance of modern science and ethics did not prevent him from expounding his "views" on these subjects at length. The honest opinions of "the people," he believed, could "settle" scientific and philosophical questions as easily as political ones.

Advancing age, as well as increasing preoccupation with revealed religion, was making Bryan less tolerant. Never one to give much thought to reasoned counterarguments, he became, in the twenties, an outspoken foe of many aspects of human freedom. He defended prohibition, refused to condemn the Ku Klux Klan, and participated eagerly in the notorious Scopes anti-evolution trial in Dayton, Tennessee, with all its overtones of censorship and self-satisfied ignorance. The final great drama of Bryan's life occurred when Clarence Darrow mercilessly exposed his simple prejudices on the witness stand. Bryan complacently maintained, among other things, that Eve was actually made from Adam's rib and that Jonah had really been swallowed by the whale. The rural audience cheered, but educated men all over the world were appalled.

Throughout his lifetime, Bryan was subject to harsh and almost continual criticism, and at least superficially he failed in nearly everything he attempted. But he was too secure in his faith to be injured by criticism, and he knew that for over two decades his influence was greater than any of his contemporaries save Theodore Roosevelt and Wilson. His life was useful and happy, for he rightly believed that he had made a lasting contribution to his country's development. Nor is it fair to condemn him for his limited intelligence and superficial understanding of his times. Other political leaders of at best ordinary intellect have done great deeds, sometimes without appreciating the meaning of events they have helped to shape. Still, there was tragedy in Bryan's career —he was unable to grow.

In 1896 he was indeed the peerless leader, vital, energetic, dedicated, and, in a measure, imaginative. He saw the problems of Nebraska farmers, realized their wider implications, and outlined a reasonable program designed to deal with them. He was almost elected President as a result, despite his youth and inexperience. Suddenly he was a celebrity; thereafter he moved into a wider world and lived there at his ease. He did not abandon his principles, and he helped achieve many important reforms, for which we must always honor him, but he soon ceased to feed upon new ideas. In a sense, despite the defeats, life's rewards came to him too easily. His magnetic voice, his charm, his patent sincerity, the memory of the heroic fight of '96—these things secured his place and relieved him of the need to grapple with new concepts.

Although he was a man of courage, strength, and endurance, Bryan was essentially lax and complacent. He preferred baggy clothes, a full stomach, the easy, undemanding companionship of small minds. For years the momentum of 1896 carried him on, but eventually the speeding world left him far behind. Fortunately for his inner well-being, he never realized what had happened. A few days after Darrow had exposed his shallowness before the world, he died peacefully in his sleep, as serene and unruffled by events as ever.

12

Here Come the Wobblies!

Bernard A. Weisberger

the Industrial Workers of the World. Their goal was to abolish the wage system, and to accomplish it, they advocated violent overthrow of the state and the creation of a national industrial syndicate run exclusively by workers. Bernard Weisberger, in an exhilarating style that matches the drama of the Wobblies themselves, describes what happened when they set out to revolutionize the American working man.

Labor unions were slow to organize in industrial America. Those that existed at the turn of the century were largely for skilled workers, such as Samuel Gompers' American Federation of Labor. While membership in Gompers' organization rose to over a million and a half in 1905, a majority of American workers—thirty million men and eight million women—remained unorganized, underpaid, and overworked.

There were several things that impeded the growth of organized labor. One was the business world itself, which bitterly opposed unionism, broke strikes with hired thugs, and associated organized labor with socialism. Another was the hostility with which American judges and lawmakers viewed labor unions, especially after the labor riots of the 1880s and the 1890s which linked unions with anarchism in the public mind. Finally there was the basic conservatism of the American worker himself, who all too often regarded unionism as anti-American and was reluctant to participate.

In 1905, a group of militant, visionary laborites met in Chicago and launched a movement designed to convert American workers to radicalism. Led by Big Bill Haywood, the group called itself

On a hot June day in 1905 William D. Haywood, a thirty-six-year-old miner, homesteader, horsebreaker, surveyor, union organizer, and Socialist, out of Salt Lake City, stood up before a large crowd in a Chicago auditorium. He gazed down at the audience with his one good eye and, taking up a loose board from the platform, impatiently banged for silence.

"Fellow workers," he shouted, "this is the continental congress of the working class. We are here to confederate the workers of this country into a working-class movement that shall have for its purpose the emancipation of the working class from the slave bondage of capitalism."

Thus, in manifesto, the working-class crusade known as Industrial Workers of the World came to birth. It grew amid storms of dissent, lived always in the blast furnace of conflict, and was battered into helplessness over forty years ago. It is still alive, but as a "church of old men" in one author's words, old men still muttering "No" to the status quo. The *Industrial Worker*, the official newspaper of the "One Big Union," still appears, still carries as its masthead motto "An injury to one is an injury to all," still valiantly runs on its editorial page the uncompromising preamble to

---

"Here Come the Wobblies!": © Copyright 1967 by the American Heritage Publishing Co., Inc. Reprinted by permission from *American Heritage*, June 1967.

the constitution adopted at that Chicago convention in 1905:

> The working class and the employing class have nothing in common. There can be no peace so long as hunger and want are found among millions of working people and the few, who make up the employing class, have all the good things of life. . . .
>
> It is the historic mission of the working class to do away with capitalism. The army of production must be organized, not only for the everyday struggle with capitalists, but also to carry on production when capitalism shall have been overthrown. By organizing industrially we are forming the structure of the new society within the shell of the old.

But the old society is still here, thriving more vigorously than ever; the workers have late-model cars, and the struggle of the I.W.W.'s young radicals to burst its bonds is history now—good history, full of poets and tramps, bloodshed and cruelty, and roads not taken by American labor. The history not merely of an organization but of an impulse that stirred men from the lower depths of the economy—vagrants, lumberjacks, harvest hands, immigrant millworkers—and set them to marching in step with Greenwich Village literary radicals to the tune of gospel hymns and innocent ballads fitted with new, class-conscious verses.

But it was not all ballads and broadsides. The I.W.W. was radical in the word's truest sense. When it denied that the working and employing classes had anything in common, it meant precisely what it said. The I.W.W. put no faith in the promises of bourgeois politicians or in the fairness of bourgeois courts. It made no contracts with employers, and it spurned other unions—like those enrolled in the American Federation of Labor—that did. It was composed of hard-working men, little known to respectability. As a result, it badly frightened millions of middle-class Americans, and it meant to.

Yet it must be understood that the I.W.W. did not grow in a vacuum. It arose out of an industrial situation for which the adjective "grim" is pallid. In the America that moved to productive maturity between 1880 and 1920, there was little room or time to care about the worker at the base of it all. It was an America in which children of ten to fourteen could and did work sixty-hour weeks in mine and factory; in which safety and sanitation regulations for those in dangerous trades were virtually unknown—and in which industrial accidents took a horrible toll each year; in which wages were set by "the market place" and some grown men with families worked ten to twelve hours for a dollar and stayed alive only by cramming their families into sickening tenements or company-town shacks; in which such things as pensions or paid holidays were unknown; lastly, it was an America in which those who did protest were often locked out, replaced by scabs, and prevented from picketing by injunction and by naked force. At Homestead, Pullman, Coeur d'Alene, Cripple Creek, Ludlow, and other places where strikers clashed with troops or police between 1892 and 1914, the record of labor's frustrations was marked with bloody palm prints. And at the bottom of the scale was the vast army of migrant workers who beat their way by rail from job to job—not only unskilled, unprotected, and underpaid but unnoticed and unremembered.

Out of such a situation grew the I.W.W. It gained much not only from the horror of its surroundings, but from the spirit of an infant century when the emancipation of almost everyone—women, workers, artists, children—from the dragons of the past seemed to be a live possibility, and "new" was a catchword on every tongue.

The opening years of the organization's life were not promising. Its founding fathers were numerous and diverse—discontented trade unionists, Socialists like Eugene V. Debs and the whiskered, professorial Daniel De Leon, and veterans of almost every other left-wing crusade of the preceding twenty years. There was among them all, a recent I.W.W. historian has written, "such a warfare as can be found only between competing radicals." They were, however, united in objecting to the craft-union principles of A.F.L. chieftain Samuel Gompers, whom Haywood described as "a squat specimen of humanity" with "small snapping eyes, a hard cruel mouth," and "a personality vain, conceited, petulant and vindictive."

Gompers' plan of organizing only skilled craftsmen and negotiating contracts aimed only at securing a better life from day to day struck the I.W.W.'s founders not only as a damper upon whatever militancy the labor movement might generate to challenge capitalism, but also as a betrayal of the unskilled laborers, who would be left to shift for themselves. The new leaders therefore created a "single industrial union," as far removed from craft divisions as possible.

All industrial labor was to be divided into thirteen great, centrally administered divisions —building, manufacturing, mining, transportation, public service, etc. Within each of these would be subgroups. But each such group would take in all employees contributing to that industry's product or service. On the steam railroads, as an instance, clerks, telegraphers, and trackwalkers would share power and glory with engineers, brakemen, and conductors. A grievance of one lowly set of workers in a single shop could bring on a strike that would paralyze a whole industry. And some day, on signal from the One Big Union, all workers in all industries would throw the "Off" switch, and the wage system would come tumbling down.

Much of the scheme came from the brain and pen of a priest, Father Thomas Hagerty, who while serving mining parishes in the Rockies had come to believe in Marx as well as Christ. He had the scheme of industrial unionism all worked out in a wheel-shaped chart, with the rim divided into the major industries and the hub labelled "General Administration." Gompers looked at a copy of it in a magazine and snarled: "Father Hagerty's Wheel of Fortune!" He did not expect it to spin very long.

Nor, during the I.W.W.'s first three years of existence, did it seem likely to. Factional quarrels wracked national headquarters and the Western Federation of Miners, the biggest single block in the entire I.W.W. structure, pulled out. By spring of 1908 the organization, whose paper strength was perhaps 5,000 but whose actual roster was probably much thinner, was broke and apparently heading toward the graveyard that seems to await all clique-ridden American radical bodies.

But the death notices were premature. The headquarters brawls were among and between trade unionists and Socialists, and the I.W.W.'s future was, as it turned out, linked to neither group. It belonged to a rank-and-file membership that was already formulating surprise tactics and showing plenty of vigor. In Schenectady, New York, for example, I.W.W.-led strikers in a General Electric plant protested the firing of three draftsmen by staying at their machines for sixty-five hours, a use of the sit-down strike thirty years before it was introduced by the auto workers as a radical measure during the Great Depression. In Goldfield, Nevada, the I.W.W. under thirty-one-year-old Vincent St. John organized the town's hotel and restaurant workers into a unit with the local silver and gold miners. This unlikely combination of hash-slingers and miners, an extreme example of industrial unionism, forced the town's employers to boost wage scales, temporarily at least, to levels of five dollars per eight-hour day for skilled underground workers, down to three dollars and board for eight hours of dishwashing by the lowly "pearl divers." It seemed to be clear proof that "revolutionary industrial unionism" could work. The fiery St. John was even able to close down the mines one January day in 1907 for a protest parade—on behalf of Haywood, Charles Moyer, and George Pettibone, three officers of the miners' union who had been arrested (they were later acquitted) in the bomb-killing of former Governor Frank Steunenberg of Idaho. St. John's parade brought three thousand unionists into the small-town streets "all wearing tiny red flags."

The real turning point came at the organization's fourth convention, in 1908. The believers in "direct action at the point of production" forced a change in the I.W.W.'s holy writ, the preamble. It had originally contained the sentence: "A struggle must go on until all the toilers come together *on the political, as well as the industrial field,* and take and hold that which they produce" (italics added). Now this "political clause" was scuttled, over the violent protests of Socialist De Leon, who helplessly denounced the change as an exaltation of "physical force." The shock troops of the direct-action group were twenty lumber workers known as the Overalls Brigade. Gathered in Portland by an organizer named Jack Walsh, they had bummed their way to Chicago in boxcars, raising grubstakes along the way at street meetings in which they sang, harangued, peddled pamphlets, and passed the hat. One of their favorite tunes, with which they regaled the convention, was "Hallelujah, I'm A Bum," set to the old hymn tune "Revive Us Again":

> O, why don't you work
> Like other men do?
> How in hell can I work
> When there's no work to do?
>
> Hallelujah, I'm a bum,
> Hallelujah, bum again,
> Hallelujah, give us a handout—
> To revive us again.

Sourly, De Leon dubbed Walsh's men The Bummery, but the day was theirs. The veteran Socialist leader retreated and organized a splinter I.W.W., which dwindled away in seven years.

It was the I.W.W.'s second split in a short history, but its most important. It gave the organization over to soapbox singers and bums, brothers in idealism who were poor in all things save "long experience in the struggle with the employer." They were to break from past labor practices and give the I.W.W. its true inwardness and dynamism; to fit it with its unique costume and role in history.

They gave it, first, a musical voice. Walsh's crusaders sang because when they sought the workers' attention on street corners they were challenged by those competing sidewalk hot-gospellers, the Salvation Army. By 1909, the press of the organization's newspaper, the *Industrial Worker*, was able to put out the first edition of *Songs of the Workers to Fan the Flames of Discontent*. More succinctly known as the "Little Red Songbook," it has gone through over thirty subsequent editions—all scarlet-covered and fitted to the size of an overalls pocket. The songbook and the preamble were to the I.W.W. membership what the hymnbook and the *Discipline of the Methodist Church* had been to frontier preachers—the sum and touchstone of faith, the pearl of revelation, the coal of fire touching their lips with eloquence. Most of the songs were the work of men like Richard Brazier, an English-born construction worker who joined up in Spokane in 1908; or Ralph Chaplin, a struggling young Chicago commercial artist who wanted to chant "hymns of hope and hatred" at the shrine of rebellion; or Joe Hill, born Joel Haaglund in Sweden, who wrote not parodies alone but also original compositions, which Chaplin described as "coarse as home-spun and as fine as silk"; or bards known simply as T-Bone Slim or Dublin Dan. The I.W.W. members soared on those songs, enjoying them as much for their mockery as anything.

To the patriotic cadences of "The Battle Hymn of the Republic" they sang "Solidarity forever, for the Union makes us strong" (a version which Ralph Chaplin had given them and which the entire labor movement took over without credit). To the sentimental notes that enfolded Darling Nelly Gray they sang of "the Commonwealth of Toil that is to be," and to the strains that had taken pretty Red Wing through ribald adventures in every barroom in the country, they roared that "the earth of right belongs to toilers, and not to spoilers of liberty." They raided the hymnbook of Moody-and-Sankey revivalism for "Hold the fort for we are coming, union men be strong," and for "There is power, there is power, in a working band" (instead of "in the blood of the Lamb"). They laughed in sharps and flats at Casey Jones, of the craft-proud Brotherhood of Railway Engineers, as a union scab who "kept his junk pile running" and "got a wooden medal for being good and faithful on the S.P. line." They sang in the hobo jungles, on the picket line, and in the jailhouse, and it was their singing especially that separated them from the A.F.L. by an abyss of spirit.

The "new" I.W.W. soon had a nickname, as derisive and defiant as its songs: the Wobblies. It is not certain how the name was born, though a popular legend declares that a Chinese restaurant owner in the Northwest was persuaded to grubstake I.W.W. members drifting through his town. His identification test was a simple question, "Are you I.W.W.?" but it emerged in Cantonese-flavored English as "Ah loo eye wobble wobble?" Whatever its origin, the name was a badge of pride.

The I.W.W.'s new leadership provided halls in the towns where a wandering Wobbly could find a warm stove, a pot of coffee, a corner in which to spread a blanket for the night, and literature: the *Industrial Worker* and *Solidarity*, leaflets by St. John or Haywood, and books like Jack London's *The Iron Heel*, Edward Bellamy's *Looking Backward*, Laurence Gronlund's *Co-operative Commonwealth*. All of them furnished material for arguments with the unorganized, and also such stuff as dreams were made on.

In 1909 the I.W.W. attracted national attention through the first of its spectacular clashes with civic authority. In Spokane a campaign was launched urging loggers to boycott the "job sharks," employment agents who hired men for work in lumber and construction camps deep in the woods, charging them a fee for the "service." Many a lumberjack who "bought a job" in this way was swindled—sent to a nonexistent camp or quickly fired by a foreman in cahoots with the shark to provide fast turnover and larger shared profits. At street meetings, the Wobblies preached direct hiring by the lumber companies. Spokane's thirty-one agencies retaliated by getting the city council to ban such meetings. The *Industrial Worker* promptly declared November 2, 1909, Free Speech Day and urged every man in the vicinity to "fill the jails of Spokane."

From hundreds of miles around, Wobblies poured in by boxcar, mounted soapboxes, and were immediately wrestled into patrol wagons. In a matter of weeks, the jail and a quickly converted schoolhouse were overflowing with five or six hundred prisoners. They came into court bloody from beatings; they were put to hard labor on bread and water, jammed into cells like sardines, and in the name of sanitation hosed with ice water and returned to unheated confinement. Three died of pneumonia. Among the prisoners was a dark-haired Irish girl from New York, Elizabeth Gurley Flynn. Eighteen years old and pregnant, she complicated her arrest by chaining herself to a lamp post. "Gurley," a proletarian Joan of Arc, was lodged with a woman cellmate who kept receiving mysterious calls to the front office. It turned out that she was a prostitute, serving customers provided by the sheriff "for good and valuable consideration." This fact was trumpeted by the I.W.W. as soon as Gurley figured it out.

Fresh trainloads of Wobblies poured relentlessly into town, while those already in jail kept the night alive with selections from the Little Red Songbook roared at full volume, staged hunger strikes, refused to touch their hammers on the rock pile, and generally discomfited their captors. In March of 1910 the taxpayers of Spokane threw in the towel, released the prisoners, and restored the right of free speech to the I.W.W. Other free-speech fights in the next few years carried the Wobbly message throughout the Far West and helped in organizing new locals among the militant.

Two years after the end of the Spokane campaign, the I.W.W. made headlines in the East. In the textile-manufacturing town of Lawrence, Massachusetts, on January 11, 1912, more than 20,000 workers struck against a wage cut that took thirty cents—the price of three loaves of bread—out of pay envelopes averaging only six to eight dollars for a fifty-four-hour week. It was an unskilled work force that hit the bitter-cold streets, and a polyglot one, too. Some twenty-five nationalities, speaking forty-five languages or dialects, were represented, including French Canadians, Belgians, Poles, Italians, Syrians, Lithuanians, Greeks, Russians, and Turks.

There was only a small I.W.W. local in Lawrence, but the tactics of One Big Union under the slogan "An injury to one is an injury to all" had never been more appropriate. I.W.W. pamphlets and newspapers in several languages had already appeared. Now the leadership deployed its best veterans in the field —Haywood, William Trautmann, Elizabeth Gurley Flynn—and in addition a big, jovial-looking Italian organizer of steelworkers, Joe Ettor, whose usual costume was a black shirt and a red tie.

For over two months, something akin to social revolution went on in Lawrence. A strike committee of fifty-six members, representing all nationalities, filled days and nights with meetings and parades. Haywood stood out like a giant. He hurdled the linguistic barrier by speeches partly in sign language (waving fingers to show the weakness of separate craft unions; balled-up fist to demonstrate solidarity), visited workers' homes, and won the women's hearts by joshing the children or smacking his lips over shashlik or spaghetti. He also shrewdly exploited the publicity that bathed Lawrence, which was near the nation's journalistic capitals. Demonstrations were called with an eye not only to working-class morale but to public opinion. It was an education for many Americans to read about "ignorant, foreign" mill girls carrying signs that said: "We Want Bread And Roses, Too."

The employers played into Haywood's hands. National Guardsmen were called out. Police arrested more than three hundred workers and, in a climax of stupidity, clubbed a group of mothers and children preparing to leave town by railroad for foster homes. In defiance of the evidence, Ettor and Arturo Giovannitti, another Italian organizer, were arrested as accessories in the shooting of a woman striker. Authorities held them for seven months before a trial. When it came, it not only let the two men go free but gave Giovannitti a chance to spellbind jury and reporters with an oration on behalf of "this mighty army of the working class of the world, which . . . is striving towards the destined goal, which is the emancipation of human kind, which is the establishment of love and brotherhood and justice for every man and every woman in this earth."

Long before that speech, in March of 1912, the bosses had given up and agreed to the strikers' terms. It was the I.W.W.'s finest hour up to then. Flushed with success, the One Big Union next answered the call of silk workers at Paterson, New Jersey, to lead them in a strike that began in February, 1913. The pattern of Lawrence seemed at first to be repeating. There were nearly fifteen hundred arrests, and in addition police and private detectives killed two workers by random gunfire. One of these, Valentino Modesto, was given a funeral at

I.W.W. strike in Lawrence, Massachusetts, in 1912. Mobilized by the I.W.W., some 20,000 textile workers struck against a wage cut that took 30¢ from pay envelopes that contained only $6 to $8 per week. "For over two months, something akin to social revolution went on in Lawrence," Weisberger writes. But when management tried to reopen the mills, the strikers clashed with militia and police, and one woman was killed. There was such nationwide sentiment for the strikers that management finally agreed to their terms. "It was," says Weisberger, "the I.W.W.'s finest hour up to then." (Courtesy Lawrence Free Public Library, Lawrence, Massachusetts.)

which twenty thousand workers filed by to drop red carnations on the coffin. But after five months even relief funds and singing rallies could not prevail over hunger. The strike was broken.

Not, however, before it produced a unique project and a strange alliance. One of the reporters who came to Paterson on an April day was John Reed—talented, charming, Harvard '10—who was enjoying life to the hilt in the Bohemian surroundings of Greenwich Village, then in its heyday. When Reed stopped to talk to a striker, a Paterson policeman on the lookout for "agitators" hustled him off to jail. There he stayed for four days, sharing smokes and food with the strikers and amiably teaching them college fight songs and French ballads in return for instruction in the arts of survival in prison. On his release he became an enthusiastic supporter of the embattled workers and brought such friends as Mabel Dodge, Hutchins Hapgood, Walter Lippmann, Lincoln Steffens, and others to hear Haywood and other Wobbly leaders speak.

Between the individualistic rebelliousness of the young artists and writers escaping their bourgeois backgrounds and the hard-shelled but dream-drenched radicalism of the I.W.W. leaders, there was instinctive connection. Reed conceived the idea of a giant fund-raising pageant to present the strikers' case. On June 7, thousands of silk workers came into New York by special train and ferry and marched to Madison Square Garden. There they watched hundreds of fellow strikers reenact the walkout, the shooting of Modesto, his funeral, and the mass meetings that followed. Staged by Reed's Harvard friend Robert Edmund Jones against a backdrop created by the artist John Sloan, the pageant was described by *Outlook* as having "a directness, an intensity, and a power seldom seen on the professional stage." Since it ran for only one night, it failed to earn any money beyond expenses, despite a full house. Yet as a moment of convergence in the currents of radicalism vitalizing American life and letters in the last days of prewar innocence, it has a historic place of its own.

The Lawrence and Paterson affairs were only forays, however. The I.W.W. ran strikes and kept footholds in the East—the dockworkers of Philadelphia were firmly organized in the I.W.W.-affiliated Marine Transport Workers Union, for example—but it lacked staying power in the settled industrial areas. As it moved into its peak years, the future of the One Big Union was in the West, where its message and tactics were suited to the style of migrant workers, and to the violent tempo of what Elizabeth Flynn recalled as "a wild and rugged country where both nature and greed snuffed out human life."

Here, in the mountains and forests, were men who needed protection even more than the unskilled rubber, textile, steel, and clothing workers receiving I.W.W. attention—men like the "timber beasts," who worked in the freezing woods from dawn to dusk and then "retired" to vermin-ridden bunkhouses, without washing facilities, where they were stacked in double tiers like their own logs. The companies did not even furnish bedding, and a lumberjack between jobs was recognizable by his roll of blankets—his "bundle," "bindle," or "balloon"—slung on his back. The bindle stiff who "played the woods," however, was only one member of an army of migrant workers, as many as a half million strong, who as the cycle of each year turned followed the harvests, the construction jobs, the logging operations, and the opening of new mines. Sometimes they got a spell of sea life in the forecastle of a merchant ship; often they wintered in the flophouses of Chicago or San Francisco; and not infrequently they spent the out-of-season months in jail on charges of vagrancy. The public mind blurred them together, and made no distinction among hoboes, bums, and tramps, assuming them all to be thieves, drunkards, and panhandlers. But the true migrant was none of these. He was a "working stiff," emphasis on the first word, and thus ripe for the tidings of class war.

The I.W.W. reached him where he lived: in the hobo "jungles" outside the rail junction points, where he boiled stew in empty tin cans, slept on the ground come wind, come weather, and waited to hop a freight bound in any direction where jobs were rumored to be. The Wobblies sent in full-time organizers, dressed in the same caps and windbreakers, but with pockets full of red membership cards, dues books and stamps, subscription blanks, song sheets, pamphlets. These job delegates signed up their men around the campfires or in the boxcars ("side-door Pullmans" the migrants called them), mailed the money to headquarters, and then followed their recruits to the woods, or to the tents in the open fields where the harvest stiffs unrolled *their* bindles after twelve hours of work in hundred-degree heat without water, shade, or toilets. But there were some whom the organizers could not reach, and the I.W.W. sent them messages in the form of "sticker-ettes." These "silent agitators" were illustrated slogans on label-sized pieces of gummed paper, many of them drawn by Ralph Chaplin. They sold for as little as a dollar a thousand, and Chaplin believed that in a few weeks a good "Wob" on the road could plaster them on "every son-of-a-bitch of a boxcar, watertank, pick handle and pitchfork" within a radius of hundreds of miles.

The stickers were simple and caught the eye. "What Time Is It? Time to Organize!" shouted a clock. "Solidarity Takes the Whole Works" explained a Bunyan-sized workingman with an armload of trains and factories. The three stars of the One Big Union (Organization, Education, Emancipation) winked bright red over a black and yellow earth. A "scissorbill"—a workingman without class loyalty—knelt on bony knees and snuffled to the sky, "Now I get me up to work, I pray the Lord I may not shirk." But the most fateful stickers to appear between 1915 and 1917, as the nation moved toward war, were those that urged: "SLOW DOWN. The hours are long, the pay is small, so take your time and buck 'em all"; and those on which appeared two portentous symbols: the wooden shoe of sabotage, and the black cat, which, as everybody knew, meant trouble.

A tough problem for the I.W.W. was how to achieve "direct action" in the migrant workers' spread-eagle world. A factory or a mine could be struck. But how could the I.W.W.'s farmhands' union, the Agricultural Workers' Organization, "strike" a thousand square miles of wheat-field divided among hundreds of farmer-employers? How could the Forest and Lumber Workers' Industrial Union tie up a logging operation spread among dozens of camps separated by lonely miles?

The answer was, as the Wobblies put it, "to bring the strike to the job," or, more bluntly, sabotage. To the average American, sabotage conjured up nightmares of violence to property: barns blazing in the night, crowbars twisting the steel and wire guts out of a machine. The word itself suggested a European tradition of radical workers' dropping their *sabots*, or wooden shoes, into the works. But the I.W.W. leaders insisted that they had something less destructive in mind—merely the slowdown, the "conscientious withdrawal of efficiency," or, in working-stiff terms, "poor pay, poor work." To "put on the wooden shoe," or to "turn loose the black kitty" or "sab-cat," meant only to misplace and misfile order slips, to "forget" to oil motors, to "accidentally" let furnaces go out. Or simply to dawdle on the job and let fruit rot on the ground or let threshing or logging machinery with steam up stand idle while farmers and foremen fumed.

I.W.W. headquarters was vague about where the limits to direct action lay. Nor did it help matters when it printed dim, oracular pronouncements like Bill Haywood's "Sabotage means to push back, pull out or break off the fangs of Capitalism." Such phrases were enough to frighten not only the capitalists, but the Socialists, who in their 1912 convention denied the red sacraments to any who advocated "crime, sabotage or other methods of violence as a weapon of the working class to aid in its emancipation." (The next year, the Socialists fired Haywood from the party's executive board, completing the divorce between the Wobblies and politics.) Still the I.W.W. leaders in the field pushed ahead with their tactics. The Agricultural Workers, to strengthen the threat of mass quittings by harvest hands, organized a "thousand-mile picket line" of tough Wobblies who worked their way through freight trains in the farm belt, signing up new members and unceremoniously dumping off any "scissorbills" or "wicks" who refused a red card. The Lumber Workers forced the camp owners to furnish clean bedding by encouraging thousands of lumberjacks to celebrate May Day, 1918, by soaking their bindles with kerosene and making huge bonfires of them.

Potentially such tactics were loaded with danger, but from 1913 to 1919 they worked. Ralph Chaplin estimated that in early spring of 1917, when the A.W.O. was signing up members at the rate of 5,000 a month, the going wage in the grain belt had jumped from two dollars for a twelve-to-sixteen-hour day to five dollars for a ten-hour day. Two years later northwestern loggers were averaging twenty-five to fifty dollars a month plus board. These facts meant more to the average reader of *Solidarity* and the *Industrial Worker* than I.W.W. theories about the overthrow of capitalism. If he thought about the shape of society after the final general strike, it was only in the vague way of a church deacon who knew there was a celestial crown reserved for him, but did not trouble his mind about it from day to day. Yet the very success of the organization anywhere stirred not only the anger of its enemies but the fears of unsophisticated Americans who were ready to believe that the Wobblies were already putting the torch to the foundations of government and justice. With war hysteria actively feeding the fires of public hostility, the I.W.W. became the victim of new and spectacular persecutions.

Perhaps it was inevitable that the blood of martyrs would splash the pages of the I.W.W.'s book of chronicles. The mine owners, lumber-camp operators, and ranchers whom the Wobblies fought were themselves hard, resourceful men who had mastered a demanding environment. They knew a challenge when they saw one, and the West, in 1915, was not too far past Indian, stagecoach, and vigilante days. Sheriffs and their deputies were ready to use any method to rid their communities of "agitators"—especially those described in the press as "America's cancer sore." The Los Angeles *Times*, for example, said that

> A vast number of I.W.W.'s are non-producers. I.W.W. stands for I won't work, and I want whisky. . . . The average Wobbly, it must be remembered, is a sort of half wild animal. He lives on the road, cooks his food in rusty tin cans . . . and sleeps in "jungles," barns, outhouses, freight cars . . . They are all in all a lot of homeless men wandering about the country without fixed destination or purpose, other than destruction.

"When a Wobbly comes to town," one sheriff told a visitor, "I just knock him over the head with a night stick and throw him in the river. When he comes up he beats it out of town." Lawmen furnished similar treatment to any hobo or "undesirable" stranger, particularly if he showed a tendency to complain about local working conditions or if, after April 6, 1917, he did not glow with the proper enthusiasm for the war to end wars. Hundreds of suspected and genuine Wobblies were jailed, beaten, shot, and tortured between 1914 and 1919, but some names and episodes earned, by excess of horror or myth-creating power, a special framing among dark memories.

There was the case of Joe Hill. He was the most prolific of the Wobbly bards; the dozens of numbers he composed while drifting from job to job after his emigration from Sweden to America (where his name transformed itself from Haaglund into Hillstrom and then into plain Hill) had done much to make the I.W.W. a singing movement. His songs had, a recent Wobbly folklorist has written, "tough, humorous, skeptical words which raked American morality over the coals." They were known and sung wherever Wobblies fought cops and bosses.

In January, 1914, Salt Lake City police arrested Hill on the charge of murdering a grocer and his son in a holdup. Circumstantial evidence was strongly against him, but Hill went through trial and conviction stoutly insisting that he had been framed. Though a popular ballad written many years afterward intones, "The copper bosses killed you, Joe," Hill was not definitely linked to any strike activity in Utah, and had been in the I.W.W. for only four years. But his songs had made him a hero to the entire radical labor movement, and he had a sure sense of drama. Through months of appeals and protest demonstrations he played—or lived—the role of Pilate's victim magnificently. On November 18, 1915, the day before a five-man firing squad shot him dead, he sent to Bill Haywood, in Chicago, a classic telegram: "Goodbye, Bill. I die like a true blue rebel. Don't waste any time mourning. Organize!" Thirty thousand people wept at his funeral. At his own request, his ashes were put in small envelopes and distributed to be scattered, the following May Day, in every state of the Union.

And there was the "Everett massacre." On October 30, 1916, forty-one Wobblies had travelled from Seattle to Everett, Washington, some forty miles away, to speak on behalf of striking sawmill workers. Vigilantes under Sheriff Donald McRae arrested them, took them to the edge of town, and forced them to run the gauntlet between rows of deputies armed with clubs, pick handles, and bats. Next morning the grass was stiff with dried blood. Five days later, two steamer loads of I.W.W. members sailed up Puget Sound from Seattle for a meeting of protest. As they approached the Everett docks singing "Hold the Fort for We Are Coming," the sheriff and his men were waiting. They opened up with a hail of gunfire, and five Wobblies were killed, thirty-one wounded; in the confused firing, two vigilantes were also killed. Seventy-four Wobblies were arrested and tried for these two deaths but were acquitted. No one was tried for killing the I.W.W. men.

The following summer Frank Little, a member of the I.W.W. executive board, died violently in Butte, Montana. Little was a dark-haired man, with only one good eye and a crooked grin. He was part Indian, and liked to josh friends like Elizabeth Gurley Flynn and Bill Haywood by saying: "I am a real Red. The rest of you are immigrants." In June, with his leg in a cast from a recent auto accident, he left Chicago headquarters for Butte to take command of the copper miners' strike, denounced by the mine owners as a pro-German uprising. On the night of August 1, 1917, six armed and masked men broke into his hotel room and dragged him at a rope's end behind an automobile to a railroad trestle, from which he was hanged, cast and all. No arrests were made by Butte police.

As a final gruesome example, there was what happened in Centralia, Washington, on Armistice Day, 1919. An American Legion parade halted before the town's I.W.W. hall, long denounced as a center of seditious efforts to stir lumberjacks to wartime strikes and already once raided and wrecked by townsmen. Now, again, a group of men broke from the line of march and swarmed toward the building. The Wobblies inside were waiting. Simultaneous shots from several directions shattered the air; three legionnaires fell dead. The marchers broke in, seized five men, and pursued a sixth. He was Wesley Everest, a young logger and war veteran. He killed another legionnaire before they captured him and dragged him, with his teeth knocked out, to jail. That night a mob broke in and took Everest to a bridge over the Chehalis River. There he allegedly was castrated with a razor and then hanged from the bridge in the glare of automobile headlights.

The hand of history struck the I.W.W. its hardest blow, however, in September of 1917. The United States government moved to cripple the One Big Union, not because it was a threat to capitalism (the government insisted, without convincing the Wobblies) but because it was impeding the prosecution of the war. Whereas Samuel Gompers had moved skillfully to entrench the A.F.L. deeper in the hearts of the middle class by pledging it fully to Wilson's crusade, the I.W.W. remained hostile. In its eyes, the only war that meant anything to a working stiff was that foretold in the preamble, between the millions who toiled and the few who had the good things of life. Wobblies had seen too many strikes broken by troops to warm to the sight of uniforms. "Don't be a soldier," said one popular stickerette, "be a man."

The General Executive Board knew the dangers of that position once war was declared. The members hedged on expressing any formal attitude toward America's entry, and when the draft was enacted, the board advised them to register as "I.W.W. opposed to war" and thereafter to consult their own consciences. (Wesley Everest had been one of many Wobblies who chose uniformed service.) But the militant I.W.W. campaigns were frank challenges to the official drive for production. Five months after the declaration of war, federal agents, under emergency legislation, suddenly descended on I.W.W. offices all over the country. They confiscated tons of books, newspapers, letters, and pamphlets—as well as wall decorations, mimeograph machines, and spittoons—as evidence, then returned to remove Wobbly officials handcuffed in pairs.

The biggest trial of Wobblies on various counts of obstructing the war effort took place in federal district court in Chicago in the summer of 1918. Relentlessly the prosecutors drew around one hundred defendants a net of rumors and accusations charging them with conspiring to burn crops, drive spikes in logs, derail trains, dynamite factories. Judge Kenesaw Mountain Landis (later to be famous as professional baseball's "czar") presided in shirt-sleeved informality over the hot courtroom as, day after day, government attorneys read into the record every savory piece of I.W.W. prose or verse from which such phrases as "direct action" and "class war" could be speared and held up for horrified scrutiny. The jury took less than an hour to consider thousands of pages of evidence and hundreds of separate alleged offenses, and returned against all but a handful of the defendants a predictable wartime verdict of "guilty" on all counts. The white-thatched Judge Landis handed out sentences running as high as twenty years, as if he were in magistrate's court consigning the morning quota of drunks to thirty days each.

The 1918 federal trials (which were followed by similar episodes in a number of states that hastily enacted laws against "criminal syndicalism") were a downward turning point for the I.W.W. In theory, the One Big Union was wholly responsive to its rank and file, and invulnerable to the destruction of its bureaucracy.* But democratic enthusiasm could not override the fact that the veteran officers and keenest minds of the I.W.W. were behind bars, and their replacements were almost totally absorbed in legal maneuvers to get them out. A pathetic Wobbly fund-raising poster compressed the truth into a single line under a picture of a face behind bars: "We are in here for you; you are out there for us." In 1920 there might still have been fifty thousand on the I.W.W. rolls, but they were riding a rudderless craft.

Other troubles beset the One Big Union. The Communist party rose on the scene and sucked into its orbit some respected veterans, including Elizabeth Gurley Flynn (though she had left the I.W.W. in 1916) and William D. Haywood himself. Released from Leavenworth while his case was on appeal, Big Bill jumped

---

* The fact was that it made valorous efforts to keep its officialdom humble. As general secretary-treasurer, Bill Haywood received thirty-five dollars a week—just twice what a field organizer took home.

bail and early in 1921 fled to the Soviet Union. Forgivably and understandably, perhaps, his courage had at last been shaken. He was fifty-one years old, seriously ill, and certain that he would die—with profit to no cause—if he had to spend any more time in jail. He was briefly publicized in Russia as a refugee from capitalism. He married a Russian woman, and for a time held a job as one of the managers of an industrial colony in the Kuznetsk Basin. But soon there was silence, and rumors of disillusionment. In May of 1928 he died. Half his ashes were sent to Chicago for burial. The other half lie under the Kremlin wall—like those of his old friend of Paterson days, John Reed (see "The Harvard Man in the Kremlin Wall" in the February, 1960, AMERICAN HERITAGE). By and large, however, Bolshevik politicians had as little appeal for old-time Wobblies as any other kind. (Yet in 1948 the leadership of what was left of the organization refused to sign Taft-Hartley non-Communist affidavits. No contract, and no deals with bourgeois governments. Principle was principle still.)

More cracks crisscrossed the surface of solidarity. Some of the more successful I.W.W. unions experienced a yearning for larger initiation fees, and for just a taste of the financial stability of the A.F.L. internationals—the stability which had never been a Wobbly strong point. They quarrelled with the General Executive Board. A few locals chafed under what they thought was too much centralization. And finally, in 1924, there was an open split and a secession of part of the organization, taking precious funds and property with it. The last great schism, in 1908, had freed the I.W.W. for vigorous growth. Now it was sixteen years later, and time and chance were playing cruel games.

Middle age was overtaking the young lions, dulling their teeth—especially those who, one by one, accepted individual offers of clemency and emerged from prison, blinking, to find a changed world. The harvest stiff no longer took the side-door Pullman. He was a "gas tramp" now, or a "flivver hobo," riding his battered Model T to the job, and beyond the reach of the thousand-mile picket line. The logger, too, was apt to be a "home-guard," living with his family and driving through the dawn hours to where the saws whined and the big ones toppled. The children of the sweated immigrants of Paterson and Lawrence were clutching their high school diplomas, forgetting their working-class background, becoming salesmen and stenographers. Even the worker who stayed in the mill or the mine was sometimes lulled into passivity by the squealing crystal set or the weekly dream-feast of the picture-show. The ferment in the unskilled labor pool was hissing out. A new society *was* being built; but Ford and the installment plan had more to do with it than the visionaries who had hotly conceived and lustily adopted the I.W.W. preamble of 1905.

There was some fight left in the old outfit. It could run a free-speech fight in San Pedro in 1923, a coal strike in Colorado in 1927–28. But it was dwindling and aging. When the Depression came, labor's dynamism was reawakened by hardship. The C.I.O. was created, and fought its battles under the pennons of "industrial unionism," the heart of the Wobbly plan for organizing the army of production. The C.I.O. used singing picket lines, too, and sit-down strikes—techniques pioneered by such men as Haywood and Vincent St. John when labor's new leaders were in knickers. The old-timers who had known Big Bill and The Saint could only look on from the sidelines as the younger generation took over. Moreover, the success of organizing drives in the thirties, and the programs of the New Deal, vastly improved the lot of millions of working people. The agony that had nourished the I.W.W.'s revolutionary temper was now abating. Ironically, the very success of labor in uplifting itself through collective bargaining and politics drove one more nail into the I.W.W.'s coffin.

But "coffin" is perhaps the wrong word. Like Joe Hill, the I.W.W. never died. In its offices scattered across the country, old-timers still sit and smoke under pictures of Frank Little and Wesley Everest, or leaf through copies of the *Industrial Worker* like the great readers they always were. They do not give up; they expect that history will knock some sense into the workers soon, and that then the cry of "One Union, One Label, One Enemy" will rise again from thousands of throats. But meanwhile, their offices are, in the words of a recent observer, haunted halls, "full of memories and empty of men."

By contrast, the steel and glass office buildings of the bigtime A.F.L. C.I.O. unions are alive with the ring of telephones, the hum of presses, the clatter of typewriters, and the clicking of secretaries' heels hurrying through the doors behind which sit organized labor's well-dressed statisticians, economists, lawyers, accountants, editors, co-ordinators, and educators. They have given much to their workers, these unions—good wages, decent hours, vacations, benefits, pensions, insurance. But they may be incapable of duplicating two gifts that the I.W.W. gave its apostles, its knights, its lovers—gifts that shine through a pair of stories. One is of the sheriff who shouted to a group of Wobblies, "Who's yer leader?" and got back a bellowed answer, "We don't got no leader, we're all leaders." The other is a recollection by an unidentified witness at the Chicago trial:

Well, they grabbed us. And the deputy says, "Are you a member of the I.W.W.?" I says, "Yes," so he asked me for my card, and I gave it to him, and he tore it up. He tore up the other cards that the fellow members along with me had. So this fellow member says, "There is no use tearing that card up. We can get duplicates." "Well," the deputy says, "We can tear the duplicates too." And this fellow worker says, he says, "Yes, but you can't tear it out of my heart."

13

Theodore Roosevelt: The Conservative As Progressive

Richard Hofstadter

In September, 1901, an assassin murdered William McKinley in Buffalo—the third time a President had been killed in less than forty years. His successor was Theodore Roosevelt, a polygonal man of aristocratic lineage who had graduated from Harvard, run a cattle ranch in the Dakotas, led the Rough Riders in the war with Spain, and served as governor of New York. "Now look," moaned a Republican Party boss, "that damned cowboy is President of the United States!"

That damned cowboy—at forty-two the youngest chief executive in United States history—brought a youthful flair and an electrifying vitality to his office; and when he left it in 1909, he had made a reputation for himself as a fighting trust-buster, an impassioned Progressive Republican who had brought industrial magnates to their knees and had made the federal government, and the presidency in particular, a watchdog for the middle and lower classes. Legends were to grow out of this image of Roosevelt. Yet behind all his tough talk, as Richard Hofstadter contends in this essay, Roosevelt's Progressivism was basically conservative and pro-business, as long as business did not grow stronger than government itself. To understand TR both as a man and a Progressive, Hofstadter guides us through Roosevelt's colorful private and public life, leaving us with an unforgettable portrait of that versatile, complicated, and explosive man.

How I wish I wasn't a reformer, oh, Senator! But I suppose I must live up to my part, like the Negro minstrel who blacked himself all over! THEODORE ROOSEVELT TO CHAUNCEY DEPEW

The coarse, materialistic civilization that emerged in the United States during the years after the Civil War produced among cultivated middle-class young men a generation of alienated and homeless intellectuals. Generally well-to-do, often of eminent family backgrounds, clubmen, gentlemen, writers, the first cluster of a native intellectual aristocracy to appear since the great days of Boston and Concord, the men of this class found themselves unable to participate with any heart in the greedy turmoil of business or to accept without protest boss-ridden politics. Money-making was sordid; politics was dirty; and the most sensitive among them made their careers in other ways. Those who were less interested in public affairs usually managed to fit themselves into the interstices of American existence. Some, like Henry James, escaped abroad or, like his brother William, immersed themselves in academic life. One, Oliver Wendell Holmes, Jr., found sanctuary on the Massachusetts bench and at length rose to the Supreme Court; another, Henry Adams, made a sort of career of bitter detachment. Some who were strong enough to overcome their distaste for business entered it without finding much personal fulfillment and left without regret. Charles Francis

---

From pp. 203–233 in *The American Political Tradition*, by Richard Hofstadter. Copyright 1948 by Alfred A. Knopf. Reprinted by permission of the publisher.

162

Adams, Jr., upon retiring from an unhappy career as a railroad executive, observed that among all the tycoons he had met, "not one . . . would I care to meet again in this world or the next; nor is one associated in my mind with the idea of humor, thought, or refinement."

Conventional politics, on the other hand, offered a choice between merely serving the business class or living off it in a sort of parasitic blackmail.[1] For the more scrupulous this was impossible; in the case of the fastidious Adamses, Brooks and Henry, even the weight of a great family tradition and an absorbing concern with political affairs was not enough to counterbalance distaste. They were, as Henry put it, "unfashionable by some law of Anglo-Saxon custom—some innate atrophy of mind." The era impelled the frustrated politician into scholarship and forced his interest in politics to find wistful expression in the writing of history. Among hardier and somewhat younger souls, however, there appeared the scholar-in-politics, a type represented by Albert J. Beveridge, John Hay, Henry Cabot Lodge, Theodore Roosevelt, and Woodrow Wilson. Such men, though hardly typical politicians, held their noses, made the necessary compromises, worked their way into politics, and bided their time until the social milieu gave them a chance to ride into power. These were the practical men of the breed, men of steady nerves, strong ambition, tenacity, and flexible scruples. The most striking among them was Theodore Roosevelt.

In his *Autobiography* Roosevelt tells how horrified his friends were when he first broached to them his determination to enter politics. "The men I knew best," he recalled, "were the men in the clubs of social pretension and the men of cultivated taste and easy life." Politics, they told him, is a cheap affair run by saloon-keepers and horse-car conductors and shunned by gentlemen. "I answered that if this were so it merely meant that the people I knew did not belong to the governing class, and that the other people did—and that I intended to be one of the governing class." And so Roosevelt began at the bottom by joining an organization that met in a spittoon-furnished hall over a barroom, the Jake Hess Republican Club of New York's 21st Assembly District.

The ends for which Roosevelt and his peers entered politics were not mere boodling or personal advancement. Searching for goals that they considered more lofty, ideals above section or class or material gain, they were bent on some genuinely national service, sought a larger theater in which to exercise their statecraft, and looked down with the disdain of aristocrats upon those who, as Roosevelt said, had never felt the thrill of a generous emotion. Adventurers in a sense they undoubtedly were, tired of "that kind of money-maker whose soul has grown hard while his body has grown soft." In an article written for the *Century* when he was only twenty-eight, Roosevelt aired his disgust at rich Americans as a political type:

> The wealthier, or, as they would prefer to style themselves, the "upper" classes, tend distinctly towards the bourgeois type, and an individual in the bourgeois stage of development, while honest, industrious, and virtuous, is also not unapt to be a miracle of timid and short-sighted selfishness. The commercial classes are only too likely to regard everything merely from the standpoint of "Does it pay? and many a merchant does not take any part in politics because he is short-sighted enough to think that it will pay him better to attend purely to making money, and too selfish to be willing to undergo any trouble for the sake of abstract duty; while the younger men of this type are too much engrossed in their various social pleasures to be willing to give up their time

---

[1] "No one wanted him," wrote Henry Adams of his own dilemma. "No one wanted any of his friends in reform; the blackmailer alone was the normal product of politics as of business."

to anything else. It is also unfortunately true ... that the general tendency among people of culture and high education has been to neglect and even to look down upon the rougher and manlier virtues, so that an advanced state of intellectual development is too often associated with a certain effeminacy of character.

But if Roosevelt was in revolt against the pecuniary values of "the glorified huckster or glorified pawnbroker type," it was not from the standpoint of social democracy, not as an advocate of the downtrodden. He despised the rich, but he feared the mob. Any sign of organized power among the people frightened him; and for many years he showed toward the labor movement an attitude as bitter as that expressed in John Hay's anonymously published novel, *The Breadwinners*. The most aggressive middle-class reformers also annoyed him. Until his post-presidential years, when he underwent his tardy but opportune conversion to radicalism, there was hardly a reform movement that did not at some time win his scorn. His writings are dotted with tart characterizations of "extremists," "radical fanatics," "muckrakers," and "the lunatic fringe." "Sentimental humanitarians," he asserted in his life of Benton, "always form a most pernicious body, with an influence for bad hardly surpassed by that of the professional criminal class."

What Roosevelt stood for, as a counterpoise to the fat materialism of the wealthy and the lurking menace of the masses, were the aggressive, masterful, fighting virtues of the soldier. "No amount of commercial prosperity," he once said, "can supply the lack of the heroic virtues," and it was the heroic virtues that he wished to make central again in American life. His admiration went out most spontaneously to the hunter, the cowboy, the frontiersman, the soldier, and the naval hero. Herbert Spencer, whose ideas were supreme in American thinking during Roosevelt's formative years, taught that Western society was passing from a militant phase, dominated by organization for warfare, to an industrial phase, marked by peaceful economic progress. Roosevelt, whom Spencer would have called atavistic, was determined to reverse this process and restore to the American spirit what he fondly called "the fighting edge." Despite his sincere loyalty to the democratic game, this herald of modern American militarism and imperialism displayed in his political character many qualities of recent authoritarianism—romantic nationalism, disdain for materialistic ends, worship of strength and the cult of personal leadership, the appeal to the intermediate elements of society, the ideal of standing above classes and class interests, a grandiose sense of destiny, even a touch of racism.

It is customary to explain Theodore Roosevelt's personality as the result of compensation for physical inferiority.[2] His sight was always poor, and at length he lost the use of his left eye. As a child he was tormented by asthma and shamed by a puny body of which he grew increasingly conscious. An encounter at the age of fourteen left an inexpugnable mark on his memory. He was riding on a stagecoach to Moosehead Lake when he met two other boys of his own age who teased him beyond endurance; and when he tried to fight back, "I discovered that either one singly could not only handle me with easy contempt, but handle me

[2] "One can state as a fundamental law that children who come into the world with organ inferiorities become involved at an early age in a bitter struggle for existence which results only too often in a strangulation of their social feelings. Instead of interesting themselves in an adjustment to their fellows, they are continually occupied with themselves and with the impression which they make on others.... As soon as the striving for recognition assumes the upper hand ... the goal of power and superiority becomes increasingly obvious to the individual, and he pursues it with movements of great intensity and violence, and his life becomes the expectation of a great triumph." Alfred Adler: *Understanding Human Nature*, pp. 69, 191.

so as not to hurt me much and yet to prevent my doing any damage whatever in return." Upon coming back to New York he began taking boxing lessons, and his life thereafter was cluttered with the paraphernalia of physical culture—boxing gloves, dumbbells, horizontal bars, and the like. From his Harvard days there survives a picture of him in boxing costume; his muscular arms are folded histrionically across his chest, and on his face there is a fierce paranoid scowl. He was still boxing in the White House at forty-three.

Possibly there is no such thing as a saturation point in such psychological compensations; but if there is, Roosevelt, above all men, should have been able to find salve for his ego. He sparred with professional prizefighters; he rode with cowboys; he led a famous cavalry charge; he hunted Spaniards and big game; he once had the exquisite pleasure of knocking out a tough in a Western barroom; he terrorized an entire police force; he defied a Pope; he became President of the United States and waved his fist under J. P. Morgan's nose. If all this was supposed to induce a sense of security, it seems to have failed badly. At the age of sixty he was still waving the flag and screaming for a regiment. One can only suspect that he was fleeing from some more persistent sense of deficiency than that induced by the obvious traumatic experiences of his childhood. He fled from repose and introspection with a desperate urgency that is sometimes pitiable. In 1886, two years after the simultaneous death of his first wife and his mother, he wrote his biography of Thomas Hart Benton in four months, during most of which he was on fourteen- or sixteen-hour ranching schedules and "pretty sleepy, all the time." In this period he poured out seven volumes of history and essays within five years, while active both in politics and on his ranch. "Get action, do things; be sane," he once raved, "don't fritter away your time; create, act, take a place wherever you are and be somebody: get action." A profound and ineluctable tendency to anxiety plagued him. His friends noticed with wonder that Roosevelt, at the time of his engagement to Alice Lee, who became his first wife, lived in a stew of fear lest someone run off with her, threatened acquaintances with duels, and actually smuggled a set of French dueling pistols through the customhouse in preparation for the event. "There were all kinds of things of which I was afraid at first," he confessed in his memoirs, ". . . but by acting as if I was not afraid I gradually ceased to be afraid."[3]

"Manly" and "masterful," two of the most common words in Roosevelt's prose, reflect a persistent desire to impose himself upon others. Such a personal motive, projected into public affairs, easily became transformed into the imperial impulse. It was no mere accident that the Rough Rider's popularity grew most rapidly as a result of his Spanish War service. The depression of the nineties found the American middle classes in an uneasy and fearful mood as they watched the trusts growing on one side and the labor and Populist movements massing on the other. For them, as for him, a fight served as a distraction; national self-assertion in the world theater gave them the sense that the nation had not lost its capacity for growth and change. The same emotions that made the people so receptive to the unnecessary Spanish War made them receptive to a man of Roosevelt's temperament. Stuart Sherman has suggested also that his popularity was due in large part to the fact that Americans, in the search for money and power that had grown so intense in the Gilded Age, had lost much of their capacity for enjoyment, and that Roosevelt, with his variety and exuberance and his perpetual air of expectation, restored the consciousness of other ends that made life worth

---

[3] Roosevelt was writing in particular about his reaction to hunting dangerous game, but the remark may illuminate a larger pattern of behavior. In many cases what the hunter hunts is nothing so much as his own fear; trophies are esteemed because they are evidence of risks undergone and fears surmounted.

living.[4] "On the whole," the colonel proclaimed in 1899, "we think that the greatest victories are yet to be won, the greatest deeds yet to be done, and that there are yet in store for our peoples and for the causes that we uphold, grander triumphs than have yet been scored."

Roosevelt himself loved the company of rough and aggressive men. Some of the most disarming writing in his *Autobiography* deals with the cowboys and hard characters he knew in the Bad Lands. "Every man," he declared in one of his essays,

> who has in him any real power of joy in battle knows that he feels it when the wolf begins to rise in his heart; he does not then shrink from blood or sweat or deem that they mar the fight; he revels in them, in the toil, the pain, and the danger, as but setting off the triumph.

The joy of battle could be found in warfare against primitive and inferior peoples. This feeling was first aroused in Roosevelt by the Indians, whom he saw with the eyes of a cowboy. He took the Western view, he confessed in 1886.

> I don't go so far as to think that the only good Indians are the dead Indians, but I believe nine out of every ten are, and I shouldn't like to inquire too closely into the case of the tenth. The most vicious cowboy has more moral principle than the average Indian.

Roosevelt's major historical work, *The Winning of the West*, which was written during his thirties, was an epic of racial conflict in which he described "the spread of the English-speaking peoples over the world's waste space" as "the most striking feature of the world's history." Only "a warped, perverse, and silly morality" would condemn the American conquest of the West. "Most fortunately, the hard, energetic, practical men who do the rough pioneer work of civilization in barbarous lands, are not prone to false sentimentality."

Roosevelt lauded the expansionist efforts of all the nations of western Europe. In September 1899 he declared at Akron:

> In every instance the expansion has taken place because the race was a great race. It was a sign and proof of greatness in the expanding nation, and moreover bear in mind that in each instance it was of incalculable benefit to mankind. . . . When great nations fear to expand, shrink from expansion, it is because their greatness is coming to an end. Are we still in the prime of our lusty youth, still at the beginning of our glorious manhood, to sit down among the outworn people, to take our place with the weak and craven? A thousand times no!

The Rough Rider was always ready for a foreign war, and did not lack the courage of his convictions; as his most discerning biographer, Henry Pringle, points out, he was a perennial volunteer. In 1886, braced at the encouraging prospect of a set-to with Mexico, he proposed to Cabot Lodge that he organize the "harum-scarum" riders of his ranch into a cavalry battalion. Nine years later, when Cleveland's quarrel with the British over the Venezuela boundary seemed likely to bring war, he was all jingo enthusiasm. Let American cities be bombarded and razed, he somewhat irrelevantly told a reporter for the New York *Sun*, rather than pay a dollar to any foe for their safety. War with England would certainly be followed by the conquest and annexation of Canada—a delightful prospect. "This country needs a war," he wrote to Lodge in December 1895, and when he was denounced by President Eliot of Harvard as a jingoist, he struck back at "the futile sentimentalists of the international arbitration type" who would bring about "a flabby, timid type of character which eats away the great fighting qualities of our race."

---

[4] It should be remembered also that his talents as a comedian were by no means slight.

A few years later he was pumping hard for the annexation of Hawaii, even at the risk of war with Japan. In June 1897, as Assistant Secretary of the Navy, he made a classic militaristic speech before the Naval War College in which he dwelt again on his pet theme of the superiority of military to pecuniary values. The most dangerous mood for the nation would be an over-pacific, not a warlike mood, he insisted. A wealthy nation "is an easy prey for any people which still retains the most valuable of all qualities, the soldierly virtues." All the "great masterful races have been fighting races."

> No triumph of peace is quite so great as the supreme triumphs of war. . . . We of the United States have passed most of our few years of national life in peace. We honor the architects of our wonderful material prosperity. . . . But we feel, after all, that the men who have dared greatly in war, or the work which is akin to war, are those who deserve best of the country.

A war with Spain, he assured a naval officer as the crisis over Cuba grew more acute, would be justified from two standpoints. First, both humanity and self-interest required interfering on behalf of the Cubans and taking another step in freeing America from "European domination." Secondly, there would be "the benefit done to our people by giving them something to think of which isn't material gain, and especially the benefit done our military force by trying both the Army and Navy in actual practice." The hesitancy of big business to launch upon a martial adventure at a time when prosperity was returning won Roosevelt's scorn. "We will have this war for the freedom of Cuba, in spite of the timidity of the commercial interests," he warned Mark Hanna.[5] Not long afterward the war began.

The Spanish War, Roosevelt believed, should be waged as aggressively as possible, and he urged that a flying squadron should be sent through Gibraltar at night to strike against Barcelona and Cádiz. Such counsels were ignored. But it was at Roosevelt's instance and without authorization from his superior, Secretary J. D. Long, that Admiral Dewey launched his attack upon the Spanish fleet in the Philippines. The extraordinary initiative Roosevelt took on this occasion has drawn sharp comment from historians; but to the chief actor himself there seemed nothing exceptionable in it. He never suffered from an over-developed sense of responsibility. Some years later he complained to Cecil Spring Rice that "our generals . . . had to grapple with a public sentiment which screamed with anguish over the loss of a couple of thousand men . . . a sentiment of preposterous and unreasoning mawkishness."

Once the fighting began, a desk job was too dull. To the despair of his friends and family—even John Hay, who thought this a "splendid little war," called him a *"wilder werwegener"* for leaving the Navy Department—Roosevelt went off to form a volunteer cavalry regiment, the famous Rough Riders. He chafed under training, fearing that the fighting would be over before the War Department delivered him to the front; but at last the great hour came; the Rough Riders reached Cuba and participated in several actions, including the so-called San Juan charge. Roosevelt was magnificent. "Are you afraid to stand up when I am on horseback?" he asked some laggards; and many years later he remembered how "I waved my hat and we went up the hill with a rush." ". . . I killed a Spaniard with my own hand," he reported to Lodge with pride—"like a Jackrabbit," was the expression he used to another. At the end came the supreme human profanity

---

[5] "The big financiers and the men generally who were susceptible to touch on the money nerve, and who cared nothing for national honor if it conflicted even temporarily with business prosperity, were against the war," he recalled in his *Autobiography*.

of his moment of triumph: the exhortation to "look at those damned Spanish dead"! Less than three years later he became President of the United States.[6]

2

It was a tortuous path that took Roosevelt to the executive chair. After serving three highly moral terms as a New York State "reform" assemblyman, he deserted the reform element during the presidential race of 1884 under Lodge's guidance, and threw his support to Blaine. Two years later he carried the Republican standard in a hopeless contest, the three-cornered New York City mayoralty campaign, in which he ran a weak third to Abram S. Hewitt and Henry George. President Harrison appointed him to the Civil Service Commission in 1889, where his zealous activity on behalf of the merit principle won him a nonpartisan reappointment from Cleveland. In 1895 he returned to New York to become president of the city's Board of Police Commissioners. At length Lodge's influence procured him the Assistant Secretaryship of the Navy under McKinley. He became a popular hero after his derring-do in the Spanish War, and was elected Governor of New York in 1898. There he proved troublesome to the Platt machine; the bosses welcomed a chance to kick him upstairs, and a combination of friends and enemies gave him the vice-presidential place on the McKinley ticket in 1900. Reluctant though he was to run for an office that seemed to promise only obscurity, Roosevelt campaigned effectively. His ultimate reward was the presidency.

Coming into the world under the best stand-pat auspices, Roosevelt had been indoctrinated with a conservatism that could be tempered only by considerable experience. His father, whom he described as "the best man I ever knew . . . a big powerful man with a leonine face, and his heart filled with gentleness for those who needed help or protection," was engaged in the glass-importing business and in banking. He held the conventional views of the big-business Republicans and had no truck with political reforms, although he engaged actively in philanthropies.

At Harvard, where J. Laurence Laughlin was preaching an extreme version of laissez-faire, Roosevelt recalled that he was exposed to orthodox canons. Beyond this he seems to have had few concrete ideas about economic policy; he admits freely that after twenty years of public life he came to the White House with only a slight background in economics. Given a college assignment on the character of the Gracchi, which could have led him to review one of the great social struggles of antiquity, he displayed, as he puts it, "a dull and totally idea-proof resistance." But the frigate and sloop actions between American and British ships during the War of 1812 fascinated him; his first historical work, begun during his senior year in college, was a loving and highly competent technical account of *The Naval War of 1812*.

---

[6] During his presidency Roosevelt showed greater restraint in the conduct of foreign policy than might have been expected. Although foreign policy remained a primary interest to him, he did not seek war. His three most significant acts—intervention in the Morocco crisis of 1905, mediation in the Russo-Japanese War, and the intrigue that led to acquisition of the Panama Canal Zone—were marked by considerable noise and a fine show of activity, but no long-range accomplishments from the standpoint of "national interest." His contribution to the settlement of the Morocco crisis, probably the most successful of his ventures, gained nothing for the United States and involved a serious risk of inciting animosity. Of his mediation in the Russo-Japanese War, Professor Samuel Flagg Bemis concludes that it "did some harm and no good to the United States." The intrigue with the Panamanian revolutionists, which brought the United States the Canal Zone on Roosevelt's terms—a source of great pride to him—has been condemned by most American historians who deal with it, on grounds of national expediency and international morality. At best it is conceded that he gained some months' time in constructing the canal, at the cost of adding tremendously to the United States' burden of ill will in Latin America.

Theodore Roosevelt, haranguing a political rally. A man of hectic action and explosive rhetoric, Roosevelt flayed away at a host of demons, from "the criminal rich" to reformers and other "members of the lunatic fringe." Because of his ability to explode in all directions at once, Hofstadter calls him "the master therapist of the middle class." (Courtesy of Brown Brothers.)

Roosevelt's determination to enter politics and become a member of "the governing class" was not inspired by a program of positive aims, but rather by a vague sense of dedication. Beyond a conviction that the pure in heart should participate more actively in politics, a disdain for purely material ends, and a devotion to the national State, one can find little deliberate ideology in the early Roosevelt. He summed up the greater part of his positive faith in a letter to his brother-in-law, Admiral William Cowles, April 5, 1896:

Although I feel very strongly indeed on such questions as municipal reform and civil service reform, I feel even more strongly on the question of our attitude towards the outside world, with all that it implies, from seacoast defense and a first-class navy to a properly vigorous foreign policy. . . . I belive it would be well were we sufficiently foresighted steadily to shape our policy with the view to the ultimate removal of all European powers from the colonies they hold in the western hemisphere.

One of the best indices of Roosevelt's place in the political spectrum was his attitude toward labor. The mid-eighties and the nineties were punctuated by hard-fought strikes. Since his own city and state were centers of the growing labor movement, he was in constant contact with organized labor pressure.

Early in his tenure in the New York Assembly Roosevelt was appointed to a commission to investigate tenement sweatshops in the New York City cigar industry. Shocked by the filthy conditions he found on his tour of inspection, he supported a bill, then considered dangerous and demagogic by his friends, designed to abolish tenement cigar-manufacturing—although he acknowledged the measure to be "in a certain sense . . . socialistic." Subsequently he voted for bills to limit the working hours of women and children in factories and for legislation dealing with industrial safety. Beyond this he would not go. His attitude toward other labor legislation won him a bad reputation in labor circles. His views at this time were well to the right of such liberal capitalists as Abram S. Hewitt and Mark Hanna. Not long after his first year in the legislature he wrote that it had been a bad year "because demagogic measures were continually brought forward in the interests of the laboring classes." Among these "demagogic" measures was one that Roosevelt was instrumental in blocking, requiring the cities of New York, Brooklyn, and Buffalo to pay their employees not less than two dollars a day or twenty-five cents an hour. Objecting to the cost it would impose on New York City, he characterized it as "one of the several score of preposterous measures that annually make their appearance purely for the purposes of buncombe." He also opposed bills to abolish contract convict labor, to raise the salaries of New York City police and firemen, and to improve enforcement of the state's eight-hour law; he indignantly fought a bill to set a twelve-hour limit on the work day of horse-car drivers in street-railway systems.

His next important contact with labor was as New York City's police commissioner. In this capacity he won applause from the labor and reform movements for getting many tenement houses condemned; he made a practice of touring the slums in the enlightening company of Jacob Riis; he began to read in the literature of housing and showed an interest in social work. But he clashed with labor time and again over his method of policing strikes. In 1895 he was quoted in the *Evening Post* as saying:

> We shall guard as zealously the rights of the striker as those of the employer. But when riot is menaced it is different. The mob takes its own chance. Order will be kept at whatever cost. If it comes to shooting we shall shoot to hit. No blank cartridges or firing over the head of anybody.

The industrial unrest stirred by the depression of the nineties was a constant torment to Roosevelt. When the notorious Bradley-Martin ball was planned in the midst of the pall of hunger and unemployment that hung over the city, the police commissioner, deeply irritated by the needless provocation the affair would give to the poor, remarked with felicitous irony: "I shall have to protect it by as many police as if it were a strike."

By 1899 Roosevelt had learned that he could assimilate some of the political strength of the labor movement (or other popular movements) by yielding to it in many practical details. As Governor he showed increasing flexibility in dealing with labor. He worked hard to get the legislature to pass a law against sweatshops; he was the first Governor ever to make a tour of the sweatshop districts; he consulted labor leaders regularly on matters affecting labor's interests; and, as though to measure the change in his philosophy, put his signature to just such a bill as he had fought most bitterly while in the Assembly, an eight-hour law for workers on government contracts. Although he identified himself closely with the authority of the State and the defense of property, he saw the justice and necessity of making authority benevolent and improving the condition of the people through social legislation. But any display of independent power by the masses, especially in the form of a strike, set off a violent reflex. He epitomized his philosophy during his governorship when he remarked of a current dispute: "If there should be a disaster at the Croton Dam strike, I'd order out the militia in a minute. But I'd sign an employer's liability law, too." He still displayed, as Howard L. Hurwitz describes it, "a trigger-like willingness to use troops.... His mind was a single track when it came to strikes, and that track always carried troops to the scene of the dispute."

Roosevelt followed events on the national scene with a similar impatience and showed the same penchant for sudden violence that appears again and again in this period of his life. At the time of the Haymarket affair he had written proudly from his ranch that his cowboys would like "a chance with rifles at one of the mobs.... I wish I had them with me and a fair show at ten times our number of rioters; my men shoot well and fear very little." The discontent of the nineties brought a new attack of hysteria. During the Pullman strike (when Mark Hanna was proclaiming before the outraged gentry of the Cleveland Union Club that "A man who won't meet his men half-way is a God-damn fool") Roosevelt wrote Brander Matthews: "I know the Populists and the laboring men well and their faults.... I like to see a mob handled by the regulars, or by good State-Guards, not over-scrupulous about bloodshed." He was among those who saw in the events of 1896 a threatened repetition of the French Revolution. "This is no mere fight over financial standards," he informed his sister in July.

> It is a semi-socialistic agrarian movement, with free silver as a mere incident, supported mainly because it is hoped thereby to damage the well to do and thrifty. "Organized labor" is the chief support of Bryan in the big cities; and his utterances are as criminal as they are wildly silly. All the ugly forces that seethe beneath the social crust are behind him.

He had not forgiven John P. Altgeld for pardoning three of the Chicago anarchists or for protesting when Cleveland sent federal troops to Illinois to break the Pullman strike. He now refused to meet Altgeld personally, because, he said, he might yet have to face him "sword to sword upon the field of battle." While Hanna was snorting at his Union Club friends: "There won't be any revolution. You're just a lot of damn fools," Roosevelt was reported as saying:[7]

> The sentiment now animating a large proportion of our people can only be suppressed as the Commune in Paris was suppressed, by taking ten or a dozen of their leaders out, standing ... them against a wall, and shooting them dead. I believe it will come to that. These leaders are plotting a social revolution and the subversion of the American Republic.

The passing of the silver crisis, the diversion of the Spanish War, and the return of prosperity did not entirely dissipate Roosevelt's worried mood. In 1899 he was still writing Lodge from Albany that the workers and small tradesmen in his state were in a mood of "sullen discontent." Brooks Adams came to visit him during the summer, and the two talked of the danger to the nation of the trade-union eight-hour movement and the possibility that the country would be "enslaved" by the organizers of the trusts. They were intrigued by the idea that Roosevelt might lead "some great outburst of the emotional classes which should at least temporarily crush the Economic Man."[8]

---

[7] Roosevelt heatedly denied having uttered these words, which were reported by Willis J. Abbot, an editor of the Democratic New York *Journal*.
[8] This was probably in reference to the distinction Adams had drawn two years earlier in *The Law of Civilization and Decay* between the imaginative, emotional, and artistic types of men and the economic man. Roosevelt wrote a significant review of this book for the *Forum*, January 1897.

Roosevelt was none too happy over McKinley's victory in 1896. Anything, of course, to beat Bryan and Altgeld; but he looked on McKinley as a weakling who could not be relied on in a "serious crisis, whether it took the form of a soft-money craze, a gigantic labor riot, or danger of a foreign conflict." The triumph of 1896 represented, after all, the victory of the type of moneybags he had always condemned, and he wrote sadly to his sister after attending the Republican celebration dinner that he was "personally realizing all of Brooks Adams' gloomiest anticipations of our gold-ridden, capitalist-bestridden, usurer-mastered future."

Because he feared the great corporations as well as the organized workers and farmers, Roosevelt came to think of himself as representing a golden mean. After he had sponsored, as Governor, a tax on public-service franchises, which alarmed the corporate interests, he was accused by the incredible Boss Platt of being too "altruistic" on labor and the trusts. Roosevelt replied that he merely wanted to show that "we Republicans hold the just balance and set our faces as resolutely against the improper corporate influence on the one hand as against demagogy and mob rule on the other." This was the conception that he brought to the presidency. He stood above the contending classes, an impartial arbiter devoted to the national good, and a custodian of the stern virtues without which the United States could not play its destined role of mastery in the world theater.

3

"Wall Street has desperate need of men like you," Brooks Adams had taunted in 1896, as he urged Theodore Roosevelt to hire himself out to the commercial interests. The thought of being such an outright mercenary was revolting to the Rough Rider, and he was doubtless uneasy in the presence of Adams's cynicism. But the more independent and statesmanlike role of stabilizer of the *status quo,* of a conservative wiser than the conservatives, appealed to him. It became his obsession to "save" the masters of capital from their own stupid obstinacy, a theme that runs consistently through his public and private writings from the time of his accession to the presidency. During his first term he was keenly aware, as Matthew Josephson remarks, that he was a "captive president" for whom it would be unwise to break the chains that bound him to the interests. "Go slow," Hanna advised him. "I shall go slow," the new President replied.[9]

The advisers to whom Roosevelt listened were almost exclusively representatives of industrial and finance capital—men like Hanna, Robert Bacon and George W. Perkins of the House of Morgan, Elihu Root, Senator Nelson W. Aldrich, A. J. Cassatt of the Pennsylvania Railroad, Philander C. Knox, and James Stillman of the Rockefeller interests. When his brother-in-law, Douglas Robinson, wrote from Wall Street to urge that he do nothing to destroy business confidence, Roosevelt answered:

> I intend to be most conservative, but in the interests of the corporations themselves and above all in the interests of the country, I intend to pursue cautiously, but steadily, the course to which I have been publicly committed . . . and which I am certain is the right course.

Toward the close of his first term Roosevelt suffered attacks of anxiety for fear that some of his policies had offended the interests, and late in 1903 he did his best to assure them that his intentions were honorable.[10] Although the

---

[9] The relationship between these two became increasingly cordial. In 1909 Philander C. Knox, asked whether he had ever witnessed an argument between them, answered that he had—just once. Roosevelt had been maintaining that the Grangers, the agrarian reformers of the seventies, were maniacs, Hanna that they were useful citizens.

[10] "The opposition to you among the capitalists is confined to a group of Wall Street and Chicago people,"

Democrats named a gilt-edged conservative candidate, Judge Alton B. Parker, Roosevelt held his own in business circles. Handsome donations poured into the treasure chest of the Republican National Committee from Morgan and Rockefeller corporations, from Harriman, Frick, Chauncey Depew, and George J. Gould. Roosevelt's opponent falsely accused him of having "blackmailed" the corporations and promising them immunity in return for their donations.[11] But Parker was overwhelmed at the polls. Roosevelt had convinced the people that he was a reformer and businessmen that he was sound.

A qualification is necessary: some business elements did fear and hate Theodore Roosevelt. And yet, by displaying their opposition, they and the conservative newspaper editors unwittingly gave him the same kind of assistance that the du Ponts later gave to Franklin D. Roosevelt: they provided the dramatic foil that enabled him to stay on the stage plausibly as a reformer. His attitudes toward many public questions were actually identical with those of the shrewder capitalists. This was particularly true where labor was concerned, and it was illustrated by Roosevelt's compromise of the formidable anthracite strike of 1902. The frame of mind of old-fashioned capitalists was expressed during that dispute by George F. Baer when he said that "the Christian men whom God in his infinite wisdom has given the control of the property interests of this country" were alone qualified to look after the welfare of the workingman. The attitude of the more statesmanlike business interests was represented by Morgan and Hanna, both of whom pressed the mine operators to accept the method of arbitration proposed by Roosevelt and Root.[12] Throughout the controversy the President fumed at the obstinacy of the mineowners. ". . . From every consideration of public policy and of good morals they should make some slight concession," he wrote to Hanna. And: "The attitude of the operators will beyond a doubt double the burden on us while standing between them and socialistic action." "I was anxious," he recalled years afterward, "to save the great coal operators and all of the class of big propertied men, of which they were members, from the dreadful punishment which their own folly would have brought on them if I had not acted. . . ."

Roosevelt worried much about the rise of radicalism during his two administrations. The prominence of the muckraking literature (which was "building up a revolutionary feeling"), the growing popularity of the socialist movement ("far more ominous than any populist or similar movements in times past"), the emergence of militant local reformers like La Follette, the persistent influence of Bryan—such things haunted him. "I do not like the social conditions at present," he complained to Taft in March 1906:

> The dull, purblind folly of the very rich men; their greed and arrogance . . . and the corruption in business and politics, have tended to produce a very unhealthy condition of excitement and irritation in the popular mind, which shows itself in the great increase in the socialistic propaganda.

Lodge reassured him, June 2, 1903, "but even in Wall Street there is a large body of men who are with you, and I do not find here on State Street any manifest hostility on account of your merger [Northern Securities] case, rather the contrary."
Senator Orville Platt of Connecticut found late in the same year that the opposition to Roosevelt came "from both ends of the party—from the moneyed influences in Wall Street and the agitators in the labor movement —one as much as the other."

[11] According to Oswald Garrison Villard's report in *Fighting Years*, Henry Clay Frick suffered from the delusion that Roosevelt had made positive commitments in return for the financial support he solicited. "He got down on his knees before us," Frick remembered angrily. "We bought the son of a bitch and then he did not stay bought!"

[12] "If it had not been for your going in the matter," Roosevelt said in thanking Morgan, "I do not see how the strike could have been settled at this time."

His dislike of "the very rich men" caused Roosevelt to exaggerate their folly and forget how much support they had given him, but his understanding of the popular excitement and irritation was keen, and his technique for draining it into the channels of moderate action was superb. (His boxing instructors had taught him not to charge into his opponents' punches but to roll with them.) In 1900 Bryan had puffed about the trusts, and Roosevelt responded in 1902 with an extremely spectacular anti-trust prosecution—the Northern Securities case. Between 1904 and 1906 Bryan agitated for government ownership of railroads, and Roosevelt answered by supporting the Hepburn bill, which made possible the beginnings of railroad rate-control by the Interstate Commerce Commission. During the fight over the bill he wrote to Lodge to deplore the activities of the railroad lobbyists: "I think they are very short-sighted not to understand that to beat it means to increase the danger of the movement for government ownership of railroads." Taking several leaves from Bryan's book, Roosevelt urged upon Congress workmen's compensation and child-labor laws, a railway hour act, income and inheritance taxes, and a law prohibiting corporations from contributing to political parties; he turned upon the federal courts and denounced the abuse of injunctions in labor disputes; he blasted dishonesty in business with some of the showiest language that had ever been used in the White House. Only a small part of his recommendations received serious Congressional attention, and in some instances —especially that of the Hepburn bill—his own part in the making of legislation was far more noteworthy for readiness to compromise than to fight against the conservative bosses of his party. But his strong language had value in itself, not only because it shaped the public image of him as a fighting radical, but because it did contribute real weight to the sentiment for reform. His baiting of "malefactors of great wealth" and the "criminal rich" also gave his admirers the satisfaction of emotional catharsis at a time when few other satisfactions were possible.

In retrospect, however, it is hard to understand how Roosevelt managed to keep his reputation as a strenuous reformer. Unlike Bryan, he had no passionate interest in the humane goals of reform; unlike La Follette, no mastery of its practical details. "In internal affairs," he confessed in his *Autobiography*, "I cannot say that I entered the presidency with any deliberately planned and far-reaching scheme of social betterment." Reform in his mind did not mean a thoroughgoing purgation; it was meant to heal only the most conspicuous sores on the body politic. And yet many people were willing and eager to accept his reform role at its face value. Perhaps the best proof that the Progressive mind was easy to please is his reputation as a trust-buster. Let it serve as an illustration:

Roosevelt became President without any clearly defined ideas or strong principles on the question of big business. As early as August 7, 1899 he had written H. H. Kohlsaat that the popular unrest over trusts was "largely aimless and baseless" and admitted frankly that he did not know what, if anything, should be done about them. But, as we have seen, he distrusted and despised the ignoble "bourgeois" spirit in politics. While bigness in business frightened the typical middle-class citizen for economic reasons, it frightened Roosevelt for political reasons. He was not a small entrepreneur, worrying about being squeezed out, nor an ordinary consumer concerned about rising prices, but a big politician facing a strong rival in the business of achieving power. He did not look forward to breaking up bigness by restoring competitive conditions. He did not have, in short, the devotion of the small man to small property that won the sympathy of such contemporaries as Brandeis, La Follette, and Wilson. Bigness in business filled him with foreboding because it presaged a day when the United States might be held in thrall by those materialistic interests he had always held in contempt, a "vulgar tyranny of mere wealth." Anti-trust action seems to have been to him partly a means of satisfying the popular demand to see the government flail big business, but chiefly a threat to hold over business to compel it to accept regulation. And regulation, not destruction, was his solution for the trust problem. Psychologically he identified himself with the authority of the State, and jealously projected his own pressing desire for "mastery" into the trust problem. The trusts must never be allowed to grow stronger than the State; they must yield to its superior moral force.

From the beginning Roosevelt expressed his philosophy quite candidly—and it is this that makes his reputation as a trust-buster such a remarkable thing. On December 2, 1902 he informed Congress:

> Our aim is not to do away with corporations; on the contrary, these big aggregations are an inevitable development of modern industrialism, and the effort to destroy them would be futile unless accomplished in ways that would work the utmost mischief to the entire body politic.... We draw the line against misconduct, not against wealth.

He repeated this theme again and again. At the beginning of his second term he declared: "This is an age of combination, and any effort to prevent all combination will be not only useless, but in the end vicious, because of the contempt for law which the failure to enforce law inevitably produces."

In his *Autobiography* Roosevelt argued with brilliant historical insight for his thesis that regulation rather than dissolution was the answer:

> One of the main troubles was the fact that the men who saw the evils and who tried to remedy them attempted to work in two wholly different ways, and the great majority of them in a way that offered little promise of real betterment. They tried (by the Sherman-law method) to bolster up an individualism already proved to be both futile and mischievous; *to remedy by more individualism the concentration that was the inevitable result of the already existing individualism.* They saw the evil done by the big combinations, and sought to remedy it by destroying them and restoring the country to the economic conditions of the middle of the nineteenth century. This was a hopeless effort, and those who went into it, although they regarded themselves as radical progressives, really represented a form of sincere rural toryism....
>
> On the other hand, a few men recognized that corporations and combinations had become indispensable in the business world, that it was folly to try to prohibit them, but that it was also folly to leave them without thoroughgoing control.... They realized that the government must now interfere to protect labor, to subordinate the big corporation to the public welfare, and to shackle cunning and fraud exactly as centuries before it had interfered to shackle the physical force which does wrong by violence....

Roosevelt did, of course, engage in a few cleverly chosen prosecutions which gave substance to his talk about improving the moral code of the corporations. The prosecution of the Northern Securities Company in 1902, near the beginning of his first term, was his most spectacular effort.

The Northern Securities holding company, organized by James J. Hill, J. P. Morgan, and others, had established a gigantic railroad monopoly in the Northwest, embracing the Northern Pacific, the Great Northern, and the Chicago, Burlington, & Quincy railroads. The roads involved had been very much in the public eye because of an extremely bitter and well-publicized rivalry between Hill and E. H. Harriman. And yet the monopoly was anything but a vital concern in the life of the business community or the affairs of the House of Morgan. To prosecute it was a brilliant stroke of publicity that could hardly have been resisted even by a more conservative politician.[13]

Nevertheless, the announcement of the Northern Securities case caused a real shock in the ranks of big business and brought Morgan himself bustling down to Washington with Senators Depew and Hanna to find out if the President was planning to "attack my other interests." He was told that this would happen only if "they have done something that we regard as wrong."

Roosevelt was never keen to find wrongdoing among the trusts. "As a matter of fact," he admitted privately toward the close of his presidential career, "I have let up in every case where I have had any possible excuse for so doing." A few outstanding cases were tried during his second term—after he had weathered the trial of re-election with the help of large donations from business—but even such obvious subjects of anti-trust action as Standard Oil and the American Tobacco Company were left untouched. There was a hundred times more noise than accomplishment. Historians have often remarked that Taft's administration brought ninety anti-trust proceedings in four years, while Roosevelt brought only fifty-four in seven years. The most intense and rapid growth of trusts in American business history took place during Roosevelt's administrations.

The ambiguity that can be seen in his trust policies came naturally and honestly to Theodore Roosevelt. In his early days it had always been his instinct to fight, to shoot things out with someone or something—imaginary lovers of his fiancée, Western Indians, Mexicans, the British navy, Spanish soldiers, American workers, Populists. But before he became President he had learned that an ambitious politician must be self-controlled and calculating. His penchant for violence, therefore, had to be discharged on a purely verbal level, appeased by exploding in every direction at once. The straddle was built like functional furniture into his thinking. He was honestly against the abuses of big business, but he was also sincerely against indiscriminate trust-busting; he was in favor of reform, but disliked the militant reformers. He wanted clean government and honest business, but he shamed as "muckrakers" those who exposed corrupt government and dishonest business. (Of course, he was all in favor of the muckrakers' revelations—but only if they were "absolutely true.") "We are neither for the rich man nor the poor man as such," he resounded in one of his typical sentences, "but for the upright man, rich or poor." Such equivocations are the life of practical politics, but while they often sound weak and halting in the mouths of the ordinary politician, Roosevelt had a way of giving them a fine aggressive surge.

Roosevelt had a certain breadth and cultivation that are rare among politicians. He read widely and enthusiastically, if not intensely, remembered much, wrote sharply at times and with a vivid flair for the concrete. He had generous enthusiasms. He invited Booker T. Washington to the White House, elevated Holmes to

---

[13] It is possible that McKinley might have undertaken such a prosecution had he lived. Hanna, who was as usual calm about the whole affair, refused to intercede: "I warned Hill that McKinley might have to act against his damn company last year. Mr. Roosevelt's done it. I'm sorry for Hill, but just what do you gentlemen think I can do?"

The prosecution, technically successful, did not restore competition. It is illuminating that Roosevelt, when he heard the news of the Supreme Court's decision in the Northern Securities case, proclaimed it "one of the great achievements of my administration. . . . The most powerful men in this country were held to accountability before the law." As Mr. Justice Holmes maliciously pointed out in his dissenting opinion, this was precisely what had not happened, for the Sherman Act logically required criminal prosecution of Messrs. Morgan, Harriman, Hill, and others involved in the company. Roosevelt never forgave Holmes.

the Supreme Court, and gave Edwin Arlington Robinson a political sinecure. Thoughtful and cultivated men found him charming, and it is hard to believe that this was merely because, as John Morley said, he was second in interest only to Niagara Falls among American natural phenomena. Yet those who knew him, from shrewd political associates like Root to men like Henry Adams and John Hay and Cecil Spring Rice, refused to take him altogether seriously as a person. And rightly so, for anyone who today has the patience to plow through his collected writings will find there, despite an occasional insight and some ingratiating flashes of self-revelation, a tissue of philistine conventionalities, the intellectual fiber of a muscular and combative Polonius. There was something about him that was repelled by thoughtful skepticism, detachment, by any uncommon delicacy; probably it was this that caused him to brand Henry James and Henry Adams as "charming men but exceedingly undesirable companions for any man not of strong nature," and to balk at "the tone of satirical cynicism which they admired." His literary opinions, which he fancied to have weight and importance and which actually had some influence, were not only intolerably biased by his political sentiments but, for all his proclaimed robustiousness, extremely traditional and genteel. Zola, for example, disgusted him with his "conscientious descriptions of the unspeakable"; Tolstoy he disliked because he preached against both marriage and war, and *The Kreutzer Sonata* he considered a "filthy and repulsive book"; Dickens, who did not like America, was no gentleman; Gorki, who came to the United States with a woman who was not his legal wife, was personally immoral, like so many Continentals, and in politics a "fool academic revolutionist."

The role in which Roosevelt fancied himself was that of the moralist, and the real need in American public life, he told Lincoln Steffens, was "the *fundamental fight for morality.*" Not long before leaving Washington he predicted to Ray Stannard Baker that economic questions —the tariff, currency, banks—would become increasingly important, but remarked that he was not interested in them. "My problems are moral problems, and my teaching has been plain morality." This was accurate enough; Roosevelt's chief contribution to the Progressive movement had been his homilies, but nothing was farther from his mind than to translate his moral judgments into social realities; and for the best of reasons: the fundamentally conservative nationalist goals of his politics were at cross-purposes with the things he found it expedient to say, and as long as his activity was limited to the verbal sphere the inconsistency was less apparent.

His mind, in a word, did not usually cut very deep. But he represented something that a great many Americans wanted. "Theodore Roosevelt," said La Follette caustically, "is the ablest living interpreter of what I would call the superficial public sentiment of a given time, and he is spontaneous in his reactions to it." What made him great, commented Medill McCormick, was that he understood the "psychology of the mutt." While Bryan had been able to do this only on a sectional basis, Roosevelt spoke the views of the middle classes of all parts of the country, and commanded the enthusiastic affection of people who had never walked behind a plow or raised a callus. He had a special sense for the realities they wished to avoid; with his uncanny instinct for impalpable falsehoods he articulated their fears in a string of plausible superficialities. The period of his ascendancy was a prosperous one, in which popular discontent lacked the sharp edge that it had had when Bryan rose to prominence. Although the middle classes, which contributed so much to the strength of progressivism, were troubled about the concentration of power in political and economic life and the persistence of corruption in government, it is doubtful that many middle-class men would have been more willing than Roosevelt to face the full implications of an attempt to unravel the structure of business power, with the attendant risk of upsetting a going concern. The general feeling was, as Roosevelt wrote Sir George Trevelyan in 1905, that "somehow or other we shall have to work out methods of controlling the big corporations *without* paralyzing the energies of the business community."

This sentence is characteristic of the essentially negative impulses behind Roosevelt's political beliefs. It was always: We shall have to do this in order to prevent that. Did he favor control of railroad rates more because he was moved to correct inequities in the existing tolls or because he was afraid of public ownership? Did he force the mine operators to make a small concession to their employees because he bled for the men who worked the mines or because he feared "socialistic action"? Did he advocate workmen's compensation laws because he had a vivid sense of the plight of the crippled wage earner or because he was afraid that Bryan would get some votes? "There were all kinds of things of which I was afraid at first," he had said of his boyhood, ". . . but by acting as if I was not afraid I gradually ceased to be afraid." But did he lose his fears, or merely succeed in suppressing them? Did he become a man who was not afraid, or merely a man who could act as though he was not afraid? His biographer Henry Pringle has pointed out how often he actually underwent attacks of anxiety. In his anxieties, in fact, and in the very negative and defensive quality of his progressivism, may be found one of the sources of his political strength. The frantic growth and rapid industrial expansion that filled America in his lifetime had heightened social tensions and left a legacy of bewilderment, anger, and fright, which had been suddenly precipitated by the depression of the nineties. His psychological function was to relieve these anxieties with a burst of hectic action and to discharge these fears by scolding authoritatively the demons that aroused them.

Hardened and trained by a long fight with his own insecurity, he was the master therapist of the middle classes.

4

Of Taft, whom he chose as his successor, Roosevelt said revealingly to Gilson Gardner: "It is true he has never originated anything that would savor of progressiveness, but he has been close enough to this Administration to know what it stands for." Taft, however, could not mold public opinion, nor run with the hare and hunt with the hounds in the Roosevelt manner. When the ex-President returned in 1910 from his self-imposed exile to Africa, he found the Republican insurgents, who had never broken so far out of line, growing bold enough to challenge Taft for control of the party. "The Administration," he complained to Nicholas Longworth, July 11, 1910, "has certainly wholly failed in keeping the party in substantial unity, and what I mind most is that the revolt is not merely among the party leaders, but among the masses of the people."[14]

Roosevelt was too young to cease to care about his reputation or to abandon political ambitions. With his customary quickness he perceived that the Progressive impulse had not yet reached its high-water mark. Starting with his famous "New Nationalism" speech of August 1910, he began to present himself as a "new" political personality. The "New Nationalism" was a transparent amalgam of the old Roosevelt doctrines with some of the more challenging Progressive ideas. Democratic ends, Roosevelt proclaimed, must now be sought through Hamiltonian means. A strong, centralized State, extended governmental interference in economic life, freedom of politics from con-

[14] La Follette remarked in his *Autobiography* that the Progressive movement in the Republican Party made greater headway in Taft's first two years than in Roosevelt's two terms. "This," he concluded, "was largely due to the fact that Taft's course was more direct, Roosevelt's devious."

cern for special interests—these were to be the main lines of development. Specifically Roosevelt endorsed the initiative, referendum, and recall, popular election of Senators, and direct primaries. He shocked conservatives by assailing the federal judiciary for obstructing the popular will, and advocated that decisions of state courts nullifying social legislation should be subject to popular recall. He supported compensation laws, limitation of the hours of labor, a graduated income tax, inheritance taxes, physical evaluation of railroad properties to enforce "honest" capitalization, and government supervision of capitalization of all types of corporations in interstate commerce.

Democracy, Roosevelt proclaimed, must be economic, not merely political. And labor? He echoed Lincoln: "Labor is the superior of capital and deserves much the higher consideration." "I wish to see labor organizations powerful," he added. But in the language of the old Roosevelt he made it clear that as they became powerful they must, like the big corporations, accept regulation by the State.

Among these proposals there were only a few things that Roosevelt had not endorsed before, and nothing for which others had not worked for at least ten years, but an appearance of newness was provided by shearing off some of the familiar Roosevelt equivocations and intensifying his paternalistic nationalism. Elihu Root found the new Roosevelt suspect: "I have no doubt he thinks he believes what he says, but he doesn't. He has merely picked up certain ideas which were at hand as one might pick up a poker or chair with which to strike." In a moment of candor Roosevelt himself declared that he was still working along familiar strategic lines. "What I have advocated," he said in 1910, ". . . is not wild radicalism. It is the highest and wisest kind of conservatism."[15]

Roosevelt's practical aims were probably centered at first on the election of 1916. Professor George Mowry suggests that he anticipated Republican defeat in 1912 and would have been happy to see Taft bear the brunt of it, leaving himself to come back to the White House at the head of a rejuvenated and reunited party in 1916, when he would be only fifty-eight. If these were his plans, he altered them as the Progressive movement came to the boiling-point.

Robert M. La Follette, by virtue of his accomplishments in Wisconsin and in the Senate, seemed the natural leader of the Progressives as they rallied for the 1912 convention. Roosevelt himself, who had written privately in 1908 of "the La Follette type of fool radicalism," praised him in 1910 for having made of his home state "an experimental laboratory of wise governmental action in aid of social and economic justice." La Follette seemed to have an excellent chance of capturing the nomination if he could get Roosevelt's backing. He subsequently charged that he had had a definite promise from Roosevelt. Although proof has never been offered, this much is certain: Roosevelt did at first give the Progressive leader informal encouragement, but withheld positive public endorsement and at length sapped the vitality of the La Follette movement by refusing to disavow his own candidacy. La Follette's friends grew indignant. "You would laugh if you were in this country now," wrote Brand Whitlock to a friend abroad, December 5, 1911, "and were to see how the standpatters are trying to bring [Roosevelt] out as a candidate for President again, in order to head off La Follette, who is a very dangerous antagonist to Taft." "The Colonel," Lincoln Steffens reported a few weeks later, "is mussing up the whole Progressive movement with his 'To be or not to be.'"

Roosevelt's seeming indecision helped to strangle the La Follette boom. By January 1912, outstanding Progressives like the Pinchots and Medill McCormick had switched to Roosevelt. In February, Fighting Bob, ill, harassed, and worried, suffered a momentary breakdown.

---

[15] On Roosevelt's Confession of Faith before the 1912 Progressive convention Frank Munsey made the charming comment: "While splendidly progressive it is, at the same time, amply conservative and sound."

Soon afterward, in response to a carefully prearranged "solicitation" by seven Progressive Governors, the ex-President threw his hat in the ring and the La Follette boom collapsed entirely. One of the most interesting comments on the mentality of the Progressives is the fact that most of them turned to Roosevelt not only without resentment but enthusiastically, and when he bolted the Republican convention to form a third party, followed him with a feeling of fervor and dedication that had not been seen since 1896. As William Allen White later recalled, "Roosevelt bit me and I went mad."[16]

Having aroused the hopes of the Progressives and having side tracked their most effective leader, Roosevelt went on to use their movement for the purposes of finance capital. One of several practical advantages that Roosevelt had over La Follette was his ability to command the support of men of great wealth. Most important among these was George W. Perkins, ex-partner in the House of Morgan, director of International Harvester, and organizer of trusts. Perkins belonged to that wing of business which was aroused by Taft's more vigorous anti-trust policy, especially by the prosecution of so vital a Morgan concern as the United States Steel Corporation.[17] He was among those who therefore preferred Roosevelt to Taft or La Follette; this preference was shared by Frank A. Munsey, the influential publisher, a large stockholder in United States Steel. Perkins and Munsey pressed Roosevelt to run, later supplied, according to the revelations of the Clapp committee, over $500,000 to his campaign, and spent even larger sums in indirect support. When Roosevelt failed to win the Republican nomination, they spurred him on to form a new party, Munsey with the grand promise: "My fortune, my magazines, my newspapers are with you." To the bitter disappointment of Progressives like Amos Pinchot, Perkins forced upon the Progressive platform a plank stating the Perkins-Roosevelt approach to the trust problem.[18]

The strong showing of the Progressives in the election—Roosevelt ran second to Wilson and almost 700,000 votes ahead of Taft—promised much for the future. But Roosevelt soon abandoned the movement. It would be impossible, he asserted, to hold the party together; there were "no loaves and fishes." Four years later when a forlorn group of Progressives again tendered him a nomination, he spurned it and tossed them a final insult by suggesting that they name his friend Henry Cabot Lodge, whose principles, if any, were thoroughly reactionary.

Roosevelt's attempt to promote Lodge was prompted by the fact that he had lost interest in the domestic aspects of the Progressive movement. War was now raging in Europe, and the colonel had little regard for the notions of foreign policy that prevailed among the more sentimental adherents of the third party. As he wrote to Lodge in the spring of 1917, the typical American Progressive was like his lib-

---

[16] It is interesting that as late as October 27, 1911 Roosevelt could have written to Hiram Johnson: "I have no cause to think at the moment that there is any real or widely extended liking for or trust in me among the masses of the people." Events proved him wrong, but it may be that this projection of dislike and distrust upon the people represented the way he imagined they might be expected to feel about him.

[17] In an address on "The Sherman Law," delivered to the Economic Club of Philadelphia in 1915, Perkins scourged Taft bitterly for having betrayed the moderate plank on trusts prepared by Roosevelt for Taft's 1908 campaign and expounded the Roosevelt-Perkins approach to the trust question.

[18] When Pinchot complained to Roosevelt about Perkins's influence in the party, Roosevelt assured him that the matter of the trust plank was "utterly unimportant" and attributed the Progressive Party's defeat to its being "too radical." At last Pinchot aired in public the rift in the party over Perkins and blamed Roosevelt for the collapse of the movement. "When I spoke of the Progressive party," replied Roosevelt to Pinchot, "as having a lunatic fringe, I specifically had you in mind."

eral brother in England—"an utterly hopeless nuisance because of his incredible silliness in foreign affairs."

Although in nominal retirement at the outbreak of the World War, Roosevelt was still in search of excitement. At first he seems to have been torn between the impulses of the hardened realist who could look upon the affairs of nations with detachment, and those of the strategist and man of action who would welcome an opportunity to engage the nation's power and see some fighting. His initial remarks on the war, although calm and impartial, were more friendly to Germany than prevailing opinion in the United States. Concerning the invasion of Belgium, which shocked so many Americans, he patiently explained that "When giants are engaged in a death wrestle, as they reel to and fro they are certain to trample on whomever gets in the way of either of the huge straining combatants." Disaster would have befallen Germany if she had not acted so resolutely in Belgium. The Germans had proved themselves "a stern, virile, and masterful people." The sole policy of the United States should be to protect her own interests and "remain entirely neutral."

As late as October 11, 1914, Roosevelt voiced a "thrill of admiration for the stern courage and lofty disinterestedness which this great crisis laid bare" in the souls of the German people, and hoped that the American public would show similar qualities should the need arise. To cripple Germany or reduce her to impotence, he warned, would be "a disaster to mankind."

Yet the preceding August Roosevelt had written to Stewart Edward White that if Germany should win, "it would be only a matter of a very few years before we should have to fight her," adding that he would consider it "quite on the cards to see Germany and Japan cynically forget the past and join together against the United States and any other power that stood in their way." By early 1915 this point of view had made its way into his public statements as he fulminated against Wilson for "supine inaction"—and for failing to help the Belgians! Thenceforth he devoted himself to baiting pacifists and scolding at Wilson's neutrality policies. The American people themselves, he once complained to Lodge, "are cold; they have been educated by this infernal peace propaganda of the last ten years into an attitude of sluggishness and timidity."

Long before the United States entered the war, Roosevelt was thinking of participating. An army officer visiting him at Oyster Bay in January 1915 found him pacing the floor, protesting American inaction, asserting his eagerness to fight. The boyish demand for excitement—"You must always remember," Spring Rice had written a decade earlier, "that the President is about six"—was as strong in him as ever. He applied to the War Department for permission to let him raise a division, and, anticipating rejection, told Ambassador Jusserand that he would lead an American division to France if the French would pay for it. Wilson's refusal to commission him brought on a new fit of rage. Wilson was "purely a demagogue," "a doctrinaire," "an utterly selfish and cold-blooded politician always."

But the last exploit was denied him. Ravaged by the strenuous life, saddened by the loss of his son Quentin at the front, he grew suddenly old and became ill. Lodge journeyed to his bedside and the two schemed to spike Wilson's League of Nations. On January 6, 1919, Roosevelt died of a coronary embolism.

14

The End of a Dream

E. David Cronon

Woodrow Wilson still ranks as one of America's most complex and paradoxical statesmen. A conservative Democrat before he took office, he became an indefatigable Progressive reformer who engineered the most sweeping legislative program since the days of Alexander Hamilton. A humane, sensitive, lonely man who wanted "the people to love me," he felt a powerful need to guard his emotions "from painful overflow." While his intellectual tradition was British (he extolled the British system of government and admired English conservatives like Burke and Gladstone), his politics were rooted in his Southern heritage. A learned, eloquent champion of democracy, he nevertheless shared the anti-Negro prejudice that prevailed among white Americans of his generation; and as president he began a policy of discrimination against blacks in federal employment.

In many ways, his foreign policy was even more paradoxical. While he had a horror of violence, he was an evangelist in foreign affairs and left the United States with a policy of military interventionism—of moralistic, gunboat diplomacy—that was to influence American statesmen for decades to come. Moreover, in spite of the pacific liberalism he had learned from British intellectuals, he led the United States into World War I on a messianic crusade to save the world for democracy. And if his League of Nations was the sanest blueprint for world peace anybody had yet contrived, he conceded that "Armed force is in the background of this programme, but it is in the background, and if the moral force of the world will not suffice, physical force of the world shall." There were some—Sigmund Freud and Mahatma Gandhi, for example—who detected the contradictions in Wilson's plan for world peace. As Erik H. Erikson put it, Freud and Gandhi "saw in Wilson, who for a brief moment in history had become the embodiment of lasting peace, the symbol instead of man's deep hypocrisy as expressed in that combination of contradictory attitudes which . . . has proven to be the greatest danger to peace: the ceaseless perfection of armament paired with that righteous and fanatic kind of moralism which ever again can pivot from peace to war."*

By almost any criteria, Wilson is a hard man to assess. Here David Cronon takes us into his life, explains how his Presbyterian upbringing gave him a sense of destiny, evaluates his progressive reforms as president, and offers a thorough account of Wilson's foreign policy. While Cronon's portrait is very sympathetic, he nonetheless presents all sides of Wilson in the context of his times, allowing readers to draw their own conclusions about him.

Shortly before noon on March 4, 1921, a black limousine left the White House and headed up Pennsylvania Avenue toward the Capitol. For one of its two occupants, genial Warren G. Harding, the short trip was in the nature of a triumphal march. Passing along the flag-draped streets, Harding smiled and waved happily to the holiday crowds come to cheer his inauguration as the twenty-ninth president of the

---

* Erik H. Erikson, *Gandhi's Truth* (New York: W. W. Norton & Co., 1969), p. 436.
E. David Cronon, "Woodrow Wilson," in Morton Bordon (Ed.), *America's Ten Greatest Presidents*, © 1961 by Rand-McNally & Company, Chicago, pp. 207–31.

United States. With the easy assurance and limited vision of a small-town Rotarian, he was confident he knew what the American people expected of him—no idealistic reforms, no emotional crusades; simply "normalcy."

In contrast, the mood of his companion, retiring President Woodrow Wilson, was serious, even a trifle grim. Ailing in body, deeply discouraged over the rejection of his dream of American leadership in a League of Nations, for Wilson the ride was a painful duty, to be endured rather than enjoyed. Wilson, if not Harding, was keenly aware that these were the final moments of an administration more vigorous and constructive, more challenged and tested, yet also more bitterly controversial, than any since that of Abraham Lincoln.

To most of those who watched the presidential limousine pass that day on its way to the Capitol, the event symbolized merely the end of an administration. Only a scattered few perceived that they were also witnessing the end of a notable era in American life.

Thomas Woodrow Wilson (he stopped using the first name after graduating from college) is remembered as a great reforming president, an imaginative statesman who exercised skillful direction over Congress, greatly strengthened the powers of his office, and left for his successors an enviable example of responsible and vigorous presidential leadership. With his administration came the climax of the Progressive Movement—that remarkable burst of reform energy which sought to transform large areas of American life in the early years of the twentieth century. Yet ironically, up to the time Wilson entered political life—only a scant two years before he was elected president—he was an avowed conservative, who distrusted governmental regulation, feared the power of organized labor and the agrarian radicals in his party, and considered the office of the presidency almost hopelessly weak for really efficient government.

Wilson was the first Southerner since Zachary Taylor to occupy the White House, though he reached it via an unlikely northern route. Born at Staunton, Virginia, on December 28, 1856, he grew up in Georgia amidst the physical wounds of Civil War and the psychological scars of Reconstruction. Yet somehow he escaped the bitterness of spirit that afflicted so many Southerners of his generation. As a young man he could confess frankly, "*because I love the South, I rejoice in the failure of the Confederacy.*" In other respects, however, Wilson showed the distinctive influence of his Southern upbringing. He was characteristically Southern in his love of family and his chivalrous attitude toward women; he inherited the upperclass Southerner's paternalistic view of the Negro; he tended to romanticize Southern history. Wilson's preacher father, the Rev. Dr. Joseph Ruggles Wilson, instilled in his children a lasting faith in the fundamentals of the Presbyterian creed. On a daily diet of prayers and Bible reading, young Tommy Wilson grew up never doubting the existence of an unalterable moral law or the ultimate triumph of God's will. In later life he would undertake a reformer's role with almost messianic zeal, supremely confident that what he did was morally right, and thus by definition must in the end prevail. But Dr. Wilson also taught his children humor and tolerance and shared with them his love of books and his lively interest in politics. He was a stickler for precision in thought and speech. "Learn to think on your feet," he would insist. "Shoot your words straight at the target. Don't mumble and fumble." Good training, this, for a future president.

Wilson's undergraduate years at Princeton (where, incidentally, he heard *The Star Spangled Banner* for the first time) marked an important turning point in his life. He found the work hard but exciting, and quickly became fascinated by the study of government and politics. He read *The Federalist*, and discovered Aristotle, Burke, Bright, Macaulay, and Bagehot. His reading of the British political theo-

Woodrow Wilson and his wife in 1920. He was still recuperating from his near fatal stroke. "With Wilson's physical collapse," says Cronon, "came the collapse of his brave new world as well." (Courtesy of Bettmann Archive, Inc.)

rists, especially Bagehot, left Wilson ever after convinced of the superiority of British parliamentary government. Many years later, as president, he would attempt with considerable success to adapt some features of the British system to American conditions—by assuming more active leadership of Congress, by developing the caucus to promote party regularity, and by taking his case on major issues directly to the people.

While still an undergraduate, Wilson managed to publish several essays; one, an article on "Cabinet Government in the United States," appeared in the *International Review* after having duly impressed that august journal's associate editor, a young Boston intellectual named Henry Cabot Lodge. At the same time Wilson gained a measure of student fame as a debater. He dreamed of going into politics, and in the privacy of his room wrote out a number of calling cards: "Thomas Woodrow Wilson, Senator from Virginia."

After graduating from Princeton in 1879, Wilson had to break the unwelcome news to his family that he felt no call to the ministry. Instead, law seemed the logical path to a desired political career, but at the University of Virginia Law School he found that he was "most terribly bored" studying it. An unremunerative year of legal practice in Atlanta further convinced him that his future lay outside the courtroom. He resolved to become a professor, even though this would probably mean the end of any hope for an active political career. For the requisite graduate training, he went to the new Johns Hopkins University in Baltimore to study history and political science under the noted Herbert Baxter Adams. In 1885, even before receiving his degree, Wilson published his Ph.D. thesis, *Congressional Government*, a brilliant and widely-acclaimed analysis of the Federal government. As the title implies, Wilson argued that the real federal power lay with Congress, which he judged inefficient and irresponsible as compared with the British cabinet system. Strangely, in the light of his own later career, he wrote off the president as weak and unimportant, a virtual nonentity.

Wilson's elation over the book's success was, characteristically, tempered with a measure of doubt and disappointment. To his future wife, Ellen Axson, he confessed that he felt "shut out from my heart's *first*—primary—ambition and purpose, ... a statesmen's career."

> I have a strong instinct of leadership, an unmistakably oratorical temperament, and the keenest possible delight in affairs; and it has required very constant and stringent schooling to content me with the sober methods of the scholar and the man of letters. I have no patience for the tedious toil of what is known as "research"; I have a passion for interpreting great thoughts to the world; I should be complete if I could inspire a great movement of opinion, if I could read the experiences of the past into the practical life of the men of today and so communicate the thought to the minds of the great mass of the people as to impel them to great political achievements.

Whatever his doubts, Wilson quickly embarked upon a distinguished academic career: three years at the brand new Bryn Mawr College, where he was the entire department of history; two years at Wesleyan University, where he published probably his best scholarly book, *The State*; and then, in 1890, the return to Princeton as professor of jurisprudence and political economy. Back amidst the familiar haunts of his alma mater, he soon became the most popular lecturer on the campus and spoke increasingly to public groups around the country. Nor did he slacken his scholarly pursuits; over the next twelve years he published nine books and thirty-five articles. His prestige was such that he was offered and declined the presidency of a number of colleges and universities. Thus when the time came to choose a new president of Princeton in 1902, it was not surprising that the trustees considered only one name. Unanimously they voted to offer the post to Woodrow Wilson.

As the first lay president in Princeton's history, Wilson experienced both impressive success and humiliating defeat. Energetically he set about revising the curriculum and overhauling the antiquated administrative structure of the university; eloquently he persuaded the trustees to approve the expensive preceptorial method of teaching undergraduates in small groups; with contagious enthusiasm he invigorated both the faculty and the student body to a new sense of dedication. Within a remarkably short time his educational reforms had made Princeton a model for other institutions and had marked Wilson as one of the outstanding educators of his time. But several of Wilson's later proposals provoked mounting opposition from influential members of the faculty, the trustees, and a vocal segment of the alumni. The critics, it might be said, objected not so much to his goals as to what they regarded as his evasive tactics and his proud and unbending stubbornness. The details of the internecine battles during Wilson's last years at Princeton are less important than the serious defects they revealed in his character. In the face of defeat he showed himself curiously unable to compromise, unduly sensitive to criticism, willing to break completely with old friends who dared to oppose him. Honest differences over issues became bitter personal quarrels in which Wilson revealed a characteristic trait of viewing his own behavior in terms of a high moral crusade. Thus his largely personal feud with Dean Andrew F. West of the Graduate School became for Wilson a great battle for democratic education against the evil forces of privilege. By 1910 he had so alienated a majority of the trustees, as well as a sizable element of the faculty and alumni, that all concerned were relieved when he resigned to run for governor of New Jersey.

Wilson's foray into the political arena at the age of fifty-three, though spurred by his difficulties at Princeton, was not a sudden or completely unexpected development. He had never lost his early interest in government, and for some time past his generally orthodox views and his growing national reputation had brought him to the attention of a group of conservative politicians anxious to rehabilitate the shattered fortunes of the Democratic party. These men were impressed both by Wilson's forensic eloquence and by his thoroughly conservative approach to the great economic issues of the day: his defense of big business, his attacks on trade unions, his denunciation of government control, and his antipathy to radicalism in any form. As early as 1906, Colonel George Harvey, the editor of the conservative *Harper's Weekly*, had begun to groom Wilson as a potential Democratic presidential nominee. Few except perhaps Wilson took the idea seriously, however, and even Harvey realized that it would first be necessary to give his candidate some political experience, and get him more in the public eye. To this end, in 1910 Harvey persuaded the Democratic bosses in New Jersey that the scholarly and principled president of Princeton was the only candidate who could win the governorship for the somewhat tarnished state Democracy. Wilson received the nomination from a well-controlled convention on the first ballot, but only over the angry protests of the reformers in the party, who quite naturally assumed that he was to be only a respectable front for continued boss rule. Two months later he was governor by an impressive fifty thousand majority, after a brilliant campaign in which he had cut loose from his early conservative and boss support and had convinced suspicious New Jersey progressives that he was heart and soul one of them.

How to account for Wilson's rather abrupt conversion to progressivism at this time is a matter that has troubled observers then and since. Undoubtedly there was an element of expediency involved, for Wilson rightly saw that without the votes of the independents and progressives of the state he could not be elected. Yet for a personality as complex as Woodrow Wilson's, expediency is by no means the entire answer. Though he had received the nomination from the bosses, no one knew better than they that Wilson was no ordinary machine candidate. In fact he had stipulated that there must be no strings attached to his candidacy. A good share of Wilson's previous conservatism stemmed from sheer ignorance; he simply had not bothered to study carefully the issues that had been agitating the progressives for the past decade and more. As he struggled to formulate his position during the campaign in response to pointed queries from the reformers, he gradually and quite sincerely found himself agreeing with them. "We are not in the same America as we were ten years ago," he explained in one campaign speech. And another time: "I'll agree not to change my mind if someone with power to do so will guarantee that if I go to bed at night I will get up in the morning and see the world in the same way." By the end of the campaign he was excoriating in the bluntest terms the very boss system to which he owed his nomination.

Wilson's acts as governor soon captured the attention of much of the nation. He swiftly beat down the bosses and established his own leadership of the Democratic party in the state, and then proceeded to cajole or coerce a reluctant legislature into enacting a whole parcel of progressive reforms: a direct primary, corrupt-practices legislation, strict regulation of railroads and public utilities, and a workmen's compensation law. In less than a year progressives in the Democratic party were rallying to Wilson as the outstanding contender for the presidential nomination in 1912, and Wilson on his part was campaigning actively throughout the country, demanding stricter control of the trusts, tariff and banking reform, and an end to special privilege. His early conservative supporters now rapidly lost interest in Wilson's presidential prospects, with George Harvey, the original Wilson man, departing with an aggrieved public blast.

The details of the political infighting at the Democratic national convention in Baltimore in June, 1912, need not concern us here. It is enough to note that Wilson, after a slow and discouraging start against Speaker Champ Clark of the House of Representatives, finally managed to win the nomination on the forty-sixth ballot. As a result the Democrats could face the country with control of the party firmly in the hand of its progressive wing. Wilson's chances were immeasurably helped, moreover, by a deep split within the Republican party. The Republican Old Guard proceeded ruthlessly to renominate William Howard Taft over the anguished howls of the party's progressive faction, led by former President Theodore Roosevelt. Roosevelt and his partisans thereupon took to the field under the banner of a new Progressive party, pledged to enact a remarkably broad and advanced program of reform. Taft was hopelessly out of the running; his candidacy seemed designed chiefly to defeat Roosevelt. This, at any event, was its effect. For when the ballots were counted, Wilson had garnered a sweeping total of 435 electoral votes to Roosevelt's 88 and Taft's 8. The popular vote told another story, however. Wilson had managed to win only a little over six million out of nearly fifteen million cast. The vote was an emphatic mandate for progressivism, but it could hardly be construed as an unrestrained endorsement of Wilson's own program of reform, his call for a New Freedom.

Few presidents have entered office better able to serve the public interest than Woodrow Wilson. His previous political experience was limited, but already he had shown himself a leader of rare ability, imagination, and boldness. His equipment was first-class: a keen analytical mind, superb oratorical and literary skill, and a thorough understanding of history and the nature of government. Neither at the Democratic convention nor during the campaign had he been forced to make any embarrassing commitments to special interests that would limit his freedom of action. His stern Presbyterian conscience demanded that he serve *all* the American people, with understanding and justice. Wilson closed his inaugural address on a note of solemn consecration:

> This is not a day of triumph; it is a day of dedication. Here muster, not the forces of party, but the forces of humanity. Men's hearts wait upon us; men's lives hang in the balance; men's hopes call upon us to say what we will do. Who shall live up to the great trust? Who dares fail to try? I summon all honest men, all patriotic, all forward-looking men, to my side. God helping me, I will not fail them, if they will but counsel and sustain me!

During the campaign Wilson and his chief rival, Theodore Roosevelt, had given the country a spirited and enlightening debate over the nature and future course of progressivism. Roosevelt's program, known as the New Nationalism, called for vigorous action by the Federal government to regulate the national economy in the interest of the many rather than the few. He demanded a variety of laws to protect the less-favored classes in American life, especially workers and farmers. Roosevelt did not condemn big business as such, for he thought it often more efficient than small business, but he proposed to control it to whatever extent was necessary to protect the public interest. Even private monopoly—suitably regulated—might in some instances be desirable, or in any event inevitable, he conceded.

Wilson, on the other hand, was in 1912 still fundamentally a states' rights Democrat who feared excessive governmental power. Though he, too, was committed to the progressive ideal of social justice, he considered laws to aid farmers and workers as wrong in principle as tariffs and other subsidies for business. Roosevelt's proposal to regulate big business through a powerful trade commission seemed to Wilson merely a move to legalize and perpetuate monopoly. Aided by the counsel of Louis D. Brandeis, a leading progressive lawyer and student of the trust problem, Wilson argued that monopoly and special privilege must be destroyed if the nation were to prosper. There could be no effective political democracy without economic democracy, he warned; the situation required not Roosevelt's paternalism, but a return to truly free enterprise, a New Freedom. "I am fighting," Wilson asserted, "not for the man who has made good, but for the man who is going to make good—the man who is knocking and fighting at the closed doors of opportunity. There is no group of men big enough or wise enough to take care of a free people."

Once in the White House, Wilson moved energetically to translate the New Freedom into reality. No sooner was he inaugurated than he called a special session of Congress, and when the lawmakers assembled he went dramatically before them to urge an end to the system of high tariff protection for "infant" industries long since grown fat and sluggish with age. Not since John Adams had a president addressed Congress in person, but Wilson, well aware of the pitfalls of tariff reform, wanted from the first to achieve a close working relationship with the legislative branch, as well as to emphasize to the country his seriousness of purpose. Afterward, driving home, Mrs. Wilson remarked that his decision to break the old precedent was the sort of thing Theodore Roosevelt would have liked to do, had he only thought of it. "Yes," chuckled her husband, "I think I put one over on Teddy."

Wilson followed up his tariff message with a series of personal conferences with congressional leaders, both at the White House and in the hitherto rarely used President's Room at the Capitol. He even had a special telephone line installed so that he could reach wavering members quickly and directly. When the protection-minded Senate, buttressed by a swarm of lobbyists, threatened to sabotage the low tariff bill passed by the House, Wilson lashed out hard. "It is of serious interest to the country," he warned in a public statement, "that the people at large should have no lobby and be voiceless in these matters, while great bodies of astute men seek to create an artificial opinion and to overcome the interests of the public for their private profit." In the end the Senate gave in before the incessant presidential pressure and actually reduced the general level of rates of the House bill, chiefly by adding certain agricultural products to the free list. Though the Underwood-Simmons Tariff of 1913 was no free trade measure (it gave an average *ad valorem* protection of about 25 per cent as opposed to the more than 40 per cent average of the Payne-Aldrich Tariff of 1909), it was nevertheless the first significant tariff reform since the Civil War and was designed to put American industry into genuine competition with European manufactures. It contained, moreover, another important progressive reform, the first graduated income tax under the new Sixteenth Amendment. Rates were low and exemptions high, but a first step had been taken to democratize the nation's tax structure.

Even while he was guiding the tariff measure through Congress, Wilson was hard at work on a much more difficult task, reform of the nation's banking and currency system. Conservatives and progressives alike agreed that it was urgently necessary to do away with the existing disorganized banking system with its immobile reserves and inelastic money supply. But they disagreed profoundly over the nature and extent of the changes to be made. The banking community favored the creation of a powerful central bank with some fifteen regional branches, able to issue currency, hold reserves, and set discount rates, with the entire system controlled by member banks on the basis of capitalization. Advanced progressives, on the other hand, insisted that the Federal government, not the bankers, must control the banking structure and that the issuance of currency must be an exclusive governmental function.

Wilson had not studied the matter carefully before his election and had no fixed opinions as to specific details, other than his general laissez faire outlook and his conviction that some reform was badly needed. Accordingly, he was at first inclined to accept a plan presented by Representative Carter Glass of Virginia, a leading member of the House Banking Committee, for the establishment of a thoroughly decentralized system of reserve banks. Glass thought the system should be run by the bankers; Wilson suggested that it should at least be supervised by a Government board. The more advanced progressives in the party were aghast at the Glass plan, which they considered hardly a reform at all. They demanded instead that the Government control both the reserve banks and the issuance of currency. The dispute became so critical that for a time it threatened to wreck party unity and thus block any banking reform whatever. After seeking Brandeis' advice, Wilson decided that the Government must control the Federal Reserve Board and must alone issue currency, and thereafter he refused to retreat in the face of outraged cries from the bankers that this was rank socialism. When a group of prominent bankers came to the White House to argue for banker representation on the Federal Reserve Board Wilson asked bluntly: "Will one of you gentlemen tell me in what civilized country of the earth there are important government boards of control on which private interests are represented? Which of you gentlemen thinks the railroads should select members of the Interstate Commerce Commission?" To this the bankers prudently made no reply.

The passage of the Federal Reserve Act on December 23, 1913, was by all odds the most important domestic achievement of the Wilson administration, and it was due largely to Wilson's great skill in holding intact his party's ranks in Congress. The measure gave the United States a banking structure well geared to modern needs, combining private operation at the local level with suitable public control. The act also pioneered in providing the first significant national economic stabilizers: an elastic currency, flexible bank reserves, and centralized control over discount rates. Subsequent experience would suggest ways to improve the Federal Reserve system, but it would remain the heart of the nation's banking structure.

Tariff and banking reform constituted a major part of the New Freedom's drive to destroy monopoly and restore competition, by removing, as Wilson told Congress, "the trammels of the protective tariff" and requiring the banks to be "the instruments, and not the masters of business and individual enterprise."

Yet there remained the job of strengthening the anti-trust laws. Wilson had argued during the campaign that since most businessmen were honest and well-meaning all that was needed was to define and proscribe by law those evil practices that led to unfair competition and monopoly. He therefore threw his influence behind a number of proposals, which were soon combined in the Clayton bill in the House of Representatives. The measure prohibited a long list of unfair trade practices, forbade interlocking directorates and stock ownership, and, to satisfy organized labor, restricted the use of injunctions in labor disputes and declared that farm and labor organizations should not be considered as illegal combinations in restraint of trade when pursuing lawful objectives.

Many progressives, however, especially Roosevelt's followers but also some Democrats, protested that this approach was both inadequate and naive, that it was impossible to foresee and spell out in precise detail all the possible roads to monopoly. In time, their criticism had an effect on the President. Not long after the Clayton bill passed the House, Wilson reversed his campaign stand and swung over to the idea of a strong trade commission with the power to inquire into business practices and issue cease and desist orders against unfair conduct. Once converted, he worked zealously to overcome the opposition, with the result that in the fall of 1914 Congress passed both measures, the Federal Trade Commission Act and a somewhat weakened Clayton Act. The President's remarkable success in securing the adoption of his domestic program led a conservative Republican, Chauncey M. Depew, to observe with wonderment: "This man who was regarded as a pedagogue, a theorist, is accomplishing the most astounding practical results."

Wilson's decision to insist upon government control over the Federal Reserve system and his acceptance of a strong trade commission showed that the line between the New Freedom and the New Nationalism was becoming blurred. By the end of his first administration it had disappeared altogether. No doubt partly because it was politically expedient, but also because he sincerely came to believe in more advanced reforms, Wilson by the summer of 1916 had taken over and shepherded through Congress the major part of the Progressive party's platform of 1912. The list was impressive: a law improving maritime safety requirements and the working conditions of seamen; a system of Federal farm loan banks to provide farmers with cheap credit; larger self-government for the Philippines; a model workmen's compensation act for Federal employees; a law prohibiting child labor; the eight-hour day for railroad employees, long a primary labor objective; and a tariff commission to review tariff rates. And although his more conservative advisers had originally talked Wilson out of offering a Cabinet post to the militant reformer Louis D. Brandeis, Wilson in 1916 overjoyed progressives by naming Brandeis to the Supreme Court and then grimly stood by him while outraged conservatives and business spokesmen tried unsuccessfully to block his confirmation.

By the time of the presidential campaign of 1916 Wilson had succeeded not only in enacting the most significant progressive legislation the country had yet known, but in the process had also managed to remake the Democratic party into a vital, unified instrument of reform, with far-reaching consequences for American politics that would extend through the New Deal and the Fair Deal a generation later. The election of 1916 demonstrated how nearly the two major parties were divided on a progressive-conservative basis. Though Wilson also benefited from the peace issue, he attracted a substantial number of the progressive Republicans who in 1912 had followed Roosevelt, along with most of the labor and farm vote. His margin over the Republican candidate, Charles Evans Hughes, was narrow—9,129,606 popular votes to 8,538,221, and a majority of only 23 electoral votes—but it was significant that the President had gained nearly three million votes over his total in 1912.

"It would be the irony of fate," Wilson had remarked to a friend shortly before his inauguration in 1913, "if my administration had to deal chiefly with foreign affairs." Grim irony, indeed! For from the very beginning of his administration the new President had to contend with a succession of urgent and critical foreign problems the like of which the nation had never before experienced.

Wilson, like most Americans, had not paid much attention to foreign affairs before entering the White House; he much preferred to apply what he sometimes jokingly described as his single track mind to domestic problems. He had traveled abroad several times, but only to vacation in the quiet English countryside. Like most of his countrymen he scarcely comprehended the profound implications of the recent emergence of the United States as a full-fledged great power. But both Wilson and his first secretary of state, William Jennings Bryan, shared certain deeply held convictions that gave a distinctive character to their diplomacy. Both were moralists who were guided by what they thought was right rather than by what was merely expedient; both had a strong sense of an American mission to civilize and uplift the world; both regarded war with horror.

The evangelistic quality of Wilson's and Bryan's diplomacy was manifested in a number of ways: the negotiation of a treaty of apology with an indemnity of 25 million dollars to Colombia for Theodore Roosevelt's aggressive role in obtaining the Panama Canal Zone in 1903 (Roosevelt's friends in the Senate blocked ratification); repeal of the tolls exemption for American ships using the Canal because it violated British rights under the Hay-Pauncefote Treaty; Bryan's great effort to arrange "cooling off" treaties with some thirty nations for the conciliation of disputes; the well-meant attempts to look out for the interests of small Latin-American states. Bryan, for example, advised the Cuban government not to accept a Wall Street loan that was not in Cuba's long range interest, and turned down an offer from Haiti of exclusive American concession rights on the ground that this might lead to the exploitation of the Haitian people.

Unfortunately, there was another, much less happy, side to the Wilson administration's moralistic diplomacy. Old-fashioned imperialism and dollar diplomacy gave way before what might be described as a new "moral" imperialism, which seemed to have the same tools and results, if different objectives and rationale. In their zeal to help spread the American ideals of freedom and democracy, Wilson and Bryan intervened on an unprecedented scale in the internal affairs of the nations of Central America and the Caribbean. Their actions were partly motivated, it is true, by the need to protect the American interest in the nearly completed Panama Canal. But equally important was their fervent belief that the United States ought to help the people of these small countries achieve stability and democracy, to protect them both from foreign dangers and themselves. By 1916 Wilson's moral impulses had led him to meddle repeatedly and disastrously in Mexican affairs, to make Nicaragua into a virtual American protectorate, and to clamp full-scale military occupations on Haiti and the Dominican Republic. Latin Americans might be pardoned for failing to distinguish between gunboats sent to help them elect good men and gunboats sent to protect foreign concessions; but Wilson, for one, was satisfied that his intervention was guided by a high moral purpose. In a sense his Mobile address in 1913 renouncing any future American territorial ambitions and his vision of a Pan-American pact guaranteeing the political independence and territorial integrity of the nations of the Western Hemisphere foreshadowed the Good Neighbor Policy of a later president. In practice, however, Wilson's Latin-American diplomacy left a legacy of distrust and bitterness that would fester for years.

Wilson's difficulties with Latin America were only a preliminary to larger and more ominous problems. While Mrs. Wilson lay dying in the White House in the summer of 1914, a Serbian student assassinated the Austrian Archduke, and one by one the great nations of Europe drifted into war. From his wife's bedside on August 4, only two days before her death, the distraught President issued an official proclamation of neutrality, and followed it with an appeal to Americans to be impartial in thought as well as in deed. This, as it turned out, proved to be an unattainable goal.

Although the vast majority of Americans were strongly opposed to any active involvement in the war before 1917, this did not prevent them from hoping, in some cases quite loudly and belligerently, for the victory of one or the other of the opposing sides. As the conflict progressed probably a majority of the American people came to favor an Anglo-French victory, though there remained a substantial hard core of German sympathizers right down to the time the United States entered the war. There were a number of reasons for this preponderance of support for the Allies. Perhaps most important, many Americans, and this included the President and most of his advisers, were horrified at Germany's callous violation of Belgian neutrality and her ruthless submarine attacks against defenseless passenger ships. Consequently they were ready even without the stimulus of Allied propaganda to believe that the British and the French were fighting to preserve Western civilization. Germany, aggressive and expansive, seemed a potential threat to American interests and security, whereas the Allies did not. Moreover, as the United States gradually became an important arsenal of the Allies, providing both needed loans and vital war supplies, the American stake in an Allied victory grew accordingly. Before 1917, however, Americans from President Wilson down overwhelmingly hoped to stay out of the war and use their influence toward a just peace.

How, then, did the United States come to enter the war? The answer lies in Wilson's fight to protect some, but not all, American neutral rights. Like Jefferson and Madison before him, Wilson found himself caught between two powerful belligerents, neither of which was willing to permit legal abstractions to stand in the way of victory. Because he was at heart sympathetic to the Allies, Wilson protested but in the end acquiesced in the various British violations of American neutral rights at sea, restrictions that effectively choked off American trade with the Central Powers. At the same time he permitted the sale of raw materials and war supplies to the Allies, on the theory that such trade was open to all belligerents even though in practice British control of the sea denied Germany access to the American market. And although the Administration at first frowned on loans by American bankers to the belligerents, in 1915, when the Allies began to run out of ready cash to continue their profitable purchases in the United States, Wilson reversed himself and allowed the bankers to extend large credits. On the other hand, when the Germans sought to check the increasingly dangerous flow of war materiel from the United States to the Allies, using the only weapon available, the submarine, Wilson reacted angrily in defense of the right of Americans and American ships to travel in safety on the high seas. The compelling difference, in the eyes of the President and many Americans, was that British actions, while oppressive and illegal, did not involve loss of life or the destruction of property, while German torpedoes accomplished both with deadly effect.

The inauguration of the German submarine blockade of the British Isles in February, 1915, faced Wilson with a painful dilemma. On the one hand, he could tacitly accept this new violation of neutral rights just as he had acquiesced in the British blockade of the Central Powers, though this might in the end insure Germany's triumph. Or he could insist that Germany respect American rights to freedom of the seas, and risk having to fight for those rights if Germany refused. Either course would favor one or the other of the belligerents. The sinking without warning of the British liner *Lusitania* on May 7, 1915, with the loss of more than 1200 lives, including 128 Americans, shocked the President and led him to take a strong stand on behalf of the right of American citizens to travel in safety in the war zones. This in turn brought the first serious rift within the Administration, for Secretary of State Bryan resigned rather than sign the second strong *Lusitania* note. Bryan argued that Americans should be warned that they traveled on belligerent ships only at their own risk, and that Wilson's firm policy toward Germany would ultimately lead to war. The President and his new secretary of state, Robert Lansing, rejected this counsel, however, determined to force a change in German policy or else break diplomatic relations. In the end the Berlin government capitulated, agreeing to sink no more passenger ships without warning and without provision for the safety of crew and passengers.

Unhappily, this diplomatic victory proved to be short-lived. In the long run, as Bryan had predicted, Wilson found it impossible to protect American neutral rights from German violation without resorting to war, for the Germans ultimately refused to abandon the use of their most effective weapon against the ever-increasing flow of American war supplies to the Allies. Early in 1917 after Germany resumed unrestricted submarine warfare against all merchant shipping in the war zone, the President saw no alternative but to fight—ironically, for the right to be neutral.

Meanwhile, Wilson had prudently begun to strengthen the nation's defenses, winning reluctant congressional approval to reorganize and enlarge the Army and greatly expand the size and strength of the Navy. At the same time he made a number of attempts to end the conflict in Europe, for he wisely saw that the best hope of an enduring peace was to gain a settlement before either side succeeded in crushing the other. Twice the President sent his trusted adviser and confidant, Colonel Edward M. House, on a round of the belligerent capitals in Europe to explore the possibility of American mediation, but House found the European leaders unwilling to give up the thought of all-out victory. On both sides the interest in Wilson's proposals varied inversely with the fortunes of the armies in the field. Shortly after his re-election in 1916, the President made one last effort at a negotiated settlement, outlining in his famous "peace without victory" speech to the Senate the kind of settlement the United States favored. It must be, he declared, a peace of justice between equals, without indemnities or annexations, a peace that would insure freedom of the seas, limitation of armaments, and the right of freedom and self-government for captive peoples.

Germany's answer came a few days later when Berlin announced the resumption of unrestricted submarine warfare. The Germans, it was clear, still hoped to enjoy the spoils of a victor's peace, and were confident that their submarines could bring Britain to her knees before any effective American intervention. Reluctantly, Wilson severed diplomatic relations, still hoping desperately that war might be averted. But events were rapidly passing out of his control. Finally, after several American ships had been sunk with heavy loss of life and the intercepted Zimmermann note had revealed German plans for an anti-American alliance with Mexico, the President on April 2, 1917, went before a special session of Congress to request a declaration of war. Sadly but with moving eloquence he concluded:

It is a fearful thing to lead this great peaceful people into war, into the most terrible and disastrous of all wars, civilization itself seeming to be in the balance. But the right is more precious than peace, and we shall fight for the things which we have always carried nearest our hearts,—for democracy, for the right of those who submit to authority to have a voice in their own Governments, for the rights and liberties of small nations, for a universal dominion of right by such a concert of free peoples as shall bring peace and safety to all nations and make the world itself at last free. To such a task we can dedicate our lives and our fortunes, everything that we are and everything that we have, with the pride of those who know that the day has come when America is privileged to spend her blood and her might for the principles that gave her birth and happiness and the peace which she has treasured. God helping her, she can do no other.

Wilson's modest preparedness program had unfortunately sufficed neither to impress the Germans nor to equip the nation to fight a major war in 1917. Yet with remarkably few failures and false starts the Administration managed to mobilize men, ships, and supplies at a rate that astonished both friend and foe alike and proved to be the decisive factor in the Allied victory in 1918. For this much of the credit was due to Wilson himself. To meet the emergency he asked for and received from Congress vastly increased presidential powers, thereby leaving for his successors both the precedents and tools necessary for strong executive leadership in time of crisis. To help pay the astronomical war cost, for example, the Wilson administration demonstrated the enormous revenue potentials of steeply graduated income, inheritance, and excess profits taxes, as well as the direct popular sale of government bonds. A selective service law raised nearly three million men for the Army with none of the confusion, riots, or scandal that had marred the operation of a similar draft measure under Lincoln. To coordinate the domestic war effort, Wilson developed a variety of controls and new administrative machinery: powerful agencies to control industrial production and conserve scarce supplies of food and raw materials, temporary nationalization of the railroads and the telegraph lines, Government operation of shipyards and a large fleet of merchant ships, boards to settle labor disputes and help place workers in vital industries, and an ambitious propaganda effort to popularize American war aims and make Americans war-conscious. Future presidents, faced with the challenge of paralyzing depression and renewed world war, would draw heavily on Wilson's wartime experience and governmental innovations.

Even before the full force of American arms had been felt on the battlefields of Europe—before, indeed, an Allied victory was assured—Wilson was hard at work on a peace settlement. The United States, he was convinced, must play the leading role in the struggle for a just and enduring peace. The other belligerents were too cynical, too embittered, too bound by tradition and previous commitments to approach the peace table with the necessary magnanimity and tolerance. Just as American military might was essential to win the war, so American morality was vital to the building of a stable world order. There were Fourteen Points in the bold peace program the President outlined before a joint session of Congress on January 8, 1918: including open diplomacy, freedom of the seas and of trade, reduction of armaments, impartial adjustment of colonial claims, self-determination for subject nationalities, and, as a capstone, a League of Nations "affording mutual guarantees of political independence and territorial integrity to great and small states alike." The Fourteen Points became at once one of the great weapons of the war, bolstering the flagging morale of the Allied peoples and seriously weakening the resolve of the enemy. As word of his liberal peace aims spread, Wilson became a great popular hero abroad. Allied leaders were skeptical, but to millions of war-weary Europeans the American President seemed to offer the best hope of a new and better world order. Nine months later when a beaten Germany sued for an armistice, its leaders appealed directly to Wilson for a peace based on his Fourteen Points.

Yet although Wilson approached the problems of peace with great intelligence and vision, he himself was partly responsible for some of the formidable obstacles in his path. In the final analysis it was, of course, his decision to take the United States into the war that made possible a dictated, rather than a negotiated, peace. Like Lincoln, Wilson's very idealism led him to underestimate the force of wartime hatred and vengeance, which ironically his own war propagandists had helped to intensify. Of even greater importance was the fact that his severe Presbyterian conscience forbade any sharp bargaining with Allied leaders over peace terms at a time when his cards were the strongest, before America's entry into the war. This would have been the ideal time to nail down Allied approval of American peace aims, not after Germany was beaten. But because Wilson tended to think of the war as a great crusade, he simply could not bring himself to demand even a high-minded *quid pro quo* as the price of American participation. Moreover, when he subsequently learned of some of the secret Allied agreements proposing to divide the spoils of victory in a manner scarcely in the spirit of the Fourteen Points, he declined to jeopardize the war effort by wielding the club of American military and economic power, trusting that the force of world public opinion would enable him to override these selfish commitments at the peace conference.

Wilson blundered, too, in failing to keep his political fences mended at home, though surely the onetime professor of government ought to have remembered that the president shares responsibility for foreign policy with a jealous Senate. Anxious to aid his party in the off-year elections of November, 1918, he called for the return of a Democratic Congress, terming the poll a personal vote of confidence in his leadership. His ill-advised appeal probably had little effect on the electorate one way or the other, but when the Republicans won control of both houses of Congress Wilson's political enemies were able to assert that by his own admission he stood repudiated by the American people. Even more serious was Wilson's failure to include any senators or prominent Republicans as members of the American delegation he took with him to the Paris Peace Conference. No doubt he ignored the Senate because he would have been obliged to invite one of his bitterest critics, Republican majority leader Henry Cabot Lodge—the same who forty years earlier had published the essay of an unknown Princeton undergraduate. Lodge had developed a consuming hatred for Wilson which was heartily reciprocated, but the President might well have avoided needless offense to the great body of moderate Republicans by including among his advisers such able and distinguished men as former President William H. Taft, Elihu Root, or Charles Evans Hughes. Wilson took with him to Paris hundreds of experts to assist in the political, economic, and ethnographical work of the conference—"Tell me what's right and I'll fight for it," he told them earnestly—yet by failing to make the undertaking truly bipartisan he greatly reduced the chances that his handiwork would survive the pitfalls of domestic politics upon his return.

Wilson has been strongly criticized for the shortcomings of the Versailles Peace Treaty, for its many failures to live up to the bright promise of his Fourteen Points. "It is incomprehensible," protested the president of the German National Assembly when the terms of the treaty were revealed, "that a man who had promised the world a peace of justice, upon which a society of nations would be founded, has been able to assist in framing this project dictated by hate." Yet the critics tend to overlook the fact that Wilson was in no position to dictate the peace terms. Inevitably he had to compromise with the less enlightened views of his chief colleagues, the shrewd, ambitious David Lloyd George of Great Britain, the cynical and vindictive Georges Clemenceau of France, and the covetous Vittorio Orlando of Italy. The wonder is not that the treaty violated some of Wilson's lofty principles but that he was able to achieve so much of his program in the face of skillful and determined opposition. Certainly Wilson's presence at the peace table was the main reason why the treaty was neither so harsh as the other Allied leaders would have liked nor indeed so ruthless as a victorious Germany would have imposed.

Wilson in fact managed to block most of the more extreme demands of his colleagues at the peace conference. For example, he set himself firmly against Clemenceau's drastic proposal to create a series of small buffer states under French control in western Germany, mollifying the French premier by agreeing to a joint Anglo-French-American defensive alliance against future German aggression. Had this defense agreement been maintained subsequently it might well have preserved the peace of Europe in the next generation. In the face of inflexible Allied demands that Germany must not regain her former overseas colonies, Wilson won an important concession that the colonies be mandates of the new League of Nations. He prevented France from annexing Germany's Saar Basin outright—which would have been a clear violation of the principle of self-determination—substituting instead temporary French control under a League mandate. He insisted that Fiume go to the new state of Yugoslavia rather than to Italy, though this action caused Orlando to withdraw for a brief sulk. In general Wilson's vigilance successfully protected the principle of self-determination in what turned out to be the most drastic reshuffling of European boundaries in over a century. Wilson made probably his most damaging concessions in the matter of reparations. Earlier he had declared that punitive damages had no place in a proper peace settlement, but at Paris he reluctantly acceded to Allied demands that Germany be saddled with a potentially astronomical reparations bill. Along with the companion war guilt clause, the heavy reparations burden insured the rise of vengeful German nationalism under a demagogue like Adolf Hitler and contributed heavily to the dangerously unstable world financial structure of the 1920's.

No one knew better than Wilson that the peace treaty fell far short of his ideals—he remarked at one point that if he were a German he thought he would never sign it—yet he was willing to accept an imperfect settlement in order to obtain what was nearest his heart, an international organization to preserve the peace. The League of Nations he felt was the heart of the post-war peace structure; it would provide the machinery through which defects in the peace settlement could gradually be remedied as wartime passions cooled. It was upon Wilson's insistence that the Covenant of the League was made an integral part of the treaty and the League entrusted with the execution of the treaty. "A living thing is born," he solemnly told the peace conference delegates when he presented the Covenant for their formal approval. "There is a compulsion of conscience throughout it. It is practical, and yet it is intended to purify, to rectify, to elevate." Yet the success of the League would be dependent upon the wholehearted support of the great powers, especially the United States. And tragically, Wilson himself would in the end bear a heavy responsibility for the American failure to join the League of Nations.

When Wilson returned with the peace treaty early in July, 1919, he faced the most difficult and most important fight of his life. The Republican majority in the Senate, led by his archenemy Senator Lodge, were bitterly resentful of what they regarded as the President's attempt to maintain a Democratic monopoly of peacemaking. Lodge, indeed, was contemptuous of even the phraseology of Wilson's cherished League Covenant. "It might get by at Princeton," he sneered, "but certainly not at Harvard." He determined to delay the vote on ratification to give time for the opposition to build up, and then to humiliate the President and win partisan advantage by attaching unacceptable reservations. Still, only twelve to fifteen bitter-end isolationist senators—the so-called "irreconcilables"—were set against any United States participation in an international organization. At all times during the debate over ratification of the treaty more than three-fourths of the Senate and the overwhelming majority of the press and articulate public opinion of the country favored joining the League with some reservations to protect American interests. The task of true statesmanship was to create a bipartisan majority for ratification without crippling amendments or reservations.

But Wilson, his Scotch stubbornness no less inflexible than the obstinacy of the irreconcilables, was temperamentally incapable of compromise with the Republican opposition. He refused to accept any but the mildest interpretive reservations, arguing that the rest would violate the nation's solemn word and reopen the treaty to wholesale amendment by other signatories. As he had done so often in the past with spectacular success, he resolved to take his case directly to the people. Surely if they understood what was at stake they would not permit the Senate to nullify his labors. His never robust health had begun to give way at Paris; his doctors protested that a strenuous speaking tour might cost him his life. "I must go," he replied earnestly. "I promised our soldiers, when I asked them to take up arms, that it was a war to end wars; and if I do not do all in my power to put the Treaty in effect, I will be a slacker and never be able to look those boys in the eye."

And so, for three weeks in September he traveled eight thousand miles through the West delivering with passionate eloquence and conviction some thirty-seven speeches to ever larger and more enthusiastic crowds. With tears in his eyes he told an audience at Pueblo, Colorado, on September 25:

> Nothing less depends upon this decision, nothing less than the liberation and salvation of the world. Now that the great mists of this question have cleared away, I believe that men will see the truth, eye to eye and face to face. There is one thing that the American people always rise to and extend their hand to, and that is the truth of justice and of liberty and of peace. We have accepted that truth and we are going to be led by it, and it is going to lead us, and through us the world, out into pastures of quietness and peace such as the world never dreamed of before.

That night, as the presidential train sped toward Wichita, Wilson's frail body gave way; his doctor cancelled the remaining speeches and ordered an immediate return to Washington. There on October 2 the President suffered a stroke that nearly killed him and left him paralyzed on the left side of his face and body.

With Wilson's physical collapse came the collapse of his brave new world as well. His meager strength jealously guarded by his physician and his devoted second wife, the ailing President was isolated and unable effectively to command the forces favoring ratification. Nor would he listen to suggestions that he compromise with his enemies. Twice the Senate voted on the treaty; twice Wilson sent word from his sickbed that his followers must not accept the Lodge reservations. After the second adverse vote had killed the treaty and with it American participation in the League of Nations, Senator

Brandegee, one of the irreconcilables, remarked gratefully to Lodge: "We can always depend on Mr. Wilson. He has never failed us."

Like Abraham Lincoln, Woodrow Wilson is a great but tragic figure among American presidents—great in his imaginative and forthright leadership, tragic in his inability to persuade his countrymen to adopt a noble dream. Wilson's—and the nation's—supreme tragedy was that his own stubbornness was at least partly responsible for his most costly defeat, the failure of the United States to take the lead in making the League of Nations a vital instrument of peace. Yet the failure should not blind us to Wilson's very real contributions. It was Wilson who demonstrated beyond question that the United States was a major world power with responsibility for mature leadership in world affairs. It was his League of Nations that pioneered in providing collective security for all countries, large and small. A later generation, after suffering the horrors of another world war, would pay tribute to Wilson's ideals by creating the United Nations, and this time only a scattered few would question the wisdom of wholehearted American participation. In other respects, too, Wilson left a tangible and living legacy: the first national economic stabilizers, democratization of the tax structure, stronger anti-trust protection, and a host of other domestic reforms. No other chief executive before him so systematically and successfully made use of the legislative powers of his office. Indeed, it might be said that he largely established the modern pattern of the president as both the leader of his party and of Congress. He greatly extended the war powers of the presidency and showed his successors how these powers might be used boldly in an emergency. He accomplished an unprecedented mobilization of the nation's military and economic resources without a major scandal touching his administration. In sum, Wilson's achievements were many and spectacular. If on occasion he also failed spectacularly, it was because, being human, he was not always capable of transforming noble dreams into reality.

V This Side of Paradise

15

The Return to Normalcy

Arthur M. Schlesinger, Jr.

The election of Warren G. Harding reflected a massive popular reaction against the missionary idealism of Woodrow Wilson and the reformist zeal of the Progressive era. Harding would take the country back to "normalcy," so that Americans might continue their "normal, onward way." Essentially, this meant that federal regulation of industry would be reduced to a minimum, that the business of government, as Calvin Coolidge put it, would be big business.

The popular stereotype of the twenties was that it was a decade of cynicism, corruption, speculative orgies, violence, and cultural decay. But in reality this decade of "normalcy" was a good deal more complex than that. True, business consolidation under Republican rule continued throughout the decade. True, there was excessive and irresponsible speculation on the New York stock exchange. True, organized crime was widespread and gang wars rocked Chicago and New York. True, as we shall see, the Ku Klux Klan—embodying the worst tendencies of racism, xenophobia, and moral absolutism—rode again. And true, as we shall also see, there was a revolution in manners and morals which challenged traditional standards and profoundly upset a number of Americans.

Yet for many contemporaries, the twenties was a time of exhilarating hope and high expectation for the United States. In fact, a number of intellectuals found much in American life to celebrate. But the most optimistic of all were the businessmen, who believed they were living in a new era. For them, it was a time not only of conservative Republican leadership in Washington, but of striking innovation and change in business itself. As industrial spokesmen happily observed, corporate managers were bringing scientific procedures and efficiency techniques to industry. And this, they contended, would raise production so high that poverty would soon be eliminated and the American dream of abundance for all at last attained. So for American businessmen the twenties seemed a golden era—a time when wise industrial magnates and their Republican allies managed the country for the benefit of all.

Still, as Arthur Schlesinger, Jr., makes clear in the following narrative, all was not so "well" and "golden" as it seemed, not even for big businessmen. For in spite of their claims of booming prosperity, in spite of Republican prophecies that America was reaching her long-cherished dream, the country was heading pell-mell toward economic disaster. Here Schlesinger examines the politics and economics of the twenties, with brilliant vignettes of the Republicans and businessmen who ran the nation during that time.

On Friday, February 1, 1919, Edward L. Doheny, the oil millionaire, was holding forth in his splendid suite on the S.S. *Aquitania*. The great danger to America, Doheny said, was socialism—socialism and its offsprings, Communism and Bolshevism. "A majority of the college professors in the United States," he said, "are teaching socialism and Bolshevism. . . . William Boyce Thompson is teaching Bolshevism and he may yet convert Lamont of J. P. Morgan and Co. Vanderlip is a Bolshevist,

From Arthur M. Schlesinger, Jr. *The Crisis of the Old Order*. Boston: Houghton Mifflin Co., 1957, pp. 49–54, 56–70, 77–89. Reprinted by permission of the publisher.

so is Charles R. Crane. . . . Henry Ford is another and so are most of those one hundred historians Wilson took abroad with him."

On Friday, March 4, 1921, Doheny should have felt better. The Bolshevists were now gone from Washington; and the new administration was one in which men like Doheny, who had contributed $25,000 to its arrival, felt at home. The change from Woodrow Wilson to Warren Gamaliel Harding, from the high-minded and lofty-visioned intellectual to the handsome small-town sport, could not have been more reassuring.

Why Harding? The Republican party had far abler men in 1920. But somehow these men —General Leonard Wood and Governor Frank Lowden, Hiram Johnson and Herbert Hoover— canceled one another out. In February 1920, Harding's intimate friend Harry Daugherty had predicted that ten or twenty weary politicians, sitting around a table in the last days of a deadlocked convention, would finally agree on Harding; and so it came to pass. The nation, fatigued with the higher idealism, accepted the decision.

Wilson, living on in Washington, watched Harding with supreme contempt. It was reported that the former President had coined the phrase "the bungalow mind" to describe his successor. And, indeed, it was not inappropriate that the year in which Sinclair Lewis published his famous novel saw Main Street take over 1600 Pennsylvania Avenue. For Harding exuded the atmosphere of a sleepy Ohio town—the shady streets, the weekly lodge meetings, the smoking-room stories, golf on Sunday morning, followed by a fried chicken dinner and an afternoon nap. Alice Roosevelt Longworth, the daughter of another Republican President and the wife of the Speaker of the House, could never forget a typical White House scene—the President's study filled with cronies; cards and poker chips on the table; whisky and tall glasses on the trays; the air thick with cigar smoke; a general atmosphere of unbuttoned vests, feet on the desk, and spittle in the cuspidor. "Harding was not a bad man," observed Alice Longworth. "He was just a slob."

Harding was not a bad man. He was kindly and amiable, devoted in friendship and without malice in antagonism. Where Wilson refused to release the Socialist Eugene Debs from his Atlanta cell, Harding had no hesitation about commuting Debs's sentence. Terre Haute and Marion, after all, were much the same. "We understand each other perfectly," exclaimed Debs, after a visit to the White House. And Harding had no illusions about himself. He was a joiner, a booster, a glad-hander. This was the life he loved, and he wanted no other. But relentlessly his wife—"the Duchess," he called her—pushed her Warren on; and in the end, against his pathetic wisps of better judgment, he found himself President of the United States.

While he drank and gambled in the presidential mansion, while he played the stock market from the presidential study (he died owing a Cleveland brokerage house $180,000), while his back-slapping friends from Ohio lined their pockets, Harding still somehow sensed the dignity of the Presidency—and sensed too his own inability ever to achieve it. In 1922, in an off-the-record speech at the National Press Club, he recalled that his father had once said to him that it was a good thing that he had not been born a girl: "you'd be in the family way all the time. You can't say No." "My God, this is a hell of a job!" Harding complained to William Allen White. "My God-damn friends, White, they're the ones that keep me walking the floor nights!" Again: "This White House is a prison. I can't get away from the men who dog my footsteps. I am in jail." And, again, to Nicholas Murray Butler, "I am not fit for this office and should never have been here."

The Presidency was more than a man. It was an institution, making its own decisions, generating its own momentum, living its own life. No matter how many afternoons the President spent on the golf course, how many evenings at the card table, the business of the Presidency went on. And in Charles Evans Hughes as Secretary of State, in Andrew Mellon as Secretary of the Treasury, in Henry C. Wallace as Secretary of Agriculture, in Herbert Hoover as Secretary of Commerce, Harding had men around him of ability and character.

But Harry Daugherty, his Attorney-General, was a small-time fixer, shrill in the field of policy, dissolute in the field of morals. When the railroad shopmen struck in 1922, Daugherty convinced himself that it was a Communist attempt to overthrow the government of the United States. "It *is* civil war," he told Harding, civil war instigated by Moscow; and he secured a sweeping injunction charging the strikers with 17,000 crimes. Hughes and Hoover found the injunction so outrageous that they attacked it in Cabinet; but when Senator Burton K. Wheeler of Montana protested publicly, the Attorney-General of the United States was quick to denounce him as "the Communist leader in the Senate." And while Daugherty labored to save the republic from such Bolsheviki as Wheeler and Donald Richberg, who was counsel for the striking unions, he applied himself with even greater diligence to manipulating the Department of Justice on behalf of old Ohio friends in the Little Green House on K Street.

The Secretary of the Interior was of similar stripe. To William Allen White, the unkempt and ill-visaged Albert B. Fall looked like a patent-medicine vendor—"a cheap, obvious faker. I could hardly believe my eyes." But Harding, who greatly admired Fall, wanted to make him Secretary of State; and Edward L. Doheny found him so irresistible that on November 30, 1921, he conveyed to Fall a satchel containing $100,000 in cash—a "loan," conceived out of fondness for an old friend, absolutely unconnected, Doheny later testified under oath, with Fall's decision to give Doheny a lease on the naval oil reserves at Elk Hills in California. Doheny at last had found a public official who was indisputably not a Bolshevist.

Daugherty and Fall were without shame. In time rumors began to spread around Washington. Then a member of the Ohio gang committed suicide just before Harding left on a trip to Alaska in the summer of 1923. The President himself began perhaps to have a sense of impending disaster. He suddenly invited his Secretary of Commerce, Herbert Hoover, to join the trip. Possibly Harding thought for a moment he wanted Hoover's counsel, but it soon seemed as if it was rather because Hoover was a good bridge player. Certainly the President played bridge compulsively in smoky, overheated rooms, from breakfast to midnight, seeking distraction in the everlasting fall of the cards. When dummy, the Secretary rushed to ship decks or observation cars to fill his lungs with fresh air.

Harding had never seemed more restless. "I cannot hope to be one of the great presidents," he said to Charles Michelson of the New York *World*, "but perhaps I may be remembered as one of the best loved." One day he finally took Hoover aside and asked him vaguely what he should do if, say, there were scandals in the administration. The apprehensions were indefinite but obsessive. By now the party was back in the Pacific Northwest, where the President, worn and haggard, resumed his speaking schedule. Soon he was sick, laid low, it was stated, by bad crabmeat (though no crabmeat was to be found on the official menu). For a day or so he seemed to rally. Then, on August 3, while his wife was reading him an article about himself from the *Saturday Evening Post*, he turned pale and gave a shudder. In a few moments he was dead. (An Associated Press reporter scored a beat on the story; his name was Steve Early, and he had worked for Franklin Roosevelt in the 1920 campaign.) The Alaska trip gave Herbert Hoover a permanent distaste for bridge. He never played again.

Slowly the funeral train made its way back to Washington, the nation struck for a moment with genuine grief, hushed crowds watching the train roll by, schoolchildren singing "Nearer My God to Thee" at stations and crossroads along the way. Harding's body lay in the East Room, a simple coffin with four wreaths of flowers standing in the center of the great room. One August night, at two in the morning, Florence Harding came down to look in the open coffin, where her husband, rouged and lipsticked, had in the dimness almost the color of life. The Duchess called for a chair and sat by him, speaking softly to him, her face close to his. "Warren," she said, "the trip has not hurt you one bit." And then: "No one can hurt you now, Warren."

. . .

It was after midnight in Plymouth, Vermont. The white cottage by the side of the road was dark, the little town still, when the clatter of an automobile suddenly broke through the night. In a moment, a Western Union messenger from Bridgewater was beating on the door of the Coolidge house. Calvin Coolidge's father sleepily lit a kerosene lamp and turned to open the telegram. In a few moments the Vice-President, hurriedly awakened, began to put on his best black suit. Soon Secretary Hughes was urging him by long-distance telephone to come to Washington for the swearing in. But Coolidge always knew what he wanted. His father was a notary public; the house had its family Bible; and, at 2.47 by the rococo Victorian clock on the mantel, Calvin Coolidge took the presidential oath.

Coolidge arrived at the Presidency at a propitious time. No one yet knew how far the corruption had gone. It was only clear that the country needed leadership which could inspire moral respect. After the slackness and indolence of Harding, it needed "character." Who could supply it better than a Vermont Yankee, reared in thrift and frugality, a fanatic for the old-fashioned virtues?

. . .

He had moved far from his rural Vermont childhood—"I never saw a man," exclaimed the British Ambassador, "who looked less like the son of a farmer." Entering law and politics in Massachusetts, he had always been competent, taciturn, and safe. The Boston police strike gave him as governor an accidental reputation for swift decision and made him Vice-President. But he had had little impact on Washington. According to a young Republican editor in Michigan named Arthur H. Vandenberg, Coolidge was "so unimpressive" that he would probably have been denied renomination.

His speeches offered his social philosophy in dry pellets of aphorism. "The chief business of the American people," he said, "is business." But, for Coolidge, business was more than business; it was a religion; and to it he committed all the passion of his arid nature. "The man who builds a factory," he wrote, "builds a temple. . . . The man who works there worships there." He felt these things with a fierce intensity. William Allen White, who knew him well, called him a mystic, a whirling dervish of business, as persuaded of the divine character of wealth as Lincoln had been of the divine character of man, "crazy about it, sincerely, genuinely, terribly crazy."

As he worshipped business, so he detested government. "If the Federal Government should go out of existence, the common run of people would not detect the difference in the affairs of their daily life for a considerable length of time." The federal government justified itself only as it served business. "The law that builds up the people is the law that builds up industry." And the chief way by which the federal government could serve business was to diminish itself; "the Government can do more to remedy the economic ills of the people by a system of rigid economy in public expenditure than can be accomplished through any other action." Economy was his self-confessed obsession; it was "idealism in its most practical form"; it was the "full test of our national character."

As President, he dedicated himself to inactivity. "No other President in my time," said the White House usher, "ever slept so much." In his dozen or so waking hours, he did as little as possible. In his *Autobiography* he singled out one rule as more important than any other: "It consists in never doing anything that someone else can do for you." In practice, he added another rule: say as little as possible. "The things I don't say," he would dryly remark, "never get me into trouble." Silence was the best defense; it baffled and defeated the outside world. Nine-tenths of the White House callers, he told Hoover, want something they ought not to have. "If you keep dead-still they will run down in three or four minutes. If you even cough or smile they will start up all over again." When a senator charged in one day demanding that something be done, Coolidge, his feet on the desk, said, "Don't you know that four-fifths of all our troubles in this life would disappear if we would only sit down and keep still?"

The main social events at the White House in Coolidge's time were his breakfasts: pancakes with Vermont maple syrup, served promptly at eight, his large white collies wandering about the room or licking the sugar out of the bottom of his coffee cup. On other mornings, he ate breakfast in his bedroom while a valet rubbed his head with Vaseline. When his faith was not involved, he watched life with a quizzical air. His humor was mordant and unpredictable. His eyes sometimes shone with the peculiar gleam of a parrot about to give someone a tweak; and then deadly remarks snapped out of compressed lips; or, in a mood of aimless mischief, he might press all the bells in his room at once and disappear to fool the servants, or he might play unfunny practical jokes on the Secret Service men. He could be irascible and nasty, straining all the understanding of his gracious wife. In the memory of the White House usher, Theodore Roosevelt in his worst rage was placid compared with Coolidge.

To some his aphoristic self-confidence represented homely folk wisdom; to others, intolerable smugness. To some his inaction was masterly restraint; to others, it was the complacent emptiness of a dull and lazy man. To some his humor was innocent fun; to others, it was sadistic meanness. To some his satisfaction with his purpose represented "character"; to others, it seemed a bankruptcy of mind and soul. To some he was the best in the American middle class. To others he was almost the worst.

William Allen White called him "a Puritan in Babylon." His frugality sanctified an age of waste, his simplicity an age of luxury, his taciturnity an age of ballyhoo. He was the moral symbol the times seemed to demand.

And he moved to make the symbolism good. As the disclosures of the Walsh investigation roused public opinion, Coolidge dismissed Daugherty as Attorney-General and began to tidy up the administration. At the same time, he quietly established his control of the Republican party—or, rather, permitted his friend William Morgan Butler to establish control on his behalf.

The rise of Butler, a Massachusetts businessman, president of the Hoosac and Quissett Mills and the West End Thread Corporation, was symptomatic. In the past, business influence in the party had been at one remove. Politicians like Henry Cabot Lodge and Boies Penrose had negotiated with business leaders as equals. Lodge, indeed, had the contemptuous feeling that businessmen were worse in politics than men of any other class; "the businessman dealing with a large political question is really a painful sight." But the North Shore patrician had not anticipated the new age. He had served the Republican party for nearly half a century; he had been permanent chairman of the convention a quarter of a century before; he had gone farther than most of his class in coming to terms with the men of trade. Yet he went to his last convention in 1924 an ordinary delegate, little noticed, never consulted, while the New Bedford textile manufacturer, backed by the cunning middle-class lawyer from Northampton, ran the show. Lodge sat through his humiliation with proud, expressionless face, aristocrat to the last, denying his enemies the satisfaction of seeing how much they had hurt him.

The Republican convention of 1924 went like clockwork. The delegates, showing no undue emotion (except when confronted by Secretary Mellon, one of the richest men in America), nominated Coolidge by virtual acclamation. After William E. Borah rejected the vice-presidential nomination ("At which end?" Borah was supposed to have said), it went to Brigadier-General Charles Gates Dawes of Illinois; and the delegates dispersed, serenely confident that the nation shared their determination to keep cool with Coolidge.

When the Democrats, after their bitter convention, nominated John W. Davis of New York, by now a conservative corporation lawyer, many liberals of both parties looked to old Bob La Follette to provide an alternative. He did so, under the standard of a new Progressive party; and it was the Progressive challenge to business supremacy, weak as this challenge was, which supplied the theme for the Republican campaign. The issue, as General Dawes declared in ringing tones, "is whether you stand on the rock of common sense with Calvin Coolidge, or upon the sinking sands of socialism with Robert M. La Follette." If this were the issue, there was no question how the American people stood.

"It was a famous victory," said William Howard Taft, meditating the results a few days after the election. Whenever the American people understand that the issue is between radicalism and conservatism, mused the Chief Justice, the answer will always be the same. "This country is no country for radicalism. I think it is really the most conservative country in the world."

In 1925, *Nation's Business*, the organ of the United States Chamber of Commerce, called the American businessman "the most influential person in the nation." The businessman now occupied, *Nation's Business* observed, "a position of leadership which the businessman has never held before." "Never before, here or anywhere else," added the *Wall Street Journal*, "has a government been so completely fused with business." From his side, Calvin Coolidge confirmed the alliance. "This is a business country," he said, ". . . and it wants a business government."

This was the essence of the Republican experiment; and, as Secretary of the Treasury, Andrew Mellon incarnated the new unity. Seventy years old in 1925, Mellon had seen in his own lifetime the transformation of a rural and colonial economy into the greatest industrial power in the world. He had entered the banking business in Pittsburgh in 1874; the great business leaders who had wrought the miraculous transformation were his contemporaries; and, as a man who remembered Bryan and Roosevelt and Wilson, he felt a shy satisfaction at the passing away of the old distrust and the national acceptance of business leadership. His own appointment to the Treasury, unthinkable in an earlier epoch, seemed to symbolize the revolution in popular attitudes.

Slight and frail, with prominent cheekbones in a grave face, he had a gentle Edwardian formality of manner and dress. His suits were dark, sober, and luxurious, with carefully buttoned coat and black tie; his hats were soft and gray. He was most himself, perhaps, among fine wines, rich cigars, antique china, and beautiful paintings. But his public face was one of perpetual weariness and worry. With a cold smile and querulous voice, he never ceased to call for government economy.

"The Government is just a business," said Mellon, "and can and should be run on business principles." The first necessity, accordingly, was to balance the budget, and the second to pay off the debt. But Mellon's greater interest, it soon developed, was somewhat inconsistently in the reduction of tax rates, especially in the highest brackets. Existing surtax rates, he felt, were intolerable. A man with an income of $1,000,000 had to pay an income tax of nearly $300,000. The consequences, he declared, were already visible on every side; everyone knew "of businesses which have not been started, and of new projects which have been abandoned, all for one reason—high surtaxes." There was a difference, he warned, between taxation and confiscation; and, to restore that difference, he proposed to establish a maximum surtax rate of 25 per cent. No one, however much money he made, should be required to pay more than one quarter of his income in surtax; otherwise it would be the end of American initiative.

A tax bill which concentrated on cutting taxes for millionaires could not command unreserved enthusiasm, even in the nineteen twenties. John Nance Garner, the wily congressman from Texas, licked Mellon's tax proposals in 1924 and forced Coolidge to sign a somewhat stiffer bill. But Mellon, ever tenacious, kept chipping away each year at rates in the upper brackets. His opponents remained notably lacking in sympathy. "Mr. Mellon himself," as George W. Norris of Nebraska observed of the Mellon bill of 1925, "gets a larger personal reduction than the aggregate of practically all the taxpayers in the state of Nebraska." But such insinuations could not daunt Mellon's crusade.

Nor was tax reduction Mellon's only resource. What he could not reduce, he could often refund—a process which had the advantage of taking place behind closed doors. Not until Garner forced the revelation of the figures in 1930 did the country know what Mellon had done. In his first eight years at the Treasury, the Secretary dispensed $3.5 billion in the shape of cash refunds, credits, and abatements. The size of these disbursements mounted steadily during the period, except in 1927 and 1930, when congressional grumbling forced the Treasury to hold back. Several million dollars went to Mellon's own companies; other millions, as Garner took pleasure in pointing out, went where they promised to do the most good to the Republican party. Thus each of the seventeen individuals contributing $10,000 to the Republican campaign in 1930 had been beneficiaries of Mr. Mellon's official generosity.

Meanwhile, Mellon himself continued an active life of speculation. Through family corporations, the Mellons shared in the grand barbecue. The *New York Times* reported in 1926 that the Secretary of the Treasury's relatives had made $300 million in the bull market on aluminum and Gulf Oil alone. Nor did this exhaust the possibilities of family corporations. "Pursuant to your request for a memorandum setting forth the various ways by which an individual may legally avoid tax," wrote the Commissioner of Internal Revenue to the Secretary of the Treasury, "I am pleased to submit the following." The following consisted of ten possible methods of tax avoidance, five of which Mellon in time admitted under oath he actually employed. The Commissioner also sent Mellon a tax expert to help prepare the Secretary's income tax return; the expert soon showed up on Mellon's personal payroll, where he turned to the Secretary's private account the knowledge accumulated in the public service.

It was this expert who set up more family corporations and, through paper losses in stock sales to and among them, enabled the Secretary to slash his tax payments at the very time when, in his official capacity, Mellon was appealing to the taxpayers to pay their own income taxes.

The Mellon tax program had—at least in the minds of skeptical observers—its contradictions in equity and ethics. And it had contradictions in economics too. For, if debt reduction and budget balancing might have constituted a useful sedative for the nervous economy, the Mellon penchant for tax reduction served to make more money available for speculation. "A decrease of taxes," as Mellon said, "causes an inspiration to trade and commerce." With this he injected a few more billion dollars into a boom which hardly needed to be further inspired.

Yet it was what the business community thought it wanted; and, across the board, this was the new test for economic policy. So Coolidge similarly cherished the high wall of protection for American industry erected in the Republican tariff of 1922. At the same time he backed Secretary of Commerce Hoover in his vigorous program to promote the sale of American manufactures abroad. Woodrow Wilson had naïvely thought a high tariff and a flourishing export trade to be incompatible. In his last official act as President, vetoing a bill to raise tariff rates, Wilson had argued that the United States was now a creditor nation, and that foreign nations could buy American goods only in three ways—through borrowing dollars from America, or selling gold to it, or selling goods to it. Wilson had rejected the first two methods. "If we wish to have Europe settle her debts," he had concluded, ". . . we must be prepared to buy from her." But Hoover, indifferent to Wilson's quandary, was content to rear the American export trade on the basis of American foreign loans. This was a project with which New York bankers were glad to cooperate. Through the twenties, billions of American dollars went abroad in private loans to subsidize the role of American goods abroad.

President Coolidge was prepared further to attest his trust in business leadership by weakening the instrumentalities through which past national governments had sought to regulate business. The regulatory commissions, inherited from more suspicious days, were quickly infused with the new spirit of unity. To the Tariff Commission, for example, were sent men who acted almost as open representatives of protected industries. When the Commission's minority, led by E. P. Costigan of Colorado, began to object that members were sitting on cases in which they or their relatives were known to have financial stakes, Coolidge upbraided them for raising prudish scruples. After all, who were better qualified to sit in such cases than men equipped by special interests with superior judgment and knowledge? In the same spirit, the White House slipped W. W. Atterbury, the president of the Pennsylvania Railroad, advance copies of the President's special message to Congress on railroad consolidation.

Coolidge, wholly honest himself, perceived no conflict of interests, and he set the model for his administration. In the years since the New Freedom, the Federal Trade Commission had been a central agency of government regulation. But, with the appointment of W. E. Humphrey in 1925, a new era began. Humphrey denounced the Wilsonian FTC as "an instrument of oppression and disturbance and injury instead of a help to business"; no longer, he said, would the Commission serve as a "publicity bureau to spread socialistic propaganda." He soon brought about drastic changes in policies and procedures. Where the FTC had been set up to discourage monopoly, it now espoused the cause of the self-regulation of business and sponsored conference after conference to encourage industry-wide agreements on trade practices.

Washington thus began to smile upon tendencies toward economic concentration, which for the better part of the century it had, in theory at least, disapproved. Hoover, recalling the War Industries Board experience, threw his Commerce Department behind the trade association movement. With Commerce Department aid, trade associations worked out "codes," which were then endorsed by the FTC and adopted by the industry. Though dedicated to the elimination of "unfair" trade practices, the codes gradually began to spill over into such questions as price-cutting and, in some cases, provided fronts behind which businessmen fraternally conspired to evade the antitrust law.

More overt forms of concentration thrived equally. Holding companies moved into the utility and transportation fields, chain stores into retail distribution; in all areas, big firms swallowed small firms and merged with other big ones. By 1930 the two hundred largest nonbanking corporations, after growing during the decade at a rate two to three times as fast as the smaller nonbanking corporations, controlled about half the total corporate wealth of the country. And from the viewpoint of government, private economic power could not have collected in more responsible hands.

Nor was this a wholly unreasonable point of view. If the merit of an economic structure was to be judged by its surface performance, then the American economy of the early twenties ranked high. The living standards of the nation steadily rose; economic opportunities steadily expanded; the flow of consumer goods steadily increased. The imagination of the American capitalist and the ingenuity of the American engineer were never more apparent in the life of the people. For a time, the country seemed to be on the edge of a new abundance.

Yet the very processes of plenty created new problems. The decisive economic fact was the extraordinary increase in technological efficiency and productivity. The output per manhour in industry rose about 40 per cent during the decade. The central economic challenge was to distribute the gains of productivity in a manner that would maintain employment and prosperity.

By the rules of orthodox economics, the reduction in production costs should have brought about either a reduction in prices or a rise in wages, or both. But the rigidities in the economy, in part the result of the process of concentration, seemed to have anaesthetized the market. The price system, so exquisitely sensitive in classical theory, was turning out to be sluggish in practice.

Denied outlet in lower prices because of accumulating rigidities, the gains of technological efficiency were equally denied outlet in higher wages or in higher farm prices because of the bargaining feebleness of the labor movement and of the farm bloc. As a result, these gains were captured increasingly by the businessmen themselves in the form of profits. Through the decade, profits rose over 80 per cent as a whole, or twice as much as productivity; the profits of financial institutions rose a fantastic 150 per cent.

The increase in profits naturally pushed up the prices of corporate securities; and, as securities rose in value, corporations found that the easiest way to obtain new cash was to issue new securities. This was cheap money, because there was no need to pay a return on stock issues as one would pay interest on bank loans. In turn, the corporations used the cash to expand plants, thereby increasing the flood of goods into an already crowded market; or, as time passed, they funneled their funds more and more into speculation. The result was to push stocks up again, repeating the whole process at a higher level. As the twenties proceeded, the stock market sucked off an increasing share of the undistributed gains of industrial efficiency.

The stock market boom in its early phases was by no means artificial. For a time it reflected solid industrial expansion. The automobile industry, in particular, had energized basic sectors of the economy—steel, machine tools, petroleum, rubber, roads, and public construction—and had encouraged innovation and research. But the very excess profits which were stimulating the boom were at the same time shortening its life. For the diversion of the gains of efficiency into profits was bound to result in a falling off of the capacity of the people as a whole to buy. The Mellon tax policy, placing its emphasis on relief for millionaires rather than for consumers, made the maldistribution of income and oversaving even worse. By 1929, the 2.3 per cent of the population with incomes over $10,000 were responsible for two-thirds of the 15 billion dollars of savings. The 60,000 families in the nation with the highest incomes saved almost as much as the bottom 25 million. The mass of the population simply lacked the increase in purchasing power to enable them to absorb the increase in goods.

The rural depression further distorted the structure of demand. The farmers had lost their foreign markets after the war; and the resulting sag in agricultural income built a basic imbalance into the economy. But the Republican administration could not get so excited over the predicament of farmers as over the predicament of business. "Farmers have never made money," Coolidge remarked philosophically to the chairman of the Farm Loan Board. "I don't believe we can do much about it." The farmers, many of them living in privation, most of them under the shadow of mortgages, were less philosophical. But when they devised measures to do for them what the protective tariff did for the manufacturer, they found no sympathy in Washington. As a result, the agricultural half of the economy could not do its share in maintaining demand.

As for city people, whose wages failed to keep pace with productivity, they found no more support in Washington than the farmers. While businessmen talked a good deal in public about the American faith in high wages, in practice they let the percentage rise of wages lag behind the rise of output and profit. Between 1923 and 1929, output per man-hour in manufacturing rose almost 32 per cent, while hourly wages rose but slightly over 8 per cent. Nor did anyone in authority see any economic value in a strong labor movement.

The unsatisfactory level of wages and of farm income meant that "prosperity" was steadily less able to generate buying power in sufficient volume to meet the steadily rising productive capacity—or, in time, to carry already available goods off the market. Still, even with a better distribution of purchasing power, the economy might have faltered as soon as the first growth of the automotive industry began to slacken. And deep structural weaknesses, especially in the banking system and on the security exchanges, rendered the future even more dubious.

Yet Wall Street and Washington had few qualms. By the middle twenties, the whole economic process began to focus on a single point—the ticker-tape machine with its endless chatter of stock market quotations. The torrent of excess money, pouring into the market, swept stock prices ever upward. And the leaders of the business community, now heedless of caution in their passion for gain, promoted new investment trusts, devised new holding companies and manipulated new pools, always with the aim of floating new securities for the apparently insatiable market. In 1923 capital issues amounted to $3.2 billion, and the annual sum rose steadily, reaching nearly $10 billion by 1927. A similar increase occurred in the volume of sales, from 236 million shares on the New York exchange in 1923 to 577 million in 1927 and 1125 in 1928. The market value of all shares on the New York Stock Exchange soared from $27 billion in 1925 to $67 billion in

Getting rich quick: a New York stock broker's office in the 1920s. As Schlesinger observes, "the whole economic process began to focus on a single point—the ticker-tape machine with its endless chatter of stock market quotations. The torrent of excess money, pouring into the market, swept stock prices ever upward. . . ." (Courtesy of Brown Brothers.)

1929. The net private debt of the nation climbed from $106 billion in 1920 to $162 billion in 1929.

In time it would appear that even the leaders of business could not decipher the intricate financial structures they were erecting. But for the moment everyone understood that here was an endless source of money and power, a roulette wheel at which no one lost. More and more the nation's passions centered on the feverish trading in the narrow streets at the lower tip of Manhattan Island. The American people learned a new vocabulary. "Brokers' loans" were loans made by the broker to the customer; they enabled customers to speculate far beyond their supply of cash. "Buying on the margin" meant that in using brokers' loans in the market the customer had to supply only a fixed proportion of the value of the shares purchased. When brokers' loans were at a 25 per cent margin, the customers' hard dollar was worth, in effect, four on the stock market. With the market steadily rising, who could lose?

Government officials meanwhile watched the speculative boom with affable approval. A decade earlier, Wilson had established the Federal Reserve System as a means of steadying the economy. The System had two chief instruments of credit policy in the twenties. Through open-market operations, it used the purchase or sale of government securities to alter the reserves of member banks and thus enlarge or contract the base of the money supply. Through the discount rate, it made the money supply tight or easy by raising or lowering the rate at which banks borrowed from the Federal Reserve.

No doubt in the twenties many exaggerated the power of monetary policy. But such power as the Federal Reserve System had was used, in the main, on the side of easy money. In part this was in deference to the situation in Europe. By keeping interest rates low and credit cheap, for example, the Board both discouraged the import of gold from Europe and made more American money available for foreign loans. Thus it believed it aided the task of European reconstruction. In the same spirit, Benjamin Strong, the vigorous governor of the Federal Reserve Bank in New York, and Montagu Norman of the Bank of England were responsible for a critical decision in the summer of 1927 to reduce the discount rate from 4 to 3.5 per cent. This act was designed to keep Britain on the gold standard to which Chancellor of the Exchequer Winston S. Churchill had rashly committed it two years earlier, and thus to avert a world-wide deflation. But the easy-money policy had the effect of accelerating the inflation in the United States. And in 1928, an election year, it was impossible to get a firm decision to check the upward spiral.

Sober businessmen began to regard the situation with discomfort. Occasionally these doubts found public expression, causing faint tremors of anxiety. But whenever the market faltered, someone in the administration could be relied on to speak words of encouragement. Nor could it be supposed that the White House or the Treasury were badly informed; for the business leaders of the country were President Coolidge's guests for lunch and dinner; and everyone knew that Secretary Mellon was himself deep in the market through his family corporation.

The doubts sometimes broke through to the President. Secretary Hoover, for example, objected periodically (though not publicly) to the buoyant Federal Reserve policy. But Coolidge's stock reply was to insist that the Board was independent of the Treasury and beyond the scope of the Executive, while Mellon seemed to dismiss his colleague's intermittent concern as much ado about nothing.

Early in 1927 William Z. Ripley, a Harvard professor, called at the White House. Ripley, who was in the tradition of Brandeis and Thorstein Veblen, though he presented his thought in a more genial vein, was much exercised by the process in which the economy was at once dispersing ownership and concentrating control. While stocks and bonds flowed from Wall Street to Main Street, power flowed from Main Street to Wall Street; and the consequence, Professor Ripley felt, was to encourage corporate secrecy and deceit—"double-shuffling, honey-fugling, hornswoggling and skulduggery." The President, his feet on his desk, a cigar clamped between his teeth, listened in increasing gloom; finally he asked, "Is there anything we can do down here?" Ripley, who did not then consider securities regulation a federal responsibility, replied, "No, it's a state matter." The President looked up, his face grateful with relief.

By the end of 1927 brokers' loans went nearly to the $4 billion mark. To many this seemed a wobbling basis for the superstructure of inflated values. Then on January 7, 1928, President Coolidge again came to the rescue. The increase in brokers' loans, he said, was a natural expansion of business in the securities market; he saw nothing wrong in it. A few weeks later, Roy Young of the Federal Reserve Board, the good friend of Secretary Hoover, told a congressional committee that he could not say whether brokers' loans were too low or too high; but "I am satisfied they are safely and conservatively made." And so the market continued to rise.

More and more in the twenties, one American emerged as the man who might bridge the gap between the ideals and the realities of the New Era. Herbert Clark Hoover was both Secretary of Commerce and a Quaker. His job placed him in the very center of economic life, while his faith identified him with the highest aspirations of service. His whole life, moreover, had been the realization of an American dream. More than anyone else in this decade, he articulated —as his career already exemplified—the ethic of American individualism, not the savage individualism of the ruthless past, but the hopeful individualism of a cooperative future.

Born in 1874 at West Branch, Iowa, Hoover had enjoyed the innocent pleasures of a classic small-town boyhood: in summer, fishing with willow poles and angleworms; in autumn, stalking pigeons and prairie chickens with bow and arrow and cooking them over a campfire; in the freezing winter dawn, tracking rabbits across snowy fields. In later years these recollections brought out a strain of unexpected lyricism in him, a memory of security. But the idyll soon came to an end. By the time he was eight years old, both his parents were dead. Soon after, he left Iowa to live with relatives in Oregon.

Something in his teens spurred him to become an engineer, and he seized the chance of training at the new university that Leland Stanford was founding in California. Finishing Stanford in 1895, a big man on campus, he set out to seek his fortune. By 1897, when twenty-three years old, he had already made his local name. The British mining firm of Bewick, Moreing and Company sent word to California that they needed an American engineer with gold-mining experience for their Australian interests. Young Hoover got the job.

His was the first generation of Americans to fan out in force across the world: the years that followed were like a series of adventures out of Richard Harding Davis. Hoover went first to Western Australia; then on to China, where, now twenty-five years old, he became chief engineer for the Chinese Bureau of Mines at $20,000 a year, helped make the natural resources of China, including the great Kaiping coal mines, safe for foreign investment, and was caught in an eddy of the Boxer Rebellion. The home office in London was quick to recognize the driving qualities of this remarkable young American. When he was only twenty-seven, Bewick, Moreing offered him a junior partnership. His business life now centered in London; but Hoover himself continued to work largely in the field, surveying mining properties, organizing new companies and syndicates, spending days and weeks on trains and steamships, a new sheaf of cables awaiting him at every stop. He traveled endlessly, from Mandalay to the Transvaal, from Egypt to the Malay States, from a turquoise mine at Mount Sinai to the foggy, gas-lit streets of the City of London.

It was a Richard Harding Davis life, but Hoover was hardly a Richard Harding Davis hero. Contained, wary, enormously capable and efficient, with round face, hazel eyes, straight mouse-colored hair, and broad shoulders, he transmuted all adventure into business, as a Davis hero would transmute all business into adventure. His manner, except among old friends to whom he had given his confidence, was forbidding; and, even among old friends, he remained reserved. Will Irwin, who had known him intimately since Stanford days, wrote in 1928: "I cannot remember that I have ever heard him laugh 'out loud.'" Something seemed to separate Hoover from human irrationality. Perhaps it was his dispassionate engineer's intelligence, concerned with solving problems rather than with relieving feelings; perhaps it was a protective coldness which an initially warm heart had to acquire at a time and in places where economic progress was purchased at such a cost in human misery.

As his reputation grew, Hoover was soon spending less and less time in actual engineering, more and more as the organizer and promoter of companies. His rise during these years could hardly have been more spectacular. The road from West Branch, Iowa, to the Red House, Hornton Street, Campden Hill, London, had been traversed with extraordinary speed. And, though he was far better known in the City of London than in Wall Street, in Rangoon and Johannesburg than in Washington, he took care to keep up his American connections. In 1907 he bought a cottage on the Stanford campus. In 1909 he joined the National Republican Club (in West Branch the only Democrat had been the town drunkard). In 1912 he contributed to Theodore Roosevelt's campaign.

By 1908 Hoover had laid the basis for a personal fortune. He decided now to strike out on his own as consulting engineer. In a short time he had offices from San Francisco to Petrograd and was a dominant figure, openly or in the shadows, in a dozen of the great international Edwardian undertakings—Russo-Asiatic Consolidated, the Inter-Argentine Syndicate, the Inter-Siberian Syndicate, Northern Nigeria Tin Mines, and many others. His interests spread from the Yukon to Tierra del Fuego and from the Altai Mountains and the Irtysh River to the Sierras. "My aggregate income from professional activities in various countries," he said of himself in 1914, "probably exceeded that of any other American engineer."

These were happy years for Hoover. Engineering and company management presented him with concrete problems that he could master with his impersonal force and intelligence. And life was rich and satisfying. "Prewar England," he later wrote, "was the most comfortable place in which to live in the whole world"; and, again, "the happiest period of all humanity in the Western World in ten centuries was the twenty-five years before the First World War." But, alas, this idyll was to be spoiled too. Hoover was in his London offices in the tense month of August 1914. War in his view was unthinkable. When it came, it appeared, he wrote, "like an earthquake. The substance and bottom seemed to go out of everything."

From the start, Hoover's organizing talent was in demand, first to take care of Americans stranded in Europe, then to administer relief in Belgium. With infinite patience and resourcefulness, he tackled the Belgian situation, negotiating problems of food, transport, finance, and diplomacy. Trips back to the United States began to re-establish him in the American scene. He made a significant impression in Washington. Wilson found him orderly and reassuring. To Brandeis he seemed "the biggest figure injected into Washington life by the war."

A few found him disconcertingly impersonal. "He told of the big work in Belgium," said Josephus Daniels, "as coldly as if he were giving statistics of production. From his words and his manner he seemed to regard human beings as so many numbers. Not once did he show the slightest feeling or convey to me a picture of the tragedies that went on." When he left, with a cold shake of the hand, Daniels felt that either Hoover had no heart or that his heart had been atrophied by his experience. But no one, not even Daniels, could gainsay Hoover's ability. As War Food Administrator, he took over in Washington with impressive mastery. "When you know me better," Hoover told General Peyton C. March, "you will find that when I say a thing is a fact it is a fact." By 1918 he was a household name in the United States. The end of the war did not terminate his responsibilities. The emphasis now shifted to the problem of averting famine and chaos abroad.

Before the war Hoover had loved the art, the literature, the magnificent cities and historic cathedrals of Europe. But war, he felt, had transformed the old continent into a "furnace of hate." Was he wrong now to perceive in the glare certain underlying European realities—forces of nationalism and imperialism, age-old hates, revenges, fierce distrusts, anxieties, fears? He did not know; he thought perhaps that the idealism of war could yet produce a European regeneration. Crossing the Atlantic from America in late 1918, Hoover, with Robert A. Taft, Lewis L. Strauss and other members of his staff, talked with anticipation. This seemed, perhaps, the moment when Europe might break with its past, when civilization itself could be reborn in the crucible of destruction.

Soon after arrival, disillusion began. Hoover attended a meeting of the Allied Ministers. They seemed to ooze, he later wrote, intrigue, selfishness, and heartlessness from every pore. As the weeks passed, it became increasingly apparent that war had not clarified the European mind or purified the European soul. Hoover fought valiantly to do his job. His representatives brought sustenance and hope to the far corners of Europe. In the discussions at Versailles, Hoover employed all his insistent force to make the statesmen forget the clash of national interest and face up to the essential facts of the European situation. He was, wrote John Maynard Keynes, "the only man who emerged from the ordeal of Paris with an enhanced reputation."

But at every turn he kept running up against emotion, prejudice, self-interest. He now succumbed to moods of deep pessimism—moods that deepened as his projects had to depend on the cooperation, not of slide rules or of hired hands, but of human equals. "He is simply reveling in gloom," wrote Colonel House to Wilson after a talk with Hoover in 1919. The treaty itself came as the shattering climax; then the troubled walk in the Paris sunrise and the meetings with Smuts and Keynes.

For Hoover the returns were in. Europe could not redeem itself, nor could America redeem it; the American destiny was separate and unique. For a long time, it was hard for him to speak of Europe without loathing. Nearly twenty years passed before he even set foot again on the European continent.

When Hoover returned to America in September 1919, he found himself a national political figure. Men of good will everywhere saw in him the largeness of character and vision which could pull the country together for the transition to peace. "I am 100 per cent for him," said Brandeis in February 1920. "High public spirit, extraordinary intelligence, knowledge, sympathy, youth, and a rare perception of what is really worth-while for the country, would, with his organizing ability and power of inspiring loyalty, do wonderful things in the Presidency." On this question, at least, Herbert Croly agreed with Brandeis; and the *New Republic* launched a campaign for Hoover. A number of younger Democrats, recalling Hoover's appeal in 1918 for a Congress that would support Wilson, assumed he was one of themselves and began to agitate for his nomination. Prominent in this group was the Assistant Secretary of the Navy, Franklin D. Roosevelt, who, after talking to Hoover late in 1919, reported with enthusiasm, "He is certainly a wonder and I wish we could make him President of the United States. There could not be a better one." According to his later memory, Roosevelt and Franklin Lane even tried to lay out a political timetable for an interested Hoover but to no avail; after a period of vacillation, Hoover decided to return to Republicanism.

Whether Hoover miscalculated in 1920 or whether he had no serious desire for either nomination is not clear from the evidence. In any case, he found no difficulty in supporting Harding; and, believing that Harding was for the League, he declared at Indianapolis that support of "the principle of an organized association of nations for the preservation of peace" was the "test of the entire sincerity, integrity and statesmanship of the Republican Party." Harding rewarded him with a choice of the Commerce or Interior Departments. Hoover chose Commerce on condition that he would have a voice in all important economic policies, whether in the field of business or labor, agriculture or finance or foreign affairs.

It is not to be supposed that Hoover made this condition out of passion for power. His return to America had precipitated in his mind a philosophy of American society—a philosophy that he felt needed expression throughout the national government. This philosophy animated the rest of his public career. In 1922 he gave it utterance in his small but important book, *American Individualism*.

American Individualism had its roots in his wartime disillusion. Hoover wished to repudiate the selfish, caste-ridden individualism of Europe. This was "individualism run riot," and it brought inequality and injustice in its train. And he wished equally to repudiate the philosophy of socialism which had arisen as Europe's answer to its arrogant individualism. This leveling equalitarianism had begun with "the claptrap of the French Revolution"; it had gained momentum with the expansion of the state during the war and "the dreamy social ferment of war emotion." Hoover had no doubt that socialism had already wrecked itself "finally" upon the rocks of "destroyed production and moral degeneracy"; look at "the ghastly failure of Russia." Still, the dangers of radicalism should not be ignored; its "destructive criticism" might well lead to revolution. Above all, beware the crowd! "The crowd only feels: it has no mind of its own which can plan. The crowd is credulous, it destroys, it consumes, it hates, and it dreams—but it never builds."

America, Hoover urged, must reject both European reaction and European radicalism; and he went on to define at length the unique mission of the new "progressive individualism" of the United States. American individualism did not have as its end "the acquisition and preservation of private property—the selfish snatching and hoarding of the common product." We had neutralized the selfish tendencies in individualism, he said, by affirming two great moral principles—the principles of equality of opportunity and of service. Equality of opportunity meant that people rose in society on their own merits. As for the "rising vision of service," which had evolved during the recent years of suffering, this great mystical force had infused society with a new sense of cooperation. Together these principles gave American individualism its spiritual setting and its moral purpose.

As Hoover looked out at America in 1922, he found that American society had already made great progress toward its ethical fulfillment. It was easy to point to undernourished and undereducated children on the one hand, petted and privileged children on the other; "but if we take the whole thirty-five millions of children of the United States, it would be a gross exaggeration to say that a million of them suffer from any of these injustices." Business organization had once been controlled by arbitrary individual ownership; now, as people acquired stock, ownership was being diffused among the population, so that "100,000 to 200,000 partners in a single concern are not uncommon." As a result, directors and managers were developing community responsibility; and business organization was "moving strongly toward cooperation."

This eloquent vision supplied an agreeable moral framework in which to interpret current tendencies toward economic concentration, increase in securities flotation, indifference to social reform, repression of radicalism. As a social philosopher, Hoover had gone far to reconcile practice and principle in the business community of the twenties. As Secretary of Commerce, he now proposed to complete the process of reconciliation.

Hoover moved into the Commerce Department as he might have into a bankrupt mining company a decade earlier. At a time when the federal government tended to languish and wither, Commerce burst into rich and vivid flower. Hoover, said S. Parker Gilbert, the banker and reparations agent, was "Secretary of Commerce and Under-Secretary of all other departments."

His greatest activity was in the foreign field. He turned the Department into a machine for promoting American sales abroad; and, with private American loans funneling dollars into foreign countries, American export trade was able for a few years to give a lively impression of prosperity. Though he expanded research in trade problems and supported the first adequate balance of payments studies, Hoover remained curiously myopic on the subject of the tariff and saw no relation between the dollar resources of foreign nations and their ability to sell in the American market. As he explained to Henry Hazlitt after the passage of the Fordney-McCumber Tariff of 1922, facts were more important than theories; and the fact was that an increasing percentage of our imports were entering duty-free. The related fact that this was because a higher tariff necessarily reduced the import of dutiable articles—that an absolutely prohibitive tariff on dutiable articles would have meant that all American imports would be duty-free—did not disturb his calculations.

In the domestic field, he sought wherever he could to give substance to his vision of service. A revolution, he felt, was taking place in our economic life: "we are passing from a period of extremely individualistic action into a period of associational activities." In the interests of this revolution, he encouraged the trade association as well as the simplification and standardization of machines and specifications; in other ways he tried to mobilize the business community into collective action against waste, "over-reckless competition" and unfair trade practices.

The boldest expression of his "progressive individualism" came in his approach to the business cycle. In the midst of the postwar slump of 1921, Hoover persuaded Harding to call a President's Conference on Unemployment. Harding opened the Conference by saying that the depression was inevitable, that anyone who thought planning might have averted it was deluding himself, and that, in particular, any plan involving government spending would only increase the trouble. The Conference itself declared flatly that unemployment was primarily a "community problem." Yet, for all these pieties, the Conference nonetheless ventured into new fields, ending with a series of recommendations about the use of public works as a stabilizing factor in the economy. Hoover, in summation, emphasized that methods had to be devised to level out the business cycle; "there is," he insisted, "a solution somewhere."

The search for a solution led to a series of basic economic studies—one, directed by Wesley C. Mitchell, on business cycles; one on stability in the construction industry; and a third, in 1928–29, on recent economic changes in America. Otto T. Mallery of the Pennsylvania State Industrial Board had been largely responsible for inducing the Conference to back the theory of a public works reserve; and in the business cycle volume he worked out his argument in greater detail. The construction study lent further support to the stabilization theory. It had been backed by the American Construction Council, whose president, Franklin D. Roosevelt, ardently supported the notion of spreading construction work through good and bad periods. We are trying, Roosevelt wrote in 1923, "to eliminate the harmful peaks of inflation, and the resulting equally harmful valleys of extreme depression. This can be done only by collective action and by the education of the public as to the facts."

In 1921 and 1923 Hoover sought with mild success to use government construction for contra-cyclical purposes, accelerating public works in the period of depression, postponing them in the period of inflation. In the meantime, Senator W. S. Kenyon of Iowa and Representative F. N. Zihlman of Maryland introduced bills in Congress calling for the expansion of public works as the remedy for periodic unemployment. Though Hoover backed these bills, they got nowhere; and two bills introduced in 1928 by Senators Wesley Jones of Washington and Robert F. Wagner of New York, both of which went farther than earlier proposals in laying down procedures for the timing of construction decisions, did no better.

The climax of these endeavors came at the Governors' Conference in New Orleans in November 1928. Governor Ralph Owen Brewster of Maine (he had not yet abandoned his first name), announcing that he was speaking on Hoover's behalf, unfolded a federal-state-municipal program for the use of public works as the balance wheel in the economy. With an annual $7 billion expenditure on construction, Brewster said, "America is in a position to stabilize prosperity to a most remarkable extent. . . . With the facts in hand, the expenditure of comparatively few millions in useful work may easily head off a depression that would cost a billion."

The Brewster plan—or the "Hoover plan," as it came to be known—differed from earlier proposals in two particulars. In the first place, while it professed to be concerned only with the timing—acceleration or postponement—of necessary public works, it contemplated a reserve fund of $3 billion, which was far larger than anything seriously suggested up to that point. In the second place, it proposed that the funds for government spending in depression should come not from tax revenues, but from government borrowing. In both these respects, it showed the imprint of the economic argument of William Trufant Foster and Waddill Catchings, whose enormously popular volume *The Road to Plenty* had come out earlier in the year. Professor Foster actually accompanied Governor Brewster to New Orleans to answer questions about the plan. But, after lengthy debate, the Governors' Conference voted to table the proposal.

Hoover's private attitude toward these ideas is hard to estimate. He gave them nominal support; but his active interest seems to have declined after the nation recovered from the postwar recession. The public works reserve schemes required, for example, rather elaborate statistical data; but Hoover did little in Commerce to set up studies on such questions as national income. He permitted the launching of the Brewster plan in his name in 1928; but nothing was heard of it thereafter, and he did not even mention the incident in his memoirs. Yet such plans seemed a further example of his constructive approach to national issues and of the new maturity he was bringing to business thought. They identified him all the more in the public mind with the idea of wisdom and foresight.

There were other forces assisting this identification. Hoover had by no means forsaken politics. He was the first President, Walter Lippmann later wrote, "whose whole public career has been presented through the machinery of modern publicity." Every item released by the Department of Commerce enhanced the picture of the master organizer, the irresistible engineer, the omniscient economist. This incessant activity did not particularly commend itself to President Coolidge, who disapproved in principle of Hoover's energy and in practice of his ambition. The President used to refer to his Secretary of Commerce sarcastically as "the wonder boy" or "the miracle worker." But he interposed no obstacles to Hoover's policies; and, as for Hoover's politics, Coolidge's objections were too feeble and oblique to have much effect.

No one knows precisely what Coolidge had in mind when he remarked cryptically in the Black Hills, "I do not choose to run for President in 1928." He may have intended to take himself out of the running; he may have hoped to shut out the other candidates by provoking a party draft for himself; or, most likely, he may with Vermont prudence have been closing the door on renomination—about three-quarters of the way. When a newspaperman asked him after his Black Hills statement whether he would be glad to retire to private life, Coolidge looked at him keenly for a few moments and then replied, "No." But whatever his intention, the effect of his delphic words was to clear the way for Hoover.

By the spring of 1928, it was evident that the Secretary of Commerce was outdistancing all rivals. It was evident too, however, that the President was increasingly unhappy about his heir-apparent. To his Secretary of Agriculture, Coolidge remarked in May of the Secretary of Commerce, "That man has offered me unsolicited advice for six years, all of it bad!" But when Senator Butler, Secretary Mellon, and others sought a go-ahead signal from him, the President relapsed into dour silence.

Three weeks before the convention, Jim Watson of Indiana made a final plea. Coolidge demurred. "The basic fact remains that I do not want the nomination," he said, as Watson remembered it. "I think I know myself very well. I fitted into the situation that existed right after the war, but I might not fit into the next one. . . . From this time on, there must be something constructive applied to the affairs of government," he continued surprisingly, "and it will not be sufficient to say, 'Let business take care of itself.'" Watson persisted. Would the President accept renomination? "Well," said Coolidge, "that is a matter for the Convention to decide." And, when it became clear three weeks later how the convention was deciding, Coolidge, hearing the news in visible distress, refused lunch and threw himself despairingly across his White House bed.

No American in 1928 could have provided a fairer test of the capacity of the business community to govern a great and multifarious nation than Herbert Hoover. And Hoover fully understood his responsibility. He had said with pride in the campaign that the Republican administration had "introduced a new basis in government relation with business." The result, he believed, was visible on every side. "Without the wise policies which the Republican Party has made effective during the past seven and one-half years the great prosperity we now enjoy would not have been possible." If the nation wanted the prosperity to last, "a continuation of the policies of the Republican Party is fundamentally necessary to the further advancement of this progress."

There were threats to prosperity, of course—above all, Democratic policies in agriculture and in public power which portended government in business, state socialism. The American people, Hoover said, had a fundamental conflict to resolve: American individualism, "rugged individualism" versus the philosophy of government operation and control. But Americans would not be beguiled from the path so clearly marked out for them by the Republicans. Confident in the wisdom of the past ("never has a political party been able to look back upon a similar period with more satisfaction"), exultant over the future ("no one can rightly deny the fundamental correctness of our economic system"), Hoover spoke repeatedly, almost ecstatically, of "the abolition of poverty."

"We in America today," said Herbert Hoover on August 11, 1928, "are nearer to the final triumph over poverty than ever before in the history of any land. The poorhouse is vanishing from among us. We have not yet reached the goal, but, given a chance to go forward with the policies of the last eight years, we shall soon with the help of God be in sight of the day when poverty will be banished from this nation."

On November 6, 1928, the American people gave Herbert Hoover the chance he sought.

16
Revolution in Manners and Morals

Frederick Lewis Allen

The sexual revolution of the twenties has become legendary; and by far the most celebrated account of the rebellion is that in Frederick Lewis Allen's *Only Yesterday*, excerpted here. But the revolt, contrary to popular belief, did not begin in the twenties themselves. As Allen points out, the initial attacks against the Victorian moral code started before America entered World War I (petting parties, for example, were going on in 1916), got a boost from that conflict, and came to full flower in the twenties.

Still, Allen's account is a bit misleading about the extent of the revolution. One might infer from his narrative that sexual permissiveness was well-nigh universal in the twenties, that almost everybody in the younger and middle generations drank bathtub gin, did the Charleston, and fornicated in closed-top cars. Thousands did, of course. But thousands more—probably a majority of both younger and middle generations—clung tenaciously to the old Victorian code. So the sexual revolution was a minority revolt, and one that enlisted more support in the cities than in the countryside. Nevertheless, throughout history minority revolutions have often had tremendous impacts on the societies that spawned them. And so it was with the sexual rebellion of the 1910s and 1920s: it brought about significant alterations in American sexual attitudes, ones that led to more revolutionary changes in the 1960s and 1970s.

A first-class revolt against the accepted American order was certainly taking place during those early years of the Post-war Decade, but it was one with which Nikolai Lenin had nothing whatever to do. The shock troops of the rebellion were not alien agitators, but the sons and daughters of well-to-do American families, who knew little about Bolshevism and cared distinctly less, and their defiance was expressed not in obscure radical publications or in soap-box speeches, but right across the family breakfast table into the horrified ears of conservative fathers and mothers. Men and women were still shivering at the Red Menace when they awoke to the no less alarming Problem of the Younger Generation, and realized that if the Constitution were not in danger, the moral code of the country certainly was.

This code, as it currently concerned young people, might have been roughly summarized as follows: Women were the guardians of morality; they were made of finer stuff than men and were expected to act accordingly. Young girls must look forward in innocence (tempered perhaps with a modicum of physiological instruction) to a romantic love match which would lead them to the altar and to living-happily-ever-after; and until the "right man" came along they must allow no male to kiss them. It was expected that some men would succumb to the temptations of sex, but

---

From "The Revolution in Manners and Morals" (pp. 88–118 hard cover ed.) from *Only Yesterday* by Frederick Lewis Allen. Copyright, 1931, by Frederick Lewis Allen. Copyright 1959 by Agnes Rogers Allen. By permission of Harper & Row, Publishers, Inc.

only with a special class of outlawed women; girls of respectable families were supposed to have no such temptations. Boys and girls were permitted large freedom to work and play together, with decreasing and well-nigh nominal chaperonage, but only because the code worked so well on the whole that a sort of honor system was supplanting supervision by their elders; it was taken for granted that if they had been well brought up they would never take advantage of this freedom. And although the attitude toward smoking and drinking by girls differed widely in different strata of society and different parts of the country, majority opinion held that it was morally wrong for them to smoke and could hardly imagine them showing the effects of alcohol.

The war had not long been over when cries of alarm from parents, teachers, and moral preceptors began to rend the air. For the boys and girls just growing out of adolescence were making mincemeat of this code.

The dresses that the girls—and for that matter most of the older women—were wearing seemed alarming enough. In July, 1920, a fashion-writer reported in the *New York Times* that "the American woman . . . has lifted her skirts far beyond any modest limitation," which was another way of saying that the hem was now all of nine inches above the ground. It was freely predicted that skirts would come down again in the winter of 1920–21, but instead they climbed a few scandalous inches farther. The flappers wore thin dresses, short-sleeved and occasionally (in the evening) sleeveless; some of the wilder young things rolled their stockings below their knees, revealing to the shocked eyes of virtue a fleeting glance of shin-bones and knee-cap; and many of them were visibly using cosmetics. "The intoxication of rouge," earnestly explained Dorothy Speare in *Dancers in the Dark*, "is an insidious vintage known to more girls than mere man can ever believe." Useless for frantic parents to insist that no lady did such things; the answer was that the daughters of ladies were doing it, and even retouching their masterpieces in public. Some of them, furthermore, were abandoning their corsets. "The men won't dance with you if you wear a corset," they were quoted as saying.

The current mode in dancing created still more consternation. Not the romantic violin but the barbaric saxophone now dominated the orchestra, and to its passionate crooning and wailing the fox-trotters moved in what the editor of the Hobart College *Herald* disgustedly called a "syncopated embrace." No longer did even an inch of space separate them; they danced as if glued together, body to body, cheek to cheek. Cried the *Catholic Telegraph* of Cincinnati in righteous indignation, "The music is sensuous, the embracing of partners—the female only half dressed—is absolutely indecent; and the motions—they are such as may not be described, with any respect for propriety, in a family newspaper. Suffice it to say that there are certain houses appropriate for such dances; but those houses have been closed by law."

Supposedly "nice" girls were smoking cigarettes—openly and defiantly, if often rather awkwardly and self-consciously. They were drinking—somewhat less openly but often all too efficaciously. There were stories of daughters of the most exemplary parents getting drunk—"blotto," as their companions cheerfully put it—on the contents of the hip-flasks of the new prohibition régime, and going out joyriding with men at four in the morning. And worst of all, even at well-regulated dances they were said to retire where the eye of the most sharp-sighted chaperon could not follow, and in darkened rooms or in parked cars to engage in the unspeakable practice of petting and necking.

It was not until F. Scott Fitzgerald, who had hardly graduated from Princeton and ought to know what his generation was doing, brought out *This Side of Paradise* in April, 1920, that fathers and mothers realized fully what was afoot and how long it had been going on. Apparently the "petting party" had been current as early as 1916, and was now widely established as an indoor sport. "None of the Victorian mothers—and most of the mothers were Victorian—had any idea how casually their daughters were accustomed to be kissed," wrote Mr. Fitzgerald. ". . . Amory saw girls doing things that even in his memory would have been impossible: eating three-o'clock, after-dance suppers in impossible cafés, talking of every side of life with an air half of earnestness, half of mockery, yet with a furtive excitement that Amory considered stood for a real moral let-down. But he never realized how widespread it was until he saw the cities between New York and Chicago as one vast juvenile intrigue." The book caused a shudder to run down the national spine; did not Mr. Fitzgerald represent one of his well-nurtured heroines as brazenly confessing, "I've kissed dozens of men. I suppose I'll kiss dozens more"; and another heroine as saying to a young man (*to a young man!*), "Oh, just one person in fifty has any glimmer of what sex is. I'm hipped on Freud and all that, but it's rotten that every bit of real love in the world is ninety-nine per cent passion and one little *soupçon* of jealousy"?

It was incredible. It was abominable. What did it all mean? Was every decent standard being thrown over? Mothers read the scarlet words and wondered if they themselves "had any idea how often their daughters were accustomed to be kissed." . . . But no, this must be an exaggerated account of the misconduct of some especially depraved group. Nice girls couldn't behave like that and talk openly about passion. But in due course other books appeared to substantiate the findings of Mr. Fitzgerald: *Dancers in the Dark, The Plastic Age, Flaming Youth*. Magazine articles and newspapers reiterated the scandal. To be sure, there were plenty of communities where nice girls did not, in actual fact, "behave like that"; and even in the more sophisticated urban centers there were plenty of girls who did not. Nevertheless, there was enough fire beneath the smoke of these sensational revelations to make the Problem of the Younger Generation a topic of anxious discussion from coast to coast.

The forces of morality rallied to the attack. Dr. Francis E. Clark, the founder and president of the Christian Endeavor Society, declared that the modern "indecent dance" was "an offense against womanly purity, the very fountainhead of our family and civil life." The new style of dancing was denounced in religious journals as "impure, polluting, corrupting, debasing, destroying spirituality, increasing carnality," and the mothers and sisters and church members of the land were called upon to admonish and instruct and raise the spiritual tone of these dreadful young people. President Murphy of the University of Florida cried out with true Southern warmth, "The low-cut gowns, the rolled hose and short skirts are born of the Devil and his angels, and are carrying the present and future generations to chaos and destruction." A group of Episcopal churchwomen in New York, speaking with the authority of wealth and social position (for they included Mrs. J. Pierpont Morgan, Mrs. Borden Harriman, Mrs. Henry Phipps, Mrs. James Roosevelt, and Mrs. E. H. Harriman), proposed an organization to discourage fashions involving an "excess of nudity" and "improper ways of dancing." The Y. W. C. A. conducted a national campaign against immodest dress among high-school girls, supplying newspapers with printed matter carrying headlines such as "Working Girls Responsive to Modesty Appeal!" and "High Heels Losing Ground Even in France." In Philadelphia a Dress Reform Committee of prominent citizens sent a questionnaire to over a thousand clergymen to ask them what would be their idea of a proper dress, and although the gentlemen of the cloth showed a distressing variety of opinion, the committee proceeded to design a "moral gown" which was endorsed by ministers of fifteen denominations. The distinguishing characteristics of this moral gown were that it was very loose-fitting, that the sleeves reached just below the elbows, and that the hem came within seven and a half inches of the floor.

Not content with example and reproof, legislators in several states introduced bills to reform feminine dress once and for all. The *New York American* reported in 1921 that a bill was pending in Utah providing fine and imprisonment for those who wore on the streets "skirts higher than three inches above the ankle." A bill was laid before the Virginia legislature which would forbid any woman from wearing shirtwaists or evening gowns which displayed "more than three inches of her throat." In Ohio the proposed limit of decolletage was two inches; the bill introduced in the Ohio legislature aimed also to prevent the sale of any "garment which unduly displays or accentuates the lines of the female figure," and to prohibit any "female over fourteen years of age" from wearing "a skirt which does not reach to that part of the foot known as the instep."

Meanwhile innumerable families were torn with dissension over cigarettes and gin and all-night automobile rides. Fathers and mothers lay awake asking themselves whether their children were not utterly lost; sons and daughters evaded questions, lied miserably and unhappily, or flared up to reply rudely that at least they were not dirty-minded hypocrites, that they saw no harm in what they were doing and proposed to go right on doing it. From those liberal clergymen and teachers who prided themselves on keeping step with all that was new came a chorus of reassurance: these young people were at least franker and more honest than their elders had been; having experimented for themselves, would they not soon find out which standards were outworn and which represented the accumulated moral wisdom of the race? Hearing such hopeful words, many good people took heart again. Perhaps this flareup of youthful passion was a flash in the pan, after all. Perhaps in another year or two the boys and girls would come to their senses and everything would be all right again.

They were wrong, however. For the revolt of the younger generation was only the beginning of a revolution in manners and morals that was already beginning to affect men and women of every age in every part of the country.

2

A number of forces were working together and interacting upon one another to make this revolution inevitable.

First of all was the state of mind brought about by the war and its conclusion. A whole generation had been infected by the eat-drink-and-be-merry-for-tomorrow-we-die spirit which accompanied the departure of the soldiers to the training camps and the fighting front. There had been an epidemic not only of abrupt war marriages, but of less conventional liaisons. In France, two million men had found themselves very close to filth and annihilation and very far from the American moral code and its defenders; prostitution had followed the flag and willing mademoiselles from Armentières had been plentiful; American girls sent over as nurses and war workers had come under the influence of continental manners and standards without being subject to the rigid protections thrown about their continental sisters of the respectable classes; and there had been a very widespread and very natural breakdown of traditional restraints and reticences and taboos. It was impossible for this generation to return unchanged when the ordeal was over. Some of them had acquired under the pressure of war-time conditions a new code which seemed to them quite defensible; millions of them had been provided with an emotional stimulant from which it was not easy to taper off. Their torn nerves craved the anodynes of speed, excitement, and passion. They found themselves expected to settle down into the humdrum routine of American life as if nothing had happened, to accept the moral dicta of elders who seemed to them still to be living in a Pollyanna land of rosy ideals which the war had killed for them. They couldn't do it, and they very disrespectfully said so.

"The older generation had certainly pretty well ruined this world before passing it on to us," wrote one of them (John F. Carter in the *Atlantic Monthly*, September, 1920), expressing accurately the sentiments of innumerable contemporaries. "They give us this thing, knocked to pieces, leaky, red-hot, threatening to blow up; and then they are surprised that we don't accept it with the same attitude of pretty, decorous enthusiasm with which they received it, way back in the 'eighties."

The middle generation was not so immediately affected by the war neurosis. They had had time enough, before 1917, to build up habits of conformity not easily broken down. But they, too, as the let-down of 1919 followed the war, found themselves restless and discontented, in a mood to question everything that had once seemed to them true and worthy and of good report. They too had spent themselves and wanted a good time. They saw their juniors exploring the approaches to the forbidden land of sex, and presently they began to play with the idea of doing a little experimenting of their own. The same disillusion which had defeated Woodrow Wilson and had caused strikes and riots and the Big Red Scare furnished a culture in which the germs of the new freedom could grow and multiply.

The revolution was accelerated also by the growing independence of the American woman. She won the suffrage in 1920. She seemed, it is true, to be very little interested in it once she had it; she voted, but mostly as the unregenerate men about her did, despite the efforts of women's clubs and the League of Women Voters to awaken her to womanhood's civic opportunity; feminine candidates for office were few, and some of them—such as Governor Ma Ferguson of Texas—scarcely seemed to represent the starry-eyed spiritual influence which, it had been promised, would presently ennoble public life. Few of the younger women could rouse themselves to even a passing interest in politics: to them it was a sordid and futile business, without flavor and without hope. Nevertheless, the winning of the suffrage had its effect. It consolidated woman's position as man's equal.

Even more marked was the effect of woman's growing independence of the drudgeries of housekeeping. Smaller houses were being built, and they were easier to look after. Families were moving into apartments, and these made even less claim upon the housekeeper's time and energy. Women were learning how to make lighter work of the preparation of meals. Sales of canned foods were growing, the number of delicatessen stores had increased three times as fast as the population during the decade 1910–20, the output of bakeries increased by 60 per cent during the decade 1914–24. Much of what had once been housework was now either moving out of the home entirely or being simplified by machinery. The use of commercial laundries, for instance, increased by 57 per cent between 1914 and 1924. Electric washing-machines and electric irons were coming to the aid of those who still did their washing at home; the manager of the local electric power company at "Middletown," a typical small American city, estimated in 1924 that nearly 90 per cent of the homes in the city already had electric irons. The housewife was learning to telephone her shopping orders, to get her clothes ready-made and spare herself the rigors of dress-making, to buy a vacuum cleaner and emulate the lovely carefree girls in the magazine advertisements who banished dust with such delicate fingers.

Women were slowly becoming emancipated from routine to "live their own lives."

And what were these "own lives" of theirs to be like? Well, for one thing, they could take jobs. Up to this time girls of the middle classes who had wanted to "do something" had been largely restricted to school-teaching, social-service work, nursing, stenography, and clerical work in business houses. But now they poured out of the schools and colleges into all manner of new occupations. They besieged the offices of publishers and advertisers; they went into tea-room management until there threatened to be more purveyors than consumers of chicken patties and cinnamon toast; they sold antiques, sold real estate, opened smart little shops, and finally invaded the department stores. In 1920 the department store was in the mind of the average college girl a rather bourgeois institution which employed "poor shop girls"; by the end of the decade college girls were standing in line for openings in the misses' sports-wear department and even selling behind the counter in the hope that some day fortune might smile upon them and make them buyers or stylists. Small-town girls who once would have been contented to stay in Sauk Center all their days were now borrowing from father to go to New York or Chicago to seek their fortunes—in Best's or Macy's or Marshall Field's. Married women who were encumbered with children and could not seek jobs consoled themselves with the thought that home-making and child-rearing were really "professions," after all. No topic was so furiously discussed at luncheon tables from one end of the country to the other as the question whether the married woman should take a job, and whether the mother had a right to. And as for the unmarried woman, she no longer had to explain why she worked in a shop or an office; it was idleness, nowadays, that had to be defended.

With the job—or at least the sense that the job was a possibility—came a feeling of comparative economic independence. With the feeling of economic independence came a slackening of husbandly and parental authority. Maiden aunts and unmarried daughters were leaving the shelter of the family roof to install themselves in kitchenette apartments of their own. For city-dwellers the home was steadily becoming less of a shrine, more of a dormitory —a place of casual shelter where one stopped overnight on the way from the restaurant and the movie theater to the office. Yet even the job did not provide the American woman with that complete satisfaction which the management of a mechanized home no longer furnished. She still had energies and emotions to burn; she was ready for the revolution.

Like all revolutions, this one was stimulated by foreign propaganda. It came, however, not from Moscow, but from Vienna. Sigmund Freud had published his first book on psychoanalysis at the end of the nineteenth century, and he and Jung had lectured to American psychologists as early as 1909, but it was not until after the war that the Freudian gospel began to circulate to a marked extent among the American lay public. The one great intellectual force which had not suffered disrepute as a result of the war was science; the more-or-less educated public was now absorbing a quantity of popularized information about biology and anthropology which gave a general impression that men and women were merely animals of a rather intricate variety, and that moral codes had no universal validity and were often based on curious superstitions. A fertile ground was ready for the seeds of Freudianism, and presently one began to hear even from the lips of flappers that "science taught" new and disturbing things about sex. Sex, it appeared, was the central and pervasive force which moved mankind. Almost every human motive was attributable to it: if you were patriotic or liked the violin, you were in the grip of sex—in a sublimated form. The first requirement of mental health was to have an uninhibited sex life. If you would be well and happy, you must obey your libido. Such was the Freudian gospel as it imbedded itself in the American mind after being filtered through the successive minds of interpreters and popularizers and guileless readers and people who had heard guileless readers talk about it. New words and phrases began to be bandied about the cocktail-tray and the Mah Jong table—inferiority complex, sadism, masochism, Œdipus complex. Intellectual ladies went to Europe to be analyzed; analysts plied their new trade in American cities, conscientiously transferring the affections of their fair patients to themselves; and clergymen who preached about the virtue of self-control were reminded by outspoken critics that self-control was out-of-date and really dangerous.

The principal remaining forces which accelerated the revolution in manners and morals were all 100 per cent American. They were prohibition, the automobile, the confession and sex magazines, and the movies.

When the Eighteenth Amendment was ratified, prohibition seemed, as we have already noted, to have an almost united country behind it. Evasion of the law began immediately, however, and strenuous and sincere opposition to it—especially in the large cities of the North and East—quickly gathered force. The results were the bootlegger, the speakeasy, and a spirit of deliberate revolt which in many communities made drinking "the thing to do." From these facts in turn flowed further results: the increased popularity of distilled as against fermented liquors, the use of the hip-flask, the cocktail party, and the general transformation of drinking from a masculine prerogative to one shared by both sexes together. The old-time saloon had been overwhelmingly masculine; the speakeasy usually catered to both men and women. As Elmer Davis put it, "The old days when father spent his evenings at Cassidy's bar with the rest of the boys are gone, and probably gone forever; Cassidy may still be in business at the old stand and father may still go down there of evenings, but since prohibition mother goes down with him." Under the new régime not only the drinks were mixed, but the company as well.

Meanwhile a new sort of freedom was being made possible by the enormous increase in the use of the automobile, and particularly of the closed car. (In 1919 hardly more than 10 per cent of the cars produced in the United States were closed; by 1924 the percentage had jumped to 43, by 1927 it had reached 82.8.) The automobile offered an almost universally available means of escaping temporarily from the supervision of parents and chaperons, or from the influence of neighborhood opinion. Boys and girls now thought nothing, as the Lynds pointed out in *Middletown,* of jumping into a car and driving off at a moment's notice—without asking anybody's permission—to a dance in another town twenty miles away, where they were strangers and enjoyed a freedom impossible among their neighbors. The closed car, moreover, was in effect a room protected from the weather which could be occupied at any time of the day or night and could be moved at will into a darkened byway or a country lane. The Lynds quoted the judge of the juvenile court in "Middletown" as declaring that the automobile had become a "house of prostitution on wheels," and cited the fact that of thirty girls brought before his court in a year on charges of sex crimes, for whom the place where the offense had occurred was recorded, nineteen were listed as having committed it in an automobile.

Finally, as the revolution began, its influence fertilized a bumper crop of sex magazines, confession magazines, and lurid motion pictures, and these in turn had their effect on a class of readers and movie-goers who had never heard and never would hear of Freud and the libido. The publishers of the sex adventure magazines, offering stories with such titles as "What I Told My Daughter the Night Before Her Marriage," "Indolent Kisses," and "Watch Your Step-Ins," learned to a nicety the gentle art of arousing the reader without arousing the censor. The publishers of the confession magazines, while always instructing their authors to provide a moral ending and to utter pious sentiments, concentrated on the description of what they euphemistically called "missteps." Most of their fiction was faked to order by hack writers who could write one day "The Confessions of a Chorus Girl" and the next day recount, again in the first person, the temptations which made it easy for the taxidriver to go wrong. Both classes of magazines became astonishingly numerous and successful. Bernarr Macfadden's *True-Story*, launched as late as 1919, had over 300,000 readers by 1923; 848,000 by 1924; over a million and a half by 1925; and almost two million by 1926—a record of rapid growth probably unparalleled in magazine publishing.

Crowding the news stands along with the sex and confession magazines were motion-picture magazines which depicted "seven movie kisses" with such captions as "Do you recognize your little friend, Mae Busch? She's had lots of kisses, but she never seems to grow *blasé*. At least you'll agree that she's giving a good imitation of a person enjoying this one." The movies themselves, drawing millions to their doors every day and every night, played incessantly upon the same lucrative theme. The producers of one picture advertised "brilliant men, beautiful jazz babies, champagne baths, midnight revels, petting parties in the purple dawn, all ending in one terrific smashing climax that makes you gasp"; the venders of another promised "neckers, petters, white kisses, red kisses, pleasure-mad daughters, sensation-craving mothers, . . . the truth—bold, naked, sensational." Seldom did the films offer as much as these advertisements promised, but there was enough in some of them to cause a sixteen-year-old girl (quoted by Alice Miller Mitchell) to testify, "Those pictures with hot love-making in them, they make girls and boys sitting together want to get up and walk out, go off somewhere, you know. Once I walked out with a boy before the picture was even over. We took a ride. But my friend, she all the time had to get up and go out with her boy friend."

A storm of criticism from church organizations led the motion-picture producers, early in the decade, to install Will H. Hays, President Harding's Postmaster-General, as their arbiter of morals and of taste, and Mr. Hays promised that all would be well. "This industry must have," said he before the Los Angeles Chamber of Commerce, "toward that sacred thing, the mind of a child, toward that clean virgin thing, that unmarked slate, the same responsibility, the same care about the impressions made upon it, that the best clergyman or the most inspired teacher of youth would have." The result of Mr. Hays's labors in behalf of the unmarked slate was to make the moral ending as obligatory as in the confession magazines, to smear over sexy pictures with pious platitudes, and to blacklist for motion-picture production many a fine novel and play which, because of its very honesty, might be construed as seriously or intelligently questioning the traditional sex ethics of the small town. Mr. Hays, being something of a genius, managed to keep the churchmen at bay. Whenever the threats of censorship began to become ominous he would promulgate a new series of moral commandments for the producers to follow. Yet of the practical effects of his supervision it is perhaps enough to say that the quotations given above all date from the period of his dictatorship. Giving lip-service to the old code, the movies diligently and with consummate vulgarity publicized the new.

Each of these diverse influences—the post-war disillusion, the new status of women, the Freudian gospel, the automobile, prohibition, the sex and confession magazines, and the movies—

had its part in bringing about the revolution. Each of them, as an influence, was played upon by all the others; none of them could alone have changed to any great degree the folkways of America; together their force was irresistible.

3

The most conspicuous sign of what was taking place was the immense change in women's dress and appearance.

In Professor Paul H. Nystrom's *Economics of Fashion*, the trend of skirt-length during the Post-war Decade is ingeniously shown by the sort of graph with which business analysts delight to compute the ebb and flow of car-loadings or of stock averages. The basis of this graph is a series of measurements of fashion-plates in the *Delineator*; the statistician painstakingly measured the relation, from month to month, of the height of the skirt hem above the ground to the total height of the figure, and plotted his curve accordingly. This very unusual graph shows that in 1919 the average distance of the hem above the ground was about 10 per cent of the woman's height—or to put it in another way, about six or seven inches. In 1920 it curved upward from 10 to about 20 per cent. During the next three years it gradually dipped to 10 per cent again, reaching its low point in 1923. In 1924, however, it rose once more to between 15 and 20 per cent, in 1925 to more than 20 per cent; and the curve continued steadily upward until by 1927 it had passed the 25 per cent mark—in other words, until the skirt had reached the knee. There it remained until late in 1929.

This graph, as Professor Nystrom explains, does not accurately indicate what really happened, for it represents for any given year or month, not the average length of skirts actually worn, but the length of the skirt which the arbiters of fashion, not uninfluenced by the manufacturers of dress goods, expected and wanted women to wear. In actual fact, the dip between 1921 and 1924 was very slight. Paris dressmakers predicted the return of longer skirts, the American stylists and manufacturers followed their lead, the stores bought the longer skirts and tried to sell them, but women kept on buying the shortest skirts they could find. During the fall of 1923 and the spring of 1924, manufacturers were deluged with complaints from retailers that skirts would have to be shorter. Shorter they finally were, and still shorter. The knee-length dress proved to be exactly what women wanted. The unlucky manufacturers made valiant efforts to change the fashion. Despite all they could do, however, the knee-length skirt remained standard until the decade was approaching its end.

With the short skirt went an extraordinary change in the weight and material and amount of women's clothing. The boyishly slender figure became the aim of every woman's ambition, and the corset was so far abandoned that even in so short a period as the three years from 1924 to 1927 the combined sales of corsets and brassières in the department stores of the Cleveland Federal Reserve District fell off 11 per cent. Silk or rayon stockings and underwear supplanted cotton, to the distress of cotton manufacturers and the delight of rayon manufacturers; the production of rayon in American plants, which in 1920 had been only eight million pounds, had by 1925 reached fifty-three million pounds. The flesh-colored stocking became as standard as the short skirt. Petticoats almost vanished from the American scene; in fact, the tendency of women to drop off one layer of clothing after another became so pronounced that in 1928 the *Journal of Commerce* estimated that in 15 years the amount of material required for a woman's complete costume (exclusive of her stockings) had declined from 19¼ yards to 7 yards. All she could now be induced to wear, it seemed, was an overblouse (2 yards), a skirt (2¼ yards), vest or shirt (¾), knickers (2), and stockings—and all of them were made of silk or rayon! This latter statement, it is true, was a slight exaggeration; but a survey published in 1926 by the National Retail Dry Goods Association, on the basis of data from department stores all over the country, showed that only 33 per cent of the women's underwear sold was made of cotton, whereas 36 per cent was made of rayon, and 31 per cent of silk. No longer were silk stockings the mark of the rich; as the wife of a workingman with a total family income of $1,638 a year told the authors of *Middletown*, "No girl can wear cotton stockings to high school. Even in winter my children wear silk stockings with lisle or imitations underneath."

Not content with the freedom of short and skimpy clothes, women sought, too, the freedom of short hair. During the early years of the decade the bobbed head—which in 1918, as you may recall, had been regarded by the proprietor of the Palm Garden in New York as a sign of radicalism—became increasingly frequent among young girls, chiefly on the ground of convenience. In May, 1922, the *American Hairdresser* predicted that the bob, which persisted in being popular, "will probably last through the summer, anyway." It not only did this, it so increased in popularity that by 1924 the same journal was forced to feature bobbed styles and give its subscribers instructions in the new art, and was reporting the progress of a lively battle between the professional hairdressers and the barbers for the cream of this booming business. The ladies' hairdressers very naturally objected to women going to barbers' shops; the barbers, on the other hand, were trying to force legislation in various states which would forbid the "hairdressing profession" to cut hair unless they were licensed as barbers. Said the *Hairdresser*, putting the matter on the loftiest basis, "The effort to bring women to barber shops for haircutting is against the best interests of the public, the free and easy atmosphere often prevailing in barber shops being unsuitable to the high standard of American womanhood." But all that American womanhood appeared to insist upon was the best possible shingle. In the latter years of the decade bobbed hair became almost universal among girls in their twenties, very common among women in their thirties and forties, and by no means rare among women of sixty; and for a brief period the hair was not only bobbed, but in most cases cropped close to the head like a man's. Women universally adopted the small cloche hat which fitted tightly on the bobbed head, and the manufacturer of milliner's materials joined the hair-net manufacturer, the hair-pin manufacturer, and the cotton goods and woolen goods and corset manufacturers, among the ranks of depressed industries.

For another industry, however, the decade brought new and enormous profits. The manufacturers of cosmetics and the proprietors of beauty shops had less than nothing to complain of. The vogue of rouge and lipstick, which in 1920 had so alarmed the parents of the younger generation, spread swiftly to the remotest village. Women who in 1920 would have thought the use of paint immoral were soon applying it regularly as a matter of course and making no effort to disguise the fact; beauty shops had sprung up on every street to give "facials," to apply pomade and astringents, to make war against the wrinkles and sagging chins of age, to pluck and trim and color the eyebrows, and otherwise to enhance and restore the bloom of youth; and a strange new form of surgery, "face-lifting," took its place among the applied sciences of the day. Back in 1917, according to Frances Fisher Dubuc, only two persons in the beauty culture business had paid an income tax; by 1927 there were 18,000 firms and individuals in this field listed as income-tax payers. The "beautician" had arrived.

As for the total amount of money spent by American women on cosmetics and beauty culture by the end of the decade, we may probably accept as conservative the prodigious figure of three-quarters of a billion dollars set by Professor Paul H. Nystrom in 1930; other estimates, indeed, ran as high as two billion. Mrs.

Christine Frederick tabulated in 1929 some other equally staggering figures: for every adult woman in the country there were being sold annually over a pound of face powder and no less than eight rouge compacts; there were 2,500 brands of perfume on the market and 1,500 face creams; and if all the lipsticks sold in a year in the United States were placed end to end, they would reach from New York to Reno—which to some would seem an altogether logical destination.

Perhaps the readiest way of measuring the change in the public attitude toward cosmetics is to compare the advertisements in a conservative periodical at the beginning of the decade with those at its end. Although the June, 1919, issue of the *Ladies' Home Journal* contained four advertisements which listed rouge among other products, only one of them commented on its inclusion, and this referred to its rouge as one that was "imperceptible if properly applied." In those days the woman who used rouge—at least in the circles in which the *Journal* was read—wished to disguise the fact. (Advertisements of talc, in 1919, commonly displayed a mother leaning affectionately over a bouncing baby.) In the June, 1929, issue, exactly ten years later, the *Journal* permitted a lipstick to be advertised with the comment, "It's comforting to know that the alluring note of scarlet will stay with you for hours." (Incidentally, the examination of those two magazines offers another contrast: in 1919 the Listerine advertisement said simply, "The prompt application of Listerine may prevent a minor accident from becoming a major infection," whereas in 1929 it began a tragic rhapsody with the words, "Spring! for everyone but her . . .")

These changes in fashion—the short skirt, the boyish form, the straight, long-waisted dresses, the frank use of paint—were signs of a real change in the American feminine ideal (as well, perhaps, as in men's idea of what was the feminine ideal). Women were bent on freedom—freedom to work and to play without the trammels that had bound them heretofore to lives of comparative inactivity. But what they sought was not the freedom from man and his desires which had put the suffragists of an earlier day into hard straw hats and mannish suits and low-heeled shoes. The woman of the nineteen-twenties wanted to be able to allure man even on the golf links and in the office; the little flapper who shingled her hair and wore a manageable little hat and put on knickerbockers for the weekends would not be parted from her silk stockings and her high-heeled shoes. Nor was the post-war feminine ideal one of fruitful maturity or ripened wisdom or practiced grace. On the contrary: the quest of slenderness, the flattening of the breasts, the vogue of short skirts (even when short skirts still suggested the appearance of a little girl), the juvenile effect of the long waist,—all were signs that, consciously or unconsciously, the women of this decade worshiped not merely youth, but unripened youth: they wanted to be—or thought men wanted them to be—men's casual and light-hearted companions; not broad-hipped mothers of the race, but irresponsible playmates. Youth was their pattern, but not youthful innocence: the adolescent whom they imitated was a hard-boiled adolescent, who thought not in terms of romantic love, but in terms of sex, and who made herself desirable not by that sly art which conceals art, but frankly and openly. In effect, the woman of the Post-war Decade said to man, "You are tired and disillusioned, you do not want the cares of a family or the companionship of mature wisdom, you want exciting play, you want the thrills of sex without their fruition, and I will give them to you." And to herself she added, "But I will be free."

4

One indication of the revolution in manners which her headlong pursuit of freedom brought about was her rapid acceptance of the cigarette. Within a very few years millions of American

Flappers on the beach in the 1920s. "The flappers wore thin dresses, short-sleeved and occasionally (in the evening) sleeveless; some of the wilder young things rolled their stockings below their knees, revealing to the shocked eyes of virtue a fleeting glance of shin-bones and knee-cap." Some flappers—like the girls shown here—revealed a good deal more than that. If their grandmothers wore voluminous swimming suits and were rolled to the water in bathhouses, the flappers went to the beach in shorts and danced the Charleston there. (National Police Gazette photo courtesy of The New York Public Library, Astor, Lenox and Tilden Foundations.)

women of all ages followed the lead of the flappers of 1920 and took up smoking. Custom still generally frowned upon their doing it on the street or in the office, and in the evangelical hinterlands the old taboo died hard; but in restaurants, at dinner parties and dances, in theater lobbies, and in a hundred other places they made the air blue. Here again the trend in advertising measured the trend in public opinion. At the beginning of the decade advertisers realized that it would have been suicidal to portray a woman smoking; within a few years, however, they ventured pictures of pretty girls imploring men to blow some of the smoke their way; and by the end of the decade billboards boldly displayed a smart-looking woman cigarette in hand, and in some of the magazines, despite floods of protests from rural readers, tobacco manufacturers were announcing that "now women may enjoy a companionable smoke with their husbands and brothers." In the ten years between 1918 and 1928 the total production of cigarettes in the United States *more than doubled*. Part of this increase was doubtless due to the death of the one-time masculine prejudice against the cigarette as unmanly, for it was accompanied by somewhat of a decrease in the production of cigars and smoking tobacco, as well as—mercifully—of chewing tobacco. Part of it was attributable to the fact that the convenience of the cigarette made the masculine smoker consume more tobacco than in the days when he preferred a cigar or a pipe. But the increase could never have been so large had it not been for the women who now strewed the dinner table with their ashes, snatched a puff between the acts, invaded the masculine sanctity of the club car, and forced department stores to place ornamental ash-trays between the chairs in their women's shoe departments. A formidable barrier between the sexes had broken down. The custom of separating them after formal dinners, for example, still lingered, but as an empty rite.

Hosts who laid in a stock of cigars for their male guests often found them untouched; the men in the dining-room were smoking the very same brands of cigarettes that the ladies consumed in the living-room.

Of far greater social significance, however, was the fact that men and women were drinking together. Among well-to-do people the serving of cocktails before dinner became almost socially obligatory. Mixed parties swarmed up to the curtained grills of speakeasies and uttered the mystic password, and girls along with men stood at the speakeasy bar with one foot on the old brass rail. The late afternoon cocktail party became a new American institution. When dances were held in hotels, the curious and rather unsavory custom grew up of hiring hotel rooms where reliable drinks could be served in suitable privacy; guests of both sexes lounged on the beds and tossed off mixtures of high potency. As houses and apartments became smaller, the country club became the social center of the small city, the suburb, and the summer resort; and to its pretentious clubhouse, every Saturday night, drove men and women (after a round of cocktails at somebody's house) for the weekly dinner dance. Bottles of White Rock and of ginger ale decked the tables, out of capacious masculine hip pockets came flasks of gin (once the despised and rejected of bartenders, now the most popular of all liquors), and women who a few years before would have gasped at the thought that they would ever be "under the influence of alcohol" found themselves matching the men drink for drink and enjoying the uproarious release. The next day gossip would report that the reason Mrs. So-and-so disappeared from the party at eleven was because she had had too many cocktails and had been led to the dressing-room to be sick, or that somebody would have to meet the club's levy for breakage, or that Mrs. Such-and-such really oughtn't to drink so much because three cocktails made her throw bread about the table.

A passing scandal would be created by a dance at which substantial married men amused themselves by tripping up waiters, or young people bent on petting parties drove right out on the golf-links and made wheel-tracks on the eighteenth green.

Such incidents were of course exceptional and in many communities they never occurred. It was altogether probable, though the professional wets denied it, that prohibition succeeded in reducing the total amount of drinking in the country as a whole and in reducing it decidedly among the workingmen of the industrial districts. The majority of experienced college administrators agreed—rather to the annoyance of some of their undergraduates—that there was less drinking among men students than there had been before prohibition and that drinking among girl students, at least while they were in residence, hardly offered a formidable problem. Yet the fact remained that among the prosperous classes which set the standards of national social behavior, alcohol flowed more freely than ever before and lubricated an unprecedented informality—to say the least—of manners.

It lubricated, too, a new outspokenness between men and women. Thanks to the spread of scientific skepticism and especially to Sigmund Freud, the dogmas of the conservative moralists were losing force and the dogma that salvation lay in facing the facts of sex was gaining. An upheaval in values was taking place. Modesty, reticence, and chivalry were going out of style; women no longer wanted to be "ladylike" or could appeal to their daughters to be "wholesome"; it was too widely suspected that the old-fashioned lady had been a sham and that the "wholesome" girl was merely inhibiting a nasty mind and would come to no good end. "Victorian" and "Puritan" were becoming terms of opprobrium: up-to-date people thought of Victorians as old ladies with bustles and inhibitions, and of Puritans as blue-nosed, ranting spoilsports. It was better to be modern,

—everybody wanted to be modern,—and sophisticated, and smart, to smash the conventions and to be devastatingly frank. And with a cocktail glass in one's hand it was easy at least to be frank.

"Listen with a detached ear to a modern conversation," wrote Mary Agnes Hamilton in 1927, "and you will be struck, first, by the restriction of the vocabulary, and second, by the higher proportion in that vocabulary of words such as, in the older jargon, 'no lady could use.'" With the taste for strong liquors went a taste for strong language. To one's lovely dinner partner, the inevitable antithesis for "grand" and "swell" had become "lousy." An unexpected "damn" or "hell" uttered on the New York stage was no longer a signal for the sudden sharp laughter of shocked surprise; such words were becoming the commonplace of everyday talk. The barroom anecdote of the decade before now went the rounds of aristocratic bridge tables. Every one wanted to be unshockable; it was delightful to be considered a little shocking; and so the competition in boldness of talk went on until for a time, as Mrs. Hamilton put it, a conversation in polite circles was like a room decorated entirely in scarlet—the result was over-emphasis, stridency, and eventual boredom.

Along with the new frankness in conversation went a new frankness in books and the theater. Consider, for example, the themes of a handful of the best plays produced in New York during the decade: *What Price Glory?*, which represented the amorous marines interlarding their talk with epithets new to the stage; *The Road to Rome*, the prime comic touch of which was the desire of a Roman matron to be despoiled by the Carthaginians; *Strange Interlude*, in which a wife who found there was insanity in her husband's family but wanted to give him a child decided to have the child by an attractive young doctor, instead of by her husband, and forthwith fell in love with the doctor; *Strictly Dishonorable*, in which a charming young girl walked blithely and open-eyed into an affair of a night with an opera-singer; and *The Captive*, which revealed to thousands of innocents the fact that the world contained such a phenomenon as homosexuality. None of these plays could have been tolerated even in New York before the Post-war Decade; all of them in the nineteen-twenties were not merely popular, but genuinely admired by intelligent audiences. The effect of some of them upon these audiences is suggested by the story of the sedate old lady who, after two acts of *What Price Glory?*, reprimanded her grandson with a "God damn it, Johnny, sit down!"

The same thing was true of the novels of the decade; one after another, from *Jurgen* and *Dark Laughter* through the tales of Michael Arlen to *An American Tragedy* and *The Sun Also Rises* and *The Well of Loneliness* and *Point Counter Point*, they dealt with sex with an openness or a cynicism or an unmoral objectivity new to the English-speaking world. Bitterly the defenders of the Puritan code tried to stem the tide, but it was too strong for them. They banned *Jurgen*—and made a best seller of it and a public reputation for its author. They dragged Mary Ware Dennett into court for distributing a pamphlet for children which explained some of the mysteries of sex—only to have her upheld by a liberal judge and endorsed by intelligent public opinion. In Boston, where they were backed by an alliance between stubborn Puritanism and Roman Catholicism, they banned books wholesale, forbade the stage presentation of *Strange Interlude*, and secured the conviction of a bookseller for selling *Lady Chatterley's Lover*—only to find that the intellectuals of the whole country were laughing at them and that ultimately they were forced to allow the publication of books which they would have moved to ban ten years before. Despite all that they could do, the taste of the country demanded a new sort of reading matter.

Early in the decade a distinguished essayist wrote an article in which she contended that the physical processes of childbirth were humiliating to many women. She showed it to the editor of one of the best magazines, and he and she agreed that it should not be printed: too many readers would be repelled by the subject matter and horrified by the thesis. Only a few years later, in 1927, the editor recalled this manuscript and asked if he might see it again. He saw it—and wondered why it had ever been disqualified. Already such frankness seemed quite natural and permissible. The aritcle was duly published, and caused only the mildest of sensations.

If in 1918 the editors of a reputable magazine had accepted a story in which one gangster said to another, "For Christ's sake, Joe, give her the gas. Some lousy bastard has killed Eddie," they would have whipped out the blue pencil and changed the passage to something like "For the love of Mike, Joe, give her the gas. Some dirty skunk has killed Eddie." In 1929 that sentence appeared in a story accepted by a magazine of the most unblemished standing, and was printed without alteration. A few readers objected, but not many. Times had changed. Even in the great popular periodicals with huge circulations and a considerable following in the strongholds of rural Methodism the change in standards was apparent. Said a short-story writer in the late nineteen-twenties, "I used to write for magazines like the *Saturday Evening Post* and the *Pictorial Review* when I had a nice innocuous tale to tell and wanted the money, and for magazines like *Harper's* and *Scribner's* when I wanted to write something searching and honest. Now I find I can sell the honest story to the big popular magazines too."

5

With the change in manners went an inevitable change in morals. Boys and girls were becoming sophisticated about sex at an earlier age; it was symptomatic that when the authors of *Middletown* asked 241 boys and 315 girls of high-school age to mark as true or false, according to their opinion, the extreme statement, "Nine out of every ten boys and girls of high-school age have petting parties," almost precisely half of them marked it as true. How much actual intercourse there was among such young people it is of course impossible to say; but the lurid stories told by Judge Lindsay—of girls who carried contraceptives in their vanity cases, and of "Caroline," who told the judge that fifty-eight girls of her acquaintance had had one or more sex experiences without a single pregnancy resulting—were matched by the gossip current in many a town. Whether prostitution increased or decreased during the decade is likewise uncertain; but certain it is that the prostitute was faced for the first time with an amateur competition of formidable proportions.

As for the amount of outright infidelity among married couples, one is again without reliable data, the private relations of men and women being happily beyond the reach of the statistician. The divorce rate, however, continued its steady increase; for every 100 marriages there were 8.8 divorces in 1910, 13.4 divorces in 1920, and 16.5 divorces in 1928—almost one divorce for every six marriages. There was a corresponding decline in the amount of disgrace accompanying divorce. In the urban communities men and women who had been divorced were now socially accepted without question; indeed, there was often about the divorced person just enough of an air of unconventionality, just enough of a touch of scarlet, to be considered rather dashing and desirable. Many young women probably felt as did the New York girl who said, toward the end of the decade, that she was thinking of marrying Henry, although she didn't care very much for him, because even if they didn't get along she could get a divorce and "it would be much more exciting to be a divorcée than to be an old maid."

The petting party, which in the first years of the decade had been limited to youngsters in their teens and twenties, soon made its appearance among older men and women: when the gin-flask was passed about the hotel bedroom during a dance, or the musicians stilled their saxophones during the Saturday-night party at the country club, men of affairs and women with half-grown children had their little taste of raw sex. One began to hear of young girls, intelligent and well born, who had spent weekends with men before marriage and had told their prospective husbands everything and had been not merely forgiven, but told that there was nothing to forgive; a little "experience," these men felt, was all to the good for any girl. Millions of people were moving toward acceptance of what a *bon-vivant* of earlier days had said was his idea of the proper state of morality —"A single standard, and that a low one."

It would be easy, of course, to match every one of these cases with contrasting cases of men and women who still thought and behaved at the end of the decade exactly as the president of the Epworth League would have wished. Two women who conducted newspaper columns of advice in affairs of the heart testified that the sort of problem which was worrying young America, to judge from their bulging correspondence, was not whether to tell the boy friend about the illegitimate child, but whether it was proper to invite the boy friend up on the porch if he hadn't yet come across with an invitation to the movies, or whether the cake at a pie social should be cut with a knife. In the hinterlands there was still plenty of old-fashioned sentimental thinking about sex, of the sort which expressed itself in the slogan of a federated women's club: "Men are God's trees, women are His flowers." There were frantic efforts to stay the tide of moral change by law, the most picturesque of these efforts being the ordinance actually passed in Norphelt, Arkansas, in 1925, which contained the following provisions:

"Section 1. Hereafter it shall be unlawful for any man and woman, male or female, to be guilty of committing the act of sexual intercourse between themselves at any place within the corporate limits of said town.

"Section 3. Section One of this ordinance shall not apply to married persons as between themselves, and their husband and wife, unless of a grossly improper and lascivious nature."

Nevertheless, there was an unmistakable and rapid trend away from the old American code toward a philosophy of sex relations and of marriage wholly new to the country: toward a feeling that the virtues of chastity and fidelity had been rated too highly, that there was something to be said for what Mrs. Bertrand Russell defined as "the right, equally shared by men and women, to free participation in sex experience," that it was not necessary for girls to deny themselves this right before marriage or even for husbands and wives to do so after marriage. It was in acknowledgment of the spread of this feeling that Judge Lindsay proposed, in 1927, to establish "companionate marriage" on a legal basis. He wanted to legalize birth control (which, although still outlawed, was by this time generally practiced or believed in by married couples in all but the most ignorant classes) and to permit legal marriage to be terminated at any time in divorce by mutual consent, provided there were no children. His suggestion created great consternation and was widely and vigorously denounced; but the mere fact that it was seriously debated showed how the code of an earlier day had been shaken. The revolution in morals was in full swing.

17

Henry Ford: Symbol of an Age

Roderick Nash

Throughout the twenties, a great many older Americans remained as old-fashioned in their moral convictions as in their politics. Chief among them was car-maker Henry Ford, whose technological genius, love of country, and traditional Americanism made him a hero to a large segment of American society. Yet, as Roderick Nash points out, Ford was also profoundly ambivalent, looking backward and forward at once, defending technology at the same time that he extolled the old rural values of a bygone time. In this respect, he symbolized the America of his age—a changing, industrial America that longed for the security of the old days as it struggled with the complexities of the new.

Few names were better known to Americans from 1917 to 1930 than that of Henry Ford. Whether one read his publications,[1] or followed his headline-making public life, or merely drove the car his company manufactured, Ford was inescapable in the twenties. Indeed it is possible to think of these years as the automobile age and Henry Ford as its czar. The flivver, along with the flask and the flapper, seemed to represent the 1920s in the minds of its people as well as its historians.

Cars symbolized change. They upset familiar patterns of living, working, recreating, even thinking. Much of the roar of the twenties came from the internal combustion engine. While providing portable bedrooms in which to enjoy the decade's alleged sexual freedom, cars also assisted gangsters and bootleggers in getting away. The image of two of them in every garage helped elect a President in 1928. The rise of widespread use of the automobile, in a word, contributed significantly to setting the twenties apart. And Henry Ford, calling machinery the "new Messiah" (as he did in 1929), seemed to herald the new era.

Beneath the surface, however, such generalizations ring hollow. Neither Ford nor the twenties merited the clichés with which each has been so frequently discussed. In the case of the man, both old and new mingled in his mind. On the one hand Ford was a builder and bulwark of the modern, mechanized nation; on the other he devoted a remarkable amount of effort and expense to sustaining old-fashioned America. In fact, the nostalgic, backward-looking Henry Ford repeatedly deplored the very conditions that Ford the revolutionary industrialist did so much to bring about. This ambivalence did not signify a lack of values so much as a superfluity. His faith was strong if bigoted and contradic-

---

[1] In all probability Henry Ford did not actually write the numerous books, pamphlets, and articles associated with his name and attributed to him in this chapter. He was not a literary man; his critics even alleged he could not read! But Ford could pay people to express his opinions for him, and there is no reason to think that the ideas these writers recorded were not those of their employer.

From pp. 153–163 of *The Nervous Generation: American Thought, 1917–1930* by Roderick Nash. Copyright © 1970 by Rand McNally College Publishing Company, Chicago. Reprinted by permission of the publisher.

236

As Nash observes, Henry Ford was "a plain, honest, old-fashioned billionaire" and "technological genius" who fretted about the new morality of the jazz age, ridiculing jazz itself as "monkey talk" and "jungle squeals" and blaming illicit liquor on a Jewish conspiracy. Still, in spite of his rural outlook and Biblical virtues, Ford was one of the most popular Americans of the roaring twenties. (Courtesy of the Ford Archives, Henry Ford Museum, Dearborn, Michigan.)

tory. His prescriptions for America were clear if simple-minded. He seemed to the masses to demonstrate that there could be change without disruption, and in so doing he eased the twenties' tensions. "The average citizen," editorialized the New Republic in 1923, "sees Ford as a sort of enlarged crayon portrait of himself; the man able to fulfill his own suppressed desires, who has achieved enormous riches, fame and power without departing from the pioneer-and-homespun tradition." In this nervous clinging to old values even while undermining them Ford was indeed a "crayon portrait" of his age.

But was Ford typical of the twenties? Can he really be said to symbolize the age? He was, after all, in his middle fifties when the decade began. However, a great many Americans were also middle-aged in the 1920s, far more in fact than the twenty-year-old collegians who have hitherto characterized these years. And at one point even a group of college students ranked Ford as the third greatest figure of all time, behind Napoleon and Jesus Christ.

The Dearborn, Michigan, into which Henry Ford was born in 1863 was a small farming community only a generation removed from the frontier. Both sides of the Ford family had agrarian backgrounds, and the children grew up on the farm. Henry's formal education began and ended in the Scotch Settlement School which he attended for eight years. The staple of his academic diet was the McGuffey reader with its moral-coated language lessons. When Ford left school to become an apprentice mechanic in Detroit, he also left the farm. But the farm never left Henry. Agrarian ideas and values shaped his thought even as he became an industrial king.

The 1880s for Ford were a time of aimlessness, his only real interest being in tinkering with watches and other engines. In 1892 he joined the Edison Company in Detroit as an engineer. During his spare time he struggled with the problem of building a gasoline engine compact enough to power a moving vehicle. By 1896 Ford had his automobile. Soon he had it doing ninety miles per hour! It required seven years more, however, for him to secure the necessary financial and administrative backing to launch the Ford Motor Company. The rest was pure Horatio Alger.

The first Model T appeared in 1908, and it soon made good Ford's boast that he could build a car for the masses. Six thousand sold the first year. Six years later, after the introduction of assembly line production, the figure was

248,000. From May to December 1920 almost 700,000 Model Ts rolled out of the Ford plants. The total for 1921 was one million. In 1923 57 per cent of all cars manufactured in the United States were Fords. Three years later the Ford Motor Company produced its thirteen millionth car. From the perspective of efficient production the Ford organization was also something of a miracle. In 1913 it required twelve hours to make a car. The following year, after the introduction of the assembly line techniques, the figure dropped to ninety-three minutes. In 1920 Ford achieved his long-time dream of building one car for every minute of the working day. And still he was unsatisfied. On October 31, 1925, the Ford Motor Company manufactured 9,109 Model Ts, one every ten seconds. This was the high point, and competition was rising to challenge Ford's preeminence, but by the end of the twenties Henry Ford was a legend, a folk hero, and reputedly the richest man who ever lived. Transcending the role of automobile manufacturer, he had become an international symbol of the new industrialism. The Germans coined a word to describe the revolutionary mass production techniques: *Fordismus*. At home Ford's popularity reached the point where he could be seriously considered a presidential possibility for the election of 1924.

Fortunately for the historian of his thought, if not always for himself, Henry Ford had a propensity for forthrightly stating his opinions on a wide variety of subjects outside his field of competence. He also had the money to publish and otherwise implement his ideas. The resulting intellectual portrait was that of a mind steeped in traditional Americanism. For Ford agrarian simplicity, McGuffey morality, and Algerian determination were sacred objects. Nationalism was writ large over all Ford did, and America was great because of its heritage of freedom, fairness, and hard, honest work. Ford's confidence in the beneficence of old-fashioned virtues verged on the fanatical. The "spirit of '76," equal opportunity democracy, rugged individualism, the home, and motherhood were Ford's touchstones of reality. He deified pioneer ethics and values. "More men are beaten than fail," he declared in 1928. "It is not wisdom they need, or money, or brilliance, or pull, but just plain gristle and bone." A decade earlier "Mr. Ford's Page" in the *Dearborn Independent* stated that "one of the great things about the American people is that they are pioneers." This idea led easily to American messianism. "No one can contemplate the nation to which we belong," the editorial continued, "without realizing the distinctive prophetic character of its obvious mission to the world. We are pioneers. We are pathfinders. We are the road-builders. We are the guides, the vanguards of Humanity." Theodore Roosevelt and Woodrow Wilson had said as much, but Ford was writing *after* the war that allegedly ended the nation's innocence and mocked its mission.

Ford's intense commitment to the traditional American faith led him to suspect and ultimately to detest whatever was un-American. The same loyalties compelled him to search for explanations for the unpleasant aspects of the American 1920s that exonerated the old-time, "native" citizen. The immigrant, and particularly the Jew, were primary targets of Ford's fire. In editorial after editorial in the *Dearborn Independent* and in several books Ford argued that aliens who had no knowledge of "the principles which have made our civilization" were responsible for its "marked deterioration" in the 1920s. They were, moreover, determined to take over the country if not the world. Spurred by such fears, Ford became a subscriber to the tired legend of an international Jewish conspiracy. When he couldn't find sufficient evidence for such a plot, Ford dispatched a number of special detectives to probe the affairs of prominent Jews and collect documentation. The search resulted in the "discovery" of the so-called "Protocols of the Learned Elders of Zion," an alleged exposition of the scheme by which the Jews planned to overthrow Gentile domination. Although the

"Protocols" was exposed as a forgery in 1921, Ford continued to use the spurious document to substantiate his anti-Semitism until late in the decade. Everything wrong with modern American civilization, from the corruption of music to the corruption of baseball, was attributed to Jewish influence. Unable to admit that America as a whole might be blamed for its problems, unwilling to question the beneficence of time-honored ways, Ford searched for a scapegoat. He found it in the newcomers who, he believed, had no conception of or appreciation for American ideals.

The tension in Henry Ford's thought between old and new, between a belief in progress and a tendency to nostalgia, is dramatically illustrated in his attitude toward farming and farmers. On the one hand he believed farm life to be a ceaseless round of inefficient drudgery. Indeed, he had abundant personal evidence, remarking at one point, "I have traveled ten thousand miles behind a plow. I hated the grueling grind of farm work." With the incentive of sparing others this painful experience, Ford addressed himself to the problem of industrializing agriculture. The farmer, in Ford's opinion, should became a technician and a businessman. Tractors (Ford's, of course) should replace horses. Mechanization would make it possible to produce in twenty-five working days what formerly required an entire year. Fences would come down and vast economies of scale take place. Ford's modern famer would not even need to live on his farm but instead could commute from a city home. To give substance to these ideals Ford bought and operated with astonishing success a nine-thousand-acre farm near Dearborn.

Still Ford, the "Father of Modern Agriculture," as he has been dubbed, was only part of the man. He also retained a strong streak of old-fashioned, horse-and-buggy agrarianism. Farming, from this standpoint, was more than a challenge in production; it was a moral act. Constantly in the twenties, even while he was helping make it possible, Ford branded the modern city a "pestiferous growth." He delighted in contrasting the "unnatural," "twisted," and "cooped up" lives of city-dwellers with the "wholesome" life of "independence" and "sterling honesty" that the farm environment offered. In Ford's view the importance of cities in the nation's development had been greatly exaggerated. Early in the 1920s the *Dearborn Independent* editorialized: "when we all stand up and sing, 'My Country 'Tis of Thee,' we seldom think of the cities. Indeed, in that old national hymn there are no references to the city at all. It sings of rocks and rivers and hills—the great American Out-of-Doors. And that is really The Country. That is, the country is THE Country. The real United States lies outside the cities."

As such a manifesto suggests, a bias toward nature and rural conditions was an important element in Henry Ford's thought. "What children and adults need," he told one reporter, "is a chance to breathe God's fresh air and to stretch their legs and have a little garden in the soil." This ideal led Ford to choose small towns instead of cities as the sites of his factories. "Turning back to village industry," as Ford put it in 1926, would enable people to reestablish a sense of community—with nature and with men— that urbanization had destroyed. Ford believed that cities were doomed as Americans discovered the advantages of country life.

Ford's enthusiasm for nature did not stop with ruralism. From 1914 to 1924 he sought a more complete escape from civilization on a series of camping trips with Thomas A. Edison. John Burroughs, the naturalist, and Harvey Firestone, the tire king, also participated. Although the equipment these self-styled vagabonds took into the woods was far from primitive, they apparently shared a genuine love of the outdoors. In the words of Burroughs, they "cheerfully endured wet, cold, smoke, mosquitoes, black flies, and sleepless nights, just to touch naked reality once more." Ford had a special fondness for birds. With typical exuberance he had five hundred birdhouses built on his Michigan farm, including one with seventy-six apartments which he called, appropriately, a "bird hotel." There were also electric heaters and electric brooders for Ford's fortunate birds. The whole production mixed technology and nature in a way that symbolized Ford's ambivalence. When he could not camp or visit his aviary, Ford liked to read about the natural world. Indeed he preferred the works of Emerson, Thoreau, and Burroughs to the Bible. Ford so admired Burroughs' variety of natural history that even before becoming acquainted with him he sent him a new Ford car.

As for roads and automobiles, Ford saw them not as a threat to natural conditions but rather as a way for the average American to come into contact with nature. The machine and the garden were not incompatible. "I will build a motor car for the great multitude...," Ford boasted, "so low in price that no man... will be unable to own one—and enjoy with his family the blessings of hours of pleasure in God's great open spaces." In *My Life and Work* of 1923 Ford again confronted the tension between nature and modern civilization. He declared that he did not agree with those who saw mechanization leading to a "cold, metallic sort of world in which great factories will drive away the trees, the flowers, the birds and the green fields." According to Ford, "unless we know more about machines and their use... we cannot have the time to enjoy the trees and the birds, and the flowers, and the green fields." Such reconciliations only partially covered Ford's nervousness about the mechanized, urbanized future. Contradictions persisted in his thinking. The same man who envisaged fenceless bonanza farms could say, "I love to walk across country and jump fences." The lover of trees could state in utmost seriousness, "better wood can be made than is grown."

Ford's attitude toward history has been subject to wide misunderstanding. The principal source of confusion is a statement Ford made in 1919 at the trial resulting from his libel suit against the *Chicago Tribune*. "History," he declared, "is more or less the bunk. It is tradition. We don't want tradition. We want to live in the present, and the only history that is worth a tinker's dam is the history we make today." On another occasion he admitted that he "wouldn't give a nickel for all the history in the world." Complementing this sentiment is Ford's reputation as a forward-looking inventor and revolutionary industrialist unsatisfied with the old processes. Here seems a man fully at home in the alleged new era of the 1920s. But in fact Ford idolized the past. His "history... is bunk" remark came in response to a question about ancient history and Napoleon Bonaparte and had reference to written history. For history itself—what actually happened in his nation's past and its tangible evidence—Ford had only praise.

The most obvious evidence of Ford's enthusiasm for history was his collector's instinct. He began with that bastion of his own youth, the McGuffey readers. Sending agents out to scour the countryside and putting aside considerations of cost, Ford owned by 1925 one of the few complete collections of the many McGuffey editions. Hoping to share his treasures with his contemporaries, Ford had five thousand copies of *Old Favorites from the McGuffey Readers* printed in 1926. The book contained such classic stories as "Try, Try Again" and "The Hare and the Tortoise." It dispensed an ideal of individualism and self-reliance at the same time that Ford's assembly lines were making men cogs in an impersonal machine.

From books Ford turned to things, and during the 1920s amassed a remarkable collection of American antiques. He bought so widely and so aggressively that he became a major factor in prices in the antique market. Everything was fair game. Lamps and dolls, bells and grandfather clocks made their way to Dearborn. Size was no problem. Ford gathered enough machines to show the evolution of the threshing operation from 1849 to the 1920s. Another exhibit traced the development of wagons in America. Eventually the entire heterogeneous collection went into the Edison Museum at Dearborn, a pretentious building designed to resemble, simultaneously, Independence Hall, Congress Hall, and the old City Hall of Philadelphia. Ford delighted in showing visitors around the five-acre layout. Asked on one occasion why he collected, Ford replied, "so that they will not be lost to America." Later, on the same tour, Ford played a few bars on an antique organ and observed, "that takes me back to my boyhood days. They were beautiful days."

This sentiment undoubtedly figured in Ford's 1920 decision to restore his boyhood home. Everything had to be exactly as he remembered it. Furniture, china, and rugs were rehabilitated or reconstructed. Ford even used archaeological techniques to recover artifacts around the family homestead. The ground was dug to a depth of six feet and the silverware, wheels, and other equipment used by his parents in the 1860s were recovered. In 1922 Ford purchased the Wayside Inn at Sudbury, Massachusetts, to preserve it from destruction. Celebrated by the poet Henry Wadsworth Longfellow, the old inn appealed to Ford as a symbol of pioneer days. He opened it for the public's edification in 1924. But a new highway ran too near. Roaring cars disturbed the horse-and-buggy atmosphere. So, turning against the age he helped create, Ford had the state highway rerouted around the shrine at a cost of $250,000. He also bought and restored the schoolhouse in Sudbury alleged to be the site where Mary and her little lamb gamboled. Naturally the shop of the "Village Blacksmith," also in Sudbury, had to be included in Ford's antique empire.

Beginning in 1926 with the construction of Greenfield Village near Dearborn, Ford embarked on a career of large-scale historical restoration. This time not a building but a whole community was the object of his attention. Greenfield, named after the Michigan hamlet in which Ford's mother grew up, was a monument to his agrarianism as well as his reverence for the past. "I am trying in a small way," Ford explained with unwarranted modesty, "to help America take a step . . . toward the saner and sweeter idea of life that prevailed in pre-war days." Greenfield Village had gravel roads, gas street lamps, a grassy common, and an old-fashioned country store. The automobile mogul permitted only horse-drawn vehicles on the premises. The genius of assembly line mass production engaged a glass blower, blacksmith, and cobbler to practice their obsolete crafts in the traditional manner. Ford dispatched his agents to seek out, purchase, and transport to Greenfield the cottages of Walt Whitman, Noah Webster, and Patrick Henry. In time they even secured the crowning glory: the log cabin in which William Holmes McGuffey had been born and raised.

History, then, was not "bunk" to Henry Ford. The speed of change seemed to increase proportionately his desire to retain contact with the past. As Ford declared in 1928, a year before completing Greenfield Village, "improvements have been coming so quickly that the past is being lost to the rising generation." To counter this tendency Ford labored to put history into a form "where it may be seen and felt." But values and attitudes were also on display. Ford looked back with nostalgia to the pioneer ethic. With it, he believed, the nation had been sound, wholesome, happy, and secure. "The Old Ways," as the *Dearborn Independent* declared, "Were Good."

Ford's opinion of the new morality of the jazz age was, not surprisingly, low. He deplored the use of tobacco and even went so far as to publish for mass circulation a tract, entitled *The Case Against the Little White Slaver*, which excoriated cigarettes. When Ford had the power he went beyond exhortation. "No one smokes in the Ford industries," their leader proclaimed in 1929. As for alcohol, Ford was equally unyielding. Twice he threatened to make his international labor force teetotalers at the risk of their jobs. In his American plants Ford enforced a policy of abstinence. Any workman detected drinking publicly or even keeping liquor at home was subject to dismissal. The prohibition policy of the 1920s, in Ford's estimation, was a great triumph. "There are a million boys growing up in the United States," he exulted in 1929, "who have never seen a saloon and who will never know the handicap of liquor." When confronted with evidence of widespread violation of the Nineteenth Amendment, Ford had a ready explanation. A Jewish conspiracy was to blame for illicit booze. The mass of real Americans, Ford believed, were, like himself, dry by moral conviction as well as by law.

Sex was too delicate a matter to be addressed directly, but Ford conveyed his opinions through a discussion of music and dancing. Few aspects of the American 1920s worried him more than the evils of jazz. The new music clashed squarely with his ruralism and Bible-belt morality. In 1921 Ford struck out in anger at "the waves upon waves of musical slush that invaded decent parlors and set the young people of this generation imitating the drivel of morons." Organized Jewry, once again, was blamed for the musical degeneracy. "The mush, the slush, the sly suggestion, the abandoned sensuousness of sliding notes," declared the *Dearborn Independent*, "are of Jewish origin." The problem, obviously, was not only musical but sexual as well. The loosening of morals in the 1920s appalled Ford. He expressed his feeling in reference to jazz: "monkey talk, jungle squeals, grunts and squeaks and gasps suggestive of cave love are camouflaged by a few feverish notes." What Ford could only bring himself to call "the thing" appeared also in song titles such as *In Room 202* and *Sugar Baby*. Pointing to the Jewish origin of these tunes (Irving Berlin was a frequent target of attacks), Ford called on his countrymen to crush the serpent in their midst.

The reform of dancing fitted nicely into Ford's campaign to elevate the nation's morals to old-time standards. His interest began with the collection of traditional folk dances. Not only the scores but the backwoods fiddlers themselves were invited to Dearborn to play *Old Zip Coon* and *Arkansas Traveler*. To Ford's delight, here was something both wholesome and historical.

He also manifested concern over social dancing, publishing in 1926 a guidebook entitled *"Good Morning": After a Sleep of Twenty-five Years Old-Fashioned Dancing is Being Revived by Mr. and Mrs. Henry Ford*. The book also endeavored to revive old-fashioned morality. It began by condemning as promiscuous the newer dances such as the Charleston and the whole flapper syndrome. "A gentleman," the book explained, "should be able to guide his partner through a dance without embracing her as if he were her lover." Proper deportment, according to Ford, minimized physical contact. "[The gentleman's] right hand should be placed at his partner's waist, thumb and forefinger alone touching her —that is, the hand being in the position of holding a pencil." There were also rules regarding gloves, handkerchiefs, and the way to request a partner for a dance. Ford's dance manual, in short, was a monument to the old conceptions of morality, decorum, and order, and the dances he and his wife hosted at Dearborn were implementations. Precisely at nine Ford's guests convened in evening dress in a lavish ballroom for a paean to Victorianism.

Ambivalence is the key to the mind of Henry Ford. He was both old and new; he looked both forward and backward. Confidently progressive as he was in some respects, he remained nervous about new ways. The more conditions changed, the more the nostalgic Ford groped for the security of traditional values and institutions. He was not lost; on the contrary, he had too many gods, at least for consistency. Neither was he dissipated and roaring. And he hated jazz. But Ford was popular, indeed a national deity, in the twenties even if his senatorial and presidential bids fell short. As a plain, honest, old-fashioned billionaire, a technological genius who loved to camp out, he seemed to his contemporaries to resolve the moral dilemmas of the age. Like Charles A. Lindbergh, another god of the age, Ford testified to the nation's ability to move into the future without losing the values of the past.

18
The Klan Rides

John Higham

The second Ku Klux Klan began as an anti-Catholic, anti-Semitic, white supremacist movement which encompassed the whole range of American nativism. In truth, the Klan was an outgrowth of racial and exonophobic hatreds—of Negroes, Catholics, Jews, and southeastern Europeans—that had been growing in America since the late Progressive era. During the twenties, as Charles C. Alexander observed in *The Ku Klux Klan in the Southwest*, the organization drew much of its support, especially in the Southwest, from rural-minded people who wanted to preserve their traditional values in a society undergoing rapid industrial and urban concentration. Many middle-class whites, Alexander contends, saw in the Klan a method to enforce their rural values and restore law and order to the towns and cities. In the latter respect, the second Klan was more than a nativist, anti-Negro movement; it became a champion of Victorian morality as well. During the twenties, in fact, the secret fraternal order strove to stamp out the kind of moral and sexual behavior which Frederick Lewis Allen described in the previous narrative. Here John Higham examines the rise and fall of the Invisible Empire, underscoring its role as an instrument of one hundred per cent Americanism and one hundred per cent moral conformity. The selection is taken from his classic study of American nativism, *Strangers in the Land*.

In Atlanta on October 16, 1915, . . . William J. Simmons conjured into being the Invisible Empire of the Knights of the Ku Klux Klan and anointed himself its Imperial Wizard. For a number of years Simmons had made a living in the rural South as a salesman and organizer of national fraternal orders. He had promoted, or at least belonged to, more than a dozen of them, including Masonry, the Knights Templar, and the Woodmen of the World; in the latter he held the rank of colonel. As befitted a southern "colonel," he had cultivated a majestic presence and a grand manner that belied his village origin. Now Colonel Simmons was launching a secret order of his own.

The idea was not wholly spontaneous. The Frank lynchers had called themselves the "Knights of Mary Phagan," and Tom Watson was currently writing about the need for a new Ku Klux Klan. In the same year a tremendously successful historical film (*The Birth of a Nation*) glorified the long-defunct Klan which ex-Confederates had organized in the Reconstruction era to intimidate Carpetbaggers and Negroes. Simmons was just the man to revive a vanished sectional institution as an instrument of modern American nationalism. His cloudy wits spun with the myths and history of the South; his heart exuded southern sentiment as a plum does juice. From his father, a small-town doctor and an ex-officer in the original Klan, Simmons heard bewitching tales of

From *Strangers in the Land, Patterns of American Nativism, 1860–1925*, John Higham. Copyright 1955 by The Trustees of Rutgers College in New Jersey. Reprinted by permission of The Rutgers University Press.

how it saved white civilization. Undoubtedly he knew also about the subsequent tradition of night-riding, by which rural bands often masked in white caps meted out informal justice upon their neighbors. He liked to trace his original inspiration to a vision that came upon him at the turn of the century not long after he returned from serving in the Spanish-American War—a vision that turned the clouds one day into white-robed horsemen galloping across the sky.

Simmons supplemented these romantic traits with an evangelical piety, a fine dramatic sense and, above all, the gift of the word. Converted by "the old-time religion" at a camp meeting, he had tried his hand at preaching before turning to the more lucrative field of fraternal work, and he remained a mellifluous orator. His first acts as Imperial Wizard were to draw up the high-sounding ritual of the Kloran, create a galaxy of Kleagles, Kligrapps, Cyclops, Geniis, and Goblins, and summon his little band of followers to Stone Mountain, where they dedicated themselves before a flaming cross and a flag-draped altar to uphold Americanism, advance Protestant Christianity, and eternally maintain white supremacy.

In modeling his little society fairly closely on the Klan of yore, Simmons had in mind the same social objective of controlling the Negroes, who were (he believed) getting "uppity" again. Even at the outset, however, there were important differences between the two organizations, and they grew more sharp as the new Klan evolved. The latter, unlike its predecessor, was formed partly as a money-making scheme; Simmons, who was half visionary and half promoter, designed his own Klan as a fraternal order in the hope of enriching himself by selling insurance benefits to the membership. Although the Klan failed to develop along such lines, it always remained something of a racket.

More importantly, it differed from the first Klan in being an avowedly *patriotic* fraternal order. Apparently the Colonel did not begin with an overtly nativist program, but his venture reflected a strong nationalist impulse. It embodied the twentieth century fusion of primitive race-feelings with Anglo-Saxon nationalism. The nineteenth century Klan, a product of sectional strife, had championed white supremacy (and white supremacy only) at a time when southern race-feelings clashed directly with nationalism. The new Klan reflected the coalescence of racial and national loyalties. Simmons' organization dramatized what the more diffuse movements of the early twentieth century had already revealed: the South was pushing into the forefront of American nativism. Thus in contrast to the first Klan, which admitted white men of every type and background, the second Klan accepted only native-born Protestant whites and combined an anti-Negro with an increasingly anti-foreign outlook. Always Anglo-Saxon nationalism remained one of the main pillars of its strength.

For five years after its founding, the Invisible Empire was far more invisible than imperial. It recruited during that time a maximum of five thousand members and attracted practically no public attention. Part of its weakness came from Simmons' impracticality. He wasted money, kept careless accounts, and generally showed no business sense. A greater impediment, however, was the temporary subsidence of racial nationalism just at the time when the Klan was forming. The war period offered very little occasion for and indeed inhibited the Klan's *raison d'être*. Significantly, the order seems to have made what little progress it did by adapting itself to the typical pattern of wartime 100 per cent Americanism. Simmons joined an auxiliary of the American Protective League, turned his followers to spy-hunting, and began to envisage the Klan not as a benevolent order but as a vast secret service agency. One of the early, if not the first, public appearances of the Klan occurred late in the war in Montgomery, Alabama, when a hundred hooded Klansmen paraded through the main

The burning cross at a Klan rally. "The flaming crosses, the altars erected at meetings, and the kneeling posture of suppliants at initiation ceremonies were central in the Klan's symbolism." (Courtesy of Ewing Galloway.)

streets warning slackers and spies to get out of town and demanding that all others aid the Red Cross and buy their share of Liberty bonds. Thereafter, wherever the Klan went and whatever it did, it persistently worked to enforce the 100 per cent American ethic of coercive conformity. The success of the Klan awaited, however, the return of a climate of opinion congenial to its own distinctive background.

The period of expansion began in the summer of 1920. Simmons joined forces with a pair of hard-boiled publicity agents, dour-faced Edward Y. Clarke and his plump partner, Mrs. Elizabeth Tyler. Both had long experience in fund-raising drives. They took over the actual management of the Klan, entering a contract with Simmons that guaranteed them $8 out of every $10 initiation fee collected by their organizers. Clarke and Tyler then launched an impressive membership campaign, operating partly through newspaper publicity, more largely through agents who usually started in a community by soliciting at the Masonic lodges. In the next sixteen months they brought in about ninety thousand members. For this accomplishment Clarke and Tyler have generally received the whole credit. The secret of their success, however, lay essentially in the mood and circumstances of 1920. The whole complex of factors—depression, prohibition, and immigration; disillusion, isolationism, and reaction—that shunted 100 per cent Americanism into the older nativistic channels contributed to the Klan's growth. Never before had a single society gathered up so many hatreds or given vent to an inwardness so thoroughgoing.

Among the special circumstances stimulating the Klan's initial surge, not least was the agricultural depression that began in 1920. As cotton prices plunged catastrophically, desperate farmers in half a dozen states resorted to the old practice of night-riding in order to check the sale of cotton. All through the fall and winter of 1920-21 masked bands roamed the countryside warning ginneries and warehouses to close until prices advanced. Sometimes they set fire to establishments that defied their edict. Occasionally there was shooting. Klan officials disavowed and apparently disapproved of this wave of economic terrorism, which indeed was soon suppressed by law enforcement officials. Like previous nativist organizations, the Klan had no economic program and rarely functioned in economic terms except to enforce a pattern of discrimination. Nevertheless the gin-burners frequently wore Ku Klux garb, and their nocturnal exploits drew attention to the potentialities of the hooded order. Night-riding of a different kind flourished within the Klan, and it seems hardly doubtful that the organization diverted farmers' economic frustrations into more socially acceptable types of aggression.

The first acknowledged public appearances of the Klan in the postwar period reflected its underlying racial spirit. On the eve of the election of 1920, Klansmen paraded in many southern towns as a silent warning against Negro voting. A large number of anti-Negro outrages were committed in the next few months under Klan auspices, provoked partly by fear that a "New Negro" had emerged from the war. (In point of fact, Negro veterans returning from France in 1919 and 1920 were often determined to stand militant and upright.) The men in white bludgeoned employers into downgrading or discharging Negro employees, intimidated Negro cotton-pickers into working for wages they would not otherwise accept, forced Negro residents out of a part of South Jacksonville coveted by whites, and branded the letters "KKK" on the forehead of a Negro bellboy. In these early months of expansion the organization presented itself very largely as a means for keeping "the nigger in his place."

White supremacy remained an important theme even when the Klan spread into the North, but it would be a mistake to regard the Negro issue as the mainspring of its career. Fear of the "New Negro" rapidly declined as he either accepted his old place or moved to northern cities. By mid-1921 the Klan was specializing in attacking white people, and thereafter the great bulk of its disciplinary activities in all parts of the country had to do with whites. This shift of emphasis by no means indicated a slackening of the racial imperative. To a considerable degree, however, it suggested that race-thinking was more and more taking a nativistic and nationalistic direction. The Klan's snowballing advance in the early twenties paralleled the upthrust of racial nativism in public opinion generally. And within the order an insistence on preserving the superiority of the old Anglo-Saxon stock over foreigners of every description became pronounced. Edward Y. Clarke exemplified this trend in 1922 by defining the Klan's mission as one of creating national solidarity by protecting "the interest of those whose forefathers established the nation." Other Klan leaders, in particularizing on the old stock's interest, called immigration restriction the most momentous legislative issue of the day, asserted that only Anglo-Saxons or Nordics had an inherent capacity for American citizenship, damned "the cross-breeding hordes" of the new immigration, and trembled lest the "real whites" fail to keep the nation "free from all mongrelizing taints." This emphatic Anglo-Saxonism did not, of course, prevent the same men from ranting loudly at foreigners as such, on the plea that America must be made safe for Americans.

If the Ku Klux Klan had mobilized only this much of the emotional ferment of the period, if it had functioned only through an Anglo-Saxon version of 100 per cent Americanism and through related fears of Jews and of foreigners generally, it would have incarnated a very large part of the current tribal spirit. Yet the Klan had another big side. By embracing the anti-Catholic tradition along with the racial tradition and the new anti-Semitism, it comprehended the whole range of post-1919 nativism. Anti-Catholicism did not prevail as widely in American public opinion as did the Anglo-Saxon ideas reflected in the organization; an urban, materialistic culture had stifled in too many Americans the religious feelings on which Protestant xenophobia fed. Due, however, to the semirural base of the Klan, within its ranks anti-Catholicism actually grew to surpass every other nativistic attitude. In fact, a religious impulse, perverted but not devoid of idealistic implications, accounts for much of the Klan's distinctive energy, both as a nativist organization and as an agent of other kinds of repressions too.

Although the Klan was Protestant from the day its first cross burned on Stone Mountain, an anti-Catholic emphasis came into the order only in the course of its expansion in 1920 and 1921. Simmons, Clarke, and Tyler had not at first expected to sell the organization as a bulwark against Rome. The Klan's stress on religious nativism, even more than the parallel expansion of its Anglo-Saxon agitation, reflected the passions of the people who joined it. By 1920 the anti-Catholic crusade that had appeared in the South and West after 1910 was reasserting itself more powerfully than ever. Under a prohibitionist governor, Alabama pointed the way as early as 1919. While laying plans for inspecting convents, the state also challenged Catholic (and secular) sentiment by requiring daily Bible reading in the public schools, thus reviving a trend begun in Pennsylvania in 1913. The following year the tide came in strongly. Tom Watson's Senatorial campaign spread about Georgia an impression that President Wilson had become a tool of the Pope; Governor Sidney J. Catts stomped up and down Florida warning that the Pope planned to invade the state and transfer the Vatican there; an able journalist reported that anti-Catholicism had become "second only to the hatred of the Negro as the moving passion of entire Southern communities"; Michigan and Nebraska debated constitutional amendments banning parochial schools; and in Missouri the once-mighty anti-Catholic weekly, *The Menace*, revived under a new name, *The Torch*.

Sentiment of this kind amounted to a standing invitation to secret societies. The first to respond prominently was not the Klan but rather the True Americans, a local southern organization. The T.A.'s acquired such influence in Birmingham in 1920 that they dominated the city administration and secured a purge of Catholic municipal employees. Before long Ku Kluxers eclipsed and very likely absorbed the True Americans. Klan propaganda, reviving all of the old stories about arms stored in Catholic church basements, began to lay special stress on the menace of Rome to the nation. Instead of relying entirely on professional organizers, the Klan engaged itinerant preachers as heralds of its message. Increasingly its arrival in a new area was signaled by public lectures on popish conspiracies to destroy *"the only truly Christian nation . . . where prophecy is being fulfilled."* As if to demonstrate that the hatred transcended rhetoric, in the summer of 1921 a Methodist minister who belonged to the Klan shot to death a Catholic priest on his own doorstep, and incendiaries destroyed a Catholic church in Illinois two hours after a monster Klan initiation.

The storm of anti-Catholic feeling, for which the Klan proved a wonderfully sensitive barometer, was closely related to the growth of fundamentalism. This militant repudiation of a liberalized gospel and a secularized culture was making itself felt in the closing years of the Progressive era, but only after the World War did it become a major force in American Protestantism. In truth, fundamentalism owed so much to the emotional aftermath of the war that one may almost define it as the characteristic response of rural Protestantism to the disillusion following America's international crusade. The wartime hope for a new and beatific world had produced nothing but crime, moral chaos, and organized selfishness on a grander scale than before. Surely here was proof that the nation had misplaced its faith, that the only true salvation for a sinful society lay in blotting out the whole spirit of innovation and returning to the theological and moral absolutism of an earlier day. Insistence on a Biblical Christianity naturally sharpened the historic lines of Protestant-Catholic cleavage, but the vigor of anti-Catholicism in the twenties could only result from the affiliations between fundamentalism and 100 per cent Americanism. The fundamentalist determination to fix and purify a Protestant orthodoxy followed the same channels and obeyed the same laws that governed the course of 100 per cent Americanism. Both epitomized a kind of crusading conformity, reacted to a common disillusion, and represented an urge for isolation from an evil world. Who can wonder that the two movements intermingled in rural areas, or that fundamentalism energized a religious version of postwar nationalism?

Simmons' religiously tinged imagination had given the Klan an appropriate structure for the anti-Catholic spirit that it absorbed and magnified. The flaming crosses burning on hillsides, the altars erected at meetings, and the kneeling posture of suppliants at initiation ceremonies were central in the Klan's symbolism. Every klavern, or local unit, had a kludd, its chaplain, who opened each meeting with a prayer; the closing ritual consisted of a "kloxology." As the Klan grew, it emphasized increasingly its militant Protestantism. Well-known hymns were modified and adopted as Klan songs. It became common practice for Klansmen to march in a silent body into a Protestant church in the middle of a Sunday service and hand the minister a donation. The organization took a close interest in compulsory Bible reading in the public schools, and in several states it lent strong support to Bible-reading bills. "Patriotism and Christianity," said one Exalted Cyclops, "are preeminently the moving principles of the Knights of the Ku Klux Klan." Another boasted: "The Klan stood for the same things as the Church, but we did the things the Church wouldn't do."

The things that the church would not do included general boycotts of Catholic businessmen, bringing pressure against Catholic public officials, and intimidation of many Catholic individuals. It would be futile, however, to try to estimate how much of this strong-arm activity applied to Catholics as opposed to foreigners, Jews, Negroes, and plain old-stock Americans. Contemporary accounts seldom identified the background of the Klan's victims, a circumstance which in itself suggests how manifold the proscriptions were. The significant fact was that the crusading, evangelical spirit behind the Klan turned it into a general instrument for moral regulation. Quite possibly (since it centered in areas where its foreign and

Catholic enemies constituted only a small minority), most of the Klan's coercions affected other native white Protestants. Certainly it differed from prewar nativist societies not only in embracing a variety of xenophobias but also in ranging far beyond nativistic limits. Somewhat like the wartime American Protective League, the Klan watched everybody.

In its function as censor and policeman of local morality, the Klan brought to a head the 100 per cent American heritage as it survived into the twenties. Impatient of legally constituted authority yet dedicated to the maintenance of law and order, local Klans saw themselves as agents for accomplishing what government was failing to do: they would work a moral regeneration by compelling all deviants or backsliders to adhere to the ancient standards of the community. Hardly any infraction of the village code seemed too petty for intervention. An undertaker refused the use of his hearse to a bereaved family unable to pay cash in advance; Klansmen drove him out of town. A businessman failed to pay a debt or practiced petty extortions; Klansmen tarred and feathered him. A husband deserted his family, or failed to support it, or maintained illicit relations with women, or gambled too much; Klansmen paid him a minatory call. A widow of doubtful virtue scandalized the neighbors; Klansmen flogged her and cut off her hair. Prohibition especially drew the order's vigilance. Its most spectacular clean-up campaign occurred in Herrin, Illinois, where lax law enforcement permitted wide-open saloons and flagrant vice, and where the large Italian Catholic population was held chiefly at fault. There the Klan carried out mass raids on homes and roadhouses, engaged in pitched battles with the bootlegging faction, and temporarily seized the city government by force. The chaos extended over a two-year period, brought twenty deaths, and subsided finally in a great religious revival.

Klan poster in the 1920s. The Klan attracted thousands of Americans in the South and Midwest because it stood for white supremacy, the Protestant faith, 100 per cent Americanism, and 100 per cent moral conformity, as this poster suggests. (Courtesy of The New York Public Library, Astor, Lenox and Tilden Foundations.)

Throughout this regulatory activity runs the war-born urge for conformity that had passed from anti-hyphenism, Americanization, and Palmer raids into fundamentalism and prohibition. No less important here is the other side of the 100 per cent American spirit, its crusading idealism. Ku Kluxers repeatedly justified their programs of action in terms of reform, though the reform consisted essentially of stabilizing the old order of things; and when first organized in a community, the Klan usually had the support of some of the "best people," intent partly on improving the local situation. In the generation before the war this evangelical zeal for reform had poured into progressivism. The war directed it partly toward an international crusade, partly toward the maintenance of homogeneity. When the disillusion that followed the war choked off any large international or progressive outlet for moral idealism, about all that remained of it in small-town America turned inward, in a final effort to preserve the values of the community against change and against every external influence. Professor Frank Tannenbaum has summed up a good part of the Klan spirit as "an attempt to destroy the 'evil' that stands in the way of the millennial hope—a hope made vivid to many souls who actually believed that the war would usher in a 'world fit for heroes to live in.'" Perhaps, in the pageant of American history, the white-robed Klansman should stand in the place of Santayana's genteel New Englander as the Last Puritan.

It was ironical but inevitable that the Klan crusade to purify and stabilize spread contamination and strife everywhere it went. The secrecy with which the order operated served to cloak many an act of private vengeance. With poetic justice it was held responsible for crimes and cruelties that others committed in its name. Still worse, the Klan rent families, communities, and states, turning husband against wife, neighbor against neighbor, and man against man, until it compacted an opposition as lawless as itself. And while hatred bred hatred outside its ranks, the poison of corruption worked within.

In 1921 the Klan crossed the Mason and Dixon Line and began to attract nation-wide attention. By the end of the year it claimed to be operating in forty-five states and enrolling a thousand members a day. Nineteen twenty-two saw a tremendous expansion, demonstrated by great public ceremonies at which a thousand or more initiates would be sworn in at once. At the same time, like its nineteenth century predecessors, the organization entered politics, not with any positive program but simply to show its strength by winning elections. In Georgia the Klan was instrumental in putting a very friendly governor in the state capitol. In Texas it spent lavishly in money and effort to send Earl Mayfield to the United States Senate. In Oregon Klan sentiment wrought a virtual political revolution, defeating a governor who had tried to suppress its activities and installing a legislature that proceeded to enact several anti-Catholic measures. Hundreds of candidates for local offices in many states were indebted to the Klan vote.

Political power greatly increased the divisive effects of the organization, partly because the Klan itself became an issue in elections, partly because law enforcement officials often dared not curb its terrorism. Thus in the latter part of 1922 local authorities in Morehouse Parish, Louisiana, proved helpless in the face of a near-civil war between the Klan-infested parish seat of Bastrop and the more leisurely and aristocratic town of Mer Rouge. Bastrop was Dry and Baptist; Mer Rouge held the Klan and all its ways in contempt. A series of whippings culminated in the abduction and murder of a well-known Mer Rouge planter's son and his companion. For months thereafter troops sent by the governor kept order while the pro-Klan sheriff and district attorney stood idle. Twice the Morehouse grand jury refused to admit that a crime had been committed.

Meanwhile internecine strife rocked the Invisible Empire. While its national officials exercised very little control over the local klaverns, an authoritarian constitution gave the members practically no control over their national leaders. For many of the latter the organization had an attraction quite different from that which drew its followers. It was immensely lucrative, and the profits to be extracted from membership fees and political corruption incited constant turmoil at the top. Clarke levied upon the Klan royally; Simmons, who was drunk or sick much of the time, was putty in his hands. When news got around in the fall of 1921 that Clarke was living with his confederate, Mrs. Tyler, this affront to Klan morality strengthened a group endeavoring to unseat him, but Simmons clung to Clarke and banished his principal enemies. Clarke held on against mounting opposition until November 1922, when a coalition of state leaders got rid of him by intimidating Simmons into retiring to an honorary position. Simmons retained a following and later tried to regain control, but the national headquarters had passed definitely into the hands of a moon-faced Texas dentist, Hiram Wesley Evans. Ultimately Simmons sold out his interest in the Klan to the Evans group for a sum which they announced as $90,000 but which he said should have been $146,000. Evans regularized financial practices somewhat, but still the money flowed richly into many pockets.

The Klan torrent rolled onward through 1923, reaching a high point late in the year. By that time the organization had enrolled an aggregate membership probably close to three million. Arkansas and Oklahoma fell vassal to it, and a spectacular expansion in the Midwest made Indiana and Ohio the leading Klan states in the nation. Except for Colorado, the order touched the Rocky Mountain states only negligibly; it left no considerable impression on the Atlantic seaboard outside of Pennsylvania and upstate New York. In Indiana and Texas, however, it could organize vast public gatherings attended by seventy-five thousand people.

The tremendous midwestern expansion in 1923 threw a new demagogue into the limelight and opened another chapter in the struggle within the Klan. D. C. Stephenson emerged as the dominant figure in the northern Klans. He could corrupt a legislator as effectively as he could organize a membership drive, and with equal ease he could convince the rural masses that the President of the United States was leaning on him for advice. He lived in bacchanalian style on an estate in Indianapolis; his political ambitions were boundless. As his power grew, he strove to wrest the national headquarters from Evans. All through 1923 the fight for control went on behind the scenes, with Stephenson perhaps partly in alliance with the disinherited Simmons faction. In November an Evans henchman murdered Simmons' attorney, supposedly to prevent an impending exposé. Somehow, that may have turned the tables against Stephenson. He surrendered his position in the national hierarchy of the Klan, but he rather than Evans retained paramount influence in Indiana.

While this internal struggle raged, opposition was mounting on all sides. All along, the urban press and urban liberals had denounced the Klan with singular unanimity. Now it was also rousing a more formidable popular resistance. Old-stock conservatives, horrified at the chaos that the Klan bred, rallied against it. So did the miscellaneous corruptionists and enraged minorities it attacked. In the winter of 1922–23 the conservative governor of Kansas opened a drive against the organization by bringing suit to restrain it from all public appearances or activities. New York, under its Catholic governor, Al Smith, took a series of legal steps that inhibited Klan operations there. Minnesota, Iowa, and Michigan passed laws forbidding the wearing of masks in public.

Oklahoma's flamboyant governor, John Walton, cast legality to the winds in trying to crush the hooded order. Although elected by a farmer-labor coalition in 1922, he soon showed greater friendliness toward grafters and big oil interests. The Klan supposedly controlled the state legislature and the Tulsa local government. Walton, in August 1923, took advantage of a series of floggings to put Tulsa County under martial law (later extended to the whole state). He imposed censorship on the leading Tulsa newspaper, forbade Klan meetings, established military courts to try Klan vigilantes, and used the National Guard to prevent the legislature from convening. When the legislature did succeed in assembling in November, it promptly impeached the governor.

At the same time, anti-Klan mobs were bebinning to lash back at the organization in areas where the immigrants were strongly entrenched. A bomb wrecked the offices of the Klan newspaper in Chicago. In a suburb of Pittsburgh an angry throng pelted a white-robed parade with stones and bottles, killing one Klansman and injuring many others. In the small industrial city of Steubenville, Ohio, a mob of three thousand attacked a meeting of one hundred Klansmen. In Perth Amboy, New Jersey, a mob six-thousand-strong, led by Jews and Catholics, closed in on a Klan meeting place, overwhelmed the entire police and fire departments, and fell upon some five hundred Ku Kluxers, kicking, stoning, and beating them as they fled.

Such, from the West Frankfort riots of 1920 to the collapse of civil government in Oklahoma three years later, from the triumphant demonstrations of racist scholarship to the nightmares of Henry Ford, were some of the fruits of nativism in a postwar world neither brave nor new.

VI "You Have Nothing to Fear but Fear Itself"

19

The Contagion of Fear

Arthur M. Schlesinger, Jr.

The crash of 1929 and the onset of depression rocked the United States to its foundations. It was the worst disaster America had faced since the Civil War, and there were voices of doubt everywhere. How had it happened? What would become of the American dream now? Would the nation disintegrate? And who was to blame? President Hoover? The Republican Party? Or capitalism itself? Arthur Schlesinger, Jr., makes it clear that a number of factors caused the crash—chief among them, inherent weaknesses in America's economic structure. He goes on to catch the contagion of fear that swept across the nation during those terrible early years of the Depression.

Crash

But the New Era knew no skepticism. The nation had reached, it seemed, a permanent plateau of prosperity. Business was expanding. Foreign trade was growing. The stock market was continuing to rise. And national leadership could not now be in more expert or safer hands. "For the first time in our history," wrote Foster and Catchings, "we have a President who, by technical training, engineering achievement, cabinet experience, and grasp of economic fundamentals, is qualified for business leadership." "I have no fears for the future of our country," said Herbert Hoover in his inaugural address in March 1929. "It is bright with hope."

There remained a few discordant voices, anxious in the main over the stock market boom. But the President regarded agricultural relief and tariff revision as the more pressing questions. In the spring of 1929, he summoned a special session of the Congress to deal with these issues. The session was not a success. Hoover's agricultural program did not satisfy the farm bloc, though Congress, after vehement debate, adopted the President's recommendations and set up a new agency, the Federal Farm Board. The Board's purpose was to control the flow of commodities to the market; one provision authorized the establishment of stabilization corporations as a means of controlling temporary surpluses. Then the session, after wrangling from April to November, adjourned without taking action on the tariff.

In other respects, Hoover as President tried to apply the policies he had developed as Secretary of Commerce. In August 1929, he moved into the conservation field, proposing that the unreserved public lands, as well as all new reclamation projects and related irrigation matters, be withdrawn from national control. The states, he said, were "more competent to manage much of these affairs than is the Federal Government," and his aim was to place the local communities—and presumably the strongest interests in them—in control of their

---

From Arthur M. Schlesinger, Jr. *The Crisis of the Old Order*. Boston: Houghton Mifflin Co., 1957, pp. 155–176. Reprinted by permission of the publisher.

own natural resources. "Well," remarked one newspaper, "conservation was a pretty dream while it lasted."

The President's attitude toward utilities regulation was similar. Certain that state regulation and private responsibility were enough, he had no misgivings about making the statutory appointment of the Secretary of War, James W. Good, the former counsel for the Alabama Power Company, as head of the Federal Power Commission. When the Commission was reorganized in 1930, staff members whose zeal had irritated the utilities were discharged; one of them, the former solicitor of the Commission, told the press that Hoover had personally intervened to prevent the rigorous application of the Federal Water Power Act to the private companies.

Yet most Americans remained more interested in the stock market than in any other economic question; and for a few interest was now beginning to turn into concern. Early in 1929, the Federal Reserve Board, under continuing pressure from the New York Federal Reserve Bank, finally consented to warn member banks that they should not lend money for speculative purposes. But this reliance on moral suasion did not satisfy conservative members of the financial community, like Dr. Adolph Miller of the Board, Paul M. Warburg of Kuhn, Loeb, and Russell Leffingwell of Morgan's. Such men wanted the Board to slow down the boom by raising the discount rate to 6 per cent.

Expansionists like Foster and Catchings, however, argued that a restrictive policy might well induce deflation. The Board had already, they felt, created "a state of mind which breeds depression." And it was certainly true that raising the interest rate was a clumsy way of combatting the boom. So long as the stock market offered the highest returns, it was bound to have first call on funds. In the short run, a higher interest rate might thus slow down real investment faster than speculation. And in the longer run, a higher interest rate would tend, through the capitalization process, to bring down the prices of all capital assets and thus to discourage real investment even further. And so the debate continued through the spring and summer. The President, preoccupied with other issues and not clear in his own mind whether he wanted to stop the easy-money policy, did little but watch the Board in its vacillating course.

By the summer of 1929 some danger signs were apparent—for example, the startling decline in building contracts. Net investment for residential construction for the entire year sank to $216 million, over a billion dollars less than 1928. At the same time, there was an alarming growth in business inventories, more than trebling from $500 million in 1928 to $1800 million in 1929. Concurrently, the rate of consumer spending was slackening; it had risen at a rate of 7.4 per cent in 1927–28 but slowed down to an inauspicious 1.5 per cent in 1928–29.

By midsummer 1929, these developments began to be discernible in production and price indexes. Industrial production reached its height in June and dropped off in July; employment rose till July, building began to fall off, and, week after week, wholesale commodity prices dropped with ominous regularity. In August the Federal Reserve Board strengthened deflationary tendencies by finally agreeing to raise the discount rate to 6 per cent.

But the stock market, riding on the impetus of half a dozen years of steady increase, paid little attention to the indexes. Early in September Stock Exchange price averages reached their highest point of all time. A.T. & T. was up to 304; General Electric up to 396, having more than tripled its price in eighteen months. By the beginning of October, brokers' loans—an index of margin buying—topped the $6 billion mark. Business leaders meanwhile competed with each other in expressions of optimism, and Washington displayed no concern.

September saw some minor setbacks. Yet through October brokers looked optimistically ahead to the moment when stocks would resume their upward climb. Then on Wednesday, October 23, there was an unexpected and drastic break, with securities suddenly unloaded in quantity, prices falling, and acute pressure on margin traders. For a moment, Wall Street was shaken, and the anxiety was suddenly infectious. The next day, selling orders began to stream down on the Stock Exchange in unprecedented volume, and prices took a frightening plunge. For a few ghastly moments the Exchange saw stocks on sale for which there were no buyers at any price. As panic spread, the Exchange decided to close the visitors' gallery; among the observers that morning had been the former British Chancellor of the Exchequer, Winston S. Churchill. The tickers fell helplessly behind in recording transactions on the floor; and, as the confusion communicated itself through the country, the instinct to unload threatened to turn into a frenzy. Down, down, down: how long could the market take it?

Around noon a group of worried men gathered in the office of Thomas W. Lamont of Morgan's; it included four of New York's great bankers (among them, Charles E. Mitchell of the National City Bank and Albert H. Wiggin of the Chase). Each was prepared to contribute $40 million on behalf of their banks to bolster the market. An hour or so later Richard Whitney, a broker for Morgan's and vice-president of the Exchange, walked onto the floor to bid 205 for 25,000 shares of U.S. Steel, then available at 193½. For a moment, backed by the bankers' pool, stability seemed to return.

The next day came a torrent of reassuring statements—from bankers, from economists, from the Treasury Department, above all, from the White House itself. "The fundamental business of the country," said President Hoover, "that is, production and distribution of commodities, is on a sound and prosperous basis." And, as prices held for the rest of the week, the bankers quietly fed back into the market the stocks they had bought on Black Thursday, strengthening their own position against further storms. (Whitney had not even bought the U.S. Steel stock; the gesture of bidding was enough.)

The weekend gave the forces of fear and liquidation time to do their work. As the banks had protected themselves against the brokers, so the brokers now sought to protect themselves against their customers, and especially against those they were carrying on the margin. The result on Monday was a new outburst of forced sales, a new explosion of gloom and panic. On that day alone, General Motors stock lost nearly $2 billion in paper value. The market closed with foreboding. The next day the Exchange had barely opened when the rout began. Soon it was like an avalanche, vast numbers rushing to get out of the market with whatever could be salvaged from the general debacle. Brokers sold stock at any price they could get. By noon 8 million shares had changed hands; by closing time, the Exchange had broken all records with an unprecedented 16 million shares. During the day, the governors of the Exchange had called a meeting, crowding into a secluded office, sitting and standing on tables, lighting cigarettes and nervously discarding them till the room was stale with smoke. Most wanted to close the Exchange. But the governors decided that it must be kept open.

For a moment October 30—Wednesday—brought new hope. The newspapers were once again plastered with optimism: Dr. Julius Klein, the President's personal economic soothsayer, John D. Rockefeller, John J. Raskob, all beamed with confidence about the future. As prices steadied, Richard Whitney took advantage of the interval of calm to announce that the Exchange would be open only briefly on Thursday and not at all for the rest of the week. But the flickering hope of stabilization turned out to be the final delusion. *Variety* summed it up in the headline of its issue on October 30: WALL ST. LAYS AN EGG.

When the Exchange reopened the next week, the downward grind resumed, leaving in its wake a trail of exploded values. By mid-November the financial community began to survey the wreckage. In a few incredible weeks, the stocks listed on the New York exchange had fallen over 40 per cent in value—a loss on paper of $26 billion. The New Era had come to its dismaying end.

As perspective has enabled economists to disentangle the causes of the collapse, the following points have come to seem most crucial:

1) Management's disposition to maintain prices and inflate profits while holding down wages and raw material prices meant that workers and farmers were denied the benefits of increases in their own productivity. The consequence was the relative decline of mass purchasing power. As goods flowed out of the expanding capital plant in ever greater quantities, there was proportionately less and less cash in the hands of buyers to carry the goods off the market. The pattern of income distribution, in short, was incapable of long maintaining prosperity.

2) Seven years of fixed capital investment at high rates had "over-built" productive capacity (in terms of existing capacity to consume) and had thus saturated the economy. The slackening of the automotive and building industries was symptomatic. The existing rate of capital formation could not be sustained without different governmental policies—policies aimed not at helping those who had money to accumulate more but at transferring money from those who were letting it stagnate in savings to those who would spend it.

3) The sucking off into profits and dividends of the gains of technology meant the tendency to use excess money for speculation, transforming the Stock Exchange from a securities market into a gaming-house.

4) The stock market crash completed the debacle. After Black Thursday, what rule was safe except *Sauve qui peut?* And businessmen, in trying to save themselves, could only wreck their system; in trying to avoid the worst, they rendered the worst inevitable. By shattering confidence, the crash knocked out any hope of automatic recovery.

5) In sum, the federal government had encouraged tax policies that contributed to oversaving, monetary policies that were expansive when prices were rising and deflationary when prices began to fall, tariff policies that left foreign loans as the only prop for the export trade, and policies toward monopoly which fostered economic concentration, introduced rigidity into the markets and anaesthetized the price system. Representing the businessmen, the federal government had ignored the dangerous imbalance between farm and business income, between the increase in wages and the increase in productivity. Representing the financiers, it had ignored irresponsible practices in the securities market. Representing the bankers, it had ignored the weight of private debt and the profound structural weaknesses in the banking and financial system. Seeing all problems from the viewpoint of business, it had mistaken the class interest for the national interest. The result was both class and national disaster.

The New Era at Bay

For eight and a half years, first as Secretary of Commerce, then as President, Herbert Hoover had a unique opportunity to study the workings and influence the policies of the American business system. No one was better placed to anticipate catastrophe. And, unless it was to be assumed that depression was inevitable under capitalism, one must assume that the depression of 1929 could have been averted by wise national policy. But if in these eight and a half years Hoover was concerned about the lag of purchasing power, about inadequate returns to farmers and workers, about regressive tax policies, about reckless stock market practices, about the piling up of private debt, about the defects of the banking system, then his concern never impelled him to effective action. And in many fields in which he did act—such as the expansion of foreign loans, the promotion of installment purchase at home, the support of economic concentration, the opposition to farm relief—his action accelerated the tendencies that caused the disaster.

Yet the fault was not Hoover's. He remained the most high-minded of the New Era leaders in the age of business. A handful of businessmen, it is true, had mumbled doubts. Paul Warburg had issued warnings. Charles G. Dawes, Vice-President under Coolidge, noted in his diary after the crash, "To me it seems that the signs of the coming of the present catastrophe were more pronounced than those of any other through which the United States has passed." But such men were in the minority. Even men like Lamont of Morgan's believed their own propaganda about the New Era.

Democratic businessmen were as fallible as Republican. In the spring of 1929 Bernard Baruch assured the readers of the *American Magazine* that they need no longer worry about the business cycle. Through the summer and fall hardly a week passed without some new dose of optimism from the chairman of the Democratic National Committee. Some obstinate dissenters had private doubts; but in the age of confidence doubt had to be phrased with caution. Thus in August 1929, Franklin D. Roosevelt, with a skeptical glance at "those business circles which can only see a fifty per cent increase in prosperity and values for every year that goes by between now and the year 2000," warily asked a banker friend, "Do you still feel as I do that there may be a limit to the increase of security values?" But Roosevelt assigned no date for the leveling-off. Even the radicals, confident of the collapse of capitalism in some far-off millennium, had no suspicion that depression might be just around the corner.

Nor, indeed, did many recognize the dimensions of the catastrophe. Andrew Mellon, who had little use for New York banks, said concisely to Hoover, "They deserved it." These "recent fluctuations," said Robert P. Lamont, Hoover's successor in the Commerce Department, would only "curtail the buying power, especially of luxuries, of those who suffered losses in the market crash. There are present today," Lamont added reassuringly, "*none* of the underlying factors which have been associated with or have preceded the declines in business in the past." Even the liberal publicist Stuart Chase regarded the stock market decline as a wholesome shakedown of inflated values. "We probably have three more years of prosperity ahead of us," said Chase, "before we enter the cyclic tailspin."

The businessmen of the nation agreed. Nor did the fall in employment in November and December seem any particular ground for alarm.

> Things are better today [November 4, 1929] than they were yesterday.
> —Henry Ford

> Never before has American business been as firmly entrenched for prosperity as it is today [December 10, 1929].
> —*Charles M. Schwab, Chairman of the Board, Bethlehem Steel*

Viewed in the longer perspective, the collapse of the inflated price structure may be

correctly regarded as a favorable development from the point of view of general business.
—*Editor of the* Guaranty Survey *of the Guaranty Trust Company of New York*

There are no great business failures, nor are there likely to be. . . . Conditions are more favorable for permanent prosperity than they have been in the past year.
—*George E. Roberts, Vice-President, National City Bank of New York*

I can observe little on the horizon today to give us undue or great concern.
—*John E. Edgerton, President, National Association of Manufacturers*

But the President was somewhat more apprehensive. He feared that the crash might induce a general wave of contraction and panic; and he conceived it his duty to assume leadership in checking downward tendencies. "Liquidate labor, liquidate stocks, liquidate the farmers, liquidate real estate," the Secretary of the Treasury had said; his only cure was to let economic forces run their downward course as they had in '73. But Hoover, convinced that the economy was basically sound, saw no reason for bringing misery to every sector of society. Where laissez-faire policy would call for putting the whole structure of prices and costs through the wringer, the New Era philosophy called for the maintenance of price levels and of spending. If this could be done, Hoover reasoned, then the stock market crash could be contained.

He unfolded his program in a series of conferences with business and community leaders in the next weeks. Through voluntary pledges from industry, he hoped to maintain wage rates and stabilize industrial prices. Through understandings with industry and local governments, he hoped to continue capital expansion and public building at a normal pace. Through Federal Reserve policy, he planned to make credit abundant for business borrowers. Through the Federal Farm Board, he aimed to prop up the agricultural sector. Through an upward revision of the tariff, he could protect American industry against foreign competition. And, with these policies under way, he hoped through persuasive exhortation and wise counsel to restore business confidence.

Of these policies, only tariff revision required new legislation. The special session of 1929 having failed on the tariff, the preparation of a new bill became the main business of Congress in the months immediately after the crash. The task was in the charge of two fervent protectionists, Senator Reed Smoot of Utah and Congressman Willis C. Hawley of Oregon, determined to attain for the United States "a high degree of self-sufficiency" (Smoot), to make the nation "self-contained and self-sustaining" (Hawley). In many respects, it was an audacious effort. When Paul Douglas drafted a statement denouncing the bill, he was able to obtain the signatures of a thousand members of the American Economic Association in ten days. But academic disapproval could not embarrass the protectionist faith. "If this bill is passed," said the Republican leader of the Senate, Jim Watson of Indiana, "this nation will be on the upgrade, financially, economically and commercially within thirty days, and within a year from this date we shall have regained the peak of prosperity." When Congress enacted the Smoot-Hawley law, President Hoover signed it with six gold pens, saying that "nothing" would so retard business recovery as continued agitation over the tariff.

As the first months passed after the crash, the administration viewed the future without visible alarm. At the turn of the year Secretary Mellon observed, "I see nothing in the present situation that is either menacing or warrants pessimism." In late January President Hoover announced that the unemployment trend had already been reversed; and early in February Secretary Lamont said that production and distribution were at normal levels; "there is nothing in the situation to be disturbed about." At the same time the Employment Service declared that "within the next sixty or ninety days the country will be on a normal employment basis," and Dr. Julius Klein exulted in the *American Magazine*, "It's Great To Be a Young Man Today." On March 4 Lamont, in a meteorological mood, was certain that "as weather conditions moderate, we are likely to find the country as a whole enjoying its wonted state of prosperity." On March 7, in his most detailed statement on the economic situation, the President declared that unemployment, such as it was, was concentrated in twelve states; that "employment had been slowly increasing" since the low point in December; that business and the state governments were spending more for construction even than in 1929. "*All* the evidences," he said, "indicate that the worst effects of the crash upon unemployment will have been passed during the next sixty days."

Hoover's position was not an easy one. He had rightly decided he could not indulge in a public pessimism that would only feed the panic. His fault lay not in taking an optimistic line, but in bending the facts to sustain his optimism, and then in believing his own conclusions. For, despite the presidential exhortations, private spending was simply not maintaining 1929 levels. Despite the presidential cheer, unemployment was increasing. The leaders of business, for all their pledges, were finding it impossible to collaborate in pegging the economy. The solemn meetings of the fall, with their professions of common purpose, had turned out to be exercises in ceremonial—"no-business meetings," in J. K. Galbraith's phrase. "There has been more 'optimism' talked and less practiced," said Will Rogers, "than at any time during our history." Some Republican leaders even began to scent conspiracy in business reactions. "Every time an administration official gives out an optimistic statement about business conditions," complained Senator Simeon Fess of Ohio, chairman of the Republican National Committee, "the market immediately drops."

The crucial period when a small amount of spending might have checked the cumulative forces of breakdown had already slipped by. But Hoover found in pledges an acceptable substitute for actions; assurances given took the place of dollars spent. "Our joint undertaking," he said, on May 1, 1930, before the United States Chamber of Commerce, "has succeeded to a remarkable degree." The intensity of the slump "has been greatly diminished." "I am convinced," Hoover said, "we have now passed the worst and with continued unity of effort we shall rapidly recover."

The Contagion of Fear

On the day before President Hoover said that all the evidence promised substantial recovery in sixty days, a group of unemployed men and women, organized by the Communist party, staged a demonstration before the White House. For a moment the President stared curiously through the window. Later the police, blackjacks in their hands, routed the crowd with tear-gas bombs. In New York City on the same day 35,000 men and women gathered to hear Communist orators in Union Square. When the Communist leader William Z. Foster called for a march on City Hall, the Police Commissioner issued sharp orders. Hundreds of policemen and detectives, swinging nightsticks, blackjacks, and bare fists, charged the crowd. The scene resounded, the *New York Times* reported, with "screams of women and cries of men with bloody heads and faces. A score of men were sprawled over the square, with policemen pummeling them." One cop, in civilian clothes, wearing a sheepskin coat and carrying a long yellow nightstick, ran wildly through the square, striking out in all directions. Two policemen pinioned a girl by the arms and smashed her face with clubs. A woman wailed, "Cossacks, murderous Cossacks."

March 6 was, by Communist decree, International Unemployment Day. The purpose of the demonstrations was to provoke police violence. In one city after another they achieved this purpose. But Communist agitation alone could not explain the impact of the riots. When else in America had Communists ever attracted crowds of 35,000? A gap was opening between the official mood in Washington and the human reality in city streets and in the countryside—between the presidential vision of accelerating private construction, declining unemployment, mounting confidence, and the actuality of privation and fear.

By the spring of 1930 at least 4,000,000 Americans were unemployed. Breadlines began to reappear in large cities for the first time since 1921—lines of embarrassed men, shuffling patiently forward for a chance at a piece of bread and a cup of coffee. In New York City it was reported in March that the number of families on relief had increased 200 per cent since the crash in October. The municipal lodging houses were now crowded; nearly half of the first 14,000 admitted were first-timers; and the city was letting homeless men sleep on the municipal barge as it tied up at the dock at night, where the icy wind whipped across the East River. In Detroit, said William Green of the A. F. of L., "the men are sitting in the parks all day long and all night long, hundreds and thousands of them, muttering to themselves, out of work, seeking work."

Across the country the dismal process was beginning, ushering in a new life for millions of Americans. In the twenties wage earners in general had found ample employment, satisfaction in life, hope for the future. Now came the slowdown—only three days of work a week, then perhaps two, then the layoff. And then the search for a new job—at first vigorous and hopeful; then sober; then desperate; the long lines before the employment offices, the eyes straining for words of hope on the chalked boards, the unending walk from one plant to the next, the all-night wait to be first for possible work in the morning. And the inexorable news, brusque impersonality concealing fear: "No help wanted here" . . . "We don't need nobody" . . . "Move along, Mac, move along."

And so the search continued, as clothes began to wear out and shoes to fall to pieces. Newspapers under the shirt would temper the winter cold, pasteboard would provide new inner soles, cotton in the heels of the shoe would absorb the pounding on the pavement, gunny sacks wrapped around the feet would mitigate the long hours in the frozen fields outside the factory gates. And in the meantime savings were trickling away. By now the terror began to infect the family. Father, no longer cheery, now at home for long hours, irritable, guilty, a little frightened. Sometimes the mother looked for work as domestic, chambermaid or charwoman; or the children worked for pennies after school, not understanding the fear that was touching them, knowing that they must do what they could to help buy bread and coffee.

As savings end, borrowing begins. If there is life insurance, borrowing on that, until it lapses; then loans from relatives and from friends; then the life of credit, from the landlord, from the corner grocer, until the lines of friendship and compassion are snapped. Meat vanishes from the table; lard replaces butter; father goes out less often, is terribly quiet; the children begin to lack shoes, their clothes are ragged, their mothers are ashamed to send them to school. Wedding rings are pawned, furniture is sold, the family moves into ever cheaper, damper, dirtier rooms. In a Philadelphia settlement house a little boy of three cried constantly in the spring of 1930; the doctor examined him and found that he was slowly starving. One

Employment office in Depression America. "Across the country," Schlesinger writes, "the dismal process was beginning, ushering in a new life for millions of Americans." First came the layoff, then "the search for a new job—at first vigorous and hopeful; then sober; then desperate; the long lines at the employment offices, the eyes straining for words of hope on the chalked boards . . . the all-night wait to be first for possible work in the morning." (Isaac Soyer. Employment Agency. 1937. Oil on canvas. 34½ x 45. Collection Whitney Museum of American Art.)

woman complained that when she had food her two small children could barely eat; they had become accustomed to so little, she said, that their stomachs had shrunk. In November the apple peddlers began to appear on cold street corners, their threadbare clothes brushed and neat, their forlorn pluckiness emphasizing the anguish of being out of work. And every night that fall hundreds of men gathered on the lower level of Wacker Drive in Chicago, feeding fires with stray pieces of wood, their coat collars turned up against the cold, their caps pulled down over their ears, staring without expression at the black river, while above the automobiles sped comfortably along, bearing well-fed men to warm and well-lit homes. In the mining areas families lived on beans, without salt or fat. And every week, every day, more workers joined the procession of despair. The shadows deepened in the dark cold rooms, with the father angry and helpless and ashamed, the distraught children too often hungry or sick, and the mother, so resolute by day, so often, when the room was finally still, lying awake in bed at night, softly crying.

This was 1930; it was, in Elmer Davis's phrase, the Second Year of the Abolition of Poverty. And it introduced thousands of Americans to a new and humiliating mode of existence—life on the relief rolls. Most of the unemployed held out as long as they could. But, with savings gone, credit exhausted, work unobtainable, there seemed no alternative save to subdue pride and face reality.

The system was, in the main, one of local poor relief, supplemented by the resources of private welfare agencies. Even in 1929 public funds paid three-quarters of the nation's relief bill; by 1932, the proportion rose to four-fifths. In larger cities, the social workers had had some success in improving standards of relief care, replacing the old "overseers of the poor" by public welfare departments. But in smaller communities, there was often no alternative to the poorhouse. And the whole patchwork system had an underlying futility: it was addressed to the care of unemployables—those who could not work in any condition—and not at all to the relief of mass unemployment.

No other modern nation had in 1930 such feeble and confused provisions for the jobless. But the President had no doubt about the adequacy of the system for the winter of 1930-31. He told the American Federation of Labor in October that his antidepression policies had had astonishing success, and that workingmen should find inspiration in the devotion "of our great manufacturers, our railways, utilities, business houses, and public officials." Later in the month, rebuking those who were demanding a special session of Congress, the President reaffirmed his confidence that the nation's "sense of voluntary organization and community service" could take care of the unemployed.

Yet, a week before, he had appointed an Emergency Committee for Employment under the direction of Colonel Arthur Woods, who had been active in the relief field during the depression of 1921. Hoover was reluctant to do even this, fearing that such action would magnify the emergency; and he informed the Committee that unemployment was strictly a local responsibility. The Committee's function in consequence became that of advice and exhortation. Colonel Woods, a man of vigor, wanted to do more. He submitted to the President a draft message to Congress calling for a public works program, including slum clearance, low-cost housing, and rural electrification. Woods and his Committee also favored Senator Robert F. Wagner's bills proposing the advance planning of public works and setting up a national employment service. But the President, rejecting the Woods program, addressed Congress with his usual optimism. Getting nowhere, Woods saw the Committee through the winter and resigned in April 1931.

Other events began to define the President's position. In the summer of 1930 a prolonged drought killed cattle and crops throughout the Southwest. This was Hoover's sort of problem—Belgium all over again, so much more concrete than the irritating and intangible issues of depression. "To overcoming the drought," reported Mark Sullivan, Hoover's intimate among the newspapermen, "President Hoover turned with something like a sense of relief, almost of pleasure." With echoes of his old confidence, he organized a program of assistance and asked Congress to appropriate money for government loans to enable farmers to buy seed, fertilizer, and cattle feed.

Democratic senators promptly sought to

apply the Hoover program to human beings as well as livestock. The old Wilsonian, W. G. McAdoo, now aspiring to the Senate from California, suggested that wheat purchased by the Farm Board be distributed to the unemployed. But Hoover reaffirmed his unwavering opposition to such proposals. The opposition, fighting back, taunted the President without mercy. He considered it wise to feed starving cattle, they said, but wicked to feed starving men, women, and children. He had fed the Belgians and the Germans, but would not feed his own countrymen. Hurt and distressed, the President, in February 1931, issued a deeply felt statement. If America meant anything, he suggested, it meant the principles of individual and local responsibility and mutual self-help. If we break down these principles, we "have struck at the roots of self-government." Should federal aid be the only alternative to starvation, then federal aid we must have; but "I have faith in the American people that such a day shall not come."

And so the nation staggered into the second winter of the depression, and unemployment began to settle into a way of life. The weather was glorious much of the winter—clear, light air, brilliant sunlight, dry, frosty snow. But the cold was bitter in unheated tenements, in the flophouses smelling of sweat and Lysol, in the parks, in empty freight cars, along the windy waterfronts. With no money left for rent, unemployed men and their entire families began to build shacks where they could find unoccupied land. Along the railroad embankment, beside the garbage incinerator, in the city dumps, there appeared towns of tarpaper and tin, old packing boxes and old car bodies. Some shanties were neat and scrubbed; cleanliness at least was free; but others were squalid beyond belief, with the smell of decay and surrender. Symbols of the New Era, these communities quickly received their sardonic name: they were called Hoovervilles. And, indeed, it was in many cases only the fortunate who could find Hoovervilles. The unfortunate spent their nights huddled together in doorways, in empty packing cases, in boxcars.

At the breadlines and soup kitchens, hours of waiting would produce a bowl of mush, often without milk or sugar, and a tin cup of coffee. The vapors from the huge steam cookers mingling with the stench of wet clothes and sweating bodies made the air foul. But waiting in the soup kitchen was better than the scavenging in the dump. Citizens of Chicago, in this second winter, could be seen digging into heaps of refuse with sticks and hands as soon as the garbage trucks pulled out. On June 30, 1931, the Pennsylvania Department of Labor and Industry reported that nearly one-quarter of the labor force of the state was out of work. Clarence Pickett of the Friends found schools where 85, 90, even 99 per cent of the children were underweight, and, in consequence, drowsy and lethargic. "Have you ever heard a hungry child cry?" asked Lillian Wald of Henry Street. "Have you seen the uncontrollable trembling of parents who have gone half starved for weeks so that the children may have food?"

And still unemployment grew—from 4,000,000 in March 1930 to 8,000,000 in March 1931. And, more and more, the community found the relief problem beyond its capacity to handle. Local fiscal sources were drying up; local credit was vanishing; towns and counties found they could tax or borrow less and less. Some states had constitutional prohibitions against the use of state funds for home relief. And states too were on the verge of exhausting their tax possibilities; the general property tax had almost reached its limit, and, as income fell, the income tax, for the few states that had it, brought in declining amounts.

The burdens of private charity were meanwhile falling ever more heavily on the poor themselves. Emergency relief committees talked virtuously of the staggering of work and the "sharing" of jobs. But men working a day less a week to provide jobs for other workers were obviously contributing a portion of their own meager wages to relief while their employers contributed nothing. And, even when employers joined in company campaigns of voluntary donations, it was too often under the principle used in the Insull group, by which all, whether top executives or unskilled workers, threw in one day's pay a month. The real recipients of the dole, wrote Professor Sumner H. Slichter of Harvard, were not the men lining up to receive a nickel from the Franciscan Fathers, but "the great industries of America," paying part of their labor overhead by taxing the wages of their employees.

As the number of unemployed grew, the standards of relief care declined. More and more it seemed as if the burden was too great for individual communities to carry longer. In the fall of 1931 Governor Franklin D. Roosevelt of New York established a state emergency relief administration; other states followed this example. Effective relief, said William Allen White in September 1931, would be "the only way to keep down barricades in the streets this winter and the use of force which will brutalize labor and impregnate it with revolution in America for a generation."

But President Hoover announced that a nationwide survey had convinced him that state and local organizations could meet relief needs in the coming winter. Giving ground slightly, he then appointed a new committee to supersede the old Woods committee. This was the President's Organization on Unemployment Relief, headed by Walter S. Gifford, president of the American Telephone and Telegraph Company. Gifford accepted the thesis of local responsibility with far more enthusiasm than Woods; and his main contribution was an advertising campaign designed to stimulate private charity. "Between October 18 and November 25," said Gifford and Owen D. Young in a joint statement, "America will feel the thrill of a great spiritual experience." Charity, the campaign hopefully suggested, could even inspire a new love between husband and wife.

On matters which might have fallen more directly within his responsibility, Gifford displayed indifference. Early in January 1932, after nearly five months in office, Gifford appeared before a committee of the Senate. There, under the incredulous questions of Robert M. La Follette, Jr., of Wisconsin and Edward P. Costigan of Colorado, Gifford disclosed imperturbably that he did not know how many people were idle, that he did not know how many were receiving aid, that he did not know what the standards of assistance were in the various states, that he did not know how much money had been raised in his own campaign, that he knew nothing of the ability of local communities to raise relief funds either through borrowing or taxation, that he did not know what relief needs were either in urban or rural areas, that he did not consider most of this information as of much importance to his job; but that, just the same, he had no question in his mind as to the capacity of the communities to meet the relief problem. "I hope you are not criticizing me for looking at life optimistically," he said plaintively. And, when Costigan asked him to supply the committee with the reports on which his optimism was based, Gifford replied, "I have none, Senator."

But on one question Gifford was clear: he was against federal aid. Should we not be concerned, asked La Follette, if the people in Philadelphia were receiving inadequate aid? As human beings, yes, said Gifford, adding incoherently, "but whether we should be concerned in the Federal Government officially with it, unless it is so bad it is obviously scandalous, and even then we would not be obliged to be concerned. I think there is grave danger in taking the determination of these things into the Federal Government." Federal aid, he said, would lessen the sense of local responsibility; it would reduce the size of private charity. His "sober and considered judgment" was that federal aid would be a "disservice" to the jobless; "the net result might well be that the unemployed who are in need would be worse instead of better off."

And so, through the winter of 1931–32, the third winter of the depression, relief resources, public and private, dwindled toward the vanishing point. In few cities was there any longer pretense of meeting minimum budgetary standards. Little money was available for shoes or clothing, for medical or dental care, for gas or electricity. In New York City entire families were getting an average of $2.39 a week for relief. In Toledo the municipal commissary could allow only 2.14 cents per meal per person per day. In vast rural areas there was no relief coverage at all. "I don't want to steal," a Pennsylvania man wrote Governor Pinchot, "but I won't let my wife and boy cry for something to eat. . . . How long is this going to keep up? I cannot stand it any longer. . . . O, if God would only open a way."

The shadow fell over the cities and towns; it fell as heavily over the countryside. Farmers had already drawn extensively on their savings before 1929. The Wall Street explosion only made their situation worse by diminishing even more the demand for farm products. And, where industry could protect its price structure by meeting reduced demand with reduced output, farmers, unable to control output, saw no way to maintain income except to increase planting. Total crop acreage actually rose in 1930 and showed no significant decline in 1931.

The burden of agricultural adjustment thus fell not on production but on price. The figures were dramatic. Between 1929 and 1934 agricultural production declined 15 per cent in volume, 40 per cent in price; industrial production 42 per cent in volume, 15 per cent in price. The relative stability of industrial prices worsened the farmers' terms of trade; the ratio of the prices the farmer received to the prices he paid plunged from 109 in 1919 (in terms of 1910–14 prices) and 89 in 1929 to 64 in 1931. Corn slid down to 15 cents, cotton and wool to 5 cents, hogs and sugar to 3 cents, and beef to 2.5 cents. A farmer who chewed one thick plug of Drummond a day required almost a bushel of wheat a day to keep him in chewing tobacco. It took 16 bushels of wheat—more than the average yield of a whole acre—to buy one of his children a pair of $4 shoes. Net farm income in 1932 was $1.8 billion—less than one-third what it had been three years earlier. So appalling a slump left many farm families with little income, and many with no income at all.

The farmer's obligations—his taxes and his debts—had been calculated in terms of the much higher price levels of the twenties. A cotton farmer who borrowed $800 when cotton was 16 cents a pound borrowed the equivalent of 5000 pounds of cotton; now, with cotton moving toward 5 cents, he must pay back the debt with over 15,000 pounds of cotton. And, while the farmer's income fell by 64 per cent, his burden of indebtedness fell a mere 7 per cent. In the meantime, fences were standing in disrepair, crops were rotting, livestock was not worth the freight to market, farm machinery was wearing out. Some found it cheaper to burn their corn than to sell it and buy coal. On every side, notices of mortgage foreclosures and tax sales were going up on gate posts and in county courthouses. William Allen White summed it up: "Every farmer, whether his farm is under mortgage or not, knows that with farm products priced as they are today, sooner or later he must go down."

The southwestern drought only intensified the sense of grievance. In January 1931, several hundred tenant farmers presented themselves at the Red Cross in England, Arkansas, and asked for food. They included whites and

Negroes, and some carried rifles. When the Red Cross administrator said that his supply of requisition blanks had been exhausted, the mob marched on the stores and seized their own flour and lard. "Paul Revere just woke up Concord," said Will Rogers, "these birds woke up America." (A New York Communist wrote a short story based on newspaper reports of the incident. Lincoln Steffens, reading Whittaker Chambers's "Can You Hear Their Voices?" wrote the young author, "Whenever I hear people talking about 'proletarian art and literature,' I'm going to ask them to . . . look at you.")

A. N. Young, president of the Wisconsin Farmers' Union, warned the Senate Agriculture Committee early in 1932: "The farmer is naturally a conservative individual, but you cannot find a conservative farmer today. He is not to be found. I am as conservative as any man could be, but any economic system that has it in its power to set me and my wife in the streets, at my age—what else could I see but red."

"The fact is today," Young told the Committee, "that there are more actual reds among the farmers in Wisconsin than you could dream about. . . . They are just ready to do anything to get even with the situation. I almost hate to express it, but I honestly believe that if some of them could buy airplanes, they would come down here to Washington to blow you fellows all up."

In country and city alike, anger was spreading. Edward F. McGrady, the conservative representative of the conservative American Federation of Labor, was testifying before a Senate committee in the spring of 1932. "The leaders of our organization," said Ed McGrady bitterly, "have been preaching patience." But preaching could not take the place of bread. "I say to you gentlemen, advisedly, that if something is not done and starvation is going to continue the doors of revolt in this country are going to be thrown open." Let the administration stop crying to the world that the most important thing to be done is to balance the budget. "There are another two B's besides balancing the Budget, and that is to provide bread and butter."

If the administration, said Ed McGrady, refused "to allow Congress to provide food for these people until they do secure work, as far as I am personally concerned, I would do nothing to close the doors of revolt if it starts.

"I say that as a man, as a citizen of the United States.

"It would not be a revolt against the Government but against the administration."

20

Franklin D. Roosevelt: The Patrician as Opportunist

Richard Hofstadter

became the hated enemy of much of the nation's business and political community. Conservatives denounced him as a Communist. Liberals said he was too conservative. The Communists castigated him as a tool of Wall Street. And the Socialists dismissed him as a reactionary. "He caught hell from all sides," recorded one observer, because nobody knew how to classify his political philosophy. Where, after all, did he fit ideologically? Was he for capitalism or against it? Was the New Deal itself revolutionary or reactionary? Was it "creeping socialism" or a bulwark against socialism? Did it lift the country out of depression, or did the economy right itself in spite of the New Deal?

Richard Hofstadter addresses himself to these and many other questions in the following portrait of F.D.R. In it, Hofstadter points out that Roosevelt was essentially non-ideological, that he rejected absolutes in favor of practical, enthusiastic experimentation. And the New Deal itself was not a coherent, far-sighted program of reform, but "a series of improvisations" which reflected Roosevelt's empirical temper.

Franklin Roosevelt swept to power in 1932, carrying every state but six in the electoral college and gathering 23 million popular votes in contrast to Hoover's 16 million. It was a bitter defeat indeed for the Republicans. But the election was even more disappointing for Norman Thomas and William Z. Foster, respective candidates for the Socialist and Communist parties. In this year of distress, with some 16 million people unemployed, Thomas collected 882,000 votes and Foster only 103,000.

Franklin Roosevelt was perhaps the most controversial President the United States ever had. For thousands of Americans, Roosevelt was a folk hero: a courageous statesman who, crippled by polio, saved a crippled nation from almost certain collapse, and whose New Deal salvaged the best features of democratic capitalism and established unprecedented welfare programs for the nation's little people. For others, Roosevelt was a tyrant, a demagogue who used the Depression to consolidate his political power, whereupon he dragged the country zealously down the road to socialism. In spite of his immense popular appeal, Roosevelt

The country needs and, unless I mistake its temper, the country demands bold, persistent experimentation. It is common sense to take a method and try it. If it fails, admit it frankly and try another. But above all, try something.
FRANKLIN D. ROOSEVELT

Once during the early years of the Wilson administration Eleanor Roosevelt and her husband, then Assistant Secretary of the Navy, were lunching with Henry Adams. Roosevelt was speaking earnestly about some governmental matter that concerned him, when his aged host turned on him fiercely: "Young man, I have lived in this house many years and seen the occupants of that White House across the

---

From pp. 311–338 in *The American Political Tradition*, by Richard Hofstadter. Copyright 1948 by Alfred A. Knopf. Reprinted by permission of the publisher.

square come and go, and nothing that you minor officials or the occupants of that house can do will affect the history of the world for long."

It was not often that Adams's superlative ironies were unintentional. Although the influence of great men is usually exaggerated, Roosevelt must be granted at least a marginal influence upon the course of history. No personality has ever expressed the American popular temper so articulately or with such exclusiveness. In the Progressive era national reform leadership was divided among Theodore Roosevelt, Wilson, Bryan, and La Follette. In the age of the New Deal it was monopolized by one man, whose passing left American liberalism demoralized and all but helpless.

At the heart of the New Deal there was not a philosophy but a temperament. The essence of this temperament was Roosevelt's confidence that even when he was operating in unfamiliar territory he could do no wrong, commit no serious mistakes. From the standpoint of an economic technician this assurance seemed almost mad at times, for example when he tossed back his head, laughed, and said to a group of silver Senators: "I experimented with gold and that was a flop. Why shouldn't I experiment a little with silver?" And yet there was a kind of intuitive wisdom under the harum-scarum surface of his methods. When he came to power, the people had seen stagnation go dangerously far. They wanted experiment, activity, trial and error, anything that would convey a sense of movement and novelty. At the very beginning of his candidacy Roosevelt, without heed for tradition or formality, flew to the 1932 nominating convention and addressed it in person instead of waiting for weeks in the customary pose of ceremonious ignorance. A trivial act in itself, the device gave the public an impression of vigor and originality that was never permitted to die. Although, as we shall see, Roosevelt had been reared on a social and economic philosophy

"The Happy Warrior": Franklin D. Roosevelt. Warm, impulsive, and flexible, Roosevelt was "a public instrument of the most delicate receptivity." (Courtesy of Franklin D. Roosevelt Library, Hyde Park, New York.)

rather similar to Hoover's, he succeeded at once in communicating the fact that his temperament was antithetical. When Hoover bumbled that it was necessary only to restore confidence, the nation laughed bitterly. When Roosevelt said: "The only thing we have to fear is fear itself," essentially the same threadbare half-true idea, the nation was thrilled. Hoover had lacked motion; Roosevelt lacked direction. But his capacity for growth, or at least for change, was enormous. Flexibility was both his strength and his weakness. Where Hoover had been remote and abstract, a doctrinaire who thought in fixed principles and moved cautiously in the rarefied atmosphere of the managerial classes, Roosevelt was warm, personal, concrete, and impulsive. Hoover was often reserved with valued associates. Roosevelt could say "my old friend" in eleven languages. He had little regard for abstract principle but a sharp intuitive knowledge of popular feeling. Because he was content in large measure to follow public opinion, he was able to give it that necessary additional impulse of leadership which can translate desires into policies. Hoover had never been able to convey to the masses a clear picture of what he was trying to do; Roosevelt was often able to suggest a clear and forceful line of policy when none in fact existed.

Raymond Moley tells an instructive story of Roosevelt's relations with Hoover in the interim between Roosevelt's election and inauguration. A conference had been arranged between the two men to discuss continuity of policy on the vexing question of foreign debts. Roosevelt, ill-informed on the facts, brought Moley with him as ballast and also carried a set of little cards in his hand as reminders of the questions he wanted to put to Hoover. Hoover talked for some time, revealing a mastery of all facets of the question which profoundly impressed Professor Moley. In contrast with the state of their information was the manner of the two men. Hoover, plainly disconcerted at this meeting with the man who had beaten him in the campaign, was shy and ill at ease and kept his eyes on the pattern of the carpet in the Red Room. Roosevelt was relaxed, informal, and cordial. That he was operating in *terra incognita* did not seem to trouble him in the least.

Roosevelt's admirers, their minds fixed on the image of a wise, benevolent, provident father, have portrayed him as an ardent social reformer and sometimes as a master planner. His critics, coldly examining the step-by-step emergence of his measures, studying the supremely haphazard way in which they were so often administered, finding how little he actually had to do with so many of his "achievements," have come to the opposite conclusion that his successes were purely accidental, just as a certain portion of a number of random shots is likely to hit a target. It is true, it is bound to be true, that there is a vast disproportion between Roosevelt's personal stature and the Roosevelt legend, but not everything that comes in haphazard fashion is necessarily an accident. During his presidential period the nation was confronted with a completely novel situation for which the traditional, commonly accepted philosophies afforded no guide. An era of fumbling and muddling-through was inevitable. Only a leader with an experimental temper could have made the New Deal possible.

Roosevelt was, moreover, a public instrument of the most delicate receptivity. Although he lacked depth, he had great breadth. A warm-hearted, informal patrician, he hated to disappoint, liked to play the bountiful friend. He felt that if a large number of people wanted something very badly, it was important that they be given some measure of satisfaction—and he allowed neither economic dogmas nor political precedents to inhibit him. The story of the WPA cultural projects illustrates his intensely personal methods and the results they yielded. When relief was being organized in the early stages of the New Deal, someone pointed out to him that a great many competent painters were poverty-stricken and desperate. Now, Roosevelt had no taste for painting, very little interest in artists and writers as a group, and no preconceived theories about the responsibility of the State for cultural welfare; but his decision to help the artists came immediately and spontaneously. "Why not?" he said. "They are human beings. They have to live. I guess the only thing they can do is paint and surely there must be some public place where paintings are wanted." And so painters were included in the benefits of CWA. Ultimately, under the WPA, relief was extended to musicians, dancers, actors, writers, historians, even to students trying to finance themselves through college. A generation of artists and intellectuals was nursed through a trying period and became wedded to the New Deal and devoted to Roosevelt liberalism.

2

James and Sara Delano Roosevelt, Franklin's parents, are reminiscent of secondary characters in Edith Wharton's novels who provide the climate of respectable and unfriendly opinion in which her unfortunate heroines live. James Roosevelt, vice-president of several corporations, was a handsome country gentleman who dabbled in Democratic politics, enjoyed a stable of trotting-horses, and lived in leisure on his Hyde Park estate. Sara Delano, James's second wife, was also from an upper-class family with deep roots in American history; her father had owned copper lands, iron and coal mines, acreage on New York harbor, and a fleet of clipper ships. When they were married Sara was twenty-six and James was fifty-two. Two years later, on January 30, 1882, an entry in James Roosevelt's diary noted the birth of "a splendid large baby boy."

The only child of a fond mother, treated like a grandson by his father, Franklin was brought up with unusual indulgence. He had governesses and tutors; his playmates were from his own class; he owned a pony and a twenty-one-foot sailboat. Eight times before his adolescence he was taken on jaunts to Europe. At fourteen he entered the Reverend Endicott Peabody's Groton School, a little Greek democracy of the elite, which, as its headmaster said, stood for "everything that is true, beautiful, and of good report." The Groton boys, about ninety per cent from social-register families, lived in an atmosphere of paternal kindness and solicitude and swallowed huge gulps of inspiration at Peabody's weekly chapel performances.

From Groton Roosevelt followed a well-beaten path to Harvard. Although he was privileged to hear James, Royce, Norton, Shaler, and other illuminati, his life flowered chiefly outside the classroom. He became a prodigious doer and joiner, with memberships in more than a half-dozen campus clubs and a position on the *Crimson* that won him a good deal of college renown. A large part of his work on the *Crimson* was devoted to petty crusades for campus reforms. At an age when many boys are kicking over the traces, flirting with heresies, defying authority, and incidentally deepening their intellectual perspectives, young Roosevelt was writing exhortations about "school spirit" and football morale. On one occasion he urged in patriarchal fashion that "the memories and traditions of our ancestors and of our University be maintained during our lives and be faithfully handed down to our children in the years to come." His most serious public interest and possibly his first manifestation of sympathy for an underdog was in a college relief drive for the Boers. He left Harvard in 1904; his youth is summed up in his mother's words: "After all he had many advantages that other boys did not have."

Since it had been decided that Franklin should become a lawyer, he entered Columbia Law School. The following year he married his distant cousin Eleanor, to whom he had secretly been engaged, and moved into a home in New York City under the managerial eye of his mother. He was not happy in law school. "I am . . . trying to understand a little of the work," he wrote plaintively to Rector Peabody. Bored by the tenuous subtleties of the law, he failed some of his courses and left school without taking a degree, although he had absorbed enough to pass bar examinations. He joined the well-known New York firm of Carter, Ledyard, & Milburn as managing clerk. In Hyde Park he assumed the public-spirited role that his position required, became a member of the local volunteer fire department, a director of the First National Bank of Poughkeepsie, and a delegate to the 1910 New York Democratic convention.

Peopled by rich gentry and their hangers-on, the Hudson Valley counties were overwhelmingly Republican. Democratic nominations were conventionally given to prominent men of means who could pay the expenses of their campaigns. In 1910 the Democratic Mayor of Poughkeepsie, who had come to like his agreeable young neighbor from up the river, got him the party nomination for state senator in a district that had elected only one Democrat since 1856. But 1910 was a bad year for Republicans, and Roosevelt, who bore the name of his wife's uncle, the popular twenty-sixth President, conducted a vigorous, unconventional campaign by automobile, ran well ahead of his ticket, and was elected on the crest of a Democratic wave.

In the legislature Roosevelt promptly became a leader among Democratic insurgents who blocked the nomination of Tammany Boss Murphy's choice for United States senator. He appeared a typical progressive in his voting record, stood for the civil service, conservation, direct primaries, popular election of Senators, women's suffrage, and social legislation. "From the ruins of the political machines," he predicted hopefully, "we will reconstruct something more nearly conforming to a democratic government." In 1911 he visited Wilson at Trenton and returned an enthusiastic supporter. He served well in the 1912 campaign and was rewarded with the Assistant Secretaryship of the Navy. Just turned thirty-one, he had had only three years of experience in politics.

From his childhood when he sailed his own knockabout, Roosevelt had been in love with ships and the sea. He collected ship models and prints, he read avidly in naval history, particularly Mahan, and had thought of entering Annapolis. During the Spanish War he had run away from Groton to enlist in the navy— an escapade cut short by a siege of scarlet fever. After his appointment Roosevelt began to campaign for naval expansion in magazine articles and speeches, revealing a somewhat nationalistic and bellicose spirit. The United States, he said, could not afford to lose control of the seas unless it was content to be "a nation unimportant in the great affairs of the world, without influence in commerce, or in the extension of peaceful civilization." Although the American people could look forward to ultimate international limitations of arms, they must in the present "keep the principles of a possible navy conflict always in mind." At the time Wilson delivered his war message to Congress, *Scribner's Magazine* was featuring a monitory article by Roosevelt entitled "On Your Own Heads," which called for quintupling the navy's personnel. No one could say, argued Roosevelt, that we were free from the danger of war. "We know that every boy who goes to school is bound sooner or later, no matter how peaceful his nature, to come to blows with some schoolmate. A great people, a hundred million strong, has gone to school." Later he demanded a system of national conscription for women as well as men. He believed that service in the navy smooths out sectionalism and class feeling and teaches equality. As an administrator Roosevelt was aggressive and efficient, cutting through red tape with genial disregard for regulations. Against the advice of most of the admirals he took an important part in promoting the unprecedented Allied mine barrage in the North Sea.

In 1920 his party, needing a good name and an effective campaigner, nominated Roosevelt as James M. Cox's running-mate. He made a grand tour of the country, delivering about a thousand speeches. On the primary issue, the League of Nations, he argued effectively, but his enthusiasm was not comparable to his energy. "The League may not end wars," he conceded, "but the nations demand the experiment." During the campaign he made one slip which indicates that his mood was one of imperialistic *Realpolitik* rather than idealistic internationalism. At Butte, answering the argument that the United States would be outvoted by the combined British Commonwealth in the League's Assembly, he said: "It is just the other way . . . the United States has about twelve votes in the Assembly." He went on to explain that Latin-American countries in the projected Assembly looked to his country as "a guardian and big brother," and that it would control their votes.

> Until last week I had two [votes] myself, and now Secretary Daniels has them. You know I had something to do with the running of a couple of little republics. The facts are that I wrote Haiti's Constitution myself, and, if I do say it, I think it a pretty good Constitution.

Immediately the opposition kicked. Roosevelt was simply voicing some of the realities of politics, but the cynicism of his remarks, which smacked so strongly of the bad neighbor, was too open. He covered himself as best he could by saying that he had only meant that the Latin-American countries had the same interests as the United States and would normally vote the same way. For the boast that an alien official had written the Constitution of a neighbor republic there could be no satisfactory explanation.[1]

But it was a campaign in which mistakes did not matter. After Harding's victory Roosevelt, now thirty-eight, became a private citizen for the first time in ten years. He resumed his slight law practice, served as an overseer of Harvard, and took up his old life. A yachting companion, Van Lear Black, gave him a position in the New York office of the Fidelity and Deposit Company of Maryland which carried a salary of $25,000. But in August 1921 it appeared that both Roosevelt's public and professional careers were over. After an exhausting spell in the heat of New York City he left for a vacation at his summer home on Campobello Island and soon found himself in the grip of severe pain, unable to move his muscles from the hips down.

3

To be sick and helpless is a humiliating experience. Prolonged illness also carries the hazard of narcissistic self-absorption. It would have been easy for Roosevelt to give up his political aspirations and retire to the comfortable privacy of Hyde Park. That he refused to relinquish his normal life was testimony to his courage and determination, and also to the strength of his ambition. From his bed he resumed as many of his affairs as possible. By the spring of 1922 he was walking on crutches, sometimes venturing to his office, and after 1924, when he found the pool at Warm Springs, he made good progress in recovering his strength. Above his enfeebled legs he developed a powerful torso.

In the long run this siege of infantile paralysis added much to Roosevelt's political appeal. As a member of the overprivileged classes with a classic Groton-Harvard career he had been too much the child of fortune. Now a heroic struggle against the cruelest kind of adversity made a more poignant success story than the usual rags-to-riches theme; it was also far better adapted to democratic leadership in a period when people were tired of self-made men and their management of affairs.

There has been much speculation about the effect of Roosevelt's illness upon his sympathies. Frances Perkins, who writes of him with intelligence and detachment and who knew him before his illness as a pleasant but somewhat supercilious young man, feels that he underwent a "spiritual transformation," in which he

---

[1] The boast was untrue as well as unwise. Roosevelt did not write the Haitian Constitution but merely approved a draft submitted to the Navy Department by the State Department.

was purged of "the slightly arrogant attitude" he had occasionally shown before. She now found him "completely warm-hearted," and felt that "he understood the problems of people in trouble." There is a further conclusion, drawn by some fabricators of the legend, that he read widely and studied deeply during his illness and developed a firm social outlook that aligned him forever with the underprivileged. This notion is not sustained by Roosevelt's history during the prosperity of the 1920's. His human capacity, enlarged though it probably was, was not crystallized in either a new philosophy or a heightened interest in reforms.

For anyone of Roosevelt's background and character to have turned to serious social study or unorthodox political views would have been most unusual. From boyhood to the time of his illness he had led an outdoor athletic life, spending his indoor leisure on such diversions as stamp collections, ship models, naval history, and the like, not on sociological literature. His way of thinking was empirical, impressionistic, and pragmatic. At the beginning of his career he took to the patrician reform thought of the Progressive era and accepted a social outlook that can best be summed up in the phrase *noblesse oblige*.[2] He had a penchant for public service, personal philanthropy, and harmless manifestoes against dishonesty in government; he displayed a broad, easygoing tolerance, a genuine liking for all sorts of people; he loved to exercise his charm in political and social situations. His mind, as exhibited in writings and speeches of the twenties, was generous and sensible, but also superficial and complacent.

Roosevelt's education in politics came in a period of progressive optimism when it was commonly assumed that the most glaring ills of society could be cured by laws, once politics fell into the hands of honest men. If women worked endless hours in sweatshops, if workingmen were haunted by fear of unemployment or stricken by accidents, if the aged were beset by insecurity, men of good will would pass laws to help them. As a state Senator and as Governor this was what Roosevelt tried to do. But the social legislation of the states, however humane and useful, was worked out in provincial theaters of action, dealt more with effects than causes, touched only the surface of great problems like unemployment, housing, taxation, banking, and relief for agriculture. The generation that sponsored these laws got from them a good deal of training in practical politics and welfare work, but no strong challenge to think through the organic ills of society.

Roosevelt's biographers have largely ignored his life in the twenties except his fight for physical recovery, his role as peacemaker in the faction-ridden Democratic Party, and his return to politics as Governor of New York. John T. Flynn, however, has pointed with malicious pleasure to his unsuccessful career in business, which certainly deserves attention, not as a reflection on his ethics or personal capacities, but on his social views during the years of prosperity. The ventures with which Roosevelt was associated—chiefly, one suspects, for the promotional value of his name—were highly speculative, and with one exception they failed. Perhaps the most illuminating of these was the Consolidated Automatic Merchandising Corporation, of which he was a founder and director along with Henry Morgenthau, Jr. This was a holding company, whose promoters were stirred by the typically American idea of a chain of clerkless stores to sell standard goods by means of automatic vending machines. In 1928 the chairman of its board announced that a large store staffed with such machines would soon be opened in New York City. Although it promised fabulous returns to investors, the firm lost over two million dollars within three years

---

[2] "Frankness, and largeness, and simplicity, and a fine fervor for the right are virtues that some must preserve, and where can we look for them if not from the Roosevelts and the Delanos?" wrote Franklin K. Lane to Roosevelt, August, 1920.

and closed its affairs in a bankruptcy court. Since Roosevelt promptly resigned his interest when he became Governor, his connection with it was brief and, in a business way, unimportant; but the social implications of the clerkless store and the jobless clerk, not to mention the loose and speculative way in which the enterprise was launched, do not seem to have troubled his mind.

In 1922 Roosevelt became president of the American Construction Council, a trade organization of the building industry. The council had been conceived in the light of Secretary of Commerce Hoover's philosophy of self-regulation by business, and Hoover presided over the meeting at which Roosevelt was chosen. In his address to the council Roosevelt endorsed the Hoover doctrine:

> The tendency lately has been toward regulation of industry. Something goes wrong somewhere in a given branch of work, immediately the public is aroused, the press, the pulpit and public call for an investigation. That is fine, that is healthy . . . but government regulation is not feasible. It is unwieldy, expensive. It means employment of men to carry on this phase of the work; it means higher taxes. The public doesn't want it; the industry doesn't want it.

Seven years later in a Fourth of July speech at Tammany Hall, Governor Roosevelt warned of dangers inherent in "great combinations of capital." But he explained that "industrial combination is not wrong in itself. The danger lies in taking the government into partnership." The chief theme of his address was summed up in the sentence: "I want to preach a new doctrine—complete separation of business and government"—which was an ironic message for the future architect of the New Deal.

Even Mr. Flynn concedes that as Governor Roosevelt was "a fair executive." On social justice and humane reform his record was strong; in matters of long-range economic understanding and responsibility it was weak. He worked earnestly and effectively with a hostile Republican legislature to extend reforms that had been started by Al Smith. He secured a program of old-age pensions, unemployment insurance, and labor legislation, developed a forthright liberal program on the power question,[3] and took the initiative in calling a conference of governors of Eastern industrial states to discuss unemployment and relief. His state was in the vanguard of those taking practical steps to relieve distress.

Along with most other Americans, however, Roosevelt had failed to foresee the depression that began when he was Governor. Six months before the crash he found New York industry "in a very healthy and prosperous condition." In his addresses and messages he ignored the significance of the depression until its effects became overwhelming. His signal failure was in the realm of financial policy.

On December 11, 1930 the Bank of United States in New York City was closed by the State Superintendent of Banks, in substantial default to 400,000 depositors, mostly people with small savings. It had long been a practice of some New York commercial banks to create special "thrift accounts," which, although much the same as ordinary savings accounts, stood outside the control of state laws regulating

---

[3] Roosevelt believed that the vast potential of the St. Lawrence should be developed to shake down the unreasonable rates of the power companies. He wanted great power sites like the St. Lawrence, Muscle Shoals, and Boulder Dam to be developed by federal or state authority so that they would "remain forever as a yardstick with which to measure the cost of producing and transmitting electricity." This yardstick could be used to test the fairness of private utility rates. He proposed that New York build power structures and market the power they generated through contracts with private companies. If the state failed to get satisfactory contracts it would go into the business of selling power directly to consumers. In 1931 the legislature created the New York Power Authority, embodying his proposals, but the necessary treaty with Canada was first blocked by the Hoover administration and later defeated by the Senate in 1934 when it failed to get the necessary two-thirds majority.

savings-bank investments and gave bankers a wide latitude with other people's money. Another device was to create bank affiliates which were manipulated in sundry complicated ways to milk depositors and stockholders for the benefit of insiders.

A few months before the collapse of the Bank of United States, the failure of the City Trust Company had led to an investigation of the State Banking Department, and in Roosevelt's absence Acting Governor Herbert Lehman appointed Robert Moses as investigator. Moses's report roundly condemned many bank practices, especially "thrift accounts" and bank affiliates, and referred to the Bank of United States as an especially flagrant case.

Roosevelt ignored the Moses report and created another commission to study the same subject, appointing as one of its members Henry Pollak—a director and counsel of the Bank of United States! Not surprisingly, the new commission rejected Moses's recommendations. Shortly afterward, when the Bank of United States failed, Roosevelt was self-assured, unabashed, impenitent. To the state legislature he boldly wrote: "The responsibility for strengthening the banking laws rests with you." Insisting that the protection of the laws be extended to depositors in thrift accounts, he waxed righteously impatient: "The people of the State not only expect it, but they have a right to demand it. The time to act is now. Any further delay is inexcusable. . . ."

This incident, particularly Roosevelt's sudden espousal of a reform he had opposed, foreshadows a great part of the history of the New Deal. There is an irresistible footnote to it. When Roosevelt came to power the banks of the nation were in paralysis. In his first press conference he was asked if he favored federal insurance of bank deposits. He said that he did not. His reason was that bad banks as well as good ones would have to be insured and that the federal government would have to take the losses. Nevertheless the Federal Deposit Insurance Corporation was soon created as a concession to a bloc of insistent Western Senators. The FDIC thus took its place among a company of New Deal reforms that add to the lustre of Roosevelt's name and will presumably be cited by historians as instances of his wise planning.

When the task of conducting a presidential campaign fell upon him, Roosevelt's background of economic innocence was dappled by only occasional traces of knowledge. "I don't find that he has read much about economic subjects," wrote Raymond Moley in a family letter, April 12, 1932. "The frightening aspect of his methods is FDR's great receptivity. So far as I know he makes no efforts to check up on anything that I or anyone else has told him." On occasion his advisers were astounded by his glib treatment of complicated subjects. Once when his campaign speeches on the tariff were being prepared, and two utterly incompatible proposals were placed before him, Roosevelt left Moley speechless by airily suggesting that he should "weave the two together." That "great receptivity" which frightened Moley, however, was the secret of Roosevelt's political genius. He became an individual sounding-board for the grievances and remedies of the nation, which he tried to weave into a program that would be politically, if not economically, coherent.

Roosevelt's 1932 campaign utterances indicate that the New Deal had not yet taken form in his mind. He was clear on two premises: he rejected Hoover's thesis that the depression began abroad, insisting that it was a home-made product, and he denounced Hoover for spending too much money. He called the Hoover administration "the greatest spending Administration in peace time in all our history." The current deficit, he charged, was enough to "make us catch our breath." "Let us have the courage," he urged, "to stop borrowing to meet continuing deficits." And yet he was "unwilling that economy should be practiced at the expense of starving people." Still, he did not indicate how he proposed to relieve starving people. Public works? They could be no more than a "stopgap," even if billions of dollars were spent on them. He was firm in ascribing the depression to low domestic purchasing power, and declared that the government must "use wise measures of regulation which will bring the purchasing power back to normal." On the other hand, he surrendered to Hoover's idea that America's productive capacity demanded a large outlet in the export market. "If our factories run even 80 per cent of capacity," he said (quite inaccurately),[4] "they will turn out more products than we as a nation can possibly use ourselves. The answer is that . . . we must sell some goods abroad."

Roosevelt made several specific promises to the farmers. There was one aspect of Hoover's farm policies that made him especially bitter—the attempt of the Farm Board to organize retrenchment in production, which Roosevelt called "the cruel joke of advising farmers to allow twenty percent of their wheat lands to lie idle, to plow up every third row of cotton and shoot every tenth dairy cow." His own program involved "planned use of the land," reforestation, and aid to farmers by reducing tariffs through bilateral negotiations. Later he backtracked on the tariff, however, promising "continued protection for American agriculture *as well as* American industry."

All Roosevelt's promises—to restore purchasing power and mass employment and relieve the needy and aid the farmer and raise agricultural prices and balance the budget and lower the tariff and continue protection—added up to a very discouraging performance to those who hoped for a coherent liberal program. The *New Republic* called the campaign "an obscene spectacle" on both sides.

Roosevelt delivered one speech at the Commonwealth Club in San Francisco, however, which did generally foreshadow the new tack that was to be taken under the New Deal. In this address Roosevelt clearly set down the thesis that the nation had arrived at a great watershed in its development. Popular government and a wide continent to exploit had given the United States an unusually favored early history, he asserted. Then the Industrial Revolution had brought a promise of abundance for all. But its productive capacity had been controlled by ruthless and wasteful men. Possessing free land and a growing population, and needing industrial plant, the country had been willing to pay the price of the accomplishments of the "ambitious man" and had offered him "unlimited reward provided only that he produced the economic plant so much desired." "The turn of the tide came with the turn of the century." As America reached its last frontiers, the demand of the people for more positive controls of economic life gave rise to the Square Deal of Theodore Roosevelt and the New Freedom of Woodrow Wilson. In 1932 the nation was still faced with the problem of industrial control.

> A glance at the situation today only too clearly indicates that equality of opportunity as we have known it no longer exists. Our industrial plant is built; the problem just now is whether under existing conditions it is not overbuilt. Our last frontier has long since been reached, and there is practically no more free land. More than half of our people do not live on the farms or on lands and cannot derive a living by cultivating their own property. There is no safety valve in the form of a Western prairie to which those thrown out of work by the Eastern economic machines can go for a new start. We are not able to invite the immigration

---

[4] "The United States," concluded the authors of *America's Capacity to Consume*, "has not reached a stage of economic development in which it is possible to produce more than the American people as a whole would like to consume."

from Europe to share our endless plenty. We are now providing a drab living for our own people. . . .

Just as freedom to farm has ceased, so also the opportunity in business has narrowed. . . . The unfeeling statistics of the past three decades show that the independent business man is running a losing race. . . . Recently a careful study was made of the concentration of business in the United States. It showed that our economic life was dominated by some six hundred odd corporations who [sic] controlled two-thirds of American industry. Ten million small business men divided the other third. More striking still, it appeared that if the process goes on at the same rate, at the end of another century we shall have all American industry controlled by a dozen corporations, and run by perhaps a hundred men. Put plainly, we are steering a steady course toward economic oligarchy, if we are not there already.

Clearly, all this calls for a re-appraisal of values. A mere builder of more industrial plants, a creator of more railroad systems, an organizer of more corporations, is as likely to be a danger as a help. The day of the great promoter or the financial Titan, to whom we granted anything if only he would build, or develop, is over. Our task now is not discovery or exploitation of natural resources, or necessarily producing more goods. It is the soberer, less dramatic business of administering resources and plants already in hand, of seeking to reestablish foreign markets for our surplus production, of meeting the problem of underconsumption, of adjusting production to consumption, of distributing wealth and products more equitably, of adapting existing economic organizations to the service of the people. The day of enlightened administration has come. . . .

As I see it, the task of government in its relation to business is to assist the development of an economic declaration of rights, an economic constitutional order. . . .

Happily, the times indicate that to create such an order not only is the proper policy of Government, but it is the only line of safety for our economic structures as well. We know, now, that these economic units cannot exist unless prosperity is uniform, that is, unless purchasing power is well distributed throughout every group in the nation.

In cold terms, American capitalism had come of age, the great era of individualism, expansion, and opportunity was dead. Further, the drying up of "natural" economic forces required that the government step in and guide the creation of a new economic order. Thus far Roosevelt had left behind the philosophy of his 1929 Tammany Hall speech. But in the Commonwealth Club speech two different and potentially inconsistent lines of government action are implied. One is suggested by the observation that the industrial plant is "overbuilt," that more plants will be "a danger," that production must be "adjusted" to consumption; the other by phrases like "meeting the problem of underconsumption," making prosperity "uniform," distributing purchasing power, and "an economic declaration of rights." The first involves a retrogressive economy of trade restriction and state-guided monopoly; the second emphasizes social justice and the conquest of poverty. In 1931 the United States Chamber of Commerce's Committee on Continuity of Business and Employment had declared in terms similar to Roosevelt's: "A freedom of action which might have been justified in the relatively simple life of the last century cannot be tolerated today. . . . We have left the period of extreme individualism." The committee then proposed a program very closely resembling the NRA as it was adopted in 1933. It is evident that Roosevelt's premises, far from being intrinsically progressive, were capable of being adapted to very conservative purposes.

His version of the "matured economy" theory, although clothed in the rhetoric of liberalism and "social planning," could easily be put to the purposes of the trade associations and scarcity-mongers. The polar opposition between such a policy and the promise of making prosperity uniform and distributing purchasing power anticipated a basic ambiguity in the New Deal.

4

At one of his earliest press conferences Roosevelt compared himself to the quarterback in a football game. The quarterback knows what the next play will be, but beyond that he cannot predict or plan too rigidly because "future plays will depend on how the next one works." It was a token of his cast of mind that he used the metaphor of a game, and one in which chance plays a very large part. The New Deal will never be understood by anyone who looks for a single thread of policy, a far-reaching, far-seeing plan. It was a series of improvisations, many adopted very suddenly, many contradictory. Such unity as it had was in political strategy, not economics.

Roosevelt had little regard for the wisdom of economists as a professional caste. "I happen to know," he declared in his third fireside chat, "that professional economists have changed their definition of economic laws every five or ten years for a long time." Within the broad limits of what he deemed "sound policy"—and they were extremely broad limits—he understood that his administration would not be politically durable unless it could "weave together" many diverse, conflicting interests. He had built a brilliantly successful career in the Democratic Party on his flair for reconciling or straddling antagonistic elements, and he was too practical to abandon a solid bedrock of political harmony in favor of some flighty economic dogma that might be abandoned in "five or ten years." Frances Perkins tells how Lord Keynes, whose spending theories were influential with some New Deal economists, paid a brief visit to the President in 1934 and talked about economic theory. Roosevelt, bewildered at Keynes's "rigamarole of figures," told his Secretary of Labor: "He must be a mathematician rather than a political economist." Keynes for his part was somewhat disappointed, remarking that he had "supposed the President was more literate, economically speaking." The Britisher's mistake is likely to become a model for Roosevelt legend-makers.

Raymond Moley, in his *After Seven Years*, has compiled a fairly long but not exhaustive enumeration of the sharp swerves and tacks in Rooseveltian policy. It will be more simple and profitable to speak only of the two New Deals that were fore-shadowed in the Commonwealth Club speech. In a sense both of them ran concurrently; but it is roughly accurate to say that the first was dominant from Roosevelt's inauguration to the spring and summer of 1935 and that the second emerged during that period and lasted until the reform energies of the nation petered out.

The first New Deal, the New Deal of 1933–4, was conceived mainly for recovery. Reform elements and humane measures of immediate relief were subsidiary to the organized and subsidized scarcity advocated by the Chamber of Commerce, the Farm Bureau Federation, and the National Grange, and incarnated in the NRA and AAA. These great agencies, the core of the first New Deal, representing its basic plans for industry and agriculture, embodied the retrogressive idea of recovery through scarcity.

The AAA was the most striking illustration of organized scarcity in action. Although successful in raising farm prices and restoring farm income, it did just what Roosevelt had found so shocking in Hoover's Farm Board. To the common-sense mind the policy seemed to have solved the paradox of hunger in the midst of plenty only by doing away with plenty. In an address at Atlanta, in November 1935, Roosevelt implicitly conceded that the whole policy was geared to the failure of the American economy. He pointed out that the average American lived "on what the doctors would call a third class diet." If the nation lived on a first-class diet, "we would have to put more acres than we have ever cultivated into the production of an additional supply of things for Americans to eat." The people lived on a third-class diet, he said candidly, because they could not afford to buy a first-class diet.[5]

The mainspring of the first New Deal was the NRA, which Roosevelt called "the most important and far-reaching legislation ever enacted by the American Congress . . . a supreme effort to stabilize for all time the many factors which make for the prosperity of the nation." Under it business received government sanction for sweeping price agreements and production quotas and in return accepted wage stipulations improving the condition of many of the poorest-paid workers.[6] It is not unfair to say that in essence the NRA embodied the conception of many businessmen that recovery was to be sought through systematic monopolization, high prices, and low production.[7] In spite of the enthusiasm with which its "planned" features were greeted, it retarded recovery, as the Brookings economists concluded, and a strong, sustained advance in business conditions began only after the Supreme Court killed it in May 1935.[8] Roosevelt was nevertheless slow to give up the NRA idea. In February 1935, asking for a two-year extension, he said that to abandon its "fundamental purposes and principles . . . would spell the return of industrial and labor chaos."

The initial New Deal was based upon a strategy that Roosevelt had called during the campaign "a true concert of interests," and that meant in practice something for everybody. Farmers got the AAA. Business got the NRA codes. Labor got wage-and-hour provisions and the collective-bargaining promise of Section 7 (a). The unemployed got a variety of federal relief measures. The middle classes got the Home Owners' Loan Corporation, securities regulation, and other reforms. Some debtors were aided by inflation. As new discontents developed they were met with new expedients.

Despite all Roosevelt's efforts, however, the nation insistently divided into right and left, and his equivocal position became more difficult to maintain. Pressure from the organized and enheartened left became stronger; but Roosevelt was also baited into a leftward turn by diehard conservatives. He was surprised and wounded at the way the upper classes turned on him. It has often been said that he betrayed his class; but if by his class one means the whole policy-making, power-wielding stratum, it would be just as true to say that his class betrayed him. Consider the situation in which he came to office. The economic machinery of the nation had broken down and its political structure was beginning to disintegrate. People

---

[5] The Ever Normal Granary Plan, enacted in 1938, was widely hailed as a more satisfactory policy. Although it promised greater price stability and other benefits, it still involved familiar plans for marketing quotas and the shadow of abundance still hung over it. Its sponsor, Henry Wallace, admitted that "several years of good weather" and good crops would "embarrass" the government.

[6] It may be necessary to say that NRA was not a universal business policy. A poll taken in 1935 showed that Chamber of Commerce members were almost three to one for continuing NRA, while NAM members opposed it three to one.

[7] NRA Administrator Hugh Johnson declared in an early press conference: "We are going to ask something in the nature of an armistice on increased producing capacity, until we see if we can get this upward spiral started. . . . We are going to plead very earnestly . . . not to use any further labor-saving devices or anything further to increase production for the present."

[8] The end of NRA was certainly not the only factor in the recovery that began in the summer of 1935, but it is beyond argument that the most sustained period of economic advance under the New Deal took place in the two years after the Blue Eagle was laid to rest.

who had anything to lose were frightened; they were willing to accept any way out that would leave them still in possession. During the emergency Roosevelt had had practically dictatorial powers. He had righted the keel of economic life and had turned politics safely back to its normal course. Although he had adopted many novel, perhaps risky expedients, he had avoided vital disturbances to the interests. For example, he had passed by an easy chance to solve the bank crisis by nationalization and instead followed a policy orthodox enough to win Hoover's approval. His basic policies for industry and agriculture had been designed after models supplied by great vested-interest groups. Of course, he had adopted several measures of relief and reform, but mainly of the sort that any wise and humane conservative would admit to be necessary. True, he had stirred the masses with a few hot words about "money changers" and chiselers, but he had been careful to identify these as a minority among businessmen. It was, after all, not Roosevelt but the terrible suffering of the depression that had caused mass discontent, and every sophisticate might be expected to know that in such times a few words against the evil rich are necessary to a politician's effectiveness.

Nothing that Roosevelt had done warranted the vituperation he soon got in the conservative press or the obscenities that the hate-Roosevelt maniacs were bruiting about in their clubs and dining-rooms. Quite understandably he began to feel that the people who were castigating him were muddle-headed ingrates. During the campaign of 1936 he compared them with the old man saved from drowning who berated his rescuer for not salvaging his hat—and again with a patient newly discharged from the hospital who had nothing but imprecations for his physician. Before 1935 Roosevelt had engaged in much political controversy, but he had generally managed to remain on friendly terms with his opponents. Surrounded from childhood with friendship, encouragement, and indulgence, he might have been able to accept criticism offered in the spirit of good-natured banter or the proposal of constructive alternatives (which he would simply have appropriated), but the malice and deliberate stupidity of his critics made him angry, and his political struggle with the "economic royalists" soon became intensely personal. Professor Moley, who in 1932 had admired his lack of "a bloated sense of personal destiny," was saddened to hear him say in 1936: "There's one issue in this campaign. It's myself, and people must be either for me or against me." In public he grew aggressive. He would like to have it said of his second administration, he stated, that in it "the forces of selfishness and of lust for power . . . met their master."

The development of Roosevelt's relation to the left is of critical importance to the Roosevelt legend. Perhaps no aspect of his public relations has been so quickly forgotten as his early labor policy. At the beginning of his administration Roosevelt was an acquaintance, not a friend, of organized labor. Although he was eager to do something about the poorest-paid workers through the NRA codes, his attitude toward unions themselves was not overcordial. The NRA itself had been rushed into shape partly to head off the strong pro-labor provisions of the Black-Connery bill. Section 7(a) of NRA, which guaranteed the right of collective bargaining, did not ban individual bargaining, company unions, or the open shop. Workers at first rallied to the NRA with enthusiasm and entered the more aggressive unions by the thousands in response to the plausible but false appeal: "The President wants you to join." But when disputes arose under Section 7(a), General Hugh Johnson and Donald Richberg handed down interpretations that, in the language of the Brookings Institution economists, "had the practical effect of placing the NRA on the side of anti-union employers in their struggle against the trade unions.... The NRA thus threw its weight against labor in the balance of bargaining power." Roosevelt stood firmly behind his administrators. Further, his last appointee as NRA administrator was a notorious foe of labor, S. Clay Williams. By early 1935, when there were few in the ranks of organized labor who had any expectation of help from the White House, workers were calling the NRA the "National Run Around." On February 2 William Green threatened that the entire labor movement would oppose Roosevelt.[9]

In the meanwhile another political threat was rising. Huey Long, who had achieved the position of a major leader of mass opinion in the hinterland through his demagogic "share-the-wealth" movement, was talking about a third party. In his *Behind the Ballots* James A. Farley recalls that the Democratic National Committee, worried about the 1936 election, conducted a secret national poll to sound Long's strength. They were dismayed at what they learned. "It was easy to conceive a situation," reports Farley, "whereby Long . . . might have the balance of power in the 1936 election." Democrats also had private reports that he would be well financed if he ran. By mid-spring Professor Moley was horrified to hear Roosevelt speak of the need of doing something "to steal Long's thunder."[10]

It was at this point that the Supreme Court broke the mainspring of the original New Deal by declaring the NRA unconstitutional. Roosevelt, looking forward to 1936, now found himself in a difficult position. The Court had torn up his entire program for labor and industry.

Labor seemed on the verge of withdrawing political support. Huey Long's popularity showed the dissatisfaction of a large part of the electorate. And no sign of a really decisive turn toward business recovery had yet come. The result was a sharp and sudden turn toward the left, the beginning of the second New Deal.

In June 1935 two striking measures were added to the President's list of "must" legislation: the Wagner labor-disputes bill and a drastic new "wealth tax" to steal Long's thunder. By the end of the 1935 legislative session the original New Deal, except for the AAA, was scarcely recognizable. In place of the NRA codes and the masquerade of Section 7(a) there was now a Labor Relations Board with a firm commitment to collective bargaining. A strong holding-company act and a stringent wealth tax stood on the books. None of these measures as they were finally enacted had been contemplated by Roosevelt at the beginning of the year. In the WPA a new relief program had been organized, with larger expenditures and a better wage scale. A Social Security Act had been passed. And at the close of the year the chief executive told Moley he was planning a "fighting speech" for his next annual message to Congress because "he was concerned about keeping his left-wing supporters satisfied."

Roosevelt's alliance with the left had not been planned; it had not even grown; it had erupted. The story of the Wagner Act, the keystone of his rapprochement with labor, and in a sense the heart of the second New Deal, is illustrative. The Wagner Act had never been an administration measure. It had been buffeted about the legislative chambers for more than a year without winning Roosevelt's interest. His Secretary of Labor recalls that he took no part in developing it, "was hardly consulted about it," and that "it did not particularly appeal to him when it was described to him." Nor did he altogether approve of the vigorous way in which it was later administered by the NLRB.

---

[9] An article in the New York *Times*, February 3, 1935, under the heading, "LABOR UNIONS BREAK WITH THE NEW DEAL," reported that labor leaders were "almost in despair of making headway toward union recognition in the face of powerful industrial interests and an unsympathetic administration."

[10] The Townsend old-age pension movement was a menace of comparable importance, although it had not taken political form.

Miss Perkins recalls that he was "startled" when he heard that the Board had ruled that no employer was to be able to file a petition for an election or ask the Board to settle a jurisdictional dispute. Yet under the stimulus of recovery and the protection of the NLRB, unions grew and flourished and provided the pressure in politics that gave the second New Deal its dynamic force. "A good democratic antidote for the power of big business," said Roosevelt.

Since Roosevelt was baited and frustrated by the right and adopted by the left, his ego was enlisted along with his sympathies in behalf of the popular point of view. During the formative period of the second New Deal he seems to have begun to feel that his social objectives demanded a crusade against the "autocracy." Early in 1936 at a Jackson Day dinner he made an elaborate and obvious comparison between Jackson and himself in which he observed of Jackson's hold on the common people: "They loved him for the enemies he had made." It is doubtful whether, even in Jackson's day, there had ever been such a close feeling of communion between a president and the great masses of the people as in the 1936 campaign. One incident that Roosevelt recalled for reporters touched him especially. He was driving through New Bedford, Massachusetts, when a young girl broke through the secret-service guards and passed him a pathetic note. She was a textile worker. Under the NRA she had received the minimum of eleven dollars a week, but had recently suffered a fifty per cent wage cut. "You are the only man that can do anything about it," her note ended. "Please send somebody from Washington up here to restore our minimum wages because we cannot live on $4 or $5 or $6 a week."[11] Here was common ground: the "resplendent economic autocracy" that imposed such a pitiful wage scale was the same interest that was flaying the President.

[11] See Roosevelt's *Public Papers*, V, 624.

Without design by either, and yet not altogether by accident, Roosevelt and the New Bedford girl had been thrown together in a league of mutual defense.

Roosevelt's second inaugural address was a lofty and benign document in which he remarked with satisfaction on the improvement of "the moral climate of America," declared that the proper test of progress is "whether we provide enough for those who have too little," and called attention to "one-third of a nation, ill-housed, ill-clad, ill-nourished." In the first two years of his second administration he sponsored, in addition to the controversial Supreme Court reform bill, four new reform measures of broad economic importance: the Housing Act of 1937, the Fair Labor Standards Act, the Farm Security Act, and an unsuccessful proposal to set up a national string of seven TVA's. But the New Deal was designed for a capitalistic economy that, as Miss Perkins says, Roosevelt took as much for granted as he did his family. For success in attaining his stated goals of prosperity and distributive justice he was fundamentally dependent upon restoring the health of capitalism. The final part of the New Deal story can be told not only in political battles and reform legislation but in jagged movements on the business-cycle graphs.

Early in 1937, administration circles, watching the rapid rise of the business index almost to 1929 levels, became fearful of a runaway boom. Federal Reserve officials put a brake upon credit, Roosevelt called upon Congress for economies, and WPA rolls were sliced in half. Roosevelt had never publicly accepted spending as a permanent governmental policy; although he had operated upon yearly deficits, he had always promised that when the national income reached a satisfactory level he would return to balanced budgets. But events proved that he had become a prisoner of the spending expedient. As Alvin Hansen has characterized it, the 1935-7 upswing was a "consumption recovery," financed and spurred by huge government outlays. When government expenditures were cut, a sharp downward trend began, which reached alarming dimensions early in 1938. Just at this time the National Resources Committee, an executive fact-finding agency, placed upon the president's desk a careful survey of consumer incomes for 1935-6. The committee estimated that 59 per cent of the families in the land had annual cash incomes of less than $1,250, 81 per cent less than $2,000. When this report reached him, Roosevelt knew that business conditions had again declined. There were still about 7,500,000 workers unemployed. Plainly something fundamental, something elusive, was wrong.

The New Deal had accomplished a heart-warming relief of distress, it had achieved a certain measure of recovery, it had released great forces of mass protest and had revived American liberalism, it had left upon the statute books several measures of permanent value, it had established the principle that the entire community through the agency of the federal government has some responsibility for mass welfare, and it had impressed its values so deeply upon the national mind that the Republicans were compelled to endorse its major accomplishments in election platforms. But, as Roosevelt was aware, it had failed to realize his objectives of distributive justice and sound, stable prosperity.[12]

In April 1938 Roosevelt adopted two expedients that signalized the severity of the crisis in the New Deal: one was a return to spending on a large scale, the other a crusade against monopoly. The first expedient solved the immediate crisis: Congress readily appropriated new funds, business conditions responded quickly, and the "Roosevelt recession" was soon liquidated. Henceforth Roosevelt took it for granted that the economy could not operate without the stimulus of government funds. In his memorable budget message of 1940 he finally accepted in theory what he had long been doing in fact, admitted the responsibility of government retrenchment for the recession, credited the revival of spending for the revival in business, and in general discussion the problem of the federal budget in Keynesian terms.[13]

The second expedient, the call for an attack upon monopoly, was a complete reversal of Roosevelt's philosophy of 1933 and the NRA policy. The message to Congress in which the crusade was announced—and which led to the fruitful TNEC investigations—was one of the most remarkable economic documents that have ever come from the White House. Roosevelt viewed the structure of economic and political power in broad social perspective. "Private power," he declared, was reaching a point at which it became "stronger than the democratic state itself." In the United States "a concentration of private power without equal in history is growing," which is "seriously impairing the effectiveness of private enterprise." "Private enterprise is ceasing to be free enterprise and is becoming a cluster of private collectivisms." A democratic people would no longer accept the meager standards of living caused by the failure of monopolistic industry to produce. "Big business collectivism in industry compels an ultimate collectivism in government." "The power of the few to manage the economic life of the Nation must be diffused among the many or be transferred to the public and its democratically responsible government."

Like Wilson, Roosevelt saw the development

[12] Cf. the comment of Professor Tugwell in *The Stricken Land*: "It was in economics that our troubles lay. For their solution his progressivism, his new deal, was pathetically insufficient. . . . I think . . . that he will be put down as having failed in this realm of [domestic] affairs."

[13] The Hoover administration, which Roosevelt had accused of extravagance in 1932, was now criticized for having failed to spend enough to fight the depression.

of big business and monopoly as a menace to democratic institutions, but like Wilson and all other politicians who touched upon the so-called trust problem, he was equivocal about how this menace was to be controlled. Although his argument carried to the brink of socialism, it was not socialism that he was proposing. Nor did he propose to reverse the whole modern trend of economic integration by trying to dissolve big business, a course of action the futility of which had been demonstrated by almost fifty years of experience. The economists whose guidance he was following believed that the rigid price structure of the semimonopolized heavy industries was throwing the whole economy out of gear. Presumably antitrust measures were not to be used to break up big corporations but to discipline their pricing policies. How the reformist state was to police the corporations without either destroying private enterprise or itself succumbing to the massed strength of corporate opposition was not made clear. Roosevelt did not tackle such problems in theory, and events spared him the necessity of facing them in practice.

Roosevelt's sudden and desperate appeal to the ancient trust-busting device, together with his failure in the fall elections of 1938 to purge the conservative elements in his party, augured the political bankruptcy of the New Deal. The reform wave had spent itself, and the Democratic Party, divided by the Supreme Court fight and the purge and hamstrung by its large conservative bloc, was exhausted as an agency of reform. Always the realist, Roosevelt rang the death knell of the New Deal in his annual message to Congress on January 4, 1939. "We have now passed the period of internal conflict in the launching of our program of social reform," he declared. "Our full energies may now be released to invigorate the processes of recovery in order to preserve our reforms." Almost three years before Pearl Harbor his experimentation had run its course. "The processes of recovery" came only with war. "Our full energies" were never successfully released for peacetime production. What would have happened to the political fortunes of Franklin D. Roosevelt if the war had not created a new theater for his leadership?

21

The Grapes of Wrath

John Steinbeck

Next to black people, to be treated later, the hardest hit by the Depression were tenant farmers in the South and on the Great Plains. As Arthur Schlesinger pointed out, farm prices fell so disastrously low that even farmers who owned their land faced financial disaster. It was worse for tenant farmers, who rented their land and could scarcely afford anything. One study of 500 tenant families revealed that their average income was about $262 a year. Many others had no money at all and they suffered severe privation.

At the same time, a terrible drought seared the Great Plains, and mighty dust storms—black blizzards, they were called—raged across the farm belt, the result not only of rainless skies but of decades of land misuse and mismanagement. The great black blizzard of November 11, 1933, darkened American skies from Chicago to Albany, New York. And still no rains came. In 1934 and 1935, dust storms swept across the Dakotas, Kansas, Oklahoma, and Texas, laying waste to thousands of square miles. To protect themselves, people in the drought regions held wet cloths to their faces and stuck oiled rags around doors and windows. But dust filtered in anyway and sullied everything. As one black blizzard raged, a farmer said he stood at his window and counted the Kansas farms as they swirled by.

In Oklahoma, the storms turned farmlands into shifting sand dunes, and the lives of Oklahoma tenants became veritable nightmares. But the worst was to come. Soon they were "tractored off the land," as owners all over the farm belt, convinced that the tenant system was wasteful and unprofitable, evicted their renters and brought in the machines. As one Oklahoma owner put it, "I had I reckon four renters and I didn't make anything. I bought tractors on the money the government give me and got shet o' my renters." With no place else to go, the displaced "Okies" headed west for California, long a symbol of hope and golden opportunity. In the Grapes of Wrath, *perhaps the best novel written about the Depression, John Steinbeck tells the story of the Okie migrants, as they set out for California with anxious hopes . . . only to discover that even California, that legendary land of beginning again, had been stricken by Depression.*

The owners of the land came onto the land, or more often a spokesman for the owners came. They came in closed cars, and they felt the dry earth with their fingers, and sometimes they drove big earth augers into the ground for soil tests. The tenants, from their sun-beaten dooryards, watched uneasily when the closed cars drove along the fields. And at last the owner men drove into the dooryards and sat in their cars to talk out of the windows. The tenant men stood beside the cars for a while, and then squatted on their hams and found sticks with which to mark the dust.

In the open doors the women stood looking out, and behind them the children—cornheaded children, with wide eyes, one bare foot on top of the other bare foot, and the toes

From *The Grapes of Wrath* by John Steinbeck. Copyright 1939, © 1967 by John Steinbeck. Reprinted by permission of The Viking Press, Inc.

working. The women and the children watched their men talking to the owner men. They were silent.

Some of the owner men were kind because they hated what they had to do, and some of them were angry because they hated to be cruel, and some of them were cold because they had long ago found that one could not be an owner unless one were cold. And all of them were caught in something larger than themselves. Some of them hated the mathematics that drove them, and some were afraid, and some worshiped the mathematics because it provided a refuge from thought and from feeling. If a bank or a finance company owned the land, the owner man said, The Bank—or the Company—needs—wants—insists—must have—as though the Bank or the Company were a monster, with thought and feeling, which had ensnared them. These last would take no responsibility for the banks or the companies because they were men and slaves, while the banks were machines and masters all at the same time. Some of the owner men were a little proud to be slaves to such cold and powerful masters. The owner men sat in the cars and explained. You know the land is poor. You've scrabbled at it long enough, God knows.

The squatting tenant men nodded and wondered and drew figures in the dust, and yes, they knew, God knows. If the dust only wouldn't fly. If the top would only stay on the soil, it might not be so bad.

The owner men went on leading to their point: You know the land's getting poorer. You know what cotton does to the land; robs it, sucks all the blood out of it.

The squatters nodded—they knew, God knew. If they could only rotate the crops they might pump blood back into the land.

Well, it's too late. And the owner men explained the workings and the thinkings of the monster that was stronger than they were. A man can hold land if he can just eat and pay taxes; he can do that.

Yes, he can do that until his crops fail one day and he has to borrow money from the bank.

But—you see, a bank or a company can't do that, because those creatures don't breathe air, don't eat side-meat. They breathe profits; they eat the interest on money. If they don't get it, they die the way you die without air, without side-meat. It is a sad thing, but it is so. It is just so.

The squatting men raised their eyes to understand. Can't we just hang on? Maybe the next year will be a good year. God knows how much cotton next year. And with all the wars—God knows what price cotton will bring. Don't they make explosives out of cotton? And uniforms? Get enough wars and cotton'll hit the ceiling. Next year, maybe. They looked up questioningly.

We can't depend on it. The bank—the monster has to have profits all the time. It can't wait. It'll die. No, taxes go on. When the monster stops growing, it dies. It can't stay one size.

Soft fingers began to tap the sill of the car window, and hard fingers tightened on the restless drawing sticks. In the doorways of the sun-beaten tenant houses, women sighed and then shifted feet so that the one that had been down was now on top, and the toes working. Dogs came sniffing near the owner cars and wetted on all four tires one after another. And chickens lay in the sunny dust and fluffed their feathers to get the cleansing dust down to the skin. In the little sties the pigs grunted inquiringly over the muddy remnants of the slops.

The squatting men looked down again. What do you want us to do? We can't take less share of the crop—we're half starved now. The kids are hungry all the time. We got no clothes, torn an' ragged. If all the neighbors weren't the same, we'd be ashamed to go to meeting.

And at last the owner men came to the point. The tenant system won't work any more. One man on a tractor can take the place of twelve or fourteen families. Pay him a wage and take all the crop. We have to do it. We don't like to do it. But the monster's sick. Something's happened to the monster.

But you'll kill the land with cotton.

We know. We've got to take cotton quick before the land dies. Then we'll sell the land. Lots of families in the East would like to own a piece of land.

The tenant men looked up alarmed. But what'll happen to us? How'll we eat?

You'll have to get off the land. The plows'll go through the dooryard.

And now the squatting men stood up angrily. Grampa took up the land, and he had to kill the Indians and drive them away. And Pa was born here, and he killed weeds and snakes. Then a bad year came and he had to borrow a little money. An' we was born here. There in the door—our children born here. And Pa had to borrow money. The bank owned the land then, but we stayed and we got a little bit of what we raised.

We know that—all that. It's not us, it's the bank. A bank isn't like a man. Or an owner with fifty thousand acres, he isn't like a man either. That's the monster.

Sure, cried the tenant men, but it's our land. We measured it and broke it up. We were born on it, and we got killed on it, died on it. Even if it's no good, it's still ours. That's what makes it ours—being born on it, working it, dying on it. That makes ownership, not a paper with numbers on it.

We're sorry. It's not us. It's the monster. The bank isn't like a man.

Yes, but the bank is only made of men.

No, you're wrong there—quite wrong there. The bank is something else than men. It happens that every man in a bank hates what the bank does, and yet the bank does it. The bank is something more than men, I tell you. It's the monster. Men made it, but they can't control it.

The tenants cried, Grampa killed Indians, Pa killed snakes for the land. Maybe we can kill banks—they're worse than Indians and snakes. Maybe we got to fight to keep our land, like Pa and Grampa did.

And now the owner men grew angry. You'll have to go.

But it's ours, the tenant men cried. We—

No. The bank, the monster owns it. You'll have to go.

We'll get our guns, like Grampa when the Indians came. What then?

Well—first the sheriff, and then the troops. You'll be stealing if you try to stay, you'll be murderers if you kill to stay. The monster isn't men, but it can make men do what it wants.

But if we go, where'll we go? How'll we go? We got no money.

We're sorry, said the owner men. The bank, the fifty-thousand-acre owner can't be responsible. You're on land that isn't yours. Once over the line maybe you can pick cotton in the fall. Maybe you can go on relief. Why don't you go on west to California? There's work there, and it never gets cold. Why, you can reach out anywhere and pick an orange. Why, there's always some kind of crop to work in. Why don't you go there? And the owner men started their cars and rolled away.

The tenant men squatted down on their hams again to mark the dust with a stick, to figure, to wonder. Their sunburned faces were dark, and their sun-whipped eyes were light. The women moved cautiously out of the doorways toward their men, and the children crept behind the women, cautiously, ready to run. The bigger boys squatted beside their fathers, because that made them men. After a time the women asked, What did he want?

And the men looked up for a second, and the smolder of pain was in their eyes. We got to get off. A tractor and a superintendent. Like factories.

Where'll we go? the women asked.

We don't know. We don't know.

And the women went quickly, quietly back into the houses and herded the children ahead of them. They knew that a man so hurt and so perplexed may turn in anger, even on people he loves. They left the men alone to figure and to wonder in the dust.

After a time perhaps the tenant man looked about—at the pump put in ten years ago, with a goose-neck handle and iron flowers on the spout, at the chopping block where a thousand chickens had been killed, at the hand plow lying in the shed, and the patent crib hanging in the rafters over it.

The children crowded about the women in the houses. What we going to do, Ma? Where we going to go?

The women said, We don't know, yet. Go out and play. But don't go near your father. He might whale you if you go near him. And the women went on with the work, but all the time they watched the men squatting in the dust—perplexed and figuring.

The tractors came over the roads and into the fields, great crawlers moving like insects, having the incredible strength of insects. They crawled over the ground, laying the track and rolling on it and picking it up. Diesel tractors, puttering while they stood idle; they thundered when they moved, and then settled down to a droning roar. Snub-nosed monsters, raising the dust and sticking their snouts into it, straight down the country, across the country, through fences, through dooryards, in and out of gullies in straight lines. They did not run on the ground, but on their own roadbeds. They ignored hills and gulches, water courses, fences, houses.

The man siting in the iron seat did not look like a man; gloved, goggled, rubber dust mask over nose and mouth, he was a part of the monster, a robot in the seat. The thunder of the cylinders sounded through the country, became one with the air and the earth, so that earth and air muttered in sympathetic vibration. The driver could not control it—straight across country it went, cutting through a dozen farms and straight back. A twitch at the controls could swerve the cat', but the driver's hands could not twitch because the monster that built the tractor, the monster that sent the tractor out, had somehow got into the driver's hands, into his brain and muscle, had goggled him and muzzled him—goggled his mind, muzzled his speech, goggled his perception, muzzled his protest. He could not see the land as it was, he could not smell the land as it smelled; his feet did not stamp the clods or feel the warmth and power of the earth. He sat in an iron seat and stepped on iron pedals. He could not cheer or beat or curse or encourage the extension of his power, and because of this he could not cheer or whip or curse or encourage himself. He did not know or own or trust or beseech the land. If a seed dropped did not germinate, it was nothing. If the young thrusting plant withered in drought or drowned in a flood of rain, it was no more to the driver than to the tractor.

He loved the land no more than the bank loved the land. He could admire the tractor—its machined surfaces, its surge of power, the roar of its detonating cylinders; but it was not his tractor. Behind the tractor rolled the shining disks, cutting the earth with blades—not plowing but surgery, pushing the cut earth to the right where the second row of disks cut it and pushed it to the left; slicing blades shining, polished by the cut earth. And pulled behind the disks, the harrows combing with iron teeth so that the little clods broke up and the earth lay smooth. Behind the harrows, the long seeders—twelve curved iron penes erected in the foundry, orgasms set by gears, raping methodically, raping without passion. The driver sat in his iron seat and he was proud of the straight lines he did not will, proud of the tractor he did not own or love, proud of the power he could not control. And when that crop grew, and was harvested, no man had crumbled a hot clod in his fingers and let the earth sift past his fingertips. No man had touched the seed, or lusted for the growth. Men ate what they had not raised, had no connection with the bread. The land bore under iron, and under iron gradually died; for it was not loved or hated, it had no prayers or curses.

. . .

In the little houses the tenant people sifted their belongings and the belongings of their fathers and of their grandfathers. Picked over their possessions for the journey to the west. The men were ruthless because the past had been spoiled, but the women knew how the past would cry to them in the coming days. The men went into the barns and the sheds.

That plow, that harrow, remember in the war we planted mustard? Remember a fella wanted us to put in that rubber bush they call guayule? Get rich, he said. Bring out those tools—get a few dollars for them. Eighteen dollars for that plow, plus freight—Sears Roebuck.

Harness, carts, seeders, little bundles of hoes. Bring 'em out. Pile 'em up. Load 'em in the wagon. Take 'em to town. Sell 'em for what you can get. Sell the team and the wagon, too. No more use for anything.

Fifty cents isn't enough to get for a good plow. That seeder cost thirty-eight dollars. Two dollars isn't enough. Can't haul it all back— Well, take it, and a bitterness with it. Take the well pump and the harness. Take halters, collars, hames, and tugs. Take the little glass brow-band jewels, roses red under glass. Got those for the bay gelding. 'Member how he lifted his feet when he trotted?

Junk piled up in a yard.

Can't sell a hand plow any more. Fifty cents for the weight of the metal. Disks and tractors, that's the stuff now.

Well, take it—all junk—and give me five dollars. You're not buying only junk, you're buying junked lives. And more—you'll see— you're buying bitterness. Buying a plow to plow your own children under, buying the arms and spirits that might have saved you. Five dollars, not four. I can't haul 'em back— Well, take 'em for four. But I warn you, you're buying what will plow your own children under. And you won't see. You can't see. Take 'em for four. Now, what'll you give for the team and wagon? Those fine bays, matched they are, matched in color, matched the way they walk, stride to stride. In the stiff pull— straining hams and buttocks, split-second timed together. And in the morning, the light on them, bay light. They look over the fence sniffing for us, and the stiff ears swivel to hear us, and the black forelocks! I've got a girl. She likes to braid the manes and forelocks, puts little red bows on them. Likes to do it. Not any more. I could tell you a funny story about that girl and that off bay. Would make you laugh. Off horse is eight, near is ten, but might of been twin colts the way they work together. See? The teeth. Sound all over. Deep lungs. Feet fair and clean. How much? Ten dollars? For both? And the wagon—Oh, Jesus Christ! I'd shoot 'em for dog feed first. Oh, take 'em! Take 'em quick, mister. You're buying a little girl plaiting the forelocks, taking off her hair ribbon to make bows, standing back, head cocked, rubbing the soft noses with her cheek. You're buying years of work, toil in the sun; you're buying a sorrow that can't talk. But watch it, mister. There's a premium goes with this pile of junk and the bay horses—so beautiful—a packet of bitterness to grow in your house and to flower, some day. We could have saved you, but you cut us down, and soon you will be cut down and there'll be none of us to save you.

And the tenant men came walking back, hands in their pockets, hats pulled down. Some bought a pint and drank it fast to make the impact hard and stunning. But they didn't laugh and they didn't dance. They didn't sing or pick the guitars. They walked back to the farms, hands in pockets and heads down, shoes kicking the red dust up.

Maybe we can start again, in the new rich land—in California, where the fruit grows. We'll start over.

But you can't start. Only a baby can start. You and me—why, we're all that's been. The anger of a moment, the thousand pictures, that's us. This land, this red land, is us; and the flood years and the dust years and the drought years are us. We can't start again. The bitterness we sold to the junk man—he got it all right, but we have it still. And when the owner men told us to go, that's us; and when the tractor hit the house, that's us until we're dead. To California or any place—every one a drum major leading a parade of hurts, marching with our bitterness. And some day—the armies of bitterness will all be going the same way. And they'll all walk together, and there'll be a dead terror from it.

The tenant men scuffed home to the farms through the red dust.

When everything that could be sold was sold, stoves and bedsteads, chairs and tables, little corner cupboards, tubs and tanks, still there were piles of possessions; and the women sat among them, turning them over and looking off beyond and back, pictures, square glasses, and here's a vase.

Now you know well what we can take and what we can't take. We'll be camping out—a few pots to cook and wash in, and mattresses and comforts, lantern and buckets, and a piece of canvas. Use that for a tent. This kerosene can. Know what that is? That's the stove. And clothes—take all the clothes. And—the rifle? Wouldn't go out naked of a rifle. When shoes and clothes and food, when even hope is gone, we'll have the rifle. When grampa came—did I tell you?—he had pepper and salt and a rifle. Nothing else. That goes. And a bottle for water. That just about fills us. Right up the sides of the trailer, and the kids can set in the trailer, and granma on a mattress. Tools, a shovel and saw and wrench and pliers. An ax, too. We had that ax forty years. Look how she's wore down. And ropes, of course. The rest? Leave it—or burn it up.

And the children came.

If Mary takes that doll, that dirty rag doll, I got to take my Injun bow. I got to. An' this roun' stick—big as me. I might need this stick. I had this stick so long—a month, or maybe a year. I got to take it. And what's it like in California?

The women sat among the doomed things, turning them over and looking past them and back. This book. My father had it. He liked a book. *Pilgrim's Progress.* Used to read it. Got his name in it. And his pipe—still smells rank. And this picture—an angel. I looked at that before the fust three come—didn't seem to do much good. Think we could get this china dog in? Aunt Sadie brought it from the St. Louis Fair. See? Wrote right on it. No, I guess not. Here's a letter my brother wrote the day before he died. Here's an old-time hat. These feathers —never got to use them. No, there isn't room.

How can we live without our lives? How will we know it's us without our past? No. Leave it. Burn it.

They sat and looked at it and burned it into their memories. How'll it be not to know what land's outside the door? How if you wake up in the night and know—and *know* the willow tree's not there? Can you live without the willow tree? Well, no, you can't. The willow tree is you. The pain on that mattress there—that dreadful pain—that's you.

And the children—if Sam takes his Injun bow an' his long roun' stick, I get to take two things. I choose the fluffy pilla. That's mine.

Suddenly they were nervous. Got to get out quick now. Can't wait. We can't wait. And they piled up the goods in the yards and set fire to them. They stood and watched them burning, and then frantically they loaded up the cars and drove away, drove in the dust. The dust hung in the air for a long time after the loaded cars had passed.

. . .

Highway 66 is the main migrant road. 66—the long concrete path across the country, waving gently up and down on the map, from the Mississippi to Bakersfield—over the red lands and the gray lands, twisting up into the mountains, crossing the Divide and down into the bright and terrible desert, and across the desert to the mountains again, and into the rich California valleys.

66 is the path of a people in flight, refugees from dust and shrinking land, from the thunder of tractors and shrinking ownership, from the desert's slow northward invasion, from the twisting winds that howl up out of Texas, from the floods that bring no richness to the land and steal what little richness is there. From all of these the people are in flight, and they come into 66 from the tributary side roads, from the wagon tracks and the rutted country roads. 66 is the mother road, the road of flight.

Clarksville and Ozark and Van Buren and Fort Smith on 64, and there's an end of Arkansas. And all the roads into Oklahoma City, 66 down from Tulsa, 270 up from McAlester. 81 from Wichita Falls south, from Enid north. Edmond, McLoud, Purcell. 66 out of Oklahoma City; El Reno and Clinton, going west on 66. Hydro, Elk City, and Texola; and there's an end to Oklahoma. 66 across the Panhandle of Texas. Shamrock and McLean, Conway and Amarillo, the yellow. Wildorado and Vega and Boise, and there's an end of Texas. Tucumcari and Santa Rosa and into the New Mexican mountains to Albuquerque, where the road comes down from Santa Fe. Then down the gorged Rio Grande to Los Lunas and west again on 66 to Gallup, and there's the border of New Mexico.

And now the high mountains. Holbrook and Winslow and Flagstaff in the high mountains of Arizona. Then the great plateau rolling like a ground swell. Ashfork and Kingman and stone mountains again, where water must be hauled and sold. Then out of the broken sun-rotted mountains of Arizona to the Colorado, with green reeds on its banks, and that's the end of Arizona. There's California just over the river, and a pretty town to start it. Needles, on the river. But the river is a stranger in this place. Up from Needles and over a burned range, and there's the desert. And 66 goes on over the terrible desert, where the distance shimmers and the black center mountains hang unbearably in the distance. At last there's Barstow, and more desert until at last the mountains rise up again, the good mountains, and 66 winds through them. Then suddenly a pass, and below the beautiful valley, below orchards and vineyards and little houses, and in the distance a city. And, oh, my God, it's over.

The people in flight streamed out on 66, sometimes a single car, sometimes a little caravan. All day they rolled slowly along the road, and at night they stopped near water. In the day ancient leaky radiators sent up columns of steam, loose connecting rods hammered and pounded. And the men driving the trucks and the overloaded cars listened apprehensively. How far between towns? It is a terror between towns. If something breaks—well, if something breaks we camp right here while Jim walks to town and gets a part and walks back and—how much food we got?

Listen to the motor. Listen to the wheels. Listen with your ears and with your hands on the steering wheel; listen with the palm of your hand on the gear-shift lever; listen with your feet on the floor boards. Listen to the pounding old jalopy with all your senses; for a change of tone, a variation of rhythm may mean—a week here? That rattle—that's tappets. Don't hurt a bit. Tappets can rattle till Jesus comes again without no harm. But that thudding as the car

Migratory workers during the Depression. "And a homeless hungry man, driving the roads with his wife beside him and his thin children in the back seat, could look at the fallow fields which might produce food but not profit, and that man could know how a fallow field is a sin and the unused land a crime against his thin children. . . ." (Courtesy of The Library of Congress.)

moves along—can't hear that—just kind of feel it. Maybe oil isn't gettin' someplace. Maybe a bearing's startin' to go. Jesus, if it's a bearing, what'll we do? Money's goin' fast.

And why's the son-of-a-bitch heat up so hot today? This ain't no climb. Le's look. God Almighty, the fan belt's gone! Here, make a belt outa this little piece of rope. Le's see how long —there. I'll splice the ends. Now take her slow —slow, till we can get to a town. That rope belt won't last long.

'F we can on'y get to California where the

oranges grow before this here ol' jug blows up. 'F we on'y can.

And the tires—two layers of fabric worn through. On'y a four-ply tire. Might get a hunderd miles more outa her if we don't hit a rock an' blow her. Which'll we take—a hunderd, maybe, miles, or maybe spoil the tube? Which? A hunderd miles. Well, that's somepin you got to think about. We got tube patches. Maybe when she goes she'll only spring a leak. How about makin' a boot? Might get five hunderd more miles. Le's go on till she blows.

We got to get a tire, but, Jesus, they want a lot for a ol' tire. They look a fella over. They know he got to go on. They know he can't wait. And the price goes up.

Take it or leave it. I ain't in business for my health. I'm here a-sellin' tires. I ain't givin' 'em away. I can't help what happens to you. I got to think what happens to me.

How far's the nex' town?

I seen forty-two cars a you fellas go by yesterday. Where you all come from? Where all of you goin'?

Well, California's a big State.

It ain't that big. The whole United States ain't that big. It ain't that big. It ain't big enough. There ain't room enough for you an' me, for your kind an' my kind, for rich and poor together all in one country, for thieves and honest men. For hunger and fat. Whyn't you go back where you come from?

This is a free country. Fella can go where he wants.

That's what *you* think! Ever hear of the border patrol on the California line? Police from Los Angeles—stopped you bastards, turned you back. Says, if you can't buy no real estate we don't want you. Says, got a driver's license? Le's see it. Tore it up. Says you can't come in without no driver's license.

It's a free country.

Well, try to get some freedom to do. Fella says you're jus' as free as you got jack to pay for it.

In California they got high wages. I got a han'bill here tells about it.

Baloney! I seen folks comin' back. Somebody's kiddin' you. You want that tire or don't ya?

Got to take it, but, Jesus, mister, it cuts into our money! We ain't got much left.

Well, I ain't no charity. Take her along.

Got to, I guess. Let's look her over. Open her up, look a' the casing—you son-of-a-bitch, you said the casing was good. She's broke damn near through.

The hell she is. Well—by George! How come I didn' see that?

You did see it, you son-of-a-bitch. You wanta charge us four bucks for a busted casing. I'd like to take a sock at you.

Now keep your shirt on. I didn' see it, I tell you. Here—tell ya what I'll do. I'll give ya this one for three-fifty.

You'll take a flying jump at the moon! We'll try to make the nex' town.

Think we can make it on that tire?

Got to. I'll go on the rim before I'd give that son-of-a-bitch a dime.

What do ya think a guy in business is? Like he says, he ain't in it for his health. That's what business is. What'd you think it was? Fella's got—See that sign 'longside the road there? Service Club. Luncheon Tuesday, Colmado Hotel? Welcome, brother. That's a Service Club. Fella had a story. Went to one of them meetings an' told the story to all them business men. Says, when I was a kid my ol' man give me a haltered heifer an' says take her down an' git her serviced. An' the fella says, I done it, an' ever' time since then when I hear a business man talkin' about service, I wonder who's gettin' screwed. Fella in business got to lie an' cheat, but he calls it somepin else. That's what's important. You go steal that tire an' you're a thief, but he tried to steal your four dollars for a busted tire. They call that sound business.

Danny in the back seat wants a cup a water.

Have to wait. Got no water here.

Listen—that the rear end?

Can't tell.

Sound telegraphs through the frame.

There goes a gasket. Got to go on. Listen to her whistle. Find a nice place to camp an' I'll jerk the head off. But, God Almighty, the food's gettin' low, the money's gettin' low. When we can't buy no more gas—what then?

Danny in the back seat wants a cup a water. Little fella's thirsty.

Listen to that gasket whistle.

Chee-rist! There she went. Blowed tube an' casing all to hell. Have to fix her. Save that casing to make boots; cut 'em out an' stick 'em inside a weak place.

Cars pulled up beside the road, engine heads off, tires mended. Cars limping along 66 like wounded things, panting and struggling. Too hot, loose connections, loose bearings, rattling bodies.

Danny wants a cup of water.

People in flight along 66. And the concrete road shone like a mirror under the sun, and in the distance the heat made it seem that there were pools of water in the road.

Danny wants a cup a water.

He'll have to wait, poor little fella. He's hot. Nex' service station. *Service* station, like the fella says.

Two hundred and fifty thousand people over the road. Fifty thousand old cars—wounded, steaming. Wrecks along the road, abandoned. Well, what happened to them? What happened to the folks in that car? Did they walk? Where are they? Where does the courage come from? Where does the terrible faith come from?

And here's a story you can hardly believe, but it's true, and it's funny and it's beautiful. There was a family of twelve and they were forced off the land. They had no car. They built a trailer out of junk and loaded it with their possessions. They pulled it to the side of 66 and waited. And pretty soon a sedan picked them up. Five of them rode in the sedan and seven on the trailer, and a dog on the trailer. They got to California in two jumps. The man who pulled them fed them. And that's true. But how can such courage be, and such faith in their own species? Very few things would teach such faith.

The people in flight from the terror behind— strange things happen to them, some bitterly cruel and some so beautiful that the faith is refired forever.

. . .

Once California belonged to Mexico and its land to Mexicans; and a horde of tattered feverish Americans poured in. And such was their hunger for land that they took the land —stole Sutter's land, Guerrero's land, took the grants and broke them up and growled and quarreled over them, those frantic hungry men; and they guarded with guns the land they had stolen. They put up houses and barns, they turned the earth and planted crops. And these things were possession, and possession was ownership.

The Mexicans were weak and fed. They could not resist, because they wanted nothing in the world as frantically as the Americans wanted land.

Then, with time, the squatters were no longer squatters, but owners; and their children grew up and had children on the land. And the hunger was gone from them, the feral hunger, the gnawing, tearing hunger for land, for water and earth and the good sky over it, for the green thrusting grass, for the swelling roots. They had these things so completely that they did not know about them any more. They had no more the stomach-tearing lust for a rich acre and a shining blade to plow it, for seed and a windmill beating its wings in the air. They arose in the dark no more to hear the sleepy birds' first chittering, and the morning wind around the house while they waited for the first light to go out to the dear acres. These things were lost, and crops were reckoned in dollars, and land was valued by principal plus interest, and crops were bought and sold before they were planted. Then crop failure, drought, and flood were no longer little deaths within life, but simple losses of money. And all their love was thinned with money, and all their fierceness dribbled away in interest until they were no longer farmers at all, but little shopkeepers of crops, little manufacturers who must sell before they can make. Then those farmers who were not good shopkeepers lost their land to good shopkeepers. No matter how clever, how loving a man might be with earth and growing things, he could not survive if he were not also a good shopkeeper. And as time went on, the business men had the farms, and the farms grew larger, but there were fewer of them.

Now farming became industry, and the owners followed Rome, although they did not know it. They imported slaves, although they did not call them slaves: Chinese, Japanese, Mexicans, Filipinos. They live on rice and beans, the business men said. They don't need much. They wouldn't know what to do with good wages. Why, look how they live. Why, look what they eat. And if they get funny—deport them.

And all the time the farms grew larger and the owners fewer. And there were pitifully few farmers on the land any more. And the imported serfs were beaten and frightened and starved until some went home again, and some grew fierce and were killed or driven from the country. And the farms grew larger and the owners fewer.

And the crops changed. Fruit trees took the place of grain fields, and vegetables to feed the world spread out on the bottoms: lettuce, cauliflower, artichokes, potatoes—stoop crops. A man may stand to use a scythe, a plow, a pitchfork; but he must crawl like a bug between the rows of lettuce, he must bend his back and pull his long bag between the cotton rows, he must go on his knees like a penitent across a cauliflower patch.

And it came about that owners no longer worked on their farms. They farmed on paper; and they forgot the land, the smell, the feel of it, and remembered only that they owned it, remembered only what they gained and lost by it. And some of the farms grew so large that one man could not even conceive of them any more, so large that it took batteries of bookkeepers to keep track of interest and gain and loss; chemists to test the soil, to replenish; straw bosses to see that the stooping men were moving along the rows as swiftly as the material of their bodies could stand. Then such a farmer really became a storekeeper, and kept a store. He paid the men, and sold them food, and took the money back. And after a while he did not pay the men at all, and saved bookkeeping. These farms gave food on credit. A man might work and feed himself; and when the work was done, he might find that he owed money to the company. And the owners not only did not work the farms any more, many of them had never seen the farms they owned.

And then the dispossessed were drawn west —from Kansas, Oklahoma, Texas, New Mexico; from Nevada and Arkansas families, tribes, dusted out, tractored out. Carloads, caravans, homeless and hungry; twenty thousand and fifty thousand and a hundred thousand and two hundred thousand. They streamed over the mountains, hungry and restless—restless as ants, scurrying to find work to do—to lift, to push, to pull, to pick, to cut—anything, any burden to bear, for food. The kids are hungry. We got no place to live. Like ants scurrying for work, for food, and most of all for land.

We ain't foreign. Seven generations back Americans, and beyond that Irish, Scotch, English, German. One of our folks in the Revolution, an' they was lots of our folks in the Civil War—both sides. Americans.

They were hungry, and they were fierce. And they had hoped to find a home, and they found only hatred. Okies—the owners hated them because the owners knew they were soft and the Okies strong, that they were fed and the Okies hungry; and perhaps the owners had heard from their grandfathers how easy it is to steal land from a soft man if you are fierce and hungry and armed. The owners hated them. And in the towns, the storekeepers hated them because they had no money to spend. There is no shorter path to a storekeeper's contempt, and all his admirations are exactly opposite. The town men, little bankers, hated Okies because there was nothing to gain from them. They had nothing. And the laboring people hated Okies because a hungry man must work, and if he must work, if he has to work, the wage payer automatically gives him less for his work; and then no one can get more.

And the dispossessed, the migrants, flowed into California, two hundred and fifty thousand, and three hundred thousand. Behind them new tractors were going on the land and the tenants were being forced off. And new waves were on the way, new waves of the dispossessed and the homeless, hardened, intent, and dangerous.

And while the Californians wanted many things, accumulation, social success, amusement, luxury, and a curious banking security, the new barbarians wanted only two things—land and food; and to them the two were one. And whereas the wants of the Californians were nebulous and undefined, the wants of the Okies were beside the roads, lying there to be seen and coveted: the good fields with water to be dug for, the good green fields, earth to crumble experimentally in the hand, grass to smell, oaten stalks to chew until the sharp sweetness was in the throat. A man might look at a fallow field and know, and see in his mind that his own bending back and his own straining arms would bring the cabbages into the light, and the golden eating corn, the turnips and carrots.

And a homeless hungry man, driving the roads with his wife beside him and his thin children in the back seat, could look at the fallow fields which might produce food but not profit, and that man could know how a fallow field is a sin and the unused land a crime against the thin children. And such a man drove along the roads and knew temptation at every field, and knew the lust to take these fields and make them grow strength for his children and a little comfort for his wife. The temptation was before him always. The fields goaded him, and the company ditches with good water flowing were a goad to him.

And in the south he saw the golden oranges hanging on the trees, the little golden oranges on the dark green trees; and guards with shotguns patrolling the lines so a man might not pick an orange for a thin child, oranges to be dumped if the price was low.

He drove his old car into a town. He scoured the farms for work. Where can we sleep the night?

Well, there's Hooverville on the edge of the river. There's a whole raft of Okies there.

He drove his old car to Hooverville. He never asked again, for there was a Hooverville on the edge of every town.

The rag town lay close to water; and the houses were tents, and weed-thatched enclosures, paper houses, a great junk pile. The man drove his family in and became a citizen of Hooverville—always they were called Hooverville. The man put up his own tent as near to water as he could get; or if he had no tent, he went to the city dump and brought back cartons and built a house of corrugated paper. And when the rains came the house melted and washed away. He settled in Hooverville and he scoured the countryside for work, and the little money he had went for gasoline to look for work. In the evening the men gathered and talked together. Squatting on their hams they talked of the land they had seen.

There's thirty thousan' acres, out west of here. Layin' there. Jesus, what I could do with that, with five acres of that! Why, hell, I'd have ever'thing to eat.

Notice one thing? They ain't no vegetables nor chickens nor pigs at the farms. They raise one thing—cotton, say, or peaches, or lettuce. 'Nother place'll be all chickens. They buy the stuff they could raise in the dooryard.

Jesus, what I could do with a couple pigs!

Well, it ain't yourn, an' it ain't gonna be yourn.

What we gonna do? The kids can't grow up this way.

In the camps the word would come whispering, There's work at Shafter. And the cars would be loaded in the night, the highways crowded—a gold rush for work. At Shafter the people would pile up, five times too many to do the work. A gold rush for work. They stole away in the night, frantic for work. And along the roads lay the temptations, the fields that could bear food.

That's owned. That ain't our'n.

Well, maybe we could get a little piece of her. Maybe—a little piece. Right down there—a patch. Jimson weed now. Christ, I could git enough potatoes off'n that little patch to feed my whole family!

It ain't our'n. It got to have Jimson weeds.

Now and then a man tried; crept on the land and cleared a piece, trying like a thief to steal a little richness from the earth. Secret gardens hidden in the weeds. A package of carrot seeds and a few turnips. Planted potato skins, crept out in the evening secretly to hoe in the stolen earth.

Leave the weeds around the edge—then nobody can see what we're a-doin'. Leave some weeds, big tall ones, in the middle.

Secret gardening the evenings, and water carried in a rusty can.

And then one day a deputy sheriff: Well, what you think you're doin'?

I ain't doin' no harm.

I had my eye on you. This ain't your land. You're trespassing.

The land ain't plowed, an' I ain't hurtin' it none.

You goddamned squatters. Pretty soon you'd think you owned it. You'd be sore as hell. Think you owned it. Get off now.

And the little green carrot tops were kicked off and the turnip greens trampled. And then the Jimson weed moved back in. But the cop was right. A crop raised—why, that makes ownership. Land hoed and the carrots eaten—a man might fight for land he's taken food from. Get him off quick! He'll think he owns it. He might even die fighting for the little plot among the Jimson weeds.

Did ya see his face when we kicked them turnips out? Why, he'd kill a fella soon's he'd look at him. We got to keep these here people down or they'll take the country. They'll take the country.

Outlanders, foreigners.

Sure, they talk the same language, but they ain't the same. Look how they live. Think any of us folks'd live like that? Hell, no!

In the evenings, squatting and talking. And an excited man: Whyn't twenty of us take a piece of lan'? We got guns. Take it an' say, "Put us off if you can." Whyn't we do that?

They'd jus' shoot us like rats.

Well, which'd you ruther be, dead or here? Under groun' or in a house all made of gunny sacks? Which'd you ruther for your kids, dead now or dead in two years with what they call malnutrition? Know what we et all week? Biled nettles an' fried dough! Know where we got the flour for the dough? Swep' the floor of a boxcar.

Talking in the camps, and the deputies, fat-assed men with guns slung on fat hips, swaggering through the camps: Give 'em somepin to think about. Got to keep 'em in line or Christ only knows what they'll do! Why, Jesus, they're as dangerous as niggers in the South! If they ever get together there ain't nothin' that'll stop 'em.

Quote: In Lawrenceville a deputy sheriff

evicted a squatter, and the squatter resisted, making it necessary for the officer to use force. The eleven-year-old son of the squatter shot and killed the deputy with a .22 rifle.

Rattlesnakes! Don't take chances with 'em, an' if they argue, shoot first. If a kid'll kill a cop, what'll the men do? Thing is, get tougher'n they are. Treat 'em rough. Scare 'em.

What if they won't scare? What if they stand up and take it and shoot back? These men were armed when they were children. A gun is an extension of themselves. What if they won't scare? What if some time an army of them marches on the land as the Lombards did in Italy, as the Germans did on Gaul and the Turks did on Byzantium? They were land-hungry, ill-armed hordes too, and the legions could not stop them. Slaughter and terror did not stop them. How can you frighten a man whose hunger is not only in his own cramped stomach but in the wretched bellies of his children? You can't scare him—he has known a fear beyond every other.

In Hooverville the men talking: Grampa took his lan' from the Injuns.

Now, this ain't right. We're a-talkin' here. This here you're talkin' about is stealin'. I ain't no thief.

No? You stole a bottle of milk from a porch night before last. An' you stole some copper wire and sold it for a piece of meat.

Yeah, but the kids was hungry.

It's stealin', though.

Know how the Fairfiel' ranch was got? I'll tell ya. It was all gov'ment lan', an' could be took up. Ol' Fairfiel', he went into San Francisco to the bars, an' he got him three hunderd stew bums. Them bums took up the lan'. Fairfiel' kep' 'em in food an' whisky, an' then when they'd proved the lan', ol' Fairfiel' took it from 'em. He used to say the lan' cost him a pint of rotgut an acre. Would you say that was stealin'?

Well, it wasn't right, but he never went to jail for it.

No, he never went to jail for it. An' the fella that put a boat in a wagon an' made his report like it was all under water 'cause he went in a boat—he never went to jail neither. An' the fellas that bribed congressmen and the legislatures never went to jail neither.

All over the State, jabbering in the Hoovervilles.

And then the raids—the swoop of armed deputies on the squatters' camps. Get out. Department of Health orders. This camp is a menace to health.

Where we gonna go?

That's none of our business. We got orders to get you out of here. In half an hour we set fire to the camp.

They's typhoid down the line. You want ta spread it all over?

We got orders to get you out of here. Now get! In half an hour we burn the camp.

In half an hour the smoke of paper houses, of weed-thatched huts, rising to the sky, and the people in their cars rolling over the highways, looking for another Hooverville.

And in Kansas and Arkansas, in Oklahoma and Texas and New Mexico, the tractors moved in and pushed the tenants out.

Three hundred thousand in California and more coming. And in California the roads full of frantic people running like ants to pull, to push, to lift, to work. For every manload to lift, five pairs of arms extended to lift it; for every stomachful of food available, five mouths open.

And the great owners, who must lose their land in an upheaval, the great owners with access to history, with eyes to read history and to know the great fact: when property accumulates in too few hands it is taken away. And that companion fact: when a majority of the people are hungry and cold they will take by force what they need. And the little screaming fact that sounds through all history: repression works only to strengthen and knit the repressed. The great owners ignored the three cries of history. The land fell into fewer hands, the number of the dispossessed increased, and every effort of the great owners was directed at repression. The money was spent for arms, for gas to protect the great holdings, and spies were sent to catch the murmuring of revolt so that it might be stamped out. The changing economy was ignored, plans for the change ignored; and only means to destroy revolt were considered, while the causes of revolt went on.

The tractors which throw men out of work, the belt lines which carry loads, the machines which produce, all were increased; and more and more families scampered on the highways, looking for crumbs from the great holdings, lusting after the land beside the roads. The great owners formed associations for protection and they met to discuss ways to intimidate, to kill, to gas. And always they were in fear of a principal—three hundred thousand—if they ever move under a leader—the end. Three hundred thousand, hungry and miserable; if they ever know themselves, the land will be theirs and all the gas, all the rifles in the world won't stop them. And the great owners, who had become through their holdings both more and less than men, ran to their destruction, and used every means that in the long run would destroy them. Every little means, every violence, every raid on a Hooverville, every deputy swaggering through a ragged camp put off the day a little and cemented the inevitability of the day.

The men squatted on their hams, sharp-faced men, lean from hunger and hard from resisting it, sullen eyes and hard jaws. And the rich land was around them.

D'ja hear about the kid in that fourth tent down?

No, I jus' come in.

Well, that kid's been a-cryin' in his sleep an' a-rollin' in his sleep. Them folks thought he got worms. So they give him a blaster, an' he died. It was what they call black-tongue the kid had. Comes from not gettin' good things to eat.

Poor little fella.

Yeah, but them folks can't bury him. Got to go to the county stone orchard.

Well, hell.

And hands went into pockets and little coins came out. In front of the tent a little heap of silver grew. And the family found it there.

Our people are good people; our people are kind people. Pray God some day kind people won't all be poor. Pray God some day a kid can eat.

And the associations of owners knew that some day the praying would stop.

And there's the end.

22

Hard Times: Personal Recollections of the Depression

Studs Terkel

What John Steinbeck did for the Okies, Studs Terkel has done for just about everybody else who suffered through the Depression. A veteran radio man, Terkel set about interviewing scores of people who lived in the thirties—businessmen, professional people, farmers, Negroes, women, students, day-laborers, and hobos. In 1970, he published their recollections in *Hard Times: An Oral History of the Great Depression*. The book is a medley of voices: the talk of people who lived through the trauma of the thirties and who recall what it was like for them. Here are a few of those people, each telling the story of Depression America from a personal, intensely human point-of-view.

A Day Laborer
[Louis Banks]

From a bed at a Veteran's Hospital, he talks feverishly; the words pour out....

"My family had a little old farm, cotton, McGehee, Arkansas. I came to Chicago, I was a little bitty boy, I used to prize-fight. When the big boys got through, they put us on there."

I got to be fourteen years old, I went to work on the Great Lakes at $41.50 a month. I thought: Someday I'm gonna be a great chef. Rough times, though. It was the year 1929. I would work from five in the morning till seven at night. Washing dishes, peeling potatoes, carrying heavy garbage. We would get to Detroit.

They was sleepin' on the docks and be drunk. Next day he'd be dead. I'd see 'em floatin' on the river where they would commit suicide because they didn't have anything. White guys and colored.

I'd get paid off, I'd draw $21 every two weeks and then comin' back I'd have to see where I was goin'. 'Cause I would get robbed. One fella named Scotty, he worked down there, he was firin' a boiler. He was tryin' to send some money home. He'd work so hard and sweat, the hot fire was cookin' his stomach. I felt sorry for him. They killed 'im and throwed 'im in the river, trying to get the $15 or $20 from him. They'd steal and kill each other for fifty cents.

1929 was pretty hard. I hoboed, I bummed, I begged for a nickel to get somethin' to eat. Go get a job, oh, at the foundry there. They didn't hire me because I didn't belong to the right kind of race. 'Nother time I went into Saginaw, it was two white fellas and myself made three. The fella there hired the two men and didn't hire me. I was back out on the streets. That hurt me pretty bad, the race part.

When I was hoboing, I would lay on the side of the tracks and wait until I could see the train

---

From *Hard Times: An Oral History of the Great Depression*, by Studs Terkel. Copyright © 1970 by Studs Terkel. Reprinted by permission of Pantheon Books, a Division of Random House, Inc.

comin'. I would always carry a bottle of water in my pocket and a piece of tape or rag to keep it from bustin' and put a piece of bread in my pocket, so I wouldn't starve on the way. I would ride all day and all night long in the hot sun.

I'd ride atop a boxcar and went to Los Angeles, four days and four nights. The Santa Fe, we'd go all the way with Santa Fe. I was goin' over the hump and I was so hungry and weak 'cause I was goin' into the d.t.'s, and I could see snakes draggin' through the smoke. I was sayin', "Lord, help me, Oh Lord, help me," until a white hobo named Callahan, he was a great big guy, looked like Jack Dempsey, and he got a scissors on me, took his legs and wrapped 'em around me. Otherwise, I was about to fall off the Flyer into a cornfield there. I was sick as a dog until I got into Long Beach, California.

Black and white, it didn't make any difference who you were, 'cause everybody was poor. All friendly, sleep in a jungle. We used to take a big pot and cook food, cabbage, meat and beans all together. We all set together, we made a tent. Twenty-five or thirty would be out on the side of the rail, white and colored. They didn't have no mothers or sisters, they didn't have no home, they were dirty, they had overalls on, they didn't have no food, they didn't have anything.

Sometimes we sent one hobo to walk, to see if there were any jobs open. He'd come back and say: Detroit, no jobs. He'd say: they're hirin' in New York City. So we went to New York City. Sometimes ten or fifteen of us would be on the train. And I'd hear one of 'em holler. He'd fall off, he'd get killed. He was tryin' to get off the train, he thought he was gettin' home there. He heard a sound. (Imitates train whistle, a low, long, mournful sound.)

And then I saw a railroad police, a white police. They call him Texas Slim. He shoots you off all trains. We come out of Lima, Ohio . . . Lima Slim, he would kill you if he catch you on any train. Sheep train or any kind of merchandise train. He would shoot you off, he wouldn't ask you to get off.

I was in chain gangs and been in jail all over the country. I was in a chain gang in Georgia. I had to pick cotton for four months, for just hoboin' on a train. Just for vag. They gave me thirty-five cents and a pair of overalls when I got out. Just took me off the train, the guard. 1930, during the Depression, in the summertime. Yes, sir, thirty-five cents, that's what they gave me.

I knocked on people's doors. They'd say, "What do you want? I'll call the police." And they'd put you in jail for vag. They'd make you milk cows, thirty or ninety days. Up in Wisconsin, they'd do the same thing. Alabama, they'd do the same thing. California, anywhere you'd go. Always in jail, and I never did nothin'.

A man had to be on the road. Had to leave his wife, had to leave his mother, leave his family just to try to get money to live on. But he think: my dear mother, tryin' to send her money, worryin' how she's starvin'.

The shame I was feeling. I walked out because I didn't have a job. I said, "I'm goin' out in the world and get me a job." And God help me, I couldn't get anything. I wouldn't let them see me dirty and ragged and I hadn't shaved. I wouldn't send 'em no picture.

I'd write: "Dear Mother, I'm doin' wonderful and wish you're all fine." That was in Los Angeles and I was sleeping under some steps and there was some paper over me. This is the slum part, Negroes lived down there. And my ma, she'd say, "Oh, my son is in Los Angeles, he's doin' pretty fair."

And I was with a bunch of hoboes, drinkin' canned heat. I wouldn't eat two or three days, 'cause I was too sick to eat. It's a wonder I didn't die. But I believe in God.

I went to the hospital there in Los Angeles. They said, "Where do you live?" I'd say,

Thousands of people, unable to pay the rent or the mortgage on their homes, were dispossessed during the Depression. On empty lots at the edges of industrial cities, they fashioned crude shelters out of packing crates, such as the one shown here. These shelters were called "Hoovervilles." (Photo by Underwood & Underwood.)

"Travelers Aid, please send me home." Police says, "O.K., put him in jail." I'd get ninety days for vag. When I was hoboing I was in jail two-thirds of the time. Instead of sayin' five or ten days, they'd say sixty or ninety days. 'Cause that's free labor. Pick the fruit or pick the cotton, then they'd turn you loose.

I had fifteen or twenty jobs. Each job I would have it would be so hard. From six o'clock in the morning till seven o'clock at night. I was fixin' the meat, cookin', washin' dishes and cleaning up. Just like you throwed the ball at one end and run down and catch it on the other. You're jack of all trade, you're doin' it all. White chefs were gettin' $40 a week, but I was gettin' $21 for doin' what they were **doin'** and everything else. The poor people had it rough. The rich people was livin' off the poor.

'Cause I picked cotton down in Arkansas when I was a little bitty boy and I saw my dad, he was workin' all day long. $2 is what one day the poor man would make. A piece of salt pork and a barrel of flour for us and that was McGehee, Arkansas.

God knows, when he'd get that sack he would pick up maybe two, three hundred pounds of cotton a day, gettin' snake bit and everything in that hot sun. And all he had was a little house and a tub to keep the water. 'Cause I went down there to see him in 1930. I got tired of hoboing and went down to see him and my daddy was all gray and didn't have no bank account and no Blue Cross. He didn't have nothin', and he worked himself to death. (Weeps.) And the white man, he would drive a tractor in there. . . . It seems like yesterday to me, but it was 1930.

'33 in Chicago they had the World's Fair. A big hotel was hirin' colored fellas as bellboys. The bellboys could make more money as a white boy for the next ten or fifteen years. I worked as a bellhop on the North Side at a hotel, lots of gangsters there. They don't have no colored bellboys at no exclusive hotels now. I guess maybe in the small ones they may have some.

Jobs were doing a little better after '35, after the World's Fair. You could get dishwashin' jobs, little porter jobs.

Work on the WPA, earn $27.50. We just dig a ditch and cover it back up. You thought you was rich. You could buy a suit of clothes. Before that, you wanted money, you didn't have any. No clothes for the kids. My little niece and my little kids had to have hand-down clothes. Couldn't steal. If you did, you went to the penitentiary. You had to shoot pool, walk all night and all day, the best you could make was $15. I raised up all my kids during the Depression. Scuffled . . . a hard way to go.

Did you find any kindness during the Depression?

No kindness. Except for Callahan, the hobo —only reason I'm alive is 'cause Callahan helped me on that train. And the hobo jungle. Everybody else was evil to each other. There was no friendships. Everybody was worried and sad looking. It was pitiful.

When the war came, I was so glad when I got in the army. I knew I was safe. I put a uniform on, and I said, "Now I'm safe." I had money comin', I had food comin', and I had a lot of gang around me. I knew on the streets or hoboing, I might be killed any time.

I'd rather be in the army than outside where I was so raggedy and didn't have no jobs. I was glad to put on a United States Army uniform and get some food. I didn't care about the rifle what scared me. In the army, I wasn't gettin' killed on a train, I wasn't gonna starve. I felt proud to salute and look around and see all the good soldiers of the United States. I was a good soldier and got five battle stars. I'd rather be in the army now than see another Depression.

POSTSCRIPT: *On recovery, he will return to his job as a washroom attendant in one of Chicago's leading hotels.*

"When I was hoboin' through the Dakotas and Montana, down there by General Custer's Last Stand, Little Big Horn, I wrote my name down, yes, sir. For the memories, just for the note, so it will always be there. Yes, sir."

A Jazz Musician
[Jimmy McPartland]

A trumpet player, he was regarded by Bix Beiderbecke as his successor. He came East, out of Chicago, in the late Twenties, along with Benny Goodman, Bud Freeman, Gene Krupa, Eddie Condon.

So many guys were jumping out of windows, you know, because they lost their money.

Goodness gracious, what for? We used to say to each other: Are they nuts? What is money? We were musicians, so what is money? That's nothing. The important thing is life and living and enjoying life. So these guys lose all their money, what the hell's the difference, we used to say, "You're still livin,' aren't ya?" They can start all over again. I mean, this is what we used to think.

Actually, we didn't think about money. I personally didn't, because I always made it. For me, things have come so easy. I'm ashamed of myself. But money never bothered me. I'd give it away, if somebody needed money.

I remember the band was out of work. This was '28, '29, before the Crash. Bix was working with Paul Whiteman's band. We were out of work, six or eight weeks. We had no money left, and, man, I'm starvin' to death, no money to eat.

They'd invite you to a party, the social set, the money set. You'd play. The best whiskey and everything like that—but no food. (Laughs.) Just all the liquor you could drink. We used to say: "You got a sandwich?"

So I got to this party on Park Avenue, we're invited: Benny Goodman and the guys. So who else is there, but the whole Whiteman band, Bix Beiderbecke and all those guys. So we're drinking and playing and jamming. Some big guy is the host. I get Bix on the side and I say, "Jesus, Bix, we aren't working. Can you lend me five bucks? I haven't eaten in two days." So God, he goes into his wallet, he had but two $100 bills and one fifty. He insisted I take the two $100 bills. I says, "No, I don't want that. All I want is $5, $10. I just want enough to buy some food." "Kid," he says, "you take this money and when you're working again, you pay me back."

Bix became ill and he left Whiteman, went home for a rest period, a dry-out actually. I was working in the show *Sons of Guns*, and I'm making $275 a week, just in the show. In the daytime I'm working in the studios, $10 an hour. Making $300, $400 a week easy. So I got plenty of money and we used to meet at Plunkett's, a speak-easy. So I come in one day and Bix is there, flat broke and sick. He said to me, "Kid, you got any money?" I said, "Sure, you want some money?" I had about $175 in my pocket. The same thing happened. I gave him one fifty. I says, "Here." If I had more, I mean, he coulda had anything I had. He said he had a job, he'd pay me back. And don't you know, he died five or six days later, '32. He got pneumonia.

In the speak-easy, we knew some guys not doing so well. What the heck, you'd take out a $50 bill or ten, twenty, and slip it in their pocket and say, "Here, use it." When they get workin' again, they pay it back. And if they don't, so what? That was the feeling we used to have. I know Teagarden was that way, Bix was that way, and a lot of other guys.

It was during Prohibition. Between sets, we'd sneak into a speak-easy for a drink. One night we couldn't get in the speak. Jeez, the police were out. Some gangsters killed about three guys. They were pretty top-flight guys, so that was the end of that speak-easy. They used to make token raids once in a while. Everything was wide open. The police, I imagine, were in on it.

One night at the Park Central Hotel, somebody came in and said, "Somebody just got shot." It was Arnold Rothstein. And we heard about the whole deal. Because we'd seen all these monkeys comin' in and out all the time. All the hoodlums in that era. They always liked us. Of course, we didn't bother with them. They'd come into the hotel, downstairs, in the basement. Dinner and dancing.

There were engagements in clubs and ballrooms throughout the country in the mid-Thirties, with various big bands and small combos. "We played nice places, the best hotels. There was dough. Some people didn't get jobs, but there was still plenty of money around. What would guys in the band talk about? Girls, mostly." (*Laughs.*) *During this period, he was master of ceremonies at a Chicago jazz club, Three Deuces.*

We had Billie Holiday in the show. She used to sing "Strange Fruit." Oh, beautiful. We got along great together, Billie and I. And I used to read in the back room sometimes to Art Tatum. He played intermission piano. 'Cause he couldn't see, you know. I used to bring books. He always talked about it: "Remember how you used to read to me, Jimmy?" He'd sit there and drink beer, and I'd read to him.

I never had this black and white feeling. Jesus, if you could sing or play, jeez, that was it. I never knew it was that bad till I went down to New Orleans in '34. Where we played, they had a gambling joint, Club Forest. They had a bunch of sheriffs around there because it could be held up. They even had a machine gun in an enclosed cage up above. They all carried guns.

One time, late at night, we were out drinking. There were three or four of these sheriffs. One of the buys said, "Hey there's that nigger son of a bitch. I'm gonna get him and blast his brains." They started towards him. He was really gonna shoot him. I pushed his hand away and I said, "Don't shoot him. I don't want to see you kill a guy." It was just a minor, simple little thing. I saved the guy's life just by pushin' this sheriff's hand away. They were gonna beat my brains out, the sheriffs. Oh, they started gettin' the pistol, one guy was gonna hit me. Another guy stopped them. Then I realized: Holy jeez, these guys are murder. They're gonna kill a guy for nothing. Just because—. . . wow, boy.

There was more camaraderie. It didn't make any difference if you were colored or white. If you were a good musician, that's all that counted. Now the colored guys say we can't play real jazz, soul music. What the hell else we play with but our soul? Every guy's soul is not the same. Know what I mean? Miles Davis thinks I'm great—he likes me, and I like him. But so many others say: the white guy can't play. He hasn't got the soul. Who they kiddin'? There's nobody with a lock-up on soul. If I let myself go and play just the way I feel, that's my soul, isn't it? Whether it be white or black, you gotta play the way you want to.

The music of the Thirties *was good*. I don't mean you stand still. I haven't. But I must play the way I feel. If my style is any good, it will endure, Thirties or Sixties. Or Seventies.

I think everybody should have a job, and the Government should see that they get a job. That WPA deal, that was a darn good idea. I was one of the lucky guys that didn't need it, but this is what I believe. Everybody should work, but do what they want. I don't mean this as a communist thing, maybe it's socialism, I don't know. Like I'm a musician. Just pay me to do concerts for nothin'. Let people listen for nothing.

The Government should work something out so people have something to do. There are so many things to be done in these cities. You feel much better if you're workin' instead of gettin' a handout. You'll get self-respect, which is number one. Drama, dancing schools, musicians. . . . You could give guys like me jobs as teachers, to teach jazz. So you perpetuate what I've learned in my lifetime. You could give that to some younger person and let them carry on, make their own choice, but at least they'd have the background. It's like studying history. It's like being part of history. . . .

A Negro
[Clifford Burke]

The Negro was born in depression. It didn't mean too much to him, The Great American Depression, as you call it. There was no such thing. The best he could be is a janitor or a porter or shoeshine boy. It only became official when it hit the white man. If you can tell me the difference between the depression today and the Depression of 1932 for a black man, I'd like to know it. Now, it's worse, because of the prices. Know the rents they're payin' out here? I hate to tell ya.

He is a pensioner. Most of his days are spent as a volunteer with a community organization in the black ghetto on the West Side of the city.

We had one big advantage. Our wives, they could go to the store and get a bag of beans or a sack of flour and a piece of fat meat, and they could cook this. And we could eat it. Steak? A steak would kick in my stomach like a mule in a tin stable. Now you take the white fella, he couldn't do this. His wife would tell him: Look, if you can't do any better than this, I'm gonna leave you. I seen it happen. He couldn't stand bringing home beans instead of steak and capon. And he couldn't stand the idea of going on relief like a Negro.

You take a fella had a job paying him $60, and here I am making $25. If I go home taking beans to me wife, we'll eat it. It isn't exactly what we want, but we'll eat it. The white man that's been making big money, he's taking beans home, his wife'll say: Get out. (Laughs.)

Why did these big wheels kill themselves? They weren't able to live up to the standards they were accustomed to, and they got ashamed in front of their women. You see, you can tell anybody a lie, and he'll agree with you. But you start layin' down the facts of real life, he won't accept it. The American white man has been superior so long, he can't figure out why he should come down.

I remember a friend of mine, he didn't know he was a Negro. I mean he acted like he never knew it. He got tied downtown with some stock. He blew about twenty thousand. He came home and drank a bottle of poison. A bottle of iodine or something like that. It was a rarity to hear a Negro killing himself over a financial situation. He might have killed himself over some woman. Or getting in a fight. But when it came to the financial end of it, there were so few who had anything. (Laughs.)

I made out during that . . . *Great* Depression. (Laughs.) Worked as a teamster for a lumber yard. Forty cents an hour. Monday we'd have a little work. They'd say come back Friday. There wasn't no need to look for another job. The few people working, most all of them were white.

So I had another little hustle. I used to play pool pretty good. And I'd ride from poolroom to poolroom on this bicycle. I used to beat these guys, gamble what we had. I'd leave home with a dollar. First couple of games I could beat this guy, I'd put that money in my pocket. I'd take the rest of what I beat him out of and hustle the day on that. Sometimes I'd come home with a dollar and a half extra. That was a whole lot of money. Everybody was out trying to beat the other guy, so he could make it. It was pathetic.

I never applied for PWA or WPA, 'cause as long as I could hustle, there was no point in beating the other fellow out of a job, cuttin' some other guy out. . . .

A Psychiatrist
[Dr. David J. Rossman]

He had studied with Freud. His patients are upper middle class. He has been practicing since the Twenties.

Millionaires would come to me for treatment of anxiety attacks. In 1933, one of them said to me, "I'm here for treatment because I have lost all my money. All I have left is one house on Long Island which is worth $750,000. I don't know what I'd get for it if I tried to sell it." He was a very aristocratic looking man. "I've always had a feeling of guilt about the money I've made."

I asked him, "Why do you feel guilty about it?" He said he was a floor trader and when he saw the market begin to fall, he would give it a big shove by selling short. At the end of the day, he had made $50–$75,000. This went on for a long time. He said, "I had always felt as if I had taken this money out of the mouths of orphans and widows."

He felt guilty after the walls caved in. He began to feel what it was like not to have any money. To give you an idea of the importance of this man: he was in a secret meeting at the J. P. Morgan bank, when they were trying to stop the decline. He had an appointment at five o'clock, and he said, "I won't be here today. But when I see you later, I'll have an important message for you."

If I had bought General Motors and Chrysler where it was in March, 1933, I could have been a multi-millionaire on the investment of $10,000. But that wasn't his message. He said, "We have decided to close the Bank of the United States because the President was truculent and insisted upon an enormously inflated price for his stock." This was a very small bank in New York. They decided to let him go to the wall. The bank failed.

This man told me to go to the bank and take all my money and get gold notes. They were yellowbacks that said on the back: Redeemable in demand at the U.S. Treasury for gold in bars. I got $10,000 in gold. I said, "What the hell am I going to do with this?" It was heavy as hell. In gold bullion. I put it in a safety deposit box. Two days later, I had to take it out because the President declared the possession of gold to be illegal. I gave it back to the bank, and they credited me with $10,000.

I learned about the crack in our economy long before the stock market crash of '29. I had a patient who was the biggest kitchen utensil distributor in America. He had a huge plant. He said: suddenly, without notice, his orders just stopped. May and June, 1929.

All of us believed a new era in finance dawned. How long was I in the stock market? From '26 to '29. I had doubled my money. I remember some of the stocks I bought. I bought Electric Bond and Share, for example. I bought it at $100 a share and sold it at $465.

That was the only way you could make any real money. Income was piddling. Physicians were the greatest amateur financiers in the world. The way in which doctors, some of my friends, became interested was they had patients in high finance. They told them which stocks to buy. They were heading for a fall.

I began to invest in 1926. At the time I was working for Veterans Administration, and I think every doctor there had his finger in some kind of stocks. Some did better than others. I was too timid. Until a couple of years later, when I got a tip to buy Montgomery Ward, and within ten days I'd made $1,000.

In May of 1929, I personally pulled out of the market. I took my money out of the house I was dealing with and entrusted it to a man who was the backer of one of the wealthiest men in the country. Thinking he was infallible. He began buying stocks. He bought me Johns-Manville, for example. It was selling at $112. He bought a hundred shares at a bargain, 105. I sold it at 50.

This man embezzled stocks in the spring of 1929, something like $3 million worth. He was in very deep trouble. He died of a coronary. There was no prosecution. He was a pawn. The man whose manager he was was worth about a hundred million. He was not injured in the Crash. He made vast fortunes in dealing with devaluating currencies in Europe. He passed tips along to his friends. A good many of them made—$6–$8 million. $6 million is a lot of money. They were cashing in on the decline in European currency.

What was happening to humans . . . ?

Nothing much. You wouldn't know a Depression was going on. Except that people were complaining they didn't have any jobs. You could get the most wonderful kind of help for a pittance. People would work for next to nothing. That's when people were peddling apples and bread lines were forming all over the city. But on the whole—don't forget the highest unemployment was less than twenty percent.

Your patients, then, weren't really affected?

Not very much. They paid fairly reasonable fees. I just came across a bankbook that I had between 1931 and 1934, and, by God, I was in those days making $2,000 a month, which was a hell of a lot of money. Then in 1934, 1935, 1936, they began coming in droves, when things began to ease up. People were looking for help. All middle class. Money loosened up. At the outbreak of the war, all psychiatrists in New York were just simply drowned with work. I saw my first patient at seven in the morning and I worked till nine at night.

He dwells on the recession of 1937, his interest in the Spanish Civil War, the disappointment in Roosevelt's embargo on Spain, the fall of Barcelona. . . . A good many of his patients were liberals, some interested in Marxism as a solution; others were "the hard core of the big merchants."

Did you have contact with the lower . . . ?

The lower classes? No. Let's take the lower middle class, a contractor. He built me a ten-room stone house for $8,500. I would pay him five cents a square foot for knotty pine that would cost you $1.50 today. Same thing. No laborer that worked in my house got more than $5 a day. I asked the contractor what he got out of it. He said, "I ate for six months." It was catch as catch can. Undersell yourself, do good work, on the hope that you would be recommended to somebody else.

In those days everybody accepted his role, responsibility for his own fate. Everybody, more or less, blamed himself for his delinquency or lack of talent or bad luck. There was an acceptance that it was your own fault, your own indolence, your lack of ability. You took it and kept quiet.

A kind of shame about your own personal failure. I was wondering what the hell it was all about. I wasn't suffering.

An outstanding feature of the Depression was that there were very few disturbances. People mass-marching, there was some. People marched in Washington and Hoover promised everything was going to be all right. People hoped and people were bewildered.

Big business in 1930 and later in '32 came hat in hand, begging Roosevelt. They have never gotten over their humiliation, and they have never forgiven him for having the wits to do something about it. Priming the pump.

Now people think it's coming to them. The whole ethos has changed. There is a great deal more hatred and free-floating aggression all over the country. We have reached unprecedented prosperity. Everybody says: "Why not *me?*" The affluent society has made itself known to people . . . how the better half lives. It's put on television, you can see it. And everybody says, "Who the hell are they? What's the matter with me? My skin is black, so what?" You don't accept responsibility for your own fate. It's the other fellow who's to blame. It's terrible. It could tear our country apart.

Do you think there might be a revolution if the Depression came upon us again?

It would be an inchoate affair. It wouldn't be organized.

Today nobody is permitted to starve. Now they think it's coming to them. As a matter of fact, it was the government that brought this idea to the people, in the Thirties. The people didn't ask the government. They ask the question they can't answer themselves: Why am *I* the goat? Why *me?* They want pie in the sky. . . .

A Woman
[Jane Yoder]

Her father was a blacksmith in a small central Illinois mining town. There were seven children. The mines closed "early, about '28 or '30." The men, among them her father, went to other towns, seeking jobs.

During the Depression, my father took a great deal of psychological abuse. Oh, tremendous. This brother-in-law that was superintendent of the mine . . . I look at these two men. . . . I really think my father had a marvelous mind. I wonder what he had the potential to become. . . .

He's like something out of Dostoevsky. My father was, I think, terribly intelligent. He learned to speak English, a couple of languages, and prided himself on not being like the rest of our neighborhood. He was constantly giving us things from either the paper or some fiction and being dramatic about it . . . "down with these people that didn't want to think." Just as proud of his kids . . . but he was schizophrenic. He could look at himself a little bit, and then just run like hell. Because what he saw was painful.

We were struggling, just desperate to be warm. No blankets, no coats. At this time I was in fourth grade. Katie* went to Chicago and bought an Indian blanket coat. I remember this incident of that Indian blanket coat. (Gasps.) Oh, because Katie came home with it and had it in her clothes closet for quite a while. And I didn't have a coat. I can remember putting on that coat in Sue Pond's house. I thought, oh, this is marvelous, gee. I took that coat home, and I waited till Sunday and wore it to church. And then everybody laughed. I looked horrid. Here was this black-haired kid, with a tendency to be overweight. My God, when I think of that. . . . But I wore that coat, laugh or not.

---
* Her older sister.

And I can remember thinking: the hell with it. I don't care what . . . it doesn't mean a thing. Laugh hard, you'll get it out of your system. I was warm.

Before that I had one coat. It must have been a terrible lightweight coat or what, but I can remember being cold, just shivering. And came home, and nothing to do but go to bed, because if you went to bed, then you put the coat on the bed and you got warm.

The cold that I've known. I never had boots. I think when I got married, I had my first set of boots. In rainy weather, you just ran for it, you ran between the raindrops or whatever. This was luxuriating to have boots. You simply wore your old shoes if it was raining. Save the others. You always polished them and put shoe trees in them. You didn't have unlimited shoe trees, either. When the shoes are worn out, they're used around the house. And of the high heels, you cut the heels down and they're more comfortable.

We tell our boys: you have a black sweater, a white sweater, and a blue sweater. You can't wear ten sweaters at once, you can only wear one. What is this thing? . . . some of the people that I know have thirty blouses. Oh, my God, I have no desire to think where I'd hang them. For what? I can't even grasp it.

If we had a cold or we threw up, nobody ever took your temperature. We had no thermometer. But if you threw up and you were hot, my mother felt your head. She somehow felt that by bringing you oranges and bananas and these things you never had—there's nothing wrong with you, this is what she'd always say in Croatian; you'll be all right. Then she gave you all these good things. Oh, gee, you almost looked forward to the day you could throw up. I could remember dreaming about oranges and bananas, dreaming about them.

My oldest brother, terribly bright, wanted to go on to school to help pay those grocery bills that were back there. But my youngest brother, Frankie, didn't know. Oh, it just overwhelms me sometimes when I think of those two younger brothers, who would want to get some food and maybe go to the store. But they would see this $900 grocery bill, and they just couldn't do it.

We all laugh now, because Frankie is now down in New Mexico, and superintendent of two mines. And we all say, "Remember, Frankie?" Frankie's *"To košta puno?"* That's "Did it cost a lot? Everything that came into the house, he'd say, *"To košta puno?"*

Did it cost much? No matter what you brought in: bread and eggs and Karo syrup. Oh, Karo syrup was such a treat. I don't remember so much *my* going to the store and buying food. I must have been terribly proud and felt: I can't do it. How early we all stayed away from going to the store, because we sensed my father didn't have the money. So we stayed hungry. And we talked about it.

I can think of the WPA . . . my father immediately got employed in this WPA. This was a godsend. This was the greatest thing. It meant food, you know. Survival, just survival.

How stark it was for me to come into nurses' training and have the girls—one of them, Susan Stewart, lived across the hall from me, her father was a doctor—their impressions of the WPA. How it struck me. Before I could ever say that my father was employed in the WPA, discussions in the bull sessions in our rooms immediately was: these lazy people, the shovel leaners. I'd just sit there and listen to them. I'd look around and realize: sure, Susan Stewart was talking this way, but her father was a doctor, and her mother was a nurse. Well, how nice. They had respectable employment. In my family, there was no respectable employment. I thought, you don't know what it's like.

How can I defend him? I was never a person who could control this. It just had to come out or I think I'd just blow up. So I would say, "I wonder how much we know until we go through it. Just like the patients we take care of. None of them are in that hospital by choice." I would relate it in abstractions. I think it saved me from just blowing up.

I would come back after that and I'd just say: Gee, these are just two separate, separate worlds.

A Big Businessman
[Robert A. Baird]

He is president of a large conglomerate in a city of the far Northwest. One of the most powerful men in the region. He engages in many charitable enterprises.

My father had been a salesman all his life, a very successful one. Even though he had only a fifth-grade education. In the great financial period of the middle Twenties, he sold bonds. The house he worked for went broke. The president of the company overextended himself and committed suicide.

My father went back to selling trucks, but there were no trucks to be sold. There were times when we didn't know whether we'd have anything to eat at night. I tell that to my children today, and they think the old man's flipped his lid.

My dad lost the house he was buying, and we rented for a while. He went through bankruptcy, which was a common thing at the time. He grubbed a great deal with all his remarkable energy, but he was plenty worried. Could he provide for his family? I have a great understanding of the Negro male today, because I saw it first-hand with my father.

But he had no doubts. He believed in the system he had grown up with. He was an inspirational man, like many good salesmen are. You have to believe in it. Because he had only a limited education, he believed all his sons and daughters should go to college. And we did.

When the Crash came, he talked about the fortunes that were lost that day. He felt there's nothing really wrong with our system. Just a few speculators. It was a popular theme in those days. He was wrong, of course. Radical changes were called for. And Roosevelt made them. But this was the kind of salesman's spirit in him.

Things kept going downhill in Detroit. The automobile plants laid off so many men. They began organizing the unions. They were organizing everything there for a while. I remember being in Stouffer's Restaurant and someone blowing a whistle and all the waitresses sitting down. People were reacting against the suffering. What could be a better way?

I can remember the trouble at Ford's, the clash at the Rouge plant.* A big demonstration. The chant of the crowd that was marching: We wanted bread, you gave us bullets. It's funny how a little thing like that sticks in your mind.

When I got out of college, I went to work at the Packard plant. I hoped eventually to get into the industrial relations end of the business. After working in the plant for six months, I could understand the men and their grievances. I was working on the assembly line. I can still remember my badge number. FSG348. This was '37.

I learned a great deal about employee relations. I learned how not to treat men. They did a lot of things at the Packard plant in those days that earned them the animosity of their workers.

They used to take a train into the plant. They'd often do it when the workers were coming to work. So you were held up fifteen or twenty minutes by the train. If you were a minute late, they docked you thirty minutes' pay. That was the way it was. There were no ifs, ands or buts about it. I can remember talking to my foreman about it. It made no difference.

We were making new models of the 1938 car for the New York Auto Show. On the assembly line, you work at a certain pace. If they change the speed, and don't tell you about it, pretty soon you're working in the next man's space trying to keep up. This chassis has gotten ahead of you. This goes all down the line. Finally, you have to shut it down. Nobody wanted to shut the line down, because you got hell if you did.

I can remember how they speeded up the line and we got in everybody's way, and finally they hollered: Shut the line down. Steve, the big foreman, weighed about three hundred pounds, came swearing all the way down the line: What was the trouble? The union was new then. The steward said: We're not working.

An hour later, out comes the plant manager with the foreman. The steward explained. The manager said he was sorry. He apologized to the men. He said, "We have a train waiting to take the cars to the New York Auto Show. Next year's business depends on us getting a good start in the show." The steward said, "Why didn't you tell us? We'll knock these cars out." They got those guys going at twice the speed. Nobody complained.

It illustrated to me something I never forgot. If you tell people what you want them to do and why you want them to do it, they're very cooperative. I've always said around here: We could sell any reasonable program to our union if we looked at it from their standpoint, and made a reasonable explanation. But if you try to push them around, they aren't going to stand for it.

I got laid off in December of 1937. It was the down draft of the Roosevelt recession. In Detroit, when the automobile industry goes down, everything goes down.

I wrote a series of letters to companies that had interviewed me when I was in college. A large mail-order house said if I wanted to come

---

* In 1937, there had been clashes at the River Rouge plant between the service men at Ford, who had been holding out against the CIO, and UAW organizers. The La Follette Committee held hearings, subsequently, and confirmed the union's charges of company violence.

to their city, they had a job for me. So I came over on the bus. It cost $6 to ride from Detroit to this city. I got the job.

I had about an hour and a half to kill before going back to the bus station. So I stopped in to see a fellow at this company. He had also interviewed me while I was at school. I thought it would be nice to know him. He talked me into working here. So I called up the other company and said no.

Peter, His Older Son

He is twenty-four. A college graduate, he works full time as an SDS (Students for a Democratic Society) organizer. He travels along the West Coast, recruiting members.

As a person, my father is a good person. He means well. His motives are all of the highest. He feels sincerely that the way you do good for the people of the world is to expand welfare capitalism. The important thing to understand about a man like my father is that in a society like this, whether a person is a nice guy or a bad guy, is irrelevant. People play certain roles. It's not so much their attitudes as the roles they play. Although he's the kind of guy you wouldn't mind having dinner with, he plays a bad role in this society.

I'm sure the Depression was important in molding my father's life. A lot of older people look at young people today and say, "Those punks, they never felt the Depression. Look at the things they're doing." I don't think this attitude makes any sense. My brother and I grew up with a certain kind of history, and he grew up with another. I don't condemn him for his experience. I condemn him for the role he plays today.

In the Depression, people were up against the wall. Fear. So when you're up against the wall like that, any kind of solution is grasped at. In the case of those people, it was military spending, war.

We didn't see the Depression. We have grown up in a time when going to school is like going to a factory. It's not totally parallel: we are materially privileged. But the conditions students face are increasingly like Depression factory conditions. We're not treated as intellectually curious beings. We're being manufactured. We're being channeled for certain roles. We're lined up, sorted into jobs . . . as well as being kept off the job market as long as possible. So growing up becomes a later and later thing.

Because of their education and the nature of communications, many young people identify with the other people of the world. We had grown up in a post-Depression, affluent society feeling this is the way it is everywhere. Then came the rude awakening: two-thirds of the world is starving and exploited by the same corporations that run our universities. My father is a member of the board of a leading university out here. He's also a board member of a bank that does lots of business with South Africa.

He's a philanthropist in many ways. That, too, is part of the approach of the individual who has made it. This is part of the whole psyche of competition: I made it—now I can help others. What competition really means is: there is a stacked deck. Some people will fight against others for a few crumbs, while the guy with the stacked deck makes most of it.

My father does want to understand us. He wants to think we're following the values he taught us. But when what we do becomes more than a childish pastime, he feels threatened. He can't really face it, because what we're saying is: We want to build a society in which roles like his are no longer possible.

(*Softly.*) He used to tell me that of all his kids—there are five of us—I could have been the one to make it. Perhaps even his successor as president of the conglomerate. He always felt I had the brains and drive to be a ruler. I think he's disappointed in me. I don't think he's quite given up hope that I'm going through a stage and will come out of it. . . .

Much of his ambition, drive and energy comes from the Depression, I'm sure. But I also have a lot of energy and I did not have that experience.

He always downgraded campus radicals in the Thirties. He called them a minority—psychologically disturbed young people. . . .

A College Student
[Robert Gard]

I set out for the University of Kansas on a September morning with $30 that I'd borrowed from my local bank. I had one suit and one necktie and one pair of shoes. My mother had spent several days putting together a couple of wooden cases of canned fruits and vegetables. My father, a country lawyer, had taken as a legal fee a 1915 Buick touring car. It was not in particularly good condition, but it was good enough to get me there. It fell to pieces and it never got back home anymore.

I had no idea how long the $30 would last, but it sure would have to go a long way because I had nothing else. The semester fee was $22, so that left me $8 to go. Fortunately, I got a job driving a car for the dean of the law school. That's how I got through the first year.

What a pleasure it was to get a pound of hamburger, which you could buy for about five cents, take it up to the Union Pacific Railroad tracks and have a cookout. And some excellent conversation. And maybe swim in the Kaw River.

One friend of mine came to college equipped. He had an old Model T Ford Sedan, about a 1919 model. He had this thing fitted up as a house. He lived in it all year long. He cooked and slept and studied inside that Model T Ford Sedan. How he managed I will never know. I once went there for dinner. He cooked a pretty good one on a little stove he had in this thing. He was a brilliant student. I don't know where he is now, but I shouldn't be surprised if he's the head of some big corporation. (Laughs.) Survival. . . .

The weak ones, I don't suppose, really survived. There were many breakdowns. From malnutrition very likely. I know there were students actually starving.

Some of them engaged in strange occupations. There was a biological company that would pay a penny apiece for cockroaches. They needed these in research, I guess. Some students went cockroach hunting every night. They'd box 'em and sell them to this firm.

I remember the feverish intellectual discussion we had. There were many new movements. On the literary scene, there was something called the Proletarian Novel. There was the Federal Theater and the Living Newspaper. For the first time, we began to get socially conscious. We began to wonder about ourselves and our society.

We were mostly farm boys and, to some extent, these ideas were alien to us. We had never really thought about them before. But it was a period of necessity. It brought us face to face with these economic problems and the rest. . . . All in all, a painful time, but a glorious time.

A Book Editor
[Ward James]

Before the Crash, I was with a small publishing house in New York. I was in charge of all the production and did most of the copy. It was a good job. The company was growing. It looked like a permanent situation. I was feeling rather secure.

I realized that people weren't secure in the publishing business. There was no tenure. We didn't have any union. That was the first move

I made, organizing the Book and Magazine Union in New York.* A lot of white collar people at the time felt unions were not for them. They were above it.

Until 1935, I had my job with this publishing house. They insisted I take a month vacation without pay and a few other things, but it wasn't really too distressing. It became tougher and tougher.

I was fired. No reasons given. I think my work with the union had a good deal to do with it, although I couldn't prove it. What hurt was that I'd gotten pretty good in writing technical books for boys. I had three published. By now, with things getting tight, no publisher wanted any book that wouldn't be a best seller.

I was out of work for six months. I was losing my contacts as well as my energy. I kept going from one publishing house to another. I never got past the telephone operator. It was just wasted time. One of the worst things was occupying your time, sensibly. You'd go to the library. You took a magazine to the room and sat and read. I didn't have a radio. I tried to do some writing and found I couldn't concentrate. The day was long. There was nothing to do evenings. I was going around in circles, it was terrifying. So I just vegetated.

With some people I knew, there was a coldness, shunning: I'd rather not see you just now. Maybe *I'll* lose my job next week. On the other hand, I made some very close friends, who were merely acquaintances before. If I needed $5 for room rent or something, it was available.

I had a very good friend who cashed in his bonus bonds to pay his rent. I had no bed, so he let me sleep there. (Laughs.) I remember getting down to my last pair of pants, which looked awful. One of my other friends had just got a job and had an extra pair of pants that fit me, so I inherited them. (Laughs.)

I went to apply for unemployment insurance, which had just been put into effect. I went three weeks in succession. It still hadn't come through. Then I discovered the catch. At that time, anybody who earned more than $3,000 a year was not paid unemployment insurance unless his employer had O.K.'d it. It could be withheld. My employer exercised his option of not O.K.'ing it. He exercised his vindictive privilege. I don't think that's the law any more.

I finally went on relief. It's an experience I don't want anybody to go through. It comes as close to crucifixion as. . . . You sit in an auditorium and are given a number. The interview was utterly ridiculous and mortifying. In the middle of mine, a more dramatic guy than I dived from the second floor stairway, head first, to demonstrate he was gonna get on relief even if he had to go to the hospital to do it.

There were questions like: Who are your friends? Where have you been living? Where's your family? I had sent my wife and child to her folks in Ohio, where they could live more simply. Why should anybody give you money? Why should anybody give you a place to sleep? What sort of friends? This went on for half an hour. I got angry and said, "Do you happen to know what a friend is?" He changed his attitude very shortly. I did get certified some time later. I think they paid $9 a month.

I came away feeling I didn't have any business living any more. I was imposing on somebody, a great society or something like that.

That ended with a telegram from Chicago, from the Illinois Writers Project. I had edited a book for the director, who knew my work. He needed a top editor to do final editorial work on the books being published, particularly the Illinois Guide. I felt we really produced something.

This was the regional office, so I worked on Guide books for four or five other states. The

---

* "I was also engaged at that time in organizing the Consumers Union. Our idea was to help people of what we now call the inner city to buy more intelligently. Advertising was even less regulated than it is today. Merchants were on the make. Now, Consumers Union, still a worthwhile organization, serves the middle class well. But I'd like to think some day it will get into the ghettos and do some real work."

Tribune said it cost two million and wasn't worth it. No matter, they were really quite good.

The first day I went on the Project, I was frightened as much as I'd ever been in my life. My confidence had been almost destroyed in New York. I didn't know a single person here. But I found there was a great spirit of cooperation, friendliness. I discovered quickly my talents were of use.

Had been in Chicago about a month or two. I remember I wanted to buy a suit on credit. I was told nobody on the WPA could get credit in any store in Chicago. It was some years later before I could establish credit of any kind.

I bought an inexpensive radio, an Emerson. My son, David, who was four or five, dictated letters to his mother to be sent to his grandmother: "We have a radio. We bought it all ourselves. Nobody gave us it all." Apparently, he had resented that he and his mother had been living rent-free in Ohio. And she may have been getting clothes from her sister. Yeah, there was an impact even on the very young.

Do you recall the sentiments of people during the depths of the Depression?

There was a feeling that we were on the verge of a bloody revolution, up until the time of the New Deal. Many people, among them, intellectuals, without knowing what else to do, worked with the Communist Party. The Communists naturally exploited this. It began to change with the New Deal and pretty much came to an end with the Russian-German pact.

I remember a very sinking feeling during the time of the Bank Holiday. I walked down to the corner to buy a paper, giving the man a fifty-cents coin. He flipped it up in the air and said, "This is no good." And he threw it in the middle of the street. (Laughs.) Some took the Holiday as a huge joke. Others had hysteria, like this newsboy: there isn't any money, there isn't anything. Most people took it calmly. It couldn't get much worse—and something was being *done*.

Everyone was emotionally affected. We developed a fear of the future which was very difficult to overcome. Even though I eventually went into some fairly good jobs, there was still this constant dread: everything would be cut out from under you and you wouldn't know what to do. It would be even harder, because you were older....

Before the Depression, one felt he could get a job even if something happened to this one. There were always jobs available. And, of course, there were always those, even during the Depression: If you wanted to work, you could really get it. Nonsense.

I suspect, even now, I'm a little bit nervous about every job I take and wonder how long it's going to last—and what I'm going to do to cause it to disappear.

I feel anything can happen. There's a little fear in me that it might happen again. It does distort your outlook and your feeling. Lost time and lost faith....

VII   The World in Flames

23
Day of Infamy

James McGregor Burns

For years a myth has flourished that Franklin Roosevelt deliberately sent the Seventh Fleet to Pearl Harbor, so that the Japanese could attack it and thereby give him an excuse to plunge the United States into World War II. Actually, as James McGregor Burns shows, Roosevelt did no such thing. In truth, the decisions and events that led to America's entry into World War II were enormously complex, involving developments in Europe as well as in Asia. Indeed, once war had broken out in Europe, Roosevelt was more preoccupied with the Nazi threat there than with Japanese expansion in Asia. Time and again he predicted that Hitler would eventually make war on the United States, and out of that belief flowed much of his European diplomacy (the destroyer-bases deal with England, Lend-Lease, and the Atlantic Charter). Still, through 1940 and 1941, as Hitler escalated the bombing of Britain and sent German armies goosestepping into Russia, the Roosevelt Administration often seemed adrift, as though the President and his advisors were confused, helplessly caught in a vortex of events over which they had no control.

Japanese intensions in the Pacific became especially perplexing. Did Japan's aggressions against China constitute an immediate threat to United States security? Was a showdown with Japan also inevitable, as United States military leaders emphatically insisted? While the United States watched Japanese movements in Asia, Congress declared economic war against Germany—this was the controversial Lend-Lease program—which gave $7 billion in military aid to embattled Britain. Soon American convoys were carrying supplies across the Atlantic. When German U-boats torpedoed several American vessels, many observers contended that war with Hitler was only a matter of time.

Meanwhile, the Japanese question had become increasingly confusing. In Tokyo, a war party led by Tojo and the military demanded that the United States be driven from the Pacific, so that Japan could establish an Asian empire free of Western influence. But Prime Minister Konoye, a moderate, wanted to negotiate with the United States and directed his American ambassador, Kichisaburo Nomuro, to present Secretary of State Cordell Hull with a set of proposals that might avoid war. At the same time, as Burns explains, the war party proceeded with a top secret plan to attack the United States navy at Pearl Harbor should negotiations fail.

These are the opening scenes of Burns's narrative, one which captures those suspense-filled days in late 1941 as the United States and Japan drifted toward a violent showdown in the Pacific.

One could sense at the end of summer 1941 that the war was rushing toward another series of stupendous climacterics. German troops had isolated Leningrad and broken through Smolensk on the road to Moscow, had surrounded and overwhelmed four Russian armies in the Kiev sector; through the two-hundred-mile gap they had torn in the south the Nazis could see

From pp. 143–167 in *Roosevelt: The Soldier of Freedom, 1940–1945*, copyright © 1970 by James McGregor Burns. Reprinted by permission of Harcourt Brace Jovanovich.

the grain of the eastern Ukraine and the oil of the Caucasus. Churchill was preparing a strong blow in North Africa and pressing for a bolder policy in Southeast Asia. Tokyo was vacillating between peace and war, under a dire timetable. Chungking's morale seemed to be ebbing away. Washington and London were stepping up the Battle of the Atlantic. And in Moscow, around the end of September, the first flakes of snow fell silently on the Kremlin walls.

Pressure from all these sectors converged on the man in the White House. Allies were stepping up their demands; enemies, their thrusts. His Cabinet war hawks battered him with conflicting advice. But Roosevelt under stress seemed only to grow calmer, steadier, more deliberate and even cautious. He joshed and jousted with the reporters even while artfully withholding news. He listened patiently while Ickes for the tenth time—or was it the hundredth?—maneuvered for the transfer of Forestry from Agriculture to Interior—an effort that the President might have found exquisitely irrelevant to the war except that he himself seemed excited by a plan to establish roe deer in Great Smoky Mountains National Park.

But Roosevelt was not impervious to the strain. More than ever before he seemed to retreat into his private world. He spent many weekends at Hyde Park, partly in settling his mother's estate. He devoted hours to planning a Key West fishing retreat for Hopkins and himself; he even roughed out a sketch for a hurricane-proof house. He found time to talk to the Roosevelt Home Club in Hyde Park, to Dutchess County schoolteachers, to a local grange. And always there were the long anecdotes about Washington during World War I days, about Campobello and Hyde Park.

Physically, too, the President was beginning to show the strain. Systolic hypertension had been noted four years earlier and not considered cause for concern; but—far more serious—diastolic hypertension was diagnosed during 1941. Dr. McIntire was no longer so rosily optimistic, though he said nothing publicly to temper his earlier statements. His patient was eating, exercising, and relaxing less, showing more strain, and carrying more worries to bed, than he had during the earlier years in the White House. But the President rarely complained and never seemed very curious about his health. Doubtless he felt that he had enough to worry about abroad.

Tension was rising, especially in the Far East. The imperial rebuke spurred Konoye to redoubled efforts at diplomacy even as the imperative timetable compelled generals and admirals to step up their war planning. The government seemed schizophrenic. All great powers employ military and diplomatic tactics at the same time; but in Japan the two thrusts were competitive and disjointed, with the diplomats trapped by a military schedule.

Subtly, almost imperceptibly, Konoye and the diplomats beat a retreat in the face of Washington's firm stand. Signals were confused: Nomura acted sometimes on his own; messages were also coming in via Grew [U.S. ambassador to Japan] and a number of unofficial channels; and Konoye and Toyoda had to veil possible concessions for fear extremists would hear of them and inflame the jingoes. The Japanese military continued to follow its own policies; amid the delicate negotiations, Washington learned that the Japanese Army was putting more troops into Indochina. The political chiefs in Tokyo, however, seemed willing to negotiate. On the three major issues Tokyo would: agree to follow an "independent" course under the Tripartite Pact—a crucial concession at this point, because America's widening confrontation with Germany raised the fateful possibility that Tokyo would automatically side with Berlin if a hot war broke out; follow co-operative, nondiscriminatory economic policies, a concession that was as salve to Hull's breast; and be willing to let Washington mediate a settlement between Japan and China.

Day after day [Secretary of State] Hull listened to these proposals courteously, discussed them gravely—and refused to budge. He insisted that Tokyo be even more specific and make concessions in advance of a summit conference. By now the Secretary and his staff conceded that Konoye was "sincere." They simply doubted the Premier's capacity to bring the military into line. That doubt did not end after the war when historians looked at the evidence, which reflected such a shaky balance of power in Tokyo that Konoye's parley might have precipitated a crisis rather than have averted it. Konoye had neither the nerve nor the muscle for a supreme stroke. Much would have depended on the Emperor, and the administration did not fully appreciate in September either his desire for effective negotiations or his ability to make his soldiers accept their outcome.

The mystery lay not with Hull, who was sticking to his principles, but with Roosevelt, who was bent on *Realpolitik* as well as morality. The President still had one simple approach to Japan—to play for time—while he conducted the cold war with Germany. Why, then, did he not insist on a Pacific conference as an easy way to gain time? Partly because such a conference might bring a showdown *too* quickly; better, Roosevelt calculated, to let Hull do the thing he was so good at—talk and talk, without letting negotiations either lapse or come to a head. And partly because Roosevelt was succumbing to his own tendency to string things out. *He* had infinite time in the Far East; he did not realize that in Tokyo a different clock was ticking.

Amid the confusion and miscalculation there was one hard, unshakable issue: China. In all their sweeping proposals to pull out of China, the Japanese insisted, except toward the end, on leaving some troops as security, ostensibly at least, against the Chinese Communists. Even the Japanese diplomats' definite promises on China seemed idle; it was as clear in Washington as in Tokyo that a withdrawal from a war to which Japan had given so much blood and treasure would cause a convulsion.

Washington was in almost as tight a bind on China as was Tokyo. During this period the administration was fearful of a Chinese collapse. Chungking* was complaining about the paucity of American aid; some Kuomintang officials charged that Washington was interested only in Europe and hoped to leave China to deal with Japan. Madame Chiang at a dinner party accused Roosevelt and Churchill of ignoring China at their Atlantic meeting and trying to appease Japan; the Generalissimo chided his wife for her impulsive outburst but did not disagree. Every fragment of a report of a Japanese-American détente set off a paroxysm of fear in Chungking. Through all their myriad channels into the administration the Nationalists were maintaining steady pressure against compromise with Tokyo and for an immensely enlarged and hastened aid program to China.

Even the President's son James, as a Marine captain, urged his father to send bombers to China, in response to a letter from Soong stating that in fourteen months "not a single plane sufficiently supplied with armament and ammunition so that it could actually be used to fire has reached China." Chiang was literally receiving the run-around in Washington as requests bounced from department to department and from Americans to British and back again. Its very failure to aid China made the administration all the more sensitive to any act that might break Kuomintang morale.

So Roosevelt backed Hull's militant posture toward Tokyo. When the Secretary penciled a few lines at the end of September to the effect that the Japanese had hardened their position on the basic questions, Roosevelt said he wholly agreed with his conclusion—even though he

---

* Located beyond the gorges of the Yangtze River, Chungking was the capital of Chiang Kai-Shek's Nationalist Government. His party was called the Kuomintang (National Peoples' Party)—Ed.

must have known that Hull was oversimplifying the situation to the point of distortion. Increasingly anxious, Grew, in Tokyo, felt that he simply was not getting through to the President on the possibilities of a summit conference. On October 2 Hull again stated his principles and demanded specifics. The Konoye government in turn asked Washington just what it wanted Japan to do. Would not the Americans lay their cards on the table? Time was fleeting; the military now were pressing heavily on the diplomats. At this desperate moment the Japanese government offered flatly to "evacuate all its troops from China." But the military deadline had arrived. Was it too late?

Not often have two powers been in such close communication but with such faulty perceptions of each other. They were exchanging information and views through a dozen channels; they were both conducting effective espionage; there were countless long conversations, Hull having spent at least one hundred hours talking with Nomura. The problem was too much information, not too little—and too much that was irrelevant, confusing, and badly analyzed. The two nations grappled like clumsy giants, each with a dozen myopic eyes that saw too little and too much.

For some time Grew and others had been warning Washington that the Konoye Cabinet would fall unless diplomacy began to score; the administration seemed unmoved. On October 16 Konoye submitted his resignation to the Emperor. In his stead Hirohito appointed Minister of War Hideki Tojo. The news produced dismay in Washington, where Roosevelt canceled a regular Cabinet meeting to talk with his War Cabinet, and a near-panic in Chungking, which feared that the man of Manchuria would seek first of all to finish off the China incident. But reassurances came from Tokyo: Konoye indicated that the new Cabinet would continue to emphasize diplomacy, and the new Foreign Minister, Shigenori Togo, was a professional diplomat and not a fire-breathing militarist. As for Tojo, power ennobles as well as corrupts. Perhaps it had been a shrewd move of the Emperor, some of the more helpful Washingtonians reflected, to make Tojo responsible for holding his fellow militarists in check.

So for a couple of weeks the President marked time. Since he was still following the diplomacy of delay, he could only wait for the new regime in Tokyo to take the initiative—and to wonder when the next clash would occur in the Atlantic.

That clash came on the night of October 16. About four hundred miles south of Iceland a slow convoy of forty ships, escorted by only four corvettes, ran into a pack of U-boats. After three ships were torpedoed and sunk, the convoy appealed to Reykjavik for help, and soon five American destroyers were racing to the scene. That evening the submarines, standing out two or three miles from the convoy and thus beyond the range of the destroyers' sound gear, picked off seven more ships. The destroyers, which had no radar, thrashed about in confusion in the pitch dark, dropping depth bombs; when the U.S.S. *Kearny* had to stop to allow a corvette to cross her bow, a torpedo struck her, knocked out her power for a time, and killed eleven of her crew. She struggled back to Iceland nursing some bitter lessons in night fighting.

At last the first blood had been drawn—and it was American blood (though the U-boat commander had not known the nationality of the destroyer he was firing at). News of the encounter reached Washington on the eve of a vote in the House on repealing the Neutrality Act's ban against the arming of merchant ships. Repeal passed by a handsome majority, 259 to 138. The bill had now to go to the Senate. On Navy Day, October 27, the President took up the incident. He reminded his listeners, packed into the grand ballroom of Washington's Mayflower Hotel, of the *Greer* and *Kearny* episodes.

"We have wished to avoid shooting. But the shooting has started. And history has recorded who fired the first shot. In the long run, however, all that will matter is who fired the last shot.

"America has been attacked. The U.S.S. *Kearny* is not just a Navy ship. She belongs to every man, woman, and child in this Nation...."

The President said he had two documents in his possession: a Nazi map of South America and part of Central America realigning it into five vassal states; and a Nazi plan "to abolish all existing religions—Catholic, Protestant, Mohammedan, Hindu, Buddhist, and Jewish alike" —if Hitler won. "The God of Blood and Iron will take the place of the God of Love and Mercy." He denounced apologists for Hitler. "The Nazis have made up their own list of modern American heroes. It is, fortunately, a short list. I am glad that it does not contain my name." The President had never been more histrionic. He reverted to the clashes on the sea. "I say that we do not propose to take this lying down." He described steps in Congress to eliminate "hamstringing" provisions of the Neutrality Act. "That is the course of honesty and of realism."

"Our American merchant ships must be armed to defend themselves against the rattlesnakes of the sea.

"Our American merchant ships must be free to carry out American goods into the harbors of our friends.

"Our American merchant ships must be protected by our American Navy.

"In the light of a good many years of personal experience, I think that it can be said that it can never be doubted that the goods will be delivered by this Nation, whose Navy believes in the tradition of 'Damn the torpedoes; full speed ahead!'"

Some had said that Americans had grown fat and flabby and lazy. They had not; again and again they had overcome hard challenges.

"Today in the face of this newest and greatest challenge of them all, we Americans have cleared our decks and taken our battle stations...."

It was one of Roosevelt's most importunate speeches, but it seemed to have little effect. After a week of furious attacks by Senate isolationists, neutrality revision cleared the upper chamber by only 50 to 37. In mid-November a turbulent House passed the Senate bill by a majority vote of only 212 to 194. The President won less support from Democrats on this vote than he had on Lend-Lease. It was clear to all—and this was the key factor in Roosevelt's calculations—that if the administration could have such a close shave as this on the primitive question of arming cargo ships, the President could not depend on Congress at this point to vote through a declaration of war. Three days after Roosevelt's Navy Day speech the American destroyer *Reuben James* was torpedoed, with the loss of 115 of the crew, including all the officers; Congress and the people seemed to greet this heavy loss with fatalistic resignation.

It was inexplicable. In this looming crisis the United States seemed deadlocked—its President handcuffed, its Congress irresolute, its people divided and confused. There were reasons running back deep into American history, reasons embedded in the country's Constitution, habits, institutions, moods, and attitudes. But the immediate, proximate reason lay with the President of the United States. He had been following a middle course between the all-out interventionists and those who wanted more time; he had been stranded midway between his promise to keep America out of war and his excoriation of Nazism as a total threat to his nation. He had called Hitlerism inhuman, ruthless, cruel, barbarous, piratical, godless, pagan, brutal, tyrannical, and absolutely bent on world domination. He had even issued the ultimate warning: that if Hitler won in Europe, Americans would be forced into a war on their own soil "as costly and as devastating as that which now rages on the Russian front."

Now—by early November 1941—there seemed to be nothing more he could say. There seemed to be little more he could do. He had called his people to their battle stations—but there was no battle. "He had no more tricks left," Sherwood said later. "The bag from which he had pulled so many rabbits was empty." Always a master of mass influence and personal persuasion, Roosevelt had encountered a supreme crisis in which neither could do much good. A brilliant timer, improviser, and manipulator, he confronted a turgid balance of powers and strategies beyond his capacity to either steady or overturn. Since the heady days of August he had lost the initiative; now he could only wait on events. And events with the massive impact that would be decisive were still in the hands of Adolf Hitler.

The crisis of presidential leadership mirrored the dilemma of national strategy in the fall of 1941. According to long-laid plans, the United States, in the event of war, would engage directly with Germany and stall off or conduct a holding action with Japan. Roosevelt was expecting a confrontation with Germany, probably triggered by some incident in the Atlantic, but he was evading a showdown with Japan. In his denunciations of Nazism he had been careful not to mention Nipponese aggression or imperialism. But Hitler still pointedly avoided final trouble in the Atlantic, while the Far Eastern front, instead of being tranquilized, was becoming the most critical one.

And if war did break out in the Pacific—what then? The chances seemed strong that the Japanese would strike directly at British or Dutch possessions, not American. Sherwood posed the question well. If French isolationists had raised the jeering cry "Why die for Danzig?" why should Americans die to protect the Kra Isthmus, or British imperialism in Singapore or Hong Kong, or Dutch imperialism in the East Indies, or Bolshevism in Vladivostok? It would no longer be enough for the United States to offer mere aid. Doubtless Roosevelt could ram through a declaration of war—but how effective would a bitter and divided nation be in the crucible of total war? And if the United States did not forcibly resist Japanese aggression against Britain and Holland, what would happen to Britain's defenses in the Far East while so heavily committed at home, in the Middle East, in North Africa, and on the seven seas?

The obvious answer was to stall Tokyo as long as possible. Eventually an open conflict with Germany must come; if Japan had not yet entered the war, perhaps it would stay out for the same reason it had kept clear of the Russo-German conflict. By November 1941 Roosevelt needed such a delay not only because of Atlantic First, but also as a result of a shift in plans for the Philippines. Earlier, the archipelago had been assumed to be indefensible against a strong enemy assault, and hence the War and Navy Departments had not made a heavy commitment there. Now, with General MacArthur's appointment as commander of U.S. forces in the Far East and the development of the B-17 heavy bomber, the Philippines were once again considered strategically viable. But time was needed, at least two or three months.

So early hostilities with Japan would mean the wrong war in the wrong ocean at the wrong time. Yet it was clear by November 1941 that the United States was faced with the growing probability of precisely this war. Why did not the President string the Japanese along further, taking care not to get close to a showdown?

This is what he did try, at least until November. It was not easy. Every time reports spread that Washington had considered even a small compromise on the central issue of a Japanese withdrawal from China, frantic cries arose from Chungking. Churchill, too, pressed insistently for a harder line toward Tokyo. At home Roosevelt had to deal with public attitudes that turned more militantly against Japan than against Germany. In early August those opposing war with Japan outnumbered those favoring it by more than three to one, while by late November twice as many as not were *expecting* war between their country and Japan in the near future.

Doubtless the basic factor, though, was one of calculation, or analysis. Churchill, still responding to the bitter lessons of Munich, contended that a policy of firmness was precisely the way to earn peace; it was the democracies' vacillation that tempted aggressors to go to war. Roosevelt was not so sure that the Asiatic mind worked in just this way. Yet he went along with Churchill's theory of peace through firmness and with Hull's insistence on adherence to principles, rather than with Stimson's and Knox's urgent advice to stall the Japanese along in order not to be diverted from Atlantic First and in order to have time to prepare in the Pacific.

Later an odd notion would arise that the President, denied his direct war with Hitler, finally gained it through the "back door" of conflict with the Japanese. This is the opposite of what he was trying to do. He wanted to avoid war with Japan because—like all the grand strategists—he feared a two-front war, and American strategy was definitely set on fighting Hitler first. In another three or six months, after the Philippines and other Pacific outposts had been strengthened, the President might well have gone through the "back door" of war—but not in late 1941. Churchill's calculations, however, were more mixed. He could assume his stand-firm posture with far more equanimity than Roosevelt; the Prime Minister could reason that a Japanese-American break would probably bring the United States into the German war as well and thus realize London's burning hope of full American involvement. But much would depend on the strength of Berlin-Tokyo solidarity and on each nation's calculus of its interest. Churchill had to face the fearsome possibility that the United States might become involved *only* in the Pacific. Hence he, too, was following the Atlantic First strategy.

It was not Roosevelt's calculation that was at fault, but his miscalculation. And because he lacked the initiative, and was assuming the imperfect moral stand of condemning Hitlerism as utterly evil and bent on world domination without openly and totally combating it, he faced a thicket of secondary but irksome troubles. Labor was restive in the fall of 1941 as it saw its chance to get in on the war boom. For many businessmen it was still business as usual. The Supply Priorities and Allocations Board had been set up on top of OPM in August, but SPAB seemed to be working with little more effectiveness than its predecessors. Congress seemed incapable of passing an effective price-control bill. Military aid to Allies, though rising, was still inadequate in the face of gigantic demands, and the orderly flow of food and munitions was disrupted by sudden emergencies and shifting needs.

Henry L. Stimson, Secretary of War, was still insisting that ills such as these could be remedied only if the President assumed clear moral leadership, took the initiative against Germany, and established definite priorities at home and abroad. But Roosevelt would not yet ask for a declaration of war. Rather, he would try by management and maneuver to swing his nation's weight into the world balance.

To relations with Moscow in particular Roosevelt applied his most delicate hand. Russia's sagging defenses in the Ukraine had produced no reversal of opinion among Congress and people, or of policy in the White House. The hard-core isolationists still opposed aid to the Soviet Union and expressed gratification that Russians and Germans were bleeding one another to death; that conflict, said the Chicago

Tribune, was the only war for a century that civilized men could regard with complete approval. Roosevelt, who was holding all negotiations with the Kremlin tightly in his own hands, was granting dollars and other aid in small dabs while recognizing that Russia needed massive help. He took care not to propose—or even discuss—bringing the Soviets under Lend-Lease until after Congress passed a big fall appropriation for the program.

The President was showing his usual respect for public opinion, which as always was shrill, divided, inchoate, and waiting for leads. He was especially wary of Catholic feeling against involvement with Bolshevism. With his implicit encouragement, at least, his friend Supreme Court Justice Frank Murphy told fellow Catholics that Communism and Nazism were equally godless but the latter was godlessness plus ruthlessness. When the President, however, suggested to reporters that Russians had some freedom of religion under their constitution, religious leaders pounced on him for his "sophistry" and ignorance. Ham Fish proposed that the President invite Stalin to Washington and have him baptized in the White House pool. Roosevelt dispatched his envoy Myron Taylor back to Rome to sound out Pope Pius and to inform him that "our best information is that the Russian churches are today open for worship and are being attended by a very large percentage of the population." Taylor carried with him a letter from President to Pope granting that the Soviet dictatorship was as "rigid" as the Nazi, but that Hitlerism was more dangerous to humanity and to religion than was Communism. The Pope was little influenced by this view, and his doctrinal expert, Monsignor Domenico Tardini, bluntly stated that Communism was and always would be antireligious and militaristic and told the Pope privately that Roosevelt was apologizing for Communism. The Vatican did respond to Roosevelt a bit by restating doctrine in such a way as to enable Catholics to make a distinction between aiding Russians and aiding Communism. Roosevelt also tried to induce Moscow to relax its antireligious posture, but with little effect.

Clearly the great opportunist was having little impact on the great doctrinaire. But if the President hardly was leading a holy crusade for a full partnership of the antifascist forces, he was at least removing some of the roadblocks and allowing events to exercise their sway. Congress defeated moves to bar the President from giving Lend-Lease aid to Russia, and at the end of October the President without fanfare told Stalin that he could have one billion dollars in supplies. Yet the President paid a price for this success. He and his colleagues had to stress not the great ideals of united nations but the expedient need to help keep the Russian armies in the fight and thus to make American military intervention less necessary. Aid was extended for crass reasons of self-interest. The only link between Americans and Russians was a common hatred and fear of Nazism.

Stalin was not deceived. He wrote to Churchill in early November that the reasons for the lack of clarity in the relations of their nations were simple: lack of agreement on war and peace aims, and no second front. He could have said the same to Roosevelt.

The whole anti-Axis coalition, indeed, was in strategic disarray by late fall of 1941, even while it was co-operating on a host of economic, military, and diplomatic matters. Churchill was almost desperate over Washington's stubborn noninvolvement. He still had serious doubts about Russia's capacity to hold out; he had to face the nightmarish possibility of Britain alone confronting a fully mobilized Wehrmacht. As it was, he had to share American aid with Russia, and while he was eager to do anything necessary to keep the Bear fighting, he found it surly, snarling, and grasping. He still feared a Nazi invasion of Britain in the spring, and he was trying to build up his North African strength for an attack to the west. Stalin was always a prickly associate. A mission to Moscow led by Lord Beaverbrook and Averell Harriman had established closer working relations with the Soviets, but no mission could solve the basic problem that Russia was taking enormous losses while only a thin trickle of supplies was arriving through Archangel, Vladivostok, and Iran. As for China, which was at best third on the waiting list for American aid, feeling in Chungking ranged between bitterness and defeatism.

So if Roosevelt was stranded in the shoals of war and diplomacy, he was no worse off than the other world leaders in 1941. All had seen their earlier hopes and plans crumble. Hitler had attacked Russia in the expectation of averting a long war on two fronts; now he was engaged in precisely that. Churchill had hoped to gain the United States as a full partner, but had gained Russia; he had wanted to take the strategic initiative long before, but had failed; he doubted that Japan would take on Britain and America at the same time, but events would prove him wrong. Stalin had played for time and lost; now the Germans, fifty miles west of Moscow, were preparing their final attack on it.

All the global forces generated by raw power and resistance, by grand strategies and counterstrategies, by sober staff studies and surprise blows—all were locked in a tremulous world balance. Only some mighty turn of events could upset that balance and release Franklin Roosevelt from his strategic plight.

On November 1, 1941, the new leaders of Japan met to decide the issues they had debated since assuming office two weeks before. Should they "avoid war and undergo great hardships"? Or decide on war immediately and settle matters? Or decide on war but carry on diplomacy and war preparations side by side? These were the alternatives as Premier Tojo framed them for his colleagues: Foreign Minister Togo, Finance Minister Okinori Kaya, Navy Minister Shigetaro Shimada, Navy Chief of Staff Osami Nagano, Planning Board Director Teiichi Suzuki. Also present were members of the military "nucleus": Army Chief of Staff General Sugiyama, the Army Vice Chief of Staff, the Navy Vice Chief of Staff, and others.

It was a long meeting—seventeen hours— and a stormy one. Pressed by a skeptical Togo and Kaya as to whether the American fleet would attack Japan, Nagano replied, "There is a saying, 'Don't rely on what won't come.' The future is uncertain; we can't take anything for granted. In three years enemy defenses in the South will be strong and the number of enemy warships will increase."

"Well, then," Kaya said, "when can we go to war and win?"

"Now!" Nagano exclaimed. "The time for war will not come later!"

The discussion went on. Finally it was agreed to pursue war preparations and diplomacy simultaneously. The burning issue was the timing of the two and their interrelation. The early deadline, said Tojo, was outrageous. A quarrel broke out so intense that the meeting had to be recessed; operations officers were called in to consider the timing question from a technical viewpoint. The military chiefs conceded that it would be all right to negotiate until five days prior to the outbreak of war. This would mean November 30.

"Can't we make it December 1?" asked Tojo. "Can't you allow diplomatic negotiations to go for even one day more?"

"Absolutely not," Army Vice Chief of Staff Tsukada said. "We absolutely can't go beyond November 30. Absolutely not."

"Mr. Tsukada," asked Shimada, "until what time on the 30th? It will be all right until midnight, won't it?"

"It will be all right until midnight."

Thus, as the army records of this session noted, a decision was made for war; the time for its commencement was set for the beginning of December; diplomacy was allowed to continue until midnight, November 30; and if diplomacy was successful by then, war would be called off. The conference then debated two alternative proposals for negotiation. The crucial point of Proposal A was that Japanese troops could be stationed in strategic areas of China until 1966. Proposal B would largely restore the *status quo ante* the July freeze: the two nations would undertake not to advance by force in Southeast Asia or the South Pacific; Japanese troops in Indochina would move to the northern part of the country; the United States would help Japan obtain resources in the Dutch East Indies and would supply annually a million tons of oil; the United States would not obstruct "settlement of the China incident." The military preferred A because it posed the crucial question of China and would settle it quickly one way or the other—but fearing that Tojo might resign and topple the whole Cabinet, they agreed also to support the broader, but hardly less severe, terms of B.

On November 5 Tojo presented this consensus to an imperial conference at the palace. All agreed that if the diplomats could not settle matters by December 1, Japan would go to war regardless of the state of negotiations at that time. The Emperor had nothing to offer on this occasion—not even verse.

It was another major step toward war, but the Japanese were still following their two-pronged approach. Nomura continued his discussions with Roosevelt and Hull and continued to receive sermons of peace, stability, and order in the Pacific. Roosevelt was still playing for time, but Hull's rigidity on principle was hardening as a result of MAGIC intercepts of Japanese coded messages indicating the dominance of the military and its timetable. Each side was now looking to its allies. Japan, which had edged away from Berlin as the Wehrmacht slowed in Russia, was now drawing closer to its partner in case of need. Hull told Nomura that he might be lynched if he made an agreement with Japan while Tokyo had a definite obligation to Germany.

The paramount issue was still China. When Nomura came back to the White House on November 17, this time with Saburo Kurusu, who had come from Tokyo as special ambassador to expedite the discussions, Roosevelt again urged the withdrawal of Japanese troops from China; once the basic questions were settled, he said, he would be glad to "introduce" Japan and China to each other to settle the details. After Kurusu failed to budge on this question Roosevelt retreated to homilies; there were no long-term differences preventing agreement, he said.

Empty words. It was becoming increasingly clear that there were few misunderstandings between the two countries, only differences. Despite much confusion the two governments understood each other only too well. Their interests diverged. They could not agree. When the Tokyo diplomats in desperation presented Proposal B, now softened a bit but still providing an end to American aid to China, Hull dismissed the contents as "of so preposterous a character that no responsible American official could ever have accepted them"—even though Tokyo meant them only as a stopgap, and Stark and Marshall found them acceptable as a way to stave off war.

Word arrived from Chungking that Chiang was completely dependent on American support and was agitated about reports of temporizing in Washington.

Undaunted, Roosevelt by now was working up a truce offer of his own. Around the seventeenth he had penciled a note to Hull:

6 Months

1. U.S. to resume economic relations—some oil and rice now—more later.
2. Japan to send no more troops to Indo-China or Manchurian border or any place south (Dutch, Brit. or Siam).

3. Japan to agree not to invoke tripartite pact if U.S. gets into European war.

4. U.S. to *introduce* Japs to China to talk things over but U.S. take no part in their conversations. Later on Pacific agreements.

This was Roosevelt's most ambitious specific truce formula in the dying days of peace, and its short life and early death summed up the intractable situation. Hull combined Roosevelt's plan with other proposals, American and Japanese, and cut the period to three months. On the twenty-second a message from Tokyo to Nomura and Kurusu was intercepted; it warned that in a week "things are automatically going to happen." Cabling Churchill the essence of the American proposal, Roosevelt added that its fate was really a matter of internal Japanese politics. "I am not very hopeful and we must all be prepared for real trouble, possibly soon." On the same day the Chinese Ambassador, Dr. Hu Shih, objected vigorously to letting Tokyo keep 25,000 men in northern Indochina. Chiang was wondering, he said, whether Washington was trying to appease Japan at the expense of China. The Dutch and the Australians were dubious about concessions.

Churchill was worried, too. ". . . Of course, it is for you to handle the business," he cabled to Roosevelt, "and we certainly do not want an additional war. There is only one point that disquiets us. What about Chiang Kai-shek? Is he not having a very thin diet? Our anxiety is about China." If it collapsed, their joint dangers would enormously increase. "We are sure that the regard of the United States for the Chinese cause will govern your action. We feel that the Japanese are most unsure of themselves." Perhaps Roosevelt would have persevered. But on the morning of the twenty-sixth Stimson telephoned him an intelligence report of Japanese troop movements heading south of Formosa.

The President fairly blew up—"jumped up into the air, so to speak," Stimson noted in his diary. To the President this changed the whole situation, because "it was evidence of bad faith on the part of the Japanese that while they were negotiating for an entire truce—an entire withdrawal (from China)—they should be sending their expedition down there to Indo-China." Roosevelt's truce formula died that day. In its stead Hull drew up a ten-point proposal that restated Washington's most stringent demands.

The whole matter had been broken off, Hull told Stimson. "I have washed my hands of it and it is now in the hands of you and Knox—the Army and the Navy." Shortly Stimson phoned the President again; the time had come, they agreed, for a final alert to MacArthur.

Diplomatic exchanges continued for a while, like running-down tops. On November 26 Hull presented Nomura and Kurusu with his ten points; Kurusu said that Japan would not take its hat off to Chiang—the proposals were not even worth sending to Tokyo. *November 27*— the President warned the two envoys at the White House that if Tokyo followed Hitlerism and aggression he was convinced beyond any shadow of a doubt that Japan would be the ultimate loser; but he was still ready to be asked by China and Japan to "introduce" them for negotiations, just as he had brought both sides together in strike situations. *November 28* —Nomura and Kurusu received word from Tokyo that they would soon have an elaboration of its position and the discussions would then be "de facto ruptured"; but they were not to hint of this. *November 29* (Tokyo time) at the liaison conference: Togo: "Is there enough time left so that we can carry on diplomacy?" Nagano: "We do have enough time." Togo: "Tell me what zero hour is. Otherwise I can't carry on diplomacy." Nagano: "Well, then, I will tell you. The zero hour is"—lowering his voice—"December 8." *November 30*—at Warm Springs for a belated Thanksgiving with the patients, the President took a telephone call from Hull urging him to return to Washington because a Japanese attack seemed imminent; he left immediately. *December 1*—Premier Tojo at the Imperial Conference: "At the moment our Empire stands at the threshold of glory or oblivion." The Chiefs of Staff asked the Emperor's permission to make war on X day. Hirohito nodded his head. He seemed to the recorder to be at ease. *December 2*—Roosevelt, through Welles, demanded of Nomura and Kurusu why their government was maintaining such large forces in Indochina. *December 3*—Tokyo handed Berlin and Rome its formal request for intervention; Mussolini professed not to be surprised considering Roosevelt's "meddlesome nature." *December 4*—the President concluded a two-hour conference with congressional leaders with the request that Congress not recess for more than three days at a time. *December 5*—some in the White House were still considering reviving the ninety-day truce proposal, if only to gain time. *December 6*—Roosevelt worked on an arresting message to Hirohito urging a Japanese withdrawal from Indochina and the dispelling of the dark clouds over the Pacific.

Almost a century before, he reminded the Emperor, the President of the United States had offered the hand of friendship to the people of Japan and it had been accepted. "Only in situations of extraordinary importance to our countries need I address to Your Majesty messages on matters of state." Such a time had come. The President dwelt on the influx of Japanese military strength into Indochina. The people of the Philippines, the East Indies, Malaya, Thailand were alarmed. They were sitting on a keg of dynamite. The President offered to gain assurances from these peoples and even from China —and offered those of his own nation—that there would be no threat to Indochina if every Japanese soldier or sailor were to be withdrawn therefrom. Clearly the President was not engaging in serious negotiation here; it was one more effort to stall off a showdown.

"I address myself to Your Majesty at this moment in the fervent hope that Your Majesty may, as I am doing, give thought in this definite emergency to ways of dispelling the dark clouds. . . ."

It was like a gigantic frieze in which all the actors move and yet there is no motion. While diplomats were deadlocked, however, the military was acting with verve and precision. In September Japanese carriers and their air groups had started specific training for Pearl Harbor, with the help of a mock-up as big as a tennis court. On October 5 one hundred officer pilots of the carrier air groups got the heady news that they had been chosen to destroy the American fleet in Hawaii early in December. On November 7 Admiral Isoroku Yamamoto set December 8 as the likely date because it was a Sunday. During mid-November the striking force of six carriers, two battleships, two cruisers, and nine destroyers put out from Kure naval base and rendezvoused in the Kuriles. On November 25 Yamamoto, from his flagship in the Inland Sea, ordered the advance into Hawaiian waters, subject to recall. On December 2 he broadcast the phrase "NIITAKE-YAMA NOBORE" (Climb Mount Niitaka)—the code for PROCEED WITH ATTACK! Meantime, other Japanese fleet units and scores of transports were moving into positions throughout the southern seas.

And Roosevelt? In this time of diplomatic stalemate and military decision he was still waiting, now almost fatalistically. "It is all in the laps of the gods," he told Morgenthau on December 1. As late as December 6 he would tell Harold Smith that "we might be at war with Japan, although no one knew." The President was pinioned between his hopes of staving off hostilities in the Pacific and his realization that the Japanese might not permit it; between his promise to avoid "foreign" wars and his deepening conviction that Tokyo was following Nazi ways and threatened his nation's security;

between his moral and practical desire to stand by the British and Dutch and Chinese and his worry that thereby he might be directly pulled into a Pacific war. He was pinioned, too, between people—between Hull, with his curious compound of moralizing and temporizing, and the militants, such as Morgenthau, who was pleading with the President not to desert China, and Ickes, who was ready to resign if he did; between the internationalists in the great metropolitan press and the isolationists in Congress; even between the "pro-Chinese" in the State Department and the "pro-Japanese," including Grew, and finally between the polled citizens who said he was going too far in intervening abroad and those who said he was doing too little.

Pinioned but not paralyzed. The President's mind was taken up by probabilities, calculations, guesses, alternatives. By the early days of December he felt that a Japanese attack south was probable. It was most likely to come, he thought, in the Dutch East Indies; next most likely in Thailand, somewhat less likely in the Philippines, and least probable—to the extent he thought about it at all—in Hawaii. If the Japanese attacked British territory he would give Churchill armed support, the nature and extent depending, much as in the Atlantic, on the circumstances; if the Japanese attacked Thailand or the East Indies, Britain would fight and Roosevelt would provide some kind of armed support; if the Japanese attacked China from Indochina, he would simply step up aid to Chungking.

At this penultimate hour Roosevelt was extending his Atlantic strategy to the Pacific. It was not a simple matter of "maneuvering the Japanese into firing the first shot," for the Japanese were probably going to fire the first shot; the question was where the United States could respond, how quickly, and how openly and decisively. What Roosevelt contemplated was a replica of his support of Britain in the Atlantic, a slow stepping-up of naval action in the southern seas, with Tokyo bearing the responsibility for escalation. He had asked and received permission from the British and Dutch to develop bases at Singapore, Rabaul, and other critical points—a repetition of his acquisition of Atlantic bases the year before. He did not concentrate on the Atlantic at the expense of the Pacific; he did not leave things unduly to Hull. He could not; the pressures were too heavy. But he did apply to the Pacific the lessons of his experience in the Atlantic.

It was a dangerous transfer, for it fostered Roosevelt's massive miscalculation as to where the Japanese would strike first. Since he had reason to believe that he was confronting another Hitlerite nation in the East, he assumed that Tokyo would follow the Nazi method of attacking smaller nations first and then isolating and encircling the larger ones. He told reporters, off the record, on November 28 that the Japanese control of the coasts of China and the mandated islands had put the Philippines in the middle of a horseshoe, that "the Hitler method has always been aimed at a little move here and a little move there," by which complete encirclement was gained. "It's a perfectly obvious historical fact today." But Roosevelt was facing a different enemy, with its own tempo, its own objectives—and its own way with a sudden disabling blow.

When general plans fail, lesser plans, miscalculations, technical procedures, and blind chance have a wider play. During the evening of December 6 the Japanese carriers reached the meridian of Oahu, turned south, and amid mounting seas sped toward Pearl Harbor with relentless accuracy. In Tokyo a military censor routinely held up the message from Roosevelt to Hirohito. If it had been in plain English he would not have dared hold up such an awesome communication; if it had been in top-priority code he would not have known enough to; but Roosevelt had sent it in gray code to save time, and it finally arrived too late. In the Japanese Embassy in Washington a many-part message began to come in from Tokyo; the parts were sent down to the coding room, but the cipher staff drifted off to a party, the fourteenth section was delayed, and the embassy closed down for the night. At the War and Navy Departments, signals experts received the first thirteen parts through their MAGIC intercept and swiftly decoded them; copies were rushed to the White House and to Knox and Navy chiefs, but not to Admiral Stark, who was at the theater, nor—inexplicably—to General Marshall, who was understood to be in his quarters.

At 9:30 P.M. a young Navy officer brought the thirteen parts to the oval study. The President was going over stamps, meanwhile chatting with Hopkins, who was sitting on the sofa. The President read rapidly through the papers. All day he had been receiving reports of Japanese convoy and ship movements in the Southwest Pacific.

"This means war," the President said as he handed the sheaf to Hopkins.

For a few moments the two men talked about likely Japanese troop movements out of Indochina. It was too bad, Hopkins said, that the Japanese could pick their own time and America could not strike the first blow.

"No, we can't do that," Roosevelt said. "We are a democracy and a peaceful people." Then he raised his voice a bit.

"But we have a good record."

In the dark early-morning hours scores of torpedo planes, bombers, and fighters soared off the pitching flight decks of their carriers to the sound of "Banzai!" Soon 183 planes were circling the carriers and moving into formation. At about 6:30 they started south. Emerging from the clouds over Oahu an hour later, the lead pilots saw that everything was as it should be—Honolulu and Pearl Harbor bathed in sunlight, quiet and serene, the orderly rows of barracks and aircraft, the white highway wriggling through the hills—and the great battlewagons anchored two by two along the mooring quays of Pearl Harbor. It was a little after 7:30 A.M., December 7, 1941. It was the time for war.

On the American ships this Sunday morning sailors were sleeping, eating breakfast, lounging on deck. Some could hear the sound of church bells. A bosun's mate noticed a flight of planes orbiting in the distance but dismissed it as an air-raid drill. Then the dive bombers screamed down, and the torpedo bombers glided in. Explosions shattered the air; klaxons squalled general quarters; a few antiaircraft guns began firing; colors were raised. Bombs and torpedoes hit the *West Virginia*, instantly knocking out power and light, disemboweling her captain, and soon sinking the ship to the shallow bottom. The *Tennessee*, protected by the *West Virginia* against torpedoes, took two bombs, each on a gun turret. The *Arizona* had hardly sounded general quarters when a heavy bomb plunged through the deck and burst in a forward magazine; more bombs rained down on the ship, one hurtling right down the stack; a thousand men burned to death or drowned as the ship exploded and listed. A torpedo tore a hole as big as a house in the *Nevada*, which nonetheless got under way to sortie, but then, under heavy bombardment, ran aground. Three torpedoes struck the *Oklahoma*; men scrambled over her starboard side as she rolled, only to be strafed and bombed. By now Japanese planes were attacking at will, pouring bombs and machine-gun fire on destroyers, seaplane tenders, minelayers, dry docks, ranging up and down the coast attacking airfields and infantry barracks.

The flash was received in Washington. AIR RAID PEARL HARBOR—THIS IS NO DRILL. "My God!" Knox exclaimed. "This can't be true, this must mean the Philippines!" He telephoned the President, who was sitting at his

The Japanese attack at Pearl Harbor caught United States army and naval forces completely by surprise. Japanese aircraft sank or severely damaged 5 battleships, 3 cruisers, and several smaller vessels, and demolished 177 airplanes. American casualties were staggering: 2,343 dead, 1,272 injured, and 876 missing. Hit by Japanese bombs and torpedoes, the West Virginia *and the* Tennessee—*as shown in this photograph—sank in a holocaust of fire and smoke. (U.S. Navy Photo.)*

desk in the oval study talking with Hopkins about matters far removed from the war. There must be some mistake, Hopkins said; surely the Japanese would not attack Honolulu. The report probably was true, Roosevelt said; it was just the kind of unexpected thing the Japanese would do. The President was calm, almost relaxed; he seemed like a man who had just got rid of a heavy burden. He had hoped to keep the country out of war, he remarked to Hopkins, but if the report was true, Japan had taken the matter out of his hands. Then, just after 2:00 P.M., he telephoned the news to Hull.

The Secretary had been at his office all morning reading intercepts of Tokyo's message. Nomura and Kurusu, whose embassy was still struggling with the translation, were due in around two. Just as they arrived, Hull received Roosevelt's telephone call. In a steady, clipped voice the President advised Hull to receive the envoys, look at their statement as though he had not already seen it, and bow them out. Hull kept the Japanese standing while he pretended to read their note. Was Nomura, he asked, presenting this document under instructions from his government? Nomura said he was. Hull fixed him in the eye. "I must say that in all my conversations with you during the last nine months I have never uttered one word of untruth.... In all my fifty years of public service I have never seen a document that was more crowded with infamous falsehoods and distortions—infamous falsehoods and distortions on a scale so huge that I never imagined until today that any Government on this planet was capable of uttering them." Nomura seemed to struggle for words. Hull cut him off with a nod toward the door.

By now the President was getting first reports on losses, calling in the War Cabinet, dictating a news release to Early. Later Churchill telephoned. The Prime Minister had been sitting with Harriman and Winant at Chequers when a vague report came in over the wireless about Japanese attacks in the Pacific. A moment later his butler, Sawyers, had confirmed the news: "It's quite true. We heard it ourselves outside...." It took two or three minutes to reach the White House. "Mr. President, what's this about Japan?" Yes, it was true. "They have attacked us at Pearl Harbor. We are all in the same boat now."

For Churchill it was a moment of pure joy. So he had won, after all, he exulted. Yes, after Dunkirk, the fall of France, the threat of invasion, the U-boat struggle—after seventeen months of lonely fighting and nineteen months of his own hard responsibility—the war was won. England would live; the Commonwealth and the Empire would live. The war would be long, but all the rest would be merely the proper application of overwhelming force. People had said the Americans were soft, divided, talkative, affluent, distant, averse to bloodshed.

But he knew better; he had studied the Civil War, fought out to the last desperate inch; American blood flowed in his veins.... Churchill set his office to work calling Speaker and whips to summon Parliament to meet next day. Then, saturated with emotion, he turned in and slept the sleep of the saved and thankful.

In Washington the shattering specifics were now coming in. So noisy and confused was the President's study that Grace Tully moved into his bedroom, where she took the calls from an anguished Admiral Stark, typed each item while Pa Watson and the others looked over her shoulder, and rushed them to her boss. She would long remember the agony and near-hysteria of that afternoon. Roosevelt's early mood of relief was giving way to solemnity and anger. He was tense, excited, shaken. Stimson and Knox were incredulous; they could not understand why Pearl Harbor was sustaining such losses. During the evening, as reports of landings in Oahu came in, Marshall said the rumors reminded him of the last war. "We're now in the fog of battle."

The President found relief in action. He went over troop dispositions with Marshall; ordered Stimson and Knox to mount guards around defense plants; asked Hull to keep Latin-American republics informed and in line; ordered the Japanese Embassy protected and put under surveillance. When the room cleared he called in Grace Tully and began dictating a terse war message. He was calm but tired.

At 8:40 Cabinet members gathered in the study. Roosevelt nodded to them as they came in, but without his usual cheery greetings. He seemed solemn, his mind wholly concentrated on the crisis; he spoke to his military aides in a low voice, as if saving his energy. The group formed a small horseshoe around their chief.

It was the most serious such session, the President began, since Lincoln met with his Cabinet at the outbreak of the Civil War. He reviewed the losses at Pearl Harbor, which by now were becoming exaggerated in the shocked

Navy reports. He read aloud a draft of his message to Congress. Hull urged that the message include a full review of Japanese-American relations, and Stimson and others wanted a declaration of war against Germany as well as Japan. The President rejected both ideas.

By now congressional leaders were crowding into the study: Speaker Sam Rayburn, Republican Leader Joseph Martin, Democrats Connally, Barkley, Bloom, Republicans McNary, Hiram Johnson, and others (but not Hamilton Fish, whom even at this juncture Roosevelt would not have in the White House). The newcomers gathered around the President's desk while the Cabinet members moved into outer seats. They sat in dead silence as the President went over the long story of negotiations with Japan. He mentioned the last Japanese note, full of "falsehoods."

"And finally while we were on the alert—at eight o'clock—half-past seven—about a quarter past—half past one [here]—a great fleet of Japanese bombers bombed our ships in Pearl Harbor, and bombed all of our airfields. . . . The casualties, I am sorry to say, were extremely heavy." Guam and Wake and perhaps Manila had been attacked, he went on. "I do not know what is happening at the present time, whether a night attack is on or not. It isn't quite dark yet in Hawaii. . . . The fact remains that we have lost the majority of the battleships there."

"Didn't we do anything to get—nothing about casualties on their side?" someone asked.

"It's a little difficult—we think we got some of their submarines but we don't know."

"Well, planes—aircraft?"

The President could offer no comfort. He seemed to Attorney General Francis Biddle still shaken, his assurance at low ebb.

The Navy was supposed to be on the alert, Connally burst out. "They were all asleep! Where were our patrols? They knew these negotiations were going on." The President did not know. But it was no time for recriminations. The fact was, he said again, that a shooting war was going on in the Pacific. When someone finally said, Well, Mr. President, this nation has got a job ahead of it, and what we have got to do is roll up our sleeves and win the war," Roosevelt quickly seized on the remark. He arranged to appear before Congress the next day, without revealing what he would say.

People had been gathering around the White House all day, pressing against the tall iron fence in front, milling along the narrow street to the west, clustering on the steps of the old State Department Building and behind the green-bronze Revolutionary War cannon and anchor. They peered at the White House, incredulous, anxious, waiting for some sign or movement. Evening came, and a misty, ragged moon. People were now five deep behind the iron railings, their faces reflecting the glow of the brightly lighted mansion; trolleys ran back and forth on Pennsylvania Avenue behind them. Reporters at the front portico watched Cabinet members and Congressmen arrive. To correspondent Richard Strout they looked grim going in, glum coming out. He watched Hiram Johnson, stern, immaculate, stalk across the little stone stage of the portico, and all the ghosts of isolationism seemed to stalk with him. By now the moon was high and the crowd was thinning. From across the White House fountain and grounds a few high, cracked voices could be heard singing "God Bless America."

Inside, in his study on the second floor, Roosevelt was gray with fatigue when he finished his emergency conferences late that night. Edward R. Murrow had won an appointment long before and expected it to be canceled, but Roosevelt called for him to share sandwiches and beer. The President was still aroused, almost stunned, by the surprise attack. He poured out to Murrow the information he had on losses. Pounding his fist on the table, he exclaimed that American planes had been destroyed "on the ground, by God, on the ground!"

Next day, round after round of applause greeted the President as he slowly made his way to the rostrum of the House of Representatives.

"Yesterday, December 7, 1941—a date which will live in infamy—the United States of America was suddenly and deliberately attacked by naval and air forces of the Empire of Japan.

"The United States was at peace with that Nation and, at the solicitation of Japan, was still in conversation with its Government and its Emperor looking toward the maintenance of peace in the Pacific. Indeed, one hour after Japanese air squadrons had commenced bombing in the American Island of Oahu, the Japanese Ambassador to the United States and his colleague delivered to our Secretary of State a formal reply to a recent American message. And while this reply stated that it seemed useless to continue the existing diplomatic negotiations, it contained no threat or hint of war or of armed attack."

The chamber was dead quiet. The President was speaking with great emphasis and deliberateness.

"It will be recorded that the distance of Hawaii from Japan makes it obvious that the attack was deliberately planned many days or even weeks ago. During the intervening time the Japanese Government has deliberately sought to deceive the United States by false statements and expressions of hope for continued peace.

"The attack yesterday on the Hawaiian Islands has caused severe damage to American naval and military forces. I regret to tell you that very many American lives have been lost. In addition American ships have been reported torpedoed on the high seas between San Francisco and Honolulu.

"Yesterday the Japanese Government also launched an attack against Malaya.

"Last night Japanese forces attacked Hong Kong.

"Last night Japanese forces attacked Guam.

"Last night Japanese forces attacked the Philippine Islands.

"Last night the Japanese attacked Wake Island.

"And this morning the Japanese attacked Midway Island."

A long pause. The chamber was still quiet.

"Japan has, therefore, undertaken a surprise offensive extending throughout the Pacific area. The facts of yesterday and today speak for themselves. The people of the United States have already formed their opinions and will understand the implications to the very life and safety of our Nation.

"As Commander in Chief of the Army and Navy I have directed that all measures be taken for our defense.

"But always will our whole Nation remember the character of the onslaught against us."

Applause broke out and quickly died away.

"No matter how long it may take us to overcome this premeditated invasion"—the President's voice was rising with indignation—"the American people in their righteous might will win through to absolute victory."

At last the chamber exploded in a storm of cheers and applause.

"I believe that I interpret the will of the Congress and of the people when I assert that we will not only defend ourselves to the uttermost but we will make it very certain that this form of treachery shall never again endanger us.

"Hostilities exist. There is no blinking at the fact that our people, our territory, and our interests are in grave danger.

"With confidence in our armed forces—with the unbounding determination of our people—we will gain the inevitable triumph—so help us God.

"I ask that the Congress declare that since the unprovoked and dastardly attack by Japan on Sunday, December 7, 1941, a state of war has existed between the United States and the Japanese Empire."

24

This Mighty Endeavor

Charles B. MacDonald

an eye toward future political developments, wanted to strike through the Balkans, Germany's "soft underbelly." Not only would this hit Germany where she was weakest; it would also keep the Russians out of Eastern Europe. But Roosevelt and Dwight Eisenhower both rejected a Balkan invasion. For them, pecking away at the perimeter of Hitler's empire seemed a waste of time and men. What American planners wanted was to strike Hitler where he was strongest—in France, along the Normandy coast—and steamroll Nazi armies in a relentless drive into Germany itself. The Russians enthusiastically endorsed the American plan, and grudgingly Churchill too came around. In top secret, the Allies began building up in England the largest invasion force in history. Here is the story of that invasion, told so vividly that one can almost feel the tossing waves and hear the roaring guns as Allied landing craft churned toward the ledges of Normandy.

On December 11, 1941, Germany and Italy declared war on the United States; and the nation found itself involved in a two-front global conflict. American strategy was to hold the line in the Pacific and to throw everything into beating Hitler first. Once Germany fell, then the United States would unleash all its might against the Japanese.

Even though the country was already in a condition of semimobilization, it took a year before the United States was ready to fight a total war. At last, in November, 1942, an American expeditionary army landed in North Africa and went on to help the British whip German Panzer divisions there. Then an Anglo-American force invaded Sicily and drove onto the Italian mainland itself.

The bloodiest fighting, though, occurred in Russia, where three German armies drove inexorably eastward. The Nazi offensive almost reached the gates of Moscow before the Russians held. There followed a series of titanic engagements which culminated in the battle of Stalingrad, where the Russians eliminated a German army of 250,000 and began to drive the invaders back toward Poland.

All along Stalin had implored the Western Allies to create an effective second front that would draw German manpower out of Russia. Churchill, with

Most of the top names assembled for the invasion were comfortably familiar: Eisenhower himself. "Beetle" Smith, experienced Chief of Staff. As deputy commander, the British airman, Tedder, who had spent 1943 as a close associate of Eisenhower's heading the Mediterranean Allied Air Forces. Commanding the 21st Army Group, General Montgomery was to serve also as over-all ground commander. (Although Eisenhower found Montgomery acceptable, he would have preferred Alexander.) Calm, dependable, though unspectacular, Omar Bradley was the top American ground officer—a result both of Bradley's proven ability and of George Patton's choler. Bradley was to head the First U.S. Army under Montgomery but was to move up to command an army group and to become Montgomery's equal once another American army under Patton came ashore. Bradley's counterpart

From "Cross-Channel Attack" in *The Mighty Endeavor* by Charles B. MacDonald. New York: Oxford University Press, 1969. Reprinted by permission of the author.

as an army commander under Montgomery was less well known: General Sir Miles Dempsey, commanding the Second British Army. Also new to the cast was Leigh-Mallory, head of the tactical air arm, and Lieutenant General Henry R. D. G. Crerar, who would command a followup force, the First Canadian Army.

A familiar figure as former British naval chief in the Mediterranean, Admiral Bertram H. Ramsay was to be Allied Naval Commander-in-Chief. While Admiral Stark remained in command of U.S. Naval Forces in Europe, the top American under Ramsay was to be Rear Admiral Alan G. Kirk, new to the top hierarchy of command but long experienced in convoy duty and a student of amphibious warfare. Kirk was to command the ships supporting American troops, called the "Western Task Force."

To deceive the Germans into believing the landings were to hit the Pas de Calais, Eisenhower's staff devised a variety of subterfuges, including a fictitious "Army Group Patton," presumably massed just across the Channel along the coast near Dover. Dummy installations, false radio traffic, dummy landing craft in the Thames estuary, deceptive information fed to known enemy agents, huge tent encampments, and a careful plan of aerial bombardment to concentrate more bombs on the Pas de Calais than anywhere else—all perpetuated a fiction that would be continued well past D Day, even after Patton himself joined the fighting.

Just how successful was the program the Allies did not know for certain until events unfolded on the beaches. In combination with the logical German mind, it was strikingly successful. None among Hitler's military high command in France and the Low Countries doubted that the invasion would strike the Pas de Calais.

Hitler himself, who substituted intuition for the shortcomings of his military education, saw it otherwise. He suddenly announced in March that the Allies were likely to land on the Cotentin and Brittany peninsulas. His naval commander in France soon echoed this appreciation, calling particular attention to the Cotentin; but once having correctly divined Allied intentions, the naval commander relaxed on the theory that, having failed to attack the coastal batteries on the Cotentin, the Allies were not yet ready to invade.

Hitler's ground commanders in France were convinced, on the contrary, that invasion was soon to come. The Commander-in-Chief in the West, Field Marshal Gerd von Rundstedt—venerable, wizened old soldier, respected paragon of all that was good and right with the German Officer Corps, he who in 1940 had sparked the penetration through the Ardennes that led to Dunkirk—looked toward the Pas de Calais. So did his top field commander, the head of *Army Group B,* the "Desert Fox," Erwin Rommel.

Like Hitler, Rundstedt and Rommel recognized that in the grave danger of invasion also lay the opportunity for turning defeat into victory. If they could thwart the invasion, the Allies would be unlikely to mount another for a long time: that would enable the Germans to shift perhaps fifty divisions to regain the initiative against the Russians and end the war in the east in time to meet a new threat in the west.

Yet there a meeting of minds ended.

Rundstedt had little faith that his troops, even when bolstered by formidable fortifications of what had become known as the "Atlantic Wall," could stop an invasion on the beaches. He believed instead in a powerful mobile reserve to be held well behind the line and rushed forward to counterattack once the Allies had revealed the site of their main landings.

Rommel, for his part, considered Allied aerial superiority too great to warrant any reliance on a mobile reserve. Repel the invaders at the water line, Rommel believed, or fail.

The divergent views might have made little difference, except that, like all holders of a marshal's baton, both Rommel and Rundstedt theoretically had direct access to Hitler, and the former had specific authority to use it. In first sending Rommel to France late in 1943, Hitler had charged him personally to plan for the defeat of the invasion and had made him responsible not to Rundstedt but directly to OKW, the Armed Forces High Command. Even after Rommel and Rundstedt agreed early in 1944 that Rommel could better serve as commander of *Army Group B* under Rundstedt, the onus of direct responsibility for repelling the invasion remained with Rommel and with it something of the special tie to OKW. Rommel, too, was the more forceful personality—energetic, assured, ready to argue with Hitler—whereas Rundstedt was disposed to avoid dispute by giving in to his volatile *Fuehrer*.

The old field marshal nevertheless could turn a trick or two. Convinced that his theory of defeating the invasion by counterattack was right, he created a special headquarters called *Panzer Group West* to command all armored units in France, subject to his command, not to Rommel's.

That prompted Rommel to a ploy of his own. If he was to be responsible for repelling the invasion—he told Hitler at a meeting of senior commanders in March of 1944—he required control not only of the armored units but of artillery reserves as well. In addition to commanding the two armies comprising *Army Group B* along the Channel coast, he required some control over two others along the southwestern and southern French coasts in case he needed to call on them for help. Hitler agreed.

For all the damage to Rundstedt's pride, it would have been better for the German cause had Hitler stuck by that decision, since that would at least have ensured a unified command in France. Yet this time Rundstedt stood up to his *Fuehrer*. The protest he put in writing drew such support from the Armed Forces High Command that Hitler relented, but only partially. He split the armored reserve, giving a portion to Rundstedt as a central reserve, assigning a portion to Rommel. Hitler thus deprived not one but both commanders of all available means for influencing the battle.

While Rundstedt continued to champion his theory of victory through counterattack (but without adequate means to achieve it), Rommel pursued his strategy of do-or-die on the beaches. He withdrew his troops from the training they sorely needed, and put them to erecting underwater obstacles, sowing mines, digging in artillery pieces, planting fields with slanting poles to counter paratroopers and gliders (*Rommelsspargel*, "Rommel's asparagus," the soldiers called them)—trying feverishly in the uncertain time left to create a barrier some four miles deep that would ensure victory by enabling the defenders to hit with full strength at the moment the invaders touched down, that moment when those coming ashore would be most vulnerable.

To a devotee of maneuver, as Rommel had proved himself to be in North Africa, it was galling to rely on a fixed defense. Yet what other choice in the face of Allied planes? The mounting Allied aerial campaign against French railroads, plus sabotage by the French Resistance, was so destructive that by June the German transportation system in France was at the point of collapse. Of two dozen bridges over the Seine River between Paris and the sea, eighteen were destroyed, three more severely damaged. What choice, too, given the quality and quantity of German troops available in France?

The divisions in France had long served as a replacement pool for the man-eating Russian front. Late in 1943, Hitler decreed that the west was no longer to be cannibalized to succor the east; but in March of 1944, as Hungary appeared about to pull out of the war, and as the Russians plunged forward two hundred miles, he modified his stand. Divisions from occupied countries that had been earmarked to move to France on first word of the invasion, left instead for the east. So did an entire SS panzer corps from France with two SS panzer divisions, plus all the assault guns of four infantry divisions.

As Hungary docilely accepted occupation, and the Soviet armies outran their supply lines, Hitler was able to repair some of the damage. Yet of the fifty-eight divisions available to Rundstedt, many were burned out from fighting in the east, others were training and so-called static divisions which the sound of Allied guns would summarily upgrade to combat status, and still others were newly formed, of which some were of creditable combat value, some only partially equipped and trained. None compared with the conquering legions of the early months of the war. Units that at one time had boasted of their all-German "racial purity," were in the spring of 1944 laced with "racial Germans" from border areas of adjacent countries, with "volunteers" from allied and occupied countries, and with auxiliaries recruited from Russian prisoners of war. Although the west had priority on tanks during the first half of 1944, the defenders who looked warily across the Channel remained far different from the force that had gazed at the same waters four years before. Moreover they could count on nothing like the grandeur they once had known in the air; the *Luftwaffe* in France was down to fewer than two hundred planes, little more than half of which could operate at any one time.

Faced with but one Allied invasion and that against the Pas de Calais, the German forces nevertheless would have been a formidable foe, perhaps superior to men stepping disorganized onto a hostile shore even in vast numbers and with strong fire support. For a long time Rundstedt and the others took comfort in that reckoning, but events in Italy made them doubt. Grossly overestimating Allied resources, they wondered why the Allies tolerated a stalemate in Italy. When late in January there came the landing at Anzio which seemed to have little tactical connection with the main front in Italy, and when John Lucas failed to push out into the Alban Hills, many on the German side were convinced that the Allies intended to attract and pin down German units with a number of subsidiary landings before striking the main blow. German commanders in France became increasingly wary of committing everything to counter an Allied invasion lest more powerful landings follow elsewhere.

That consideration served to color Rundstedt's and Rommel's thinking when in late April, Hitler began to insist that the invasion would hit the Cotentin and demanded that forces there be strengthened. His field commanders at last saw some merit in Hitler's concern, but not much. On the theory that the Allies might make subsidiary landings in the Cotentin, probably airborne landings, they sent there a few battalions and an infantry division. The main landings, they continued to believe, would strike the Pas de Calais. Even the German naval commander, for all his earlier prescience, came around to that view.

As D Day neared, the German order of battle was much as Allied intelligence pictured it. In keeping with an assigned responsibility for the critical Pas de Calais, the *Fifteenth Army*, with nineteen divisions, was the stronger of the two armies along the Channel coast. Charged with defense of the Cotentin and Brittany peninsulas, the *Seventh Army* had thirteen divisions, but only six of them in Normandy. Five panzer divisions stood behind the *Fifteenth Army*, only one behind the *Seventh Army*, and two in southern France.

As May turned into June, the Germans remained ignorant of the time and place of the invasion. An agent in the British Embassy in Ankara had reported the code name—OVERLORD—but nothing more. German intelligence also had learned that the BBC would broadcast the first line of a poem by the nineteenth-century French poet, Paul Verlaine, as a signal to the French Resistance that invasion was imminent, while broadcast of the second line would mean invasion within forty-eight hours. Yet few German commanders had faith in that information. As Field Marshal von Rundstedt's intelligence officer put it, the Allies would be absurd to announce over the radio in advance when they were coming.

One who did believe was the intelligence officer of the *Fifteenth Army* in the Pas de Calais, Lieutenant Colonel Hellmuth Meyer. On the night of June 1 one of Meyer's monitors picked up the first message, the first line of Verlaine's "Chanson d'Automne"—*Les sanglots longs des violons de l'automne.* Meyer was anxiously awaiting the second line when on the night of the third his men monitored the message that the negligent apprentice teletype operator had sent from London:

EISENHOWER'S HQ ANNOUNCED
ALLIED LANDINGS IN FRANCE.

That threw Meyer for a moment, but not for long. His continuing vigil at last paid off when on the night of June 5 the BBC finally came through with the second line of Verlaine's poem: *Blessent mon coeur d'une langueur monotone.*

Meyer burst excitedly with the news into a room where the *Fifteenth Army* commander, Generaloberst Hans von Salmuth, was playing bridge. Salmuth failed to share Meyer's excitement but, to be prudent, he ordered his army to the alert. Then he went back to his cards.

Rundstedt's and Rommel's headquarters also got the word, but neither put out a general alert. They considered it unlikely that the messages actually meant anything out of the ordinary, while the weather augury for an invasion was anything but favorable. Rundstedt's staff in a blockhouse in the Paris suburb of St.-Germain-en-Laye continued planning for an inspection trip the Commander-in-Chief was to make to Normandy the next day. Rommel had left his command post in a chateau at La Roche-Guyon, along the Seine, for a visit with his wife in Germany. Furthermore, the German navy was not worried: with gale-force winds lashing the Channel, nobody would attempt an invasion. Also unperturbed, the *Luftwaffe* in France went on with the process of transferring its feeble fighter squadrons to airfields closer to Germany, where they might help combat the great aerial armadas that were pummeling the Reich.

Only the *Seventh Army* along the coasts of Normandy and Brittany failed to learn of the messages on the BBC. Because of the foul weather the *Seventh Army* commander, Generaloberst Friedrich Dollmann, canceled a practice alert for the night of June 5. At a corps headquarters in St. Lô, only a few miles from the Cotentin coast, the corps staff readied a surprise midnight birthday party for the commander. They had to celebrate early because their chief was leaving before dawn for Brittany, where he was to join General Dollmann and a number of division commanders in a war game to be fought on maps.

In the concrete bunkers and blockhouses of the Atlantic Wall, looking out on squall-drenched beaches and a raging surf, sentries of the *Seventh Army's* forward divisions relaxed, as confident as were their commanders that nobody would try to come ashore on a night like that.

On the other side of the Channel, General Eisenhower early in May had set the date for June 5: that day when the vanguard of more than four million Allied troops was, as the Combined Chiefs had ordered, to "enter the continent of Europe and ... undertake operations aimed at the heart of Germany and the destruction of her armed forces."

Late in May they had begun to brief lower-level commanders and the troops themselves on what they were to do. In the process they sealed them in great barbed-wire enclosures along the southern coast of England and detailed some two thousand counterintelligence agents to guard them. All contact by the men inside was severed with a countryside already cordoned off from the rest of the world.

The vast paraphernalia for staging the most complex military operation of all time was waterproofed and ready. Much of the material had become commonplace—the artillery, antiaircraft guns, DUKW's, ambulances, jeeps, trucks, halftracks, tanks, bulldozers, observation planes, landing craft, steel mesh mats for footing on sand and for constructing airfields, field kitchens, aid stations, hospital tents. Ready for early followup were such big items as locomotives and rolling stock. To transport and provide fire support for the invaders, the Allies had assembled almost 5,000 ships, the largest armada the world has ever seen: landing craft, troop transports, Liberty ships, coasters, mine sweepers, almost 900 warships ranging from torpedo boats to battle wagons, even midget submarines to guide assault craft through early morning darkness to the beaches. American air strength alone totaled almost 13,000 planes, including more than 4,500 big bombers.

There were special devices as well. Lest the Germans employ gas, all men carried gas masks and wore uniforms impregnated with a malodorous chemical that made the clothing stiff and hot until it got wet; then it became soggy and slimy. Some tanks wore canvas bloomers so they could swim. Ready for laying on the floor of the Channel were great coils of big rubber hose for piping fuel to feed hungry trucks and tanks—PLUTO, for "Pipe Line Under the Ocean." Ready for towing across the Channel was the most revolutionary device of all—two artificial, prefabricated harbors with the code name MULBERRY. They consisted of an inner breakwater constructed of hollow, floating concrete caissons six stories high, which were to be sunk and anchored in position, and a floating pier which would rise and fall with the tide while fixed on concrete posts resting on the bottom of the sea. Ponton-supported treadway bridging would connect the piers with the shore, while old cargo ships were to be sunk to provide an outer breakwater.

On May 30 the troops began to climb gangways to landing craft and transports in harbors all along the southern and southwestern coasts of England. By the third day of June all who were to go by sea were crammed aboard. Those that were to go by air stood on close alert, reading, writing letters, playing cards or dice, some shaving their heads to look like Indian braves, daubing war paint on their faces.

All was ready but the weather. The prophet upon whom General Eisenhower depended to predict that, Group Captain J. M. Stagg of the Royal Air Force, had been optimistic at first; but the night of Saturday, June 3, all optimism vanished. The day Eisenhower had chosen for the invasion, Stagg revealed, would be overcast and stormy with high winds and a cloud base too low for flying. Furthermore, Stagg went on, conditions were so unsettled that he could venture no forecast more than twenty-four hours ahead.

The first step was to call back convoys that already had put to sea, then to face the terrible dilemma that Stagg's revelation posed. June 5 was out. As Eisenhower pondered the alternatives on Sunday, the fourth (the day the Fifth Army entered Rome), wind and rain swirled around his command trailer. If they were unable to go on Tuesday, the sixth, the next three days still would provide reasonable tidal conditions; but getting off on any of those days was doubtful, since convoys already at sea would have to be recalled and refueled. The next time when tides would be right was June 19, but that date would afford no moonlight for the airborne troops. The nineteenth and the first possible date in July would mean disembarking troops already briefed and keyed up for the invasion. Even if morale might be sustained, what of security? What, too, of the loss of that much more good campaigning weather on the Continent? What of the perils if the enemy brought new, revolutionary weapons to bear? Already a special arm of British intelligence had warned that the Germans might be capable of contaminating the beaches with a curtain of radioactive materials.

As Eisenhower and the other principals gathered that Sunday night in the library of Southwick House—Admiral Ramsay's headquarters near Portsmouth—rain continued to fall, the wind to blow. When Group Captain Stagg began his briefing, faces were tense.

He had no good news, Stagg revealed quickly,

but he had encouraging news. His meteorologists, he said, had spotted a new weather front which should move up the Channel the next day. The rains would stop, the winds would decrease but not desist, the cloud cover would rise enough for bombers to operate much of the night of the fifth and the morning of the sixth. The cloud base at H hour on the sixth might be just high enough to enable observers to spot for naval gunfire. Later in the day the clouds would thicken, the weather would deteriorate again.

To the eager questions that followed, Stagg could say only that the weathermen had done their best. They could make no guarantee of even those merely tolerable conditions.

Eisenhower had little time left to decide. If D Day was to be Tuesday, the sixth, convoys carrying American troops from ports in southwestern England would have to get the order within half an hour.

One by one Eisenhower polled his subordinates.

His Chief of Staff, "Beetle" Smith, said without qualification to go. Conscious of their immense responsibility for helping put the ground troops ashore, the airmen were less definite. At best, said Leigh-Mallory and Tedder, an assault on the sixth would be "chancy."

When it came to the ground commander, General Montgomery, he hesitated not a moment. "I would say—go!"

Yet the final decision could only be made by the Supreme Commander himself. At 9:45 P.M., Eisenhower spoke. "I'm quite positive we must give the order. I don't like it, but there it is. I don't see how we can possibly do anything else."

At a final briefing after midnight to review the weather situation in case it had taken a turn for the worse, Eisenhower confirmed the decision. After three and one-half years of waiting, D Day for Operation OVERLORD, the invasion of the Nazi-held Continent, at last was set. Airborne troops would begin dropping before daylight. Seaborne American troops would start arriving on French beaches at 6:30 A.M.; within the next hour, depending upon tidal conditions, British and Canadian troops on beaches farther east.

The decision was irrevocable.

D Day was to be Tuesday, the sixth of June.

A little before 9 P.M. on the fifth, more than a dozen little British and American mine sweepers approached so close to the Norman coast that men aboard could make out scattered villas on the waterfront. Nobody in the big blockhouses on the shore spotted them. Their job done, the little craft moved back to sea—all but one, the U.S.S. *Osprey*, which detonated a mine, caught fire, and sank with OVERLORD's first losses, six American sailors. Out in the Channel the mine sweepers found a gusty wind still blowing at twelve to twenty knots and stirring up waves five feet high.

D Day was fifteen minutes old when the first Allied soldiers came to Normandy. They were pathfinders and special assault teams of three airborne divisions, the vanguard of 18,300 who were to arrive by air. One division was British, ordered to seal off the left flank of the Allied beachhead by seizing bridges over the Orne River near Caen and by destroying others. Two were American—the 82d and the 101st—with the assignment of assuring success on the Allied right flank by capturing exits of causeways leading across two miles of marshland from a sloping stretch of sand that would forever after be known as "UTAH Beach."

As intrepid men and women of the Resistance moved to appointed secret tasks all over France, Allied planes sowed paratroopers broadcast. Trying to evade antiaircraft fire which rose in ever-increasing volume, pilots shifted and shunted their vulnerable, slow-flying C-47 transport planes this way and that. Black clouds interfered, too; and many a pathfinder had failed to reach the drop zone he was to have marked.

The men came down like pollen scattered by the winds, some as much as thirty-five miles from where they were supposed to land. Hun-

The Normandy Invasion, June 6, 1944. Men and supplies pour onto Omaha Beach, while ships of the gigantic Allied fleet are anchored off shore. Barrage balloons (visible in the background) were to protect against German air attacks. (Courtesy of The National Archives.)

dreds plummeted into vast stretches of lowland that the Germans had flooded to augment their defenses; weighted down by their equipment, trapped in their harness, unknown numbers drowned. Many landed full on German positions. Twenty came down in or close to the town square of Ste.-Mère-Église, behind UTAH Beach. One man dangled by his harness for more than two hours from the church steeple, playing dead, until the Germans finally cut him down and captured him. Two British troopers landed just beyond the veranda of a house that served as headquarters for a German division. The division commander himself helped capture them. Here, there, and everywhere men played out thousands of intense individual dramas—sometimes living through them, sometimes not. Many an American trooper held his breath time after time while he snapped a toy metal cricket to identify himself. The response might be a reassuring two snaps from another American, or it might be death from German guns.

Through it all Allied fighters and bombers ranged up and down the coast, hitting coastal batteries, radar sites, headquarters towns, traffic choke points. Before the day was out, Allied planes had flown 11,000 sorties and dropped nearly 12,000 tons of bombs. In keeping with the deception plan, a preponderance of the bombs again was reserved for the Pas de Calais.

As in Sicily, the dispersal of the airborne troops had a positive effect which to some degree offset the negative: it added immeasurably to a confusion that plagued the German foe. Excited cries of *"Fallschirmjaeger! Fallschirmjaeger!"* early began to pour into various German headquarters in such volume that it was impossible to fit into a pattern the places where the paratroopers were reported to be dropping.

Dummy paratroopers fused with firecrackers served for a time to deceive many German commanders. Others thought the real paratroopers were crewmen bailing out of ailing bombers. For some time that was the view at Rommel's headquarters, *Army Group B*. The dummies temporarily persuaded Rundstedt's staff that all the excitement signified nothing more than a raid or at worst a diversionary attack, certainly not the invasion. At one division headquarters the commander thought it the work of the French Resistance. Sentries in the blockhouses along the coast still could discern no evidence of invasion by sea, and those radar stations that survived Allied bombing reported no unusual traffic in the Channel.

Most of those who from the first were convinced the invasion was upon them were within the *Seventh Army*, those who had least expected to be hit. At the corps headquarters in St. Lô, where members of the staff were honoring their commanding general's birthday, first reports put a quick end to the revelry. As the corps passed on the word to army headquarters in Brittany, the Chief of Staff promptly ordered the entire *Seventh Army* to full alert. Yet some of those scheduled to engage in the map exercise early the next day already had left their commands or still did so, despite the alert. The commander of the *91st Division*, which had only recently come to Normandy in response to Hitler's concern about the Cotentin, died on the way at the hands of an American paratrooper.

The *Seventh Army's* Chief of Staff, who was sure that the invasion had begun and correctly pinpointed it from Caen to Ste.-Mère-Église, ordered the *91st Division* to counterattack. Since his superiors at *Army Group B* and Rundstedt's headquarters remained unconvinced, that was the only action higher German commanders took for several hours. The only panzer division along the threatened front, the *21st*, located southeast of Caen, stood to its guns and vehicles, but no orders came to move.

Hundreds of confused local combats were raging when shortly before dawn there came again the drone of planes, followed by a strange fluttering of gliders brushing the air. Men in the frail plywood craft closed their eyes, locked arms, and steeled themselves for the impact of landing. Most of the gliders of the British division made it to the proper landing zones, where they crash-landed in incredible disarray but nonetheless deposited the bulk of their passengers intact. Those of the 101st Airborne Division also made it for the most part, though *Rommelsspargel* and hedgerows of thick earth interlaced with trees and brush took an inevitable toll. The gliders bringing men of the 82d Airborne Division were harder hit. Fewer than half made the correct landing zone. The others crashed into hedgerows or buildings or carried their heavily laden occupants to watery deaths in the flooded marshes.

The first of the gliders was yet to come when Field Marshal von Rundstedt, at his headquarters in St.-Germain-en-Laye, became convinced that some kind of Allied assault was under way, probably a diversionary attack in support of larger landings to hit the Pas de Calais. Yet even diversionary attacks had to be defeated. Somewhere around 4 A.M., Rundstedt ordered two panzer divisions from positions behind the south wing of the *Fifteenth Army*—the closest to the threatened sector of the divisions under his as opposed to Rommel's control—to head for Caen and prepare to counterattack.

Having issued the orders, Runstedt reported what he had done to OKW, the Armed Forces High Command. Two hours later word came back to halt the divisions pending approval from Hitler. That approval would be a long time coming, for members of Hitler's staff at the retreat in the Bavarian Alps at Berchtesgaden saw no reason yet to disturb their leader's sleep: they might invoke one of those neurotic tantrums they all dreaded. Although Rundstedt as a field marshal and theater commander could have appealed directly to Hitler, he was too unsure himself whether the situation warranted commiting the armor to venture a personal call.

At the *Seventh Army*'s headquarters in Brittany, in the meantime, the persistent Chief of Staff had become more certain than ever that the invasion was at hand. A little before 5 A.M. he telephoned Rommel's headquarters to report without qualification that Allied ships were concentrating from the mouth of the Orne River near Caen to the mouth of the Vire River near Ste.-Mère-Église. The information prompted Rommel's own Chief of Staff to act in the name of his absent commander and order the waiting *21st Panzer Division* to head for Caen, but the division was destined to encounter crucial delays.

The job of defeating a seaborne invasion thus fell, as with the airborne invasion, primarily to those German soldiers already in position in the fortifications of the Atlantic Wall or in close reserve in coastal villages and towns. Many of them were aware that something was up, that this time the alert was no practice. They had heard the planes, the word that *Fallschirmjaeger* had landed behind them; but looking out into the gusty Channel where Allied ships were assembling, they still could discern no foe.

It was close to 5:30 A.M. when gathering light first began to reveal form in the mist over the sea. As yet more moments passed, men with field glasses glued to their eyes turned to their comrades in shocked incredulity. The sea, the entire horizon, had begun to come alive with ships, more ships than they would have believed possible for man to assemble in one place.

Fifteen minutes later the naval bombardment began: thundering salvos chewed the bluffs, crushed the villas, rocked the blockhouses. Then overhead roared more planes, wave after wave of bombers.

Out in the Channel, off forty miles of beach, organized pandemonium reigned. Men overburdened with ammunition, guns, and gear moved like automatons across slippery decks, then down rope ladders to landing craft bobbing treacherously in the water below. Officers everywhere were yelling commands of one kind or another; others shouted words or slogans meant for encouragement. Public address systems crackled. Men shook hands with companions. Many prayed, some silently, some aloud. Others were vomiting, miserable in a way that only he who has known a rough crossing of the Channel can comprehend.

Amid the seething mass of men and ships the throb of motors, the clank of landing craft against unyielding steel plates of the mother ships, big naval guns belched with such noise and vehemence toward the hostile shore that the ships appeared to rock deep in the water from the convulsive effort. Here and there angry coastal batteries tried to return the fire, but it was a one-sided duel. From behind a smokescreen three German torpedo boats tried briefly but generally ineffectively to inflict some hurt. Only one found a mark, a Norwegian destroyer; thereupon the torpedo boats scurried back to base, thus ending the German navy's sole contribution to D Day.

Out of the confusion somehow—few could say how—some kind of order emerged. The circles of churning landing craft increased in size as boats newly filled with humanity joined the formations; and amid the tossing waves they formed into rows and headed beneath the curtain of shellfire toward a shore that was but a dim, distant haze, a shore that planning officers long ago had subdivided and accorded peculiar names like "Easy Red," "Fox Green," "Dog White."

At UTAH Beach—that stretch of sloping sand lying between sea and marshes from which causeways led up to Ste.-Mère-Église—men of the U.S. 4th Division were lucky. For all the propaganda boasts, the Atlantic Wall was not everywhere the line of steel and concrete Hitler would have had the world believe. UTAH was one of the weak points, and a strong coastal current carried the landing craft over a mile from the planned landing site to a still weaker spot. In less than three hours men of the 4th Division were in full control of UTAH Beach and had begun to push over the causeways toward firm ground where paratroopers and glidermen anxiously awaited their arrival. The day's losses were remarkably low: 197 killed and wounded, plus another 13 dead when shore batteries sank a destroyer, the U.S.S. *Corry*.

Almost ten miles up the coast to the east the story was strikingly different. There on steep scrub-covered bluffs more than 150 feet high, behind a wide stretch of sand and a narrow carpet of stone shingle, the Atlantic Wall was much closer to being what Hitler had boasted it to be everywhere. Embedded in the sand below the high-tide mark was a devil's delight of obstacles designed to wreck landing craft—hedgehogs, tetrahedra, Belgian Gates, concrete cones, slanting poles topped with mines—the whole draped in barbed wire. In the sand, and particularly in narrow draws leading up through the bluffs, there were quilts of antitank and antipersonnel mines. At various levels on the bluffs and in the draws there were casemates, bunkers, blockhouses; many were equipped with big field pieces, others with multiple machine guns sighted through narrow slits to cover almost every inch of the sand below.

It was the added misfortune of the men who came ashore along that stretch of sand to find manning the defenses the *352d Infantry Division,* one of the best divisions in Normandy and one that Allied intelligence had failed to detect until the last moment. There, too, were high seas, for no land mass like the tip of the Cotentin peninsula which protected UTAH Beach existed to either left or right.

This was OMAHA Beach, a name destined to become a symbol for all that was risky, for all that was grim and terrible, about coming ashore on a hostile fortified beach on the coast of France that sixth day of June. There landed two regiments of the 1st Division and one of the 29th.

During the ten-mile run from mother ships to shore, misery piled upon misery for the thirty-odd men crammed with their fighting gear into each of the landing craft. The boats pitched and rolled; waves broke over the gunwales. Gagging, nothing left to vomit, some men lay awash on the floor of the boats, too miserable to care what happened to them. At least ten boats sank, too far away for the men to swim ashore; and those in the other boats had strict orders to get on with their task, leaving survivors to be picked up by rescue craft coming later.

As the other boats neared the shore, a rain of machine-gun fire peppered their bows. German field pieces, which nobody had believed could survive the pounding of the big naval guns, also opened fire, sending water skyward in geysers. Mortar shells, too, poured down.

Some landing craft went up in flames, the victims of shells or mines. Men slipped over the sides of others whenever they reached water shallow enough for wading—sometimes, to their regret, before—in order to avoid that agonizing moment when the ramp would drop and expose the guts of the small craft to the enemy's machine guns. Other men somehow found the courage to race down the ramps. Some miraculously lived to plow slowly through the water, weighted down by waterlogged uniforms and equipment. Some made it—perhaps one-third of them, maybe a few more—to gain hazardous cover at the base of a low sea wall or behind a line of dunes. Hundreds of others died— drowned, cut down as they left the landing craft, hit as they plodded through the surf or across the sea-washed sand.

Lest in the smoke and confusion supporting shells hit the men coming ashore, the naval fire had to lift, thus leaving the Germans free to turn full fury on the pathetic but frightening panorama below them. The little knots of infantrymen and engineers struggling like turtles across the sand could return little fire of their own, other than with rifles or an occasional machine gun or a mortar that somebody had managed to lug laboriously through the surf. The tanks with canvas bloomers which were to have provided early fire support were missing. At least half had sunk, victims of the turbulent sea. Only with the second wave of landing craft did any tanks touch down.

A spectator of the fractured formations arriving on OMAHA Beach during the early hours of June 6 would have deduced that the invasion had failed, or was about to fail. The first wave had been so shattered by the German fire that the next wave seemed almost to be making the first run. Most of the men who made it through the surf and across the sand were bunched along the sea wall, the line of dunes, or the fringe of shingle, in no position to neutralize any of the German guns. A strong coastal current had pulled many units from their appointed landing positions, so that there were many stretches of beach on which no American soldier had yet landed. German fire cut down one engineer after another who tried to get on with the task of demolishing the beach obstacles. Even those who managed to fix explosives to the obstacles found that they could not blow them lest they kill wounded infantrymen seeking cover behind them.

Many men had hoped to find an occasional bomb crater for cover, but the weather had disappointed them. Forced to bomb by instrument through the overcast, bombardiers in B-24 Liberators had delayed their bomb release for several seconds for safety's sake. That was too long. Not a single bomb struck either the beaches or the forward German defenses.

Amid the confusion other landing craft continued to arrive, some to take direct shell hits and go up in flame, others to find no path through the obstacles, but still others to grind their metal noses into the sand. Grass fires started by naval rockets or shells obscured German vision along some parts of the beach, enabling occasional boatloads to reach the edge of the shingle unscathed. Other men simply gritted their teeth and dashed through the German fire as fast as they could. While many fell, others made it, surprised at how much small-arms fire a man can pass through without getting hit.

A few tanks made it too: some of those with canvas floats came under their own power; others churned off landing craft that had managed to get close enough to shore to enable the tanks to disembark. An occasional bulldozer also arrived.

Three companies of Rangers meanwhile were attempting a mission deemed vital to successful landings at OMAHA Beach. They were to knock out a battery of six 155-mm. howitzers believed to be in position a few hundred yards to the west atop an almost sheer cliff called Pointe du Hoe, which towered one hundred feet above a narrow stretch of rocky beach. There it was job enough even to reach the beach without being pounded to pieces by the surf against outcroppings of rock. Touching down, the Rangers fired rockets carrying grapnels attached to ropes and rope ladders to hook into the top of the cliff. As the men began to climb, some Germans at the top opened fire, while others tried to cut the ropes. Having spotted the threat, a destroyer hove perilously close to shore to rake the cliff top with fire.

Less than five minutes after reaching shore, the first Rangers were throwing themselves over the lip of the cliff and clearing haggard, shell-shocked Germans from trenches and gun emplacements that proved to be empty of guns. The howitzers they discovered later in a grove of trees a few hundred yards inland, but the crews had fled. Elated, the Rangers spiked the guns; but hardly had they begun to dig to protect their little enclave when counterattacking Germans closed in. Not until two long days later did other American troops arrive to relieve the Rangers, whose strength of 225 was cut by half.

Back at embattled OMAHA Beach, German

observers were sending optimistic reports to their superiors. Debarkation, one said, had ceased. Dead and wounded littered the sand. Bodies bobbed in and out with the action of breaking waves. Men were cowering behind beach obstacles, as the advancing tide nipped at their heels. By 11 A.M. the commander of the *352nd Division* was so convinced he had won at OMAHA that he diverted local reserves to the east, where British troops were hitting his division's right flank.

Much of what the Germans reported was true and echoed many of the same fragmentary reports that were reaching American commanders offshore aboard the flagship U.S.S. *Augusta*. The beach was jammed with men, and enemy fire was obviously still highly effective. LCT's were milling around in the water like "a stampeded herd of cattle." Looking anxiously toward a shoreline barely discernible through haze and smoke, a grim-faced Omar Bradley began to lay plans for evacuating the beachhead and diverting subsequent waves to UTAH or British beaches.

But the drama of OMAHA Beach was not yet finished. Among those who crouched for cover along the sea wall and the shingle walked an intrepid few—officers, noncoms, privates, men of all ranks—who rose to the occasion. "They're murdering us here!" shouted a colonel amid the 29th Division's lone assault regiment at the west end of the beach. "Let's move inland and get murdered!" That division's assistant commander strode calmly here and there, encouraging men to rise, to begin the slow, frightening climb up the bluffs.

Near the other end of the beach in the sector of the 1st Division, a colonel exhorted his men with threat and hope. "Two kinds of people are staying on this beach," he yelled, "the dead and those who are going to die. Now let's get the hell out of here." Others tended to even more forthright persuasion. "Get your ass up that hill!" yelled a sergeant.

Here and there grim-faced men began to move. A few naval fire-support parties were ashore now and could bring the big guns to bear again without fear of killing their own men. Some destroyers came so close to shore that they risked grounding, and raked obvious enemy strongpoints. Here a bazooka man knocked out a pillbox; there a machine gunner neutralized another with rattling bursts of fire. In the surf valiant commanders of two circling landing craft decided to end their futile peregrinations and ram a way through the obstacles. Guns blazing, they made it. Seeing it could be done, others did it, too.

Up the bluffs the men climbed, slowly, painfully, some falling but others continued to inch forward. The more heavily defended draws, vital for getting vehicles off the beach, remained in German hands, but what mattered for the moment was that men were moving. German positions were collapsing. By noon small, disorganized parties were astride a little highway that runs along the bluffs, only a few hundred yards inland, but inland nevertheless.

Crisis still reigned at OMAHA, but defeat no longer mocked the men full in the face: courage, like fear, is contagious.

No such crisis arose up the coast to the east at British and Canadian beaches. There on strips of sand christened GOLD, JUNO, and SWORD, a Canadian and two British divisions operating under General Dempsey's Second British Army stormed ashore from half an hour to an hour later than the landings at UTAH and OMAHA. The men on these beaches benefitted from the additional naval bombardment the delays afforded. They benefitted, too, from the fact that the beaches sloped gently and had no towering bluffs behind, that German defenses were markedly weaker than at OMAHA, and that no top-ranked German division stood in the way. There stood a static division which included in its ranks impressed foreigners from eastern Europe. Early in the fighting, one battalion of foreigners broke, opening a gaping hole in the line.

Men died at all three of these beaches, many in as cruel a way as at OMAHA; but most pressed quickly inland. There, too, almost all the swimming tanks made it ashore early to provide the close, coordinated fire support the infantry required. There also the *Luftwaffe* made its lone strike of the day against ground troops, a single fruitless strafing run by two Focke-Wulf 190's. Some 250 sorties flown against the invasion armada were equally fruitless.

Before the day was out, British and Canadians were several miles inland; they were short of their assigned objectives of Bayeux and Caen, but sturdy tank and artillery support backed them up. Linkup was achieved with the paratroopers and glidermen who had taken and held bridges over the Orne and had knocked out a deadly German battery which might have enfiladed the landing sites. The defending German division was crushed. The commander, who earlier had helped capture two paratroopers at the edge of his veranda, was reduced to tears.

All the while the German *21st Panzer Division* was moving to counterattack the landings, and its commander and his superiors were secure in the knowledge that their predawn decision to send the panzers toward Caen was right. The greater numbers of British and Canadians employed in the assault wave, the depth they had penetrated—those facts were testament enough that here was the Allied main effort, the *Schwerpunkt* that every German officer was trained to search for.

It was noon before the panzer columns reached Caen, there to find streets piled high with debris from the day's bombings. French civilians further clogged the streets, walking, pushing perambulators filled with belongings, riding their omnipresent bicycles, trying somehow to escape a city almost sure to feel again the fury of Allied bombers. Over the Orne in Caen still stood only one bridge. Moving an entire panzer division across it and through the choked streets would take hours, perhaps days. The commander reluctantly ordered his columns to countermarch and bypass the city to the west.

At four o'clock in the afternoon the *21st Panzer Division* was finally in a position to attack. By that time a British division had established a firm hold on commanding ground four miles inland. When the British called in fire support from three of His Majesty's battleships standing offshore, one German column lost ten tanks in a matter of minutes. Although a company of panzer grenadiers slipped between JUNO and SWORD beaches to reach an observation point above the coast, there to gaze in awe at the naval power massed below, the rest of the *21st Panzer Division* ground painfully to a halt.

It was four o'clock in the afternoon, too, when Hitler at long last approved Rundstedt's employing the two other panzer divisions that the Commander-in-Chief in the west had tried to commit early in the day. By that time the clouds and the overcast that might have screened the tanks from Allied planes had blown away, and the tanks would be able to move only after dark. Because Hitler had slept and then vacillated, the power of those two divisions had been denied at a time when it well might have proved decisive.

Also impotently standing aside as Allied troops poured ashore was the rest of the armored reserve in France—five divisions. Just as impotent were the nineteen divisions of the *Fifteenth Army* in the Pas de Calais. These Rundstedt was saving for the main invasion that was yet to come. He who had focused attention on the Cotentin as the site of the invasion—Adolf Hitler—inexplicably agreed that Rundstedt was right.

Returning from Germany by automobile, Erwin Rommel had no part in the proceedings.

As the climactic day came to an end, the Allied beachheads fell far short of what Eisenhower and his associates had hoped for. They had sought holdings averaging six miles deep; yet at only a few points were Allied troops as much as five miles inland. Although seaborne British troops from SWORD Beach had linked with the British airborne division, and Canadians on JUNO and British on GOLD were in firm contact, nowhere else were any of the five beachheads joined. Because of a German pocket on the coastal side of Ste.-Mère-Église, the American 4th Division, for all the relative ease of coming ashore, had yet to link with the two American airborne divisions.

So widely scattered in the night drop, the airborne troops had waged a host of separate and small but nonetheless costly fights. Although a few bands of paratroopers had crossed the little Merderet River in hope of holding a bridgehead that might be exploited later to cut the neck of the Cotentin peninsula and isolate the port of Cherbourg, they were under a state of seige from the enemy's *91st Division*, and overall control of the airborne troops was yet to be established. Four thousand of them still had failed to join their units after the drop.

The 1st and 29th Divisions on OMAHA Beach held a precarious toehold on the enemy shore which was nowhere more than a mile and a half deep. Yet even at OMAHA optimism prevailed. Almost all the first tier of coastal villages was in hand: obscure Norman hamlets which in normal times smelled of cow manure, dairy products, new-mown hay but now gave off a brown odor of smoldering rubble and straw, a yellow smell of burned gunpowder, a green smell of death. They had names indelibly stamped into the senses of the men who fought there: Vierville-sur-Mer, Colleville, St. Laurent, les Moulins, le Grand Hameau.

The beach itself was still a shambles and was raked from time to time by German shelling, even occasionally by machine-gun and sniper fire from bypassed Germans reluctant to give up. Somewhere out in the surf rested twenty-six big artillery pieces and more than fifty tanks. Bodies still bobbed in the water. Wrecked landing craft, knocked-out tanks, abandoned bulldozers, and assorted residue of war littered the sand and the fringe of the sea. Men and supplies nevertheless continued to get ashore through the carnage, in considerable numbers even if not as many as the planners had envisaged. A regiment of the 29th Division which had been scheduled to land only on D plus 1, pushed in ahead of time to help extend the beachhead line. Much remained to be done if Allied troops were to stay ashore in Normandy, but hardly anybody on the Allied side was talking of failure.

Had the Allies known of the near bankruptcy on the German side, they would have had more cause for encouragement. General Dollmann's *Seventh Army* already had thrown into the battle every major unit that stood in the Cotentin, including the *21st Panzer Division*. Committing units from Brittany and elsewhere would take time and, as Rommel had been so aware, would expose them to the omnipresent *jabos,* the Allied fighter-bombers. Dollmann was reluctant in any case, in the same way Rundstedt and Hitler were reluctant about the Pas de Calais, to move much from Brittany lest the Allies stage a second landing there.

In the critical hour of trial in the west, a German army that had bled in North Africa, Sicily, Italy, and on the plains of Russia, had had to stand alone, with almost no help from the navy and the *Luftwaffe.* Although the adversary had been weak as he moved from sea to land, the German army had been weaker. It was an army that failed the tests of viligance and of intelligence. Combined with these failures, Allied power in the aggregate had prevailed.

Allied losses in some places were high. Possibly 2,500 men fell at bloody OMAHA. Once all the stragglers had made their way in, the American airborne divisions set their toll at 2,499 (some had predicted airborne losses of 80 per cent; these were losses of 15 per cent). The Canadians lost 1,047 men; the British, approximately 3,000. The Allied total was probably a little more than 9,000 of which probably one-third was killed.

What mattered more at the moment was that as many as 100,000 other Allied troops had made it safely ashore. That turned the casualty figures into something Allied commanders could accept.

Back in England a relieved Dwight D. Eisenhower authorized a message to be broadcast to the world: "Under the command of General Eisenhower, Allied naval forces, supported by strong air forces, began landing Allied armies this morning on the northern coast of France." (He is reputed to have torn up a note he had written to be released if the landings failed.)

Most people in Britain got the news at work. For many it was a relief—confirmation of something they had suspected, what with all the naval activity off the south coast, the steady drone of planes through the preceding night. Some groups burst spontaneously into singing "God Save the King." Others prayed. Church bells pealed. At noon, before a packed House of Commons, a shrewd Winston Churchill fed German apprehension by calling the invasion "the first of a series of landings in force upon the European Continent."

In the United States the news came in the middle of the night—on the east coast at 3:33 A.M.; on the west coast at 12:33 A.M. Here and there in a sleepy town lights nevertheless came on. People turned on their radios, went to the telephone, knelt in prayer. In America, too, church bells rang.

On the evening of June 6 in Britain, George VI spoke over the BBC. "The Lord will give strength unto his people," he quoted from the Book of Psalms; "the Lord will bless his people with peace."

Franklin Roosevelt called his people to prayer. "Almighty God—Our sons, pride of our nation, this day have set upon a mighty endeavor...."

25

The Falling Sun

Fletcher Knebel and
Charles W. Bailey II

Normandy was indeed the beginning of the end for Hitler's Third Reich. Thanks to incredible German errors and to masterful Allied planning and execution, the invasion was a miraculous success. With a foothold at Normandy, American, British, and French armies drove a wedge into German defenses and poured inland. As the Western Allies pushed toward Germany from the West, Russian armies drove in from the East. By May 1945—less than a year after D Day—German resistance had collapsed and the once mighty Reich was a smoldering ruin.

Meanwhile the United States had moved from a holding action in the Pacific to an aggressive, two-pronged island-hopping campaign. It began in June, 1943, with Admiral Chester Nimitz' forces attacking at Tarawa and Kwajalein and General Douglas MacArthur's command breaking through the Bismarcks Barrier. Eventually, MacArthur recaptured the Philippines and drove toward Manila, while Nimitz pushed toward Japan from the central Pacific.

Japan fought back desperately, sending out Kamikaze planes to slow the American advance. They took a terrible toll: 34 American ships sunk and 288 damaged. But the "Divine Wind" vengeance which the Kamikazes represented also cost the Japanese heavily: their losses were estimated at from 1,288 to 4,000 planes and pilots. Moreover, they could not stop American army and naval forces which moved on relentlessly, capturing Iwo Jima and then Okinawa, located just south of Japan itself.

From Okinawa, the United States planned to launch an all-out invasion of the Japanese home islands, to begin sometime in November, 1945. MacArthur himself thought relatively light casualties would be sustained in the initial fighting. But ultimately the losses would be staggering—especially if it took a year to break Japanese resistance, as some experts predicted. General Marshall, for his part, estimated that the invasion would cost the United States a half million men.

But the invasion never took place, because the United States soon had an awesome and terrible alternative. On July 16, 1945, after three years of top-secret development and production, American scientists successfully detonated an atomic bomb out on the New Mexico desert. Some scientists involved in the project urged privately that a demonstration bomb be dropped on an uninhabited island. But an advisory committee of scientists opposed any such demonstration and recommended that the bomb be used against Japan at once. Secretary of War Harry L. Stimson emphatically agreed: while the bomb would kill thousands of civilians, he argued, it would nevertheless shock Japan into surrender and save a half million American lives.

The final decision lay with Harry Truman, who had become President after Roosevelt had died of a brain hemorrhage back in April, 1945. "I regarded the bomb as a military weapon and never had any doubt that it should be used," Truman later wrote. "The top military advisers to the president recommended its use, and when I talked to Churchill he unhesitatingly told me that he favored the use of the atomic bomb if it might aid to end the war." On July 25, Truman ordered that atomic bombs be dropped on or about August 3, unless Japan surrendered before that date. Then the United States, Great Britain, and China sent the Japanese an ultimatum which demanded unconditional surrender. But the Japanese made no official reply. When August 3 passed and Japan fought on, Truman's fateful orders went into effect, and American B-29's unleashed two of those "superhuman fireballs of destruction"—one on Hiroshima and the other on Nagasaki—and brought the Pacific War to an abrupt and decisive end.

Since then, many people have questioned the wisdom of Truman's decision. What, after all, was the big hurry to drop the bomb? Was it merely to save American lives? Or was there some deeper, hidden motive behind Truman's orders? Several critics now contend that the bomb was not the only alternative open to Truman in July and August. They point out that the invasion of Japan was not scheduled until November, so Truman had plenty of time "to seek and use alternatives." He could have sought a Russian declaration of war, or he could have ignored the advisory committee of scientists and dropped a demonstration bomb to show Japan what an apocalyptic weapon it was. There was still time, these critics insist, to develop another bomb should the Japanese remain unimpressed. But Truman, in a remarkable display of "moral insensitivity," used the bomb because it was there to be used, and never questioned his position.

Other critics maintain that Truman employed the bomb with an eye toward postwar politics. In their view, the President wanted to end the war in a hurry, before Russia could get into the conflict, seize territory, and threaten America's role in the postwar balance of power. Still others contend that the United States could have offered the Japanese conditional surrender, or found other ways to demonstrate the bomb, and so could have ended the war before Russia entered it.

Many analysts, on the other hand, still defend Truman—still insist that his decision was a wise one which avoided a prolonged land invasion in which hundreds of thousands of people would have died. But for the people of Hiroshima and Nagasaki, the questions of political motivation and grand strategy did not matter. Nothing mattered to them but that searing flash of light which killed over 100,000 people, scarred and twisted thousands more, and left Hiroshima and Nagasaki alike a smoking, radioactive rubble.

Since then, a number of books have appeared about the atomic explosions at Hiroshima and Nagasaki. Among the best are John Hersey's *Hiroshima* (1946) and *No High Ground,* by Fletcher Knebel and Charles W. Bailey II. The latter volume recounts the entire history of the first atomic bomb at Hiroshima, from Truman's decision to use it, to the flight of the *Enola Gay* (the B-29 that dropped "Little Boy," as the bomb was called), down to the actual explosion and its cataclysmic results. Here Knebel and Bailey describe that explosion, narrating the experiences of several people who somehow lived through it. Their experiences have universal appeal, with implicit lessons about the horror of atomic war that speak directly to us in our own nuclear age.

The sounding of the all-clear signal in Hiroshima at 7:13 A.M. on August 6 made little change in the tempo of the city. Most people had been too busy, or too lazy, to pay much attention to the alert. The departure of the single, high-flying B-29 caused no more stir than its arrival over the city twenty-two minutes earlier.

As the plane flew out over the sea, Michiyoshi Nukushina, a thirty-eight-year-old fire-truck driver at the Hiroshima Army Ordinance Supply Depot, climbed onto his bicycle and headed for home. He had received special permission to quit his post half an hour before his shift ended. Wearing an official-duty armband to clear himself through the depot gates, and carrying a new pair of wooden clogs and a bag of fresh tomatoes drawn from the depot commissary, he headed home through the narrow streets of Hiroshima.

Nukushina crossed two of the seven river channels that divided the city into fingerlike islands and finally arrived at his home in Kako-

---

From pp. 135–155 in *No High Ground* by Fletcher Knebel and Charles W. Bailey II. Copyright © 1960 by Fletcher Knebel and Charles W. Bailey II. Reprinted by Harper & Row, Publishers, Inc.

machi precinct a little more than half an hour after leaving the firehouse. Propping his bicycle by an entrance to his small combination home and wineshop he walked inside and called to his wife to go get the tomatoes.

At this same instant, in a comfortable house behind the high hill that made Hijiyama Park a welcome variation in the otherwise flat terrain of Hiroshima, a mother named Chinayo Sakamoto was mopping her kitchen floor after breakfast. Her son Tsuneo, an Army captain fortunately stationed right in his home town, had left for duty with his unit. His wife Miho had gone upstairs. Tsuneo's father lay on the straw mat in the living room, reading his morning paper.

Off to the east and south of the city, a few men in air defense posts were watching the morning sky or listening to their sound-detection equipment. At the Matsunaga lookout station, in the hills east of Hiroshima, a watcher filed two reports with the air defense center. At 8:06, he sighted and reported two planes, headed northwest. At 8:09, he saw another, following some miles behind them, and corrected his report to include it.

At 8:14, the telephone talker at the Nakano searchlight battery also made a report. His sound equipment had picked up the noise of aircraft engines. Unidentified planes were coming from Saijo, about fifteen miles east of Hiroshima, and were heading toward the city.

The anti-aircraft gunners on Mukay-Shima Island in Hiroshima harbor could now see two planes, approaching the eastern edge of the city at very high altitude. As they watched, at precisely seventeen seconds after 8:15, the planes suddenly separated. The leading aircraft made a tight, diving turn to the right. The second plane performed an identical maneuver to the left, and from it fell three parachutes which opened and floated slowly down toward the city.

The few people in Hiroshima who caught sight of the two planes saw the parachutes blossom as the aircraft turned away from the city. Some cheered when they saw them, thinking the enemy planes must be in trouble and the crews were starting to bail out.

For three quarters of a minute there was nothing in the clear sky over the city except the parachutes and the diminishing whine of airplane engines as the B-29's retreated into the lovely blue morning.

Then suddenly, without a sound, there was no sky left over Hiroshima.

For those who were there and who survived to recall the moment when man first turned on himself the elemental forces of his own universe, the first instant was pure light, blinding, intense light, but light of an awesome beauty and variety.

In the pause between detonation and impact, a pause that for some was so short it could not register on the senses, but which for others was long enough for shock to give way to fear and for fear in turn to yield to instinctive efforts at self-preservation, the sole impression was visual. If there was sound, no one heard it.

To Nukushina, just inside his house, and to Mrs. Sakamoto, washing her kitchen floor, it was simply sudden and complete blackness.

For Nukushina's wife, reaching for the bag of tomatoes on her husband's bicycle, it was a blue flash streaking across her eyes.

For Dr. Imagawa, at his patient's city home, it again was darkness. For his wife, in the suburban hills to the west, it was a "rainbow-colored object," whirling horizontally across the sky over the city.

To Yuko Yamaguchi, cleaning up after breakfast in the rented farmhouse where she and her in-laws now lived, it was a sudden choking black cloud as the accumulated soot and grime of decades seemed to leap from the old walls.

Hayano Susukida, bent over to pick up a salvaged roof tile so she could pass it down the line of "volunteer" workers, did not see anything. She was merely crushed to the ground as if by some monstrous supernatural hand. But her son Junichiro, lounging outside his dormitory at Otake, saw a flash that turned from white to pink and then to blue as it rose and blossomed. Others, also at a distance of some miles, seemed to see "five or six bright colors." Some saw merely "flashes of gold" in a white light that reminded them—this was perhaps the most common description—of a huge photographic flashbulb exploding over the city.

The duration of this curiously detached spectacle varied with the distance of the viewer from the point in mid-air where the two lumps of U-235 were driven together inside the bomb. It did not last more than a few seconds at the most.

For thousands in Hiroshima it did not last even that long, if in fact there was any moment of grace at all. They were simply burned black and dead where they stood by the radiant heat that turned central Hiroshima into a gigantic oven. For thousands of others there was perhaps a second or two, certainly not long enough for wonder or terror or even recognition of things seen but not believed, before they were shredded by the thousands of pieces of shattered window glass that flew before the blast waves or were crushed underneath walls, beams, bricks, or any other solid object that stood in the way of the explosion.

For everyone else in history's first atomic target, the initial assault on the visual sense was followed by an instinctive assumption that a very large bomb had scored a direct hit on or near the spot where they were standing.

Old Mr. Sakamoto, who a moment before had been lounging on the living-room floor with his newspaper, found himself standing barefoot in his back yard, the paper still in his hand. Then his wife staggered out of the house, and perhaps half a minute later his daughter-in-law Miho, who had been upstairs, groped her way out also.

Dr. Imagawa had just reached for his medical satchel to begin the examination of his patient. When the blackness lifted from his senses, he found himself standing on top of a five-foot pile of rubble that had been the sickroom. With him, surprisingly, were both the sick man and the patient's young son.

Mrs. Susukida, flat on the ground amid the pile of old roof tiles, was left all but naked, stripped of every piece of outer clothing and now wearing only her underwear, which itself was badly torn.

Mrs. Nukushina had just time to throw her hands over her eyes after she saw the blue flash. Then she was knocked insensible. When she recovered consciousness, she lay in what seemed to her to be utter darkness. All around her there was only rubble where a moment earlier there had been her home and her husband's bicycle and the bag of fresh tomatoes. She too was now without clothing except for her underwear. Her body was rapidly becoming covered with her own blood from dozens of cuts. She groped around until she found her four-year-old daughter Ikuko. She saw no trace of her husband. Dazed and terrified, she took the child's hand and fled.

But Michiyoshi Nukushina was there, and was still alive, though buried unconscious inside the wreckage of his home. His life had been saved because the blast blew him into a corner where two big, old-fashioned office safes, used in the family wine business, took the weight of the roof when it fell and thus spared him from being crushed. As he came to, raised his head and looked around, everything seemed strangely reddened. He discovered later that blood from cuts on his head had gushed down over his eyelids, forming a sort of red filter over his eyes. His first conscious thought was that the emergency water tank kept on hand for fire-bombing protection was only one-third full. As his head cleared, he called for his wife and daughter. There was no reply. Getting painfully to his feet—his left leg was badly broken—he found a stick for a crutch and hobbled out of the rubble.

Hold out your left hand, palm down, fingers spread, and you have a rough outline of the shape of Hiroshima. The sea is beyond the fingertips. The back of the hand is where the Ota River comes down from the hills to the north. The spot where the bomb exploded is about where a wedding ring would be worn, just south of the main military headquarters and in the center of the residential-commercial districts of the city. Major Ferebee's aim was nearly perfect. Little Boy was detonated little more than two hundred yards from the aiming point on his target chart, despite the fact that it was released from a fast-moving aircraft over three miles to the east and nearly six miles up in the air.

Dropped with such precision, the bomb performed better than its makers had predicted. Several factors combined by chance to produce even more devastation than had been expected.

First was the time of the explosion. All over Hiroshima, thousands of the charcoal braziers that were the stoves in most households were still full of hot coals after being used for breakfast cooking. Almost every stove was knocked over by the massive blast wave that followed the explosion, and each became an incendiary torch to set fire to the wood-and-paper houses. In addition, where Oppenheimer had estimated casualties on the assumption that most people would be inside their air-raid shelters, almost no one in Hiroshima was sheltered when the bomb actually fell. The recent all-clear, the fact that it was a time when most people were on their way to work, the mischance by which there had been no new alert when the *Enola Gay* approached the city, the fact that small formations of planes had flown over many times before without dropping bombs, all combined to leave people exposed. Thus more than seventy thousand persons instead of Oppenheimer's estimate of twenty thousand were killed outright or so badly injured that they were dead in a matter of hours.

The initial flash spawned a succession of calamities.

First came heat. It lasted only an instant but was so intense that it melted roof tiles, fused the quartz crystals in granite blocks, charred the exposed sides of telephone poles for almost two miles, and incinerated nearby humans so thoroughly that nothing remained except their shadows, burned into asphalt pavements or stone walls. Of course the heat was most intense near the "ground zero" point, but for thousands of yards it had the power to burn deeply. Bare skin was burned up to two and a half miles away.

A printed page was exposed to the heat rays a mile and a half from the point of explosion, and the black letters were burned right out of the white paper. Hundreds of women learned a more personal lesson in the varying heat-absorption qualities of different colors when darker parts of their clothing burned out while lighter shades remained unscorched, leaving the skin underneath etched in precise detail with the flower patterns of their kimonos. A dress with blue polka dots printed on white material came out of the heat with the dark dots completely gone but the white background barely singed. A similar phenomenon occurred in men's shirts. Dark stripes were burned out while the alternate light stripes were undamaged. Another factor that affected injury was the thickness of clothing. Many people had their skin burned except where a double-thickness seam or a folded lapel had stood between them and the fireball. Men wearing caps emerged with sharp lines etched across their temples. Below the line, exposed skin was burned, while above it, under the cap, there was no injury. Laborers working in the open with only undershirts on had the looping pattern of shoulder straps and armholes printed on their chests. Sometimes clothing protected the wearer only if it hung loosely. One man standing with his arm bent, so that the sleeve was drawn tightly over his elbow, was burned only around that joint.

The heat struck only what stood in the direct path of its straight-line radiation from the fireball. A man sitting at his desk writing a letter had his hands deeply burned because the heat rays coming through his window fell directly on them, while his face, only eighteen inches away but outside the path of the rays, was unmarked. In countless cases the human body was burned or spared by the peculiarity of its position at the moment of flash. A walking man whose arm was swinging forward at the critical instant was burned all down the side of his torso. Another, whose moving arm happened to be next to his body, was left with an unburned streak where the limb had blocked out the radiation. In scores of cases people were burned on one side of the face but not on the other because they had been standing or sitting in profile to the explosion. A shirtless laborer was burned all across his back—except for a narrow strip where the slight hollow down his spine left the skin in a "shadow" where the heat rays could not fall.

Some measure of the heat's intensity can be gained from the experience of the mayor of Kabe, a village ten miles outside the city. He was standing in his garden and even at that distance distinctly felt the heat on his face when the bomb exploded.

After the heat came the blast, sweeping outward from the fireball with the force of a five hundred-mile-an-hour wind. Only those objects that offered a minimum of surface resistance—handrails on bridges, pipes, utility poles—remained standing. The walls of a few office buildings, specially built to resist earthquakes, remained standing, but they now enclosed nothing but wreckage, as their roofs were driven down to the ground, carrying everything inside down under them. Otherwise, in a giant circle more than two miles across, everything was reduced to rubble. The blast drove all before it. The stone columns flanking the entrance to the Shima Surgical Hospital, directly underneath the explosion, were rammed straight down into the ground. Every hard object that was dislodged, every brick, every broken timber, every roof tile, became a potentially lethal missile. Every window in the city was suddenly a shower of sharp glass splinters, driven with such speed and force that in hundreds of buildings they were deeply imbedded in walls—or in people. Many people were picking tiny shards of glass from their eyes for weeks afterward as a result of the shattering of their spectacles, or trying to wash out bits of sand and grit driven under their eyelids. Even a blade of grass now became a weapon to injure the man who tended it. A group of boys working in an open field had their backs peppered with bits of grass and straw which hit them with such force that they were driven into the flesh.

Many were struck down by a combination of the heat and the blast. A group of schoolgirls was working on the roof of a building, removing tiles as the structure was being demolished for a firebreak. Thus completely exposed, they were doubly hurt, burned and then blown to the ground. So quickly did the blast follow the heat that for many they seemed to come together. One man, knocked sprawling when the blast blew in his window, looked up from the floor to see a wood-and-paper screen across the room burning briskly.

Heat and blast together started and fed fires in thousands of places within a few seconds, thus instantly rendering useless the painfully constructed firebreaks. In some spots the ground itself seemed to spout fire, so numerous were the flickering little jets of flame spontaneously ignited by the radiant heat. The city's

Hiroshima after the atomic bomb. When the bomb exploded, thousands of people "were simply burned black and dead where they stood by the radiant heat that turned central Hiroshima into a gigantic oven. For thousands of others there was perhaps a second or two . . . before they were shredded by the thousands of pieces of shattered window glass that flew before the blast waves or were crushed underneath walls, beams, bricks, or any other solid object that stood in the way of the explosion." (Courtesy of Magnum Photos, Inc. Photo by Shunkichi Kikuchi.)

fire stations were crushed or burned along with everything else, and two-thirds of Hiroshima's firemen were killed or wounded. Even if it had been left intact, the fire department could have done little or nothing to save the city. Not only were there too many fires, but the blast had broken open the city's water mains in seventy thousand places, so there was no pressure. Between them, blast and fire destroyed every single building within an area of almost five square miles around the zero point. Although the walls of thirty structures still stood, they were no more than empty shells.

After heat, blast and fire, the people of Hiroshima had still other ordeals ahead of them. A few minutes after the explosion, a strange rain began to fall. The raindrops were as big as marbles—and they were black. This frightening phenomenon resulted from the vaporization of moisture in the fireball and condensation in the cloud that spouted up from it. As the cloud, carrying water vapor and the pulverized dust of Hiroshima, reached colder air at higher altitudes, the moisture condensed and fell out as rain. There was not enough to put out the fires, but there was enough of this "black rain" to heighten the bewilderment and panic of people already unnerved by what had hit them.

After the rain came a wind—the great "fire wind"—which blew back in toward the center of the catastrophe, increasing in force as the air over Hiroshima grew hotter and hotter because of the great fires. The wind blew so hard that it uprooted huge trees in the parks where survivors were collecting. It whipped up high waves on the rivers of Hiroshima and drowned many who had gone into the water in an attempt to escape from the heat and flames around them. Some of those who drowned had been pushed into the rivers when the crush of fleeing people overflowed the bridges, making fatal bottlenecks of the only escape routes from the stricken islands. Thousands of people were simply fleeing, blindly and without an objective except to get out of the city. Some in the suburbs, seeing them come, thought at first they were Negroes, not Japanese, so blackened were their skins. The refugees could not explain what had burned them. "We saw the flash," they said, "and this is what happened."

One of those who struggled toward a bridge was Nukushina, the wine seller turned fireman whose life had been saved by the big office safes in his house just over a half mile from "zero," the point over which the bomb exploded. Leaning on his stick, he limped to the Sumiyoshi bridge a few hundred yards away, where, with unusual foresight, he kept a small boat tied up, loaded with fresh water and a little food, ready for any possible emergency.

"I found my boat intact," he recalled later, "but it was already filled with other desperate victims. As I stood on the bridge wondering what to do next, black drops of rain began to splatter down. The river itself and the river banks were teeming with horrible specimens of humans who had survived and come seeking safety to the river."

Fortunately for Nukushina, another boat came by, operated by a friend who offered to take him on board.

"With his assistance, I climbed into the boat. At that time, they pointed out to me that my intestines were dangling from my stomach but there was nothing I could do about it. My clothes, boots and everything else were blown off my person, leaving me with only my loincloth. Survivors swimming in the river shouted for help, and as we leaned down to pull them aboard, the skin from their arms and hands literally peeled off into our hands.

"A fifteen- or sixteen-year-old girl suddenly popped up alongside our boat and as we offered her our hand to pull her on board, the front of her face suddenly dropped off as though it were a mask. The nose and other facial features suddenly dropped off with the mask, leaving only a pink, peachlike face front with holes where the eyes, nose and mouth used to be. As the head dropped under the surface, the girl's black hair left a swirling black eddy. . . ."

Here Nukushina mercifully lost consciousness. He came to five hours later as he was being transferred into a launch that carried him, with other wounded, to an emergency first-aid station set up on the island of Ninoshima in the harbor. There he found safety, but no medical care. Only twenty-eight doctors were left alive and able to work in a city of a quarter million people, fully half of whom were casualties.

When Hayano Susukida tried to get up off the ground onto which she and the other members of her tile-salvaging labor gang had been thrown, she thought she was going to die. Her whole back, bared by the blast, burned and stung when she moved. But the thought of her four-year-old daughter Kazuko, who had been evacuated from the city after Hayano's husband was sent overseas and the family home had been marked for destruction in the firebreak program, made her try again. This time she got to her feet and staggered home. The blast had not leveled her house, about a mile and a quarter from the zero point, and the fire had not yet reached it. Hurriedly she stuffed a few things—a bottle of vegetable oil, some mosquito netting, two quilts, a small radio—into an old baby carriage, and started wheeling it toward the nearest bomb shelter. After going a few feet, she had to carry the carriage, for the street was choked with debris. She reached the shelter and passed the oil around to those inside, using the last of it to salve her own burns, which had not blistered or peeled but were nevertheless strangely penetrating and painful. She wondered what time it was. Her wrist watch was gone, so she walked home again to get her alarm clock. It was still running; it showed a little after ten. Back at the shelter, she just sat and waited. At noon someone handed out a few rice balls. As the survivors ate, an Army truck miraculously appeared and carried them to the water front, just beyond the edge of the bomb's destruction. Then they were ferried over to the emergency hospital on Ninoshima Island.

Dr. Imagawa, a little further from the center of the blast, was not seriously injured, although he was cut by flying glass in a number of places. His first reaction was annoyance. His clothes were in tatters, and he wondered how he would find the new pair of shoes which he had left at his patient's front door. Helping the small boy down off the five-foot rubble pile that had been the sickroom, he asked the youngster to take him to the front door. Oddly enough, they could not even find where the front of the house had been. Imagawa, much to his disgust, was out a new pair of shoes. At an artesian well with a pump that was still operating, he washed as best he could and set out for suburban Furue where his wife and children should be. He stopped frequently in response to appeals for help from the injured. One was a woman who wandered aimlessly in the street holding her bare breast, which had been split open. She pleaded with him to tell her whether she would live. The doctor, although positive she could not survive, assured her that a mere breast injury would not be fatal. Later, he drew water for a score of wounded from another well pump. Down the street, a trolley car burned briskly. Finally he got clear of the city and climbed the hill to Furue, where he found his family safe and uninjured. The walls of the house had cracked and in some places fallen, but his wife and the two little children had escaped injury, while the oldest girl had walked home from school without a scratch after the blast. The doctor ate, washed thoroughly, painted his cuts with iodine and worked till dark with his wife cleaning up their house. That evening the somewhat sybaritic physician sat down to dinner and then relaxed, as he had done the night before in Hiroshima—twenty-four hours and an age earlier—over a few cups of wine.

The doctor sipping his wine that night had one thing in common with Mrs. Susukida and Michiyoshi Nukushina, both lying injured and untended in the emergency hospital on Ninoshima Island. None of them knew what it was that had destroyed their city. Nor did they yet have either time or inclination to wonder.

But others, outside Hiroshima, were anxiously trying to find out what the *Enola Gay* had dropped on the city. The search for information was a frustrating one.

At first there had been no indication that anything unusual had happened in Hiroshima. A moment after 8:16 AM., the Tokyo control operator of the Japanese Broadcasting Corporation noticed that his telephone line to the radio station in Hiroshima had gone dead. He tried to re-establish his connection, but found that he could not get a call through to the western city.

Twenty minutes later the men in the railroad signal center in Tokyo realized that the mainline telegraph had stopped working. The break seemed to be just north of Hiroshima. Reports began to come in from stations near Hiroshima that there had been some kind of an explosion in the city. The railroad signalmen forwarded the messages to Army General Headquarters.

It was almost ten o'clock when Ryugen Hosokawa, managing editor of the *Asahi* vernacular newspaper in Tokyo, received a telephone call at his home. It was the office, reporting that Hiroshima had "almost completely collapsed" as the result of bombing by enemy planes. Hosokawa hurried to the office and sifted through the reports collected by *Asahi*'s relay room. Every one of them sounded to him like something quite different from any previous bombing. This must have been caused, he thought to himself, by very unusual bombs.

At about the same time Major Tosaku Hirano, a staff officer of the II Army Corps, was in General Headquarters in Tokyo. He had come up from Hiroshima a week earlier to report on the status of military supplies in the port city, and had been scheduled to fly back on Sunday. But he had put his departure off for a day or two and thus was still in the capital.

Now his telephone rang. It was a call from Central Command Headquarters in Osaka, an installation under the control of the II Army Corps in Hiroshima, reporting that its communications to Hiroshima and points west had failed.

Tokyo GHQ tried several times to raise the Hiroshima communications center, in the earth-and-concrete bunker next to the moat of the old castle, but could not get through. There was no explanation. The succession of reports from the radio network, from the railroad signal center, from *Asahi*'s newsroom and from Osaka indicated that something serious had happened, but no one could find out what it was.

Then, shortly after 1 P.M., General Headquarters finally heard from the II Army Corps. The message was short but stunning: "Hiroshima has been annihilated by one bomb and fires are spreading."

This flash came not from Corps Headquarters but from the Army shipping depot on the Hiroshima water front, which was outside the blast area and was not reached by the fire that followed. There was considerable damage at the shipping depot, something in the neighborhood of 30 per cent, but officers there were able to get a message out as far as Kure, where the naval station relayed it to Tokyo. There was no word at all from the II Army Corps Headquarters at the old castle in the northern part of town.

Reports continued to trickle in. By the middle of the afternoon, the Army knew that only three enemy planes had been over Hiroshima when the bomb exploded. It had been told that two of these did not drop any bombs. This information supported the startling assertion in the first flash that there had been only one bomb exploded. Something very big, and very frightening, had hit Hiroshima.

In mid-afternoon the managing editors of the five big Tokyo newspapers, plus their counterpart in the Domei news agency, were called to the office of the government Information and Intelligence Agency, which had charge of press and radio censorship. An Army press officer addressed the little group of newsmen:

"We believe that the bomb dropped on Hiroshima is different from an ordinary one. However, we have inadequate information now, and we intend to make some announcement when proper information has been obtained. Until we issue such an announcement, run the news in an obscure place in your papers and as one no different from one reporting an ordinary air raid on a city."

In other words, the lid was on. The Army already had a strong suspicion that the Hiroshima bomb might be an atomic weapon. Japanese Naval intelligence had reported U.S. work on the bomb in late 1944, noting the interest of the American government in buying up all available pitchblende (uranium ore). Thus, although the best scientists in Japan had agreed that there was no chance of the United States producing a fission bomb in less than three to five years, there was now immediate suspicion that an atomic bomb had fallen. But the Army, anxious to keep the war going so it could fight a showdown hand-to-hand battle with the Americans on Japanese soil, was determined to withhold the news from the Japanese people as long as it could.

The editors protested mildly, but the decision stood. At six o'clock that evening, the radio gave the people of Japan their first hint that Hiroshima had been chosen for a place in history as the spot where man first proved he could tear apart the basic structure of his world. A listener, however, would have been hard put to deduce the true story from the first news item as it was read:

> A few B-29s hit Hiroshima city at 8:20 A.M. August 6, and fled after dropping incendiaries and bombs. The extent of the damage is now under survey.

This cryptic item was repeated several times between six and nine o'clock without further explanation. On the nine o'clock program in Osaka, the sound of the musical chime that signaled the switch from national to local news was followed by this item:

> An announcement by the Osaka railway bureau in regard to changes in various transportation organs and changes in handling of passenger baggage:
> First of all, the government lines. Regarding the down train, trains from Osaka will turn back from Mihara on the Sanyo line. From Mihara to Kaitichi, the trains will take the route around Kure. . . .

Mihara was about halfway from Osaka to Hiroshima. Kaitichi was on the southeastern edge of Hiroshima. Trains headed there from Osaka on the main line ordinarily ran through the Hiroshima yards and station before swinging back to the smaller community.

The morning *Asahi* in Tokyo on August 7 carried a long front-page story with a sizable headline reporting "Small and Medium Cities Attacked by 400 B-29s." At the end of this story, there was a four-line item tacked on. It read:

> *Hiroshima Attacked by Incendiary Bombs*
> Hiroshima was attacked August 6th by two B-29 planes, which dropped incendiary bombs.
> The planes invaded the city around 7:50 A.M. It seems that some damage was caused to the city and its vicinity.

Those who survived in Hiroshima still did not know what it was that had struck them so viciously the day before. They did not have much time for thinking about it. Merely keeping alive was a full-time job. Some thought, as they fled the burning city, that the Americans had deluged their homes with "Molotov flower baskets," as the unhappily familiar incendiary clusters were nicknamed. Others, sniffing the air and detecting a strong "electric smell," decided that some kind of poison gas had been dropped. Another explanation was that a magnesium powder had been sprayed on the city, exploding wherever it fell on trolley wires and other exposed electrical conductors.

The prefectural government did what it could to bring order into the city. Somehow almost two hundred policemen were found for duty on August 7. They set to work, with whatever help they could commandeer, to clear the streets of bodies and debris. Police stations became emergency food depots, doling out hastily gathered supplies of rice, salt, pickled radishes, matches, canned goods, candles, straw sandals and toilet paper.

The governor of Hiroshima prefecture, Genshin Takano, issued a proclamation:

> People of Hiroshima Prefecture: Although damage is great, we must remember that this is war. We must feel absolutely no fear. Already plans are being drawn up for relief and restoration measures. . . .
>
> We must not rest a single day in our war effort. . . . We must bear in mind that the annihilation of the stubborn enemy is our road to revenge. We must subjugate all difficulties and pain, and go forward to battle for our Emperor.

But most people in Hiroshima, if they could overcome their pain on this second day of the atomic age, were more concerned with finding their loved ones than with battling for their Emperor.

Yuko Yamaguchi, waiting out the war in the rented suburban farmhouse while her husband served overseas in the Army, was unhurt. So were her three little children. But her father-in-law, who had driven into the city Sunday for the meeting of his gas company board of directors, and her mother-in-law, who had left early Monday morning to fetch more supplies from their requisitioned city house, had not been heard from since the bomb fell. Yuko had had no word, either, from her own parents.

So at 6:30 this Tuesday morning, she left her children and set out for the city, walking the whole way because the suburban rail lines were not running. It was a long walk. By the time she reached the Red Cross hospital, where she thought her in-laws might have been taken, it was noon.

Yuko did not find her husband's parents there. But, by sheerest chance, she found her own father, lying untended on the floor with an ugly wound in the back of his head. He begged his grief-stricken daughter for some water. When she did her best and filled a broken cup with stagnant water from a nearby pond, the delirious eye specialist was furious, insisting that ice and a slice of lemon be added to make it more palatable. Somehow, she found both in the wrecked hospital kitchen and made him as comfortable as possible. Then she started through the littered, jammed wards and halls to search for her other relatives. Again she found no trace of her in-laws, but at five o'clock she came on her own mother, lying unconscious, her face smashed almost beyond recognition and her intestines bared by a savage stomach wound.

Daughter dragged mother through the corridors to her father's side so the two could at least be together. There was little enough time. Near dusk the mother died, and Yuko had to carry the body outside, build a crude pyre and cremate it herself. At about dawn her father also died. This time, there were enough other corpses on hand so the hospital arranged a makeshift mass cremation, and Yuko left. She spent the day searching again for her husband's parents, but there was no trace of them, and she finally walked home to the hills to join her children. It was to be more than a month before she found any trace of her in-laws. Then she got only the stub of a commutation ticket bearing her mother-in-law's name, recovered from the wreckage of the train she had been riding at 8:16 A.M. Monday. A few charred bones uncovered still later in the burned-out office of the gas company president were the only trace ever found of her father-in-law.

Some who survived seemed to accept with stoicism the death of their loved ones. Miho Sakamoto, who with her husband's parents had escaped the blast and fire because their home was protected by the city's only high hill, was told on August 7 that her husband's military unit had been completely wiped out. She shed no tears and showed no emotion. Four days later, she visited the ruins of the building in which he had died, found a bent ash tray which she recognized as his and brought it home. That night, she seemed in good spirits when she went upstairs to the room she had shared with her Tsuneo. The next morning she did not come down to breakfast. Her mother-in-law found her lying in front of a little altar, the ash tray in front of her beside a photograph of her dead husband, the razor with which she had cut her throat still clutched in her hand. She left a note of apology to "My Honorable Father and Mother":

> What I am about to do, I do not do on sudden impulse; nor is it due to temporary agitation. It is a mutual vow exchanged with my husband while he still lived. This is the road to our greatest happiness and we proceed thereon. Like a bird which has lost one wing, we are crippled birds who cannot go through life without one another. There is no other way. Please, do not bewail my fate. Somewhere both of us will again be living happily together as we have in the past. . . . My honorable Tsuneo must be anxiously awaiting me and I must rush to his side.

Sixteen-year-old Junichiro Susukida, at his factory-school dormitory in Otake, sixteen miles west of Hiroshima, had seen the fireball and the great cloud that rose over the city Monday morning. When the first refugees arrived with the news that the city had been badly hit, he was one of many students who demanded permission to go to their homes, and he was one of five finally allowed to go into the city to contact authorities at the main school building and seek news of the students' families.

By the time they reached Miya-jima, on the southwestern edge of the city, the students could see the fires still burning in the bright late afternoon. As they came closer, they began to realize the full extent of the calamity. It was dark before the boys reached their home neighborhood and began their search for relatives. Junichiro, though unable to find either his mother or younger brother, did at least encounter neighbors who told him his brother had survived, though wounded, and had been taken to the home of other relatives in Fuchu. He could learn nothing about his mother, however, and finally headed back to his dormitory in Otake. Dead tired when he arrived at 2 A.M., he was nevertheless too distraught to sleep. He sat in the school auditorium and incongruously played the piano until fatigue finally subdued his nerves just before dawn on Tuesday, August 7.

Junichiro was not the only one who did not sleep that night. In Tokyo, the truth about Hiroshima was beginning to be revealed in ways that made it clear that the facts could not be kept from the people of Japan much longer.

A little before midnight on the sixth, the Tokyo office of Domei, the quasi-governmental news agency that served the whole nation, much as the Associated Press or Reuters do in the west, received a bulletin from Okayama prefecture, just east of Hiroshima. It was followed by a longer dispatch: the first eye-witness account of the bombing by a professional newsman.

Bin Nakamura, subchief of Domei's Hiroshima bureau, had been eating breakfast in his suburban garden when the bomb's explosion lifted him off the straw mat on which he was sitting and sent a wave of "immense" heat washing over his face. Once Nakamura discovered that the concussion and heat had not been caused by the nearby explosion of a "blockbuster"—his first reaction had been the typical one—he went to work as a reporter. On his bicycle and on foot, he spent the day in the city and talking to the refugees who streamed through his suburb. Then, at 10 P.M., like the experienced press-association man he was, he found communications at the suburban Haramura radio station and dictated a story to Okayama, the only point he could reach. In his dispatch, he said there was no way to tell what kind of a bomb had caused such havoc.

But before the night was much older the editors of Domei, and the leaders of Japan, had a way of telling much more about the bomb. In Saitama prefecture outside Tokyo, Domei operated a big monitoring station where nearly fifty workers, many of them Nisei girls born in the United States, listened to broadcasts from American stations. About 1 A.M. on the 7th of August (noon on the 6th in Washington, D.C.), Hideo Kinoshita, chief of the monitoring room, was awakened by the Japanese youth who had charge of the operation that night. The boy reported that U.S. stations were all broadcasting a statement by President Truman, describing the weapon that had been dropped on Hiroshima as "an atomic bomb." Kinoshita listened to the account and the boy's explanation of what "atomic bomb" might mean. Then he quickly called his own superior, Saiji Hasegawa, Domei's foreign news chief. Hasegawa was asleep in his hotel. When he was told of an "atomic bomb," he had no idea what it was, but although he was irritated at being awakened he hustled to his office. When he saw the text transcripts that were beginning to come through from the Saitama monitors, he was glad he had come to work. He reached for his telephone and called Hisatsune Sakomizu, chief secretary of the cabinet.

Sakomizu sleepily answered his bedside telephone, then came suddenly wide awake as he listened to the Domei executive. He already knew, from the first confused reports on the 6th, that the Americans had used some kind of new weapon. Now, learning that it was an atomic bomb, something the cabinet had discussed briefly almost a year earlier, he knew it meant just one thing: the war was over.

Sakomizu quickly called Prime Minister Suzuki, with whom he had been working in the effort to arrange a peace settlement by negotiation. They knew immediately, he said later,

> ... that if the announcement were true, no country could carry on a war. Without the atomic bomb it would be impossible for any country to defend itself against a nation which had the weapon. The chance had come to end the war. It was not necessary to blame the military side, the manufacturing people, or anyone else—just the atomic bomb. It was a good excuse.

The Army, however, was unwilling to accept this attitude, despite the urgings of the peace group that the bomb gave military leaders a chance to save face by blaming the "backwardness of scientific research" for Japan's inability to counter the new American bomb. The generals, sitting in an emergency cabinet meeting on the seventh, pointedly recalled an old Japanese legend about an Army commander who became a laughingstock because he mistook the fluttering of a flight of birds for the sound of an approaching enemy and fled. They argued that the bomb was not atomic but was merely a huge conventional projectile. They flatly refused Foreign Minister Togo's proposal to take up for immediate consideration the possibility of surrender on the terms of the Potsdam ultimatum, and insisted on keeping the Truman atomic statement from the Japanese people until the Army could conduct an "investigation" on the ground at Hiroshima.

The military had already started such a check. Major Hirano, the staff officer from the Hiroshima headquarters whose desire to spend a couple of extra nights in Tokyo had saved his life, called Yoshio Nishina, the nation's ranking nuclear scientist. He told him of the Truman claims and asked him to ride down to Hiroshima in his little liaison plane to investigate the matter. Nishina agreed to make the trip. The scientist was already pretty well convinced, on the basis of Hirano's report and further excerpts from the Truman statement given him a few minutes later by a reporter, that the bomb had indeed been the fission weapon which he and his colleagues had believed the United States could not manufacture so quickly. Truman's claim of a destructive power equal to twenty thousand tons of TNT coincided exactly with theoretical calculations made recently by one of Nishina's laboratory associates on the yield of an atomic bomb.

But the Army high command was keeping the lid on tight. When the Tokyo managing editors met again with the Information Agency censors that afternoon, they all had seen the text of Truman's statement. But they got nowhere with requests for permission to print it. The Army grudgingly allowed use of the phrase "a new-type bomb," but not the word "atomic." The editors argued hard this time, but to no avail. The end result of the wrangle was this communiqué from Imperial General Headquarters at 3:30 P.M. on Tuesday, August 7:

> 1. A considerable amount of damage was caused by a few B-29s which attacked Hiroshima August 6th.
> 2. It seems that the enemy used a new-type bomb in the raid. Investigation of the effects is under way.

By evening, the newsmen were stretching the Army embargo as far as they could. A home service broadcast at 7 P.M amplified the cryptic communiqué by adding that "a considerable number of houses were reduced to ashes and fires broke out in various parts of the city . . . investigations are now being made with regard to the effectiveness of the bomb, which should not be regarded as light." The broadcast went on to attack the Americans for "inhuman and atrocious conduct" and to urge Japanese not to be "misled" by "exaggerated propaganda" such as "an announcement regarding the use of a new-type bomb" by Truman.

One man who was not likely to be "misled" by any announcement that night was Major Hirano, who finally had started back to Hiroshima in his five-seater liaison plane late in the afternoon. He had arrived at the Tokyo airport with the hurriedly assembled team of investigators earlier in the day, but had been ordered to wait until afternoon to avoid the U.S. Navy fighter planes that were now operating over Japan daily. There was some top brass in the inspection group which apparently was not anxious to hasten the day of personal contact with American invaders. Thus it was almost seven in the evening when Hirano's plane came down over Hiroshima. It was still light, however, so he got the full picture with shocking suddenness:

> Being a soldier, my eye had been inured to the effects of bombing by that time. But this was a different sight. *There were no roads in the wastes that spread below our eyes:* that was my first impression. In the case of a normal air raid, roads were still visible after it was over. But in Hiroshima, everything was flattened and all roads were undiscernibly covered with debris.

When Hirano stepped from his plane, the first person he saw was an Air Force officer who came out on the runway to meet the team from Tokyo. His face was marked by a sharp dividing line right down the middle. One side was smooth and unhurt. The other, the one that had been toward the explosion, was burned, blistered, blackened. The investigators picked their way through the city to the wreckage of II Army Corps headquarters. Nobody was there. They finally found what was left of the headquarters—a few officers holed up in a hillside cave. By the time they began their formal investigation the next morning, the men from Tokyo knew the truth anyway. Hirano, in fact, had known it the moment he caught sight of what was left of Hiroshima from his circling plane. . . .

VIII   Balance of Terror

26

Truman's Cold War Crusade

James Paul Warburg

"We are going to win the war," Roosevelt declared after Pearl Harbor, "and we are going to win the peace that follows." The Allies won the war, but it was a victory without peace. For out of the muck and rubble of World War II emerged a Cold War between Russia and the West which threatened the very survival of mankind. Indeed, the genesis of the Cold War (what Churchill called "the Balance of Terror") goes back to the early days of World War II and involved control of Eastern Europe. Russia and the Western Allies clashed over that area, and their rival strategies for the domination of Eastern Europe influenced most of the wartime Big Three conferences. The West, for its part, hoped to establish capitalistic regimes in Eastern Europe, ones that might well look to Russia for leadership but that would retain their land and factory owners and permit Western investment. It was an impossible program, for the massive Red Army overran Eastern Europe; and Stalin vowed to maintain Soviet supremacy there. He did so not to export world Communism, but to ensure Russian security from the West—to make certain that no Western army could ever sweep through Poland and invade Russia again. Once the Red Army occupied Eastern Europe, Roosevelt did the only thing he could do: he acknowledged Soviet hegemony in the region, but pressed Stalin to hold free elections in the countries he controlled. Mainly to hold the wartime alliance together, Stalin promised free elections for Eastern Europe. But obsessed as he was with Russian security, the Soviet boss never kept his promise, instead setting up Russian puppet states from the Baltic to the Adriatic.

The West, of course, felt betrayed. By the time Roosevelt died and Truman came to power, the United States and many of her Allies increasingly saw Stalin as a mad and devious Marxist dictator out to spread Communism across the globe. In the United States especially, a profound fear of Russia and world Communism swept over Washington in the waning days of World War II, and Truman himself was one of the first to feel the fear. Unlike Roosevelt, who had tried to conciliate the Russians, Truman adopted a get-tough policy that was to form the basis of United States foreign policy for years to come. At the Potsdam Conference, where the final plans for the occupation of Germany were worked out, Truman confronted the Soviets about the spheres of influence they had established in Eastern Europe, particularly in Poland. The Russians did not know what to make of this belligerent little man from Missouri. "He told the Russians just where they got off," said a happy Winston Churchill, "and generally bossed the whole meeting." Although Truman compromised and eventually recognized Poland's Communist government, he still hoped to roll the Soviets out of Eastern Europe.

Meanwhile Truman received word that the atomic bomb had been successfully exploded in New Mexico. The President was delighted. Not only could he use this terrible weapon to end the war with Japan (which he did), but he could also employ it "as a hammer against those boys"—the Russians. It is highly possible that Truman wanted to use the bomb as an implied threat, in order to curtail Russia's influence and force her to accept American policies, especially those regarding Eastern Europe.

Most writers have praised Truman's militant policy toward the Russians and the rest of the "Communist World." In the conventional view of the Cold War, the Russians were out for nothing less than total world conquest, and the only way to stop them was to contain the Soviet Union with American military and economic power. Conventional analysts have applauded Truman for doing just that, contending that his policy of containment saved much of the "free world" from Communism.

A number of other critics—and their number has swelled in recent years—have questioned the conventional wisdom about Truman's diplomacy. In their judgment, the United States both overestimated and misinterpreted Soviet intentions in foreign affairs. By relying on force and atomic threats to deal with the Communist bloc, these critics contend, America too must be held accountable for the escalation of the Cold War in the late 1940s and 1950s. One of the first such critics was James Paul Warburg, a maverick American banker and public servant who in the Truman years sharply attacked the policy of containment and the militant anti-Communism that underlay it. Warburg's writings anticipated the modern "revisionist" critique of American foreign policy that flourished in the late 1960s and the 1970s. But while Warburg's argument provides a much-needed corrective to the conventional view, those who want to examine both interpretations should consult the accounts of the Truman years in Herbert Agar's *The Price of Power* or in the foreign policy studies of Herbert Feis.

Harry Truman was a man far more characteristic of the American people as a whole than the paternalistic Hudson Valley patrician whom he succeeded in the White House. Truman's people were small farmers in the Middle West. His four grandparents had been born in Kentucky and had moved to Missouri in 1840. One was German, the three others came of English–North Irish stock.

Born at Independence in 1884, Truman attended public school, went to work at seventeen, first for the *Kansas City Star* and then as a timekeeper and helper in Kansas City banks. In 1905, aged twenty-one, he joined the Missouri National Guard and tried to enter West Point but was rejected because of defective eyesight. From 1906 until the United States entered the war, he ran his family's farm. In 1917, he entered the Field Artillery School at Fort Sill, Oklahoma, was commissioned a lieutenant and then captain in the 129th Field Artillery, was sent overseas and served in the Argonne and St. Mihiel actions with the American Expeditionary Corps. He was discharged as a major in 1919.

Then, for about three years, he ran a not very successful haberdashery and became interested in courthouse politics, obtaining an appointment as judge of the Jackson County Court in 1922. After attending the Kansas City School of Law for two years, he ran, first unsuccessfully and then successfully, for the office of presiding judge. In 1934, at the age of fifty, he became a United States Senator and, in 1944, was chosen by Roosevelt to become Vice President, succeeding to the Presidency at Roosevelt's death in April 1945. He was then sixty-one but possessed the energy and spirit of a much younger man.

This was the man who, within two weeks of his succession to the Presidency, decided to have a showdown with Josef Stalin. And this was the man who, after waging a Cold War for almost three years, was endorsed and re-elected by the American people.

What elements in the American society, what characteristics of the American people did he reflect?

1. Like many young Americans who came from a Middle West farming background and could see no particularly bright future for themselves in agriculture or business, Truman tried for an appointment to West Point at the age of twenty-one. Had he not been rejected because of weak eyesight, one can easily imagine him as having become a professional soldier rather than a politician. His wartime experience as a field officer in the artillery was one which he enjoyed

---

From pp. 10–13, 37–38, 40–51 in *The United States in the Postwar World* by James P. Warburg. Copyright © 1966 by James P. Warburg. Reprinted by permission of Atheneum Publishers.

and looked back upon with pride. From it, he acquired a respect for discipline, an admiration for successful generals and admirals, and something of the spirit which pervades such veterans' organizations as the American Legion.

2. Brought up in the Baptist religion, Truman acquired, like many young Americans, a fundamentalist faith in the Bible and an unhesitating conviction of revealed truth as to "right" and "wrong." On the other hand, experience with Missouri courthouse politics in the days of the notorious Pendergast machine taught him the practical value of choosing a "side" and, by loyal service to that side, achieving advancement. The two influences combined, as they do with many Americans, to make him a strong and loyal partisan with an unshakable belief in the "rightness" of the faction, political party or nation to which he belonged.

Strong partisanship, whether for nation or political party, tends to create a black-and-white view in which it becomes difficult to attribute any virtue to the other side and easy to ascribe virtue to one's own.

3. Coming from a border state in which there had been strong sympathy for the South (his mother's family had been sympathetic to the Confederacy), Truman drifted toward friendship with Southern Senators, most of them ardent believers in "white supremacy." These Southerners controlled important committee chairmanships. On the other hand, his religious convictions made Truman keenly conscious of the injustice being done to Negroes and left him with an ambivalent feeling toward the issue of race relations. It was significant that he chose as his first Secretary of State James F. Byrnes, a South Carolinian white-supremacist and apostate Roman Catholic, whom Roosevelt had rejected as a running-mate in 1944 largely because of his religion and his racial prejudice.

If one adds up these characteristics, plus an almost total unfamiliarity with the world outside of the United States, one obtains some insight into the factors which made Harry Truman adopt a simplistic and, as the writer sees it, a distorted view of the foreign-policy problems that he faced when he became President.

. . .

On March 5, 1946, Winston Churchill, now no longer Prime Minister, made his famous speech at Fulton, Missouri, with President Truman sitting by his side and apparently beaming approval. Shorn of its characteristic embellishments, the speech amounted to this:

The world is divided into communist and capitalist blocs. To check the expansion of the communist bloc, the English-speaking peoples—a sort of latter-day "master race"—must sooner or later form a union. They should immediately form an alliance and coordinate their military establishments. They must lead "Christian civilization" in an anti-communist crusade. They must hold on to the secret of the atomic bomb, for only thus, said Churchill, could a probable war be averted. Stalin, he said, respected strength and would probably come to terms with a powerful and determined alliance. What Churchill was really saying was that the United States must underwrite the British Empire—and this at the very moment when Clement Attlee's Labour Government had repudiated Churchill's old-fashioned imperialism.

The speech was immediately disavowed by London and was widely criticized here and abroad. There was much speculation as to whether, by his apparent sponsorship, the President had meant to convey his agreement or approval. The White House denied any such intention but the curious circumstances in which the speech had been delivered left a question mark. A year later, the question would be answered. At the time, Churchill's speech was considered an unfortunately disturbing factor in the then current effort to win Congressional approval for a loan to Britain.

It is a widely held belief that the Fulton speech prepared the way for the policy which

Truman was to announce in March 1947 (The Truman Doctrine). Actually, Truman was already thinking and acting in the manner Churchill recommended, except that he was not thinking of an anti-communist crusade conducted by the English-speaking people but, rather, of an anti-communist crusade conducted by the United States. Truman was no more interested than Roosevelt had been in preserving the British Empire.

While Byrnes was concentrating on the Balkan treaties, a Soviet attempt to maintain control of northern Iran was blocked by a prompt appeal to the United Nations which succeeded in forcing the withdrawal of Soviet troops in accordance with a wartime agreement. But the Western powers were able to do little more than protest against continuing Soviet penetration of the Balkans. The Rumanian treaty returned Bessarabia to the Soviet Union and ceded North Bukovina which had never been Russian. Western protests against Soviet-dominated governments lost much of their force because they were based upon the ambiguous promise of "free elections" obtained from Stalin at Yalta. What were "free elections" in countries like Rumania and Bulgaria where no such elections had ever been held? What, for that matter, was "freedom" or "democracy" where none had ever existed? The Big Three had used these words in their wartime agreements, but had left them undefined.

. . .

While the offensive against Stalin in Europe had been showing unsatisfactory results, a dangerous situation had been developing in the Far East. In spite of lavish American aid in the form of money, transportation and military supplies, Chiang Kai-shek's Nationalist troops were being steadily pushed southward by the Chinese Communists. In the hope of inducing both Chiang and Mao Tse-tung to end the civil war and to form some sort of coalition government, Truman sent General Marshall to try to mediate the conflict. The effort failed, partly because Mao already sensed complete victory and perhaps even more because Chiang refused to undertake a reform of his corrupt and oppressive regime which might have enabled him to arrest its loss of popular allegiance. There was at this time no evidence to suggest that Stalin had gone back on his treaty with the Nationalists by giving aid to the Chinese Communists. The latter were obtaining arms chiefly by capturing American weapons from Chiang's forces.

In the November elections of 1946, Truman lost majority control of the Congress to the Republicans. Partly because he now needed a Secretary of State who would command Republican as well as Democratic support and partly because of his great and well-merited confidence in the wartime Chief of Staff, Truman now asked for Byrnes's resignation and appointed General Marshall to take his place. His first assignment would be to attend the Moscow Conference on Germany and Austria, scheduled to take place in early March 1947.

With Dean Acheson as Under Secretary, Marshall set about creating a more orderly procedure in a Department of State that had suffered from Byrnes's habit of "carrying around the department in his briefcase on his frequent travels." Marshall expressed the view that the United States must assume a "more military posture." The opportunity to do so was not long in presenting itself.

A communist-led revolt against the Greek monarchy—aided not, as was thought, by Stalin but by Tito's Yugoslavia—had assumed proportions with which Britain was no longer able to cope. Simultaneously, the Soviet Union was making threatening gestures toward Turkey, demanding control of the Black Sea Straits and a cession of Turkish territory.

Just as Marshall was preparing to leave for Moscow, the British Government informed Washington that it would no longer be able to carry out the obligations assumed by Churchill in his spheres-of-influence deal with Stalin, and that both Greece and Turkey required military and economic aid beyond Britain's ability to provide. When Truman sent for the Congressional leaders to propose that the United States extend $400 million worth of aid, he was told that to obtain Congressional approval, he would have to "scare hell out of the Congress and the country." The task of drafting an appropriate message to Congress was assigned to Presidential assistant Clark Clifford and Under Secretary Acheson.

The message, delivered on March 12, 1947, set forth the need for aiding Greece and Turkey. Both were, at the time, governed by right-wing dictatorships. In Greece, the communist-led revolt was against the military dictatorship resulting from Churchill's restoration of the monarchy. The Turkish government was the same regime which had declined to enter the war against the Axis and had, in fact, sold chromium to the Germans.

Going far beyond a recommendation of the specific actions required, the President then proclaimed a global policy which quickly became known as "The Truman Doctrine." He declared that henceforth the United States would come to the aid of any country threatened from within or without by totalitarian conspiracy or aggression. Since it was obvious that the term "totalitarian" did not apply to the existing governments in Greece and Turkey, nor to the fascist governments of Spain and Portugal, nor to the dictatorships which ruled a number of Latin American states, it was clear that the Truman Doctrine amounted to a declaration of global ideological war upon communism.

Thus far, Truman's offensive against the Soviet Union had been confined to Europe, except for the American-sponsored United Nations action in Iran. Now, however, the new doctrine proclaimed the unilateral assumption by the United States of global responsibility for the containment of communism—a commitment undertaken outside of the United Nations and without the assured support of any allies. That "containment" was the right word became clear when the doctrine was spelled out by a high-ranking foreign service officer, George F. Kennan, writing anonymously as "Mr. X" in the April 1947 issue of *Foreign Affairs*.

While the containment policy under Truman and Eisenhower became essentially a military policy designed to prevent physical encroachment, its author, Kennan, had in mind a somewhat different aim. Unlike Truman, he did not seek to extirpate communism but to hold the Soviet regime in check until, in the course of time, it would mellow and become less aggressive. Kennan did not share the view that the world could not exist "half-slave and half-free"; and his belief that the Soviet regime would mellow as Russia became more and more of a "have" nation was proved right by later developments.

Six days before enunciating the Truman Doctrine, Truman had made a little-noticed but important speech at Baylor University on the subject of foreign economic policy. "We are," he said, "the giant of the economic world. Whether we like it or not, the future pattern of economic relations depends upon us. The world is waiting and watching to see what we shall do." The President then discussed the need for freeing world trade from artificial barriers and restrictions and, having asserted that the pattern of world trade rested in American hands, proceeded to outline what he thought that pattern ought to be. The text warrants careful study. Briefly, what Truman said was this:

Political freedom is bound up with freedom of individual enterprise; that pattern of international trade which promotes individual enterprise and leaves the direction of the international movement of goods and services to private individual initiative is the pattern which leads to peace; that pattern in which governments direct or control the flow of goods and services between nations is the pattern which leads to war. Therefore, we, the economic giant, are go-

Harry Truman (left) and General George Marshall in 1948. Tough, blunt, and profane, Truman sharply defended his containment policy and the Marshall Plan, and extolled Marshall himself as somebody "you could count on to be truthful in every way, and when you find somebody like that, you have to hang on to them. You have to hang on to them." In later years, Truman insisted that the Marshall Plan saved Europe from Russia's grasp. (Courtesy of United Press International.)

ing to use our power to set a world pattern of free-enterprise capitalism.

Mr. Truman was not merely reaffirming the American belief in the American system as the best system for America. He made it quite clear that he believed that the whole world should adopt the American system, first, because it was the best system and, second, because the American system could survive in America only if it became the world system.

This was an unequivocal challenge not merely to those governments and peoples who believed in the Marxist doctrine but also to the far greater number of nations which had come either to believe in or to accept as necessary some form of national economic planning and some degree of government control over their respective economies. The challenge, though little noticed or understood at the time in this country, was very much noted abroad and formed an important part of the background against which the more spectacular Truman Doctrine was interpreted.

As might have been expected, Stalin's reaction to the Truman Doctrine, announced on the eve of the Moscow Conference on Germany, was a reinforced policy of *"Nyet."* Germany had now become merely one battleground in a global ideological conflict. It was all the easier for Stalin to take a negative attitude because the three Western powers had failed to arrive at a common policy regarding the political and economic future of Germany. Returning to Washington, Marshall dispassionately reported on the failure of his mission.

Marshall and Acheson now set about developing a new approach to the problems of Europe. They recognized, as Byrnes had not, that the basic threat to European stability resided not in Moscow's aggressive intentions but in the social and economic weakness of both Eastern and Western Europe—a weakness that gave rise to mass discontent easily exploited by communist propaganda. In a speech at Cleveland, Mississippi, on May 8, 1947, Acheson outlined a policy of economic aid which was then more fully developed by Marshall in his famous speech at Harvard University on June 5. As stated by Marshall, the new American policy offered economic assistance to *all of Europe,* communist or non-communist. It was a policy "not directed against any country or doctrine but against hunger, poverty, desperation and chaos."

Coming only three months after the Truman Doctrine, the European Recovery Program, which was offered to all the European countries provided only that they would cooperate in mutual aid and self-help, seemed like an almost unbelievable reversal of American policy. It was enthusiastically welcomed by the nations of Western Europe which had been shocked and frightened by the belligerent Truman Doctrine, and it was hailed by many Americans, including the writer, as a return to sanity. Stalin's reaction, however, was one of skepticism. From his point of view, the Marshall Plan probably seemed merely a more intelligent (and therefore more dangerous) form of waging the Cold War. Nevertheless, he sent Molotov to the Paris meeting to explore what the Americans had in mind. Two East European countries, Poland and Czechoslovakia, accepted the American proposal. For a few days, it looked as if the Cold War might end and a new period of East-West cooperation might set in.

In Washington, there were mixed feelings. Some of the Administration advisers, including above all Secretary Marshall, hoped that the Russians would accept the unprecedented American offer. Others hoped that Stalin would reject it—some because they feared that the Congress would refuse to ratify a plan which involved aid to the communist countries; others because they were more sympathetic to the belligerent anti-communism expressed by the Truman Doctrine than to the conciliatory shift in policy sponsored by Secretary Marshall. Britain's Foreign Secretary, Ernest Bevin, who presided over the Paris meeting, made it clear that he, for one, had no desire to see the Russians accept the proposal. This, undoubtedly, was one reason why Molotov decided to walk out of the meeting on July 14; more importantly, Stalin probably realized that participation in the American program would require too great a disclosure of the Soviet economic weakness. Had Stalin decided to join the Marshall program, he might well have wrecked it, because it was more than likely that the Congress, inflamed by the Truman Doctrine, would have refused ratification. As it was, a sigh of relief emanated from many quarters in Washington when Molotov withdrew from the conference.

The fact that Poland and Czechoslovakia had joined the European Recovery Program (ERP) was now hailed by the American press as a breakaway on the part of these two East European countries from Soviet control. Shortly afterward, when the Foreign Ministers of Poland and Czechoslovakia visited Moscow and announced the withdrawal of their countries from the ERP, American headlines proclaimed that the Iron Curtain had descended upon these two countries, making them helpless satellites of the Soviet Union.

With Stalin's rejection of the unprecedentedly generous Marshall offer, Europe was now definitely divided into a Western and Eastern economic orbit, with the United States underwriting the rehabilitation of the Western countries and the Soviet Union organizing the economy of those countries which lay east of the dividing line. This focused the Cold War even more sharply upon Germany, lying as it did between the two orbits and as yet not under the control of either camp.

Until early 1947, Washington's chief concern had centered on Eastern Europe, the security of the Western countries being taken more or less for granted in spite of mounting economic distress and the existence of powerful communist parties in Italy and France. Recovery from the devastation and dislocation caused by the war was extremely slow, not only because the food, fuel, machinery and tools urgently required could be obtained only in the United States in exchange for scarce American dollars but also because European recovery was severely hampered by the lack of German coal and steel, the production of which had all but ceased under four-power occupation.

The Marshall Plan was developed primarily in order to meet the increasingly urgent needs of Western Europe and only incidentally as a modification of the anti-communist crusade launched by the Truman Doctrine. When participation was rejected by Moscow, it became a powerful adjunct to the Western prosecution of the Cold War, saving Western Europe from threatened starvation and economic chaos and thus locking the door against communist subversion or penetration. It is important to recall that, at this time, there was no fear of Soviet military action against Western Europe; that came only later, with the Berlin Blockade and the communist coup in Czechoslovakia.

However, by this time a powerful sentiment of distrust and hatred of the Soviet regime had been generated in the United States, nourished by official pronouncements. So far as is known, Truman himself had drawn little if any distinction during the early days of the war between Hitler's fascism and Stalin's communism. Both were totalitarian, oppressive, atheistic and aggressive. Both were our enemies and the enemies of Western civilization. It apparently made no difference to Truman that Stalin had been the first to oppose Nazi aggression (in the League of Nations and in the Spanish Civil War), had been eager to come to Czechoslovakia's assistance at the time of Munich, and had "ganged up with Hitler" only after he had failed to enlist Western support in stopping him. And when Hitler turned upon Russia in June 1941, Truman—then a senator from Missouri—was reported in the *New York Times* to have expressed the view that if Hitler seemed likely to win, the United States should help Stalin, and if Stalin seemed about to win, the United States should help Hitler. This sentiment was one that was widely held among Americans at the time.

On the other hand, once Russia had become an ally, her tremendous contribution to allied victory created a strong pro-Russian feeling in the United States. For the most part, this was not a pro-communist sentiment although a certain amount of actual pro-communism had been engendered in the 1930's by disgust at Western appeasement and admiration of Soviet opposition to the Axis, especially during the Spanish Civil War. This pro-communist sentiment had decreased sharply when the American Communist Party and its European counterparts performed their overnight somersaults on June 21, 1941, proclaiming that what had been a "capitalist imperialist war" had now become a crusade for freedom.

Roosevelt had never wholly equated Nazism and Communism, even during the period of the Molotov-Ribbentrop Pact. Like most Americans, he loathed the totalitarian police-state, deplored official atheism and rejected the Marxist dogma, but he never lost sight of the fact that Hitler and Mussolini, not Stalin, had begun a war of conquest. And, when the Soviet Union emerged from the war as the strongest power in Europe, having at great sacrifice made a tremendous contribution to victory, Roosevelt felt that the United States and Britain must come to terms with the power-political realities in the interests of preserving the hard-won peace. By persuasion and the extension of much-needed economic assistance, he had hoped to lighten the lot of the East European peoples whom the conduct of the war had brought under Soviet domination. Churchill, too, once he had failed to gain support for his preferred strategy of invading the continent through the Balkans, was reconciled to the need for coming to terms with Stalin, and did so in his spheres-of-influence deal with respect to Southeastern Europe. Neither Roosevelt nor Churchill seriously considered going to war with Russia in order to liberate Eastern Europe. It was true that Britain had gone to war over Poland, but, later, Churchill's primary concern had been not so much the liberation of all Eastern Europe as the preservation of the British Empire and its lifeline through the Mediterranean.

In contrast to the pragmatic idealism of Roosevelt and the shrewd realism of Churchill, Truman combined a benevolent idealism with a cocky confidence that he knew what was good for the world and that he had the power to impose it. In addition, he possessed a short temper and a great capacity for moral indignation. The combination of these characteristics led him to take a simplistic view of the world somewhat like the dualistic theology of the ancient Persian philosopher Manichaeus, according to which the world was governed by Powers of Light and Powers of Darkness. During the war, the Axis Powers had represented the seat of all evil. As Truman saw it, the postwar world was polarized between a benevolent Washington and a malevolent Moscow.

The conviction that only the Soviet Union stood in the way of his imposing a benevolent design for peace upon the world created in Truman an angry hostility toward the Soviet Union. This, in turn, created counter-hostility in Stalin and a vicious circle of mutual suspicion, distrust and hatred. Thus, Truman and Stalin came to expect the worst of each other and thereby caused the worst to happen.

Unlike Roosevelt, Truman confused Russian nationalistic expansionism with what he conceived to be a worldwide communist conspiracy. As Truman saw it, the Devil who dwelt in the Kremlin was a spider in the center of a worldwide communist web plotting world revolution, whereas in reality Stalin was an old-fashioned, ruthless, Machiavellian nationalist using Marxist-Leninist ideology as a tool. To be sure, this ideology proclaimed the inevitable triumph of communism throughout the world, but this had been a prophecy rather than a program of conquest; and Stalin was far more interested in the power-political future and security of Mother Russia than in a realization of the Marxist dream.

The fact that Truman made communism, rather than Soviet imperialism, the target of his hostility had a number of fateful consequences. It automatically caused him to consider all communist governments and communist political parties as enemies of the United States; to identify socialism with communism; and to regard all anti-communist governments and political parties as friends and potential allies, including the most oppressive dictatorships and feudal oligarchies. It caused him to define as "free" any nation whose government was not communist-dominated, no matter how anti-democratic that government might be. And, finally, his identification of a worldwide communist conspiracy as the primary threat to American security caused him to issue a Loyalty Order aimed at discovering communists in the United States which reversed the established American principle that an individual shall be considered innocent until proved guilty, shifting the burden of proof upon the accused.

27

Eisenhower, Dulles, and the Irreconcilable Conflict

Stephen E. Ambrose

From 1947 on, Containment was the cornerstone of American foreign policy toward "the Communist world." Containment dictated that the United States get tough with China, too, after the Communists took over there in 1949 and drove Chiang Kai-shek into exile on Formosa. Containment also provided the rationale for sending United States combat forces to South Korea after it was invaded by North Korean Communists. And so the United States became involved in a controversial "limited" war there that lasted from 1950 to 1953 and that ended in stalemate. While the Republicans attacked Truman's war in Korea and disparaged Containment as "a treadmill policy," they ended up adopting it, too, and with modifications that doctrine persisted through both Eisenhower administrations. In the following essay, Stephen Ambrose examines Eisenhower's foreign policy, as it was formulated largely by Secretary of State John Foster Dulles. Like Bernstein, Ambrose rejects much of the conventional wisdom about the Cold War; he is especially critical of Dulles, whose nuclear brinkmanship exacerbated tensions between the United States and the Communist bloc. Ambrose shows that Eisenhower also believed in atomic force to protect American interests and "deter aggression." But Eisenhower did oppose military intervention in the internal struggles of other nations, especially Vietnam.

'We can never rest,' General Eisenhower declared during his 1952 campaign for the Presidency, 'until the enslaved nations of the world have in the fulness of freedom the right to choose their own path, for then, and then only, can we say that there is a possible way of living peacefully and permanently with communism in the world.' Like most campaign statements, Eisenhower's bowed to both sides of the political spectrum. For the bold he indicated a policy of liberation, while the cautious could take comfort in his willingness to someday live peacefully with the communists. Since the Americans believed, however, that no one would freely choose communism, Eisenhower's statement had a major internal contradiction.

The emphasis, therefore, was on liberation. John Foster Dulles, the Republican expert on foreign policy, author of the Japanese peace treaty, and soon to be Secretary of State, was more explicit than Eisenhower. Containment, he charged, was a treadmill policy 'which, at best might perhaps keep us in the same place until we drop exhausted.' It cost far too much in taxes and loss of civil liberties and was 'not designed to win victory conclusively'. One plank in the Republican platform damned containment as 'negative, futile and immoral', for it abandoned 'countless human beings to a despotism and Godless terrorism'. It hinted that the Republicans, once in power, would roll back the atheistic tide, a hint that Dulles made into a promise when in a campaign speech he said that Eisenhower, as President, would use 'all

---

From pp. 217–227, 234–245 in *Rise to Globalism* by Stephen E. Ambrose. Baltimore: Penguin Books, Inc., 1971. Reprinted by permission.

means to secure the liberation of Eastern Europe'. Rollback would come not only in East Europe but also in Asia. The platform denounced the 'Asia last' policy of the Democrats and said, 'We have no intention to sacrifice the East to gain time for the West.'

The Eisenhower landslide of 1952 was a compound of many factors, the chief being the General's enormous personal popularity. Corruption in the Truman administration, and the McCarthy charges of communist infiltration into the government ('There are no Communists in the Republican Party,' a platform plank began), also helped. So did Eisenhower's promise to go to Korea and end the war there, not through victory but through negotiation. But one of the major appeals of the Eisenhower–Dulles team was its rejection of containment. The Republican pledge to do something about communist enslavement—it was never very clear exactly what—brought millions of former Democratic voters into the Republican fold, especially those of East European descent. Eisenhower reaped where McCarthy sowed. Far from rejecting internationalism and retreating to isolationism, the Republicans were proposing to go beyond containment. They would be more internationalist than Truman.

Republican promises to liberate the enslaved, like nineteenth-century abolitionist programs to free the Negro slaves, logically led to only one policy. Since the slaveholders would not voluntarily let the oppressed go, and since the slaves were too tightly controlled to stage their own revolution, those who wished to see them freed would have to fight. In the second half of the twentieth century, however, war was a much different proposition than it had been a hundred years earlier. Freeing the slaves would lead to the destruction of much of the world; most of the slaves themselves would die in the process.

There was another major constraint on action. The Republicans had accepted some of the New Deal, but essentially they were wedded to conservative fiscal views that stressed the importance of balancing the budget and cutting taxes. All of Eisenhower's leading cabinet figures, save Dulles, were businessmen who believed that an unbalanced federal budget was immoral. Government expenditures could be reduced significantly, however, only by cutting the Defense Department budget, which the Republicans proceeded to do. The cuts made liberation even more difficult.

In practice, then, Eisenhower and Dulles continued the policy of containment. There was no basic difference between their foreign policy and that of Truman and Acheson. Their campaign statements frequently haunted them, but they avoided embarrassment over their lack of action through their rhetoric. 'We can never rest,' Eisenhower had said, but rest they did, except in their speeches, which expressed perfectly the assumptions and desires of millions of Americans.

Better than anyone else, Dulles described the American view of communism. A devout Christian, highly successful corporate lawyer, something of a prig, and absolutely certain of his own and his nation's goodness, Dulles's unshakable beliefs were based on general American ideas. They differed hardly at all from those of Truman, Acheson, Main Street in Iowa, or Madison Avenue in New York City. All the world wanted to be like America; the common people everywhere looked to America for leadership; communism was unmitigated evil imposed by a conspiracy on helpless people, whether it came from the outside as in East Europe or from the inside as in Asia; there could be no permanent reconciliation with communism for 'this is an irreconcilable conflict'. In January 1953, Dulles told the Senate Foreign Relations Committee that communism 'believes that human beings are nothing more than somewhat superior animals . . . and that the best kind of a world is that world which is organ-

John Foster Dulles and Dwight Eisenhower. "Better than anyone else," writes Ambrose, "Dulles described the American view of communism. A devout Christian, highly successful corporate lawyer, something of a prig, and absolutely certain of his own and his nation's goodness, Dulles's unshakable beliefs were based on general American ideas. . . . All the world wanted to be like America; the common people everywhere looked to America for leadership; communism was unmitigated evil . . . (and) there could be no permanent reconciliation with communism for 'this is an irreconcilable conflict.' " (Courtesy of Wide World Photos.)

ized as a well-managed farm is organized, where certain animals are taken out to pasture, and they are fed and brought back and milked, and they are given a barn as shelter over their heads.' This was somewhat more sophisticated than the way Eisenhower usually described the ideology that had millions of adherents, and far more sophisticated than the description employed by newspaper editors and television commentators, but it accurately summed up the American view of communism.

The Eisenhower administration, like its predecessor, based its policy on the lessons of history, or at least on one lesson, which was that appeasement was a disaster. The verbiage of the thirties helped shape the policies of the fifties. When the Chinese moved to capture tiny islands held by Chiang, for example, and America's N.A.T.O. allies indicated that they did not want to start World War III over such a trifling matter, Eisenhower talked incessantly about Munich and compared the Russian and Chinese leaders to Hitler. He could never understand why the Europeans could not see the threat as clearly as he did.

The Eisenhower–Dulles speeches helped hide the fact that they did nothing about their promise to liberate the enslaved, but perhaps more important to their popularity was their unwillingness to risk American lives, for here too they were expressing the deepest sentiments of their countrymen. On occasion the Republicans rattled the saber and always they filled the air with denunciations of the communists, but they also shut down the Korean War, cut corporate taxes, and reduced the size of the armed forces. Despite intense pressure and great temptation, they entered no wars. They were willing to supply material, on a limited scale, to others so that they could fight the enemy, but they would not commit American boys to the struggle. Like Truman they did their best to contain communism; unlike him they did not use American troops to do so. They were unwilling to make peace but they would not go to war. Their speeches provided emotional satisfaction but their actions failed to liberate a single slave. No one had a right to complain that the Republicans had been misleading, however, for the policy had been clearly spelled out in the campaign. The vague and militant talk about liberation was balanced by specific promises to end the war in Korea—without liberating North Korea, much less China—and balance the budget.

When General Marshall was Secretary of State he had complained that he had no muscle to back up his foreign policy. Truman agreed and did all he could to increase the armed forces. Dulles did not make such complaints. He worked with what was available—which was, to be sure, far more than Marshall had at hand in 1948—for he shared the Republican commitment to fiscal soundness.

The extent of the commitment was best seen in the New Look, the term Eisenhower coined to describe his military policy. It combined domestic, military, and foreign considerations. The New Look rejected the premise of N.S.C. 68* that the United States could spend up to 20 per cent of its G.N.P. on arms; it rejected deficit financing; it maintained that enough of N.S.C. 68 had been implemented to provide security for the United States and to support a policy of containment. It came into effect at a time of lessening tension. The Korean War had ended and Stalin's death (March 1953) made the world seem less dangerous. The New Look was based in large part on the success of the N.S.C. 68 program, for the first two years of the New Look were the high-water mark of relative American military strength in the Cold War. As Samuel Huntington has noted, 'The basic military fact of the New Look was the overwhelming American superiority in nuclear weapons and the means of delivering them.' Between 1953 and 1955 the United States could have effectively destroyed the Soviet Union with little likelihood of serious reprisal. The fact that America did not do so indicated the basic restraint of the Eisenhower administration, as opposed to its verbiage.

The New Look became fixed policy during a period of lessened tensions and American military superiority, but it did not depend on either for its continuation. In its eight years of power, the Eisenhower administration went through a series of war scares and it witnessed the development of Soviet long-range bombers, ballistic missiles, and nuclear weapons. Throughout,

---

* This was the National Security Council Report, written in 1950 during the Truman Administration, which included the major premises and applications of the Containment Policy.—Editor

however, Eisenhower held to the New Look. His Defense Department expenditures remained in the $35 to $40 billion range.

In 1956, when the Soviets had nearly caught up to the American Armed Services, the Eisenhower administration subjected the New Look to careful scrutiny. Three alternatives were examined. Admiral Arthur W. Radford, Chairman of the Joint Chiefs, proposed to continue the existing level of military spending but to maintain a clear superiority in nuclear forces by major cutbacks in conventional strength. He wanted to begin by cutting the Army by nearly a half-million men. The Democrats in Congress went beyond Radford's proposal. They insisted on maintaining conventional strength at current levels while increasing Air Force appropriations by nearly $1 billion. Eisenhower chose a third course. Like Radford, he wanted to stabilize military expenditures; like the Senate Democrats he was opposed to reducing conventional forces. He disagreed with both on the fundamental question—should the United States maintain superiority? Eisenhower's answer was no. For him, and thus for the country, sufficiency was enough. He refused either to reduce the Army or to increase the Air Force. In fact, America retained superiority, but only because the Soviets did not increase their armament as rapidly as expected.

The key to the New Look was the American ability to build and deliver nuclear weapons. Put more bluntly, Eisenhower's military policy rested on America's capacity to destroy the Soviet Union. Soviet strides in military technology gave them the ability to retaliate, but not to defend Russia, which was the major reason Eisenhower could accept sufficiency. The United States did not have to be superior to the Soviet Union to demolish it.

To give up superiority was not easy, however, and it rankled with many Americans, especially in the military. Eisenhower had his greatest difficulties with the Army, for it suffered most from his refusal to increase the Defense Department budget. Three Army Chiefs of Staff resigned in protest and one of them, Maxwell Taylor, later became the chief adviser on military affairs to Eisenhower's successors and saw his views triumph. The Army wanted enough flexibility to be able to meet the communist threat at any level. The trouble with Eisenhower's New Look, the Army Chiefs and some Democrats argued, was that it locked the United States into an all-or-nothing response. Wherever and whenever conflict broke out, the Chiefs wanted to be capable of moving in. To do so, they needed a huge standing army, with specialized divisions, elite groups, a wide variety of weapons, and an enormous transportation capacity.

Eisenhower insisted that the cost of being able to intervene anywhere, immediately, was unbearable. 'Let us not forget,' the President wrote a friend in August of 1956, 'that the Armed Services are to defend a "way of life", not merely land, property or lives.' He wanted to make the Chiefs accept the need for a 'balance between minimum requirements in the costly implements of war and the health of our economy . . .'. As he told the American Society of Newspaper Editors on 16 April 1953, 'Every gun that is made, every warship launched, every rocket fired signifies, in the final sense, a theft from those who hunger and are not fed, those who are cold and are not clothed.' The cost of one destroyer was equal to the cost of new homes for 8,000 people.

Still, the Army Chiefs had put their finger on the most obvious limitation of the New Look and massive retaliation. Eisenhower and Dulles tried to make up the deficit by signing up allies, as in World War II, who would do the ground fighting that had to be done. Eisenhower offered one reason when he pointed out that while 'it cost $3,515 to maintain an American soldier each year, for a Pakistani the price was $485, for a Greek, $424'. This was good economics, but poor politics, since the Pakistanis and the Greeks were not anxious to fight America's wars. They were more concerned with improving their own standards so that it would cost more to maintain their soldiers.

The New Look meant that Eisenhower had abandoned his former advocacy of universal military training, with its assumption that the next war would resemble World War II. More fundamentally, he had abandoned the idea of America fighting any more Korean wars. Eisenhower's policy emphasized both the importance of tactical nuclear weapons and the role of strategic airpower as a deterrent to aggression. He used technology to mediate between conflicting political goals. Big bombers carrying nuclear weapons were the means through which he reconciled lower military expenditures with a foreign policy of containment.

The New Look shaped foreign policy. Since it was almost his only weapon, Dulles had to flash a nuclear bomb whenever he wanted to threaten the use of force. To make the threat believable, the United States developed smaller atomic weapons that could be used tactically on the battlefield. Dulles then attempted to convince the world that the United States would not hesitate to use them. The fact that the N.A.T.O. forces were so small made the threat persuasive, for there was no other way to stop the Red Army in Europe. Both Dulles and Eisenhower made this explicit. If the United States were engaged in a major military confrontation, Dulles said, 'those weapons would come into use because, as I say, they are becoming more and more conventional and replacing what used to be called conventional weapons.' Eisenhower added, 'Where these things are used on strictly military targets . . . I see no reason why they shouldn't be used just exactly as you would use a bullet or anything else.'

Dulles called the policy massive retaliation. In a speech in January 1954, he quoted Lenin and Stalin to show that the Soviets planned to overextend the free world and then destroy it with one blow. Dulles held that the United States should counter the strategy by maintaining a great strategic reserve in the United States and that the free world should be 'willing and able to respond vigorously at places and with means of its own choosing'. The Eisenhower administration had made a decision 'to depend primarily upon a great capacity to retaliate, instantly, by means and at places of our own choosing'.

Dulles used massive retaliation as the chief instrument of containment. In 1956 he called his overall method brinkmanship, which he explained in an article in *Life* magazine. 'You have to take chances for peace, just as you must take chances in war. Some say that we were brought to the verge of war. Of course we were brought to the verge of war. The ability to get to the verge without getting into the war is the necessary art . . . . If you try to run away from it, if you are scared to go to the brink, you are lost. We've had to look it square in the face . . . . We walked to the brink and we looked it in the face. We took strong action.'

Dulles implicitly recognized the limitations on brinkmanship. He never tried to use it for liberation and he used it much more sparingly after the Soviets were able to threaten the United States itself with destruction. It was a tactic to support containment at an acceptable cost, within a limited time span under a specific set of military circumstances, not a strategy for protracted conflict.

In the *Life* article, Dulles cited three instances of going to the brink. All were in Asia. The first came in Korea. When Eisenhower took office, the truce talks were stalled on the question of prisoner of war repatriation. The Chinese wanted all their men held by the U.N. command returned, while the Americans insisted on voluntary repatriation, which meant that thousands of Chinese and North Koreans would remain in South Korea, for they did not want to return to communism. Truman and Acheson had first raised the issue. They could have had peace early in 1952 had they accepted the usual practice, firmly established in international law, of returning all prisoners, but they decided to offer a haven to those prisoners who wished to defect. The talks, and the war, continued. The Chinese would not give.

After his election, but before his inauguration, Eisenhower made a trip to Korea. He returned on 14 December, convinced more than ever that involvement in a land war in Asia was a disaster for America. Determined to cut losses and get out, but locked into Truman's policy on prisoners—after Truman had made such an issue out of it, Eisenhower could hardly hand over the Chinese P.O.W.'s who did not want to return—Eisenhower warned that unless the war ended quickly, the United States might retaliate 'under circumstances of our own choosing'. On 2 February, in his first State of the Union message, the President said there was no longer 'any sense or logic' in restraining Chiang, so the U.S. Seventh Fleet would 'no longer be employed to shield Communist China'. Chiang then began bombing raids against the China coast. Armistice talks, which had broken down, recommenced in April, but again there was no progress. Dulles then warned Peking, through India, that if peace did not come the United States would bring in atomic weapons. Eleven days later the two sides agreed to place the question of prisoner repatriation in the hands of international, neutral authorities.

In its first test, massive retaliation had won a victory. Ominous portents for the future, however, soon appeared. Dulles's policy was based on a bipolar view of the world, which in his rhetoric was good *v.* evil or free *v.* slave but which in practice meant that Moscow and Washington ruled the world. He believed that the United States could make the major decisions for the free world while Russia would make them for the communists. He refused to accept, or perhaps even recognize, the diversity of the world, for he thought all important issues were related to the Cold War and was impatient with those who argued that the East–West struggle was irrelevant to many world problems. His negative expression of this belief in bipolarity was his denunciation of neutrality, which he characterized as immoral.

Syngman Rhee was no neutral, and he was willing to participate in the Cold War when it suited his purposes, but he refused to be a pawn in the State Department's hands. Peace in Korea meant the end of Rhee's hopes for ruling all of the peninsula. The end of the war may have signified victory for containment, but it also spelled defeat for Rhee. He refused, therefore, to accept any truce. To make one impossible, on 18 June 1953 he released 27,000 communist prisoners, who scattered over the countryside. On the 20th he threatened to pull his forces out of the U.N. command if a truce were signed.

China and America co-operated in putting pressure on Rhee. The Chinese launched a major offensive against South Korean troops, driving them to the south and demonstrating that Rhee could never fight on alone against them. The Americans sent high-level officials to Korea to plead with Rhee not to commit national suicide. Rhee remained recalcitrant, but eventually gave in when the American, British, and French Foreign Ministers all promised to fight side-by-side with Rhee if the communists should renew their aggression. On 27 July 1953, a military armistice was signed. Rhee had not been able to keep the United States committed to war in Asia against its will, but he had come close, and he had demonstrated how small nations could force the hands of great powers. He had also shown the limitations of massive retaliation. Dulles could hardly threaten to drop nuclear bombs on the Chinese because Rhee allowed Chinese prisoners of war to escape.

Some of the same general issues emerged in the second application of brinkmanship, which came in Vietnam. Vietnam also illustrated the continuity of policy between the Truman and Eisenhower administrations, based as they were on the same assumptions. In December 1952, the lame-duck Truman administration approved $60 million for support of the French effort against Ho Chi Minh's Vietminh. Truman, and later Eisenhower, labeled Ho a communist agent of Peking and Moscow, characterizing the war in Vietnam as another example of communist aggression.

When Eisenhower moved into the White House, the State Department presented him with a background paper on Vietnam that succinctly summed up the American position not only on Vietnam but on the entire Third World. In 1949 France had broken up Indochina and granted Laos, Cambodia, and Vietnam 'independence within the French Union'. All objective observers recognized this as a heavy-handed attempt to buy off the Vietminh without giving anything of substance in return. Even the U.S. State Department could not totally ignore the obvious sham, but it did its best to dismiss it.

In the background presentation to Eisenhower, the State Department said that 'certain symbols of the former colonial era remain'. These 'certain symbols' included total French control over 'foreign and military affairs, foreign trade and exchange, and internal security. France continues to maintain a near monopoly in the economic life' of Vietnam. The State Department told Eisenhower that French control of the reality of power in its former colonies was 'disliked by large elements of the native population', but said it was 'justified' because the French were bearing the major burden of 'defending the area'. But the only non-native troops in Vietnam were French and even State admitted that the bulk of the population 'disliked' French rule. American policy was to encourage an end to colonialism; yet in the face of all this State could still seriously assert that France retained 'certain symbols' of power and was 'defending the area'. Against whom, and for what?

Such nonsense could have meaning only to those who believed that the challenge to French rule came not from the Vietnamese but from the Chinese communists, acting in turn as proxies for the Kremlin, with the ultimate purpose of world conquest. If these beliefs were true, there was little point in fighting what Eisenhower called the tail of the snake, the Vietminh. Better to cut off the neck in Peking, or even the head in Moscow. Dulles tried that, warning the Chinese that if their troops entered Vietnam the United States would use nuclear weapons against China. The Chinese sent no troops, but they had never planned to anyway and Dulles's threat had absolutely no effect on the war in Vietnam.

While he served as Supreme Commander at N.A.T.O. Headquarters in Europe, and again in his first year in the White House, Eisenhower continually urged the French to state unequivocally that they would give complete independence to Vietnam upon the conclusion of hostilities. He made 'every kind of presentation' to the French to 'put the war on an international footing', i.e., to make it a clear Cold War struggle rather than a revolt against colonialism. If France promised independence, and Ho continued to fight, Eisenhower reasoned that the Vietminh could no longer pretend to be national liberators and would stand revealed as communist stooges. At that point, Britain and the United States could enter the conflict to halt aggression.

Eisenhower was badly confused about the nature of the war, but the French were not. Like Rhee, they were willing enough to talk about the communist menace in order to receive American aid, but they had no intention of giving up Vietnam. They knew perfectly well that their enemies were in the interior of Vietnam, not in Peking or Moscow, and they were determined to retain the reality of power. If the Americans wanted to fight communists, that was fine with the French; their concern was with continuing the exploitation of the Vietnamese.

Unfortunately the war did not go well for the French. By early 1954 the Vietminh controlled over half the countryside. The French put their best troops into an isolated garrison north of

Hanoi, called Dien Bien Phu, and dared the Vietminh to come after them. They assumed that in open battle the Asians would crumble. The results, however, were the other way around, and by April it was the garrison at Dien Bien Phu that was in trouble. War weariness in France was by then so great, and the French had attached so much prestige to Dien Bien Phu, that it was clear that the fall of the garrison would mean the end of French rule in Vietnam. Eisenhower and Dulles saw such an outcome as a victory for communist aggression and a failure of containment.

On 3 April 1954, Dulles and Radford met with eight Congressional leaders. The administration wanted support for a congressional resolution authorizing American entry into the war. The Congressmen, including Senator Lyndon B. Johnson of Texas, the Senate majority leader, were aghast. They remembered all too well the difficulties of the Korean War and they were disturbed because Dulles had found no allies to support intervention. Congressional opposition hardened when they discovered that one of the other three Joint Chiefs disagreed with Radford's idea of saving Dien Bien Phu through air strikes.

Eisenhower was as adamant as the Congressional leaders about allies. He was anxious to shore up the French but only if they promised complete independence and only if Britain joined the United States in intervening. Unless these conditions were met he would not move, but he was worried about what would happen if the French lost. On 7 April he introduced a new political use for an old word when he explained that all Southeast Asia was like a row of dominoes. If you knocked over the first one what would happen to the last one was 'the certainty that it would go over very quickly'.

To make sure the dominoes stood, Eisenhower went shopping for allies. He wanted 'the U.S., France, United Kingdom, Thailand, Australia, and New Zealand et al to begin conferring at once on means of successfully stopping the Communist advances in Southeast Asia'. He proposed to use the bulk of the French army already there, while 'additional ground forces should come from Asiatic and European troops'. America would supply the material, but not the lives. The policy had little appeal to Britain, Australia, New Zealand, et al, but it was consistent with the approach of both Eisenhower's predecessors. The trouble was it had no chance of success. The proposed allies figured that if America would not fight in Korea, they would not fight in Vietnam. Even when Eisenhower wrote Churchill and compared the threat in Vietnam to the dangers of 'Hirohito, Mussolini and Hitler', the British would not budge.

The Vice President, Richard M. Nixon, then tried another tack. On 16 April he said that 'if to avoid further Communist expansion in Asia and Indochina, we must take the risk now by putting our boys in, I think the Executive has to take the politically unpopular decisions and do it'. Nixon was evidently confused about the premises of the New Look, which made his suggestion impossible, since there were no troops available. In any case, the storm that followed his speech was so fierce that the possibility of using 'our boys' in Vietnam immediately disappeared from the suggestion pile. Eisenhower would never have supported it anyway, and his Army Chief of Staff, Matthew Ridgway, was firmly opposed to rushing into another ground war in Asia.

What to do? The question was crucial because a conference on Vietnam was scheduled to begin in Geneva on 26 April*. Like Truman in

---

*The conference had been called at the end of the Berlin Conference of Foreign Ministers in February 1954, the first meeting of the Foreign Ministers in nearly five years. The Berlin Conference came about because the West wanted to see how honest the Soviet successors to Stalin were in their professions of peaceful intent. Molotov at the Berlin Conference proposed that Germany be evacuated by foreign troops and the country neutralized, then unified. The West proposed German unity first, by free elections, rejecting any role for the East German Democratic Republic, after which a peace treaty could be drawn up. Dulles refused to

Korea, the Eisenhower administration was flatly opposed to a negotiated peace at Geneva which would give Ho Chi Minh any part of Vietnam. The United States was paying 75 per cent of the cost of the war, an investment too great simply to abandon. But the French position at Dien Bien Phu was deteriorating rapidly. Air Force Chief of Staff Nathan Twining had a solution. He wanted to drop three small atomic bombs on the Vietminh around Dien Bien Phu 'and clean those Commies out of there and the band could play the Marseillaise and the French would come marching out... in fine shape'. Eisenhower was opposed to using atomic bombs for the second time in a decade against Asians, but he did consider a conventional air strike. Dulles flew to London a week before the Geneva Conference to get Churchill's approval. Churchill would not approve, and Eisenhower did not act. Brinksmanship had failed.

On 7 May 1954, Dien Bien Phu fell. Still there was no immediate progress in Geneva and the Americans withdrew from the conference. At the insistence of the N.A.T.O. allies Eisenhower eventually sent his close friend, Walter B. Smith, as an observer. Dulles himself refused to return and the negotiations dragged on. The break came when the French government fell and, in mid-June, the Radical-Socialist Pierre Mendès-France assumed the position of Foreign Minister as well as of Premier. On the strength of his pledge to end the war or resign by 20 July, he had a vote of confidence of 419 to 47. Mendès-France immediately met Chinese Premier Chou En-lai privately at Berne, which infuriated the Americans, and progress towards

---

discuss West German rearmament or Germany's role in N.A.T.O. Neither side would bend and the conference did not lead to any agreement. The French, however, insisted on another meeting; the great war weariness within France could be held in check only through the promise of a Foreign Ministers' meeting to discuss Vietnam. The Americans went along because it was necessary to prolong the life of the Laniel government in Paris; behind Laniel loomed the shadow of Mendès-France, the advocate of peace in Vietnam.

peace began. Eisenhower, Dulles, and Smith were helpless bystanders. On 20–21 July two pacts were signed, the Geneva Accords and the Geneva Armistice Agreement.

The parties agreed to a truce and to a temporary partition of Vietnam at the 17th parallel, with the French withdrawing south of that line. Neither the French in south Vietnam nor Ho Chi Minh in the north could join a military alliance or allow foreign military bases on their territory. There would be elections, supervised by a joint commission of India, Canada, and Poland, within two years to unify the country. France would stay in the south to carry out the elections. The United States did not sign either of the pacts, nor did any South Vietnamese government. The Americans did promise that they would support 'free elections supervised by the United Nations' and would not use force to upset the agreements. Ho Chi Minh had been on the verge of taking all of Vietnam, but he accepted only the northern half because he needed time to repair the war damage and he was confident that when the elections came he would win a smashing victory. All Western observers agreed with his prediction on how the vote would go.

Desperate to save something from the débâcle, in July 1954 Dulles, Radford and Twining, along with others at the Pentagon, worked out an invasion scheme calling for a landing at Haiphong and a march to Hanoi, which American troops would then liberate. Again, Ridgway opposed, arguing that the adventure would require at least six divisions even if the Chinese did not intervene, and again Eisenhower refused to act.

The New Look had tied Dulles's hands in Vietnam, so after Geneva and Eisenhower's refusal to invade North Vietnam the Secretary of State moved in two ways to restore some flexibility to American foreign policy. One of the major problems had been the lack of allies for an intervention. Dulles tried to correct this before the next crisis came by signing up the allies in advance. In September 1954, he persuaded Britain, Australia, New Zealand, France, Thailand, Pakistan, and the Philippines to join the Southeast Asian Treaty Organization (S.E.A.T.O.), in which the parties agreed to consult if any signatory felt threatened. They would act together to meet an aggressor if they could unanimously agree on designating him and if the threatened state agreed to action on its territory. Protection for Cambodia, Laos, and South Vietnam was covered in a separate protocol. Thus quickly did the United States undermine the Geneva Accords by implicitly bringing the former French colonies into an alliance system. The absence of India, Burma, and Indonesia was embarrassing, as was the presence of so many white men. Clearly this was no N.A.T.O. for Southeast Asia, but rather a Western—especially American—effort to regulate the affairs of Asia from the outside. Once again the hoary old Monroe Doctrine had been extended. The United States, as Dulles put it, had 'declared that an intrusion [in Southeast Asia] would be dangerous to our peace and security', and America would fight to prevent it.

Not, however, with infantry. Dulles assured a suspicious Senate that the New Look policies would continue, that the American response to aggression would be with bombs, not men. This solved one problem but left another. What if the aggression took the form of internal communist subversion directed and supported from without? In such an event, it would be difficult to get the S.E.A.T.O. signatories to agree to act. Dulles was aware of the danger and assured the Cabinet that in such an event he was ready to act alone. He took a different tack in the Senate Foreign Relations Committee, where he stated that 'if there is a revolutionary movement in Vietnam or in Thailand, we would consult together as to what to do about it . . . but we have no undertaking to put it down, all we have is an undertaking to consult'. Reassured, the Senate passed the treaty by a vote of 82 to 1.

Dulles's other major post-Geneva move was unilaterally to shore up the government of South Vietnam. In so doing, he revealed much about American attitudes towards revolution in the Third World. Dulles grew almost frantic when he thought about the colored peoples of the world, for he realized that the struggle for their loyalty was the next battleground of the Cold War and he knew that American military might was almost useless in the struggle. Russia had a tremendous initial advantage, since the Third World did not regard the Russians as white exploiters and colonists. Further, the Russian example of how a nation could build its economy through controlled production and consumption rather than by waiting for the slow accumulation of capital through the profits of free enterprise had great appeal to the emerging nations. Finally, the oppressed of the world were not overthrowing their white masters merely in order to substitute local rulers with the same policies. The revolutionaries were just what they said they were, men determined to change the entire social, political, and economic order. It was this radicalism that separated the post–World War II revolutions from the American Revolution and made the American talk about an identity between George Washington and the Third World just so much cant.

America could neither accept nor adjust to radicalism, either psychologically or economically. Dulles accused the Soviets of being the real imperialists of the modern world, but in East Europe at least the Russians encouraged industrial development and they were never shocked by, and in fact encouraged, radical action in the Third World. All the colored peoples had to do to see what America regarded as a proper role for the emerging nations was to look at the Mid-East or Latin America, where the Western-owned corporations retained their position, the economy was extractive, the rulers lived in splendor, and the masses of the people remained in poverty. Truman's Point Four ensured the continuation of these conditions.

Given the American emotional need to define

social change as communist aggression, given the needs of American business to maintain an extractive economy in the Third World, and given the military desire to retain bases around Russia and China, the United States had to set its face against revolution. 'American policy was designed to create maximum change behind the Iron Curtain and to prevent it elsewhere', Norman Graebner has written. 'On both counts, this nation placed itself in opposition to the fundamental political and military realities of the age'. In 1960 V. K. Krishna Menon of India invited the American delegation to the United Nations to read the Declaration of Independence. 'Legitimism cannot be defended', he declared, 'and if you object to revolutionary governments, then you simply argue against the whole of progress'. But America did object to revolution. In 1958 Senator Fulbright summed up the Truman and Eisenhower approach when he said that the United States 'has dealt with princes, potentates, big business, and the entrenched, frequently corrupt, representatives of the past'.

Fulbright had accurately described Dulles's post-Geneva policy in South Vietnam. In September 1954, Dulles announced that henceforth American aid would go directly to the South Vietnamese and not through the French. In November, American military advisers began training a South Vietnamese Army. Fulbright had warned that 'there are few of the newly independent countries in the world in which we have an understanding of the motivations of the common man', but Dulles was sure that the United States could do what the French could not. The Americans gave power in South Vietnam to Ngo Dinh Diem, who drew his support from the landlords and had good relations with the French plantation owners, and Eisenhower pledged American economic aid to Diem. The President hedged by requiring social and economic reforms from Diem, but from the first it was understood that Diem could do as he wished as long as he remained firmly anti-communist.

By July 1955, the French had left Vietnam, where they were supposed to stay to supervise the elections promised at Geneva, and with American support Diem announced that the elections would not be held. Diem and Dulles both knew that Eisenhower was correct in predicting that in an election Ho Chi Minh would win 80 per cent of the vote. In May 1955, Dulles had told reporters that the United States would recognize an anti-Diem government in the south only if 'it seems to be expressive of the real will of the people and if it is truly representative'. Since the President himself had admitted that an overwhelming majority of the people wanted Ho, Dulles had to cover himself by arguing that the people of South Vietnam could not make a real choice since they did not understand the alternative to Ho and did not realize that Ho was an agent of international communism. Dulles was willing to abide by election results after the Vietnamese had learned how much more Diem had to offer. The Russians had used an identical argument to justify the absence of elections in East Europe.

American aid then began to pour into Diem's hands as the United States tried to promote South Vietnam as a model for Third World development. Brinksmanship had failed to prevent the loss of North Vietnam and was of little or no help in dealing with the problems of the underdeveloped nations, so Dulles offered the Diem example as a method of handling what he regarded as the most important problem of the era. Whether it would be a convincing example or not remained to be seen.

If brinksmanship failed to halt or even shape the revolution of rising expectations, it could still be used to protect what was already clearly America's. Dulles faced his third major challenge, and used brinksmanship for the third time, in the Formosa Straits, where he did succeed in achieving his objective.

In January 1953, Eisenhower had unleashed Chiang. The Nationalist Chinese then began a series of bombing raids, in American-built planes, against mainland shipping and ports. The pin-prick war was just enough to keep the Chinese enraged without injuring them seriously.* In January 1955, the Chinese were ready to strike back. They began by bombing the Tachen islands, 230 miles north of Formosa and held by a division of Chiang's troops. The Chinese also began to build up strength and mount cannon opposite Quemoy and Matsu, small islands sitting at the mouths of two Chinese harbors and garrisoned by Nationalist divisions. Eisenhower—although not some of his advisers—was willing to write off the Tachens, which were soon evacuated, but he was determined to hold Quemoy and Matsu as he believed they were integral to the defense of Formosa itself. His reasoning, as he explained during a 1958 crisis over the same issue, was that if Quemoy and Matsu fell, Formosa would follow, which would 'seriously jeopardize the anti-Communist barrier consisting of the insular and peninsular position in the Western Pacific, e.g., Japan, Republic of Korea, Republic of China, Republic of the Philippines, Thailand and Vietnam'. Indonesia, Malaya, Cambodia, Laos, and Burma 'would probably come fully under Communist influence'.

Summing up, Eisenhower declared, 'the consequences in the Far East would be even more far-reaching and catastrophic than those which followed when the United States allowed the Chinese mainland to be taken over by the Chinese Communists, aided and abetted by the Soviet Union'. The statement was not, it is important to note, campaign propaganda. It was not even intended for the public. It was a position paper drafted by Dulles and edited by Eisenhower, which indicated that it represented their honest opinion. Aside from revealing their astonishing attitude towards the reasons for Chiang's loss of China, it accepted for the purposes of policy the idea that if the Chinese were not fought on Quemoy and Matsu, America would have to fight them in San Francisco.

To avoid the 'catastrophic consequences' of the loss of Quemoy and Matsu, on 24 January 1955 Eisenhower went before Congress to ask for authority to 'employ the armed forces of the United States as he [the President] deems necessary for the specific purpose of protecting Formosa and the Pescadores against armed attack', the authority to include protection for 'related positions', which meant Quemoy and Matsu. Eisenhower feared that if the Chinese moved and he had to go to Congress for authority to act it would be too late, so the asked for a blank check on which he could draw at will. As the legal adviser of the Department of State who helped draft the resolution remarked, it was a 'monumental' step, for 'never before in our history had anything been done like that'. Nevertheless, there was hardly a debate. The House passed the Resolution by 409 to 3, while it went through the Senate by 85 to 3.

A major war scare then ensued. As the Chinese began to bombard Quemoy and Matsu, the Eisenhower administration seriously considered dropping nuclear weapons on the mainland. At no other time in the Cold War did the United States come so close to launching a preventive war. Had the Chinese actually launched invasions of the islands, it is possible, perhaps even probable, that the United States would have struck. In a speech on 20 March, Dulles referred to the Chinese in terms usually reserved for use against nations at war. The Secretary said the Chinese were 'an acute and imminent threat, ... dizzy with success'. He compared their 'aggressive fanaticism' with Hitler's and said they were 'more dangerous and provocative of war'.

---

*Eisenhower was once asked what the United States would have done in 1865 if Jefferson Davis, Robert E. Lee, and the Confederate Army had escaped to Cuba, if they had then mounted raids against Florida, and if the British Navy had stationed a fleet between Florida and Cuba to prevent the United States from over-running the island and driving the Confederates off. Eisenhower replied that the analogy was not a good one, since the Confederate government had never been legitimate.

To stop them, he threatened to use 'new and powerful weapons of precision, which can utterly destroy military targets without endangering unrelated civilian centers', which meant tactical atomic bombs. Eisenhower backed him up by saying he regarded the small atomic bombs as no different than bullets or any other military weapons.

On 25 March, the Chief of Naval Operations, Admiral R. B. Carney, briefed correspondents at a private dinner. He said the President was considering acting militarily on an all-out basis 'to destroy Red China's military potential and thus end its expansionist tendencies'. Dulles told the President that before the problem was solved, 'I believe there is at least an even chance that the United States will have to go to war'. Dulles thought that small air bursts, with minimal civilian casualties, would do the job quickly and 'the revulsion might not be long-lived'. Eisenhower, however, began to doubt that the operation could be limited in time or scope, and he set his face against preventive war. On 28 April, at a press conference, he said he had a 'sixth-sense' feeling that the outlook for peace had brightened and revealed that he had been in correspondence with his old wartime friend, Marshal Zhukov, one of the current Soviet rulers. Chinese pressure on Quemoy and Matsu lessened and the crisis receded. Brinksmanship had held the line.

In the process, however, it had scared the wits out of people around the globe, perhaps even members of the Eisenhower administration itself. The nuclear weapons of the fifties were at least a thousand times more destructive than the atomic bombs of the forties—one American bomber carried more destructive power than all the explosives set off in all the world's history put together—and everyone was frightened. The small, tactical atomic bombs Dulles was talking about were much larger than those dropped on Japan. Ever since the first American tests of the new fission bomb, Winston Churchill had been urging the United States and the Soviets to meet at the summit to try to resolve their differences. The Americans had consistently rejected his calls for a summit meeting, but by mid-1955, as the Russians began to improve both the size of their bombs and their delivery capabilities, and as the Formosa crisis made the United States face squarely the possibility of a nuclear exchange, Eisenhower and Dulles were more amenable.

Eisenhower's decision to go to the summit meant the end of any American dreams of winning the Cold War by military means. The Russians had come so far in nuclear development that Eisenhower himself warned the nation that an atomic war would ruin the world. There could be no 'possibility of victory or defeat', only different degrees of destruction. As James Reston reported in the *New York Times*, 'Perhaps the most important single fact in world politics today is that Mr. Eisenhower has thrown the immense authority of the American Presidency against risking a military solution of the cold war'. Since Eisenhower would not lead the nation into a nuclear war, and since he did not have the troops to fight a limited war, nor could he get them from his allies, and since the Republicans were more determined to balance the budget and enjoy the fruits of capitalism than they were to support a war machine, the only alternative left was peace of some kind with the Russians. Eisenhower was not willing to give in on any of the crucial questions, like the unification of Germany or Vietnam or Korea, but he was willing to talk with the new Russian leaders.

Eisenhower's readiness to go to Geneva and sit down with the Russians—the first meeting in a decade between leaders of the two nations—also represented his and Dulles's assumption that between them Moscow and Washington could rule the world, which in turn rested on the American notion that revolutionary activities in the Third World were directed by the Kremlin. A good illustration of the attitude, held in Moscow as well as in Washington, came at the height of the Formosan crisis, when Dulles talked to Molotov about easing tensions. Dulles reported that America was putting pressure on Chiang to cool down and asked Molotov to do the same to Mao. The American Secretary said that 'we needed a situation where as in Germany, Korea and Vietnam, it was agreed that unification would not be sought by force', which was another way of saying that the Chinese—both in Peking and on Formosa—should forget their own aspirations, pride, and national interests because Washington and Moscow had decided the time had come to calm the waters, not in the interests of the Chinese but in the interests of America and Russia. Molotov more or less agreed and suggested a summit conference.

Events broke rapidly in the late spring of 1955, helping to drive Eisenhower and the Russians to the summit. On 9 May, West Germany became a formal member of N.A.T.O. On 14 May the Soviet Union and the Eastern European nations signed the Warsaw Pact, the communist military counter to N.A.T.O. The next day Russia and America finally solved one of the long-standing problems of World War II by signing the Austrian treaty, which gave Austria independence, forbade union with Germany, and made Austria a permanent neutral. Both sides had been responsible for various delays. The Russians signed because they wanted to ease tensions and advance to the summit while the Americans accepted it as a reasonable solution for the Austrian problem. Dulles was unhappy. As Eisenhower later recalled, 'Well, suddenly the thing was signed one day and [Dulles] came in and he grinned rather ruefully and he said, "Well, I think we've had it." '

What Dulles feared was misinterpretation. The fear was justified, for columnists and pundits began to advocate a similar solution for Germany. Actually, far from being a step towards German unity and neutrality, the Austrian treaty was a step towards making German division permanent. Russia and America in effect agreed that neither of the Germanies would get Austria.

On 19 May, in an air show, the Soviets displayed impressive quantities of their latest long-range bombers. A week later the new top Russian leaders, Nikita Khrushchev and Nikolai Bulganin, flew to Yugoslavia, where in true Canossa style they apologized for Stalin's treatment of Tito and begged Tito's forgiveness. The Soviets were also initiating an economic assistance program for selected Third World nations. Clearly Russia had emerged from the confusion that followed Stalin's death and was on the offensive.

Some ground rules for the Cold War, of spirit if not of substance, were obviously needed. America's N.A.T.O. allies were adamant about the need, insistently so after N.A.T.O. war games in June showed that if conflict started in Europe (and if the war game scenario were accurate), 171 atomic bombs would be dropped on West Europe. For the United States to continue to take a stance of unrestrained hostility towards Russia was intolerable. This deeply felt sentiment in Europe, plus Eisenhower's personal dedication to peace, were the main factors in making the summit meeting at Geneva possible.

The Geneva meeting was not the result of any political settlement. Neither side was willing to back down from previous positions. Dulles made this perfectly clear when he drew up the American demands on Germany. His first goal was unification 'under conditions which will neither "neutralize" nor "demilitarize" united Germany, nor subtract it from N.A.T.O.'. There was not the slightest chance that the Russians would accept such a proposal. Neither would they ever agree to the only new American offer, Eisenhower's call for an 'open skies' agreement, for to them that was only another heavy-handed American attempt to spy on Russia. Bulganin, who fronted for Khrushchev at Geneva, was no more ready to deal than the Americans were. His position on Germany was to let things stand as they were.

On 18 July 1955 the summit meeting began. It had been called in response to the arms race and it was no surprise that there was no progress towards political settlements. What Dulles had feared most, however, did happen—there emerged a 'spirit of Geneva'. Before the meeting, Dulles had warned Eisenhower to maintain 'an austere countenance' when being photographed with Bulganin. He pointed out that any pictures taken of the two leaders smiling 'would be distributed throughout the Soviet satellite countries', signifying 'that all hope of liberation was lost and that resistance to communist rule was henceforth hopeless'. But the pictures were taken, and 'Ike' could not restrain his famous grin, and the photographs were distributed.

Dulles had been unable to prevent this symbolic recognition of the failure of Republican promises for liberation of communist satellites. The Soviets had almost caught up militarily and brinksmanship was dead. Geneva did not mean the end of the Cold War but it did put it on a different basis. The West had admitted that it could not win the Cold War, that a thermonuclear stalemate had developed, and that the *status quo* in Europe and China (where tensions quickly eased) had to be substantially accepted.

Dulles was bitter but helpless. He was especially infuriated because the battleground now shifted to the areas of economic and political influence in the Third World, a battleground on which Russia had enormous advantages. Dulles warned the N.A.T.O. Foreign Ministers in December 1955 that the Soviets would hereafter employ 'indirect' threats 'primarily developed in relations to the Near and Middle East and South Asia'. To fight back, Dulles needed two things—money, and an American willingness to accept radicalism in the emerging nations. He had neither. Republicans who resented giving money to West Europe through the Marshall Plan were hardly likely to approve significant sums for non-white revolutionaries.

Like his spiritual ancestors, the nineteenth-century abolitionists, Dulles was forced to retreat to what the abolitionists used to call moral suasion. He would talk the Soviets out of East Europe. This provided emotional satisfaction but little else. His chances for success were indicated by the aftermath of Geneva. In September, the Soviets worked out formal diplomatic relations with West Germany and a week later they gave East Germany full powers in foreign affairs. In January 1956, East Germany entered the Warsaw Pact.

Adjusting to the new realities was not easy. Dulles had denounced containment but had been unable to go beyond Truman's policy. He had promised liberation and had failed. Neither brinksmanship nor moral suasion had freed a single slave or prevented North Vietnam from going communist. But despite Geneva and the new realities, Dulles would not quit without a fight. On Christmas Day, 1955, the White House sent its usual message to the peoples of Eastern Europe to 'recognize the trials under which you are suffering' and to 'share your faith that right in the end will bring you again among the free nations of the world'. When Khrushchev complained that this 'crude interference' was not in accord with the spirit of Geneva, the White House pointed out that the goal of liberation was permanent. The statement said, 'The peaceful liberation of the captive peoples is, and, until success is achieved, will continue to be a major goal of United States foreign policy'.

28
Years of Shock

Eric Goldman

A veritable anti-Communist hysteria swept over the United States in the Truman and early Eisenhower years, as Americans saw Red conspiracies at home as well as abroad. It had happened before. In 1919, two years after Russia had fallen to Bolshevism, American patriots warned that a Bolshevik plot was under way to overthrow the United States, too. Convinced that this was so, Attorney-General A. Mitchell Palmer—"the fighting Quaker"—announced that he would round up all Bolsheviks and deport them to Russia on a special ship called *The Soviet Ark*. Authorities then set about apprehending hundreds of suspicious-looking people; and newspapers ran pictures of what a Bolshevik looked like (he was bearded, bespectacled, and sinister) so that Americans might root out any such conspirators in their churches, their schools, and their homes. Finally the Red scare subsided, but not before many innocent people had suffered.

Now in the 1940s and 1950s—in another postwar period—it was happening again, as thousands of insecure Americans began to suspect that many of their fellow countrymen had succumbed to Communism. And out of their fears emerged a conspiracy view of history, which held that since 1932 a Communist plot had been under way to take over the United States from within and to hand the country over to Moscow. The chief agent in this plot was Franklin Roosevelt; and the cast of villains also included the Brains Trusters and most of the New Dealers in the Cabinet and the Congress. The New Deal itself, with all its welfare measures, seemed part of a sinister world conspiracy directed by Moscow. Truman, too, in spite of his tough-guy stance toward the Russians, was linked to the Great Conspiracy. Had he not been Roosevelt's vice-president? And look at his Fair Deal domestic program, the patriots said. It consisted of such "socialistic" programs as civil rights legislation for Negroes, federal aid to schools, federal health insurance, and public housing. From the American Right, where the patriots were clustered, came resounding accusations that the Truman Administration was brimming with traitors and that all liberals were Communists.

The Communist scare, however, was not confined to the American Right. The fact was that Truman and the liberals were obsessed with Communism, too, and out of that obsession, as we have seen, came nuclear diplomacy and the Containment Policy. Furthermore, it was the liberals who went to war against Communism, first in Korea and later in Vietnam. At home, moreover, Truman instituted a sweeping loyalty oath program and began extensive security checks for federal employment. In truth, the liberals' preoccupation with Communism helped create a national mood in which hysterical anti-Communism flourished.

And flourish it did. Thousands of conservative and moderate Americans were very much afraid that Communists had infiltrated the schools, the churches, and the federal government itself. The House Un-American Activities Committee only fanned the flames when it unearthed alleged Communists in the universities and out in Hollywood. Then came the sensational trial of Alger Hiss.

Hiss had been a New Deal luminary and an official in the State Department. In 1948, Whittaker Chambers stood before the House Un-American Activities Committee and accused Hiss of being a Communist spy during the thirties. Chambers, turning state's evidence, admitted that he had belonged to the Communist Party and insisted that

Hiss had given him classified State Department documents. When Hiss sued him for libel, Chambers produced microfilms of the papers. In 1949 Hiss came to trial on a charge of perjury (the statute of limitations prevented him from being charged with espionage). The first trial ended in a hung jury, but the second found him guilty of perjury—and by implication of treason.

For many Americans, the Hiss trial was unchallengeable proof that the New Deal had been alive with Communists in government, proof that the conspiracy thesis was true, proof that the United States was in danger of being overthrown from within. There were other developments in 1949—that "year of shocks"—which convinced thousands of Americans (Republicans and Democrats alike) that disaster was imminent. First, China fell to Communism. Then came the stunning news that Russia also had the atomic bomb. 1950 came on. "For the frightened and embittered," writes Eric Goldman, "there was only more incitement to fright and bitterness."

On January 31, Presidential Press Secretary Charles Ross handed reporters a statement from President Truman: "It is part of my responsibility as Commander in Chief of the armed forces to see to it that our country is able to defend itself against any aggressor. Accordingly I have directed the Atomic Energy Commission to continue its work on all forms of atomic weapons, including the so-called hydrogen or super-bomb." Once again a terrifying announcement had been made with all the studied toning down of a mimeographed sheet—this time the President even saw to it that he was casually lunching at Blair House when Ross met the reporters. Once again nothing could really cushion the news. Not only

From pp. 135–279 in *The Crucial Decade—And After*, by Eric Goldman. Copyright © 1956, 1960 by Eric Goldman. Reprinted by permission of Alfred A. Knopf, Inc.

would a hydrogen bomb have one hundred to one thousand times the power of the largest atomic weapon. Twelve distinguished scientists immediately issued a joint statement which pointed out that "in the case of the fission bomb the Russians required four years to parallel our development. In the case of the hydrogen bomb they will probably need a shorter time."

Some Americans talked tough. Secretary of Defense Louis Johnson told an alumni gathering at the University of Virginia: "I want Joe Stalin to know that if he starts something at four o'clock in the morning, the fighting power and strength of America will be on the job at five o'clock in the morning." Other Americans raised harsh, portentous questions. Senator Brien McMahon, chairman of the Joint Congressional Committee on Atomic Energy, brought solemn handshakes from both sides of the chamber by a speech in which he asked: "How is it possible for free institutions to flourish or even to maintain themselves in a situation where defenses, civil and military, must be ceaselessly poised to meet an attack that might incinerate fifty million Americans—not in the space of an evening, but in the space of moments?" The most authoritative voice of all talked doom. Albert Einstein went on television, the simple sweater jacket, the scraggly gray hair, the childlike face with the brilliant eyes all adding to the aura of an otherworldly wisdom beyond the power of ordinary mortals. With the order of President Truman to produce an H-bomb, Einstein said, "radioactive poisoning of the atmosphere and hence annihilation of any life on earth has been brought within the range of technical possibilities. . . . General annihilation beckons."

Another four days and another jolting headline. On February 3 the British government announced the confession of Dr. Klaus Fuchs, a high-level atomic scientist. The descriptions of Fuchs sitting behind the cast-iron grill of the prisoner's dock in Bow Street police court, plainly dressed, bespectacled, quiet-mannered, gave him every inch the appearance of the dedicated scientist—"the last man in the world you would expect to be a spy," as one English reporter commented. Yet Fuchs's confession stated that from 1943 through 1947, while engaged in government atomic research in the United States and Britain, he had systematically passed over to Soviet agents the inmost scientific secrets of the Western powers. "I had complete confidence in Russian policy," he told the police, "and I had no hesitation in giving all the information I had." The knowledge Fuchs handed over, his superior, Michael Perren stated, had been "of the highest value to a potential enemy," and no doubt speeded up the Russian production of an atom bomb "at least a year."

Senator Homer Capehart of Indiana stood up in the Senate and stormed: "How much more are we going to have to take? Fuchs and Acheson and Hiss and hydrogen bombs threatening outside and New Dealism eating away the vitals of the nation. In the name of Heaven, is this the best America can do?" The applause was loud and long, from the floor and from the galleries.

That afternoon the regular plane from Washington to Wheeling, West Virginia, began loading. The stewardess did her duty, noted a United States Senator on the passenger list, and greeted him with a smiling, "Good afternoon, Senator McCarthy." The reply was a bit plaintive. "Why, good afternoon—I'm glad somebody recognizes me."

Getting recognized was no new concern of Joseph McCarthy. The Irish settlement in northern Wisconsin where he grew up respected money and looks; the McCarthys were a struggling brood of nine and Joe was the ugly duckling, barrel-chested and short-armed with thick eyebrows and heavy lips. Mother Bridget McCarthy threw a special protective wing around the shy, sulky boy and when the rough teasing came, he sought out her big warm apron. "Don't you mind," she would console. "You be somebody. You get ahead."

Joe took heed. He would get back; he would show everybody. The shy sulkiness turned into a no-holds-barred ambition curiously mixed with a gawky, grinning likability. The boy worked so furiously on the family farm that neighbors joked he must have spent his babyhood wearing overalls instead of diapers. Starting his education late, he talked, wheedled, and shoved his way through Marquette University with so much corner-cutting that Wisconsin educators still gasp at the record.

Associates noted the fierce, blinding drive in everything McCarthy did. When he boxed and his awkwardness was getting him cut to pieces, he would keep coming in, slashed and bleeding but flailing away in the hope of striking a knockout blow. When he played poker, he played all-or-nothing. He had the "guts of a burglar," one friend remembers. "He was brutal. He'd take all the fun out of the game, because he took it so seriously." When he ran for office in college, he dropped his homework, cut school for weeks at a time, devoted night and day to buying coffees and cokes and making lavish promises. He and his opponent agreed that each would vote for the other until the election was decided. The first ballot was a tie. On the next McCarthy won by two votes.

"Joe," the defeated candidate said, "did you vote for yourself?"

McCarthy grinned his big, disarming, tail-between-the-legs grin. "Sure. You wanted me to vote for the best man, didn't you?"

Once out of Marquette, he bashed his way to a Wisconsin Circuit Judgeship and soon converted it into a political stump, knocking off divorces in five minutes or less, racing around to please people by trying as many cases as possible. After Pearl Harbor he entered the Marine Corps, turning the whole Pacific Theater of War into a headquarters of McCarthy for United States Senator, blithely giving himself the name of "Tail-gunner Joe" although most of the time he was actually serving as an intelligence officer and doing the paper work for a squadron of pilots. Elected to the Senate in 1946, he thrashed about for ways to secure his political hold. McCarthy served the interests of the Pepsi-Cola Company so faithfully he became known to fellow Senators as the "Pepsi-Cola Kid." He delighted the real-estate interests in Wisconsin by battling public housing and he pleased some of his large German-American constituency by defending the Nazis on trial for the murders of Malmédy.

It was a great life, this being a United States Senator. "Pretty good going for a Mick from the backwoods, eh?" McCarthy would grin at the cocktail parties and the ladies thought he was awfully cute—"such an engaging primitive," as one debutante put it. But there was a problem and the engaging primitive was no more patient with a problem than he had ever been.

On January 7, 1950 McCarthy sat having a troubled dinner at the Colony Restaurant in Washington. The get-together had been arranged by Charles H. Kraus, a professor of political science at Georgetown University, and William A. Roberts, a well-known Washington attorney. Kraus in particular had been seeing a good deal of the Senator and had been suggesting books for him to read—especially the potent anti-Communist volume *Total Power* by Father Edmund A. Walsh, vice-president of Georgetown and regent of its School of Foreign Service. (McCarthy was hardly a book-lover but he did like to skim hurriedly and he had spoken of his desire "to read some meaty books.") The prime purpose of the dinner was to permit the Senator to meet Father Walsh, whom both Kraus and Roberts profoundly admired.

McCarthy soon brought the conversation around to what was uppermost in his mind. His situation was bad, the Senator said. Here it was already the beginning of 1950, with his term running out in two years, and he had neither the national publicity which would attract Wisconsin voters nor any specific issue likely to stir them.

Within months Kraus, Roberts, and Walsh were all to repudiate McCarthy but at this time they were well disposed toward the youthful Senator. Kraus and Roberts were also Marine veterans of World War II; everyone at the table was a Catholic; the Senator's shaggy affability could attract men as well as women. Eager to help McCarthy, the group threw out suggestions.

"How about pushing harder for the St. Lawrence seaway?" Roberts proposed.

McCarthy shook his head. "That hasn't enough appeal. No one gets excited about it."

The Senator then thought aloud about a Townsend-type pension plan for all elderly Americans. Why not start a campaign to pay one hundred dollars a month to everybody over sixty-five years of age? But the three other men agreed that the idea was economically unsound.

After dinner the group went to Roberts's office in the adjoining DeSales Building and continued the discussion. McCarthy and Roberts, both voluble men, did most of the talking but at one point Father Walsh spoke at length. He emphasized the world power of Communism and the danger that it would infiltrate any democratic government. He was sure, Walsh declared, that vigilance against Communism was of such importance that it would be an issue two years hence.

The Senator's face brightened. Communist infiltration—wasn't this what everybody was talking about? And wasn't this, after all, a *real* issue? The priest's remarks touched chords that reached far back into McCarthy's life. In the 1930's, the Irish settlement of northern Wisconsin voted for Franklin Roosevelt; the farms were in too desperate a condition for anything else. But the New Dealism had its own Midwestern, new-immigrant, Irish-Catholic coloration. It was filled with suspicion of Easterners, "radicals," "aristocrats," the British, and the "striped-pants fellows" of the State Department. McCarthy had started in politics a New Deal Democrat but as soon as the prosperity came he shifted to a more congenial Taft Republicanism. Whether a Democrat or a Republican, he had always more or less consciously assumed that the big trouble with America, as his boyhood neighbor Jim Heegan used to put it, was "those Leftists."

McCarthy cut in on Father Walsh. "The Government is full of Communists. The thing to do is to hammer at them."

Roberts, a longtime liberal attorney, spoke a sharp warning. Such a campaign would have to be based on facts; the public was weary of "Wolf! Wolf!" cries about "Reds." The Senator said offhandedly he would get the facts.

Lincoln's Birthday, the traditional time for Republican oratory, was approaching, and McCarthy—probably at his own request—was assigned by the Senate Republican Campaign Committee to speak on the topic, "Communism in the State Department." The Senator's office put together some materials drawn mostly from hearings and staff investigations of a House Appropriations subcommittee. Three weeks after Hiss was convicted, ten days after President Truman ordered work on the H-bomb, six days after the British announced the Fuchs confession, on February 9, 1950, McCarthy took the plane to deliver his speech before the Women's Republican Club in Wheeling, West Virginia. He would give it a try. He would see if he could not get someone besides polite airline stewardesses to recognize the name Joseph McCarthy.

"The reason why we find ourselves in a position of impotency [in international affairs]," the Senator told the club, "is not because our only powerful potential enemy has sent men to invade our shores, but rather because of the traitorous actions of those who have been treated so well by this Nation...." Where was the situation most serious? "Glaringly" so in the State Department. And what kind of men were the offenders? "The bright young men who are born with silver spoons in their mouths are the ones who have been worst.... In my opinion the State Department, which is one of the most important government departments, is thoroughly infested with Communists." Most dangerous of all was Dean Acheson, that "pompous diplomat in striped pants, with a phony British accent."

McCarthy had always believed that a speaker had to get specific in order to make his points stick. Near the end of his speech he talked about a list "I hold here in my hand." Exactly what he said about the list will probably never be known with certainty. James E. Whitaker and Paul A. Myers, news editor and program director respectively of the Wheeling radio station that broadcast the speech, WWVA, later swore in an affidavit that McCarthy's words were: "I have here in my hand a list of 205—a list of names that were known to the Secretary of State as being members of the Communist Party and who nevertheless are still working and shaping the policy in the State Department." The Senator's friends later insisted that his point was something like: "I have here in my hand 57 cases of individuals who would appear to be either card-carrying members or certainly loyal to the Communist Party, but who nevertheless are still helping to shape our foreign policy." One man who would never be sure what he had said was Joseph McCarthy. Frederick Woltman, the responsible reporter for the Scripps-Howard newspapers, has described how "on a number of occasions —mostly in my apartment at the Congressional —I heard McCarthy and his advisors wrack their brains for some lead as to what he said in that Wheeling speech. He had no copy; he had spoken from rough notes and he could not find the notes.... The Senator's staff could find no one who could recall what he'd said precisely. He finally hit on the idea of appealing to ham radio operators in the area who might have made a recording of the speech. He could find none."

For the moment there was no such interesting problem. There was only another plane to catch, another polite stewardess to greet Senator McCarthy. The speech seemed to disappear; it was not even reported except in the Wheeling newspapers and in the *Chicago Tribune*. The Senator kept flailing away. On February 10, in Salt Lake City, he made a speech similar to his Wheeling talk and charged that there were "57 card-carrying members of the Communist Party" in the State Department. The next day he repeated substantially the same talk in Reno and wired President Truman demanding that the White House do something.

Things began to happen. Newspapers in many parts of the country headlined the Salt Lake City and Reno charges. President Truman and Secretary of State Acheson issued angry statements of denial. The Senate stirred, authorizing a subcommittee of the Foreign Relations Committee to investigate the Senator's statements.

But what was happening did not seem to bode well for Joseph McCarthy. The materials that he had used for his speeches were largely old and none too sturdy charges. The Senate subcommittee, chairmanned by the militantly Democratic Millard Tydings of Maryland, kept McCarthy pinned in the worst possible light. Veteran Republican Senate leaders were plainly hesitant about backing this rambunctious upstart.

Then, gradually, support came. By an instinct born of the whole climate of ideas in which he had grown up, McCarthy was attacking precisely in the way most likely to capture the groups in America who were most disturbed about foreign policy—the whole conspiracy theory of international affairs down to the last suspicion of Dean Acheson's striped pants. By the same instinct, he kept broadening the sense of conspiracy, catching more strands of the rebelliousness abroad in the country. Within a month after his Wheeling speech he was assailing as Communists the "whole group of twisted-thinking New Dealers [who] have led America near to ruin at home and abroad." Many others had been saying these things. No one had kept naming names, dozens of specific, headline-making names. And no one had attacked with such abandon—McCarthy politicking as he had done everything else, ignoring the rules, always walking in, taking his beatings, endlessly throwing wild, spectacular punches. Shortly after the Tydings subcommittee did its most telling job on the charge of fifty-seven card-carrying Communists in the State Department, the Senator closed his eyes completely and swung so hard he shook the country.

He would "stand or fall on this one," McCarthy let it be known. He was naming "the top Russian espionage agent" in the United States and a man who had long been "one of the top advisers on Far Eastern policy"—Owen Lattimore. In the ensuing uproar only the most informed Americans could make out the fact that Lattimore was a non-Communist liberal who had been called into consultation infrequently by the State Department and whose suggestions had been almost totally ignored.

By late March private contributions were pouring into the Senator's office. The awards began. The Marine Corps League of Passaic, New Jersey, announced that it had selected Joseph McCarthy to receive its 1950 citation for Americanism. Leading Taft Republicans, including Senator Taft himself, the two powerhouses, Senators Kenneth Wherry and Styles Bridges, and the chairman of the Republican National Committee, Guy Gabrielson, were giving a respectful and cooperative attention to the rambunctious upstart. Various groups which had their own special uses for McCarthy's kind of anti-Communism came to his support—including the potent manipulators who were soon known as the "China Lobby."

Now the grin was as broad as Mother Bridget's apron. The Senator was affable, endlessly affable. In the course of a discussion in McCarthy's apartment, Mrs. Frederick Woltman asked testily: "Tell me, Senator, just how long ago did you discover Communism?"

The Senator grinned. "Why, about two and a half months ago."

In the office of Herbert Block, the strongly New Dealish cartoonist of the *Washington Post*, there was no grinning. Herblock angrily sketched a harassed Republican elephant, being pushed and pulled by Taft, Wherry, Bridges, and Gabrielson toward a stack of buckets of tar with an extra big barrel of tar on top. The cartoonist hesitated for a moment, thinking over possible one-word labels. Then he was satisfied. On the large barrel of tar he printed the letters, McCARTHYISM.

Immediately, and so naturally that people promptly forgot where the term had first been used, the word McCarthyism passed into the language. The revolt set off by the shocks of 1949 had its name and the expression of its most violent, most reckless mood.

. . .

The shocks of 1949 had given Senator Joseph McCarthy his start. The frustrations of 1950 and 1951 blasted wide his road to power. With America tangled in deadlocks at home and abroad, the man with the simple answer, the furious, flailing answer, had his day. In early 1951 Mickey Spillane's *One Lonely Night* started on its way to selling more than three million copies. The hero, Mike Hammer, gloated: "I killed more people tonight than I have fingers on my hands. I shot them in cold blood and enjoyed every minute of it. . . . They were Commies, Lee. They were red sons-of-bitches who should have died long ago. . . . They never thought that there were people like me in this country. They figured us all to be soft as horse manure and just as stupid." Hammer's tough-guy certainty that he was solving the world's problems by bludgeoning Communists hardly hurt the sales of *One Lonely Night*. It was a day for Mike Hammerism, in books or in politics.

Week after week Senator McCarthy became bolder and more reckless. For years General of the Army George Marshall, the over-all architect of victory in World War II, had been one of the most generally esteemed figures in the United States. But Marshall was associated with the Truman policy in the Far East and on June 14, 1951 McCarthy stood up in the Senate and delivered a sixty-thousand-word speech which charged that Marshall was part of "a conspiracy so immense, an infamy so black, as to dwarf any in the history of man. . . . [a conspiracy directed] to the end that we shall be contained, frustrated and finally fall victim to Soviet intrigue from within and Russian military might from without." The more reckless McCarthy became, the more his influence mounted. Fewer and fewer Senators rose to gainsay him. Pollsters found that steadily increasing percentages of Americans were ready to answer yes to questions like, Do you in general approve of Senator McCarthy's activities?

Outside of politics, the flood of McCarthyism mounted—the people who were chasing alleged Communists, the men and the institutions who were abetting McCarthyism by acquiescing in its attitudes. Some of the furor was simply ridiculous. Monogram Pictures canceled a movie about Henry Wadsworth Longfellow. Hiawatha, the studio explained, had tried to stop wars between the Indian tribes and people might construe the picture as propaganda for the Communist "peace offensive." Wheeling,

West Virginia, staged the kind of comic-opera terror that was going on in scores of cities. In Wheeling the hubbub began when a policeman announced his discovery that penny-candy machines were selling children's bonbons with little geography lessons attached to the candies. The very tininess of the messages, half the size of a postage stamp, was suspicious; most rousing of all was the revelation that some of the geography lessons bore the hammer-and-sickle Soviet flag and the message: "U.S.S.R. Population 211,000,000. Capital Moscow. Largest country in the world." City Manager Robert L. Plummer thundered: "This is a terrible thing to expose our children to." Stern measures were taken to protect the candy-store set from the knowledge that the Soviet Union existed and that it was the biggest country in the world.

Much of the furor, far from being ridiculous, was sinister. The United States Government was tainting the names of innocent men and costing itself the services of invaluable specialists. Senator McCarthy decided that Philip Jessup, a distinguished professor of international law at Columbia and a skilled diplomat, was a man with "an unusual affinity for Communist causes"; supinely a subcommittee of the Senate Foreign Relations Committee turned down Jessup's nomination as a delegate to the UN General Assembly. Trying to fight off McCarthyism, the Truman Administration adopted loyalty procedures that were increasingly dubious. In or out of government, utterly innocent people were losing their jobs. Irene Wicker, the "Singing Lady" of television, who was soon to have an audience with the Pope and be given a special blessing for her work with children, found her TV contract canceled. The McCarthy-type magazine *Counterattack*, which was connected with the pressure to dismiss her, made everything clear. The *Daily Worker* had listed Miss Wicker as a sponsor of a Red councilmanic candidate in New York and "the *Daily Worker* is very accurate; they never make a mistake."

Everywhere in the United States, the fury against Communism was taking on—even more than it had before the Korean War—elements of a vendetta against the Half-Century of Revolution in domestic affairs, against all departures from tradition in foreign policy, against the new, the adventurous, the questing in any field. Self-confident Yale University felt it necessary to appoint a committee of distinguished alumni to protect itself against a recent undergraduate, William F. Buckley, who talked, in the same burst of indignation at the Yale faculty, about the menace of Communism and the threat of "atheists" and of men who criticized "limited government" or economic "self-reliance." For most of 1951 the best-seller lists of the country included *Washington Confidential* by two newspapermen, Jack Lait and Lee Mortimer. The book was a jumble of breathless revelations about "Communism" in Washington, quotations like the one from an unnamed Negro dope peddler who told an unnamed federal agent "You can't arrest me. I am a friend of Mrs. Roosevelt," and such observations as "Where you find an intellectual in the District you will probably find a Red." In a number of cities, educators reported, anything "controversial" was being stripped from the schools—and more than a few times the "controversial" writing turned out to be factual information about UNESCO or New Deal legislation. A battle over a textbook in Council Bluffs, Iowa, produced the kind of statement that was commonplace. Ex-Congressman Charles Swanson opened the meeting with a roaring denunciation of "all these books. . . . They should be thrown on a bonfire—or sent to Russia. Why according to this book, Jefferson, Jackson, Wilson and Franklin Roosevelt were outstanding Presidents —what about William Howard Taft?"

In Washington, William Howard Taft's son Robert was in a new phase of his career. "The sad, worst period," his sympathetic biographer, William S. White, has called it. Certainly Senator Robert Taft was moving closer to McCarthyism. Even before the Korean War, in March, 1950, several responsible reporters asserted that Taft had remarked: "McCarthy should keep talking and if one case doesn't work out he should proceed with another." The Senator protested that this quotation misrepresented him but there can be no question about the meaning of statements he made after the Korean intervention. Taft complained that Truman had the bad habit to *"assume the innocence* of all the persons mentioned in the State Department." He also declared: "Whether Senator McCarthy has *legal evidence,* whether he has overstated or understated his case, is of lesser importance. The question is whether the Communist influence in the State Department *still exists."* (Italics added.) "This sort of thing," William White could only sadly comment, "was not the Taft one had known."

In domestic affairs the Senator's attacks became sharper and edged closer to the argument that Fair Dealism was a conspiracy of socialists. In foreign affairs, all the matters that were "open to question" in Taft's speech at the time the United States entered the Korean War were now settled and settled against the Administration. The American intervention was "an unnecessary war," an "utterly useless war," a war "begun by President Truman without the slightest authority from Congress or the people." And in explaining the international policy of the Administration the Senator was more and more using phrases that suggested a plot on the part of—to use a 1951 statement of Taft —"men who did not and do not turn their backs on the Alger Hisses."

If the Senator was going far, a large part of the GOP was moving in the same direction. In part this trend represented out-and-out McCarthyism. More of it came from the feeling—to use the phrase current then—that "I don't like some of McCarthy's methods but his goal is good." To the largest extent the development resulted from a fundamental disquietude with foreign and domestic affairs that showed itself in a violent anti-Trumanism, particularly on the issue of Far Eastern policy.

. . .

General Republicans, Taftite Republicans, McCarthyite Republicans, McCarthyite Democrats, and the millions of Americans who fitted none of these categories—in late 1951 and 1952 much of the nation was restlessly, irritably seeking to break through the sense of frustration. People flailed Harry Truman as a caged animal lashes at its bars. The President's Gallup rating sank to a minuscule twenty-six per cent and the personal attacks were so extreme the pro-Truman *New York Post* found itself pleading: "After all, the President of the United States is a member of the human race." Men and women were looking for some bright shining light, some road without endless roadblocks.

. . .

[For a majority of Americans that "bright, shining light" was Republican Dwight Eisenhower, who assumed office in 1953. But the fears of Communist subversion remained; and even Eisenhower had to worry about Joe McCarthy.]

On Capitol Hill Senator Joseph McCarthy was asked his judgment of the new Administration and he smiled loftily. The Administration's record on anti-Communism, he said, was "fair."

Circumstances were hardly such as to curb the arrogance of Joseph McCarthy. The Republican capture of the Senate in 1952 had made him for the first time the chairman of his own committee—the powerful Committee on Government Operations—and he also headed its formidable subcommittee, the Permanent Subcommittee on Investigations. With a handful of exceptions the whole Senate treated him with respect or at least with care. He seemed to have proved what a politician respects most—an awesome ability to affect votes. He himself had been re-elected in 1952 by a majority of more than 140,000. No less than eight of the men in the Senate—six who had been elected in 1952—were thought to owe their seats largely to his campaigning. Around the country his name had an increasing potency. A belligerent if small pro-McCarthy faction was making itself heard even among the group which had shown the most solid bloc resistance to him, the intellectuals of the United States.

Probably most important of all, the man in the White House had a conception of his role which very specifically ruled out openly battling McCarthy. Eisenhower not only wanted to respect the Constitutional division between the Executive and legislative divisions. He was keenly aware that he was the head of a divided party and anxious to unite it along the lines of his own thinking. Whatever the President's own tendencies toward the right, his views were quite different from those of the right-wingers, who for the most part were bitter anti-New Dealers, all-out isolationists with respect to Europe, all-out interventionists with respect to Asia, and enthusiasts for the kind of anti-Communism represented by McCarthy. These men followed the President reluctantly when they followed him at all and Eisenhower wanted to do nothing to increase the friction. It was the President's "passion," his aide C. D. Jackson remarked, "not to offend anyone in Congress" and this attitude soon permeated most of his subordinates.

Month after month McCarthy went to further extremes and month after month the Administration sidestepped, looked the other way, or actually followed his bidding. At the beginning of the Administration McCarthy declared that he believed there were still Communists in the State Department and that Dulles could go a long way toward rooting them out by naming a good security officer. The Secretary named a good security officer—Scott McLeod, widely assumed to be a McCarthy disciple. March 1953 and the Senator announced that he had negotiated with Greek shipowners to stop trading at Soviet and satellite ports. Director of Mutual Security Harold Stassen angrily pointed out that this was a flagrant Senatorial interference with the functions of the Executive Branch and that by negotiating with a small group "you are in effect undermining and are harmful to our objective" of stopping the general trade with the Communists. Immediately a mollifying statement came from Frank Nash, Assistant Secretary of Defense for international affairs, and Secretary of State Dulles and McCarthy got together for a congenial lunch. At his press conference, the President did the final smoothing over by suggesting that both McCarthy and Stassen had gone a bit far. The Senator had probably made a "mistake" and the Director of Mutual Security probably meant "infringement" rather than "undermining."

All the while McCarthy was stepping up his campaign against the State Department's overseas information program. The country began to hear about the two 27-year-olds, Roy Cohn, the Subcommittee's chief counsel, and G. David Schine, an unpaid Subcommittee consultant. They left on an eighteen-day whirl through western Europe to ferret out "subversion" in the overseas program. Seventeen hours in Bonn, twenty hours in Berlin, nineteen hours in Frankfurt—these and a sprinkling of other stops and McCarthy was proclaiming "appalling infiltration." The State Department reacted dutifully. It asked for resignations—including those of men like Theodore Kaghan who had probably dabbled with radicalism in the late 1930's and who now was known through central Europe as one of the most effective organizers of anti-Communist propaganda. (When the Subcommittee made its charges Leopold Figl, the ultraconservative former Chancellor of

Austria, wrote Kaghan: "What goes on? After all, April Fool's day has long passed by. . . .") The State Department also issued a new directive banning from American information activities all "books, music, paintings, and the like . . . of any Communists, fellow travelers, *et cetera*" and ordering that "librarians should at once remove all books and other material by Communists, fellow travelers, *et cetera*, from their shelves and withdraw any that may be in circulation."

Many librarians, taking no chance on having a work by an *et cetera* on their shelves, removed the books of authors like Bert Andrews, chief of the Washington bureau of the Republican *New York Herald Tribune;* Walter White, head of the anti-Communist National Association for the Advancement of Colored People; Richard Lauterbach, former European correspondent of *Time;* Clarence Streit, chief figure in the strongly democratic movement for a federal union of the North Atlantic democracies; and Foster Rhea Dulles, a decidedly anti-Communist professor at Ohio State and cousin of the Secretary of State. Some librarians stored the books they removed; others burned them.

. . .

McCarthy rampaged on. With the opening of 1954 he and his staff concentrated increasingly on the Department of the Army and a number of top Army officials tried hard to work with them. In January the Senator began to hammer on the case of Major Irving Peress, a New York dental officer. Peress had been permitted to receive his regularly due promotion and granted an honorable discharge after he had refused to sign an Army loyalty certificate and after he had refused, on the grounds of possible self-incrimination, to answer a number of questions at a Subcommittee hearing. In a letter to McCarthy, Secretary of the Army Robert Stevens acknowledged that the Peress case had been mishandled and stated that if he found the promotion had been anything but routine he would discipline the officers involved. He also ordered that in the future Reserve officers who refused to sign a loyalty certificate were to be given an other than honorable discharge.

Unappeased, the Senator summoned Peress and a group of Army officials, including Brigadier General Ralph Zwicker, to a Subcommittee hearing. At one point, when the hearing was in executive session, McCarthy demanded that Zwicker answer questions concerning the processing of the Peress case and Zwicker replied that such information was inviolate under a Presidential order. The Senator was furious. According to Zwicker, McCarthy shouted at the General: "You are a disgrace to the uniform. You're shielding Communist conspirators. You are going to be put on public display next Tuesday. You're not fit to be an officer. You're ignorant."

Zwicker was a highly esteemed officer who was obviously simply following orders. The Army seethed with resentment. Secretary Stevens heatedly accused McCarthy of humiliating Zwicker and of undermining Army morale, and ordered two officers not to appear before the Senator's Subcommittee. McCarthy promptly replied that Stevens was an "awful dupe" and summoned the Secretary himself to testify. Stevens decided to go and prepared a strong statement which he intended to read at the hearing. But the statement was never read. Instead Stevens met with McCarthy and other members of the Subcommittee and accepted a "Memorandum of Agreement." When the memorandum was released few commentators, pro- or anti-McCarthy, interpreted it as anything but complete and abject surrender on the part of the Secretary of the Army.

That afternoon the White House was filled with glum discussions of ways to do something about the Stevens debacle. In the Capitol a reporter passed by the hearings room of the Subcommittee, noticed the door open, and looked in. He saw McCarthy and Roy Cohn sitting at the end of the table and "laughing so hard," the newsman remembered, "that the room seemed to shake."

. . .

From the day of the Memorandum of Agreement the Administration moved against McCarthy, sometimes indirectly but steadily. Secretary Stevens countered the Memorandum with a strong statement and the President made plain that he backed his Secretary "one hundred percent." On March 11, 1954 the Army attacked with the charge that Senator McCarthy, Roy Cohn, and Francis Carr, the Subcommittee staff director, had sought, separately and collectively, by improper means, to obtain preferential treatment in the Army for G. David Schine, the Subcommittee consultant who was now a private in the Army. McCarthy and "associates" promptly replied with forty-six charges against the Army, of which the key one was that Secretary Stevens and John Adams, the department counselor, had tried to stop the Subcommittee's exposure of alleged Communists at Fort Monmouth and that they used Private Schine as a "hostage" to this end. Four more days and the Subcommittee voted to investigate the Army-McCarthy clash, with TV cameras in the room and with McCarthy temporarily replaced by the next ranking Republican, Senator Karl Mundt of South Dakota. Once again a TV spectacle would transfix the country and once again television would have a major part in shaping opinion on a critical national issue.

Shortly after 10 a.m. on April 22, 1954 the red lights in the cameras went on amid the florid Corinthian columns and the brocaded curtains of the large Senate Caucus Room. Senator Mundt tapped his big pipe, leaned forward, and delivered a little speech about how everything was going to be done with "dignity, fairness, and thoroughness." The ranking Democrat, John McClellan, said a few words to the same effect.

"Thank you very much, Senator McClellan," Chairman Mundt declared. "Our counsel, Mr. Jenkins, will now call the first witness." Ray Jenkins opened his mouth but the words came from down along the table. "A point of order, Mr. Chairman," McCarthy was saying. "May I raise a point of order?"

For thirty-six days and more than 2,000,000 words of testimony the hearings went on. A thousand impressions were driven into the public mind—Senator Mundt, roly-poly and pliable and so torn between his McCarthyite sympathies and the fact that he was supposed to be an impartial chairman that someone thought to call him the "tormented mushroom"; the Subcommittee's special counsel, Ray Jenkins, the homicide lawyer from Tellico Plains, Tennessee, chin stuck forward, intoning away with his questions; Senator John McClellan of Arkansas, the real terror of the Subcommittee, cadaverous and saturnine and pursuing everyone with a rasping logic; Robert Stevens, earnest and decent but having to pour out his, the Secretary of War's, pathetic attempts to mollify the friends of buck private G. David Schine; Roy Cohn, leaning over to make a point to McCarthy with a mouth that seemed perpetually pouting, obviously tremendously attached to Schine, obviously tremendously attached to Roy Cohn; Cohn and Schine, endlessly Cohn and Schine. But with each passing day one impression was having an increasingly potent effect on the millions at their TV sets. It was Joseph McCarthy, full-life, acting precisely like Joseph McCarthy.

"Point of order, point of order, Mr. Chairman," the Senator would interrupt in his scowling, sneering way until the children of the United States were imitating him on the streets.

Senator Joseph McCarthy, chairing a Senate investigation into alleged Communist subversion in government. At right is his aid Roy Cohn. McCarthy's anti-communist crusade in the early 1950s terrorized people both in and out of government. His major weapon, as Richard Rovere put it, was "the multiple untruth"—a mendacious charge so complicated and so grandiose that it seemed to defy rational refutation. (Courtesy of Wide World Photos.)

He repaid loyalty, like that of bumbling Senator Henry Dworshak of Idaho, by riding contemptuously over what the supporter was trying to say. He seized the floor from opponents by physical force, repeating in his strong, singsong voice until the opponent wearily gave way. McCarthy flung smears and constantly accused others of smearing; his aides tried to use a cropped photograph and he cried deceit at the Army; he sidetracked, blatantly sidetracked, and demanded the end of "diversionary tactics." Day after day he was still Joe McCarthy of the boyhood fights, ceaselessly, recklessly swinging for the knockout.

The more reckless McCarthy became, the more strongly the Administration opposed him. In mid-May the President threw the Constitution of the United States at him. McCarthy became involved in demands that were flagrant violations of the rights of the Executive and from the White House came a blunt statement of those rights, which "cannot be usurped by any individual who may seek to set himself above the laws of our land." No one, not even the President of the United States, not even a President of his own party, was immune to the Senator's standard weapon, the charge of softness toward Communism. McCarthy's answer to Eisenhower was to talk once again of "the evidence of treason that has been growing over the past twenty—" Then he paused and added darkly: "twenty-one years."

The hearings ground on. The changing national mood, the Presidential opposition, and the appearance McCarthy was making on TV were costing the Senator heavily in public support. But he was still not a ruined man. The evidence was certainly not giving either side a clear-cut victory in the issues immediately at stake. Had the McCarthy group sought preferential treatment for Schine? Clearly they had. Had the Army tried to stop McCarthy's investigation at Fort Monmouth? Equally clearly it had—though it was emphasizing that it was anxious to get "that type" of hearing ended because it demoralized the Army. Other charges and countercharges were tangled in a maze of conflicting testimony. Throughout the country a good many pro-McCarthy or anti-anti-McCarthy people were wavering but they were only wavering. The Senator could have emerged from the hearings partially intact if he had now made some moves to present himself as a reasonable, responsible person. But Joseph McCarthy was not interested in being partially intact. He went on looking for the haymaker and the right man was present to see to it that when the Senator swung his wildest, he swung himself flat on his face.

The chief Army counsel, Joseph Welch, was a senior partner of the eminent Boston law firm of Hale and Dorr and he had a well-deserved reputation as an infinitely shrewd trial lawyer. But friends emphasized more Welch's innate sense of human decency and his gift of ironic laughter. They associated him with his spacious colonial home in Walpole, where he puttered around studying his thermometers (there were twelve in the house), spending a day fishing or an evening in a game of carom or cribbage, delighting more than anything else in kindly, bantering talk about the cosmos. Mrs. Welch had a favorite story about the whimsicality of the man. She liked to tell how she had urged him to take up gardening, which he loathed, and he countered that he would garden if she would drink beer, which she detested. So on weekends the two would alternately garden in the broiling sun and stop for a beer in the shade, both grinning through their periods of suffering.

At the hearings Welch sat questioning away, his long, drooping face quizzical, his questions softly spoken and deftly insidious, dropping a damaging little jest and looking utterly surprised when people laughed. The sessions were only eight days old when the Army counsel drew blood. Welch was driving hard at a photograph which the McCarthy forces had produced, cropped to show only Stevens and Schine together although the original photograph contained two other men. The Army counsel brought out that the original had hung on Schine's wall and he questioned James Juliana, a Subcommittee employee who had arranged the cropping, as to why he had not brought the whole picture.

> JULIANA: "I wasn't asked for it. . . ."
> WELCH: ". . . You were asked for something different from the thing that hung on Schine's wall?"
> JULIANA: "I never knew what hung on Schine's wall. . . ."
> WELCH: "Did you think this came from a pixie? Where did you think this picture that I hold in my hand came from?"
> JULIANA: "I had no idea."

There was a stir of voices and McCarthy interrupted. "Will counsel for my benefit define—I think he might be an expert on that—what a pixie is?"

Welch's face was beatific. "Yes. I should say, Mr. Senator, that a pixie is a close relative of a fairy. Shall I proceed, sir? Have I enlightened you?"

The spectators roared. Roy Cohn's pouting lips hardened into angry lines. The Senator glowered.

In the world of Joseph McCarthy nothing was more alien than the deft, and the Senator's feeling about Welch steadily mounted. He denied the Army counsel, or was wary of giving him, what he considered the ordinary camaraderie. McCarthy would walk up to friends and opponents alike, hand extended and the other hand grasping an arm, but he moved a wide circle around Joseph Welch. He first-named almost everybody—Secretary Stevens was "Bob" and the obviously hostile Senator Stuart Symington was "Stu." Welch was "Mr. Welch" or "the counsel."

Eight days before the hearings ended, on June 9, the Army counsel led Roy Cohn through a mocking, destructive cross-examination and McCarthy sat fuming. Now Welch was pressing Cohn as to why, if subversion was so serious at Fort Monmouth, he had not come crying alarm to Secretary Stevens. When Welch went ahead along this line, McCarthy began to grin broadly.

The Army counsel got in another dig at Cohn: "May I add my small voice, sir, and say whenever you know about a subversive or a Communist or a spy, please hurry. Will you remember these words?"

McCarthy broke in, bashed his way to attention. "In view of Mr. Welch's request that the information be given once we know of anyone who might be performing any work for the Communist Party, I think we should tell him that he has in his law firm a young man named Fisher whom he recommended, incidentally, to do work on this committee, who has been for a number of years a member of an organization which was named, oh, years and years ago, as the legal bulwark of the Communist Party...."

The Senator was grinning ever more broadly, pausing now and then to lick his lips and savor his words. Roy Cohn sat in the witness chair, his legs dangling apart, the blood drained from his face, and once his lips seemed to be forming the words "Stop, stop." McCarthy went on: "Knowing that, Mr. Welch, I just felt that I had a duty to respond to your urgent request.... I have hesitated bringing that up, but I have been rather bored with your phony requests to Mr. Cohn here that he personally get every Communist out of government before sundown....

"I am not asking you at this time to explain why you tried to foist him on this committee. Whether you knew he was a member of that Communist organization or not, I don't know. I assume you did not, Mr. Welch, because I get the impression that, while you are quite an actor, you play for a laugh, I don't think you have any conception of the danger of the Communist Party. I don't think you yourself would ever knowingly aid the Communist cause. I think you are unknowingly aiding it when you try to burlesque this hearing in which we are trying to bring out the facts, however."

Welch was staring at McCarthy with the look of a man who was watching the unbelievable. The puck was gone; his face was white with anger. "Senator McCarthy," Welch began, "I did not know—"

McCarthy turned away contemptuously and talked to Juliana. Twice the Army counsel demanded his attention and the Senator talked to Juliana in a still louder voice, telling him to get a newspaper clipping about Fisher so that it could be put in the record.

Welch plunged ahead. "You won't need anything in the record when I have finished telling you this.

"Until this moment, Senator, I think I never

really gauged your cruelty or your recklessness. Fred Fisher is a young man who went to the Harvard Law School and came into my firm and is starting what looks to be a brilliant career with us.

"When I decided to work for this committee I asked Jim St. Clair . . . to be my first assistant. I said to Jim, 'Pick somebody in the firm who works under you that you would like.' He chose Fred Fisher and they came down on an afternoon plane. That night, when we had taken a little stab at trying to see what the case was about, Fred Fisher and Jim St. Clair and I went to dinner together. I then said to these two young men, 'Boys, I don't know anything about you except that I have always liked you, but if there is anything funny in the life of either one of you that would hurt anybody in this case you speak up quick.'

"Fred Fisher said, 'Mr. Welch, when I was in law school and for a period of months after, I belonged to the Lawyers Guild.' . . . I said, 'Fred, I just don't think I am going to ask you to work on the case. If I do, one of these days that will come out and go over national television and it will just hurt like the dickens.'

"So Senator, I asked him to go back to Boston.

"Little did I dream you could be so reckless and so cruel as to do an injury to that lad. It is true that he is still with Hale & Dorr. It is true that he will continue to be with Hale & Dorr. It is, I regret to say, equally true that I fear he shall always bear a scar needlessly inflicted by you. If it were in my power to forgive you for your reckless cruelty, I would do so. I like to think I am a gentle man, but your forgiveness will have to come from someone other than me."

The Senate Caucus Room was hushed. McCarthy fumbled with some papers, began saying that Welch had no right to speak of cruelty because he had "been baiting Mr. Cohn here for hours."

Welch cut off McCarthy. "Senator, may we not drop this? We know he belonged to the Lawyers Guild, and Mr. Cohn nods his head at me." Cohn was quite plainly nodding.

WELCH: "I did you, I think, no personal injury, Mr. Cohn."
COHN: "No, sir."
WELCH: "I meant to do you no personal injury, and if I did, I beg your pardon."

Cohn nodded again. The Army counsel turned back to McCarthy and his emotion was so great that on the TV screens his eyes seemed to be filling with tears. "Let us not assassinate this lad further, Senator. You have done enough. Have you no sense of decency, sir, at long last? Have you left no sense of decency?"

McCarthy tried to ask the Army counsel a question about Fisher. Welch cut him off again. He had recovered his composure now and his voice was cold with scorn. "Mr. McCarthy, I will not discuss this with you further. You have sat within 6 feet of me, and could have asked me about Fred Fisher. You have brought it out. If there is a God in heaven, it will do neither you nor your cause any good. I will not discuss it further. I will not ask Mr. Cohn any more questions. You, Mr. Chairman, may, if you will, call the next witness."

For a long few seconds the hush in the room continued. One of the few rules Chairman Mundt had tried hard to enforce was the one against demonstrations and six policemen were present to assist him. But suddenly the room shook with applause. For the first time in the memory of Washington observers, press photographers laid aside their cameras to join in the ovation for Welch. Chairman Mundt made no effort to interfere and instead soon called for a five-minute recess.

Joseph McCarthy sat slouched in his chair, breathing heavily. Spectators and reporters avoided him. Finally he found someone to talk to. He spread out his hands in a gesture of puzzlement and asked: "What did I do wrong?"

Joseph McCarthy would never know. And

that June day, 1954, millions at their TV sets learned once and for all that Joseph McCarthy would never know.

McCarthy died in 1957 and with him died the worst flames of the Communist scare that had produced him. Still, McCarthyism retained a powerful hold on thousands of Americans, who regarded the late Senator as "the finest American who ever lived." Nor did the country at large reject him as rapidly as many historians have contended. In fact, as Robert Griffith observes in *The Politics of Fear*, thirty-six per cent of the American people still approved of McCarthy after the Army-McCarthy hearings. And in the 1960s, when a national television network re-ran the hearings, the network received countless letters wanting to know where McCarthy was now that America needed him.

IX The Fire Next Time

29

The Mobilization of Black Strength

equality for now and to learn skills and trades to support themselves. He told his fellow Negroes that emphasizing economic opportunities and material progress—and earning the friendship of upper-class whites—offered them more than agitation and protest. The latter would only get them killed.

Not all Negroes heeded Washington's advice. In 1905, a handful of well-educated, bold, and unhappy black men met at Niagara and drafted a manifesto which demanded justice and equality for American Negroes. This "Niagara platform" marked a turning point in the black man's attitude toward American white society, and it launched a Negro protest movement that is still going on. The following narrative, taken from *Life Magazine*'s distinguished series, "The Search for a Black Past," traces the Negro resistance and protest movement from Niagara down to the 1960s.

In the twentieth century, as in the nineteenth, the race issue remained America's most vexing social problem. At the turn of the century, blacks were universally discriminated against, in the North as well as the South. In fact, when the great "black migration" began out of the South, Negroes discovered to their shock and dismay that the North was no more a land of equality than was the South. Flocking by the thousands into Northern cities, they were herded into ghettos and kept there by a host of municipal and real estate codes. Thereafter when Negroes went North, as James Baldwin observed, they did not go to New York City, they went to Harlem. They did not go to Chicago, they went to the South Side. They did not go to Los Angeles, they went to Watts. But Northern whites, priding themselves for abolishing slavery in the Civil War, insisted that they had no "Negro problem." *That* existed only in the *South* . . . and it was a problem best left to Southern whites to work out by themselves.

Initially blacks submitted to living as third-class citizens in a white man's country: in that period of reaction, of course, there was little else they could do. Most followed the advice of Booker T. Washington, who in Atlanta in 1895 urged American Negroes to forget about political and social

In July 1905 a small band of Negro professional men met in the Canadian city of Niagara Falls and drew up a platform for Negro resistance and protest that is still making American history. The tactics announced by the Niagara platform—to stand up and give battle for the Negro's "manhood rights," to denounce bad laws and fight to get rid of them, to "assail the ears" and the consciences of white Americans "so long as America is unjust"—marked a turning point in the Negro's attitude toward the nation's white majority. The 29 founders of the Niagara Movement . . . represented a new wave of talented, mostly college-educated Negroes who had come of age after Reconstruction, and had seen the failure of Negro hopes based on moderation and compromise. Their leaders was William Edward Burghardt DuBois, a brilliant historian, sociologist and poet,

---

From "The Mobilization of Black Strength," *Life Magazine*, December 6, 1968. Reprinted by permission.

whose black pride and militancy carried on the tradition of the pre-Civil War Frederick Douglass and rejected the conciliatory methods of the turn-of-the-century Booker T. Washington.

The group held its first meeting in Canada because hotels on the New York State side of the Falls did not admit Negroes. "We refuse to allow the impression to remain that the Negro American assents to inferiority, is submissive under oppression and apologetic before insults," said the Niagara platform which DuBois largely wrote. The platform listed some of the wrongs inflicted on Negroes in the less than 30 years since Reconstruction: Jim Crow laws and the loss of voting rights in the South, segregated and inferior public schools, the Southern convict system of leasing chained gangs of Negroes to contractors, denial of equal jobs and protection to Negroes by employers and labor unions everywhere, exclusion of black youths from West Point and Annapolis, the federal government's abject failure to enforce rights guaranteed to Negroes by the 14th and 15th Amendments. There were now 10 million black Americans, the platform noted—more than double the number when the slaves were emancipated—and they had sizable resources of money, property, institutions, intelligence and executive ability. It called on them to unite this strength for the betterment of their race.

The Niagara platform was a virtual blueprint for the first large-scale nationwide organization dedicated to fighting for fair treatment of Negroes. The National Association for the Advancement of Colored People (NAACP) was founded in 1909, the centennial year of Abraham Lincoln's birth. It was a result, in part, of the agitation begun at Niagara and it was a sequel, also, of a particularly revolting race riot in 1908 in which Negroes were lynched within half a mile of Lincoln's old home city of Springfield, Ill. DuBois and seven other Niagara leaders were on the NAACP's original board of directors, along with 19 white liberals whose crusading zeal traced back to the abolitionist era—Oswald Harrison Villard, an NAACP founder, was the grandson of the abolitionist editor William Lloyd Garrison. DuBois was the NAACP's first director of research and editor of its magazine, *Crisis*.

The NAACP began at once its courageous and effective campaign to uphold and establish the rights of Negroes by legal action and court battles. These involved hundreds of cases at local, state and federal court levels, and enlisted scores of lawyers and experts during the next 50-odd years. The first major victory for NAACP lawyers came in 1915, when the U.S. Supreme Court declared null and void the "Grandfather Clause" in the state constitutions of Oklahoma and Maryland, by which Negroes were barred from voting unless they could prove that their grandfathers had voted. When the Ku Klux Klan raised its hooded heads again in the 1920s, the NAACP harassed and exposed its bigotry. To mobilize public opinion against racial savagery, the NAACP investigated race riots and lynchings, and relentlessly documented them. It also sponsored a pioneer study, "Thirty Years of Lynching in the United States, 1889–1918," which listed 3,224 victims in the period of whom about 80% were Negroes. In only 19% of the cases was rape or any other sex offense alleged, although Southern editors sometimes wrote approvingly of lynching as a "necessary" weapon to protect white womanhood. The NAACP campaign against it continued for years. Whenever a lynching occurred a black flag with a white inscription, A MAN WAS LYNCHED YESTERDAY, hung outside NAACP headquarters in New York City. In 1926 the flag appeared 30 times, and in 1935 there were 20 lynchings.... After that they declined dramatically as the NAACP's campaign and public opinion combined to erase such disgrace from the American scene.

The growing restiveness of black America

was accompanied and fed by a mass migration of Southern Negroes to Northern cities. In the war years of 1916–1918 alone a half million Negroes moved North, mostly to fill a labor shortage caused by booming war industry and curtailed immigration from Europe. Many of the migrants were poor and found themselves living in big city ghettos. But in the North they could vote, attend better schools, look for higher wages or—as one of them said— eat ice cream inside the ice cream parlor instead of outside on the sidewalk.

The Negroes left the South for many stated reasons: in fear of violence (after every lynching there was a local exodus), to escape menial drudgery, to stop saying "yes ma'am" or "yes sir" to all white people, to get away from the Southern sharecropper-debt system that kept black farmers in virtual peonage. To help them adjust to crowded life in the cities, a second major organization, the National Urban League, was founded in 1911, staffed by professional social workers who stayed close to the ghetto and its problems.

Among the migrants were able young men who became leaders of their race. James Weldon Johnson, first Negro to be executive secretary of the NAACP (in 1920), was the son of a headwaiter in Florida. He had taught in Jacksonville schools and written a song for schoolchildren—*Lift Ev'ry Voice and Sing*, which became a Negro "national anthem." Walter Francis White, who succeeded Johnson and directed the NAACP until 1955, was born and educated in Atlanta. One summer Saturday in 1906 he was riding his father's mail truck, helping pick up mail, when a howling white mob surged into Peachtree Street and trampled a lame Negro shoeshine boy to death before their eyes. Robert S. Abbott, whose Chicago *Defender* recruited migrants with the slogan, "To die from the bite of the frost is far more glorious than that of the mob," was a migrant from Georgia. In 1928, when Chicago's black residents numbered nearly a quarter million, they elected Oscar DePriest as the first Negro congressman since 1901—and the first ever elected from the North.

In the 1920s two forceful leaders worked to mobilize race pride and direct the attention of American Negroes once more toward their ancestral African motherland. Marcus Garvey, the flamboyantly uniformed "provisional President of Africa," and W. E. B. DuBois, the bearded intellectual organizer of Pan-African Congresses, were as different as two men can be. Garvey was born and raised in Jamaica, where his pure Negro blood consigned him to the lowest level of a class system based on relative lightness of skin. Self-educated Garvey worked as a printer, a timekeeper on a banana plantation, a newspaperman in Panama and a magazine writer in London. In 1914, aged 27, he founded in Jamaica his Universal Negro Improvement Association, which had as its purpose to "take Africa, to organize it, develop it, arm it and make it the defender of Negroes the world over." The U.N.I.A.'s membership boomed after Garvey moved to Harlem in 1916. Preaching the gospel of "Black is beautiful"—which endears him to young Negroes today—Garvey wrote an ode to *The Black Woman*, beginning

> Black queen of beauty, thou
>   hast given color to the world
> Among other women thou art
>   royal and the fairest . . .

and he urged all shades of Negroes to "combine to re-establish the purity of their own race . . . rather than seeking to lose their identities through miscegenation and social intercourse with the white race." As the commercial arm of his back-to-Africa crusade he organized in 1919 a Black Star Line of steamships "owned, controlled and manned by Negroes to reach the Negro people of the world."

Garvey once claimed 11 million members for U.N.I.A., but his Negro critics—of whom there were many—conceded him only from 9,700 to 80,000. Recent study suggests that one to four million Negroes may have supported Garvey at the peak of his career. His downfall came in 1923 when he insisted on being his own lawyer in a trial for mail fraud in selling shares of the Black Star Line. He was convicted and sentenced to five years in federal prison. Pardoned after 30 months, he returned to Jamaica and died in London in 1940.

Garvey and DuBois had nothing but scorn for each other. Garvey condescendingly called the light-skinned DuBois "the mulatto." DuBois, who was born in Massachusetts and rigorously trained in scholarship at Fisk, Harvard and the University of Berlin, dismissed Garvey's muddled revival of old African colonization schemes as "spiritual bankruptcy and futility." In 1917 DuBois proposed that German colonies conquered in World War I and the Belgian Congo be joined in a new, independent African state. In 1919, with NAACP backing, DuBois went to Paris and convened the first Pan-African Congress, with African, West Indian and U.S. delegates, to push this scheme during the Paris Peace Conference. The Pan-African Congresses continued at intervals until they were succeeded, in 1958, by a historic All-Africa Conference at Accra in Ghana.

But DuBois' main concern, all the while, was for the welfare of the American Negro. He edited *Crisis,* wrote poetry, novels, led student walkouts at Negro universities, resigned from the NAACP in 1934 after he advocated a go-it-alone ("voluntary segregation") policy for Negroes instead of all-out integration, made pilgrimages to Moscow and Peking, and joined the Communist party in 1961, when he was 93. Like Garvey, he was indicted by the government (in 1950, on a charge of failing to register as a foreign agent), but he was promptly acquitted in a directed verdict. Unlike Garvey—who never set foot in Africa—DuBois died there in 1963, angry and bitter, after renouncing his United States citizenship and becoming a citizen of Ghana.

On the outer beat of that indigenous American music, jazz, and the inward beat of their own pride and self-esteem came a sudden outpouring of art by Negroes. These were the New Negroes, emancipated and flexing their minds, and they converged on the largest black community in the world, Harlem. So vivid was their creativity that they formed what has quite properly been called ever since the Harlem Renaissance. They spoke first as men and then as black men. Though their art was accepted without question everywhere, it is perhaps most important because it touched a responding sense of pride and self-confidence in the Negro community.

The scattered black peasantry had concentrated in the cities, gone into business, developed its own middle-class patterns and a bourgeois society from which an intelligentsia could arise. This occurred in many American communities, but it focused in Harlem, which drew Negroes from all over America as well as Africa and the West Indies into a crucible of black culture. New York already was the cultural center of America and it offered a unique cosmopolitan milieu. It could not insulate the black man from the slights to which his rising intellectuality made him ever more vulnerable, but it could unlock his talents.

Harlem became a popular, romantic place in the white mind. Downtowners went "uptown," to the Savoy and the Cotton Club, and reveled in jungle-beat revues. It was the frantic, frenetic Twenties, and the mixture of lighthearted fun and the exotic that touched the Negro theater was made to order for the times. In 1921 the first big Negro musical, *Shuffle Along,* ran a year in New York and two on the road. There was *Chocolate Dandies* with Josephine Baker, and *Africana* with Ethel Waters. But entertainment was not necessarily aimed at the white world—Bessie Smith, known as the Empress of the Blues and probably the finest blues singer in the world, played entirely to Negro audiences. The circumstances of her death in 1937 were not entirely clear, but they spawned a legend that was a sobering reminder of the reality of Negro life in America: that she had bled to death after an auto accident when a white hospital in Mississippi refused to admit her.

The core of the Harlem Renaissance, however, lay in a group of writers whose work, largely in poetry and the novel, articulated the anguish of the New Negro and his determination to be heard. In a sense it was protest literature but in quality it rose above its environment and entered the mainstream of a particularly productive period of American letters.

Men like Claude McKay, Jean Toomer and Countee Cullen were considered leading poets and novelists of their day. James Weldon Johnson, himself a poet, also served as the chronicler and historian of the movement. The incomparable Langston Hughes, whose first book of poems, *Weary Blues,* appeared in 1926, became one of America's most prolific writers. By the time he died in 1967 a host of fine Negro writers had become famous—men like Richard Wright, Ralph Ellison, James Baldwin. The Renaissance writers were iconoclasts. Skeptical and critical, they represented the new, emancipated Negro in defying the old, turn-of-the-century attitudes. Like their white counterparts—but with the added bitterness of highly intelligent men in a hostile society—many of them eventually sought exile abroad.

The Renaissance spanned the arts. There was painting, sculpture, theater, and, above all, jazz. It began with Negro musicians in the South and moved to Chicago, where it was played as intimate music in small groups, its genius a wild improvisation. It flowered in New York in the '20s, but there it appeared in big bands, which meant special arrangements instead of improvising. From 1928 on, the best and most original jazz band in America was led by Duke Ellington. He played the Cotton Club in Harlem and was recognized all over the world. He was composer, arranger, band leader and pianist, famous for the subtlety and the richness of his music, which as time went on grew ever more refined and sophisticated. Like Langston Hughes, he gave the Harlem Renaissance continuity and carried it forward into today.

Through the years Negroes had placed their faith in Presidents who let them down. Theodore Roosevelt's friendship with Booker T. Washington proved only a token and ultimately meant little. Wilson, a high-minded Southern liberal, turned out to be much more Southern than liberal; he deliberately segregated the civil service. So when Franklin Roosevelt in 1932 spoke of a "New Deal" for all Americans, black voters were skeptical and few Negroes—who were by tradition Republican—voted for F.D.R. But this time they were wrong. The Depression, which hurt black people more than anyone else, turned the federal government into an unexpected ally. Almost immediately F.D.R. formed what came to be called his "Black Cabinet"—a group of Negro administrators who advised in Negro affairs and traveled the country to ensure impartiality in the application of new federal aid programs.

Negroes had also been skeptical of labor unions, most of which, for all their concern for the workingman, had banned Negroes from membership. When the C.I.O. in 1935 began to organize millions of workers, both white and black, Negroes were reluctant to join. But they found that the C.I.O. gave them a fair shake, and by joining Negroes found a new way to exert their strength.

Skilled Negro workers were still walking the streets when the approach of World War II brought massive defense contracts to industry. The government did nothing. It was a Negro who forced action. Declaring his own war on Roosevelt's administration, A. Philip Randolph of the Brotherhood of Sleeping Car Porters prepared to lead 100,000 Negroes in a march on Washington. F.D.R. tried to force Randolph to call it off but, in the end, he had to capitulate. He issued the famous Executive Order 8802: "There shall be no discrimination in the employment of workers in defense industry or government. . . ." By the end of the war most industries had at least a token number of black employes.

But Executive Order 8802 did not apply to the armed forces. The million black men and women who served during the war were segregated in camps, military posts and in their fighting units. As in every American war there were Negro soldiers and units who served with distinction. But only a few Negroes were allowed to fight. Most of them served—as they had in every war—in service battalions.

Once again they had fought for this country, their country, in a war which, among other things, was a fight against racism. Opposition to racism had thus become a part of American patriotism and a part of the ideological baggage of Americans in and out of uniform. That was still no guarantee that it would have much effect in the courts, schools and streets of America. But it was something, and it stirred a new spirit among American Negroes. Also, Negroes had left the South by the hundreds of thousands, and many had found industrial jobs at wages undreamed of by their brothers still confined within the borders of the rural South. The Northern and Western migration of Southern Negroes was and is a constant current throughout the 20th century, but it accelerated dramatically during and after the war. American Negroes became what they are today—overwhelmingly urban.

They had learned, too, that the impetus for change had to come from them, that they themselves had to keep the pressure on. The NAACP and other predominantly black organizations intensified the drive for full equality after the war, and they soon discovered that they had a critically important ally in President Harry Truman. Truman's commitment to black Americans was probably stronger than any President before or since has demonstrated. "The constitutional guarantees of individual liberties and of equal protection under the laws," he said in 1946, "clearly place on the federal government *the duty to act*, when state or local authorities abridge or fail to protect these constitutional rights."

Truman appointed a committee on civil rights which, in broad and strong terms, recommended ways of striking at discrimination and segregation in voting, employment, housing and other fields. But Congress was unmoved; no new legislation was passed. In 1948, the President took it upon himself, as commander in chief of the armed forces, to order full integration of the services. By the time the Korean war broke out in 1950, military integration was a fact. It was limited integration but still an important step.

Truman's decision to put the authority and prestige of the Presidency behind the Negro struggle for equality represented a great historic shift—"the crucial turning point," Professor John Hope Franklin has called it, "in viewing the problem of race as a national problem in the United States." It was the first step away from the smug delusion that bigotry was peculiar to the South, the first full acceptance of federal responsibility, the first occasion when the racists found themselves on the defensive. The next step took longer, but when it came it was an enormous one: the Supreme Court decision outlawing school segregation.

The decision was the culmination of a long and frustrating battle by the NAACP Legal Defense Fund led by Thurgood Marshall (who became, in 1967, the first Negro to sit on the Supreme Court). When Chief Justice Earl Warren wrote, in 1954, that "separate educational facilities are inherently unequal," American Negroes had won their greatest victory of the century. Down came the whole intricate and devious legal underpinning for the idea of segregation, down came a century and a half of tortuous rationalizations supporting an untenable creed, that the Negro was inherently inferior. "To separate [students] solely because of their race, generates a feeling of inferiority as to their status in the community that may affect their hearts and minds in a way unlikely ever to be undone," Warren wrote, and the psychological consequences of segregation were at last acknowledged.

The segregationists labeled the day of the decision "Black Monday," but they didn't react immediately. "For the first few months . . . there was mainly silence," Dan Wakefield wrote in *Revolt in the South*. "It was a time like the one that separates the moments when a person is burned and when, in the fraction of a second that it takes for his body to absorb and react to the pain, he opens his mouth and screams." But the screams came in many forms. In Sunflower County, Miss. the first of hundreds of White Citizens Councils was formed. In the Congress, 101 Southern senators and congressmen signed a manifesto attacking the decision and pledging to reverse it by "all lawful means." Means less than lawful were left to the renascent Ku Klux Klan and random terrorism. Lynchings, beatings and bombings increased.

The next act belonged to the Southern blacks. The names, with a few vivid exceptions such as Reverend Martin Luther King Jr. and Reverend Ralph Abernathy, have been all but lost in the tide of events that has rushed past since the middle and late 1950s—names like Mrs. Daisy Bates, the NAACP leader in Little Rock, Ark., Elizabeth Eckford, the black teen-ager who braved a mob to enter Little Rock's Central High School, and Autherine Lucy, the first Negro to attend the University of Alabama. Most of all, the name of Mrs. Rosa Parks of Montgomery, Ala. What Mrs. Parks did, simply, was to refuse to get up and give her seat in a Montgomery bus to a white man. She was tired, and she was fed up. "It just happened," she explained later, "that the driver made a demand and I just didn't feel like obeying his demand."

So began the Montgomery bus boycott of 1955–56, led by Martin Luther King. For 381 days Negroes refused to ride Montgomery buses, and the boycott ended only after a Supreme Court decision ruling bus segregation illegal. But the boycott had a more immediate —and more profound—effect in influencing what was just coming to be known as the "civil rights movement." Mrs. Parks's refusal to yield her seat was an act of nonviolent resistance. The boycott was the first nonviolent mass action aimed at breaking down segregation and discrimination. It thrust King, then an obscure Montgomery minister, into Negro leadership and national prominence. Most important, it showed that black Americans recognized that court decisions were not enough, that something more was needed to break down a system of repression that showed few signs of weakening.

The Supreme Court's order to desegregate schools had been sweeping and explicit but Southern compliance was minimal. In Prince Edward County, Va. public schools were closed for five years to avoid integration. Alabama and Mississippi stalled it for nine and ten years, respectively. The bitterest clash of all came in Little Rock, where President Eisenhower had to dispatch Army troops to enforce a court order integrating the schools.

As pieces of freedom and equality were won here and there—as interstate transportation was ordered desegregated in 1955, as more Negroes were elected to Congress from Northern ghettos—black impatience with the delays in gaining real equality grew more intense. The emergence of independent black nations in Africa heightened the mood, giving American

Negroes pride in the achievements of other Negroes—and providing an international audience that grew critical and scornful of the American double standard of democracy.

The decade of nonviolence, set off by the bus boycott, began. It was bracketed by the names of two Alabama cities, Montgomery in 1955 and Selma in 1965. Demonstrations. Marches. The leader was King, the anthem was *We Shall Overcome,* and the battle ribbons bore such names as Greensboro, N.C., Albany, Ga., Birmingham and Bogalusa, La. It was in Greensboro, in February 1960, that "sit-in" entered the language. Four freshmen from all-Negro North Carolina A&T College sat down at the lunch counter of a dime store, ordered coffee, and waited coffeeless until the store closed. "It just didn't seem right," said one of the four later, "that we [could] buy notebook paper and toothpaste in a national chain store and then not be able to get a bite to eat and a cup of coffee at the counter." Sit-ins had been tried years earlier, but this time they caught on. Within a few months lunch counter sit-ins had been staged in every Southern state, there had been "wade-ins" at segregated public beaches and "freedom rides" had tested integration on interstate trains and buses. Black and white students went south by the thousands. Dr. King broadened his campaign to attack voting and job discrimination. And in the spring of 1960 there was a new organization—the Student Nonviolent Coordinating Committee (SNCC), destined to go through a succession of transformations as it responded to the passionate demands of militant black youth.

Southern protesters violated local laws and went to jail, to make the point that the laws were unjust. They found now that the whole country was watching them, and many whites were feeling a growing sense of shame and guilt. When three hundred and fifty students were penned in an open-air stockade in Orangeburg, S.C. after a protest march, television viewers saw them praying and singing *The Star-Spangled Banner.* TV was present again to show the crude brutality of Birmingham police, under chief "Bull" Connor, using fire hoses and dogs on protesting Negroes. It documented the recurrent Southern violence–the murder of Medgar Evers, the killing of three civil rights workers near Philadelphia, Miss., the tragedy of the four young black girls killed when a Birmingham church was bombed.

In Washington, the arena for civil rights decisions had moved to the branch of government which had been least responsive—the legislative. Congress, stalled principally by the filibuster technique, had done little. A weak civil rights bill in 1957 contributed a U.S. Commission on Civil Rights, but not much else. The first strong civil rights law had to wait until 1964. Finally voting to break a filibuster, the Senate passed a new law that forbade discrimination in most "public accommodation" facilities and authorized the withdrawal of federal money from programs where discrimination was practiced. A follow-up bill permitting federal examiners to assure fair registration was passed in 1965. "We intend to fight this battle where it should be fought—in the courts, in the Congress, and in the hearts of men," President Johnson told Congress. Then, borrowing the Negroes' own cry, he concluded, "And we shall overcome."

Nonviolence put on its last impressive display in 1965, with the Selma-to-Montgomery march. By that time the restless stirring within the black community, the feeling that demonstrations and nonviolence simply weren't working, weren't getting them anywhere, was becoming obvious. "You can only sing *We Shall Overcome* so many times," a young black said, "before you realize that it's not the way to overcome."

The center of the Negroes' struggle was moving north, where the ghettos were, where

Marching from Selma to Montgomery, Alabama, during voter registration drive in 1965. (Photograph of the March on Selma taken by James Karales. Copyright © Cowles Communications, Inc. 1965.)

blacks could easily see the white world that was still denied them—fertile ground for the rising militance. The day of peaceable marches beginning at cinder-block Southern churches and ending in damp Southern jails was past. In Northern cities, black patience was wearing thin, and frustration was reaching the boiling point. The larger problem had always lain in the North, ignored by most whites who paid only lip service to the ideal of equality.

With a few minor exceptions, every legal safeguard that could be enacted had been enacted. But residential segregation was intact in most of the North, job discrimination remained pervasive, Negro poverty was severe, *de facto* school segregation was common. Despite the entry of Negroes into such formerly all-white preserves as the Senate, the Cabinet and the Supreme Court, there was a widespread feeling of powerlessness and the average black man saw little change in his daily life.

Out of that wash of frustration came the black nationalism of Malcolm X, the "black power" of Stokely Carmichael and H. Rap Brown, the emphasis on *blackness*, on "soul food" and African hair styles, on black history and culture. White offers of help, however well intended, were rejected. A new ideology seemed to be developing; young Negroes were thinking of themselves as Afro-Americans, identifying with the oppressed peoples of the world, directing abuse and hatred at the white society.

Out of that same hopelessness came the riots. They began in New York in 1964, escalated violently in Watts in 1965, and reached a crescendo in Newark and Detroit [in 1967]. The black rage was expressing itself however it could—by throwing a rock at a window, cursing a policeman, looting a store.

Writing almost a quarter century after the war, Historian Joanne Grant declared, "Today, the situation for the majority of Negroes has not changed, except in this all-important aspect: a major aim of the current movement, with all of its changes and floundering and periods of inactivity during which direction and goals seem to have been lost sight of, has been fulfilled. The masses of Negroes have been stirred, there is a widespread will to fight, a new-found ability to organize, and a substantial decrease of fear." *A substantial decrease of fear.* That in itself was a monumental accomplishment.

In ways that are just becoming clear, the last 25 years of black history have also had a profound effect on whites. Black methods of nonviolent protest inspired whites to attack laws they deemed unjust in the same ways. The black tactics of unlawful protest, of civil disobedience have been taken up by whites—especially the young—for their own causes. The moral commitment and willingness to sacrifice demonstrated by blacks impressed an activist minority of the white community, and led students, ministers and intellectuals to follow their example. In this respect, the Negro's struggle for himself has caused an interaction which has had considerable impact on today's America.

30

Uncle Tom's Children

Richard Wright

Born in Mississippi in 1908, Richard Wright grew up in a white supremacist South which remained virtually unchanged from the turn of the century until recent years. He worked at odd jobs there and then migrated to Chicago like thousands of other Southern blacks. When the Depression came on, he went jobless and hungry until finding employment with the New Deal Federal Writers' Project. Along with many other Americans in the thirties, Wright joined the American Communist party, only to abandon the organization in disillusionment and despair. In 1940 he published *Native Son*, a brilliant novel about a young black's experiences in Chicago. Wright went on to become the leading black writer of his generation, dying in Paris at the age of fifty-two. Here, in a sketch that appeared in *Uncle Tom's Children* in 1937, he recalled his education in how to live as a Negro in the Jim Crow South. But given the racial prejudice that also flourished in the North and West, Wright's experiences could have happened almost anywhere in the country at that time.

I

My first lesson in how to live as a Negro came when I was quite small. We were living in Arkansas. Our house stood behind the railroad tracks. Its skimpy yard was paved with black cinders. Nothing green ever grew in that yard. The only touch of green we could see was far away, beyond the tracks, over where the white folks lived. But cinders were good enough for me and I never missed the green growing things. And anyhow cinders were fine weapons. You could always have a nice hot war with huge black cinders. All you had to do was crouch behind the brick pillars of a house with your hands full of gritty ammunition. And the first woolly black head you saw pop out from behind another row of pillars was your target. You tried your very best to knock it off. It was great fun.

I never fully realized the appalling disadvantages of a cinder environment till one day the gang to which I belonged found itself engaged in a war with the white boys who lived beyond the tracks. As usual we laid down our cinder barrage, thinking that this would wipe the white boys out. But they replied with a steady bombardment of broken bottles. We doubled our cinder barrage, but they hid behind trees, hedges, and the sloping embankments of their lawns. Having no such fortifications, we retreated to the brick pillars of our homes. During the retreat a broken milk bottle caught me behind the ear, opening a deep gash which bled profusely. The sight of blood pouring over my face completely demoralized our ranks. My fellow-combatants left me standing paralyzed in the center of the yard, and scurried for their homes. A kind neighbor saw me and rushed me to a doctor, who took three stitches in my neck.

From "The Ethics of Living Jim Crow" (pp. 3–15) in *Uncle Tom's Children* by Richard Wright. Copyright 1937 by Richard Wright; renewed 1965 by Ellen Wright. Reprinted by permission of Harper & Row, Publishers, Inc.

I sat brooding on my front steps, nursing my wound and waiting for my mother to come from work. I felt that a grave injustice had been done me. It was all right to throw cinders. The greatest harm a cinder could do was leave a bruise. But broken bottles were dangerous; they left you cut, bleeding, and helpless.

When night fell, my mother came from the white folks' kitchen. I raced down the street to meet her. I could just feel in my bones that she would understand. I knew she would tell me exactly what to do next time. I grabbed her hand and babbled out the whole story. She examined my wound, then slapped me.

"How come yuh didn't hide?" she asked me. "How come yuh awways fightin'?"

I was outraged, and bawled. Between sobs I told her that I didn't have any trees or hedges to hide behind. There wasn't a thing I could have used as a trench. And you couldn't throw very far when you were hiding behind the brick pillars of a house. She grabbed a barrel stave, dragged me home, stripped me naked, and beat me till I had a fever of one hundred and two. She would smack my rump with the stave, and, while the skin was still smarting, impart to me gems of Jim Crow wisdom. I was never to throw cinders any more. I was never to fight any more wars. I was never, never, under any conditions, to fight *white* folks again. And they were absolutely right in clouting me with the broken milk bottle. Didn't I know she was working hard every day in the hot kitchens of the white folks to make money to take care of me? When was I ever going to learn to be a good boy? She couldn't be bothered with my fights. She finished by telling me that I ought to be thankful to God as long as I lived that they didn't kill me.

All that night I was delirious and could not sleep. Each time I closed my eyes I saw monstrous white faces suspended from the ceiling, leering at me.

From that time on, the charm of my cinder yard was gone. The green trees, the trimmed hedges, the cropped lawns grew very meaningful, became a symbol. Even today when I think of white folks, the hard, sharp outlines of white houses surrounded by trees, lawns, and hedges are present somewhere in the background of my mind. Through the years they grew into an overreaching symbol of fear.

It was a long time before I came in close contact with white folks again. We moved from Arkansas to Mississippi. Here we had the good fortune not to live behind the railroad tracks, or close to white neighborhoods. We lived in the very heart of the local Black Belt. There were black churches and black preachers; there were black schools and black teachers; black groceries and black clerks. In fact, everything was so solidly black that for a long time I did not even think of white folks, save in remote and vague terms. But this could not last forever. As one grows older one eats more. One's clothing costs more. When I finished grammar school I had to go to work. My mother could no longer feed and clothe me on her cooking job.

There is but one place where a black boy who knows no trade can get a job, and that's where the houses and faces are white, where the trees, lawns, and hedges are green. My first job was with an optical company in Jackson, Mississippi. The morning I applied I stood straight and neat before the boss, answering all his questions with sharp yessirs and nosirs. I was very careful to pronounce my *sirs* distinctly, in order that he might know that I was polite, that I knew where I was, and that I knew he was a *white* man. I wanted that job badly.

He looked me over as though he were examining a prize poodle. He questioned me closely about my schooling, being particularly insistent about how much mathematics I had had. He seemed very pleased when I told him I had had two years of algebra.

"Boy, how would you like to try to learn something around here?" he asked me.

"I'd like it fine, sir," I said, happy. I had visions of "working my way up." Even Negroes have those visions.

A white planter with his black workers in Jim Crow Mississippi. Richard Wright, who received a good part of his "Jim Crow education" there, observed that "there is but one place a black boy who knows no trade can get a job, and that's where the houses and faces are white." (Courtesy of The Library of Congress.)

"All right," he said. "Come on."

I followed him to the small factory.

"Pease," he said to a white man of about thirty-five, "this is Richard. He's going to work for us."

Pease looked at me and nodded.

I was then taken to a white boy of about seventeen.

"Morrie, this is Richard, who's going to work for us."

"Whut yuh sayin' there, boy!" Morrie boomed at me.

"Fine!" I answered.

The boss instructed these two to help me, teach me, give me jobs to do, and let me learn what I could in my spare time.

My wages were five dollars a week.

I worked hard, trying to please. For the first month I got along O.K. Both Pease and Morrie seemed to like me. But one thing was missing. And I kept thinking about it. I was not learning anything and nobody was volunteering to help me. Thinking they had forgotten that I was to learn something about the mechanics of grinding lenses, I asked Morrie one day to tell me about the work. He grew red.

"Whut yuh tryin' t' do, nigger, get smart?" he asked.

"Naw; I ain' tryin' t' git smart," I said.

"Well, don't, if yuh know whut's good for yuh!"

I was puzzled. Maybe he just doesn't want to help me, I thought. I went to Pease.

"Say, are yuh crazy, you black bastard?" Pease asked me, his gray eyes growing hard.

I spoke out, reminding him that the boss had said I was to be given a chance to learn something.

"Nigger, you think you're *white,* don't you?"

"Naw, sir!"

"Well, you're acting mighty like it!"

"But, Mr. Pease, the boss said . . ."

Pease shook his fist in my face.

"This is a *white* man's work around here, and you better watch yourself!"

From then on they changed toward me. They said good-morning no more. When I was just a bit slow in performing some duty, I was called a lazy black son-of-a-bitch.

Once I thought of reporting all this to the boss. But the mere idea of what would happen to me if Pease and Morrie should learn that I had "snitched" stopped me. And after all the boss was a white man, too. What was the use?

The climax came at noon one summer day. Pease called me to his work-bench. To get to him I had to go between two narrow benches and stand with my back against a wall.

"Yes, sir," I said.

"Richard, I want to ask you something," Pease began pleasantly, not looking up from his work.

"Yes, sir," I said again.

Morrie came over, blocking the narrow passage between the benches. He folded his arms, staring at me solemnly.

I looked from one to the other, sensing that something was coming.

"Yes, sir," I said for the third time.

Pease looked up and spoke very slowly.

"Richard, *Mr.* Morrie here tells me you called me *Pease.*"

I stiffened. A void seemed to open up in me. I knew this was the show-down.

He meant that I had failed to call him Mr. Pease. I looked at Morrie. He was gripping a steel bar in his hands. I opened my mouth to speak, to protest, to assure Pease that I had never called him simply *Pease,* and that I had never had any intentions of doing so, when Morrie grabbed me by the collar, ramming my head against the wall.

"Now, be careful, nigger!" snarled Morrie, baring his teeth. "*I* heard yuh call 'im *Pease!* 'N' if yuh say yuh didn't, yuh're callin' me a *lie,* see?" He waved the steel bar threateningly.

If I had said: No, sir, Mr. Pease, I never called you *Pease,* I would have been automatically calling Morrie a liar. And if I had said: Yes, sir, Mr. Pease, I called you *Pease,* I would have been pleading guilty to having uttered the worst insult that a Negro can utter to a southern white man. I stood hesitating, trying to frame a neutral reply.

"Richard, I asked you a question!" said Pease. Anger was creeping into his voice.

"I don't remember calling you *Pease,* Mr. Pease," I said cautiously. "And if I did, I sure didn't mean . . ."

"You black son-of-a-bitch! You called me *Pease,* then!" he spat, slapping me till I bent sideways over a bench. Morrie was on top of me, demanding:

"Didn't yuh call 'im *Pease?* If yuh say yuh didn't, I'll rip yo' gut string loose with this bar, yuh black granny dodger! Yuh can't call a white man a lie 'n' git erway with it, you black son-of-a-bitch!"

I wilted. I begged them not to bother me. I knew what they wanted. They wanted me to leave.

"I'll leave," I promised. "I'll leave right *now.*"

They gave me a minute to get out of the

factory. I was warned not to show up again, or tell the boss.

I went.

When I told the folks at home what had happened, they called me a fool. They told me that I must never again attempt to exceed my boundaries. When you are working for white folks, they said, you got to "stay in your place" if you want to keep working.

II

My Jim Crow education continued on my next job, which was portering in a clothing store. One morning, while polishing brass out front, the boss and his twenty-year-old son got out of their car and half dragged and half kicked a Negro woman into the store. A policeman standing at the corner looked on, twirling his nightstick. I watched out of the corner of my eye, never slackening the strokes of my chamois upon the brass. After a few minutes, I heard shrill screams coming from the rear of the store. Later the woman stumbled out, bleeding, crying, and holding her stomach. When she reached the end of the block, the policeman grabbed her and accused her of being drunk. Silently, I watched him throw her into a patrol wagon.

When I went to the rear of the store, the boss and his son were washing their hands at the sink. They were chuckling. The floor was bloody and strewn with wisps of hair and clothing. No doubt I must have appeared pretty shocked, for the boss slapped me reassuringly on the back.

"Boy, that's what we do to niggers when they don't want to pay their bills," he said, laughing.

His son looked at me and grinned.

"Here, hava cigarette," he said.

Not knowing what to do, I took it. He lit his and held the match for me. This was a gesture of kindness, indicating that even if they had beaten the poor old woman, they would not beat me if I knew enough to keep my mouth shut.

"Yes, sir," I said, and asked no questions.

After they had gone, I sat on the edge of a packing box and stared at the bloody floor till the cigarette went out.

That day at noon, while eating in a hamburger joint, I told my fellow Negro porters what had happened. No one seemed surprised. One fellow, after swallowing a huge bite, turned to me and asked:

"Huh! Is tha' all they did t' her?"

"Yeah. Wasn't tha' enough?" I asked.

"Shucks! Man, she's a lucky bitch!" he said, burying his lips deep into a juicy hamburger. "Hell, it's a wonder they didn't lay her when they got through."

III

I was learning fast, but not quite fast enough. One day, while I was delivering packages in the suburbs, my bicycle tire was punctured. I walked along the hot, dusty road, sweating and leading my bicycle by the handle-bars.

A car slowed at my side.

"What's the matter, boy?" a white man called.

I told him my bicycle was broken and I was walking back to town.

"That's too bad," he said. "Hop on the running board."

He stopped the car. I clutched hard at my bicycle with one hand and clung to the side of the car with the other.

"All set?"

"Yes, sir," I answered. The car started.

It was full of young white men. They were drinking. I watched the flask pass from mouth to mouth.

"Wanna drink, boy?" one asked.

I laughed as the wind whipped my face. Instinctively obeying the freshly planted precepts of my mother, I said:

"Oh, no!"

The words were hardly out of my mouth before I felt something hard and cold smash me between the eyes. It was an empty whisky bottle.

I saw stars, and fell backwards from the speeding car into the dust of the road, my feet becoming entangled in the steel spokes of my bicycle. The white men piled out and stood over me.

"Nigger, ain' yuh learned no better sense'n tha' yet?" asked the man who hit me. "Ain' yuh learned t' say *sir* t' a white man yet?"

Dazed, I pulled to my feet. My elbows and legs were bleeding. Fists doubled, the white man advanced, kicking my bicycle out of the way.

"Aw, leave the bastard alone. He's got enough," said one.

They stood looking at me. I rubbed my shins, trying to stop the flow of blood. No doubt they felt a sort of contemptuous pity, for one asked:

"Yuh wanna ride t' town now, nigger? Yuh reckon yuh know enough t' ride now?"

"I wanna walk," I said, simply.

Maybe it sounded funny. They laughed.

"Well, walk, yuh black son-of-a-bitch!"

When they left they comforted me with:

"Nigger, yuh sho better be damn glad it wuz us yuh talked t' tha' way. Yuh're a lucky bastard, 'cause if yuh'd said tha' t' somebody else, yuh might've been a dead nigger now."

IV

Negroes who have lived South know the dread of being caught alone upon the streets in white neighborhoods after the sun has set. In such a simple situation as this the plight of the Negro in America is graphically symbolized. While white strangers may be in these neighborhoods trying to get home, they can pass unmolested. But the color of a Negro's skin makes him easily recognizable, makes him suspect, converts him into a defenseless target.

Late one Saturday night I made some deliveries in a white neighborhood. I was pedaling my bicycle back to the store as fast as I could, when a police car, swerving toward me, jammed me into the curbing.

"Get down and put up your hands!" the policemen ordered.

I did. They climbed out of the car, guns drawn, faces set, and advanced slowly.

"Keep still!" they ordered.

I reached my hands higher. They searched my pockets and packages. They seemed dissatisfied when they could find nothing incriminating. Finally, one of them said:

"Boy, tell your boss not to send you out in white neighborhoods after sundown."

As usual, I said:

"Yes, sir."

V

My next job was a hall-boy in a hotel. Here my Jim Crow education broadened and deepened. When the bell-boys were busy, I was often called to assist them. As many of the rooms in the hotel were occupied by prostitutes, I was constantly called to carry them liquor and cigarettes. These women were nude most of the time. They did not bother about clothing, even for bell-boys. When you went into their rooms, you were supposed to take their nakedness for granted, as though it startled you no more than a blue vase or a red rug. Your presence awoke in them no sense of shame, for you were not regarded as human. If they were alone, you could steal side-long glimpses at them. But if they were receiving men, not a flicker of your eyelids could show. I remember one incident vividly. A new woman, a huge, snowy-skinned blonde, took a room on my floor. I was sent to wait upon her. She was in bed with a thick-set man; both were nude and uncovered. She said she wanted some liquor and slid out of bed and waddled across the floor to get her money from a dresser drawer. I watched her.

"Nigger, what in hell you looking at?" the white man asked me, raising himself upon his elbows.

"Nothing," I answered, looking miles deep into the blank wall of the room.

"Keep your eyes where they belong, if you want to be healthy!" he said.

"Yes, sir."

VI

One of the bell-boys I knew in this hotel was keeping steady company with one of the Negro maids. Out of a clear sky the police descended upon his home and arrested him, accusing him of bastardy. The poor boy swore he had had no intimate relations with the girl. Nevertheless, they forced him to marry her. When the child arrived, it was found to be much lighter in complexion than either of the two supposedly legal parents. The white men around the hotel made a great joke of it. They spread the rumor that some white cow must have scared the poor girl while she was carrying the baby. If you were in their presence when this explanation was offered, you were supposed to laugh.

VII

One of the bell-boys was caught in bed with a white prostitute. He was castrated and run out of town. Immediately after this all the bell-boys and hall-boys were called together and warned. We were given to understand that the boy who had been castrated was a "mighty, mighty lucky bastard." We were impressed with the fact that next time the management of the hotel would not be responsible for the lives of "trouble-makin' niggers." We were silent.

VIII

One night, just as I was about to go home, I met one of the Negro maids. She lived in my direction, and we fell in to walk part of the way home together. As we passed the white night-watchman, he slapped the maid on her buttock. I turned around, amazed. The watchman looked at me with a long, hard, fixed-under stare. Suddenly he pulled his gun and asked:

"Nigger, don't yuh like it?"

I hesitated.

"I asked yuh don't yuh like it?" he asked again, stepping forward.

"Yes, sir," I mumbled.

"Talk like it, then!"

"Oh, yes, sir!" I said with as much heartiness as I could muster.

Outside, I walked ahead of the girl, ashamed to face her. She caught up with me and said:

"Don't be a fool! Yuh couldn't help it!"

This watchman boasted of having killed two Negroes in self-defense.

Yet, in spite of all this, the life of the hotel ran with an amazing smoothness. It would have been impossible for a stranger to detect anything. The maids, the hall-boys, and the bell-boys were all smiles. They had to be.

IX

I had learned my Jim Crow lessons so thoroughly that I kept the hotel job till I left Jackson for Memphis. It so happened that while in Memphis I applied for a job at a branch of the optical company. I was hired. And for some reason, as long as I worked there, they never brought my past against me.

Here my Jim Crow education assumed quite a different form. It was no longer brutally cruel, but subtly cruel. Here I learned to lie, to steal, to dissemble. I learned to play that dual role which every Negro must play if he wants to eat and live.

For example, it was almost impossible to get a book to read. It was assumed that after a Negro had imbibed what scanty schooling the state furnished he had no further need for books. I was always borrowing books from men on the job. One day I mustered enough courage to ask one of the men to let me get books from the library in his name. Surprisingly, he consented. I cannot help but think that he consented because he was a Roman Catholic and felt a vague sympathy for Negroes, being himself an object of hatred. Armed with a library card, I obtained books in the following manner: I would write a note to the librarian, saying: "Please let this nigger boy have the following books." I would then sign it with the white man's name.

When I went to the library, I would stand at the desk, hat in hand, looking as unbookish as possible. When I received the books desired I would take them home. If the books listed in the note happened to be out, I would sneak into the lobby and forge a new one. I never took any chances guessing with the white librarian about what the fictitious white man would want to read. No doubt if any of the white patrons had suspected that some of the volumes they enjoyed had been in the home of a Negro, they would not have tolerated it for an instant.

The factory force of the optical company in Memphis was much larger than that in Jackson, and more urbanized. At least they liked to talk, and would engage the Negro help in conversation whenever possible. By this means I found that many subjects were taboo from the white man's point of view. Among the topics they did not like to discuss with Negroes were the following: American white women; the Ku Klux Klan; France, and how Negro soldiers fared while there; French women; Jack Johnson; the entire northern part of the United States; the Civil War; Abraham Lincoln; U. S. Grant; General Sherman; Catholics; the Pope; Jews; the Republican Party; slavery; social equality; Communism; Socialism; the 13th and 14th Amendments to the Constitution; or any topic calling for positive knowledge or manly self-assertion on the part of the Negro. The most accepted topics were sex and religion.

There were many times when I had to exercise a great deal of ingenuity to keep out of trouble. It is a southern custom that all men must take off their hats when they enter an elevator. And especially did this apply to us blacks with rigid force. One day I stepped into an elevator with my arms full of packages. I was forced to ride with my hat on. Two white men stared at me coldly. Then one of them very kindly lifted my hat and placed it upon my armful of packages. Now the most accepted response for a Negro to make under such circumstances is to look at the white man out of the corner of his eye and grin. To have said: "Thank you!" would have made the white man *think* that you *thought* you were receiving from him a personal service. For such an act I have seen Negroes take a blow in the mouth. Finding the first alternative distasteful, and the second dangerous, I hit upon an acceptable course of action which fell safely between these two poles. I immediately—no sooner than my hat was lifted—pretended that my packages were about to spill, and appeared deeply distressed with keeping them in my arms. In this fashion I evaded having to acknowledge his service, and, in spite of adverse circumstances, salvaged a slender shred of personal pride.

How do Negroes feel about the way they have to live? How do they discuss it when alone among themselves? I think this question can be answered in a single sentence. A friend of mine who ran an elevator once told me:

"Lawd, man! Ef it wuzn't fer them polices 'n' them ol' lynch-mobs, there wouldn't be nothin' but uproar down here!"

31

Letter from Birmingham Jail

Martin Luther King, Jr.

In 1955, as "The Mobilization of Black Strength" indicated, all hell broke loose in the South in spite of the police and the lynchings. That was the year of the Montgomery bus boycott, an event that launched the nonviolent Negro protest movement of the fifties and sixties. Though a great many people rose to prominence in the movement, Martin Luther King became its most popular and most eloquent spokesman. For twelve tumultuous years he led nonviolent demonstrations in the South and North alike, assailing racial injustice with a haunting eloquence that would never be forgotten by those who heard him.

In 1963, on the one hundredth anniversary of the Emancipation Proclamation, King turned up in Birmingham, Alabama, to help blacks protest against the city's rigid racial caste system. The demonstration began just before Easter, with columns of unarmed blacks marching and singing in the streets. At the same time, the blacks boycotted white-owned stores in Birmingham, intending to hurt the whites' pocketbooks if not their consciences. Though the demonstration remained nonviolent, the Birmingham police, led by bull-necked Eugene Connor, turned fire hoses and police dogs on the blacks, shocked them with cattle prods, and dragged them beaten and bleeding off to jail.

King also demonstrated and also ended up in jail. While languishing there, he received a public declaration from eight white Alabama clergymen, who castigated outsiders like King for stirring up trouble in Alabama and implored blacks there to denounce the Birmingham demonstrations. King responded with his now classic "Letter from Birmingham Jail," regarded as the most eloquent expression of the goals and philosophy of the nonviolent civil rights movement ever written.

April 16, 1963

MY DEAR FELLOW CLERGYMEN:

While confined here in the Birmingham city jail, I came across your recent statement calling my present activities "unwise and untimely." Seldom do I pause to answer criticism of my work and ideas. If I sought to answer all the criticisms that cross my desk, my secretaries would have little time for anything other than such correspondence in the course of the day, and I would have no time for constructive work. But since I feel that you are men of genuine good will and that your criticisms are sincerely set forth, I want to try to answer your statement in what I hope will be patient and reasonable terms.

I think I should indicate why I am here in Birmingham, since you have been influenced by the view which argues against "outsiders coming in." I have the honor of serving as president of the Southern Christian Leadership Conference, an organization operating in every southern state, with headquarters in Atlanta, Georgia. We have some eighty-five affiliated organizations across the South, and one of them is the Alabama Christian Movement for Human Rights. Frequently we share staff, educational and finan-

---

"Letter from Birmingham Jail—April 16, 1963" from *Why We Can't Wait* by Martin Luther King, Jr. Copyright © 1963 by Martin Luther King, Jr. Reprinted by permission of Harper & Row, Publishers, Inc.

cial resources with our affiliates. Several months ago the affiliate here in Birmingham asked us to be on call to engage in a nonviolent direct-action program if such were deemed necessary. We readily consented, and when the hour came we lived up to our promise. So I, along with several members of my staff, am here because I was invited here. I am here because I have organizational ties here.

But more basically, I am in Birmingham because injustice is here. Just as the prophets of the eighth century B.C. left their villages and carried their "thus saith the Lord" far beyond the boundaries of their home towns, and just as the Apostle Paul left his village of Tarsus and carried the gospel of Jesus Christ to the far corners of the Greco-Roman world, so am I compelled to carry the gospel of freedom beyond my own home town. Like Paul, I must constantly respond to the Macedonian call for aid.

Moreover, I am cognizant of the interrelatedness of all communities and states. I cannot sit idly by in Atlanta and not be concerned about what happens in Birmingham. Injustice anywhere is a threat to justice everywhere. We are caught in an inescapable network of mutuality, tied in a single garment of destiny. Whatever affects one directly, affects all indirectly. Never again can we afford to live with the narrow, provincial "outside agitator" idea. Anyone who lives inside the United States can never be considered an outsider anywhere within its bounds.

You deplore the demonstrations taking place in Birmingham. But your statement, I am sorry to say, fails to express a similar concern for the conditions that brought about the demonstrations. I am sure that none of you would want to rest content with the superficial kind of social analysis that deals merely with effects and does not grapple with underlying causes. It is unfortunate that demonstrations are taking place in Birmingham, but it is even more unfortunate that the city's white power structure left the Negro community with no alternative.

In any nonviolent campaign there are four basic steps: collection of the facts to determine whether injustices exist; negotiation; self-purification; and direct action. We have gone through all these steps in Birmingham. There can be no gainsaying the fact that racial injustice engulfs this community. Birmingham is probably the most thoroughly segregated city in the United States. Its ugly record of brutality is widely known. Negroes have experienced grossly unjust treatment in the courts. There have been more unsolved bombings of Negro homes and churches in Birmingham than in any other city in the nation. These are the hard, brutal facts of the case. On the basis of these conditions, Negro leaders sought to negotiate with the city fathers. But the latter consistently refused to engage in good-faith negotiation.

Then, last September, came the opportunity to talk with leaders of Birmingham's economic community. In the course of the negotiations, certain promises were made by the merchants—for example, to remove the stores' humiliating racial signs. On the basis of these promises, the Reverend Fred Shuttlesworth and the leaders of the Alabama Christian Movement for Human Rights agreed to a moratorium on all demonstrations. As the weeks and months went by, we realized that we were the victims of a broken promise. A few signs, briefly removed, returned; the others remained.

As in so many past experiences, our hopes had been blasted, and the shadow of deep disappointment settled upon us. We had no alternative except to prepare for direct action, whereby we would present our very bodies as a means of laying our case before the conscience of the local and the national community. Mindful of the difficulties involved, we decided to undertake a process of self-purification. We began a series of workshops on nonviolence, and we repeatedly asked ourselves: "Are you able to accept blows without retaliating?" "Are you able to endure the ordeal of jail?" We decided to schedule our direct-action program for the Easter season, realizing that except for Christ-

Martin Luther King (right foreground), leading a march in Birmingham in direct violation of a court order. After white police jailed him, Ralph Abernathy (at King's right), and fifty-one others, King wrote his celebrated "Letter from Birmingham Jail." (Courtesy of United Press International.)

mas, this is the main shopping period of the year. Knowing that a strong economic-withdrawal program would be the by-product of direct action, we felt that this would be the best time to bring pressure to bear on the merchants for the needed change.

Then it occurred to us that Birmingham's mayoral election was coming up in March, and we speedily decided to postpone action until after election day. When we discovered that the Commissioner of Public Safety, Eugene "Bull" Connor, had piled up enough votes to be in the run-off, we decided again to postpone action until the day after the run-off so that the demonstrations could not be used to cloud the issues. Like many others, we waited to see Mr. Connor defeated, and to this end we endured postponement after postponement. Having aided in this community need, we felt that our direct-action program could be delayed no longer.

You may well ask: "Why direct action? Why sit-ins, marches and so forth? Isn't negotiation a better path?" You are quite right in calling for negotiation. Indeed, this is the very purpose of direct action. Nonviolent direct action seeks to create such a crisis and foster such a tension that a community which has constantly refused to negotiate is forced to confront the issue. It seeks so to dramatize the issue that it can no longer be ignored. My citing the creation of tension as part of the work of the nonviolent-resister may sound rather shocking. But I must confess that I am not afraid of the word "tension." I have earnestly opposed violent tension, but there is a type of constructive, nonviolent tension which is necessary for growth. Just as Socrates felt that it was necessary to create a tension in the mind so that individuals could rise from the bondage of myths and half-truths to the unfettered realm of creative analysis and objective appraisal, so must we see the need for nonviolent gadflies to create the kind of tension in society that will help men rise from the dark depths of prejudice and racism to the majestic heights of understanding and brotherhood.

The purpose of our direct-action program is to create a situation so crisis-packed that it will inevitably open the door to negotiation. I therefore concur with you in your call for negotiation. Too long has our beloved Southland been bogged down in a tragic effort to live in monologue rather than dialogue.

One of the basic points in your statement is that the action that I and my associates have taken in Birmingham is untimely. Some have asked: "Why didn't you give the new city administration time to act?" The only answer that I can give to this query is that the new Birmingham administration must be prodded about as much as the outgoing one, before it will act. We are sadly mistaken if we feel that the election of Albert Boutwell as mayor will bring the millennium to Birmingham. While Mr. Boutwell is a much more gentle person than Mr. Connor, they are both segregationists, dedicated to maintenance of the status quo. I have hope that Mr. Boutwell will be reasonable enough to see the futility of massive resistance to desegregation. But he will not see this without pressure from devotees of civil rights. My friends, I must say to you that we have not made a single gain in civil rights without determined legal and nonviolent pressure. Lamentably, it is an historical fact that privileged groups seldom give up their privileges voluntarily. Individuals may see the moral light and voluntarily give up their unjust posture; but, as Reinhold Niebuhr has reminded us, groups tend to be more immoral than individuals.

We know through painful experience that freedom is never voluntarily given by the oppressor; it must be demanded by the oppressed. Frankly, I have yet to engage in a direct-action campaign that was "well timed" in the view of those who have not suffered unduly from the disease of segregation. For years now I have heard the word "Wait!" It rings in the ear of every Negro with piercing familiarity. This "Wait" has almost always meant "Never." We must come to see, with one of our distinguished jurists, that "justice too long delayed is justice denied."

We have waited for more than 340 years for our constitutional and God-given rights. The nations of Asia and Africa are moving with jet-like speed toward gaining political independence, but we still creep at horse-and-buggy pace toward gaining a cup of coffee at a lunch counter. Perhaps it is easy for those who have never felt the stinging darts of segregation to say, "Wait." But when you have seen vicious mobs lynch your mothers and fathers at will and drown your sisters and brothers at whim; when you have seen hate-filled policemen curse, kick and even kill your black brothers and sisters; when you see the vast majority of your twenty million Negro brothers smothering in an airtight cage of poverty in the midst of an affluent society; when you suddenly find your tongue twisted and your speech stammering as you seek to explain to your six-year-old daughter why she can't go to the public amusement park that has just been advertised on television, and see tears welling up in her eyes when she is told that Funtown is closed to colored children, and see ominous clouds of inferiority beginning to form in her little mental sky, and see her beginning to distort her personality by developing an unconscious bitterness toward white people; when you have to concoct an answer for a five-year-old son who is asking: "Daddy, why do white people treat colored people so mean?"; when you take a cross-country drive and find it necessary to sleep night after night in the uncomfortable corners of your automobile because no motel will accept you; when you are humiliated day in and day out by nagging signs reading "white" and "colored"; when your first name becomes "nigger," your middle name becomes "boy" (however old you are) and your last name becomes "John," and your wife and mother are never given the respected title "Mrs."; when you are harried by day and haunted by night by the fact that you are a Negro, living constantly at tiptoe stance, never quite knowing what to expect next, and are plagued with inner fears and outer resentments; when you are forever fighting a degenerating sense of "nobodiness"—then you will understand why we find it difficult to wait. There comes a time when the cup of endurance runs over, and men are no longer willing to be plunged into the abyss of despair. I hope, sirs, you can understand our legitimate and unavoidable impatience.

You express a great deal of anxiety over our willingness to break laws. This is certainly a legitimate concern. Since we so diligently urge people to obey the Supreme Court's decision of 1954 outlawing segregation in the public schools, at first glance it may seem rather paradoxical for us consciously to break laws. One may well ask: "How can you advocate breaking some laws and obeying others?" The answer lies in the fact that there are two types of laws: just and unjust. I would be the first to advocate obeying just laws. One has not only a legal but a moral responsibility to obey just laws. Conversely, one has a moral responsibility to disobey unjust laws. I would agree with St. Augustine that "an unjust law is no law at all."

Now, what is the difference between the two? How does one determine whether a law is just or unjust? A just law is a man-made code that squares with the moral law or the law of God. An unjust law is a code that is out of harmony with the moral law. To put it in the terms of St. Thomas Aquinas: An unjust law is a human law that is not rooted in eternal law and natural law. Any law that uplifts human personality is just. Any law that degrades human personality is unjust. All segregation statutes are unjust because segregation distorts the soul and damages the personality. It gives the segregator a false sense of superiority and the segregated a false sense of inferiority. Segregation, to use the terminology of the Jewish philosopher Martin Buber, substitutes an "I–it" relationship for an "I–thou" relationship and ends up relegating persons to the status of things. Hence segregation is not only politically, economically and sociologically unsound, it is morally wrong and sinful. Paul Tillich has said that sin is separation. Is not segregation an existential expression of man's tragic separation, his awful estrangement, his terrible sinfulness? Thus it is that I can urge men to obey the 1954 decision of the Supreme Court, for it is morally right; and I can urge them to disobey segregation ordinances, for they are morally wrong.

Let us consider a more concrete example of just and unjust laws. An unjust law is a code that a numerical or power majority group compels a minority group to obey but does not make binding on itself. This is *difference* made legal. By the same token, a just law is a code that a majority compels a minority to follow and that it is willing to follow itself. This is *sameness* made legal.

Let me give another explanation. A law is unjust if it is inflicted on a minority that, as a result of being denied the right to vote, had no part in enacting or devising the law. Who can say that the legislature of Alabama which set up that state's segregation laws was democratically elected? Throughout Alabama all sorts of devious methods are used to prevent Negroes from becoming registered voters, and there are some counties in which, even though Negroes constitute a majority of the population, not a single Negro is registered. Can any law enacted under such circumstances be considered democratically structured?

Sometimes a law is just on its face and unjust in its application. For instance, I have been arrested on a charge of parading without a permit. Now, there is nothing wrong in having an ordinance which requires a permit for a parade. But such an ordinance becomes unjust when it is used to maintain segregation and to deny citizens the First-Amendment privilege of peaceful assembly and protest.

I hope you are able to see the distinction I am trying to point out. In no sense do I advocate evading or defying the law, as would the rabid segregationist. That would lead to anarchy. One who breaks an unjust law must do so openly, lovingly, and with a willingness to accept the penalty. I submit that an individual who breaks a law that conscience tells him is unjust, and who willingly accepts the penalty of imprisonment in order to arouse the conscience of the community over its injustice, is in reality expressing the highest respect for law.

Of course, there is nothing new about this kind of civil disobedience. It was evidenced sublimely in the refusal of Shadrach, Meshach and Abednego to obey the laws of Nebuchadnezzar, on the ground that a higher moral law was at stake. It was practiced superbly by the early Christians, who were willing to face hungry lions and the excruciating pain of chopping blocks rather than submit to certain unjust laws of the Roman Empire. To a degree, academic freedom is a reality today because Socrates practiced civil disobedience. In our own nation, the Boston Tea Party represented a massive act of civil disobedience.

We should never forget that everything Adolf Hitler did in Germany was "legal" and everything the Hungarian freedom fighters did in Hungary was "illegal." It was "illegal" to aid and comfort a Jew in Hitler's Germany. Even so, I am sure that, had I lived in Germany at the time, I would have aided and comforted my Jewish brothers. If today I lived in a Communist country where certain principles dear to the Christian faith are suppressed, I would openly advocate disobeying that country's antireligious laws.

I must make two honest confessions to you, my Christian and Jewish brothers. First, I must confess that over the past few years I have been gravely disappointed with the white moderate. I have almost reached the regrettable conclusion that the Negro's great stumbling block in his stride toward freedom is not the White Citizen's Counciler or the Ku Klux Klanner, but the white moderate, who is more devoted to "order" than to justice; who prefers a negative peace which is the absence of tension to a positive peace which is the presence of justice; who constantly says: "I agree with you in the goal you seek, but I cannot agree with your methods of direct action"; who paternalistically believes he can set the timetable for another man's freedom; who lives by a mythical concept of time and who constantly advises the Negro to wait for a "more convenient season." Shallow understanding from people of good will is more frustrating than absolute misunderstanding from people of ill will. Lukewarm acceptance is much more bewildering than outright rejection.

I had hoped that the white moderate would understand that law and order exist for the purpose of establishing justice and that when they fail in this purpose they become the dangerously structured dams that block the flow of social progress. I had hoped that the white moderate would understand that the present tension in the South is a necessary phase of the transition from an obnoxious negative peace, in which the Negro passively accepted his unjust plight, to a substantive and positive peace, in which all men will respect the dignity and worth of human personality. Actually, we who engage in nonviolent direct action are not the creators of tension. We merely bring to the surface the hidden tension that is already alive. We bring it out in the open, where it can be seen and dealt with. Like a boil that can never be cured so long as it is covered up but must be opened with all its ugliness to the natural medicines of air and light, injustice must be exposed, with all the tension its exposure creates, to the light of human conscience and the air of national opinion before it can be cured.

In your statement you assert that our actions, even though peaceful, must be condemned because they precipitate violence. But is this a logical assertion? Isn't this like condemning a robbed man because his possession of money precipitated the evil act of robbery? Isn't this like condemning Socrates because his unswerving commitment to truth and his philosophical inquiries precipitated the act by the misguided populace in which they made him drink hemlock? Isn't this like condemning Jesus because his unique God-consciousness and never-ceasing devotion to God's will precipitated the evil act of crucifixion? We must come to see that, as the federal courts have consistently affirmed, it is wrong to urge an individual to cease his efforts to gain his basic constitutional rights because the quest may precipitate violence. Society must protect the robbed and punish the robber.

I had also hoped that the white moderate would reject the myth concerning time in relation to the struggle for freedom. I have just received a letter from a white brother in Texas. He writes: "All Christians know that the colored people will receive equal rights eventually, but it is possible that you are in too great a religious hurry. It has taken Christianity almost two thousand years to accomplish what it has. The teachings of Christ take time to come to earth." Such an attitude stems from a tragic misconception of time, from the strangely irrational notion that there is something in the very flow of time that will inevitably cure all ills. Actually, time itself is neutral; it can be used either destructively or constructively. More and more I feel that the people of ill will have used time much more effectively than have the people of good will. We will have to repent in this generation not merely for the hateful words and actions of the bad people but for the appalling silence of the good people. Human progress never rolls in on wheels of inevitability; it comes through the tireless efforts of men willing to be co-workers with God, and without this hard work, time itself becomes an ally of the forces of social stagnation. We must use time creatively, in the knowledge that the time is always ripe to do right. Now is the time to make real the promise of democracy and transform our pending national elegy into a creative psalm of brotherhood. Now is the time to lift our national policy from the quicksand of racial injustice to the solid rock of human dignity.

You speak of our activity in Birmingham as extreme. At first I was rather disappointed that fellow clergymen would see my nonviolent efforts as those of an extremist. I began thinking about the fact that I stand in the middle of two opposing forces in the Negro community. One is a force of complacency, made up in part of Negroes who, as a result of long years of oppression, are so drained of self-respect and a sense of "somebodiness" that they have adjusted to segregation; and in part of a few middle-class Negroes who, because of a degree of academic and economic security and because in some ways they profit by segregation, have become insensitive to the problems of the masses. The other force is one of bitterness and hatred, and it comes perilously close to advocating violence. It is expressed in the various black nationalist groups that are springing up across the nation, the largest and best-known being Elijah Muhammad's Muslim movement. Nourished by the Negro's frustration over the continued existence of racial discrimination, this movement is made up of people who have lost faith in America, who have absolutely repudiated Christianity, and who have concluded that the white man is an incorrigible "devil."

I have tried to stand between these two

forces, saying that we need emulate neither the "do-nothingism" of the complacent nor the hatred and despair of the black nationalist. For there is the more excellent way of love and nonviolent protest. I am grateful to God that, through the influence of the Negro church, the way of nonviolence became an integral part of our struggle.

If this philosophy had not emerged, by now many streets of the South would, I am convinced, be flowing with blood. And I am further convinced that if our white brothers dismiss as "rabble-rousers" and "outside agitators" those of us who employ nonviolent direct action, and if they refuse to support our nonviolent efforts, millions of Negroes will, out of frustration and despair, seek solace and security in black-nationalist ideologies—a development that would inevitably lead to a frightening racial nightmare.

Oppressed people cannot remain oppressed forever. The yearning for freedom eventually manifests itself, and that is what has happened to the American Negro. Something within has reminded him of his birthright of freedom, and something without has reminded him that it can be gained. Consciously or unconsciously, he has been caught up by the *Zeitgeist*, and with his black brothers of Africa and his brown and yellow brothers of Asia, South America and the Caribbean, the United States Negro is moving with a sense of great urgency toward the promised land of racial justice. If one recognizes this vital urge that has engulfed the Negro community, one should readily understand why public demonstrations are taking place. The Negro has many pent-up resentments and latent frustrations, and he must release them. So let him march; let him make prayer pilgrimages to the city hall; let him go on freedom rides—and try to understand why he must do so. If his repressed emotions are not released in nonviolent ways, they will seek expression through violence; this is not a threat but a fact of history. So I have not said to my people: "Get rid of your discontent." Rather, I have tried to say that this normal and healthy discontent can be channeled into the creative outlet of nonviolent direct action. And now this approach is being termed extremist.

But though I was initially disappointed at being categorized as an extremist, as I continued to think about the matter I gradually gained a measure of satisfaction from the label. Was not Jesus an extremist for love: "Love your enemies, bless them that curse you, do good to them that hate you, and pray for them which despitefully use you, and persecute you." Was not Amos an extremist for justice: "Let justice roll down like waters and righteousness like an ever-flowing stream." Was not Paul an extremist for the Christian gospel: "I bear in my body the marks of the Lord Jesus." Was not Martin Luther an extremist: "Here I stand; I cannot do otherwise, so help me God." And John Bunyan: "I will stay in jail to the end of my days before I make a butchery of my conscience." And Abraham Lincoln: "This nation cannot survive half slave and half free." And Thomas Jefferson: "We hold these truths to be self-evident, that all men are created equal . . ." So the question is not whether we will be extremists, but what kind of extremists we will be. Will we be extremists for hate or for love? Will we be extremists for the preservation of injustice or for the extension of justice? In that dramatic scene on Calvary's hill three men were crucified. We must never forget that all three were crucified for the same crime—the crime of extremism. Two were extremists for immorality, and thus fell below their environment. The other, Jesus Christ, was an extremist for love, truth and goodness, and thereby rose above his environment. Perhaps the South, the nation and the world are in dire need of creative extremists.

I had hoped that the white moderate would see this need. Perhaps I was too optimistic; perhaps I expected too much. I suppose I should have realized that few members of the oppressor race can understand the deep groans and passionate yearnings of the oppressed race, and still fewer have the vision to see that injustice must be rooted out by strong, persistent and determined action. I am thankful, however, that some of our white brothers in the South have grasped the meaning of this social revolution and committed themselves to it. They are still all too few in quantity, but they are big in quality. Some—such as Ralph McGill, Lillian Smith, Harry Golden, James McBride Dabbs, Ann Braden and Sarah Patton Boyle—have written about our struggle in eloquent and prophetic terms. Others have marched with us down nameless streets of the South. They have languished in filthy, roach-infested jails, suffering the abuse and brutality of policemen who view them as "dirty nigger-lovers." Unlike so many of their moderate brothers and sisters, they have recognized the urgency of the moment and sensed the need for powerful "action" antidotes to combat the disease of segregation.

Let me take note of my other major disappointment. I have been so greatly disappointed with the white church and its leadership. Of course, there are some notable exceptions. I am not unmindful of the fact that each of you has taken some significant stands on this issue. I commend you, Reverend Stallings, for your Christian stand on this past Sunday, in welcoming Negroes to your worship service on a nonsegregated basis. I commend the Catholic leaders of this state for integrating Spring Hill College several years ago.

But despite these notable exceptions, I must honestly reiterate that I have been disappointed with the church. I do not say this as one of those negative critics who can always find something wrong with the church. I say this as a minister in its bosom; who has been sustained by its spiritual blessings and who will remain true to it as long as the cord of life shall lengthen.

When I was suddenly catapulted into the leadership of the bus protest in Montgomery, Alabama, a few years ago, I felt we would be supported by the white church. I felt that the white ministers, priests and rabbis of the South would be among our strongest allies. Instead, some have been outright opponents, refusing to understand the freedom movement and misrepresenting its leaders; all too many others have been more cautious than courageous and have remained silent behind the anesthetizing security of stained-glass windows.

In spite of my shattered dreams, I came to Birmingham with the hope that the white religious leadership of this community would see the justice of our cause and, with deep moral concern, would serve as the channel through which our just grievances could reach the power structure. I had hoped that each of you would understand. But again I have been disappointed.

I have heard numerous southern religious leaders admonish their worshipers to comply with a desegregation decision because it is the law, but I have longed to hear white ministers declare: "Follow this decree because integration is morally right and because the Negro is your brother." In the midst of blatant injustices inflicted upon the Negro, I have watched white churchmen stand on the sideline and mouth pious irrelevancies and sanctimonious trivialities. In the midst of a mighty struggle to rid our nation of racial and economic injustice, I have heard many ministers say: "Those are social issues, with which the gospel has no real concern." And I have watched many churches commit themselves to a completely otherworldly religion which makes a strange, un-Biblical distinction between body and soul, between the sacred and the secular.

I have traveled the length and breadth of Alabama, Mississippi and all the other southern states. On sweltering summer days and crisp autumn mornings I have looked at the South's beautiful churches with their lofty spires pointing heavenward. I have beheld the impressive outlines of her massive religious-education buildings. Over and over I have found myself asking: "What kind of people worship here? Who is their God? Where were their voices when the lips of Governor Barnett dripped with words of interposition and nullification? Where were they when Governor Wallace gave a clarion call for defiance and hatred? Where were their voices of support when bruised and weary Negro men and women decided to rise from the dark dungeons of complacency to the bright hills of creative protest?"

Yes, these questions are still in my mind. In deep disappointment I have wept over the laxity of the church. But be assured that my tears have been tears of love. There can be no deep disappointment where there is not deep love. Yes, I love the church. How could I do otherwise? I am in the rather unique position of being the son, the grandson and the great-grandson of preachers. Yes, I see the church as the body of Christ. But, oh! How we have blemished and scarred that body through social neglect and through fear of being nonconformists.

There was a time when the church was very powerful—in the time when the early Christians rejoiced at being deemed worthy to suffer for what they believed. In those days the church was not merely a thermometer that recorded the ideas and principles of popular opinion; it was a thermostat that transformed the mores of society. Whenever the early Christians entered a town, the people in power became disturbed and immediately sought to convict the Christians for being "disturbers of the peace" and "outside agitators." But the Christians pressed on, in the conviction that they were "a colony of heaven," called to obey God rather than man. Small in number, they were big in commitment. They were too God-intoxicated to be "astronomically intimidated." By their effort and example they brought an end to such ancient evils as infanticide and gladiatorial contests.

Things are different now. So often the contemporary church is a weak, ineffectual voice with an uncertain sound. So often it is an archdefender of the status quo. Far from being disturbed by the presence of the church, the power structure of the average community is consoled by the church's silent—and often even vocal—sanction of things as they are.

But the judgment of God is upon the church as never before. If today's church does not recapture the sacrificial spirit of the early church, it will lose its authenticity, forfeit the loyalty of millions, and be dismissed as an irrelevant social club with no meaning for the twentieth century. Every day I meet young people whose disappointment with the church has turned to outright disgust.

Perhaps I have once again been too optimistic. Is organized religion too inextricably bound to the status quo to save our nation and the world? Perhaps I must turn my faith to the inner spiritual church, the church within the church, as the true *ekklesia* and the hope of the world. But again I am thankful to God that some noble souls from the ranks of organized religion have broken loose from the paralyzing chains of conformity and joined us as active partners in the struggle for freedom. They have left their secure congregations and walked the streets of Albany, Georgia, wth us. They have gone down the highways of the South on tortuous rides for freedom. Yes, they have gone to jail with us. Some have been dismissed from their churches, have lost the support of their bishops and fellow ministers. But they have acted in the faith that right defeated is stronger than evil triumphant. Their witness has been the spiritual salt that has preserved the true meaning of the gospel in these troubled times. They have carved a tunnel of hope through the dark mountain of disappointment.

I hope the church as a whole will meet the challenge of this decisive hour. But even if the church does not come to the aid of justice, I have no despair about the future. I have no fear about the outcome of our struggle in Birmingham, even if our motives are at present misunderstood. We will reach the goal of freedom in Birmingham and all over the nation, because the goal of America is freedom. Abused and scorned though we may be, our destiny is tied up with America's destiny. Before the pilgrims landed at Plymouth, we were here. Before the pen of Jefferson etched the majestic words of the Declaration of Independence across the pages of history, we were here. For more than two centuries our forebears labored in this country without wages; they made cotton king; they built the homes of their masters while suffering gross injustice and shameful humiliation—and yet out of a bottomless vitality they continued to thrive and develop. If the inexpressible cruelties of slavery could not stop us, the opposition we now face will surely fail. We will win our freedom because the sacred heritage of our nation and the eternal will of God are embodied in our echoing demands.

Before closing I feel impelled to mention one other point in your statement that has troubled me profoundly. You warmly commended the Birmingham police force for keeping "order" and "preventing violence." I doubt that you would have so warmly commended the police force if you had seen its dogs sinking their teeth into unarmed, nonviolent Negroes. I doubt that you would so quickly commend the policemen if you were to observe their ugly and inhumane treatment of Negroes here in the city jail; if you were to watch them push and curse old Negro women and young Negro girls; if you were to see them slap and kick old Negro men and young boys; if you were to observe them, as they did on two occasions, refuse to give us food because we wanted to sing our grace together. I cannot join you in your praise of the Birmingham police department.

It is true that the police have exercised a degree of discipline in handling the demonstrators. In this sense they have conducted themselves rather "nonviolently" in public. But for what purpose? To preserve the evil system of segregation. Over the past few years I have consistently preached that nonviolence demands that the means we use must be as pure as the ends we seek. I have tried to make clear that it is wrong to use immoral means to attain moral ends. But now I must affirm that it is just as wrong, or perhaps even more so, to use moral means to preserve immoral ends. Perhaps Mr. Connor and his policemen have been rather nonviolent in public, as was Chief Pritchett in Albany, Georgia, but they have used the moral means of nonviolence to maintain the immoral end of racial injustice. As T. S. Eliot has said: "The last temptation is the greatest treason: To do the right deed for the wrong reason."

I wish you had commended the Negro sit-inners and demonstrators of Birmingham for their sublime courage, their willingness to suffer and their amazing discipline in the midst of great provocation. One day the South will recognize its real heroes. They will be the James Merediths, wih the noble sense of purpose that enables them to face jeering and hostile mobs, and with the agonizing loneliness that characterizes the life of the pioneer. They will be old, oppressed, battered Negro women, symbolized in a seventy-two-year-old woman in Montgomery, Alabama, who rose up with a sense of dignity and with her people decided not to ride segregated buses, and who responded with ungrammatical profundity to one who inquired about her weariness: "My feets is tired, but my soul is at rest." They will be the young high school and college students, the young ministers of the gospel and a host of their elders, courageously and nonviolently sitting in at lunch counters and willingly going to jail for conscience' sake. One day the South will know that when these disinherited children of God sat down at lunch counters, they were in reality standing up for what is best in the American dream and for the most sacred values in our Judaeo-Christian heritage, thereby bringing our nation back to those great wells of democracy which were dug deep by the founding fathers in their formulation of the Constitution and the Declaration of Independence.

Never before have I written so long a letter. I'm afraid it is much too long to take your precious time. I can assure you that it would have been much shorter if I had been writing from a comfortable desk, but what else can one do when he is alone in a narrow jail cell, other than write long letters, think long thoughts and pray long prayers?

If I have said anything in this letter that overstates the truth and indicates an unreasonable impatience, I beg you to forgive me. If I have said anything that understates the truth and indicates my having a patience that allows me to settle for anything less than brotherhood, I beg God to forgive me.

I hope this letter finds you strong in the faith. I also hope that circumstances will soon make it possible for me to meet each of you, not as an integrationist or a civil-rights leader but as a fellow clergyman and a Christian brother. Let us all hope that the dark clouds of racial prejudice will soon pass away and the deep fog of misunderstanding will be lifted from our fear-drenched communities, and in some not too distant tomorrow the radiant stars of love and brotherhood will shine over our great nation with all their scintillating beauty.

Yours for the cause of Peace and Brotherhood,
MARTIN LUTHER KING, JR.

Five years later, while leading a protest in behalf of black garbage collectors in Memphis, Tennessee, King was shot and killed by a sniper. White authorities blamed the assassination on a petty white thief named James Earl Ray and finally apprehended him after an extensive manhunt across North America and Europe. On the advice of his lawyer, Percy Foreman of Houston, Ray pleaded guilty and went to prison for life. Ray, however, soon recanted his testimony, insisting that he was innocent of King's murder and that he had been "set up" by his own criminal associates, by white authorities, or both. Ray's dramatic claim generated tremendous public interest, and a number of books and magazine articles came out about him and the confused and often contradictory events that surrounded King's death and Ray's own arrest and imprisonment. As this volume goes to press, it is still unclear whether Ray murdered King alone, whether he did it with others, or whether he was indeed a dupe in a conspiracy to assassinate the famed civil rights leader.

X The Ordeal of Modern America

32

"They've Killed the President!"

Robert Sam Anson

When John Fitzgerald Kennedy was elected president in 1960, many observers hailed his victory as the beginning of a new era in American politics. Kennedy was not only the youngest man—he was forty-three in 1960—but the first Roman Catholic elected to the presidency. And his youthful flair seemed to support the contention that a new era had indeed begun—a time when the United States turned to a new generation, one born in this century, for enlightened political leadership.

Kennedy had style, to be sure. His youth and glamour—and his lovely wife—made him an idol among young and old alike. But his presidency, for the short time it lasted, did not usher in a golden new age in American politics. In foreign affairs, he accepted the basic assumptions of Truman's containment policy and Dulles' domino theory; he escalated American involvement in Vietnam, approved the disastrous Bay of Pigs invasion of Cuba, and took the nation to the brink of nuclear war in the Cuban missile showdown with Khrushchev. While his administration did negotiate a nuclear test ban treaty and did establish the Peace Corps, his other programs—federal aid to schools, a civil rights act, medicare, and tax reform—were blocked by a conservative-dominated Congress.

Had he lived, he might have done more, a great deal more. For when Kennedy was assassinated in Dallas on November 22, 1963, he had been in office only two years and ten months; and it was simply not enough time to accomplish the goals set forth in his inaugural address. And in any case, the shocking manner of his death tended to overshadow the record of his brief administration. People the world over were stunned that so young a statesman could have been shot down in the prime of life, and nobody who watched the aftermath on television would ever forget the sight of Jacqueline Kennedy, still dressed in bloodstained clothes, flying back to Washington with her husband's coffin ... would ever forget the spectacle of Jack Ruby, Dallas strip-joint operator, shooting the alleged assassin Lee Harvey Oswald just two days after Kennedy's murder—and doing so in a crowded Dallas police station in front of a national television audience ... would ever forget the heartbreaking grandeur of Kennedy's funeral itself—the drums that shattered the sunlit day, the riderless horse, the farewell salute John Jr. gave his father's coffin, the eternal flame wavering at his grave in Arlington National Cemetery. Afterward, millions of Americans, especially the young, remembered John Fitzgerald Kennedy as an elegant and idealistic young president who had a noble dream of how to make America—and the world—a better place for mankind. And his death left them bitterly disillusioned, a mood intensified when Martin Luther King, Jr., and Robert Kennedy, the president's brother, subsequently fell by assassins' bullets.

Still, troubling questions about the president's assassination remained. Was Lee Harvey Oswald the only gunman—or even the real one? Was the president's killer linked to the American right? To the left? To Cuba? To the Soviet Union? To dispel all the rumors that crawled through the country, the new president, Lyndon B. Johnson, set up a blue-ribbon commission under Chief Justice Earl Warren to investigate the assassination. In haste to put the matter to rest, the Warren Commission relied heavily on an F.B.I. report that Lee Harvey Oswald had fired all the shots in Dallas that day. According to the F.B.I., Oswald had armed himself with a twenty-one-dollar, Italian-made rifle and had waited for Kennedy in the School Book Depository which overlooked Dealey Plaza in downtown Dallas. When the presidential limousine swept by with Kennedy and his wife in back and Governor John Connally of Texas and his wife in front, Oswald opened fire, squeezing off shots in rapid succession at the back of the receding car. The F.B.I. contended that three of Oswald's bullets found their mark: the first struck Kennedy in the back, the second hit Connally, and the third smashed into the president's head, inflicting a mortal wound. The commission found this an entirely feasible explanation: Oswald and Oswald alone had killed the president.

Then disturbing new evidence came to light in the form of a film taken by bystander Abraham Zapruder. Although the Warren Commission conceded that it took at least 2.3 seconds for Oswald to fire his first bullet at Kennedy and his second at Connally, the Zapruder film demonstrated that only 1.6 seconds elapsed between the time Kennedy was first hit and the time Connally was shot. Did this indicate, then, that two gunmen were involved, one firing from the School Book Depository and one (or even more) from somewhere else? There were eyewitnesses who swore they heard gunshots sounding in other directions than the depository and who thought they saw additional gunmen in the area.

Warren and his colleagues, though, clung steadfastly to the single-assassin theory. To explain the discrepancy between the F.B.I. report and the Zapruder film, the commission decided that the F.B.I. was wrong in claiming that three of Oswald's bullets had found their mark. Actually only two of them had done so, the commission asserted, and the first bullet had struck both men, which explained how both were hit in the space of 1.6 seconds. In the commission's view, this so-called superbullet had pierced Kennedy's back and passed out his neck, and then had tunneled through Connally, severely wounding his chest, crushing his wrist bone, and lodging finally in his thigh.

Yet there were major problems with the superbullet hypothesis. For one thing, the bullet itself, recovered at Dallas' Parkland Hospital, was virtually undamaged. This seemed impossible for a missile that had supposedly smashed up two men. It seemed even more impossible when the commission had a similar bullet fired into the wrist of a cadaver, and the bullet came back with its tip "severely flattened and mangled," as one critic noted. And the single-assassin, superbullet explanation seemed even weaker when the finest marksmen in the country tried to duplicate the assassination as the commission reconstructed it, but failed to fire the alleged murder weapon with the accuracy ascribed to Oswald. Moreover, the Zapruder film also showed that Kennedy's head jerked violently backward after the final shot, a motion which suggested that the last bullet came from the front of the car and not from the back in the direction of the School Book Depository. Nevertheless, the Warren Commission stuck to its interpretation and on September 24, 1964, submitted its report to President Johnson.

After the report was published, a veritable procession of books and magazine articles came out which challenged its conclusions. Although a lot of the critical literature was cheaply sensational, some of it provided serious and responsible analyses of the Warren Report, pointing out its weaknesses and inconsistencies and all the troubling questions that remained. How could Oswald, at best only a fair shot, have fired with such deadly skill a rusted Italian rifle distinguished mainly for its inaccuracy and equipped with a defective scope? How could the Warren Commission accept such "incriminating" evidence as photographs of Oswald holding the alleged murder weapon in one hand and Communist propaganda in the other, when even to the casual eye the photographs appear to be forgeries, with Oswald's head superimposed on somebody else's body? How, too, could the commission disregard evidence of Oswald's Cuban connection? Of the possibility that he might have been a U.S. espionage agent, given his marine background, his defection to Russia, and his association with both pro- and anti-Castro Cubans? How could the commission dismiss the possibility that there might have been an Oswald look-alike to implicate Oswald himself in the slaying (on several occasions Oswald was at two different places at the same time)? Though critics of the Warren Report disagree as to who beyond Oswald might have been involved in the assassination, most suggest that it has all the marks of a professional "hit" job. Some now think it the work of pro-Castro Cubans, who were out to avenge the C.I.A.'s abortive attempts to murder Castro.

Others, though, speculate that Kennedy was killed by a secret coalition of C.I.A. men, organized crime, and groups of anti-Castro Cuban exiles, all of whom were enraged when Kennedy softened toward Cuba after the missile crisis.

On the other hand, a great many respected critics disparage all this as speculative nonsense and insist that the Warren Report must be believed until disproved by conclusive evidence. But given recent revelations about the covert operations of the C.I.A. and the F.B.I. and given the spate of assassinations and assassination attempts in recent times, the House of Representatives voted in September, 1976, to reopen the investigation of Kennedy's assassination, as well as that of Martin Luther King, Jr.

Maybe we shall never know the full truth about the murder of John F. Kennedy. But Robert Sam Anson, a noted critic of the Warren Report and a prominent New York journalist, has tried with painstaking thoroughness to reconstruct the details of that grim and terrible day in Dallas. Based on the evidence now available, Anson's is an astute, brilliantly written, disturbing narrative which invites readers to draw their own conclusions about the role of Lee Harvey Oswald and the possibility of a conspiracy to kill the president.

I am sure that all but a handful of our citizens will cordially welcome the President of the United States to Dallas.

JESSE CURRY, CHIEF OF POLICE
NOVEMBER 1963

It rained Friday morning in Dallas, the kind of sudden storm that sweeps over the Texas plains, and just as quickly disappears. That is how it was with this rain: quick, violent, gone. By 9:30 the clouds had disappeared, and a bright November sun was climbing in the sky. It was a perfect day for a parade.

The city prepared. In slightly more than two hours, the President of the United States would arrive.

There had been no choice for John Kennedy. He had to make this trip. One reason had brought him to Texas: politics. There was none more compelling. In less than a year he would, by his calculation, as well as that of the political experts—and of his enemies—be elected to a second term with a handy majority. Only disaster could prevent it. But Kennedy was taking no chances. He wanted to run his vote total as high as he could. The paper-thin margin of his first victory had cramped his style, made him unaccustomedly cautious, had helped him blunder into mistakes. Now the worst errors were behind him. He was gaining confidence. There was much, however, that was left to do, and many who would seek, who had already sought to block him. Kennedy would need all the strength he could muster. Which is why he had come to Texas. Because Texas was important. And Texas was a problem.

The state's Democratic party was, as usual, badly split, between the dominant conservatives of the Connally-Johnson wing of the party, and the small but noisy group of liberals led by Senator Ralph Yarborough. Yarborough and Connally were not even on speaking terms. There were other problems. Kennedy's brand of liberalism did not go down well in conservative Texas. Cuba, the test-ban treaty, the administration's initiatives in civil rights, and now the move to repeal the sacrosanct 27½ percent oil depletion allowance were, to say the least, not popular in this, the largest oil-producing state in the nation, which had one of the most massive defense establishments. If the election were held this November, Kennedy would probably lose Texas. And he knew it.

There had been talk of coming to Texas for more than a year, but the decision was finally pinned down in early June, at a meeting between

---

"One Sunny Day" from *"They've Killed the President!": The Search for the Murderers of John F. Kennedy;* copyright © 1975 by Robert Sam Anson. Reprinted by permission of Bantam Books, Inc.

Kennedy, Connally, and Johnson in El Paso. It was agreed: the President would come to Texas in late November. One of his stops would be Dallas. By mid-September the President's upcoming trip was already well known in the city. In October a motorcade was added to the schedule. In early November the planning of the exact motorcade route, and the selection of the site where the President would speak, began. By and large, it was an exercise in irrelevance. Once it became known that the President would come to Dallas and speak to a large luncheon crowd there was, for all practical purposes, only one site that made sense. That was the spanking new Trade Mart, west of downtown, out on the Stemmons Freeway. And since the President would be driving downtown so that a maximum number of people could see him, there was only one route the motorcade could travel: through the suburbs, then downtown on Main Street, right onto Houston, then left onto Elm and through the Triple Underpass that led to Stemmons Freeway and the Trade Mart beyond.

Everything had been set, and so far all had gone well. On Thursday the President had arrived in San Antonio, then gone on to Houston, and finally to Fort Worth to spend the night. The crowds had been large and friendly, the reception uniformly warm. The Kennedy magic was working. Even Connally and Yarborough had begun talking to each other. Friday morning the President spoke to a prayer breakfast of the Fort Worth Chamber of Commerce. Now, there was only one stop left before heading home. Dallas.

The city was a worry. A week before Kennedy's visit, Ambassador Adlai Stevenson had come to Dallas to speak to a local UN Association luncheon. When Stevenson emerged from the Adolphus Hotel, where the luncheon had been held, a group of noisy right-wing protesters were waiting for him. At the sight of Stevenson there was a small riot. The demonstrators shoved and spat on and cursed Stevenson. At least one picket hit him on the head with a sign. Stevenson was left shaken by the incident. He called Arthur Schlesinger and asked him to warn Kennedy not to go to Dallas. The city seemed to foster extremists. But Adlai Stevenson was not taken seriously by John Kennedy, or his aides. He had a record, after all, of shrinking from confrontation. During the missile crisis, it had been he who had urged accommodation with the Russians most forcefully. Besides, not visiting Dallas, the most important city in the state, was unthinkable.

When Kennedy picked up the *Dallas Morning News* in his hotel room Friday morning he saw that Stevenson was not kidding. There, emblazoned in bold black type, was a full-page advertisement suggesting in so many words that the President was a Communist and a traitor. The ad was signed: "American Fact–Finding Committee." Kennedy was appalled, and angry. "How can people write such things?" he demanded. Then he began to reflect on the ultimate extremism. If people wanted to badly enough, if they hated him sufficiently, they could kill him. He mused on how it could be done. Put a man in a high building; give him a high-powered rifle with a telescopic sight; ensure that he was willing to trade his life for the President's, and then—well, all the security in the world couldn't save the President. Kennedy was not worried. He had an Irish sense of fatalism. Danger was one of the things that went with the job.

Lee Harvey Oswald was up and dressed while his wife, Marina, still lay in bed. Their marriage had not been going well. They had been quarreling for more than a year, almost from the moment Lee brought her to the United States from her home in Russia. The couple had separated for long periods at a time, but always Lee came drifting back. This time, though, they seemed to be heading for divorce. Lee was talking of going back to Russia, where he had lived for two years after getting out of the Marine Corps. Marina would hear none of it. The rowing had gotten fiercer, and five weeks before, Lee had moved out again, this time into a rooming house in the Oak Cliff section of Dallas. Marina and the children had stayed in nearby Irving, Texas, living at the home of her friend Ruth Paine. Lee continued to visit her on weekends. This week, though, he had broken his routine. He came to the Paine home Thursday night to pick up a package to take to work the next day at the School Book Depository in downtown Dallas, where to his embarrassment, he labored as a stock boy for $1.25 per hour. The clock read 7:15 when Lee walked through the kitchen toward the back door. In his right hand he carried the package that had brought him home to Irving, a long, bulky brown bag tapered at one end. Buell Frazier, a friend and coworker from the Book Depository, met him at the back door. They walked across the street and got into Frazier's car. Lee put the bag on the back seat. "What's the package, Lee?" Frazier asked. "Curtain rods," Oswald answered.*

---

*This reconstruction of the events of November 22 is based on the testimony and public recollections of *credible* eyewitnesses. From this category the accounts of a number of witnesses, including some who support the single-assassin thesis as well as some who contradict it, are purposely excluded. Thus, for example, the testimony of Mrs. Helen Markham, who told the Commission she spoke to Officer Tippit *after* he had been instantly killed, is omitted, as is that of nearsighted Howard Brennan, who claimed to have seen Oswald firing the rifle from the sixth-floor window, yet was unable to pick him out of a police lineup. By the same token Julia Ann Mercer's account of a man carrying what appeared to be a gun case up the grassy knoll several hours before the assassination is also passed over, since investigations by the Dallas police and the FBI found that no such man ever existed. Moreover, Mrs. Mercer raised serious doubts about her credibility when, during the Garrison trial, she put Jack Ruby near the grassy knoll as well. The accounts which are included stand on their own even though some witnesses contradict each other. It is clear, for instance, that Oswald carried a package with him to work on November 22. It is not at all certain that this package, despite the Commission's claims, contained the Mannlicher-Carcano. In the same vein, the cars which Lee

The morning passed uneventfully at the Book Depository. As he did every day, Oswald worked filling orders, moving boxes and cartons back and forth to the shipping room. On the sixth floor a work crew labored to install a new flooring. They broke for lunch about 11:45 and, in a playful mood, ran to the building's two elevators. The game was to see which elevator could race the fastest to the ground floor. The workers climbed aboard the cars, slammed the gates, and started down. As one of the elevators passed the fifth floor, some of the workers saw Oswald standing in the doorway, evidently getting ready to break for lunch. "Hey, guys," he yelled as they passed by, "how about an elevator for me?" As the car disappeared down the shaft, Oswald shouted after them: "When you get downstairs, close the gate!" Lee Oswald didn't want to be kept waiting. If the gate wasn't closed, he couldn't call the car back up. It was a long walk down to the first-floor lunchroom.

At first it was just a dark speck in the brilliant blue Texas sky. The speck got larger and larger, the roar louder and louder, and at last the silver, red, white, and blue Boeing swooped down on the runway at Love Field. As the big plane emblazoned with the seal of the President of the United States rolled up to Gate 28I, a cheer went up from the waiting crowd. Excited schoolgirls waved tiny American flags. Home-made signs bobbed above the welcomers. "We Love You Jack!" "Welcome to Texas, Mr. President!" "We Love *You*, Jackie!" The President and first lady were obviously pleased. Mrs. Kennedy, resplendent in a pink suit and pillbox hat, smiled widely when she was presented with a large bouquet of long-stemmed red roses. The President grinned and plunged into the crowd, shak-

---

Bowers saw cruising the area near the Book Depository before the assassination could have been doing so innocently. They may just as well have contained assassins. The conclusions are left for you to draw.

John and Jacqueline Kennedy, a few days before the president's assassination in Dallas. On the morning of that grim and terrible day, Kennedy reflected on the possibility of assassination. "If people wanted to badly enough, if they hated him sufficiently, they could kill him. He mused on how it could be done. Put a man in a high building; give him a high-powered rifle with a telescopic sight; ensure that he was willing to trade his life for the president's, and then—well, all the security in the world couldn't save the president. Kennedy was not worried. He had an Irish sense of fatalism. Danger was one of the things that went with the job." (Courtesy of United Press International.)

ing hands, touching, reaching out to the hands that reached after him.

The plane had touched down at 11:37. Minutes slipped by and the President was still working the crowd. This, after all, is why he had come. But the Secret Service were getting anxious. The agents were worried by the chief executive's prolonged exposure in the open. Already they were late. By the time the motorcade wound through Dallas, they would be later still. Finally the President broke away from the crowd and waved one last time. The motorcycles roared to life. Red lights blinking and sirens screaming, the motorcade slowly rolled away, pilot car in the lead, then the motorcade lead car, then the presidential limousine, the Secret Service follow-up car immediately behind it, then cars containing the vice-president, local dignitaries, and the press.

The crowds had long since been forming in downtown Dallas. By the time *Air Force One* touched down at Love Field they were stacked up on Main Street seven and eight deep. They were in a festive, buoyant mood. Earlier, some men had moved among the crowds passing out handbills with the President's picture on them. "Wanted for Treason," the headline read. The leaflet ticked off seven particulars, among them a charge that the President was appointing "anti-Christians to Federal office," that he had given "support and encouragement to Communist inspired racial riots," that he had been soft on Communists—"betraying our friends (Cuba, Katanga, Portugal) and befriending our enemies (Russia, Yugoslavia via Poland)." Most people threw the leaflets in the street, with the other trash. Today, Dallas was friendly.

Toward 12:30 Mrs. R. E. Arnold, one of the secretaries in the Book Depository, got up from her desk to join the crowd outside waiting for the President. She went outside and stood in front of the doorway. She turned around for a moment and glimpsed one of the employees standing in the hallway between the front door and the double doors that led to the warehouse. She caught only a fleeting look at the man, and she could not be sure, but she thought it was one of the new boys. Lee was his name. Lee Harvey Oswald.

The crowd in Dealey Plaza numbered several hundred, and more were coming by the minute. Dealey Plaza was a good place to catch a look. Unlike the downtown streets, now packed with people, the plaza was wide open. The several-acre-sized plaza, which had been named after the founder of the *Dallas Morning News,* was a gently sloping V-shaped bowl dissected by several main business arteries. The streets formed a pitchfork. On one side, curving away to the east, was Commerce Street. On the other, curving down toward the west, was Elm Street. Running down the middle was Main Street. All the streets came together at the base of the plaza beneath a railroad overpass. At the top of the plaza, two hundred yards away, ran Houston Street. On the right ride of Houston, away from the plaza, were several tall buildings, the last of them, at the corner of Houston and Elm, the School Book Depository. Once the President's motorcade passed through Dealey Plaza, it would be out on the freeway. The plaza was the last chance to see the President up close.

Atop his tower in the Union Terminal railroad yards, Lee Bowers looked out to watch the motorcade. The time was nearly 12:30. The President would be passing at any moment. From his tower Bowers could see virtually everything that moved into, out of, or around the parking lot behind the grassy knoll atop Elm Street. Two and a half hours before, around 10:00, Bowers had spotted two cars moving into the area. The first had been a mud-smeared 1959 blue and white Oldsmobile station wagon. All that distinguished it was out-of-state plates and a Goldwater for President sticker on its bumper. The car drove in front of the School Book Depository, down across two or three sets of tracks, and then circled the area in front of his tower, as if searching for a way out. A few moments later another car appeared, this one a 1957 black Ford. The driver, Bowers noticed, appeared to be holding a microphone to his mouth. After three or four minutes of cruising the area, the black car departed the same way the Olds had. Now Bowers saw a third car. This one was a Chevrolet. But in many ways it was identical to the Oldsmobile Bowers had seen earlier. The Chevy had the same out-of-state plates, the same Goldwater bumper sticker; even the red mud that covered the car's sides was the same as that which had smeared the Olds. The car circled in front of Bowers and slowly cruised back toward the School Book Depository.

Abraham Zapruder was nervous. He had bought his Bell and Howell 8-mm movie camera only the day before, for the express purpose of filming the motorcade, and Zapruder was worried that, what with the newness of it, something would go wrong. Zapruder, who ran a dressmaking company in the nearby Dal-Tex Building, was an unabashed admirer of John

Kennedy's, which made him a distinct rarity among Dallasites. When Zapruder drove to work Friday morning the skies were dark and threatening. Figuring that the day would be poor for picture taking, he had left his camera at home. But as the sun broke through the clouds, Zapruder changed his mind. He hurried back home and grabbed his camera. When he returned to Dealey Plaza the crowds had already lined Houston Street. With that vantage point gone, Zapruder next tried the window of his office, across the street from the Book Depository. But the camera angle there was too narrow. Finally, with Marilyn Sitzman, his receptionist, tagging along behind him, he walked outside and spotted the perfect position: a four-foot-high concrete pedestal on the pergola overlooking Elm Street. Shortly before 12:30, the motorcade pilot car hove into view. Zapruder could hear the cheering coming from Main Street. He set the lens selector on telephoto, brought the camera up to his eye, focused on the lead motocycle, and pressed the shutter release.

Carolyn Walther, too, had been waiting for the parade to come by. Standing across the street from the Book Depository, she cocked her head at the sound of the approaching motorcycles, and then absently gazed up at the building in front of her. To her surprise she saw two men standing in the corner window of one of the upper stories. Both were looking south up Houston Street, as if they were waiting too. The dirt on the windowpanes obscured her view of one man, but Mrs. Walther could see the other clearly. He was wearing a white shirt, and his hair was light or blond. And he was holding something. It was a rifle, that much Mrs. Walther could be sure of, but one like she had never seen before: a weapon with a short barrel and something that seemed large around the stock—just what she couldn't tell. She guessed that it was a machine gun, and that the men were in the window to protect the President. Before she could think more of it, someone in the crowd shouted, "Here they come."

Moments before, Bob Edwards had seen a man in the Book Depository too, standing in the sixth-floor corner window, a low wall of cartons behind him. Edwards and a friend, Ronald Fischer, were standing near a reflecting pool on the southwest corner of Houston and Elm. Edwards had spotted the man in the window by chance, but there was something about him that captured his attention. The man, who wore a light-colored sport shirt, seemed uncomfortable. Edwards poked Fischer and told him to look up at the window. Fischer saw the man, too. Oddly, the man in the window wasn't watching the parade. Instead, he was looking away toward the Triple Underpass. The man stared at it, seemingly transfixed.

Arnold Rowland saw the man too, the same figure in a light-colored sport shirt open at the collar. From where he stood on Houston Street, midway between Main and Elm, Rowland could see something else as well: a rifle, mounted with a telescopic sight, cradled in the man's arms.

The turn from Houston onto Elm was sharp and oblique. To negotiate it the long presidential limousine had to come almost to a dead halt directly beneath the sixth-floor window on the southeast corner of the School Book Depository. The car paused and began its turn. The Secret Service agents, some of them weary from a long night before, looked ahead, to the rear, and to both sides. Everywhere but up.

As the presidential limousine rounded the sharp corner, a gust of wind caught the President's hair and he reached up with his right hand to pat it back into place. Nellie Connally, the governor's wife, turned to Mrs. Kennedy, pointed to the underpass and said, "We're almost through; it's just beyond that." Jacqueline Kennedy looked at the tunnel and smiled, thinking it would be cool inside, away from the Texas sun. No one had guessed it would go so well. The crowds had been big, enthusiastic. Nellie was proud of the city. She smiled at Kennedy. "Well, Mr. President, you can't say

Dallas doesn't love you." There was no answer, only a sharp, popping noise, a sound, someone thought, like exploding firecrackers.

In the jump seat in front of Kennedy, John Connally sensed immediately what the sound meant. He turned to his left to look over his shoulder, and seeing nothing, faced around and was beginning to turn to his right when, all at once, what felt like a tremendous punch slammed into the right side of his back. Connally's handsome tanned face contorted in pain, his cheeks puffed, and his hair flew askew. As he slumped into Nellie's arms, he yelled in pain, "Oh, my God, they are going to kill us all."

Nellie Connally did not recognize the crack of a gunshot, only that the noise she heard was loud and frightening. She turned around and saw the President contort in pain. The expression on his face revealed nothing, only a trace of puzzlement. An instant later, her husband crumpled into her arms like a wounded animal. As she nestled him close to her chest, she heard a third and final shot, and felt a fine mist fall over her. For a moment, she thought it might be chaff from buckshot. Then she realized that the mist came from what had been John Kennedy's brains.

Glen Bennett, one of the Secret Service men riding in the follow-up car behind the presidential limousine, had seen it all. They had just rounded the oblique corner at Houston and Elm when he heard the crack of rifle fire and saw the bullet go into the President's back, four inches beneath the right shoulder. Then Connally had been hit. Twenty yards ahead of him, much farther than it should have been, the limousine slowly coasted downhill. Bennett and the other agents watched, stunned, immobile.

In the car with them, Dave Powers watched too. Powers was the President's professional funny man, the Boston Irishman whose duty was making his chief relax. Powers always had a story or a quip. Even in the worst moments he could bring John Kennedy back to the easier days when John was a skinny U.S. representative from Brookline. What Dave Powers heard and saw now filled him with horror. As the motorcade swung down Elm, Powers heard what he thought was an exploding firecracker. He looked ahead and saw the President going down. There was a second pop, and Connally disappeared from view. Then the third shot. From the sound Powers thought the shots had come from overhead, and perhaps one from the front. The impact of the final round could be heard distinctly. To Powers it sounded like a grapefruit being splattered against a wall.

On the fifth floor of the Depository three workers were spending their lunch hour watching the motorcade from the windows. As the presidential limousine cruised by beneath them, Harold Norman, one of the workers, thought he saw Kennedy bring up his right arm in a salute to the crowd. Then he heard something that convinced him Kennedy wasn't waving. He turned to Jim Jarman and Bonnie Ray Williams, who were watching the parade with him, and exclaimed, "I believe someone is shooting at the President." Then Norman heard another sound, the noise of shell casings dropping on the floor above him. There was another shot, and the whole building seemed to shake. Jarman noticed that Williams had some kind of fine, white dust on his head. And then it dawned on him. It was plaster, shaken loose from the ceiling above. He stuck his head out the window and looked up.

Bob Jackson, a photographer for the *Dallas Times Herald*, looked up from the motorcade and saw Norman and Williams standing in the window, craning to see something above them. Jackson's eyes panned up and he saw what they were looking for. "Look up in the window," he yelled to the reporters in the car with him. "There's the rifle."

Zapruder had not seen the President being hit. The Stemmons Freeway sign to his left had blocked his view. But when the limousine emerged from behind the sign it was obvious that something was terribly wrong. Kennedy was slumping forward, his face a mask of pain, his arms coming up to his throat. Connally had looked back, and then he too had gone down. Instinctively Zapruder followed the scene through the viewfinder. Only yards in front of him, the limousine glided down the hill. In the front seat the Secret Service agent driver turned and looked back at the President, turned forward, and then turned back again. Still the car coasted, as if frozen in time. The seconds slipped by... one one thousand... two one thousand... three one thousand... four one thousand... five one thousand. Then, behind him and to his right, Zupruder heard an awful roar and felt a bullet whistle past his right ear. What he saw through the viewfinder sickened him: an explosion of blood and brains completely obscuring the President's head. For an instant it jerked him forward, and then, like a blow from a giant sledgehammer, drove Kennedy's body backward into his wife's arms, only now the entire left portion of his skull was missing. "They killed him," Zapruder cried. "They've killed the President!"

Riding in the lead car of the motorcade, Jesse Curry, the Dallas police chief, could hear but not see the shots. He grabbed at the mircophone of his radio transmitter and barked an order: "Get a man on top of that triple underpass and see what happened up there." In the Secret Service follow-up car, chief Dallas agent Forrest Sorrels had heard the shots as well, and turned to look to where he thought they had come— above and to the right, toward the knoll. Several of the agents riding with Sorrels were sure that the final explosion had been a double impact, one shot followed instantly by another. But only one agent moved.

Clint Hill was off the follow-up car and running at the sound of the final shots. A favorite of Mrs. Kennedy, Hill had not been scheduled to make the Dallas trip until, at the last moment, she had personally requested he come along. Now Hill could see Mrs. Kennedy's arm reach back, trying to grasp something that flew off the top of her husband's head. In a moment she was on the back of the car, crawling after it. Just then Hill reached the limousine. It lurched forward and he lunged after it, grabbing one of the handrails and vaulting in, pushing Mrs. Kennedy backward into the car. In the front seat, Secret Service Agent Roy Kellerman was yelling into the microphone to the lead car: "We are hit. Get us out of here." Hill had only to glance at the form that lay on the seat before him, amid the blood and scattered roses, to know that now escape was too late. As the accelerating Lincoln emerged from beneath the underpass, agents in the car behind could see Hill beating his fists on the trunk, in anger and frustration.

The impact of the final bullet spattered motorcycle officer Bobby Hargis with blood and sticky gray tissue, nearly knocking him off his bike. The force was so violent that for a moment Hargis thought he had been hit. As it was, the windshield of the motorcycle he had been riding to the left and rear of the presidential limousine was covered with blood. He had no doubt where the shots had come from. Hargis jumped off his bike and, gun drawn, joined the crowd that was racing up the grassy knoll.

Bill and Gayle Newman were lying flat on the ground as Hargis charged by them. Newman, a decorated infantry officer in World War II, knew when he heard the shots ring out that somebody was firing from behind him, from behind and atop the knoll. He saw a bullet rip into Kennedy's right temple and blow out the back of his head. He yelled to his wife to get down and threw himself face forward so he would not be hit.

James Tague was not as lucky. He had been standing nearly a hundred yards away from the presidential limousine, watching the motorcade from the right side of Commerce Street, at the mouth of the Triple Underpass, when the shots struck the President. Somehow Tague was struck too. A bullet had gone wild and hit the curb in front of him, chipping the concrete and sending a shard of stone into his face. The stone nicked him in the cheek and Tague was bleeding. It had been a near thing. Tague was glad to be alive.

Atop the Triple Underpass, S. M. Holland and half a dozen workers from the railroad had been watching the motorcade pass. Holland heard four shots, and after the report of the final round looked down and to his left, past the trees, to a stockade fence atop the knoll. The last shot had been as loud as the first three, and as Holland looked to the point from which he thought it had come he saw a puff of smoke wafting out from beneath the trees. Some of the other workers saw the smoke too. Now, together, they ran into the parking lot behind the knoll. The lot was jammed with cars, and after a few moments of clambering over bumpers and hoods Holland and the other workers, joined by a deputy sheriff, finally reached the fence. Whoever had been there was gone. They saw only the traces: some footprints, a few crushed cigarette butts, a dirty car bumper smeared by someone cleaning mud off his shoes. The footprints seemed to belong to more than one man. They were in a tight grouping, as if people had been walking back and forth, pacing like tigers in a cage.

As Holland and the other workers scrambled toward the fence, J. C. Price had seen someone running from it. Price had been watching the motorcade from the roof of the Terminal Annex Building, across Dealey Plaza from the knoll. After the shots he saw a young man in a dress white shirt and khaki trousers running toward the cars parked along the railroad siding. Price finally lost sight of him, but before he did he saw the running man was carrying something in his hand.

Within moments the parking lot and the area behind the knoll were swarming with people. On Police Chief Curry's order, lawmen were checking cars, looking for a trace of the assassin. One of the police officers doing the searching was Joe Marshall Smith. Smith had been directing traffic at Houston and Elm when a woman ran to him, yelling, "They're shooting the President from the bushes." When Smith got to the parking lot he could still smell spent gunpowder hanging in the air. As he moved from car to car he encountered a stranger in a business suit. Smith leveled his gun and demanded identification. The stranger obligingly reached into his jacket and pulled out his credentials. They read: "United States Secret Service." Feeling foolish, Smith lowered his weapon and moved on. Though he could not know it then, all the Secret Service men had gone on with the motorcade.

Moments before, Lee Bowers had seen two men standing behind the fence atop the grassy knoll. His attention had been drawn to them because of all the people he could see from the railroad tower these were the only strangers. One was middle-aged and heavyset. The other, who Bowers judged was in his mid-twenties, was wearing a plaid jacket. Bowers's attention was then distracted by the approach of the motorcade. When the shots rang out Bowers looked and saw that the two men were still there. Something else caught his eye, something he could not identify, perhaps a flash of light.

Orville Nix had seen something too, but at that moment he didn't know it. He had been standing on the greensward that divides Elm from Main, across the street from Zapruder. Like Zapruder, Nix had brought along a movie camera to record the motorcade. Later, when Nix's film was developed, a tiny white hump would appear behind a light-colored station wagon parked atop the grassy knoll. The FBI would decide that the hump was nothing more than shadows and light. But careful blowups of the frame in Orville Nix's film would, to some, reveal something very different. Though the lines were grainy the outline was plain. It was the figure of a man, carefully sighting something in his hand.

Dealey Plaza was a scene of panic and confusion. Sirens were wailing. People were racing everywhere, or cowering on the ground, afraid that they too would be shot. In the midst of the chaos one man remained icily calm. He was dressed in a dark business suit and he seemed to be middle-aged. There was one other thing about him. On this sunny, windy day he was carrying a large black umbrella. The man had found the ideal vantage point from which to observe the President: on the curb along Elm Street, immediately behind the Stemmons Freeway sign. When the motorcade turned onto Houston, his umbrella stayed furled. But when it came down Elm, beneath the Depository and toward the grassy knoll, the man suddenly raised it up. As the President emerged from behind the freeway sign, hit but not fatally wounded, the umbrella was clearly visible to anyone on the grassy knoll. It stayed there, almost like a marker, until the final, fatal shots. Then the man furled it again, paused for a moment, looked after the departing limousine, and unhurriedly began to walk up Elm toward the Depository.

By now almost everyone else was running—policemen, guns at the ready, toward the knoll, others to the Triple Underpass, and still others to the Book Depository, where the Hertz time sign blinked 12:32. Marion Baker was the first police officer to reach the building. Baker had been riding a motorcycle in the middle of the motorcade. At the sound of the shots he looked up and saw pigeons scattering from their roosts in the Book Depository. He wheeled his bike around and gunned it toward the building. Arriving, he found Roy Truly, the building manager, and together they raced up the stairs toward the upper floors, where people had already reported shots fired. On the second-floor landing Baker encountered a thin young man wearing a white shirt, leaning against a soft-drink machine, calmly sipping a Coke. Less than two minutes had elapsed since the final shots. Baker poked his gun in the young man's stomach. Baker turned to Truly. "Do you know this man, does he work here?" "Yes," Truly answered. Baker lowered his pistol and rushed by.

Lee Harvey Oswald finished drinking his Coke and slowly walked downstairs and outside, looking for a bus.

He found one within moments. But the shooting had tied up traffic. The bus was hopelessly enmeshed in cars. Oswald waited for a few minutes, then got up and left the bus and walked to the nearby Greyhound Bus Terminal. There he hailed a cab. But as the cab pulled up to the curb Oswald saw that an elderly woman was waiting for a ride too, and he graciously offered his cab to her. The lady declined, Oswald got in, and they headed off toward Oak Cliff. The cab drove off. Oswald was gone. Within fifteen minutes, police would issue an alert for a suspect matching his description as the perpetrator of the crime of the century.

As Oswald strolled away, attention was turning to the Dal-Tex Building, behind and across the street from the Book Depository. Here too, police were conducting a floor-by-floor search, looking for anything suspicious, anyone out of place. In the course of their hunt they discovered two people. One was a boy, who had been in the building, as the police report later put it, "without a good excuse." No one would ever know anything more about him. After his arrest and transfer to the sheriff's office, he simply disappeared.

Quite a lot was known about the other suspect. The name he gave the officers who arrested him on the second floor of the Dal-Tex Building was his alias, Jim Braden; he was better known to the police as Eugene Hale Brading. A self-described oilman, Braden told police he had merely happened to be in the area at the time of the assassination, and had gone into the Dal-Tex Building in search of a phone. The cops, not knowing that the files of the Los Angeles police department listed him as a long-time associate of organized crime, took him at his word.* Within hours of his arrest Braden was released.

*The information on Brading's criminal background and police record throughout is reported by Peter Noyes, *Legacy of Doubt.*

Across the street in the School Book Depository, the search was beginning to turn up clues. On the sixth floor in the extreme southeast corner, behind a shield of packing cases, the police had found three shell cases scattered around the floor. Not long after the shell cases were found a high-powered rifle, mounted with a telescopic scope, was discovered near an opposite wall, wedged between some packing cases. The Book Depository was quickly sealed, trapping three men who were not employees inside. Two were newsmen. The other was Captain James W. Powell, an army intelligence officer.

There was action outside the Depository as well. Like many witnesses to the assassination, James Worrell was frightened, worried that perhaps the shooting was not over. He ran from Elm, where he had watched the motorcade, past the Depository onto Houston. He did not stop until he reached the corner of Pacific Street, a hundred yards from the Depository. As he paused to catch his breath, he saw a man burst from the back door of the Depository. From where Worrell stood the man seemed to be young, dark-haired, medium height and build, wearing light pants and a dark sport jacket. That was all that Worrell could see. The man was running away.

Richard Carr saw someone leaving the Depository too. Carr thought he had seen him before; in fact, only moments before, in one of the upper windows of the Book Depository. From his perch on a metal stairway of the new county courthouse then a-building at the corner of Houston and Commerce, Carr could now see him more clearly. He was heavy-set, wore a hat, horn-rimmed glasses, and a tan coat. As Carr watched, the man walked very fast south along Houston Street. He turned east on Commerce and walked a block to Record Street. There he got into a late model gray Rambler station wagon, parked just north of Commerce on Record. The car bore Texas plates, and a dark young man was at the wheel. The station wagon pulled away, heading north.

Marvin Robinson saw the car again when it stopped on Elm, down from the Depository at the base of the grassy knoll. At the time, Robinson himself had been driving south on Elm. He had just crossed the intersection at Houston, directly in front of the Depository, when he spotted the station wagon. It paused only for a moment, just long enough for a man to come down the grassy knoll and climb inside. The station wagon then drove off, heading in the direction of Oak Cliff.

By now John Kennedy's motorcade had come to its final destination, the emergency entrance of Parkland Memorial Hospital. Inside the building, a frantic call went out for doctors to report to trauma room 1. A foul-up in police communications had sidetracked the message that the gravely wounded President would soon be reaching the hospital. It was too late in any case. In the limousine, Jacqueline Kennedy pulled her husband's shattered body close to her. Clint Hill's suit jacket had been draped over the President's head to keep the curious from viewing the hideous wound. Now Hill told Mrs. Kennedy that the President would have to be brought inside. "You know he's dead, Mr. Hill," she replied, and pulled his body even closer. Gently, other arms pulled him from her grasp and lifted his limp body onto a stretcher. In the jump seat John Connally, still conscious, tried to rise, but collapsed from excruciating pain. There was a large jagged wound in his chest. His lung had collapsed and his left wrist had been smashed. Finally the attendants succeeded in lifting him from the car and placing him on a stretcher.

In trauma room 1, Dr. William Kemp Clark, the young physician on duty, took one look at his patient and knew that the prognosis was terminal. It did not stop him. Quickly, but methodically he examined the President's wounds. There were two that he could see: a gaping gash on the right side of the head, from which oozed blood and brain matter, and a small neat hole just over the Adam's apple. The heartbeat and pulse were faint and irregular, but still there was life. The President needed air. The bullet that Clark judged had entered the President's throat had punctured his windpipe. Taking a scalpel, Clark cut into the throat wound and enlarged it, providing an air passage. Other resuscitory measures were taken. A blood transfusion was begun. As Kennedy's heart began to fail, Malcolm Perry, another one of the doctors, desperately began pumping his chest to keep the rhythm going. Other doctors inserted tubes in Kennedy's chest and in his leg. They did everything. Everything was not enough. After twenty minutes one of the doctors turned to Perry and said, "It's too late, Mac." Perry brought up his hands from John Kennedy's chest. A priest was summoned to perform the last rites of the Catholic Church. At 1:00 p.m. (CST) the President of the United States was pronounced dead.

Outside, in the hospital corridors, the Secret Service were struggling to maintain a semblance of security, for the new president had been taken to Parkland as well. With each passing moment the crowds around the hospital grew larger. The White House press corps had also arrived. One of the first reporters on the scene was Seth Kantor, a writer for the *Dallas Times Herald*. At 1:30 Kantor was hurrying to a briefing by Assistant White House Press Secretary Malcolm Kilduff, who would announce that John Kennedy was dead. As Kantor walked through the hospital corridor he felt a tug on the back of his jacket and turned to face an old acquaintance. Kantor was tempted to keep going, but the friend stuck out his hand. "Isn't this a terrible thing?" the friend asked the reporter. Kantor agreed gravely that it was, and anxiously started to pull away. But the friend had another question: "Should I close my place for the next three nights, do you think?" Kantor said he had to go, that he was late for the briefing, leaving his friend, Jack Ruby, to ponder his own question.

As John Kennedy lay dying, Lee Oswald was hurrying home. He walked through the front door, brushed past his housekeeper, Earlene Roberts, and disappeared into his room. In a few moments he emerged, now wearing a dark zippered jacket. Beneath it, tucked in his pants, was a .38 caliber revolver. Without speaking to Mrs. Roberts, he went back through the front door and walked to the street. He lingered there for a few moments, looking down the street as if he were waiting for something. Then he started pacing briskly up the street in the direction of a local movie theater. A few moments later Mrs. Roberts heard a car horn toot outside, looked through the window and saw a Dallas police cruiser parked at the curb. The car idled a few minutes as if it too were waiting for someone, and then drove off. Later, authorities would be able to find no record of a police cruiser going to the Beckley Avenue address.

There was at least one policeman in the area, however. His name was J. D. Tippit. At the time of the assassination, Tippit, a veteran of eleven undistinguished years on the force, had been on patrol on the outskirts of Dallas. At 12:45 his radio crackled to life. The police dispatcher told him to proceed to central Oak Cliff, miles from his position, and "be at large for any emergency that might arise." At 12:54 Tippit radioed that he was moving into position. At 1:00, as Oswald prepared to leave his rooming house, the dispatcher tried to raise Tippit again. This time there was no answer. Eight minutes later, as Oswald was walking away from his home, Tippit tried twice to signal the dispatcher. Now the dispatcher was silent. Tippit cruised on. He had just begun to head east on East 10th Street when something he saw caused him to pull to the curb.

Acquila Clemmons, who was walking nearby, saw Tippit get out of the cruiser. She also saw two men, one short and somewhat heavy, the other tall and thin. The thin man was wearing light khaki trousers and a white shirt. As Tippit walked to the front of his car the short, heavyset man pulled out a pistol and fired several times. Four of the bullets struck Tippit in the head, and the officer fell to the pavement, killed instantly. The killer then waved to the other man, and they ran off in different directions.

A few minutes earlier, Domingo Benavides, a mechanic at Dootch Motors, had driven off in the company pickup truck to bring back a part from an auto supply dealer. He was driving west on 10th when he saw Tippit's police cruiser pull to the curb. When the shots rang out, Benavides was only fifteen feet away. He saw the killer standing on the right side of the car. The man was wearing a light-colored zippered jacket and dark slacks. After the shots Tippit's killer walked back to the sidewalk, unloaded his gun, and threw the shells on the ground. He then started off toward Patton Street at a trot, the gun still in his hand.

William Scoggins witnessed the murder, too. A cabdriver, Scoggins had just finished having lunch in a restaurant at the corner of Patton and 10th, and was getting back into his cab, when he saw Tippit's car drive slowly down 10th. Scoggins headed that way as well. He saw Tippit stop his car, get out, and begin to walk to the front of the cruiser when a man in a light jacket fired at the officer several times. Tippit went down, clutching at his stomach. Scoggins pulled his cab over and got out. For an instant the killer glanced over at him, and Scoggins ducked, afraid that he would be seen. The killer then began to run away in the direction from which Scoggins had come. As he rushed by, Scoggins heard him mutter, "Poor dumb cop."

Just then T. F. Bowley turned his car east onto 10th Street. He saw Tippit's body lying in the road and pulled over. Inside the cruiser Benavides was trying to work Tippit's police radio with no success. Bowley grabbed the mike and turned in the alarm. It was 1:16 p.m. Blocks away, Lee Harvey Oswald was heading toward a rendezvous at the Texas Theatre.

Warren Reynolds was in his used-car dealership on Patton Street, just a block from where Tippit had fallen. Reynolds heard the shots and ran outside to see what happened. He saw a man with a pistol in his hand running south on Patton toward Jefferson. Reynolds loped along behind him, but lost him when the man disappeared behind some buildings.

The shots had brought many people into the streets. A number of them had seen a man fleeing the scene. One of the witnesses eventually found another police officer, H. W. Summers, cruising by. At 1:22, Summers relayed the witness's description of the killer to police headquarters. "I got an eyeball witness to the getaway man, that suspect in this shooting," Summers reported. "He is a white male, twenty-seven, five feet eleven inches, 165, black wavy hair, fair-complected, wearing light grey Eisenhower-type jacket, dark trousers and a white shirt . . . apparently armed with a .32 caliber dark finish, automatic pistol which he had in his right hand."

Within minutes police cars were converging on the area. There were several reports of suspicious men. First they surrounded the fundamentalist church where Reynolds had seen the man with the gun disappear. But before they could go in they were called off, and sent in pursuit of yet another suspicious man, this one at a local library. This time a man was found, but he explained he had run inside to tell the people in the library that the President had been shot. The police were satisfied. In any case, they had no time to linger. For there was another report. A man had rushed into the nearby Texas Theatre without paying.

Johnny Brewer saw him first. Brewer was the manager of Hardy's Shoestore on West Jefferson, a few doors east of the Texas Theatre, and eight blocks away from the spot where J. D. Tippit had been murdered. On the afternoon of November 22 Brewer was in his shop listening to the radio reports on the assassination of the President when suddenly a bulletin cut in that a police officer had been shot in his neighborhood. Almost at that moment Brewer heard the first wail of police sirens. As he looked out to the street he saw a man duck into his doorway. The man appeared to be about 5'9". His hair was brown, and he wore a brown sport shirt, partly unbuttoned. For some reason Brewer thought he looked funny. As the police sirens died away, the man walked away from Brewer's store and toward the theater. Brewer followed him and saw him walk inside without paying. By now Brewer was highly suspicious. When he had first seen the man he looked as if he had been running. His shirt was untucked and his hair was disarranged. He had a scared look. Entering the theater without buying a ticket completed the picture. Brewer informed the ticket taker, who called the police. Brewer, meanwhile, walked inside, told his story to an usher, and together they proceeded to check the exits. None appeared to have been used. He asked the operator of the concession stand if he had seen a man in a brown sport shirt enter the theater. He hadn't. The concession stand man and Brewer then searched the balcony. A dozen, perhaps two dozen people were in the theater. In the dark, Brewer could not pick out the man he had seen by his store. By now it didn't matter. The police were arriving.

The call about the theater had drawn everyone's attention. Jerry Hill, the police sergeant who had commanded the search on the sixth floor of the Book Depository, was there. So apparently was Bill Alexander, the assistant district attorney who would later want to charge Oswald with being part of an "international Communist conspiracy," and later still would successfully prosecute Jack Ruby. Now Alexander and several other officers, guns drawn, waited outside the building, covering the exits, while still more officers went inside.

The house lights went up. For a few moments the movie, a war picture, played on, dancing across the figures in dark blue who strode across the stage. N. M. McDonald, one of the officers, looked out over the rows of seats. There were twelve or fifteen people sitting on the lower level. McDonald couldn't be sure who he was supposed to be looking for. As McDonald scanned the theater, a man sitting near the front spoke up quietly. The man the police were looking for, he said, was sitting on the ground floor, in the center, about three rows from the back. McDonald unholstered his pistol, climbed down from the stage, and started walking slowly toward the back, his eyes fixed on the suspect. He stopped after about ten rows and told two men who were sitting there to get up. McDonald searched them for weapons and found none. All the while, he never took his eyes off the man in the rear. The man looked back, his face expressionless. McDonald moved toward him in a crouch. As he got to the row, Lee Harvey Oswald, the man he had been staring at, suddenly got up, and said, "It's all over now." McDonald pounced on him. As he did Oswald struck him in the face and reached down for the revolver in his trousers. McDonald grappled for it. The other officers closed in. Both Oswald's and McDonald's hands were on the gun. There was a click as a hammer fell down on a defective round. Now the other officers were swarming over Oswald, punching and grabbing him. "Kill the President, will you," one of them shouted as Oswald went down beneath his seat. When they yanked him up he was twisting and squirming. In a loud voice, so that everyone in the theater heard him, Oswald said: "I am not resisting arrest! I am not resisting arrest!"

The police had their man. As they led him away the man in the front row who had fingered him rose from his seat, walked outside, and quietly disappeared.

33

Vietnam—Time of Illusion

Jonathan Schell

The Vietnam War was surely one of the most controversial episodes in United States history. American involvement in that conflict began with Truman and persisted through Democratic and Republican administrations alike (as Ambrose's narrative pointed out), although the largest escalation took place under Lyndon Johnson. In truth, the war was a logical outgrowth of the Containment Policy and the domino theory; and people who accepted these without question likewise endorsed American intervention in Vietnam. As Johnson himself phrased it, the United States had the choice of fighting Communism in Indochina or "pulling back our defenses to San Francisco." And so the Johnson administration sent waves of bombers roaring over North Vietnam, and it sharply increased the number of United States troops in the South. By 1968 more than 500,000 American troops were fighting to prevent South Vietnam from falling to a coalition of North Vietnamese and South Vietnamese Communists (the latter calling themselves the National Liberation Front), who were struggling to unify the country.

Yet even as the United States sought a military solution to Vietnam, hoping that American power could simply crush the North Vietnamese and their southern allies, there were unmistakable signs that the original premise for American intervention in Indochina was erroneous. The domino theory, based as it was on the assumption of a worldwide, monolithic Communist conspiracy directed by Moscow, seemed more and more implausible. For one thing, China and Russia developed an intense and bitter ideological feud that sharply divided the Communist world, and they almost went to war over their disputed boundary. The Sino-Soviet split exploded the notion of a Communist monolith out for world dominion, and so did the fierce independence of North Vietnam itself. Though Hanoi received aid from both Russia and China, North Vietnam was far less dependent on them than South Vietnam was on the United States. Moreover, with the historic hatred and mistrust the Vietnamese held for China, North Vietnam apparently never asked China to intervene in the struggle (and apparently China never offered to do so). The truth was that North Vietnam was fighting to unite the country under Hanoi's leadership rather than Peking's or Moscow's.

Back in the United States, meanwhile, the war became increasingly unpopular, with protest rallies springing up in Washington, D.C., and on college campuses across the land. By 1968, as Jonathan Schell observed in *The Time of Illusion*, the war "had installed itself at the center of the nation's political life." It forced Lyndon Johnson from office and helped bring Richard Nixon to the White House because he promised to end the conflict. But Nixon seemed to take up where Johnson left off. Like his predecessors, Nixon worried about "American credibility," about what would happen to American prestige if the United States sold out her South Vietnamese ally; and in 1970 he sent American troops into contiguous Cambodia to exterminate Communist hide-outs there. The Cambodian invasion brought campus protest to a tragic climax, as Ohio National Guardsmen opened fire on protesting students at Kent State University and killed four of them. With the campuses in turmoil and the country divided and adrift, Nixon gradually disengaged American ground troops in Vietnam and sought détente with both Russia and China. Though the Nixon administration continued to speak of "peace with honor" in Indochina and though it continued to bomb Hanoi, it was clear nevertheless that American involvement in the

Vietnamese civil war was a tragic and costly mistake. At last, in top-secret negotiations in Paris, Secretary of State Henry Kissinger and North Vietnam's Le Duc Tho worked out a peace agreement. Eventually the United States removed its combat forces, and in 1975 South Vietnam's corrupt and repressive regime fell to the North Vietnamese and the National Liberation Front. After almost two decades of bitter civil war and the loss of more than a million lives, Vietnam was now united under Hanoi's Communist government, something that would probably have happened without further violence had general elections been held in 1956, according to the Geneva agreements of two years before.

Why did the United States remain entangled in Vietnam for so many years? Why did American planners feel obliged to continue military operations in that fire-scarred land long after the original reason for going there had become untenable? In the following selection, Jonathan Schell provides a trenchant analysis of American policy in Vietnam and offers provocative insights into America's ordeal of power there.

From January of 1961, when John Kennedy took office, until August of 1974, when Richard Nixon was forced to leave office, the unvarying dominant goal of the foreign policy of the United States was the preservation of what policymakers throughout the period called the credibility of American power. (And, indeed, since President Nixon's fall the preservation of American credibility has remained the dominant goal of United States foreign policy.) The various policymakers phrased the aim in many ways. To have a formidable "psychological impact . . . on the countries of the world" is how the Joint Chiefs of Staff put it in a memo to Secretary of Defense Robert McNamara in January of 1962. To prevent a situation from arising in which "no nation can ever again have the same confidence in American promise or in American protection" is how President Johnson put it at a news conference in July of 1965. To "avoid humiliation" is how Assistant Secretary of Defense John McNaughton put it in a memo in January of 1966. To shore up "the confidence factor" is how Assistant Secretary of State William Bundy put it in a speech in January of 1967. To prevent "defeat and humiliation" is how President Nixon put it in a speech in November of 1969. To demonstrate America's "will and character" is how President Nixon put it in a speech in April of 1970. To prevent the United States from appearing before the world as a "pitiful, helpless giant" is another way that President Nixon put it in that speech. To maintain "respect for the office of President of the United States" is how President Nixon put it in a speech in April of 1972. To win an "honorable" peace or a "peace with honor" is how President Nixon put it from time to time. But, whatever words it was couched in, the aim was always the same: to establish in the minds of peoples and their leaders throughout the world an image of the United States as a nation that possessed great power and had the will and determination to use it in foreign affairs. In the name of this objective, President Kennedy sent "advisers" to Vietnam in the early nineteen-sixties, and President Johnson escalated the Vietnam war in secrecy and persisted in carrying on the war in the face of growing public opposition. In the name of this objective, also, President Nixon sent planes and troops into Cambodia, sent an aircraft carrier into the Indian Ocean at the time of the India-Pakistan war, mined North Vietnamese ports in the spring of 1972, and carpet-bombed North Vietnam during the Christmas season of 1972. In the pursuit of this objective, massacres were condoned, hundreds of thousands of lives were lost, dictatorial governments were propped up, nations friendly to the United States were turned into adversaries, the

---

From pp. 341–387 of *The Time of Illusion* by Jonathan Schell. Copyright © 1975 by Jonathan Schell. Reprinted by permission of Alfred A. Knopf, Inc.

domestic scene was thrown into turmoil, two Presidents were forced from office, the Constitution was imperilled, and the entire world was repeatedly brought to the verge of war.

The doctrine of credibility, far from being a fanatical ideology, was a coldly reasoned strategic theory that was designed to supply the United States with effective instruments of influence in an age dominated by nuclear weapons. The doctrine did not take shape all at once but evolved gradually as the full sweep of American military policy, including, especially, nuclear policy, was subjected to a reëxamination, which got under way outside the government in the late nineteen-fifties and was carried forward within the government in the early nineteen-sixties, after President Kennedy took office. When Kennedy entered the White House, the nation's nuclear policy had remained all but unchanged since the end of the Korean war, in 1953. In fact, although the conditions under which men lived and conducted their politics were altered more drastically by the invention of nuclear weapons than by any previous single invention, nuclear weapons had never become the subject of intensive public debate. In the aftermath of the Second World War, the United States had made a brief effort at the United Nations to bring the new weapons under some form of international control, but the atmosphere of the Cold War had soon settled in and the effort had been abandoned. Then, in the nineteen-fifties, the nation's attention had been further distracted from the new peril by rising levels of consumption, which quickly climbed beyond the highest expectations. In the United States, unprecedented wealth and ease came to coexist with unprecedented danger, and a sumptuous feast of consumable goods was spread out in the shadow of universal death. Americans began to live as though on a luxuriously appointed death row, where one was free to enjoy every comfort but was uncertain from moment to moment when or if the death sentence might be carried out. The abundance was very much in the forefront of people's attention, however, and the uncertainty very much in the background; and in the government as well as in the country at large the measureless questions posed by the new weapons were evaded. As far as any attempt to find a way out of the nuclear dilemma was concerned, the time was one of sleep. But in the late nineteen-fifties, as the reëxamination of the American military position gathered momentum, a few men began to think through the whole subject of nuclear strategy anew. Among them were two men whose writings proved to be of special importance, not only because the ideas expressed were influential in themselves but because each man was to take a high post in government in the years ahead. One was Henry Kissinger, who was a professor at Harvard during the nineteen-fifties and nineteen-sixties, and whose book *Nuclear Weapons and Foreign Policy* appeared in 1957. The other was General Maxwell Taylor, who was the Army Chief of Staff under President Eisenhower, and whose book *The Uncertain Trumpet* appeared in 1960.

Both men were disturbed by a paradox that seemed to lie near the heart of the nuclear question. It was that nuclear weapons, the most powerful instruments of violence ever invented, tended to immobilize rather than strengthen their possessors. This paradox was rooted in the central fact of the weapons' unprecedented destructive force, which made mankind, for the first time in its history, capable of annihilating itself. Nuclear weapons, Kissinger and Taylor realized, were bound to have a chilling effect on any warlike plans that their possessors, including the United States, might entertain. Wars were supposedly fought for ends, but a war fought with nuclear arms might well obliterate any end for which a war could be fought. Not only that but it might obliterate all means as well, and, for that matter, obliterate the only earthly creature capable of thinking in terms of means and ends. As Kissinger put it in his book, "the destructiveness of modern weapons deprives victory in an all-out war of its historical meaning." He decided that "all-out war has therefore ceased to be a meaningful instrument of policy." Thenceforward, the United States would be in the position of having to fear its own power almost as much as it feared the power of its foes. Taylor, in his book, described his doubts about the usefulness of nuclear weapons in somewhat different language. The notion that "the use or the threatened use of atomic weapons of mass destruction would be sufficient to assure the security of the United States and its friends," he wrote, was "The Great Fallacy" in the prevailing strategic thinking of the day. The new strategists were saying that nuclear weapons, instead of making the nuclear powers more formidable, appeared to be casting a pall of doubt over their military policies. The doubt did not concern the amounts of military power at their disposal; it concerned their willingness, in the face of the dread of extinction, to unleash that power. Kissinger wrote, "Both the horror and the power of modern [nuclear] weapons tend to paralyze action: the former because it will make few issues seem worth contending for; the latter because it causes many disputes to seem irrelevant to the over-all strategic equation"—which had to do with the victory of one side or the other. In strength, it had turned out, lurked weakness; in omnipotence, impotence.

Kissinger and Taylor, working separately, set out to frame a foreign policy that would take into account the implications of nuclear weapons. Each of them began to think through a policy that would accommodate two broad aims. One aim was to prevent the extinction of the world in a nuclear war, and the other aim was to prevent the domination of the world—naturally, including the domination of the United States—by Communist totalitarian forces. It was clear to the two men that these aims conflicted at many points. The aim of preventing human extinction, which was peculiar to the nuclear age, seemed to call for unprecedented restraint in military matters, but the aim of preventing global Communist totalitarian rule seemed to call for unceasing military efforts on an unprecedented scale. On the one hand, nuclear dread inhibited the United States from using its military power aggressively; on the other hand, the ambitions, ideals, and fears that have traditionally impelled powerful nations onto the world stage impelled the United States to use its military power aggressively. Kissinger wrote, "The dilemma of the nuclear period can, therefore, be defined as follows: the enormity of modern weapons makes the thought of war repugnant, but the refusal to run any risks would amount to giving the Soviet rulers a blank check." The aim of standing firm in the face of Soviet power, which, of course, corresponded to the broad aim of preventing world domination by Communist totalitarian forces, struck a responsive chord in the thinking of American politicians of the late nineteen-fifties. American political life had been dominated at least since the decade began by a conviction that the freedom and independence of nations all over the world was threatened by a unified, global Communist conspiracy that was under the control of the Soviet Union. Since then, "anti-Communism" not only had been the mainspring of American foreign policy but for a time—when Senator Joseph McCarthy hunted for Communists in the United States—had also been the central preoccupation of domestic politics. In this atmosphere, a reluctance to give Soviet leaders "a blank check" was quickly understood. However, the second aim recognized by Kissinger and Taylor—the avoidance of a nuclear catastrophe—was harder for the politicians of that time to grasp; and it was in championing this aim that the two men had to do the greater part of their explaining. (Something that helped them greatly in getting a hearing on the nuclear question was the fact that the anti-Communism of each of them was so strong as to be above suspicion.) The military, in particular, was difficult to persuade. The notion that an increase in military strength might, in effect, enfeeble the nation was a paradox not to the liking of the military mind. It was therefore difficult at first for the military to agree that, as Kissinger put it, in the nuclear age "the more powerful the weapons ... the greater becomes the reluctance to use them"—in other words, the greater the power, the greater the paralysis...

Kissinger, employing a word that was just beginning to come into vogue, observed that a threat to use nuclear weapons in each minor crisis around the world would lack "credibility." What worried him was not only that the United States might make a misstep at the brink; it was also that the Communists might not be adequately deterred by a threat of massive nuclear retaliation. He was afraid that the Communists would find it implausible that the United States should be willing to risk nuclear annihilation merely to serve some minor purpose thousands of miles from home, and that they would therefore be unafraid to oppose the United States. For in the strategy of massive retaliation the government seemed to take the use of nuclear force almost lightly, as though nuclear weapons were ordinary, readily usable instruments of policy rather than engines of doom. The danger was, as Kissinger saw it, that "every move on [the Soviet bloc's] part will ... pose the appalling dilemma of whether we are willing to commit suicide to prevent encroachments, which do not, each in itself, seem to threaten our existence directly but which may be steps on the road to our ultimate destruction." Kissinger was attempting to work out the implications of the distressing fact that once both adversaries were armed with nuclear weapons, a decision to use nuclear weapons was as dangerous to oneself as it was to the foe, for the result might be "suicide." And a threat to commit suicide was not a very convincing way of deterring a foe. Kissinger was suggesting that the policy of brinksmanship menaced the world with both great dangers of the period: global totalitarianism *and* human extinction. On the one hand, that policy threatened to transform every small crisis into a major nuclear crisis, and, on the other hand, it left the United States without "credible" instruments of force in situations where the stakes were too small to justify any risk of "suicide." The need was for a policy that would steer a middle course between the two dangers —for a policy that would, in Kissinger's words, "provide a means to escape from the sterility of the quest for absolute peace, which paralyzes by the vagueness of its hopes, and of the search for absolute victory, which paralyzes by the vastness of its consequences."

A middle course was available, both Kissinger and Taylor believed, in a strategy of limited war. "A strategy of limited war," Kissinger wrote, "would seek to escape the inconsistency of relying on a policy of deterrence [that is, massive retaliation], whose major sanction involves national catastrophe." And Taylor wrote, "The new strategy would recognize that it is just as necessary to deter or win quickly a limited war as to deter general war." Kissinger, for his part, believed that even in the nuclear age the freedom actually to use force rather than merely to threaten the use of force was indispensable to the maintenance of international order. He derided "the national psychology which considers peace as the 'normal' pattern of relations among states," and, while granting that "the contemporary revolution cannot be managed by force alone," he maintained that "when there is no penalty for irresponsibility, the pent-up frustrations of centuries may seek an outlet in the international field." Therefore, "to the extent that recourse to force has become impossible the restraints of the international order may disappear as well." In his view, dangerous as the use of force was in the nuclear age, the United States would have to overcome its uneasiness and thus "face up to the risks of Armageddon." And limited war, he believed, was both a more acceptable and a more effective way of facing up to these risks than was massive retaliation. For a strategy of limited war would rescue the use of force from nuclear paralysis. It would provide "credible" means of threatening the foe. It would make the world safe again for war.

More specifically, there were, in Kissinger's view, "three reasons...for developing a strategy of limited war." He listed them as follows: "First, limited war represents the only means for preventing the Soviet bloc, at an acceptable cost, from overrunning the peripheral areas of Eurasia. Second, a wide range of military capabilities may spell the difference between defeat and victory even in an all-out war. Finally, intermediate applications of our power offer the best chance to bring about strategic changes favorable to our side." (By "victory even in an all-out war" Kissinger meant the survival after nuclear war of enough conventional forces in the United States to impose America's will on the surviving remnant of the Soviet population.) His reference to "the best chance to bring about strategic changes favorable to our side" had to do with what he saw as the possibility that on occasion limited war might be used offensively as well as defensively, and would place the United States in a position to reduce "the Soviet sphere." These aims—the defense of a perimeter, the attainment of "victory" in all-out hostilities, and the attainment of improved strategic positions that would reduce "the Soviet sphere" —were straightforward military aims of a tradional kind. They can be called the tangible objectives of limited war.

One aim of the strategy of limited war, then, was to free the use of military force from nuclear paralysis, so that the United States might still avail itself of its arms to stop Communism from spreading around the globe. But there was also a second aim. It was to help in preventing a nuclear war. It was Kissinger's hope that the new policy could "rescue mankind from the horrors of a thermonuclear holocaust by devising a framework of war limitation." Or, in Taylor's words, the new policy "is not blind to the awful dangers of general atomic war; indeed, it takes as its primary purpose the avoidance of that catastrophe." By assigning largely to limited war the achievement of the tangible objectives in the fight against Communist enemies, the policy opened the way to a crucial shift in the mission of the American nuclear force. Secretary of State Dulles had sought to use the threat of nuclear war to work America's will in small crises around the world, but if limited-war forces could take over this job, the nuclear force, relieved of its provocative, belligerent role, could be retired into the purely passive one of deterring nuclear attack. Thereafter, the role of the nuclear force would simply be that of threatening retaliation in order to dissuade the Soviet Union from using its nuclear force in a first strike. Neither Taylor nor Kissinger spelled out the possibility of this shift, but it was implicit in their writings, and was later adopted as policy, under the name of deterrence. The strategy of limited war was thus a necessary companion to the policy of deterrence. In fact, it had been designed, in part, to wean the United States from its perilous sole reliance on the threat of massive nuclear retaliation. The policies of nuclear deterrence and limited war represented a division of labor, in which nuclear weapons would take on the defensive role in military policy and the limited-war forces would take on the offensive role. Taylor, describing a proposal along these lines he had made to the National Security Council in 1958, wrote, "Our atomic deterrent forces would be the shield under which we must live from day to day with the Soviet threat. This shield would provide us protection, but not a means of maneuver. It was rather to the so-called limited-war forces that we henceforth must look for the active elements of our military strategy."

The limited-war strategy would dovetail with nuclear strategy in another way, too. It would give the United States a new opportunity to make demonstrations of its "will" or "resolve" to use force in the world. It would, that is, give the nation a chance to demonstrate its credibility. This objective of limited war can be called the psychological objective.

. . .

By advertising America's strength to the world at levels below the brink, it would hold the world a few steps back from nuclear extinction and at the same time would deter the Communists from aggressive moves. New room for military maneuvering would open up. Whereas under the strategy of massive retaliation there was only one step on the ladder between peace and the holocaust, under the strategy of limited war there would be many steps, and at each step the superpowers would have the opportunity to take stock of each other's intentions, to send each other clear signals of their "resolve," and, perhaps, to draw back before things got out of hand. In a passage that compared the opportunities for demonstrating credibility which were offered by the strategy of massive retaliation (in which only threats were possible) with the opportunities offered by a strategy of limited war (in which actual military efforts were possible), Kissinger wrote, "It is a strange doctrine which asserts that we can convey our determination to our opponent by reducing our overseas commitments, that, in effect, our words will be a more effective deterrent than our deeds." Under the policy he was proposing, America's deeds—its actions in limited wars—would "convey our determination." Taylor similarly underscored the psychological importance of limited war, writing, "There is also an important psychological factor which must be present to make this retaliatory weapon [the nuclear deterrent force] effective. It must be clear to the aggressor that we have the will and determination to use our retaliatory power without compunction if we are attacked. Any suggestion of weakness or indecision may encourage the enemy to gamble on surprise." And the best way to prevent "any suggestion of weakness or indecision" from appearing, he thought, was to prepare for limited war. The strategy would, in his words, guard against the danger that "repeated [Communist] success in creeping aggression may encourage a Communist miscalculation that could lead to general war."

The psychological objective was to be sharply distinguished from the tangible objectives. The tangible objectives grew out of an effort to escape the paralyzing influence of nuclear strategy, but the psychological objective was part and parcel of the nuclear strategy. In the new scheme, the attainment of the tangible objectives would belong wholly to the limited-war forces, but the attainment of the psychological objective of maintaining credibility, though it was also an important aim of limited war, would still belong primarily to the nuclear retaliatory force. For it was the inherent futility of ever using the nuclear retaliatory force—a futility that threatened military paralysis—that had driven the policymakers to rely so heavily on credibility in the first place. It was dread of extinction in a nuclear war that had placed in doubt the "will" of the United States to use its undeniably tremendous nuclear arsenal. Of course, there were additional factors that might paralyze America's will to use its military forces. One was the element of isolationism that had long existed in American political life, and another was the natural revulsion of any peaceful people against warfare. Yet these obstacles had been overcome in times of danger in the past. The dread of nuclear war was a paralyzing influence of new dimensions. Now, even if the public should develop a will to victory, a clear upper limit had been placed on the usefulness of violence as an instrument in foreign affairs. The strategists were preoccupied with the question of how to demonstrate America's will—or "resolve," or "determination," or "toughness," as it was variously put. How to make demonstrations of credibility was, above all, a problem of public relations, since what counted was not the substance of America's strength or the actual state of its willingness but the image of strength and willingness. . . . The strategy of massive retaliation had been one way of maintaining credibility —the technique in that case being to attest to America's will to go to war by *almost* going to war—but it was in the doctrine of nuclear deterrence that the doctrine of credibility found its purest expression. The deterrent force was real, but its entire purpose was to *appear* so formidable that the Soviet Union would hesitate to take aggressive actions that might provoke the United States into retaliating. The deterrent was not meant for use, because its use would lead to the utter futility of mutual extinction. Appearances, therefore, were not merely important to deterrence—they were everything. If the deterrent was used, deterrence would have failed. If the image did not do its preventive work and there was a resort to action, the whole purpose of the policy would have been defeated, and the human race, with all its policies and purposes, might be lost.

. . .

Since the whole system was so shaky, with its cross-currents of belligerence and dread of annihilation, it was perhaps not surprising that the strategists turned in any direction they could, including the direction of limited war, to find theatres where the crucial but elusive quantity of "credibility" might be demonstrated. Certainly limited wars were among the last places where the appearance of "weakness or indecision" which Taylor feared so much could be tolerated. For, in this system, if the credibility of American power should be destroyed in a limited war, then the middle ground between global extinction and global totalitarianism would be lost, and the government would be forced once again to choose between the risk of giving the Soviet leaders "a blank check" and the risk of committing suicide.

In considering the origins and the character of the war in Vietnam, the extent of the theoretical preparations for limited war in general must be kept in mind. Today, the notion that the war was a "quagmire" into which successive Administrations were sucked, against their will, has won wide acceptance. The metaphor is apt insofar as it refers to the policymakers' undoubted surprise, year after year, at the way their policies were turning out in Vietnam, and to the evident reluctance of both President Kennedy and President Johnson to get involved there; but it is misleading insofar as it suggests that the United States merely stumbled into the war, without forethought or planning. In 1960, Taylor recommended the establishment of a "Limited War Headquarters"—and this was before the nation began fighting in Vietnam. Rarely has such a large body of military theory been developed in advance of an outbreak of hostilities. The war in Vietnam was, in a sense, a theorists' war *par excellence.* The strategists of the late nineteen-fifties were only slightly interested in the question of which country or countries might be the scene of a limited war. When they turned their attention to questions of geography—which they did only rarely— they tended to speak blurrily of "peripheral areas" around the Soviet Union and China which stretched from Japan, in the east, through India and the Middle East, in the south, to Europe, in the west. A reader in the nineteen-seventies of Kissinger's and Taylor's books is struck by how seldom Vietnam is mentioned. Today, the very word "Vietnam" is so rich in association and so heavily laden with historical significance that an atmosphere of inevitability —almost of fate—hangs over it, and it is difficult to imagine oneself back in a time when few Americans even knew of that nation's existence. Instead of speaking in terms of particular wars, whether in Vietnam or elsewhere, the theorists tended to speak in terms of types of wars.... [One] type of limited war that the new strategists recommended would rely on conventional forces that could be flown to troubled areas around the globe at a moment's notice in a fleet of special transport planes, whose construction the strategists counselled. In virtually all the planning for limited war, the speed of the American reaction was seen as crucial. The strategists of the time apparently believed that limited war would be not only limited but short.

Once one has worked out the strategy and the goals of a war, and has gone as far as to contemplate setting up a "headquarters" from which to fight it, the step to actual hostilities is not necessarily a very large one; in the early nineteen-sixties the abstractions in Kissinger's and Taylor's books came to life in the hostilities in Vietnam. John Kennedy found the arguments of the limited-war strategists persuasive, and in February of 1960, while he was still a senator, he stated, "Both before and after 1953 events have demonstrated that our nuclear retaliatory power is not enough. It cannot deter Communist aggression which is too limited to justify atomic war. It cannot protect uncommitted nations against a Communist takeover using local or guerrilla forces. It cannot be used in so-called brushfire peripheral wars. In short, it cannot prevent the Communists from gradually nibbling at the fringe of the free world's territory and strength, until our security has been steadily eroded in piecemeal fashion—each Red advance being too small to justify massive retaliation, with all its risks.... In short, we need forces of an entirely different kind to keep the peace against limited aggression, and to fight it, if deterrence fails, without raising the conflict to a disastrous pitch." Kennedy was saying that the limited-war forces would accomplish the two great objectives of policy that Kissinger and Taylor had set forth in their books: the prevention of global totalitarianism and the prevention of human extinction. By using limited forces to push back "limited aggression," the United States would be able to oppose the spread of Communism, and at the same time avoid confrontation at the brink. Kennedy, moreover, had become persuaded that the outcome of a limited war would be important not only for tangible objectives that might be attained but for the psychological objective of demonstrating America's "will" to oppose Communism, and after he became President he often referred to the hostilities in Vietnam as a "test case" of America's determination to protect its allies.

. . .

One of the members of President Kennedy's staff was Maxwell Taylor, who had been appointed Military Representative of the President, and in the fall of 1961 he was sent to Vietnam to take stock of the situation there. In Vietnam, the strategists of limited war, who had been thinking mainly in global terms, found themselves face to face with the challenge of guerrilla warfare. They quickly set about devising techniques to meet the challenge. Turning to the manuals of the Communist foe for guidance, they came up with the concept of "counterinsurgency" war. Men in the Pentagon began to regard themselves as potential guerrilla soldiers, and soon they were repeating such Maoist phrases as "The soldiers are the fish and the people are the sea." And in the early nineteen-sixties it was not only in the military area that the theories of professors were being translated into governmental policy in the struggle against Communism. During that period, a new breed of professor, trained in the social sciences and eager to test theories in the laboratory of real societies, came forward to offer "models" of economic and social development with which the government could rival the Communist "model."

In spite of all the expertise that was being brought to bear on the war, however, the reports from the field in Vietnam, when they began to come in, were discouraging. The long, sad tale of optimistic predictions followed by military reverses, to be followed, in turn, by increasingly drastic military measures, began to unfold, and by the mid-nineteen-sixties it was plain that the war would be far longer and far more difficult to end than any of the professors or policymakers had foreseen. The theory of limited war had been abstract and general, but Vietnam was a particular country, with a particular history and a particular society, and these particularities turned out to be more important than the strategists had ever dreamed they could be. Awed, perhaps, by the magnitude of America's global power and global responsibilities, the strategists had overlooked the possibility that purely local events, not controlled by a centralized, global conspiracy, might pose serious obstacles to their plans. Yet it was on the local events, and not on the balance of nuclear forces, that the outcome in Vietnam was proving to depend. For Vietnamese life had its own tendencies, which not even the power of the United States could alter. Moreover, the strategic theory had it that human beings behaved according to certain laws—that if people were punished sufficiently, they could be deflected from their goals, even if they had not been defeated outright. Accordingly, the strategists had fashioned a policy known as escalation, in which the level of violence would be raised, notch by notch, until the foe, realizing that America's instruments of pain were limitless and its will to inflict pain unshakable, would reach the breaking point and desist. The Vietnamese revolutionaries, however, did not behave in this way at all. Their will stiffened under punishment. And many Americans at home, too, behaved in an unexpected way. Their will to inflict the punishment began to falter. The material resources for inflicting punishment were indeed nearly limitless, but the capacity of the American spirit for inflicting punishment, although great, did have limits. The stubborn uniqueness of the situation in Vietnam was perhaps even more devastating to the plans of the theorists than the unexpected stiffness of the opposition. It meant not only that the war was going to be difficult to win but that it was not the war they had thought it was—that the United States might have sent its troops into the wrong country altogether. For if the Vietnam war was primarily a local affair, rather than a rebellion under the control of World Communism, then it was not a test case of anything. Then, instead of being one of those limited wars between global forces of freedom and global forces of totalitarianism which the theorists had foreseen in their books, it was just a civil war in a small country.

If the war had been planned only to achieve the tangible objectives that Kissinger assigned to limited war in 1957, the unexpected intractability of Vietnamese affairs and the revelation that the Vietnamese forces were not under the control of World Communism might well have inspired a reappraisal of the American effort, and perhaps a withdrawal. After all, even if Vietnam *had* been the right place to oppose World Communism, only a limited tangible advantage could have been gained there: at best, the freedom of one-half of one small country could be protected. And when the situation had deteriorated to the point where the possible strategic gains were outweighed by the manifold costs of the war effort, a strict accounting logic would have dictated that the United States should cut its losses and leave. In the mid-nineteen-sixties, that point was apparently reached. However, the war was not being fought only for the tangible objectives. It was being fought also for the psychological objective of maintaining American credibility—an aim that was bound up in the strategists' thinking with the prevention of nuclear war and the prevention of global totalitarianism. The war had a symbolic importance that was entirely separate from any tangible objective that might or might not be achieved. The policy-makers were divided on many points, but they were united on this one. In both their private and their public statements, they unwaveringly affirmed the absolute necessity of preserving the integrity of America's image in the fighting in Vietnam. . . . For President Johnson, in a speech in April of 1965, the United States was in Vietnam because it had "a promise to keep." He went on, "We are also there to strengthen world

South Vietnamese children watching American tanks. For thirteen years, Jonathan Schell contends, the United States fought in Vietnam mainly to preserve "what policy-makers throughout the period called the credibility of American power." (U.P.I. photo by Nik Wheeler.)

order. Around the globe, from Berlin to Thailand, are people whose well-being rests in part on the belief that they can count on us if they are attacked. To leave Vietnam to its fate would shake the confidence of all these people in the value of an American commitment and in the value of America's word. The result would be increased unrest and instability, and even wider war." By 1966, the aim of upholding credibility had become virtually the sole aim of the war. In January of that year, McNaughton wrote the memo in which he said, "*The present U.S. objective in Vietnam is to avoid humiliation.* The reasons why *we went into* Vietnam to the present depth are varied; but they are now largely academic. Why we have *not withdrawn* is, by all odds, *one* reason. (1) To preserve our reputation as a guarantor, and thus to preserve our effectiveness in the rest of the world...." The aim of upholding American credibility superseded any conclusions drawn from a single accounting of tangible gains and tangible losses, and it dictated that the war must go on, for it was on American credibility, the strategists thought, that the safety of the whole world depended. Secretary of State Dean Rusk wrote in a letter to a hundred student leaders in January of 1967, "We are involved in Vietnam because we know from painful experience that the minimum condition for order on our planet is that aggression must not be permitted to succeed. For when it does succeed, the consequence is not peace, it is the further expansion of aggression. And those who have borne responsibility in our country since 1945 have not for one moment forgotten that a third world war would be a nuclear war." Nor did the question of whether or not Vietnam was the wrong country to be fighting in matter much in this thinking. The fact that the United States was fighting there made it the right country; America's presence in Vietnam invested the war with the global significance that it lacked intrinsically, for if the United States involved itself in a war, its credibility was by that very action placed at stake....

Limited war had been conceived in part as a way for the United States to do bold things in an age when nuclear dread made the doing of bold things—particularly if they were violent things—especially dangerous. But now all hope of *doing* anything was abandoned. That aim was now considered to be, in McNaughton's phrase, "largely academic." What remained was proving something, to friends and foes alike: America's will and determination. The tangible objectives of limited war had been completely eclipsed by the psychological objective. The war had became an effort directed entirely toward building up a certain image by force of arms. It had become a piece of pure theatre. The purpose of the enterprise now was to put on a performance for what John McNaughton called "audiences." In the memo in which he mentioned the need to avoid harmful appearances, he went on to say, "In this connection, the relevant audiences are the Communists (who must feel strong pressures), the South Vietnamese (whose morale must be buoyed), our allies (who must trust us as 'underwriters'), and the US public (which must support our risk-taking with US lives and prestige)." The triumph of the doctrine of credibility had introduced into the actual conduct of the war the gap between image and substance which characterized the doctrine of nuclear deterrence. The whole aim of having a nuclear retaliatory force for deterrence was to create an image of the United States as a nation not to be trifled with, and so to forestall challenges that could lead to a nuclear holocaust. Now a real and bloody war was being fought for precisely the same end. As the paper of the National Security Council "working group" put it, the loss of South Vietnam could lead to "the progressive loss of other areas or to taking a stand at some point where there would almost certainly be major conflict and perhaps the great risk of nuclear war." Those who were opposed to the war tirelessly pointed out the disparity between the Johnson Administration's depiction of South Vietnam as a free country battling international Communist aggression and their own impression that the South Vietnamese government was a corrupt dictatorship that, supported by foreign arms and foreign money, was fighting a civil war against indigenous Communist forces. What those opposed to the war did not know was that the Johnson Administration had largely lost interest in Vietnam *per se*. What primarily interested the Johnson Administration from the mid-sixties on was not what was going on in Vietnam but how what was going on in Vietnam was perceived by what the Joint Chiefs referred to as the "countries of the world." In fact, so important were appearances in the official thinking that as things went from bad to worse on the battlefield the policymakers began to dream of completely separating the nation's image from what happened in the war, in order that even in the face of failure the desired image of American "will" might be preserved. The effort to rescue the national image from the debacle conditioned the tactics of the war from the mid-nineteen-sixties on. On one occasion in 1965, McGeorge Bundy, a special assistant to the President for national-security affairs, discussing a plan for *"sustained reprisal against North Vietnam,"* wrote, "It may fail.... What we can say is that even if it fails, the policy will be worth it. At a minimum, it will damp down the charge that we did not do all that we could have done, and this charge will be important in many countries, including our own. Beyond that, a reprisal policy—to the extent that it demonstrates U.S. willingness to employ this new norm in counterinsurgency—will set a higher price for the future upon all adventures of guerrilla warfare." To Bundy, a disastrous war effort was better than no war effort, because even a disastrous war effort would "demonstrate" the crucial "willingness" to use force in the nuclear age, and so would enhance American credibility....

The men in charge of the government were struggling to work out what the uses of military force might be in the age of nuclear weapons. The dilemma in which they found themselves was expressed in a memo that Walt Rostow, chairman of the State Department Policy Planning Council, wrote to Secretary of State Rusk in November of 1964, in which he mentioned "the real margin of influence... which flows from the simple fact that at this stage of history, we are the greatest power in the world—if we behave like it." Rostow's qualifying phrase "if we behave like it" summed up the maddening predicament of the great power in the nuclear age. For in reality "the fact" that the United States was "the greatest power in the world" was not "simple" at all. It was endlessly complicated, and contained deep, and perhaps irreconcilable, ambiguities. The reality was that the United States could by no means "behave like" the greatest power in the world if that meant acting the way great powers had acted on the world stage in the past. And it was not only idealism or moral scruple that stood in the way (although one can hope that these factors, too, did have a restraining influence) but also the unprecedented destructiveness, and self-destructiveness, of nuclear war.... [This] nuclear predicament forced the great powers to take military action only within a narrowed sphere, and always to behave with extreme caution and trepidation, not because they were weak but because they were too strong, and it taught them to rely more on the reputation of power—on show—than on the use of power. Still, the level of show was not without its possibilities. It provided the military strategists with what they regarded as an entire new sphere of action—the image world, in which battles were fought not to achieve concrete ends but to create appearances. Through actions taken to buttress the image of the United States, the strategists believed, the nation might still lay claim to the "margin of influence" that flowed from being the greatest power in the world. The United States might still have its way in international affairs, they thought, by fighting the admittedly militarily useless but presumably psychologically effective war in Vietnam. The image world was not the world of borders defended, of strategic positions won or lost, of foes defeated in great and bloody battles; it was the world of "reputations," of "psychological impact," of "audiences." It was, in a word, the world of credibility.

In the late nineteen-sixties, the war began to come home. The very nature of the war aims made a political struggle in the United States inevitable. Any long war, and particularly one that is poorly understood and is a failure besides, is likely to stir up opposition in the home country. But when the war, in addition, is being fought to uphold the nation's image, the strife at home takes on a deeper significance. When a government has founded the national defense on the national image, as the United States did under the doctrine of credibility, it follows that any internal dissension will be interpreted as an attack on the safety of the nation. The strain of such a situation on a democratic system is necessarily great. An authoritarian government has the means to project a single, self-consistent image of itself to its own people and the world, unchallenged by any disruption from within, but the image of the government of a free country is vulnerable to assault from every side on the home front. In a democracy, where anyone can say whatever he wants to say, and can frequently get on television saying it, the national image is the composite impression made by countless voices and countless deeds, all of them open to inspection by the whole world. It is not only the President and his men who form the image but anyone who wants to get out on the street with a sign. If the Vietnam war was one aspect of the nation's image, then the political process at home was the very essence of the nation's image. After all, in the United States the public, and not the government, *was* the nation. If the standing of the United States as the greatest power in the world was conditional upon its behaving like the greatest power in the world, then the way the public, in its scores of millions, was seen to behave at home was far more important to the national defense than the way a few hundred thousand soldiers were seen to behave nine thousand miles away. The soldiers in Vietnam could hardly demonstrate that America possessed the "will" to use force freely in the world while America itself denied it. When a war is being fought as a demonstration of the nation's "will and character," as President Nixon put it, what better way is there to oppose the war than to mount a demonstration of one's own—a demonstration, for instance, in which thousands of people march through the streets of the nation's capital in protest against the war? What better way is there to oppose a public-relations war than with a public-relations insurrection? The anti-war movement was often taken to task for its "theatricality." The fact is that it was precisely in its theatricality that its special genius lay. The war had been conceived as theatre—as a production for multiple "audiences"—and the anti-war movement was counter-theatre, and very effective counter-theatre. The demonstrations at home, if they were large enough, said as much about the nation's will and character as the demonstrations that the government was staging in Vietnam with B-52s. And the "psychological impact" of the demonstrations at home was probably greater around the world than that of the demonstrations in Vietnam, because the ones at home were voluntary, whereas the ones in Vietnam were backed by the coercive power of the government. Officials of the government often objected that the demonstrations at home undermined the war effort by giving encouragement to the enemy and by spreading demoralization among the troops. The opposition denied the charges, but here the government was probably right. Yet even the government never fully articulated why domestic dissent had such a devastating effect on the war cause. The fact is that the demonstrations at home struck at the very foundation of the larger aims for which the war was being fought. They struck a crippling blow at the credibility on which the whole strategy was based. In considering the shattering impact of the anti-war movement on the government, and the drastic responses of both the Johnson Administration and the Nixon Administration, it is important to recall that the nation's credibility was not an afterthought of the strategists of national defense but, rather, the linchpin of the deterrence strategy on which the government rested its hopes for avoiding the alternatives of global totalitarianism and nuclear extinction. A blow to the image of "toughness" was not just a blow to the pride of the men in government, or a political setback for them, or a blow to the war policy; it was a blow to the heart of the national defense. The aim of the war was to say something to the "countries of the world" about America's willingness to use force in the world, but the demonstrations at home tended to show the countries of the world that Americans were unwilling to use it. The war was meant to show that America was "tough," but the anti-war movement tended to show that it was "soft." The purpose of the war was to say one thing; the anti-war movement said the opposite thing. Some of the demonstrators took to wearing old Army uniforms, as though to parody the real Army; and they *were* a counter-army, which undid at home the work that the Army was doing in the field. . . . Under these circumstances, even if the war could somehow be won militarily, the whole purpose of the war would be destroyed: in the process of fighting the war abroad the all-important appearance of a willingness to fight many more wars of this kind would have been lost at home. On the other hand, if the public were to suffer the war in silence, or were to make some show of supporting the war, then even if the war should be lost militarily, the image of a "tough" nation, unafraid to use its power in the nuclear age, might still be salvaged from the debacle, and McGeorge Bundy's "new norm" might yet be established. In fact, if the public were to go on supporting a disastrous policy indefinitely, that might be the most impressive display of will there could be. What could be tougher than a nation that, as it loses one war, is eager for the next? In this war, it was literally true that the battle at home for public opinion was more crucial to the war aims than the battle in the field against the foe.

The uproar at home over the war took the Johnson Administration by surprise. None of the theorists or practitioners of limited war had foreseen the domestic implications of their policy; their thinking had been restricted to the foreign sphere. President Johnson therefore attempted to cope with his domestic difficulties in a loose and improvisatory—and often a repressive—way, such as when he sent out the F.B.I., the C.I.A., and the military to spy on and harass the opposition. Yet, for all his rage at his opponents, when he saw that his war policy was threatening the fundamental health of the body politic he resisted the temptation to turn an election into a contest between the representatives of order in the White House and disloyal anarchists in the streets; instead, he made his decision to quit political life and offered to open negotiations on the war. Thus, Lyndon Johnson remained devoted to the domestic well-being of the nation, even to the extent of being willing to risk reverses in foreign policy. It was not until President Nixon came to power that the full impact of the war policy made itself felt at home, and put the democratic system in jeopardy. For when President Nixon saw the domestic opposition to the war policy taking shape again, he accepted the challenge: he made national division the principal theme of national politics, and sought to reorganize the national life around the issue of the war and around such issues subsidiary to the war as the news coverage of the war and the protesters' response to the war. And when he saw that the domestic strife was starting to quiet down, he took covert steps to whip it up again: he launched his secret program of "exacerbating" divisive issues. Here was the basic difference between the two Presidents. President Johnson, a man of great cunning, vanity, and pride, who had no love for the rebels opposing him, and who was not above deceptions and manipulations of all kinds, and who remained convinced up to the end that his Vietnam policy was correct, nevertheless withdrew from politics and altered his course when he saw that, somehow, his policy was leading the nation toward a ruinous political crisis. President Nixon, when he saw the same crisis mounting, set about "exacerbating" it, and eventually had to be driven from office in mid-term. . . .

At first, President Nixon . . . promised the openness, the decentralization of power, the easing of tempers, and, above all, the withdrawal from the war which a full recovery of the democracy required. But his commitment to the war, and to the doctrine of credibility that was the principle justification for the war, was deep, and before long he was speaking of "peace with honor," and the like, and the domestic strife was revived with a new fury. The President then embarked on his effort—which was to continue throughout his remaining years in office—to make himself the unchallenged scenarist of American political life. Vietnam was one stage on which the credibility of American power was being demonstrated, and American life, if he had his way, would be another. Under his Administration, the separation of substance and image which characterized nuclear policy, and had come to characterize the war policy, now grew to characterize virtually all the policies of the Administration, including its domestic policies. After all, what was the use of fighting a war abroad to establish credibility when that same credibility was under challenge at home? How could foreign governments be taught to have "respect for the office of President of the United States" when the Americans themselves had not learned to respect it?

President Nixon's anxiety that the powers of his office were inadequate was reinforced by another worry that grew directly out of the nuclear dilemma: his fear that the United States was threatened with impotence in world affairs. The fear of impotence was a recurrent one in his public statements. President Nixon dreaded that the country might "tie the hands" of the President, that it would "cut off the President's legs," that the nation would be turned into a "pitiful, helpless giant." If the separation of substance and image was the form that the doctrine of credibility took, the fear of impotence—of "softness"—was its content. Everywhere the President looked, at home as well as abroad, he saw "appeasement," "passive acquiescence," Americans inclined to "whine and whimper about our frustrations" and "turn inward." In the courts, in the schools, and in the home, no less than in foreign affairs, he saw signs that the will on which everything now depended was eroding. His uneasiness on this score led him to his belief that the Congress, the courts, the press, the television networks, the federal bureaucracies, and the demonstrators in the streets were usurping powers that were rightfully his, and it fed his apparently insatiable appetite for new powers—powers that would destroy the independence of the other branches of the government and cancel out the rights of the people. It also led him to try to attempt to compensate for the lack of will he found among the people with a fierce will of his own, which would operate independently of the people. Some observers tended to see the roots of President Nixon's fear of impotence in the psychological idiosyncrasies of his character, and certainly these abounded. He was, however, far from being the first occupant of the White House to fear that the Presidency was in danger of becoming crippled. The fear of executive impotence in world affairs had been one of the deepest themes of nuclear politics for some fifteen years, having been powerfully augmented by the fear of nuclear paralysis which had worried Kissinger as far back as 1957....

There was one more characteristic of the Nixon Presidency which had its roots in the nuclear dilemma: President Nixon's apparent isolation from the world around him. Presidential isolation, like the Presidential preoccupation with images and the Presidential fear of impotence, had a history at least as long as the war in Vietnam. The fact that whoever was President was alone required to concern himself from day to day with the practical and moral problems of survival while his countrymen thought, for the most part, about pleasanter things was at the source of his isolation. The strategists in the White House regarded the war as one way of "facing up to the risks of Armageddon," but the public remained largely unaware of this function. The fundamental principles of the foreign policy of the time had grown out of an elaborate theoretical structure that was meant to accommodate the two broad aims of opposing the spread of Communism and coping with the risk of nuclear war, but the policymakers, in their public statements, tended to give the aim of opposing Communism far the greater emphasis. The aim of preventing nuclear war, when it was brought up at all, tended to be mentioned only in passing. This anomalous state of affairs, in which the government was cultivating a grim "resolve" to brave the risks of annihilation, and was preparing itself for terrible sacrifices and for getting "bloodied," while the public lacked any such sentiments, was partly of the government's own making. Kissinger had warned in his 1957 book that the policy he was proposing would require "a public opinion which has been educated to the realities of the nuclear age"—by which he meant a public that had been educated to accept the need for limited wars. But no such education ever took place. Instead, the executive branch sent American forces into the limited war in Vietnam by stealth while promising to stay out. One reason for the government's failure to apprise the public of the full importance of nuclear strategy in its war policy may have been simply the peculiar combination of abstractness and horror which made the subject so forbidding to think about. An aura almost of obscenity surrounded the calculations of how many millions might be killed and in what manner, and this may have helped cause public figures to shun the whole topic when they could. Another reason for their reticence, certainly, was the political vitality of the anti-Communist position, which made it very dangerous for any politician with national ambitions to suggest policies that smacked in any way of weakness or lack of resolve in the fight against Communism. . . .

In the second half of his first term, as President Nixon went on disengaging American ground troops from the fighting in Vietnam and inaugurated his policy of détente with the Soviet Union, hopes were raised that a spirit of disengagement and détente might come to prevail in the domestic wars, too. It had been these hopes, after all, that carried Mr. Nixon into office in 1968. But just the opposite occurred. The anger in the White House intensified, the President's isolation deepened, and the campaign to humble the Congress, the press, and the other powers in the society which rivalled the executive branch was stepped up. Once again, the public, never having been adequately informed about the imperatives of the doctrine of credibility, had failed to take them into account. For, according to the doctrine, if the President was going to risk American credibility by withdrawing from a war, it became all the more important to uphold credibility on the home front. A period of military retrenchment was no time to allow suggestions of "weakness or indecision" to crop up in domestic affairs. Instead, dramatic and unmistakable demonstrations of firmness were required. And the withdrawal itself could not be rushed or panicky. It would have to be stately and slow. It would have to be accompanied by many awesome displays of unimpaired resolve —displays such as the invasion of Cambodia, the invasion of Laos, the mining of the ports of North Vietnam, and the carpet-bombing of North Vietnam in the Christmas season of 1972. In an era in which the President was haunted by a fear of seeming impotent, a withdrawal was the most delicate of operations. Under no circumstances could it be allowed to appear an expression of weakness or loss of will. The Nixon Administration's resolution of its dilemma was the one suggested by John McNaughton and McGeorge Bundy years earlier— that of trying to maintain an image of toughness in the face of failure by mounting futile but tough-seeming military campaigns. McNaughton had written in 1965 that it was important for the United States to get bloodied even as it failed in Vietnam, and this is exactly what happened. The United States did fail in Vietnam, and it did get bloodied, in Vietnam and at home as well.

If withdrawal from ground operations in Vietnam increased the pressures for militancy in other spheres of Presidential action, the policy of détente increased them even more. The apparent contradiction between the militancy both in Vietnam and at home and the spirit of friendly coöperation at the summit conferences with the Russians and the Chinese baffled the public. For a moment, as President Nixon proclaimed that "America's flag flies high over the ancient Kremlin fortress" while Americans were dying in Southeast Asia in an attempt to counter the Kremlin's influence, the fighting in Vietnam came to look like something without precedent in military history: a war in which the generals on the opposing sides had combined into a joint command. But President Nixon's split policy was in keeping with the fundamental requirements of American strategy as they had been conceived by men in the White House at least since the time of President Kennedy. Throughout the sixties and the early seventies, White House strategists had sought to balance each move toward peace in the nuclear sphere with militancy in other spheres of competition with the Communists. In the early nineteen-sixties, the move toward peace in the nuclear sphere came in the shift from the provocative doctrine of massive retaliation to the passive doctrine of nuclear deterrence, and the balancing display of anti-Communism came in the adoption of the aggressive strategy of limited war. Now, in the early nineteen-seventies, an Administration was once again taking a step away from the brink in the nuclear sphere—this time by its conclusion of agreements on the limitation of strategic arms at the Moscow summit meeting of May, 1972— and was once again seeking out other spheres in which to shore up the President's reputation as a fierce anti-Communist: to give him opportunities for the expression of his "ruthless" side, to quote the fourth, and final, draft of the speech by Kissinger to Soviet Communist Party Secretary Leonid Brezhnev a few weeks before the summit meeting. In the framework of Kissinger's thinking, it made perfect sense to move toward the summit, and so toward peace, in the sphere of direct relations with the Soviet Union while simultaneously moving toward confrontation, and so toward intensified war, in the sphere of Vietnam policy. As far back as 1957, Kissinger had noted and deplored "the notion that war and peace, military and political goals, were separate and opposite." Now, under his guidance, war and peace were being pursued simultaneously. At the summit, the President would work for a relaxation of nuclear tension (what he now called a "generation of peace"), and in the "peripheral areas" he would continue to make demonstrations of his credibility (what he now called "respect for the office of President of the United States"). . . .

During [Nixon's] years in office, it became a cliché to point out that only a seemingly determined anti-Communist like President Nixon could afford the political risks of visiting China and of establishing a policy of détente wth the Soviet Union. But even President Nixon, with his impeccable anti-Communist credentials, nevertheless felt obliged to reaffirm his militancy, and he and other members of his Administration often hinted darkly to journalists that a "humiliating defeat" in Vietnam might lead to a dangerous right-wing backlash at home. Politically as well as strategically, therefore, the policy of détente created a pressure to find places where the credibility of American power could be affirmed, and in the early nineteen-seventies those places were Vietnam and the domestic politics of the United States.

If the record of American statesmanship in the Vietnam years, with its sheer mendacity, fumbling, and brutality—not to mention the apparent dementia in the White House which first made its appearance in the Johnson years and emerged fully into public view in President Nixon's last days in office—has a tragic aspect as well, it lies in the fact that in those years the nation experienced the defeat of its first sustained, intellectually coherent attempt to incorporate the implications of nuclear weaponry into national policy. For today it is clear that the doctrine of credibility has failed. It has failed not only in the terms of those who opposed it but also in its own terms. The doctrine of credibility did not provide the United States with an effective means of promoting its interests and ideals at levels of violence below the brink of nuclear war; instead, it provided the notorious quagmire in Vietnam into which the United States poured its energy and power uselessly for more than a decade. The doctrine of credibility, though different from the doctrine of massive retaliation, did not spare mankind from confrontations at the brink between the nuclear powers; far from freezing hostilities at a low level of the escalatory ladder, it led the United States up the ladder, step by step, until, in May of 1972, President Nixon felt obliged to lay down a frontal challenge to the Soviet Union and China by mining North Vietnamese ports against their ships. Finally, the doctrine of credibility failed to enhance American credibility; instead of enabling the United States to "avoid harmful appearances" and to create "respect for the office of President of the United States," it engendered appearances that were supremely harmful to the United States—appearances not only of helplessness, irresolution, and incompetence but of duplicity and ruthlessness—and precipitated a wave of disrespect for a particular President which culminated in his forced resignation from office. Nor did the doctrine of credibility merely fail; it was a catastrophe in its own right, which led to the needless devastation of the Indo-Chinese peninsula and the assault on Constitutional government in the United States.

. . .

The fact that the inception of nuclear weapons coincided with the launching of a worldwide crusade by the United States against the spread of Communist influence; the fact that the President's exclusive control over the nuclear arsenal tended to concentrate other kinds of power in his hands; and the fact that nuclear strategy enclosed the White House in a hermetic world of theories and images which was all but impervious to real events and which fostered an atmosphere of unreality in the White House—all these were circumstances that belonged to a distinct phase of the nuclear story. The boastfulness, the hypocrisy, the hardheartedness, the obsession with outward appearance and the neglect of inward substance, and the nervous insecurity in spite of matchless power which marred American policy in the Vietnam years may all be seen as aspects of one contortion in the nation's writhing in the grip of the nuclear dilemma. With the fall of President Nixon and the end of the war in Vietnam, this particular episode in the story of the nuclear dilemma has apparently come to an end, and, with it, some of the special problems of that time may have come to an end as well. What will not come to an end is the nuclear dilemma itself. Nor does it seem likely that the decisive influence of the nuclear dilemma on the American Presidency—whatever form that influence may take as time goes on—will come to an end. For the advent of nuclear weapons has done nothing less than place the President in a radically new relation to the whole of human reality. He, along with whoever is responsible in the Soviet Union, has become the hinge of human existence, the fulcrum of the world. He lives and works astride the boundary that divides the living world from universal death. Surveyed from where he stands, the living creation has no more permanence than a personal whim. He or his Soviet counterpart can snuff it out as one might blow out a candle. If Presidents in recent years have lost touch with reality, bringing disaster to their Administrations and to the nation, may it not be because their grip on what is literally human reality—on the continued existence of mankind—is so tenuous and shaky? When the whole of human existence is trembling in one's grasp, it may be difficult to train one's attention on each detail. And, measured against the extinction of the whole, almost anything that does not contribute directly to the current scheme for survival may seem to be a detail. If President Nixon, then, slipped into the habit of treating the world as though it were nothing but a dream, may it not have been because the world's continued existence did rest on the foundation of his thoughts, his moods, his dreams? And if a false atmosphere of emergency came to pervade White House thinking on every issue that arose, surely it was in part because the men there lived with a vast, perpetual, genuine emergency. And, finally, if the President tended to gather tremendous new power into his hands, to violate the rights of others, to break the law, and generally to ride roughshod over every obstacle, the reason, at bottom, may have been much the same. He had discovered a rationalization without limits in the altogether real aim of protecting mankind from extinction. For what right, what law, what fact, what truth, what aspiration could be allowed to stand in the way of the imperative of human survival, in which all rights, laws, facts, truths, and aspirations were grounded? The first question of the age was how to guarantee survival. Another question was the one that the strategists asked themselves in the nineteen-fifties—how a great power can exercise its influence in the face of the paralyzing effects of nuclear dread. And still other questions that were posed by the ruinous experience of the Vietnam years were how, in the face of the nuclear imperatives, other human aims and human qualities, including freedom and sanity, could be preserved. For thirty years, the burden of nuclear weapons has rested upon the nation with a crushing weight. Their presence has corrupted the atmosphere in which the nation lives, distorted its politics and coarsened its spirit. The questions they raised have all outlasted the Presidency of Richard Nixon and the nation's reaffirmation of its Constitution and its laws. They are questions on which the framers of the Constitution and all other counsellors from other centuries are silent. The questions are unprecedented, they are boundless, they are unanswered, and they are wholly and lastingly ours.

34
Presidential Sin from Jefferson to Nixon

Fawn M. Brodie

As the United States passed through the crisis of Vietnam, so it also went through a constitutional crisis at home, as the Nixon administration resorted to appalling abuses of power that in the public mind became known simply as "Watergate." Perhaps, as Jonathan Schell suggests in *The Time of Illusion*, Vietnam and Watergate were symptomatic of the crushing burdens a modern American president must bear, as he tries to lead a mighty nuclear power in a complex and dangerous world menaced with the specter of human extinction. Even so, there can be little doubt that Nixon brought the Watergate disaster on himself, not only by hiring dishonest assistants but by persistently lying about his own complicity in Watergate and abusing the powers of his office worse than did any President in history. Although Nixon had promised in 1968 to "bring us together again," he and his advisors clearly viewed a great many Americans—newsmen, northeastern Republicans, liberal Democrats, and protesting students—as mortal enemies of the president and therefore of the Republic itself. For Nixon and his men, domestic politics became a desperate battlefield between *them* and *us*, with the Nixon White House increasingly identifying *them* as traitors and *us* as the only patriots and true saviors of America. In the name of the Republic, the Nixon administration compiled an "enemies list," used the Internal Revenue Service to harass political opponents, wiretapped government officials and private citizens, established an elaborate spy system inside the White House, collected hundreds of thousands of dollars in illegal campaign contributions, hired thugs to ransack the psychiatry files of a prominent antiwar dissident, authorized a burglary of Democratic national headquarters at the Watergate complex in Washington, D.C., and then tried to cover up the crime through payoffs, lies, and a systematic obstruction of justice. The Watergate scandal, exposed by Carl Bernstein and Bob Woodward of the *Washington Post,* shocked people regardless of political persuasion and eventually brought Nixon's presidency crashing down.

Nixon's fall came after a bitter struggle over tapes the president had secretly recorded of his own White House meetings and conversations. When the existence of the tapes became known, congressional committees and special prosecutors investigating Watergate subpoenaed the White House for the tapes. But Nixon steadfastly refused to surrender them until the Supreme Court, by a vote of 8–0, ordered him to do so. The president had good reason to cling to his tapes, for they revealed his own involvement in the Watergate cover-up (despite his repeated pronouncements that he had no knowledge of any such cover-up). By the summer of 1974, Congress had had enough: the House Judiciary Committee began impeachment proceedings, and Nixon's support on Capitol Hill evaporated. "The president," raged Republican Senator Barry Goldwater, "has lied to me for the last time and lied to my colleagues for the last time." With an impeachment conviction all but assured in the Senate, Nixon spared the nation the ordeal of a trial, and in August, 1974, he resigned his office, the first American president in history to do so.

Like Vietnam, Watergate is an unhappy chapter in the story of modern America which should be confronted openly and honestly, for the mark of a great people is surely their ability to admit mistakes in their leaders as well as in themselves. In order to understand Nixon's downfall, it seems best to view his "presidential sin" in historical perspective, which is what biographer Fawn M. Brodie sets out to do in her lively and informed essay. For Nixon's only crime was not, as many Americans contend, that he simply got caught doing what other presidents had done. As historian C. Vann Woodward has observed in *Responses of the President to Charges of Misconduct*, "Heretofore, no president has been proved to be the chief coordinator of the crime and misdemeanor charged against his own administration. . . . Heretofore, no president has been held to be the chief personal beneficiary of misconduct in his administration or of measures taken to destroy or cover up evidence of it. Heretofore, the malfeasance and misdemeanor have had no confessed ideological purpose, no constitutionally subversive ends. Heretofore, no president has been accused of extensively subverting and secretly using established government agencies to defame or discredit political opponents and critics, to obstruct justice, to conceal misconduct and protect criminals, or to deprive citizens of their rights and liberties. Heretofore, no president has been accused of creating secret investigative units to engage in covert and unlawful activities against private citizens and their rights." If there is any way to guard against such abuses in the future, perhaps it is the concluding remarks of Brodie's own essay.

A deposed president, like a deposed king, presents prickly problems to his successor. When Richard II was forced off the throne in 1399 by Bolingbroke, he was sent to Pontefract Castle, where he died six months later of what some historians believe was self-imposed starvation. Shakespeare, however, had him assassinated. In the final scene of Richard II we see the murderer, Piers Exton, presenting his body to the new king, Henry IV, who says:

From the Davis Memorial Lecture, III, with permission of the History Department of Gonzaga University, Spokane, Washington.

Exton, I thank thee not; for thou has wrought
A deed of slander, with thy fatal hand,
Upon my head and all this famous land.

President Ford, instead of banishing Richard Nixon, our own abdicated monarch, treated him with great compassion, pardoned him for sins as yet undiscovered as well as for those made evident by the tapes and tape transcripts, and, at least in the beginning, made him custodian over all his papers, including the fatal tapes that had brought him crashing down from Olympus. This modern abdication presents prickly problems, too, for the historian. President Ford, for his compassion, was accused by many of being an accessory to the coverup. Still the spectacle of the crippled, depressed, and what seemed for a time a possibly dying man at San Clemente compelled compassion. Representative Dan Kuykendall on August 26, 1974, reported that the anxious ex-president had asked him by telephone, "Do you think these people want to pick the carcass?" And those journalists and historians who continued to attack Richard Nixon in the face of ever mounting evidence of his "presidential sin" were denounced by Nixon supporters as vultures delighting in dissection and mutilation.

Early in the deliberations of the House Judiciary Committee, Chairman Peter Rodino called C. Vann Woodward, eminent historian of American History at Yale University, and asked him to prepare an historical study for the use of his staff, "a study of misconduct in previous administrations and how previous Presidents had responded to charges of misconduct." He emphasized that the study should be "factual and non-interpretive." Given the deadline of July 1, 1974, Woodward called fourteen historians who "dropped everything instantly and plunged into their assignments." The result is a remarkable book, *Responses of the Presidents to Charges of Misconduct*. What is no less remarkable is the request itself. Representative Rodino was intent on seeing that his own staff have a proper perspective on the history of presidential sin. His aim was not compassion but perspective. What were the precedents in presidential history, he wanted to know, concerning corruption, malfeasance, and abuse of power? No one could properly judge the Nixon record, he believed, save against the records of the past, and the collection was intended to illuminate the present by way of the past in the hope that the impeachment proceedings would be both judicious and fair.

Though the volume will serve historians and students, will it serve to lessen the harshness of the judgments already pronounced? Richard Nixon's release of the "smoking gun" transcript and his subsequent resignation stopped the impeachment process, but it did not stop the venomous political obituaries. He was called "shabby," "foul-mouthed," "conspiratorial," "manipulative," "synthetic," "vindictive," "power-hungry," and "morally bankrupt." The editors of *Time* said "he gave undue aid and comfort to the narrow and mean spirited," and the editors of *Newsweek* said he had "a harsh instinct for guerilla politics," and that "nothing so honored his Presidency as his leaving of it." George V. Higgins called him "a virtuoso of deception," and John Galbraith said he had "a deeply bogus streak." Arthur Miller wrote that Nixon "marched instinctively down the crooked path." Jack McCurdy, who polled the leading campuses for judgments on the fallen president, found no real compassion. He quoted Richard Neustadt, expert on the presidency, as predicting that future disagreement "would be between those who regard this as the most inept of presidential performances and those who will regard it as the most vicious."

Historians were almost uniformly harsh. Henry Steele Commager called Nixon "the first dangerous and wicked president," and Arthur Schlesinger Jr. said that his resignation had saved the presidency "from the man who did more to discredit and endanger it than any other President in our history." Emmet John Hughes, biographer of Eisenhower, said flatly, "In the life of the presidency, the awful smell of political smut has ended." In reading these judgments one is reminded of Milton's Lucifer falling from heaven, pelted by a hailstorm of derision and calumny.

Even President Ford in his inaugural address pronounced an implicit negative judgment on Nixon when he said, "The long nightmare of the nation is over." And in the statement later in which he pardoned the former president he returned again to the same theme. "I cannot," he said, "prolong the bad dreams." Father John J. McLaughlin, stout defender of Nixon in the White House, admitted after the resignation, "The incubus has been lifted from our backs."

In his resignation speech the former president told us how he hoped to be evaluated by history, saying that he had resigned simply because he had lost his political base in Congress, as if he visualized himself as our prime minister, meeting an unexpected no-confidence vote. His loyal son-in-law, David Eisenhower, said within a month after the resignation that "fifteen years hence the offense is going to look pretty small." Nixon, he said, had simply "acquiesced in the non-prosecution of aides who covered up a little operation into the opposition's political headquarters, which is a practice that was fairly well established in Washington for a long time and that no one took all that seriously." There will be "other grounds," he said, "on which to judge the administration." And he suggested that his father-in-law might eventually run for the Senate from California. Andrew Johnson, it will be remembered, was elected to the Senate from his home state of Tennessee seven years after his impeachment trial, though he died of a paralytic stroke two months after his return to Washington. Whether the judgments upon Nixon will become more compassionate as we pass the nation's bicentennial, or ever more pejorative, depends partly upon Nixon's memoirs, and upon future exposures, if any, not yet brought to light.

The bicentennial inevitably invites fantasies about what the founding fathers would say were they to return to the United States today. Jefferson left such an immense legacy of letters that it is possible to speculate without too great foolishness what he might think of Watergate. Imagine his being confronted, without any previous briefing, with the spectacle of Richard Nixon in isolation at San Clemente, accused of massive lying, bribery, coverup, suborning a judge, subverting the electoral process, curtailing freedom of speech and the press, misuse of public funds, illegal manipulation of the CIA, FBI, and IRS, the grossest abuse of power in presidential history? Would he ask in consternation, as did young William Cohen of Maine, on the House Judiciary Committee, "How did we get from the Federalist Papers to the tape transcripts?"

Were Jefferson to tour San Clemente and be told its financial history, he would certainly remember that when he had left Washington after eight years as president he was so much in debt that he had been forced to borrow $8,000 to pay his Washington creditors. This was because he had overspent his salary on good food and French wine in hundreds of White House dinners, entertaining both Republicans and Federalists in a ceaseless effort to ease the abrasive party hostilities. Had he asked for a presidential pension, or funds to ease the transition back into private life, it would then have been considered an affront to the Republic.

"Let us begin by committing ourselves to the truth—to see it like it is, and tell it like it is—to find the truth, to speak the truth, and to live the truth. The time has come for honesty in government." So said Richard M. Nixon in his acceptance speech at the Republican National Convention in 1968. Over the next six years, Nixon lied and abused the powers of his office more than any other president before him. (Photo by Hiroji Kubota, courtesy of Magnum Photos.)

Jefferson would not, however, be as shocked as we might think at the decline and fall of Richard Nixon. One of his first questions, I suspect, would be, "How many other presidents have been forced to resign? How many have been impeached in the House and convicted in the Senate? He might well be astonished to learn that only Andrew Johnson was impeached, and that when it came to resignations, Richard Nixon was the first. We are so accustomed to trusting our presidents of whatever party to be decent and well-meaning, if sometimes misguided or foolish, that we are inclined to forget that the founding fathers took it for granted that it was in the nature of man to abuse power, and that corruption was a natural accompaniment of high office. Washington in his famous "Political Testament" of June 8, 1783, described the new republic as "giving a fairer opportunity for political happiness than any other Nation has ever been favored with." But he warned that it was in the people's choice "and depends upon their conduct, whether they will be respectable and prosperous, or contemptible and miserable as a Nation."

None of the founding fathers was certain that the system would work for long. Benjamin Franklin in the Constitutional Convention of 1789 said, "This government is likely to be well administered for a course of years, and can only end in despotism, as other forms have done before, when the people shall become so corrupted as to need despotic government, being incapable of any other." He was here implying that the need for despotism could indeed develop within the framework of a democracy. Hamilton was certain that the republic would lapse quickly into anarchy, thus inviting a Julius Caesar, and he seems to have had fantasies of playing the role himself, though in his actions he remained firmly committed to "propping up" what he called "the frail and worthless fabric," the American Constitution.

Jefferson in his *Notes on the State of Virginia* warned that "in every government on earth is some trace of human weakness, some germ of corruption and degeneracy, which cunning will discover, and wickedness insensibly open, cultivate and improve. Every government degenerates when trusted to the rulers of the people alone." He hoped that the electoral system itself, buttressed by universal education, would ensure the surfacing of what he called an aristocracy of talent and virtue, believing that a constitutional system could be devised with machinery not only to throw the rascals out, but also to ensure that they did not get elected. "The time to guard against corruption and tyranny," he wrote in the *Notes* in 1782, "is before they have gotten hold of us. It is better to keep the wolf out of the fold than to trust to drawing his teeth and talons after he shall have entered."

To a friend, Mann Page, he wrote on August 30, 1795, "I do not believe . . . that fourteen out of fifteen men are rogues. . . . But I have always found that the rogues would be uppermost." As president he warned, in another famous letter to a friend, "Bad men will sometimes get in, and with such an immense patronage, make great progress in corrupting the public mind and principles." He particularly distrusted the rich, insisting to John Adams that no laws were necessary to protect them, "because enough of these will find their way into every branch of government to protect themselves."

But Jefferson when president was himself accused of political error and private sin. A resolution by Representative Josiah Quincy to impeach him on the frivolous and untrue charge that he had failed to let the collector of the Port of Boston resign, was voted down 117–1. He was accused in the press of atheism, though he was a deist not an atheist. He was accused of being an anarchist, though no man has believed more consistently in the orderly processes of republican government. He was accused of violating the Constitution by spending fifteen million dollars for the Louisianna Purchase, this by the same Federalists who had earlier urged him to send an army to take New Orleans by force.

The charge that he had mishandled the funds of his widowed sister was as false as the charge that he had behaved as a coward when British dragoons tried to capture him at Monticello during the Revolution. The accusation that he had taken to bed the quadroon slave, Sally Hemings, half sister to his dead wife, which found its way into the press of 1802, has, however, overwhelming evidence to support it. He met the press accounts with dignified public silence, not denial, but there is evidence of private anguish of spirit during this crisis of public revelation.

The phrase "private sin," which is here

applied to Jefferson, is generally considered inappropriate for modern historians, who are supposed to avoid value judgments having to do with the commandments of God. The whole concept of presidential sin may be attacked as unhistorical and anachronistic. Henry Adams wrote long ago that honesty could be only a private virtue, that business and diplomacy inevitably involve lying and intrigue. Many historians would agree that dirty tricks have been routine in American politics. David Wise's *The Politics of Lying* has documented deception not only on the part of Nixon but also Eisenhower, Kennedy, and Johnson. Many Nixon defenders agree privately with Gordon Liddy, who told Mike Wallace in a TV interview in January, 1975, that the former President's only error was in not being ruthless enough, by failing to destroy the tapes.

Despite widespread contemporary cynicism, there are still historians and biographers who use the word "virtue" in judging presidents of the past. James T. Flexner, author of an excellent biography of George Washington, has summed up the essence of our first president in the phrase "political virtue." But members of the profession are less comfortable with the word "sin." Classifications of sin, like the Ten Commandments and the seven deadly sins, are associated with religion not politics. Still, until very recent times, they exerted a subtle influence on political judgments. Now the words "covetousness," "lust," "wrath," "envy," "sloth," and "pride," when hurled at either the godless or the godly, have lost their impact. Envy and covetousness are considered essential for the health of the economy; a glutton goes to Weight Watchers instead of the priest; explosions of wrath are considered an antidote for ulcers; pride and lust are presumably necessary components of a strong ego and a healthy sexuality.

Campus phrases like "hung up," "spaced out," or "freaked out," which might be considered modern substitute words for sins, are not, I am assured, value judgments of the young but mere descriptions, though my own daughter stated, in clarifying these definitions, "we would not want to see a freaked out president. There we are more interested in sanity than in sin." Clinical words like "schizoid" or "paranoid" are so common they have become vitiated by careless use, even when applied to our former president. To use the word "paranoid" to describe the president is something new in American history, but it is not very terrifying. Students throw the accusation at each other in a friendly fashion, as do husbands and wives. Perhaps we should return to another ancient word which though misused still has an impact, and say instead—if the evidence warrants it— "The president is mad." Fear of this in regard to Richard Nixon seems to have been unfounded, but it was palpable during the nuclear alert of October 24–25, following the so-called "Saturday Night Massacre" after the firing of prosecutor Archibald Cox. That the fear returned in earnest during Nixon's last weeks in office was hinted at by Secretary of Defense James Schlesinger, when he permitted an aide to say after the president's resignation, that he and Secretary of State Kissinger had earlier issued orders that all military commands emanating from the White House be channeled through them.

The sins of Watergate are real, but how they will be classified by historians, whether in religious or clinical terms, is not yet clear. Are they venial or mortal? Are they venial or venal? Venal sins—purchasability, accessibility to bribery and other monetary corruption—certainly permeated the Nixon White House. David Eisenhower would dismiss these sins as venial—easily forgiven—but few historians would agree. Venial sin, in any case, for most Americans suggests "sins of the flesh," what the social scientists coldly codify as "libidinal behavior."

There are many examples of sins of the flesh among our past presidents. The discovery by historians that George Washington had had a tender affection for his neighbor's wife, Sally Fairfax, came late. It helped to humanize a man who had become a monument, and did not denigrate either the first president or his amiable wife. Jefferson was the first chief of state whose sexual life was used as a bludgeon for attack by his political enemies. Bawdy ballads about Long Tom and his slave Dusky Sally peppered the Federalist press for several years, and their editors scolded Jefferson for not marrying a nice white girl. Still, if one looks at the election of 1804, when Jefferson won all but two states, it would seem that the liaison with the slave mistress did not cost him votes. True there were no opinion polls at the time to measure this, but it does appear that Americans chose either not to believe the story or to forgive the lonely widower this lapse from what was considered socially acceptable behavior. What would have been real political sin in the eyes of many in the North and almost everyone in the South would have been for Jefferson to have acknowledged the liaison publicly and to have defended it. This would have meant social ostracism and political annihilation.

Marriage between whites and blacks was of course forbidden. Moreover, Jefferson could not without publicity free Sally Hemings, for by Virginia law she would have been automatically banished from the state, unless Jefferson publicly petitioned the legislature to permit her to remain as a reward for "meritorious service." In any case, a liaison with a free black woman was much more damaging socially and politically than with a slave. There are historians today who continue to deny the validity of the psychological as well as the material evidence of the Sally Hemings story, and who denounce it as "a scandal," when they should be emphasizing instead that the real scandal was slavery, which enforced secrecy, punished and degraded love between white and black, and made public recognition of the offspring of miscegenation a grave social sin.

Grover Cleveland frankly acknowledged his illegitimate child in advance of his election; his honesty seems to have served to win more votes than the indiscretion cost him. With Warren Harding revelations about his two mistresses, and a child born out of wedlock, became public only after his death, as did most of the details of the Teapot Dome scandal. The timing of his dying was fortuitous. Biographers and historians waited a decent interval until both Eleanor Roosevelt and Lucy Mercer Rutherford were dead before publishing in detail the evidence of a long relationship saddening to those who had thought the Roosevelt marriage to be fulfilling in every aspect. But this story, as told with great sensitivity by biographer Joseph Lash in *Eleanor and Franklin* did not diminish the heroic image of Franklin Roosevelt, who accomplished "prodigies of salvage" during the depression, and who helped to save the world from the spread of the most monumental tyranny in world history.

Neither Kay Summersby nor Dwight Eisenhower was damaged by Merle Miller's release of a Harry Truman tape documenting their special friendship. In fact the persistence of folklore about the mistresses of the presidents is so tenacious, even when there seems to be no foundation for it, that one suspects there is something at work here beyond the normal malice and envy directed toward the powerful. Europeans always delighted in the amours of their kings, just as the poorest Moslems who could not afford the four wives permitted by Mohammed gloried in the sheer numbers of their rulers' concubines. There have always been Puritan punishers, but many Americans compassionately and quietly enjoy what seems to be evidence of masculinity in their leaders.

But what about mortal sins, those which—in that troubling canonical phrase—cause "the death of the soul"? In looking at the history of presidential sin, I think it fair to say that for the first time in our two hundred years we have truly been witnessing the death of a soul of the president. The rich religious imagery evoked by this phrase becomes especially meaningful when we remember that this president as a child was brought up to be a devout Quaker for whom the "soul" had real meaning.

Representative Kuykendall, among others, has likened the fall of Richard Nixon to Greek tragedy. Some hold that there can be no great tragedy where there is no nobility, and that there never has been nobility in Richard Nixon. Whether you agree with this or not, all must concede that there has been high drama in the dying. It has held spellbound friend and foe alike. The drama still continues as we contemplate the incredible decline from the jubilant president in the victory of 1972 to the man of San Clemente, no longer a giant, but simply pitiful and helpless.

After Watergate broke, Paul Conrad, cartoonist of the *Los Angeles Times*, portrayed Richard Nixon as Richard II in his abdication, doleful and wretched, with the marvelously appropriate lines from Shakespeare's play underneath, lines that become more appropriate with each passing day:

> O that I were as great
> As is my grief, or lesser than my name!
> Or that I could forget what I have been,
> Or not remember what I must be now.

No president has left to history so meticulously detailed a record of the worst of himself. Nixon, surreptitiously recording slander in his closet, has been his own Duc de Saint Simon, hostile diarist of Louis XIV's court, and he may well go down in history as the supreme informer —both on himself and others—of all time. It seems most unlikely, even if he completes his memoirs, which are said to be planned in two volumes, one on Watergate and one on his efforts to bring peace, that he will be able to restore the balance of good against evil in his own record. Ulysses S. Grant, not himself guilty of corruption but shockingly guilty of tolerating it in his aides, including his brother-in-law, won back much of his shattered reputation with a remarkable two-volume memoir, written when he was dying of cancer of the throat. The books did not, however, cover his scandal-ridden years as president but only his record as the general who saved the Union. And it should be noted that Lyndon Johnson failed to win converts in his memoir, *The Vantage Point*, and that Herbert Hoover—condemned for ineptness not malfeasance—never succeeded by his own writings in recovering his original reputation for administrative skill.

Richard Rovere, political analyst for *The New Yorker*, crystalized a common judgment when he said that Nixon "is the first president to my knowledge who has really been a crook." But few would deny that Nixon is no ordinary "wicked" man, no ordinary liar or crook. Along with the unique negative legacy he has left a record of positive accomplishments, notably détente with the Soviet Union begun by John F. Kennedy, and the new understanding with China. And into the scales on the positive side the historian must place also the record of the Nixon fantasies—fantasies of being a great president like his heroes Theodore Roosevelt and Woodrow Wilson, fantasies of bringing truth to government, law and order to society, and peace to the world.

In his acceptance speech at the Republican National Convention in Miami Beach in 1968 he said, "Let us begin by committing ourselves to the truth—to see it like it is, and tell it like it is—to find the truth, to speak the truth, and to live the truth. The time has come for honest government in America." In this same speech we see his fantasy for the bicentennial:

> Eight years from now, in the second term of the next President, we will celebrate the 200th anniversary of the American Revolution. By our decision in this election, we will determine what kind of a world America will live in in the year 2000. This is the kind of a

day I see for America on that glorious Fourth—eight years from now.

I see a day when Americans are once again proud of their flag.... I see a day when the President of the United States is respected and his office honored because it is worthy of respect and honor....

I see a day when every child in this land, regardless of color or background, has a chance for the best education our wisdom and talents will take him.... I see a day when we can look back on massive breakthroughs in solving the problems of the slums, pollution and traffic which are choking our cities to death.... I see a day when our nation is at peace.... and everyone on earth—those who hope, who aspire and those who crave liberty—will look to America as a living example of hopes realized and dreams achieved....

We know from Nixon's biographers that this speech was not ghost-written, and that the idealism in it helped make him president.

In a speech on February 12, 1974, President Nixon pointed wistfully to the ancient vilification of Lincoln, implying that in time the aspersions of his own enemies would disappear and that he would emerge triumphant in the history books as a man of truth and peace. It is true that the judgment of the textbooks is generally more compassionate than the worst of what is said about a president when he is still alive. But this judgment does not represent something original and new but rather the considered choice among the many made at the time at best refined and sharpened by accumulated data. Even the negative record of Richard Nixon is still incomplete. And the overwhelmingly hostile judgments of the present, especially among historians, augur ill for the concensus of the future. In the parlor game historians and political scientists sometimes play, listing the presidents from best to worst, Richard Nixon's name would seem to be securely at the bottom.

Until now four presidents have been competing candidates for the lowest rung of the ladder, James Buchanan, Andrew Johnson, Ulysses S. Grant, and Warren G. Harding, with Franklin Pierce always a possible fifth. In every case it was not personal sins—sins of the flesh—that destroyed them but political sins. Buchanan made great pretensions to public morality, announcing that he would receive no gift, however small. But as C. Vann Woodward has written, during his administration "corruption of the public press and the election process and of government agencies was uncovered in appalling amounts. Buchanan had made no serious attempt to stop known malfeasance in custom houses, navy yards, post office and public printing contracts, and he vehemently resisted congressional investigation." Moreover, his failure to stop the seceding states from taking federally owned forts, mints, ammunition dumps, and ships into the Confederacy—his indulgence in passivity, handwringing and praying instead of Jacksonian action in the face of the breakup of the Union—can more properly be described not as political sin but as political imbecility.

Andrew Johnson, obstinately racist, refused to accept the political and civil rights for black people which the Republican Party believed them entitled to as a result of the Civil War, and vetoed bill after bill written to ensure these rights, including what became the great Fourteenth Amendment. He went so far in distortion of political reality as to place the blame for a massacre of over forty blacks in New Orleans in 1866, carried out by the city police, upon the radical wing of the Republican Party in Congress. For this and numerous other acts that were deemed political sin at the time, he was impeached, but in the Senate trial he failed to be convicted, the decision hanging on a single vote. Harding, like Grant, seems not to have been personally corrupt, but tried to hide the corruption of his aides, and his reputation was shattered in their trials after his death. Three of his appointees, including one cabinet officer, went to jail, and his attorney general barely escaped the same fate.

Some presidents have one or two stains on a record otherwise exemplary, like Franklin D. Roosevelt and his internment of the west coast Japanese during World War II, or his failure to lend greater assistance to the European Jews during Hitler's reign of terror. John Adams, who had been called by Jefferson "the colossus" of the Continental Congress, damaged his record in history by encouraging the passage of the notorious Alien and Sedition Acts, gross violations of the Bill of Rights. The Alien Act discriminated against refugees from the French Revolution, whom Adams feared as anarchists, and the Sedition Act made it a criminal offense to criticize the president. During Adams' term several editors and one member of Congress went to jail. Historians abominate the Acts but are gentler with Adams than one might expect, pointing out that like many patriots of his day he retained a fondness for certain practices of the British monarchy. He wanted George Washington to be called His Most Benign Highness, an idea Washington thought preposterous. And he believed in all good faith that the president should be above political attack, like the British king. Later he ruefully admitted his error.

President James K. Polk, who was so scrupulous about accepting gifts that he would accept nothing worth more than the price of a book or a cane, nevertheless told one lie which in its consequences was more momentous even than Lyndon Johnson's celebrated deception concerning the attack on a United States warship in the Gulf of Tonkin. Polk told the American people that Mexican soldiers had attacked United States troops on our own soil. Actually our soldiers had crossed the border into Mexico. But Polk was bent on war, and who now living in California, New Mexico, Arizona, Utah, or Nevada would penalize him for mendacity if he could?

The most consistent presidential sin in the eyes of many historians and practically all blacks and American Indians has been the sin of racism. A new word, but an old concept, and certainly in today's world among the young a consequential—if not mortal—sin. All our presidents have been guilty of some racist statements and only a handful have seriously urged legislation on behalf of blacks or Indians. Although every president from Washington to John Quincy Adams favored emancipation, none worked actively for it. Andrew Jackson set a new trend by openly defending slavery, and he violated the First Amendment by permitting his Postmaster General to confiscate abolitionist literature. His active participation in the destruction of the American Indians makes for chilling reading.

No president between Jackson and Lincoln lifted a finger for black people. Lincoln did far more for them than any president, but it is one of the exasperating ironies of our own day that no president is under so much attack for his so-called racism as the Great Emancipator. Militant modern denunciations are based on a highly selective reading of the Lincoln record, with emphasis on a few unfortunate statements made during the Lincoln-Douglas debates. There is in truth ambivalence in the Lincoln record of spoken words, but the chronicle of Lincoln action, which is generally ignored, remains the most heartening record of liberation in our history save for the American Revolution itself.

The most sobering presidential sin in our own time is not racism—which is always with us—but the enormity of the Vietnam War. Whether historians in the end will agree that it was or was not totally evil depends in part on whether or not democracy ever comes to South Vietnam. At the moment nothing could seem less likely. Even with a non-Communist government it has not yet come to South Korea. The war destroyed Lyndon Johnson as president and clouded a reputation that might have been excellent. The historical judgment on Richard Nixon as peacemaker in Indochina, presently controversial, will depend ultimately on whether or not historians agree that four years was a long time for getting us removed from a small but hideously costly war which we never should have entered at all.

If Thomas Jefferson and the other founding fathers were able to look at the Vietnam record in its entirety they would, one suspects, be more appalled by it than by anything in our history. They would be outraged to see that the war-making power had been usurped from the Congress by the president, and that Congress itself had permitted 57,000 Americans to die in a war it had never declared. Taking the war-making power out of the hands of the king—or chief executive of the state—and giving it to Congress, theoretically to the people, had been one of the great triumphs of the American Constitution.

Jefferson as president managed with what Henry Adams called his "genius for peace" to keep the young republic out of the Napoleonic wars, which Madison did not. He counselled against involvement in what we call the War of 1812 right up to the moment of Madison's declaration, and in words that suggest what he might say were he now alive and faced with the debacle in Indochina:

> For us to attempt, by war, to reform all Europe, and bring them back to the principles of mortality, and a respect for the equal rights of nations, would show us to be only maniacs of another character. We should indeed have the merit of the good intentions as well as the folly of the hero of La Mancha.

It is fair to assume that he would have had from the beginning a certain sympathy with the anti-colonial revolution in Vietnam. He would also have detested Communist tyranny, and been torn by the dilemma all Americans faced. But I suspect that he might well have agreed with one of the later counsels of John F. Kennedy, that for the United States it is imperative not that we try to save the whole world from Communism, but only that we "make the world safe for diversity."

Richard Nixon's orchestration of lying in the secret bombing of Cambodia before our so-called "incursion" of that unfortunate small state—lying that also involved men in the departments of State and Defense, generals as well as pilots, and that included fabrication of reports, lying to the press, to members of Congress and to all the American people—would, one suspects, have horrified Jefferson far more than Watergate. Let us remember that Jefferson, in his first great letter to King George III deploring the abuses of the British ministers, "A Summary View of the Rights of British America," a paper that got him on the enemies list in London, wrote, "The whole art of government is the art of being honest." Later, in a letter to his nephew, Peter Carr, he said:

> ...he who permits himself to tell a lie once, finds it much easier to do it a second time, and a third time, till at length it becomes habitual; he tells lies without attending to it, and truths without the world's believing him. This falsehood of the tongue leads to falsehood of the heart, and in time depraves all its good dispositions.

Thus we return to the rich old concepts, "falsehood of the heart" and "death of the soul." In Richard Nixon I believe we have had both. And we have had something in addition, and intimately related to them—the odor of psychopathology. The constitution, with its various amendments, was written with considerable skill to control the abuse of power in the president, but it was not written to control the problem of psychopathology. Even though King George III was mad in 1789 when the constitution was being written—mad from a disease we now know as an inherited defect of metabolism called porphyria—no one in the young American republic seemed seriously concerned about madness in a future president. In our own time Dr. Arnold Hutschnecker, Nixon's New York physician, who later became a psychiatrist but who has denied treating Nixon for anything but "how to deal with the stresses of his office" as vice-president, wrote an illuminating article in the *New York Times* of July 4, 1973. He described "frightened small men," men who "seem to have difficulty in dealing with the first law of morality: 'Truth' "—men of emotional immaturity, with "an obvious identification with an image of power," men whose own "voracious ambition or irrational fears of imaginary attacks cause them to plot holy wars in the name of self-defense." Although ostensibly he was writing about Nixon's staff, and not the president, such lines could seem to constitute a thinly transparent and frightening diagnosis of Nixon himself. Dr. Hutschnecker in his recently published *Drive for Power* tells us that Nixon's political advisers recommended that he stop treating the vice-president, and that "Mr. Nixon and I yielded." In several articles written during Nixon's presidency he urged that a resident psychiatrist be retained at the White House. Nobody seems to have realized that the doctor may have been trying, within the severe limitations of the doctor-patient confidential relationship, to warn the nation about our president's mental health.

Obviously no historians will have, or should have, access to any of Nixon's psychiatric records. But they should bring to the study of the president some understanding of the clinical significance of wholesale lying, especially when it is accompanied by an almost obsessive reiteration that one is telling the truth. Someone must explain how the president could say to Rabbi Baruch Korff at late as May 13, 1974:

> ... The most important factor is that the individual must know, deep inside, that he is right. He must believe that. If, for example,

these charges on the Watergate and the coverup, et cetera, were true, nobody would have to ask me to resign. I wouldn't serve for one minute if they were true. But I know they are not true, and therefore I will stay here....

Even in his farewell speech to his staff, the morning after his resignation, Nixon said:

> No man or no woman ever came into this administration and left it with more of the world's goods than when he came in. No man or no woman ever profited at the public expense or the public till.... Mistakes yes. But for personal gain, never.

Not Agnew. Not himself. Denial of the ugly about himself, long a political technique, had now accelerated into an almost total denial of reality.

Who is to resolve the multiple contradictions and paradoxes? With no president has there been such a huge disparity between word and deed. None has used the word truth so often, and left such a reputation for untruth. This president, who used the words "law and order" more than any other, has ended up presiding over the greatest breakdown of law and order the executive branch of our government has ever seen. How did it happen that it was our Quaker president who chose to decorate his presidential office with 307 battle streamers, commemorating battles from Ticonderoga to Vietnam? That it was our Quaker president who said repeatedly, "Amnesty, never!" for the traditional Quaker heroes, the men who will not fight in war?

It was our Quaker president who ordered more bombs dropped than any man in history. And it was he who, in ordering the Christmas carpet bombing of North Vietnam, said to his aides, "Try and get the weather, damn it, if any of you know of any prayers, say them. Let's get the weather cleared up. The bastards have never been bombed like they're going to be bombed this time."

There has been much speculation about the self-destructive as well as the destructive impulses in Richard Nixon. By his failure to destroy the tapes it would seem that he had indeed programmed himself for his Luciferian fall. As T. R. B. put it in *The New Republic* of August 24, 1974, "Nobody has so trapped himself for self-destruction since Shylock and his pound of flesh." These thin strips of tape like the microfilm that convicted Hiss of perjury and catapulted Nixon into the vice-presidency, are intricately bound up with his own doom.

After the resignation Rev. Joseph S. Stephens, pastor of the San Clemente Presbyterian Church, observed that "God has a tape recorder of all that is going on." The idea of a deity keeping a record in heaven as a tool for future punishment is as old as it is primitive. Arthur Miller has already speculated that Nixon, in taping himself, might have desired not only to have a secure weapon against betrayal but also to "monumentalize himself" by playing God. Nixon, he wrote, in partaking secretly of "that godhead which remembers everything thereby holds control." There is evidence in the farewell speech that Nixon had enjoyed active fantasies of omnipotence. In apologizing to his cabinet and staff for his former aloofness, he said, "I should have been by your offices and shaking hands and I'd love to have talked to you and found out how to run the world." Not run the country, but *run the world*.

But there is great danger in believing that the past was inevitable. The psychobiographers in particular must remember Freud's warning, "It takes a sophisticated person to believe in chance." Of all our presidents none has been so importantly affected by accident as Richard Nixon. Without the accidents of two assassinations he would never have become president. The accidents of Watergate—the crude tape on the door noticed by Frank Wills, the alert night watchman, the failure of E. Howard Hunt's walkie-talkie, and later the accident of the offhand question to Alexander Butterfield that revealed the existence of the tapes—these were the little accidents that led to the toppling of the king.

Still, the historian must not ignore Plutarch's dictum that character is fate. Nixon had options almost to the date of his resignation. Exactly how it happened remains to be explored, but the historians must record that it was the same man who as an ebullient candidate in 1968 promised us at Miami Beach to "find the truth, to speak the truth and to live the truth," in the end, by not destroying the tapes, gave us the truth about the worst of himself.

The self-hatred of Richard Nixon may ultimately prove to be the most significant clue to the cause, evolution, and nature of his presidential sins. Someone, perhaps Nixon himself in his memoirs, will explain why, three and one half years after winning one of the largest landslides in United States electoral history, he could say to John Dean, "Nobody is a friend of ours. Let's face it." He gave us an indirect answer to this mystery in his farewell speech when he said, "Never be petty, always remember that others may hate you but those who hate you don't win, unless you hate them. And then you destroy yourself."

To hate is not one of the seven deadly sins. Nor is it expressly forbidden in the Ten Commandments. But it is certainly a Quaker sin.

A final general word about presidential sin. The one-hundred-eighty-six year record, except in regard to racism, is astonishingly good. Very few presidents have lied to the American people on important issues, and over the years there have been indefatigable journalists and historians, as well as enemies of the presidents, who have been keeping a record. Still so pervasive is our cynicism today that a poll taken in early

1975 showed 69% of Americans believing that their government consistently lies to them. Whether this is alarming or healthy will depend on the nature of the reforms growing out of the Nixon presidency. As Tom Paine put it long ago, "Those who expect to reap the blessing of freedom must, like men, undergo the fatigue of supporting it."

Jefferson, suspicious though he was of men in power, could write cheerfully to John Adams October 28, 1813, of the American people, "In general they will elect the really good and wise." Later, January 6, 1816, he wrote to Charles Yancey, "Where the press is free, and every man is able to read, all is safe." This should be amended for our own time, "*If* the press is free, and every man *does* read, all is safe." Perhaps, too, we should read not only what is in the newspapers but also something about the psychopathology of lying. Just to be safer.

35

The Counter-Culture

William L. O'Neill

The sixties and early seventies was a time of profound change in fashions, artistic expression, and sexual behavior not just in America, but in Europe as well. Except that in America the changes did not suddenly begin in 1960. As William O'Neill makes clear, the so-called counter-culture ("a vague and elastic substitute" for youth culture or youth rebellion against "The Establishment") grew out of the bohemian life-style of the previous decade. In a larger sense, the counter-culture had roots that stretched back to the revolution in manners and morals during the 1920s, a rebellion described by Frederick Lewis Allen earlier in this volume. In fact, if one reads Allen's and O'Neill's accounts together, one gets a tremendous sense of historical continuity. For the Charleston, the saxophone, the bobbed hair, the short skirts, the gin and cigarettes —weapons of revolt during the twenties—were forerunners of the frug, the electric guitar, the long hair, the mini-skirts, and the drugs which characterize the counter-culture revolt of our time. Although O'Neill does not hazard such a comparison, he has written a sparkling narrative, with enough opinions about heroes and happenings in the counter-culture that most readers can find something here that will make them angry.

Counter-culture as a term appeared rather late in the decade. It largely replaced the term "youth culture," which finally proved too limited. When the sixties began, youth culture meant the way adolescents lived. Its central institutions were the high school and the mass media. Its principal activities were consuming goods and enacting courtship rituals. Critics and students of the youth culture were chiefly interested in the status and value systems associated with it. As time went on, college enrollments increased to the point where colleges were nearly as influential as high schools in shaping the young. The molders of youthful opinion got more ambitious. Where once entertainers were content to amuse for profit, many began seeing themselves as moral philosophers. Music especially became a medium of propaganda, identifying the young as a distinct force in society with unique values and aspirations. This helped produce a kind of ideological struggle between the young and their elders called the "generation gap." It was the first time in American history that social conflict was understood to be a function of age. Yet the young were not all rebellious. Most in fact retained confidence in the "system" and its norms. Many older people joined the rebellion, whose progenitors were as often over thirty (where the generation gap was supposed to begin) as under it. The attack on accepted views and styles broadened so confusingly that "youth culture" no longer described it adequately. Counter-culture was a sufficiently vague and elastic substitute. It meant all things to all men and embraced everything new from clothing to politics. Some viewed the counter-culture as mankind's best, maybe only, hope; others saw it as a portent of civilization's im-

---

Reprinted by permission of Quadrangle Books from *Coming Apart: An Informal History of America in the 1960's* by William L. O'Neill, copyright © 1971 by William L. O'Neill.

minent ruin. Few recalled the modest roots from which it sprang.

Even in the 1950's and very early sixties, when people still worried about conformity and the silent generation, there were different drummers to whose beat millions would one day march. The bohemians of that era (called "beatniks" or "beats") were only a handful, but they practiced free love, took drugs, repudiated the straight world, and generally showed which way the wind was blowing. They were highly publicized, so when the bohemian impulse strengthened, dropouts knew what was expected of them. While the beats showed their contempt for social norms mostly in physical ways, others did so intellectually. Norman Mailer, in "The White Negro," held up the sensual, lawless hipster as a model of behavior under oppressive capitalism. He believed, according to "The Time of Her Time," that sexual orgasm was the pinnacle of human experience, perhaps also an approach to ultimate truth. Norman O. Brown's *Life Against Death*, a psychoanalytic interpretation of history, was an underground classic which argued that cognition subverted intuition. Brown called for a return to "polymorphous perversity," man's natural estate. The popularity of Zen Buddhism demonstrated that others wished to slip the bonds of Western rationalism; so, from a different angle, did the vogue for black humor.

The most prophetic black humorist was Joseph Heller, whose novel *Catch-22* came out in 1960. Though set in World War II the book was even more appropriate to the Indochinese war. Later Heller said, "That was the war I had in mind; a war fought without military provocation, a war in which the real enemy is no longer the other side, but someone allegedly on your side. The ridiculous war I felt lurking in the future when I wrote the book." *Catch-22* was actually written during the Cold War, and sold well in the early sixties because it attacked the perceptions on which that war, like the Indochinese war that it fathered, grew. At the time reviewers didn't know what to make of *Catch-22*. World War II had been, as everyone knew, an absolutely straightforward case of good versus evil. Yet to Heller there was little moral difference between combatants. In fact all his characters are insane, or carry normal attributes to insane lengths. They belong to a bomber squadron in the Mediterranean. Terrified of combat, most hope for ground duty and are free to request it, but: "There was only one catch and that was Catch-22, which specified that a concern for one's own safety in the face of dangers that were real and immediate was the process of a rational mind. Orr was crazy and could be grounded. All he had to do was ask; and as soon as he did, he would no longer be crazy and would have to fly more missions. Orr would be crazy to fly more missions and sane if he didn't, but if he was sane he had to fly them. If he flew them he was crazy and didn't have to; but if he didn't want to he was sane and had to."

The squadron's success depends more on having a perfect bomb pattern than hitting the target. Milo Minderbinder is the key man in the Theater, though only a lieutenant, because he embodies the profit motive. He puts the entire war on a paying basis and hires the squadron out impartially to both sides. At the end Yossarian, the novel's hero, resolves his dilemma by setting out for neutral Sweden in a rubber raft. This was what hundreds of real deserters and draft evaders would be doing soon. It was also a perfect symbol for the masses of dropouts who sought utopian alternatives to the straight world. One day there would be hundreds of thousands of Yossarians, paddling away from the crazed society in frail crafts of their own devising. *Catch-22* was not just black comedy, nor even chiefly an anti-war novel, but a metaphor that helped shape the moral vision of an era.*

Although children and adolescents watched a great deal of television in the sixties, it seemed at first to have little effect. Surveys were always showing that youngsters spent fifty-four hours a week or whatever in front of the tube, yet what they saw was so bland or predictable as to make little difference. The exceptions were news programs, documentaries, and dramatic specials. Few watched them. What did influence the young was popular music, folk music first and then rock. Large-scale enthusiasm for folk music began in 1958 when the Kingston Trio recorded a song, "Tom Dooley," that sold two million records. This opened the way for less slickly commercial performers. Some, like Pete Seeger, who had been singing since the depression, were veteran performers. Others, like Joan Baez, were newcomers. It was conventional for folk songs to tell a story. Hence the idiom had always lent itself to propaganda. Seeger possessed an enormous repertoire of message songs that had gotten him blacklisted by the mass media years before. Joan Baez cared more for the message than the music, and after a few years devoted herself mainly to peace work. The folk-music vogue was an early stage in the politicalization of youth, a forerunner of the counter-culture. This was hardly apparent at the time. Folk music was not seen as morally reprehensible in the manner of rock and roll. It was a familiar genre. Folk was gentle music for the most part, and even when sung in protest did not offend many. Malvina Reynolds' "What Have They Done to the Rain?" complained of radioactive fallout which all detested. Pete Seeger's anti-war song "Where Have All the Flowers Gone?" was a favorite with both pacifists and the troops in Vietnam.

Bob Dylan was different. Where most folk singers were either clean-cut or homey looking, Dylan had wild long hair. He resembled a poor white dropout of questionable morals. His songs were hard-driving, powerful, intense. It was hard to be neutral about them. "The Times They Are a-Changing" was perhaps the first song to exploit the generation gap. Dylan's life was as controversial as his ideology. Later he dropped politics and got interested in rock music. At the Newport Jazz Festival in 1965 he was booed when he introduced a fusion of his own called "folk-rock." He went his own way after that, disowned by the politically minded but admired by a great cult following attracted as much, perhaps, by his independent life as by his music. He advanced the counter-culture in both ways and made money too. This also was an inspiration to those who came after him.

Another early expression, which coexisted with folk music, though quite unlike it, was the twist. Dance crazes were nothing new, but the twist was remarkable because it came to dominate social dancing. It used to be that dance fads were here today and gone tomorrow, while the two-step went on forever. Inexpert, that is to say most, social dancers had been loyal to it for generations. It played a key role in the traditional youth culture. Who could imagine a high school athletic event that did not end with couples clinging to one another on the dimly lit gym floor, while an amateur dance band plodded gamely on? When in 1961 the twist became popular, moralists were alarmed. It called for vigorous, exhibitionistic movements. Prurient men were reminded of the stripper's bumps and grinds. They felt the twist incited lust. Ministers denounced it. Yet in the twist (and its numerous descendants), bodies were not rubbed together as in the two-step,

---

* Lenny Bruce was a more tragic harbinger of change. He was a successful night club comedian who created an obscene form of black comedy that involved more social criticism than humor. Bruce was first arrested for saying "motherfucker" on stage in 1962. Later he was busted for talking dirty about the Pope and many lesser offenses. He may have been insane. He died early from persecution and drug abuse, and then became an honored martyr in the anti-Establishment pantheon. He was one of the spiritual fathers of the yippies.

which had embarrassed millions of schoolboys. Millions more had suffered when through awkwardness they bumped or trod on others. The twist, by comparison, was easy and safe. No partner was bothered by the other's maladroitness. It aroused few passions. That was the practical reason for its success. But there was an ideological impulse behind it also. Amidst the noise and tumult each person danced alone, "doing his own thing," as would soon be said. But though alone, the dancer was surrounded by others doing their own thing in much the same manner. The twist celebrated both individuality and communality. This was to become a hallmark of the counter-culture, the right of everyone to be different in much the same way. The twist also foretold the dominance of rock, to which it was so well suited.

No group contributed more to the counter-culture than the Beatles, though, like folk music and the twist, their future significance was not at first apparent. Beatlemania began on October 13, 1963, when the quartet played at the London Palladium. The police, caught unawares, were hardly able to control the maddened throngs. On February 9, 1964, they appeared on U.S. television. The show received fifty thousand ticket requests for a theater that seated eight hundred. They were mobbed at the airport, besieged in their hotel, and adored everywhere. Even their soiled bed linen found a market. Their next recording, "Can't Buy Me Love," sold three million copies in advance of release, a new world's record. Their first movie, *A Hard Day's Night* (1964), was both a critical and a popular success. Some reviewers compared them with the Marx brothers. They became millionaires overnight. The Queen decorated them for helping ease the balance-of-payments deficit. By 1966 they were so rich that they could afford to give up live performances.

For a time the Beatles seemed just another pop phenomenon, Elvis Presley multiplied by four. Few thought their music very distinguished. The reasons for its wide acceptance were hard to fathom. Most felt their showmanship was the key factor. They wore their hair longer than was fashionable, moved about a lot on stage, and avoided the class and racial identifications associated with earlier rock stars. Elvis had cultivated a proletarian image. Other rock stars had been black, or exploited the Negro rhythm-and-blues tradition. The Beatles were mostly working class in origin but sang with an American accent (like other English rock stars) and dressed in an elegant style, then popular in Britain, called "mod." The result was a deracinated, classless image of broad appeal.

The Beatles did not fade away as they were supposed to. Beatlemania continued for three years. Then the group went through several transformations that narrowed its audience to a smaller but intensely loyal cult following in the Dylan manner. The group became more self-consciously artistic. Their first long-playing record took one day to make and cost £400. "Sergeant Pepper's Lonely Hearts Club Band" took four months and cost £25,000. They were among the first to take advantage of new recording techniques that enabled multiple sound tracks to be played simultaneously. The Beatles learned new instruments and idioms too. The result was a complex music that attracted serious inquiry. Critics debated their contributions to musicology and argued over whether they were pathfinders or merely gifted entrepreneurs. In either case, they had come a long way aesthetically from their humble beginnings. Their music had a great effect on the young, so did their styles of life. They led the march of fashion away from mod and into the hairy, mustached, bearded, beaded, fringed, and embroidered costumes of the late sixties. For a time they followed the Maharishi, an Indian guru of some note. They married and divorced in progressively more striking ways.

Some were arrested for smoking marijuana. In this too they were faithful to their clientele.

John Lennon went the farthest. He married Yoko Ono, best known as an author of happenings, and with her launched a bizarre campaign for world peace and goodness. Lennon returned his decoration to the Queen in protest against the human condition. Lennon and Ono hoped to visit America but were denied entry, which, to the bureaucratic mind, seemed a stroke for public order and morality. They staged a bed-in for peace all the same. They also formed a musical group of their own, the Plastic Ono Band, and circulated nude photographs and erotic drawings of themselves. This seemed an odd way to stop the war in Indochina, even to other Beatles. The group later broke up. By then they had made their mark, and, while strange, it was not a bad mark. Whatever lasting value their music may have, they set a good example to the young in most ways. Lennon's pacifism was nonviolent, even if wildly unorthodox. At a time when so many pacifists were imitating what they protested against, that was most desirable. They also worked hard at their respective arts and crafts, though others were dropping out and holding up laziness as a socially desirable trait. The Beatles showed that work was not merely an Establishment trick to keep the masses in subjection and the young out of trouble.

Beatlemania coincided with a more ominous development in the emerging counter-culture—the rise of the drug prophet Timothy Leary. He and Richard Alpert were scientific researchers at Harvard University who studied the effects of hallucinogenic drugs, notably a compound called LSD. As early as 1960 it was known that the two were propagandists as well as scientists. In 1961 the University Health Service made them promise not to use undergraduates in their experiments. Their violation of this pledge was the technical ground for firing them. A better one was that they had founded a drug cult. Earlier studies of LSD had failed, they said, because the researchers had not themselves taken the drug. In order to end this "authoritarian" practice, they "turned on" themselves. Their work was conducted in quarters designed to look like a bohemian residence instead of a laboratory. This was defended as a reconstruction of the natural environment in which social "acid-dropping" took place. They and many of their subjects became habitual users, not only of LSD but of marijuana and other drugs. They constructed an ideology of sorts around this practice. After they were fired the *Harvard Review* published an article of theirs praising the drug life: "Remember, man, a natural state is ecstatic wonder, ecstatic intuition, ecstatic accurate movement. Don't settle for less."

With some friends Leary and Alpert created the International Foundation for Internal Freedom (IF-IF) which published the *Psychedelic Review*. To advertise it a flyer was circulated that began, "Mescaline! Experimental Mysticism! Mushrooms! Ecstasy! LSD-25! Expansion of Consciousness! Phantastica! Transcendence! Hashish! Visionary Botany! Ololiuqui! Physiology of Religion! Internal Freedom! Morning Glory! Politics of the Nervous System!" Later the drug culture would generate a vast literature, but this was its essential message. The truth that made Western man free was only obtainable through hallucinogenic drugs. Truth was in the man, not the drug, yet the drug was necessary to uncover it. The natural state of man thus revealed was visionary, mystical, ecstatic. The heightened awareness stimulated by "consciousness-expanding" drugs brought undreamed-of sensual pleasures, according to Leary. Even better, drugs promoted peace, wisdom, and unity with the universe.

Alpert soon dropped from view. Leary went on to found his own sect, partly because once

LSD was banned religious usage was the only ground left on which it could be defended, mostly because the drug cult *was* a religion. He wore long white robes and long blond hair. And he traveled about the country giving his liberating message (tune in, turn on, drop out) and having bizarre adventures. His personal following was never large, but drug use became commonplace among the young anyway. At advanced universities social smoking of marijuana was as acceptable as social drinking. More so, in a way, for it was better suited to the new ethic. One did not clutch one's solitary glass but shared one's "joint" with others. "Grass" made one gentle and pacific, not surly and hostile. As a forbidden pleasure it was all the more attractive to the thrill-seeking and the rebellious. And it helped further distinguish between the old world of grasping, combative, alcoholic adults and the turned-on, cooperative culture of the young. Leary was a bad prophet. Drug-based mystical religion was not the wave of the future. What the drug cult led to was a lot of dope-smoking and some hard drug-taking. When research suggested that LSD caused genetic damage, its use declined. But the effects of grass were hard to determine, so its consumption increased.

Sometimes "pot" smokers went on to other drugs—a deadly compound called "speed," and even heroin. These ruined many lives (though it was never clear that the lives were not already ruined to begin with). The popularity of drugs among the young induced panic in the old. States passed harsher and harsher laws that accomplished little. Campaigns against the drug traffic were launched periodically with similar results. When the flow of grass was interrupted, people turned to other drugs. Drug use seemed to go up either way. The generation gap widened. Young people thought marijuana less dangerous than alcohol, perhaps rightly. To proscribe the one and permit the other made no sense to them, except as still another example of adult hypocrisy and the hatred of youth. Leary had not meant all this to happen, but he was to blame for some of it all the same. No one did more to build the ideology that made pot-smoking a morally constructive act. But though a malign influence, no one deserved such legal persecution as he experienced before escaping to Algeria from a prison farm.

In Aldous Huxley's prophetic novel *Brave New World,* drug use was promoted by the state as a means of social control. During the sixties it remained a deviant practice and a source of great tension between the generations. Yet drugs did encourage conformity among the young. To "turn on and drop out" did not weaken the state. Quite the contrary, it drained off potentially subversive energies. The need for drugs gave society a lever should it ever decide to manipulate rather than repress users. Pharmacology and nervous strain had already combined to make many adult Americans dependent on drugs like alcohol and tranquilizers. Now the young were doing the same thing, if for different reasons. In a free country this meant only that individual problems increased. But should democracy fail, drug abuse among both the young and old was an instrument for control such as no dictator ever enjoyed. The young drug-takers thought to show contempt for a grasping, unfeeling society. In doing so they opened the door to a worse one. They scorned their elders for drinking and pill-taking, yet to outsiders their habits seemed little different, though ethically more pretentious. In both cases users were vulnerable and ineffective to the extent of their addiction. Of such ironies was the counter-culture built.

Another sign of things to come was the rise and fall of Ken Kesey and his Merry Pranksters. Kesey graduated from college in Oregon in 1958 and came to Stanford University. There he studied creative writing and absorbed the local bohemian atmosphere, which was still pretty traditional. People drank wine, lamented the sad state of American culture, and looked to Europe for relief in the classic manner. Kesey found work in a mental hospital, which was the subject of his first published novel, *One Flew over the Cuckoo's Nest*. It enjoyed a great success in 1962. He also figured in medical experiments conducted at the hospital. One of the drugs tested on him was LSD. Soon he was moving in psychedelic drug circles. In 1963, with the profits from his book, he bought a log house and some land near La Honda, about fifteen miles from Palo Alto.

Among the restless types who joined him was Neal Cassidy, a legendary figure who had been the model for Dean Moriarty in Jack Kerouac's famous beat-generation novel *On the Road*. The Merry Pranksters, as they became known, developed a unique life style. Sex played a part in it (a lean-to called the Screw Shack was added to the cabin for this purpose), but music and drugs more so. Everyone was also involved in The Movie—a continuing film record of their experiences. In the spring of 1964 the Pranksters bought a school bus, fitted it out with camping facilities, loaded the refrigerator with orange juice and acid, painted it in psychedelic colors, wired it for sound, and set off for the World's Fair in New York. One freaked out along the way (suffered a drug-induced breakdown) and was lost, but the rest made it to New York and then to Timothy Leary's borrowed estate in Millbrook. Leary refused to see them, but the contrast in drug subcultures was strikingly demonstrated all the same. Leary's League for Spiritual Discovery was cool and devotional. He was, literally, the high priest of a religious movement. The Pranksters were hot and crazy on principle. They visited the meditation rooms in Leary's basement and promptly termed it the Crypt Trip. They also made fun of the Tibetan Book of the Dead, one of the Learyites' most revered texts. Though a fiasco in one sense, the trip to New York helped define the Pranksters' secular identity in the semi-mystical drug world.

They went back to La Honda and wired it ever more extravagantly for light and sound. The Movie got more elaborate. The group expanded. Then, on April 23, 1965, they entered history with the most psychedelic drug bust ever. The county sheriff, federal agent Wong, eight police dogs, and wave upon wave of cops and squad cars stormed La Honda and arrested thirteen unarmed drug freaks. Eventually charges were dropped against all but Kesey, who was tagged for possession of marijuana. Overnight his status as a folk hero was established. In August he went so far as to invite the Hell's Angels to La Honda, and to everyone's amazement the visit came off nicely. There was only one gang-bang, and that voluntary. The Angels left without smashing everything up, even though high on beer and acid. It was practically an unnatural event. Soon after, Kesey was invited to the annual California Unitarian Church conference, where he seduced the young and appalled the old. An appearance at Berkeley's Vietnam Day in October was less successful. He had a theory about ending the war by having everyone turn his back on it. The Vietnam Day Committee thought stronger measures were in order.

What really put Kesey at the center of the new culture, however, were the "acid tests." These were big public gatherings with light shows, rock music, mad dancing, and, of course, acid-dropping. "Can you pass the acid test?" was their motto. These were the first important multimedia happenings, combining light shows, tapes, live rock bands, movie and slide projectors, strobe lights, and other technical gimmicks. Their climax was reached at the San Francisco Tripps Festival in January 1966. It was meant to release all the new forms of expression in the cultural underground. Bill Graham, who had managed the San Francisco

Mime Troupe, was its organizer. Kesey and the Pranksters gave the acid test. The Tripps Festival was a great success. Several rock groups (The Grateful Dead and Big Brother and the Holding Company) proclaimed the emergence of a new musical genre—acid rock. Graham began staging such affairs regularly in the Fillmore Auditorium in San Francisco. Out of this came the "San Francisco Sound," which made the city a provincial capital in the music industry. Hippie culture, with its drugs, rock groups, psychedelic folk art, and other apparatus, was well and truly launched.

None of this did Kesey himself much good. Just before the Tripps Festival he was arrested for possession again. To escape a stiff jail term he fled to Mexico. Thereafter the new culture had to do without him. Mexico was a bad trip and he returned a chastened man. He talked about "going beyond acid" and gave a poorly received Acid Test Graduation. Many thought he was just copping out to avoid prison. Thanks to good lawyers and hung juries he finally got only six months at a work camp near his old place in La Honda. On being released he went back to Oregon with his family and started another novel. (His third. The second, *Sometimes a Great Notion*, was published while he was still a Prankster. It is a lovely book, though not so successful as his first.)

Kesey was not well known outside of California at the time except as a novelist. He owed his nonliterary folk-freak reputation to Tom Wolfe's book *The Electric Kool-Aid Acid Test*, which came out afterward. Hence Kesey was not so much influential as archetypal. His progression from student to artist to acidhead and crazy commune leader to jail and repentance was a course many would later take, in part anyway. He foreshadowed the hippies and yippies. He also showed how hazardous the psychedelic drug life was. Kesey lost his freedom for a while, and only time would tell what remained of his talent. Yet the somber end of his trip did not have much effect. The local media gave his revels much publicity, their dénouement relatively little. Wolfe, his Boswell, added to the Kesey legend by writing it up in the breathless, adulatory, highly colored prose of the "new journalism." It made insanity seem romantic and the tawdry glamorous. Nothing contemporary was alien to it if sufficiently bizarre, Wolfe's book was a best-seller. Kesey's activities sold a lot of newspapers. Everyone made money from his adventures but Kesey himself. This moral was not lost on the folk heroes who came after him. A striking feature of the mature counter-culture was the facility with which its leading figures made deviance pay off, usually by writing nonbooks. Even so, their profits were small compared with what the rock kings made.

Though Kesey and his friends had different hopes for it, the Tripps Festival proved to be a turning point in the history of rock. Bill Graham and other promoters took the idea and institutionalized it. Rock and light shows attracted big audiences for years afterward and helped launch counter-cultural music groups into the pop culture mainstream. "Acid rock" and such brought deviant values to a national audience. Sex, dope, and anti-social notions became so common that many radio disc jockeys finally gave up trying to censor the music, though TV managed to stay pure. Radio did try to draw the line at revolutionary exhortations. Thus in 1968 many disc jockeys played the Beatles' "Revolution No. 1" because of its counterrevolutionary lyrics ("But if you're carrying a picture of Chairman Mao, you ain't going to make it with anyone anyhow") but did not play the Rolling Stones' rebuttal which insisted that "the time is right for fighting in the streets."

But rock as an idiom was more concerned with social and sexual freedom than politics.

The Rolling Stones' subversive appeal was more formalistic than not. The group's real power derived from its sexuality. Mick Jagger hopped about, whacking the stage with a leather belt. Jim Morrison of the Doors was arrested twice for indecent exposure. More articulate than most rock stars, Morrison described his group's function this way: "A Doors' concert is a public meeting called by us for a special kind of dramatic discussion and entertainment." And, further, "We make concerts sexual politics. The sex starts with me, then moves out to include the charmed circle of musicians on stage. The music we make goes out to the audience and interacts with them: they go home and interact with the rest of reality, then I get it all back by interacting with that reality, so the whole sex thing works out to be one big ball of fire." Their listeners took the message perfectly. Morrison was famous in the rock underground for supposedly being able to hold an erection through a two-hour performance. The performers attracted young camp followers known as "groupies." Something like the bobby-soxers of an earlier day, the groupies were more obviously sensual. One legendary (perhaps mythical) team of groupies, known as the Chicago Plaster Casters, carried rock-phallic worship to its logical conclusion by making plaster casts of the performers' sex organs.

But not all rock fans were overstimulated teenie-boppers. At its most pretentious the cult laid great moral responsibilities on the backs of rock groups. When the Beatles released a new album late in 1968 (called simply "The Beatles"), one student critic announced that having transformed the male image and performed other great services, it was now their duty to "forge a cultural revolution." There was broad agreement on this, but rock revolutionaries differed otherwise. Some thought the Beatles more truly revolutionary than the Rolling Stones, despite the latters' enthusiasm for streetfighting. The San Francisco music critic Ralph Gleason thought that "Revolution No. 1" and its variations proved they had sold out to the Establishment. The Stones were not only ideologically more correct but sexier too. The Beatles' defenders insisted, however, that such songs as "Why Don't We Do It in the Road?" were more profoundly sexual than anything the crude Rolling Stones were capable of.

To see how far the youth culture had progressed in a few years, one had only to compare the careers of Joan Baez and Janis Joplin. Miss Baez remained as delicately beautiful and as clear-voiced as ever. In 1964 she and Bob Dylan had been the "fantasy lovers of the folk revival." But by 1968 her vogue was long since gone. She still sang in much the same manner as before. She was even more dedicated to peace and nonviolence. Miss Baez was a tax resister on moral grounds, and she married a draft resister who went to prison rather than accept induction. Yet neither her music nor her beliefs nor her style of life was "relevant" to young people any longer. The place she once occupied was taken by Janis Joplin, a wholly different kind of woman. Miss Joplin was a hard-drinking, tough-talking, ugly but dynamic power singer with roots in the blues tradition. She became famous as the singer for a San Francisco rock band called Big Brother and the Holding Company. A wild, passionate, totally involved performer, she was not much different as a person. Miss Joplin was what the groupies would have become if talented. She did exactly what she pleased, took lovers freely, owned a psychedelic sports car and a closet full of costumes, and, when her reputation eclipsed that of Big Brother and the Holding Company, struck out on her own. "If I miss," she told a reporter, "I'll never have a second chance on nothing. But I gotta risk it. I never hold back, man. I'm always on the outer limits of probability." What was her philosophy of life? "Getting stoned, staying happy, and having a good time. I'm doing just what I want with my life, enjoying it." She burned her candle at both ends and it did not last the night.

Miss Joplin was far more candid than many rock stars. One of their most tiresome habits was insisting on having it both ways. They wanted to be rich and famous while also radical and culturally momentous. What made the Beatles so attractive was that having become rich beyond the dreams of avarice, they abandoned it. And (Lennon excepted) they did not moralize much, however seriously they took themselves. The Rolling Stones, on the other hand, called for revolution in 1968 and the following year made millions with a whirlwind tour of the U.S. As time went on, the commercial aspects increasingly dominated rock. Few went so far as the coalition of groups in St. Louis who refused demands that they offer free, or at least reduced-price, tickets to the needy because doing so would be contrary to the American principle of free enterprise. But time was on their side. The evolution of the San Francisco Sound showed how quickly culture could give way to commerce. At their inception the hippie rock groups were products of the Haight-Ashbury subculture and dedicated to its precepts. But those who prospered soon succumbed to the cash nexus. Bill Graham got rich from his rock palaces, the Fillmore West in San Francisco and Fillmore East in New York. The Carousel Ballroom in San Francisco, funded by the indigenous Grateful Dead and the Jefferson Airplane, went broke. Before long San Francisco was only a regional music center, the New Rock's Nashville, as one critic put it. It was not so much an independent musical capital as a branch office of the music industry. As rock became less a movement and more a business, its impact, though not its popularity, declined. It seemed unlikely that rock would soon become a television staple. But some day its fans would be middle-aged, so even that possibility could not be permanently excluded.

The counter-culture's influence on fashion was nearly as great as on rock. Fashions began to change radically even before the hippies and other such groups appeared. An early sign of this was Rudi Gernreich's topless bathing suit for women in 1964. Designed more in fun than avarice, this curious garment (knitted trunks suspended from a cord around the neck) actually sold. Only a few gallant models really bared their breasts in public, yet it was clearly an idea whose time had come. Discothèques (night clubs featuring recorded music) were starting up, and they inspired customers with writhing "go-go" girls who demonstrated the new dance routines. Some of these went topless, and before long, in California at least, others followed. The first thing one saw on leaving the Los Angeles airport was a sign reading "Topless Bowling." This did not mean that customers went half-nude but that cocktail waitresses did. Later bottomlessness was added, even in such unlikely places as Madison, Wisconsin. Although only performers went this far, as a rule, a new exposure prevailed. Rudi Gernreich raised his skirts three inches above the knee and introduced the no-bra bra, a wispy creation appropriate to the new designs.

In London things had already gone further. Skirts were so short that some were calling them "mini-skirts." Young designers like Mary Quant were making Carnaby Street synonymous with fashion. The "mod" look would soon reach New York. Bikinis were now seen on American beaches in sizable numbers. Less abbreviated than the European models, they still astonished people accustomed to the reinforced swimsuits of the fifties. Before long they would be standard among girls and young women. The most striking thing about these changes was that they came from below. Fashion had always been dictated from above, by Parisian couturiers and other authorities. It was a monopoly of the rich. But in the sixties it was the young and relatively unknown designers like Quant and Gernreich who catered to them, who set the pace. Young people did the twist first, shortened their skirts first, and made being "kicky" and "switched on" desirable. More expensive versions of their styles were then designed for the modish rich. Not since the 1920's had women's clothing changed so radically. No one could remember when the flow of fashion had been reversed on such a scale.

This was all to the good. Few tendencies in the sixties were entirely wholesome. Some were very dangerous. But the breakdown of fashion authority and the stylistic anarchy that followed were wonderful. While skirts went up, they also went down. When the ankle-length "maxi-skirt" came in, the mini did not go out. The result was that a woman might wear a mini-skirt under a maxi-coat, or a late Victorian top over either length. Hair could be long or short. Necklines might touch the throat or the navel. Every kind of color, pattern, and design flourished. Wigs of many shades followed. Even the sober eyeglass became a fashion accessory, being sometimes huge and dark, other times small and wire-framed. Not everyone made intelligent use of her new freedom. As always in modern times, designers liked the young and thin. Less favored people could not always resist wearing styles inappropriate to them. But only individual bad taste or perversity was responsible for this. Fashion's door opened so wide that, properly worn, almost anything went. Never before had women such a range of garments to choose from. Many, particularly older ones, failed to profit from this. They went on wearing conventional garments whether suited to them or not. It was the rare elderly woman who looked good in deepnecked, bare-armed evening dresses, yet few took advantage of the formal pants suits and party pajamas that enabled older people to be in style without exposing the ravages of time. It was the young, who had no need of them, who ordinarily wore such outfits. The ideal strategy would be to expose oneself when young and firm, and then cover up as needed later. For the first time it became theoretically possible to do this. If such freedom persisted, women might learn to take advantage of it.

By mid-decade even the great couturiers had accepted the new wave. Yves St. Laurent included utterly transparent—save for a few opaque bands—dresses in one collection. Other designers cut large circles out of their garments, usually around the midriff. In 1964 Christian Dior had plunged necklines below the waist. The next year armholes dipped also. André Courrèges developed the first true pop-fashion line. It involved white boots, zombie glasses, astronaut baby bonnets, and a short, boxy silhouette in stark white, pastel, or checked fabrics. One critic thought it resembled architecture more than textiles.

Few girls next door wore clothes that extreme. But in modified and low-priced versions the new styles were very popular. Mini-skirts became common. With them girls wore knee boots and short A-line coats. Boots made whips a suitable fashion accessory. Sadomasochism in dress was further encouraged by one firm which sold a leather or vinyl garment called "The Story of O" dress, after a chic pornographic novel by that name. Betsy Johnson developed the do-it-yourself dress, a clear plastic shell with separate designs to be stuck on as the wearer pleased.

Male clothing changed too. In 1962 Cardin introduced a male line to complement his clothes for women. At first his tight-waisted, long-jacketed suits seemed peculiar. Only the slightly precious wore them. The Beatles helped change that in 1964 with their Prince Valiant hairdos, suits buttoned to the chin, visored caps, and extravagant haberdashery. Though they later went hippie, the original effect persisted. Young males began to flower. Older ones emulated them, more discreetly of course. Frilly, vivid clothes on the model of Carnaby Street appeared in U.S. department stores. Bonwit Teller added a Cardin male boutique in 1966. The same year fur coats for men appeared, though they were rare until football superstar Broadway Joe Namath bought a mink two years later. Ties, collars, and cuffs widened. Trouser legs flared and belled. Shirts got darker; ties lighter. Sideburns sprouted. Some styles were transient, like the all too forgettable Nehru coats of 1968. But generally male fashions followed the women's lead. Not since the eighteenth century had men been so colorfully arrayed. They never smelled better either. By the mid-sixties American males were spending nearly half a billion dollars yearly on scents and beauty aids. They became almost as gorgeous and sexy as women. Where once at parties men resembled penguins, they now emulated the peacock. And best of all, unlike so much else in the decade, no one was the worse for it.

The rebellion against traditional fashion went in two directions, though both were inspired by the young. The line of development just described emphasized brilliant or peculiar fabrics and designs. Here the emphasis was on costuming in a theatrical sense. People wore outfits that made them look like Mongols or cavaliers or whatever. These costumes, never cheap, were often very costly, though not more so than earlier styles. They were worn by others besides the young. What they owed to the emerging counter-culture was a certain freedom from constraint, and a degree of sensuality. Though the mini-skirt became a symbol of rebellious youth, it was so popular that wearing it was not an ideological statement, even if Middle Americans often thought so.

The other direction clothing took was more directly related to counter-cultural patterns. This mode had two seemingly incompatible elements—surplus military garments and handcrafted ones. Army and navy surplus clothing was the first style to be adopted by young people looking for a separate identity. Socially conscious youths began wearing army and navy jackets, shirts, and bell-bottom trousers in the early sixties. This was not meant to show contempt for the military, for anti-war sentiment was then at a low ebb, but as a mark of ostentatious frugality in the high-consumption society. As these garments became more in demand, the price went up and more expensive commercial imitations appeared. Wearing them accordingly meant less, but a certain flavor of austere nonconformity stuck to them all the same. They remained favorites of dissenting youths thereafter, even though worn by the merely fashionable too.

The hippies made handcrafted items popular. The implication here was that the wearer had made them, thus showing his independence and creativity. In the beginning this may often have been so. Soon, however, the market was so large and the people with skill and patience so limited that handcrafted items were commercially made and distributed, frequently by entrepreneurs among the young, sometimes through ordinary apparel channels. Bead shops and hippie boutiques became commonplace. Though their products were often quite costly, the vogue persisted among deviant youths anyway, partly because it was clear that whatever they wore would soon be imitated, partly because the message involved was too dear to abandon. Wearing beads, bangles, leather goods, fringes, colorful vests, and what all showed sympathy for American Indians, who inspired the most common designs, and fitted in with the popular back-to-nature ethic. When combined with military surplus garments they enabled the wearer to touch all the counter-cultural bases at once. Thus these fashions transmitted, however faintly, signals meaning peace, love, brotherhood, noble savagery, community, folk artistry, anti-capitalism and anti-militarism, and, later, revolutionary zeal.

This hippie *cum* military surplus mode also had a functional effect. It was a great leveler: when everyone wore the same bizarre costumes, everyone looked alike. Even better, it gave the ugly parity with the beautiful for the first time in modern history. Most of these costumes were pretty ghastly. A string of beads or an Indian headband did not redeem faded blue jeans and an army shirt. Long stringy hair or an untrimmed beard only aggravated the effect. Yet the young called such outfits beautiful. In effect, aesthetics were exchanged for ethics. Beauty was no longer related to appearance but to morality. To have the proper spirit, though homely, was to be beautiful. This was a great relief for the poorly endowed and a point in the counter-culture's favor. Yet it enraged adults. Once the association between beads, beards, and military surplus goods on the one hand, and radicalism and dope on the other, was established, Middle America declared war on the counter-culture's physical trappings. School systems everywhere waged a relentless struggle against long hair. To dress this way in many places was a hostile act which invited reprisals. The style became a chief symbol of the generation gap, clung to fanatically by youngsters the more they were persecuted for it, as fiercely resisted by their elders. The progress of the generational struggle could almost be measured by the spread of these fashions.

No doubt older people would have resented the new styles in any case, but the way they emerged made them doubly offensive. They were introduced by young bohemians, mainly in New York and San Francisco, whose deviant attributes were highly publicized. New York hippies were concentrated in a section called the East Village. (Greenwich Village, the traditional bohemian refuge, had gotten too commercial and expensive.) By the mid-sixties a sizable community of radicals, dropouts, youthful vagrants, unrecognized avant-garde artists, and others were assembling there and a variety of cults beginning to flourish. One of the odder was called Kerista. It was a religio-sexual movement that planned to establish a colony in the Caribbean. "Utopia Tomorrow for Swingers," its publication, the *Kerista Speeler*, proclaimed. Kerista invoked a murky, perfectionist theology revolving around sexual love. Sometimes the members engaged in bisexual gropes to advance the pleasure principle. This sounded like more fun than it actually was, according to visitors.

The mainstream of East Village cultural life was more formally political and artistic. The many activities of Ed Sanders suggest the range of enterprises generated there. He was editor and publisher of *Fuck You: A Magazine of the Arts*. A typical editorial in it began: "Time is NOW for TOTAL ASSAULT ON THE MARIJUANA LAWS. It is CLEAR to us that the cockroach theory of grass smoking has to be abandoned. IN THE OPEN! ALL THOSE WHO SUCK UP THE BENEVOLENT NARCOTIC CANNABIS, TEENSHUN!! FORWARD, WITH MIND DIALS POINTED: ASSAULT! We have the facts! Cannabis is a nonaddictive gentle peace drug! The marijuana legislations were pushed through in the 1930's by the agents and goon-squads of the jansensisto-manichean fuckhaters' conspiracy. Certainly after 30 years of the blight, it is time to rise up for a bleep blop bleep assault on the social screen. . . . But we can't wait forever you grass cadets to pull the takeover: grass-freak senators, labor leaders, presidents, etc.! The Goon Squads are few and we are many. We must spray our message into the million lobed American brain IMMEDIATELY!"

Sanders was also head of the East Village's most prominent rock group, The Fugs. They sang obscene songs of their own composition, and created equally obscene instruments for accompaniment (such as the erectophone, which appeared to be a long stick with bells on it). Among their better efforts were "What Are You Doing After the Orgy?" and the memorable "Kill for Peace." *The Fugs Song Book* described their music thusly:

> The Fug-songs seem to spurt into five areas of concentration:
> a) nouveau folk-freak
> b) sex rock and roll
> c) dope thrill chants
> d) horny cunt-hunger blues
> e) Total Assault on the Culture (anti-war/anti-creep/ anti-repression)
> ... The meaning of the Fugs lies in the term BODY POETRY, to get at the frenzy of the thing, the grope-thing, The Body Poetry Formula is this:
> The Head by the way of the Big Beat to the genitals
> The Genitals by way of Operation Brain Thrill to the Body Poetry.

In his spare time Sanders made pornographic movies. His most epic work, *Mongolian Cluster Fuck!*, was described in *Fuck You* as a "short but searing non-socially redeeming porn flick featuring 100 of the lower east side's finest, with musical background by Algeron Charles Swinburne & THE FUGS." Though more versatile and creative than most, Sanders was typical of the East Village's alienated young artists. Tiny papers like *Fuck You* were springing up everywhere. All tried to be obscene, provocative, and, it was thought, liberating. They despised form, caring only for the higher morality and aesthetics it was their duty to advance. Some were more political (porno-political usually) than others. Collectively they were soon to be known as the "underground press."

Several cuts above the underground press were the flourishing little magazines. They were avant garde in the traditional sense and aimed, in their way, for greatness. By 1966 there were at least 250 of these (as against sixty or so in the 1920's). The better financed (*Outsider, Steppenwolf*) were tastefully composed and printed; others were crudely photo-offset (*Kayak, Eventorium Muse*). The *Insect Trust Gazette,* an annual experiment, once published an issue in which the original manuscripts were simply photographed and printed without reduction. About a third of the "littles" were mimeographed. There was even a little magazine for scientists, the *Worm-Runners' Digest*, edited by a droll researcher at the University of Michigan for people of like taste.

Older cultural rebels contributed to the ferment. George Brecht's musical composition "Ladder" went as follows: "Paint a single straight ladder white/Paint the bottom rung black/Distribute spectral colors on the rungs between." Even more to the point was "Laugh Piece" by John Lennon's future wife, Yoko Ono. It went "Keep laughing for a week." Nam June Paik composed a work known as "Young Penis Symphony." He was also an underground film producer and put on elaborate performances resembling *the* late happenings. One such was given at the Film-Makers Cinematheque using film, live music, and the cellist Charlotte Moorman. The audience saw short segments of a film by Robert Breer, alternating with views of Miss Moorman, silhouetted by backlighting behind the projection screen, playing short phrases of a Bach cello sonata. On completing each phrase she removed a garment. Another film clip would then be shown. This continued until she was lying on the floor, completely nude, playing her cello which was now atop her. Miss Moorman, "the Jeanne d'Arc of New Music," as she was called, appeared in other Paik compositions. She had been trained at the Juilliard School and was a member of Leopold Stokowski's American Symphony Orchestra.

As these few examples suggest, the East Village gained from its proximity to the New York avant garde. The mature counter-culture owed a lot to this relationship, but even in its early stages the East Village suffered from the influx of teenie-boppers and runaways who were to spoil both it and the Haight-Ashbury for serious cultural radicals. The people who were soon to be called hippies meant to build alternatives to the straight world. Against the hostile competitive, capitalistic values of bourgeois America they posed their own faith in nonviolence, love, and community. Drugs were important both as means to truth and advancers of the pleasure principle. The early hippies created institutions of sorts. Rock bands like the Jefferson Airplane, the Grateful Dead, Country Joe and the Fish flourished, as did communal societies, notably the Diggers. They were inspired by the seventeenth-century communists whose name they took. In practice they were a hip version of the Salvation Army.

Hippies lived together, in "tribes" or "families." Their golden rule was "Be nice to others, even when provoked, and they will be nice to you." In San Francisco their reservation was the Haight-Ashbury district near Golden Gate Park. They were much resented in the East Village by the natives, poor ethnics for the most part. In the Hashbury, on the other hand, they were welcome at first. Though peculiar, they were an improvement over the petty criminals they displaced. Even when freaked-out in public from drugs, a certain tolerance prevailed. After all, stepping over a drooling flower child on the street was better than getting mugged. Civic authorities were less open-minded. The drug traffic bothered them especially, and the Hashbury was loaded with "narks" (narcotics agents). Hunter S. Thompson wrote that "love is the password in the Haight-Ashbury, but paranoia is the style. Nobody wants to go to jail."

The fun-and-games era did not last long, perhaps only from 1965 to 1966. The hippie ethic was too fragile to withstand the combination of police surveillance and media exposure that soon afflicted it. The first hippies had a certain earnestness. But they were joined by masses of teen-age runaways. Nicholas von Hoffman observed that the Hashbury economy that began as a fraternal barter system quickly succumbed to the cash nexus. It became the first community in the world to revolve entirely around the buying and selling and taking of drugs. Marijuana and LSD were universal; less popular, but also commonplace, were LSD's more powerful relative STP, and amphetamines. "Speed kills" said the buttons and posters; speed freaks multiplied anyhow. To support themselves some hippies worked at casual labor or devised elaborate, usually unsuccessful schemes to make money out of hippie enterprises. Panhandling was popular, so was theft, disguised usually as communism.

Bohemians invariably deplore monogamy, and the hippies were no exception. As one member of the Jefferson Airplane put it "The stage is our bed and the audience is our broad. We're not entertaining, we're making love." Though committed to sexual freedom on principle, and often promiscuous in fact, the hippies were not really very sexy. Timothy Leary notwithstanding, drugs seemed to dampen the sexual urge. And the hippies were too passive in any case for strenuous sex play. Conversely, the most ardent free lovers, like those in the Sexual Freedom League, had little interest in drugs. Among hippies the combination of bad diets, dope, communal living, and the struggle to survive made for a restricted sex life. Of course the hippies were always glad of chances to shock the bourgeoisie, which made them seem more depraved than they were. Then too, people expected them to be sexually perverse, and the more public-spirited hippies tried to oblige. Like good troupers they hated to let the public down, though willing to put it on.

Hippie relations with black people were worse than might have been supposed. Hippies owed blacks a lot. Their jargon was derived from the ghetto. They admired blacks, as certain whites always have, for being more emotional, sensual, and uninhibited. But there were very few black hippies. Superspade, a beloved Negro drug pusher, was an exception. Most hippies were frightened of blacks. "Spades are programmed for hate" was the way many put it. The Hashbury was periodically swept by rumors of impending black attacks. Some hippies looked to the motorcycle outlaws to protect them from black rage. This was not without a certain logic. Outlaws hated blacks and loved to fight. But they played their role as hippie militiamen uneasily. In truth they were more likely to destroy a hippie than defend him.

In the end it was neither the bikers nor the blacks but the media that destroyed hippiedom. The publicity given the summer of love attracted countless thousands of disturbed youngsters to the Hashbury and the East Village in 1967. San Francisco was not burdened with the vast numbers originally expected. But many did come, bringing in their train psychotics, drug peddlers, and all sorts of criminals. Drug poisoning, hepatitis (from infected needles), and various diseases resulting from malnutrition and exposure thinned their ranks. Rapes, muggings, and assaults became commonplace. Hippies had little money, but they were irresistibly easy marks. Hippie girls were safe to assault. They reacted passively, and as many were drug users and runaways they could not go to the police.

So the violence mounted. On the West Coast one drug peddler was stabbed to death and his right forearm removed. Superspade's body was found hanging from a cliff top. He had been stabbed, shot, and trussed in a sleeping bag. On October 8 the nude bodies of Linda Rea Fitzpatrick, eighteen, and James Leroy "Groovy" Hutchinson, twenty-one, were discovered in an East Village boiler room. They had been murdered while high on LSD. Though pregnant, Miss Fitzpatrick had also been raped. That was how the summer of love ended. Two days earlier the death and funeral of a hippie had been ritually observed in San Francisco's Buena Vista Park. But the killing of Linda and Groovy marked its real end. The Hashbury deteriorated rapidly thereafter. Bad publicity drove the tourists away, and the hippie boutiques that serviced them closed. Some local rock groups dissolved; others, like the Jefferson Airplane and even the Grateful Dead, went commercial. The hippies and their institutions faded quietly away. The Hashbury regained something of its old character. The East Village, owing to its more diverse population and strategic location, changed less.

At its peak the hippie movement was the subject of much moralizing. Most often hippies were seen as degenerate and representative of all things godless and un-American. A minority accepted them as embodying a higher morality. The media viewed them as harmless, even amusing, freaks—which was probably closest to the truth. But before long it was clear that while the hippie movement was easily slain, the hippie style of life was not. Their habit of dressing up in costumes rather than outfits was widely imitated. So was their slang and their talk of peace, love, and beauty. The great popularity of ex-hippie rock groups was one sign of the cultural diffusion taking place, marijuana another. Weekend tripping spread to the suburbs. While the attempt to build parallel cultures on a large scale in places like the Hashbury failed, the hippies survived in many locales. Isolated farms, especially in New England and the Southwest, were particularly favored. And they thrived also on the fringes of colleges and universities, where the line between avant-garde student and alienated dropout was hard to draw. In tribes, families, and communes the hippies lived on, despite considerable local harassment wherever they went.

Though few in number, hippies had a great effect on middle-class youth. Besides their sartorial influence, hippies made religion socially acceptable. Their interest in the supernatural was contagious. Some of the communes which sprang up in the late sixties were actually religious fellowships practicing a contemporary monasticism. One in western Massachusetts was called the Cathedral of the Spirit. Its forty members were led by a nineteen-year-old mystic who helped them prepare for the Second Coming and the new Aquarian Age when all men would be brothers. The Cathedral had rigid rules against alcohol, "sex without love," and, less typically, drugs. Members helped out neighboring farmers without pay, but the commune was essentially contemplative. Its sacred book was a fifty-seven-page typewritten manuscript composed by a middle-aged bus driver from Northfield, Massachusetts, which was thought to be divinely inspired. Another commune in Boston, called the Fort Hill Community, was more outward looking. Its sixty members hoped to spread their holy word through the mass media.

Some of the communes or brotherhoods sprang from traditional roots. In New York City a band of young Jews formed a Havurah (fellowship) to blend Jewish traditions with contemporary inspirations. They wanted to study subjects like "the prophetic mind; new forms of spirituality in the contemporary world; and readings from the Jewish mystical tradition." At the University of Massachusetts a hundred students celebrated Rosh Hashanah not in a synagogue but in a field where they danced and sang all night. Courses in religion multiplied. At Smith College the number of students taking them grew from 692 in 1954 to nearly 1,400 in 1969, though the student body remained constant at about 2,000. Columbia University had two hundred applicants for a graduate program in religion with only twenty openings.

Students saw traditional religion as a point of departure rather than a place for answers. Comparatively few joined the new fellowships, but large numbers were attracted to the concepts they embodied. Oriental theologies and the like grew more attractive, so did magic. At one Catholic university a coven of warlocks was discovered. They were given psychiatric attention (thereby missing a great chance. If only they had been exorcised instead, the Establishment would have shown its relevance). When a Canadian university gave the studentry a chance to recommend new courses they overwhelmingly asked for subjects like Zen, sorcery, and witchcraft. A work of classic Oriental magic, *I Ching* or the *Book of Changes*, became popular. The best edition, a scholarly product of the Princeton University Press, used to sell a thousand copies a year. In 1968 fifty thousand copies were snapped up. Sometimes magic and mysticism were exploited more in fun than not. The Women's Liberation Movement had guerrilla theater troupes calling themselves WITCH (Women's International Terrorist Conspiracy from Hell). During the SDS sit-in at the University of Chicago they cursed the sociology department and put a hex on its chairman.

But there was a serious element to the vogue for magic. Teachers of philosophy and religion were struck by the anti-positivist, anti-science feelings of many students. Science was discredited as an agent of the military-industrial complex. It had failed to make life more attractive. Whole classes protested the epistemology of science as well as its intellectual dominion. Students believed the Establishment claimed to be rational, but showed that it was not. This supported one of the central truths of all religion, that man is more than a creature who reasons. Nor was it only the young who felt this way. Norman Mailer was something of a mystic, so was Timothy Leary. And the most ambitious academic effort to deal with these things, Theodore Roszak's *The Making of a*

Counter Culture, ended with a strong appeal to faith. Like the alienated young, Roszak too rejected science and reason—"the myth of objective consciousness" as he called it. Instead of empiricism or the scientific method he wanted "the beauty of the fully illuminated personality" to be "our standard of truth." He liked magic as "a matter of communion with the forces of nature as if they were mindful, intentional presences." What he admired most in the New Left was its attempt, as he thought, to revive shamanism, to get back to the sanity and participatory democracy of prehistoric society. But he urged the left to give up its notion that violence and confrontation would change the world. What the left must do to influence the silent majority "was not simply to muster power against the misdeeds of society, but to transform the very sense men have of reality."

The anti-war movement was strongly affected by this new supernaturalism. On Moratorium Day in 1969 a University of Massachusetts student gave an emotional speech that brought the audience to its feet shouting, "The war is over." "He went into a dance, waving his arms," a campus minister said. "It was the essence of a revival meeting, where the audience makes a commitment to Christ at the end." The great peace demonstrations in 1969 were full of religious symbolism. In Boston 100,000 people gathered before a gigantic cross on the Common. In New York lighted candles were carried to the steps of St. Patrick's Cathedral. Candles were placed on the White House wall during the November mobilization. At other demonstrations the shofar, the ram's horn sounded by Jews at the beginning of each new year, was blown. Rock, the liturgical music of the young, was often played. So was folk music, which continued as a medium of moral expression after its popular decline.

Theology reflected the new supernaturalism, just as it had the aggressive secularism of a few years earlier. Harvey Cox, most famous of the contemporary theologians, published a study of the extra-institutional spiritual revival called *The Feast of Fools* in 1969. "God Is Dead" gave way to the "Theology of Hope," after Jurgen Moltmann's book by that title. A German theologian, Moltmann argued that the trouble with Christian theology was that it ignored the future. "The Church lives on memories, the world on hope," he remarked elsewhere. Though he was a Protestant, Roman Catholic theologians in Germany and America agreed with him. Institutional churches responded to the new by absorbing as much of it as they could. Church happenings, rock masses, light shows, and readings from Eastern mystics were used by Protestants and Catholics alike. The home mass gained popularity among Catholics. It gave to formal worship something of the intimate fellowship that the young found so compelling. Thus while church attendance declined from the high levels of the 1950's, this did not mean a decrease in religious enthusiasm. The most striking aspect of the "religious revival" of the 1950's, after all, had been the absence of devotion. Going to church then was more a social than a religious act. In the late sixties faith was expressed by not going to church.

There were many ways of responding to this spiritual revival. Orthodox churchgoers were offended by it, and even more by the efforts of their denominations to win the inspirited young. More flexible religious leaders saw it as a great opportunity. Secular radicals and educators were more often depressed by it. Men whose lives were dedicated to the pursuit of truth through reason were not about to become shamans. If it was true that science and scholarship had not yet brought the millennium, this did not seem good cause for abandoning them.

The most surprising man to protest this new turn was Paul Goodman. Goodman's life and work were more nearly of a piece than most people's. He was a secular anarchist, but while hoping to wreck the old order, he believed that the old tools—reason, expertise, science—

would still be needed. Hence, though he was one of the chief intellectual mentors of the counter-culture, its growing spiritualism, indeed anti-intellectualism, disturbed him.

Late in 1969 he wrote that this first became clear to him while giving a graduate seminar on "professionalism." He hoped to teach the difference between careerism and fidelity to a professional calling. To his astonishment the class rejected the notion that there was such a thing as a true profession. All decisions were made by the power structure. Professionals were merely peer groups formed to delude the public and make money. "Didn't every society, however just, require experts?" he asked. No, they insisted; it was only important to be human, and all else would follow.

> Suddenly I realized that they did not really believe that there was a nature of things. Somehow all functions could be reduced to interpersonal relations and power. There was no knowledge, but only the sociology of knowledge. They had so well learned that physical and sociological research is subsidized and conducted for the benefit of the ruling class that they did not believe there was such a thing as the simple truth. To be required to learn something was a trap by which the young were put down and co-opted. Then I knew that I could not get through to them. I had imagined that the world-wide student protest had to do with changing political and moral institutions, to which I was sympathetic, but I now saw that we had to do with a religious crisis of the magnitude of the Reformation in the fifteen hundreds, when not only all institutions but all learning had been corrupted by the Whore of Babylon.

This was a strange confession from one who specialized in youth and its discontents, as Goodman fully realized. His most influential book, *Growing Up Absurd* (1960), dealt with generational alienation. But he had thought it a specialized deviance then, and was heartened by the new student radicals "who made human sense and were not absurd at all. But the alienating circumstances had proved too strong after all; here were absurd graduate students, most of them political activists." "Alienation," he continued, "is a powerful motivation of unrest, fantasy, and reckless action. It leads . . . to religious innovation, new sacraments to give life meaning. But it is a poor basis for politics, including revolutionary politics." Mere confrontation was not the answer to society's ills, especially when done hatefully. Gandhi's great point had been that the confronter aims at future community with the confronted. Yet many New Leftists did not regard their enemies as members of the same species. "How can the young people think of a future community when they themselves have no present world, no profession or other job in it, and no trust in other human beings? Instead, some young radicals seem to entertain the disastrous illusion that other people can be compelled by fear. This can lead only to crushing reaction."

The young knew nothing of society's institutions, how they worked, where they came from, what had made them what they were. For many, history began in 1968. "I am often hectored to my face," Goodman said, "with formulations that I myself put in their mouths, that have become part of the oral tradition two years old, author prehistoric." They didn't trust people over thirty because they didn't understand them and were too conceited to try. "Having grown up in a world too meaningless to learn anything, they know very little and are quick to resent it." The most important thing to the young was being together, en masse if possible. At the rock festivals they found the meaning of life which, as they explained it, consisted of people being nice to each other. A group of them passing a stick of marijuana behaved like "a Quaker meeting waiting for the spirit." And, Goodman concluded, "in the end it is religion that constitutes the strength of this generation, and not, as I used to think, their morality, political will, and common sense." Neither moral courage nor honesty was their salient trait, but rather "metaphysical vitality."

Goodman's argument was an exceptionally brave one. No one who had done less for the young could in good conscience have spoken so bluntly of them. And religion as an organizing principle for making sense of the serious young seemed useful. But it didn't help to distinguish what was durable and what merely fashionable in the counter-culture. The term itself was hard to define as it embraced almost everything new and anti-Establishment, however frivolous. On its deepest level the counter-culture was the radical critique of Herbert Marcuse, Norman O. Brown, and even Paul Goodman. It also meant the New Left, communes and hippie farms, magic, hedonism, eroticism, and public nudity. And it included rock music, long hair, and mini-skirts (or, alternatively, fatigue uniforms, used clothes, and the intentionally ugly or grotesque). Most attacks on the counter-culture were directed at its trivial aspects, pot and dress especially. Pot busts (police raids), often involving famous people or their children, became commonplace. The laws against pot were so punitive in some areas as to be almost unenforceable. Even President Nixon, spokesman for Middle American morality that he was, finally questioned them. Local fights against long hair, beards, and short skirts were beyond number. The American Civil Liberties Union began taking school systems to court for disciplining students on that account. New York City gave up trying to enforce dress codes. It was all the more difficult there as even the teachers were mod. At one school the principal ordered women teachers to wear smocks over their minis. They responded by buying minismocks.

Nor were athletics—the last bastion of orthodoxy, one might think—exempt, though coaches struggled to enforce yesterday's fashions. At Oregon State University one football player, the son of an Air Force officer, went hippie and dropped the sport. His coach said, "I recruited that boy thinking he was Jack Armstrong. I was wrong. He turned out to be a free-thinker." At the University of Pennsylvania a star defensive back showed up for summer practice with shoulder-length hair, sideburns down to the neck, beads, bells, thonged sandals, and a cloth sash round his waist. He was the only man on the team to bring a pet dog and a stereo set to the six-day camp. After a war of nerves culminating in an ultimatum from the coach, he grudgingly hacked a few inches off his mane. And so it went all over America.

Both sides in this struggle took fashion and style to be deadly serious matters, so political conflicts tended to become cultural wars. In the fall of 1969 the most important radical student group at New York University was called Transcendental Students. At a time when SDS could barely muster twenty-five members, five hundred or more belonged to TS. It began the previous semester when a group protesting overcrowding in the classroom staged a series of freak-outs in classrooms. This proved so attractive a custom that it was institutionalized. Rock, pot, and wine parties had obvious advantages over political action. The administration shrewdly made a former restaurant available to TS for a counter-cultural center. The students welcomed it as a haven for "guerrilla intellect" where the human spirit could breathe free. The administration saw it as just another recreational facility, which, of course, it was. And what dean would not rather have the kids singing out in a restaurant than locking him in his office? Sometimes culture and politics were united. When the $12 million center for the performing arts opened in Milwaukee, Wisconsin, on September 18, 1969, six hundred students disrupted the inaugural concert. They rubbed balloons, blew bubble pipes, threw rolls of toilet paper, and demanded that 20 per cent of the seats be given free to welfare recipients.

"The greatest event in counter-culture history"—the Woodstock Festival in Bethel, New York, August 15, 1969. (Courtesy of Magnum Photos, Inc. Photo by Burk Uzzle.)

The greatest event in counter-cultural history was the Woodstock Festival in Bethel, New York. It was organized on the pattern of other large rock festivals. Big-name groups were invited for several days of continuous entertaining in the open. A large crowd was expected, but nothing like the 300,000 or 400,000 youngsters who actually showed up on August 15, 1969. Everything fell apart in consequence. Tickets could not be collected nor services provided. There wasn't enough food or water. The roads were blocked with abandoned autos, and no one could get in or out for hours at a time. Surprisingly, there were no riots or disasters. The promoters chartered a fleet of helicopters to evacuate casualties (mostly from bad drug trips) and bring in essential supplies. Despite the rain and congestion, a good time was had by all (except the boy killed when a tractor accidentally drove over his sleeping bag). No one had ever seen so large and ruly a gathering before. People stripped down, smoked pot, and turned on with nary a discouraging word, so legend has it. Afterward the young generally agreed that it was a beautiful experience proving their superior morality. People were nicer to each other than ever before. Even the police were impressed by the public's order (a result of their wisely deciding not to enforce the drug laws).

But the counter-culture had its bad moments in 1969 also. Haight-Ashbury continued to decay. It was now mainly a slum where criminals preyed on helpless drug freaks. Worse still was the Battle of Berkeley, which put both the straight culture and the counter-culture in the worst possible light, especially the former. The University of California owned a number of vacant lots south of the campus. The land had been cleared in anticipation of buildings it was unable to construct. One block lay vacant for so long that the street people—hippies, students, dropouts, and others—transformed it into a People's Park. Pressure was brought on the University by the local power structure to block its use, which was done. On May 15 some six thousand students and street people held a rally on campus, then advanced on the park. County sheriffs, highway patrolmen, and the Berkeley police met them with a hail of gunfire. One person died of buckshot wounds, another was blinded. Many more were shot though few arrested. Those who were arrested were handled so brutally that the circuit court enjoined the sheriff to have his men stop beating and abusing them. Disorders continued. Governor Reagan declared a state of emergency and brought in the National Guard. Five days later one of its helicopters sprayed gas over the campus, thus making the educational process at Berkeley even more trying than usual.

Of course the Establishment was most to blame for Vietnamizing the cultural war. But the meretricious aspects of the counter-culture were evident too. If the police were really "fascist pigs," as the street people said, why goad and defy them? And especially why harass the National Guardsmen who didn't want to be in Berkeley anyhow? This was hardly on the same order as murdering people with shotguns. Yet such behavior was stupid, pointless, and self-defeating, like so much else in the counter-culture. The silent majority was not won over. Nor was the People's Park saved. A year later the area was still fenced in. (Though vacant. The University, having pretended to want it as a recreational area, tried to make it one. But as the students thought it stained with innocent blood, they avoided it.)

The rock festival at Altamont that winter was another disaster. It was a free concert that climaxed the Rolling Stones' whirlwind tour of the U.S. They called it their gift to the fans. Actually it was a clever promotion. The Stones had been impressed with the moneymaking potential of Woodstock. While Woodstock cost the promoters a fortune, they stood to recoup their losses with a film of the event. This inspired the Stones to do a Woodstock themselves. At the last minute they obtained the use of Dick Carter's Altamont Raceway. It had been doing porly and the owner thought the publicity would help business. Little was done to prepare the site. The police didn't have enough notice to bring in reserves, so the Stones hired a band of Hell's Angels as security guards (for $500 worth of beer). The Stones did their thing and the Angels did theirs.

The result was best captured by a *Rolling Stone* magazine photograph showing Mick Jagger looking properly aghast while Angels beat a young Negro to death on stage. A musician who tried to stop them was knocked unconscious, and he was lucky at that. Before the day was over many more were beaten, though no others fatally. Sometimes the beatings were for aesthetic reasons. One very fat man took off his clothes in the approved rock festival manner. This offended the Angels who set on him with pool cues. No one knows how many were clubbed that day. The death count came to four. Apart from Meredith Hunter, who was stabbed and kicked to death, they mostly died by accident. A car drove off the road into a clump of people and killed two. A man, apparently high on drugs, slid into an irrigation canal and drowned. The drug freak-outs were more numerous than at Woodstock. The medical care was less adequate. Not that the physicians on hand didn't try; they just lacked the support provided at Woodstock, whose promoters had spared no expense to avert disaster. Oddly enough the press, normally so eager to exploit the counter-culture, missed the point of Altamont. Early accounts followed the customary rock festival line, acclaiming it as yet another triumph of youth. In the East it received little attention of any kind.

It remained for *Rolling Stone*, the rock world's most authoritative journal, to tell the whole story of what it called the Altamont Death Festival. The violence was quite bad enough, but what especially bothered *Rolling Stone* was the commercial cynicism behind it. That huge gathering was assembled by the Stones to make a lucrative film on the cheap. They could have hired legitimate security guards, but it cost less to use the Angels (At Woodstock unarmed civilians trained by the Hog Farm commune kept order.) They were too rushed for the careful planning that went into Woodstock, too callous (and greedy) to pour in the emergency resources that had saved the day there. And, appropriately, they faked the moviemaking too so as to have a documentary of the event they intended, not the one they got. *Rolling Stone* said that a cameraman was recording a fat, naked girl freaking out backstage when the director stopped him. "Don't shoot that. That's ugly. We only want beautiful things." The cameraman made the obvious response. "How can you possibly say that? Everything here is so ugly."

Rolling Stone thought the star system at fault. Once a band got as big as the Stones they experienced delusions of grandeur, "ego trips" in the argot. And with so much money to be made by high-pressure promotions, "the hype" became inevitable. Others agreed. The *Los Angeles Free Press*, biggest of the underground papers, ran a full-page caricature of Mick Jagger with an Adolf Hitler mustache, arm draped around a Hell's Angel, while long-haired kids gave them the Nazi salute. Ralph Gleason of the *San Francisco Chronicle* explained Altamont this way: "The name of the game is money, power, and ego, and money is first as it brings power. The Stones didn't do it for free, they did it for money, only the tab was paid in a different way. Whoever goes to the movie paid for the Altamont religious assembly."*

Quite so. But why did so many others go along with the Stones? The Jefferson Airplane, and especially the Grateful Dead, reputedly the most socially conscious rock bands, participated. So did counter-culture folk heroes like Emmet Grogan of the Diggers. Here the gullibility—innocence, perhaps—of the deviant young was responsible. Because the rock bandits smoked pot and talked a revolutionary game, they were supposed to be different from other entertainers. Even though they made fortunes and spent them ostentatiously, their virtue was always presumed. What Altamont showed was that the difference between a rock king and a robber baron was about six inches of hair.**

If Altamont exposed one face of the counter-culture, the Manson family revealed another. Late in 1969 Sharon Tate, a pregnant movie actress, and four of her jet-set friends were ritually murdered in the expensive Bel-Air district of Los Angeles. Though apparently senseless, their deaths were thought related to the rootless, thrill-oriented life style of the Beautiful People. But on December 1 policemen began

---

* Gleason was the best writer on popular music and the youth culture associated with it, which he once admired greatly. For an earlier assessment see his "Like a Rolling Stone," *American Scholar* (Autumn 1967).

** This is to criticize the singer, not the song. Whatever one might think of some performers, there is no doubt that rock itself was an exciting musical form. Adults rarely heard it because rock seldom was played on television, or even radio in most parts of the country. Rock artists appeared mainly in concerts and clubs, to which few over thirty went. Not knowing the music, there was little reason for them to buy the records that showed rock at its most complex and interesting. Like jazz, rock became more sophisticated with time and made greater demands on the artist's talent. Even more than jazz, rock produced an army of amateur and semi-professional players around the country. Though often making up in volume what they lacked in skill, their numbers alone guaranteed that rock would survive its exploiters.

arresting obscure hippies. Their leader, Charles Manson, was an ex-convict and seemingly deranged. Susan Atkins, a member of his "family," gave several cloudy versions of what had happened. On the strength of them Manson was indicted for murder. Though his guilt remained unproven, the basic facts about his past seemed clear. He was a neglected child who became a juvenile delinquent. In 1960 he was convicted of forgery and spent seven years in the penitentiary. On his release he went to the Hashbury and acquired a harem of young girls. After floating through the hippie underground for a time, he left the Hashbury with his family of nine girls and five boys early in 1968. They ended up at Spahn's Ranch in the Santa Susana Mountains, north of the San Fernando Valley. The owner was old and blind. Manson terrified him. But the girls took care of him so he let the family stay on. They spent a year at the ranch before the police suspected them of stealing cars. Then they camped out in the desert until arrested.

Life with the Manson family was a combination of hippieism and paranoia. Manson subscribed to the usual counter-cultural values. Inhibitions, the Establishment, regular employment, and other straight virtues were bad. Free love, nature, dope, rock, and mysticism were good. He believed a race war was coming (predicted in Beatle songs) and armed his family in anticipation of it. Some of the cars they stole were modified for use in the desert, where he meant to make his last stand. And, naturally, he tried to break into the rock music business. One reason why he allegedly murdered Miss Tate and her friends was that they were in a house previously occupied by a man who had broken a promise to advance Manson's career. The Manson family was thought to have killed other people even more capriciously. Yet after his arrest most of the girls remained loyal to Manson. Young, largely middle class, they were still "hypnotized" or "enslaved" by him. Those not arrested continued to hope for a family reunion. Of course hippies were not murderers usually. But the repressed hostility, authoritarianism, perversity, and mindless paranoia that underlay much of the hippie ethic were never displayed more clearly. The folkways of the flower children tended toward extremes. At one end they were natural victims; at the other, natural victimizers. The Manson family were both at once.

Taken together the varieties of life among deviant youths showed the counter-culture to be disintegrating. What was disturbing about it was not so much the surface expression as its tendency to mirror the culture it supposedly rejected. The young condemned adult hypocrisy while matching its contradictions with their own. The old were materialistic, hung up on big cars and ranch houses. The young were equally devoted to motorcycles, stereo sets, and electric guitars. The old sought power and wealth. So did the young as rock musicians, political leaders, and frequently as salesmen of counter-cultural goods and services. What distinguished reactionary capitalists from their avant-garde opposite numbers was often no more than a lack of moral pretense. While condemning the adult world's addiction to violence, the young admired third-world revolutionaries, Black Panthers, and even motorcycle outlaws. The rhetoric of the young got progressively meaner and more hostile. This was not so bad as butchering Vietnamese, but it was not very encouraging either. And where hate led, violence followed.

Adults pointed these inconsistencies out often enough, with few good results. Usable perceptions are always self-perceptions, which made the *Rolling Stone* exposé of Altamont so valuable. This was a small but hopeful sign that the capacity for self-analysis was not totally submerged, despite the flood of self-congratulatory pieties with which the deviant young described themselves. The decline of the New Left was another. Once a buoyant and promising thing, it became poisoned by hate, failure, and romantic millennialism. Its diminished appeal offered hopes of sobriety's return. So did the surge of student interest in environmental issues at the decade's end. These were not fake problems, like so many youthful obsessions, but real ones. They would take the best efforts of many generations to overcome. No doubt the young would lose interest in them after a while as usual. Still, it was better to save a forest or clean a river than to vandalize a campus. No amount of youthful nagging was likely to make adults give up their sinful ways. It was possible that the young and old together might salvage enough of the threatened environment to leave posterity something of lasting value. The generations yet unborn were not likely to care much whether ROTC was conducted on campus or off. But they will remember this age, for better or worse, with every breath they take.

One aspect of the counter-culture deserves special mention: its assumption that hedonism was inevitably anti-capitalist. As James Hitchcock pointed out, the New Left identified capitalism with puritanism and deferred gratifications. But this was true of capitalism only with respect to work. Where consumption was concerned, it urged people to gratify their slightest wish. It exploited sex shamelessly to that end, limited only by law and custom. When the taboos against nudity were removed, merchants soon took advantage of their new freedom. Naked models, actors, even waitresses were one result, pornographic flicks another. Who doubted that if marijuana became legal the tobacco companies would soon put Mexican gold in every vending machine? It was, after all, part of Aldous Huxley's genius that he saw how sensual gratification could enslave men more effectively than Hitler ever could. Victorian inhibitions, the Protestant Ethic itself were, though weakened, among the few remaining defenses against the market economy that Americans possessed. To destroy them for freedom's sake would only make people more vulnerable to consumerism than they already were. Which was not to say that sexual and other freedoms were not good things in their own right. But there was no assurance that behavioral liberty would not grow at the expense of political freedom. It was one thing to say that sex promoted mental health, another to say it advanced social justice. In confusing the two young deviants laid themselves open to what Herbert Marcuse called "repressive desublimation," the means by which the socioeconomic order was made more attractive, and hence more durable. Sex was no threat to the Establishment. Panicky moralists found this hard to believe, so they kept trying to suppress it. But the shrewder guardians of established relationships saw hedonism for what it partially was, a valuable means of social control. What made this hard to get across was that left and right agreed that sex was subversive. That was why the Filthy Speech Movement arose, and why the John Birch Society and its front groups divided a host of communities in the late sixties. They insisted that sex education was a communist plot to fray the country's moral fiber. They could hardly have been more wrong. As practiced in most schools, sex education was anything but erotic. In fact, more students were probably turned off sex than on to it by such courses. The Kremlin was hardly less orthodox than the Birch Society on sexual matters, sexual denial being thought a trait of all serious revolutionaries. But the sexual propaganda of the young confirmed John Birchers in their delusions. As elsewhere, the misconceptions of each side reinforced one another.

Still, the counter-culture's decline ought not to be celebrated prematurely. It outlasted the sixties. It had risen in the first place because of the larger culture's defects. War, poverty, social and racial injustice were widespread. The universities were less human than they might have been. The regulation of sexual conduct led to endless persecutions of the innocent or the pathetic to no one's advantage. Young people had much to complain of. Rebellious youth had thought to make things better. It was hardly their fault that things got worse. They were, after all, products of the society they meant to change, and marked by it as everyone was. Vanity and ignorance made them think themselves free of the weaknesses they saw so clearly in others. But adults were vain and ignorant too, and, what's more, they had power as the young did not. When they erred, as in Vietnam, millions suffered. The young hated being powerless, but thanks to it they were spared the awful burden of guilt that adults bore. They would have power soon enough, and no doubt use it just as badly. In the meantime, though, people did well to keep them in perspective.

The dreary propaganda about youth's insurgent idealism continued into the seventies. So did attempts to make them look clean-cut. American society went on being obsessed with the young. But all popular manias are seasonal. Each era has its own preoccupations. The young and their counter-culture were a special feature of the 1960's and would probably not be regarded in the old way for very long afterward. And, demographically speaking, youth itself was on the wane. The median age of Americans had risen steadily in modern times, reaching a peak of thirty years of age in 1952. The baby boom reversed this trend, like so many others. In 1968 the median age was only 27.7 years. But as the birthrate fell the median age began to rise. By 1975 it would be over twenty-eight. By 1990 it should be back up to thirty again, putting half the population beyond the age of trust. Their disproportionate numbers was one reason why youth was so prominent in the sixties. It was reasonable to suppose they would become less so as their numbers declined in relation to older people.

Common sense suggested that work and the pleasure principle would both continue. Once life and work were thought to be guided by the same principles. In the twentieth century they had started to divide, with one set of rules for working and another for living. The complexities of a postindustrial economy would probably maintain that distinction. The discipline of work would prevail on the job. The tendency to "swing" off it would increase, and the dropout community too. The economy was already rich enough to support a substantial leisure class, as the hippies demonstrated. The movement toward guaranteed incomes would make idleness even more feasible. A large dependent population, in economic terms, was entirely practical—perhaps, given automation, even desirable. How utopian to have a society in which the decision to work was voluntary! Yet if economic growth continued and an effective welfare state was established, such a thing was not unimaginable, however repugnant to the Protestant Ethic. Perhaps that was what the unpleasant features of life in the sixties pointed toward. Later historians might think them merely the growing pains of this new order. A Brave New World indeed!

A further reason for taking this view was the rise of an adult counter-culture. Americans have always been attracted to cults and such. No enthusiasm, however bizarre, fails to gain some notice in so vast and restless a country. Crank scientists and religious eccentrics are especially welcomed. In the 1960's this was more true than ever, and there seemed to be more uniformity of belief among the cults than before. Perhaps also they were more respectable. The Esalen Institute in northern California was one of the most successful. It offered three-day seminars conducted by Dr. Frederick S. Perls, the founder of Gestalt therapy. When his book by that title was published in 1950 it won, as might have been expected, little attention. But in the sixties it flourished to the point where perhaps a hundred Gestalt therapists were in practice. As employed at Esalen, Gestalt therapy involved a series of individual encounters within a group context. Perls tried to cultivate moments of sudden insights that produced a strong awareness of the present moment. Unlike psychoanalysis, Gestalt therapy was directive. The therapist diagnosed the ailment and organized its cure in short bursts of intensive treatment. People were encouraged to act out dreams so as to discover their hidden message. The emphasis was on sensuality, spontaneity, and the reduction of language which was seen as more a barrier to understanding than a means of communication. There was much role-playing, aggression-releasing exercises, and "unstructured interaction." Esalen itself, with its hot sulphur baths where mixed nude bathing was encouraged, combined the features of a hip spa, a mental clinic, and a religious center. It brought social scientists and mystics together in common enterprises. By 1967 Esalen grossed a million dollars a year. Four thousand people attended its seminars. Twelve thousand used its branch in San Francisco.

Though Esalen was the most celebrated center of "Third Force Psychiatry," it was hardly alone. Encounter groups, T-groups, sensitivity groups all practiced variations of the same theme. So, in a more intense way, did Synanon. Synanon was founded in 1958 by an ex-alcoholic named Charles E. Dederich. It began as a way of reclaiming alcoholics, and especially drug addicts, through communal living and group therapy. It aimed to peel away the defenses that supported addiction. The cure was a drastic one and the Synanon ethic extremely authoritarian, as a treatment based not on clinical experience but actual street life would naturally be. Synanon's most popular feature was the Synanon game, a kind of encounter group open to outsiders. From its modest beginning Synanon expanded rapidly into a network of clinics and small businesses operated by members to support the therapeutic program. Already a corporation by the decade's end, Dederich expected it to become a mass movement in time. Others thought so too. Abraham Maslow of Brandeis University declared that "Synanon is now in the process of torpedoing the entire world of psychiatry and within ten years will completely replace psychiatry."

Esalen and Synanon got much publicity, but, though substantial efforts, they were only the tip of the iceberg. Beneath them were literally thousands of groups dedicated to better mental health through de-sublimation, often sponsored by businesses and universities. In a sense what they did was rationalize the counter-cultural ethic and bend it to fit the needs of middle-class adults. For some, expanding their consciousness meant little more than weekend tripping, with, or more commonly without, drugs. If most didn't give up work in the hippie manner, they became more relaxed about it. Some thought less about success and more about fun. Some found new satisfaction in their work, or else more satisfying work. The range of individual response was great, but the overall effect was to promote sensuality, and to diminish the Protestant Ethic. As with the counter-culture, an inflated propaganda accompanied these efforts. Ultimate truth, complete harmony with self, undreamed-of pleasures, and the like were supposed to result from conversation. De-sublimation did not mean license, of course. As the Haight-Ashbury showed, without self-denial there is self-destruction. The cults tried to develop more agreeable mechanisms to replace the fears and guilts undergirding the old morality. They wanted people to live more rich and immediate social lives, but they didn't propose to do away with restraint entirely. Mystic cults promoted self-discipline through various austere regimes. Psychiatric cults used the group as a control. One learned from his fellows what was appropriate to the liberated spirit.

The sensuality common to most of these groups was what the sexual revolution was all about. Properly speaking, of course, there was no sexual revolution. Easy divorce, relatively free access to contraceptives, and tolerated promiscuity were all well established by the 1920's. Insofar as the Kinsey and other reports are historically reliable, there had been little change since then in the rate of sexual deviance. What had changed was the attitude of many people toward it. In the 1960's deviance was not so much tolerated as applauded in many quarters. Before, college students having an affair used discretion. Later they were more likely to live together in well-advertised nonmarital bliss. Similarly, adults were not much more promiscuous in the sixties than in the forties or fifties, but they were more disposed to proclaim the merits of extra-marital sexuality. The sexualization of everyday life moved on. This was often desirable, or at least harmless, except for the frightening rise in the incidence of VD after the Pill made condoms seemingly obsolete.

Fornication, though illegal in most places, was not usually regarded as actionable. But there remained many laws against sexual behavior that were enforced, if erratically. Contraceptives were difficult to get in some places, especially for single women. Legal abortions were severely limited. Homosexuals were persecuted everywhere. Attempts to change these laws were part of the new moral permissiveness. Few legal reforms were actually secured in the sixties. Liberalized abortion laws were passed in Colorado and elsewhere to little effect. Abortions remained scarce and expensive. The overwhelming majority continued to be illegal. Contraceptive laws did not change much either, though in practice contraceptives became easier to get. Nor were the laws prohibiting homosexuality altered much. Here too, though, changes in practice eased conditions. The deliberate entrapment of homosexuals declined in some cities. Some police forces, as in San Francisco, made more of an effort to distinguish between harmless (as between consenting adults) and anti-social perversions.

More striking still was the willingness of sexual minorities to identify themselves. Male homosexuals were among the first to do so. In the Mattachine Society and later organizations they campaigned openly for an end to discriminatory laws and customs. The Daughters of Bilitis did the same for lesbians. Even the most exotic minorities, like the transvestites and transsexuals (men, usually, who wanted to change their sex surgically), became organized. Most of the groups were, their sexual customs excepted, quite straight. The creation of homosexual churches, like the Metropolitan Community Church of Los Angeles, testified to that. They hoped mainly to be treated the same as heterosexuals. But in the Gay Liberation Front the sexual underground produced its own New Left organization. Its birth apparently dated from the night of June 28, 1969, when police raided a gay bar in Greenwich Village called the Stonewall Inn. Homosexuals usually accepted arrest passively. But for some reason that night it was different. They fought back, and for a week afterward continued to agitate, ending with a public march of some one thousand people.

More sober homosexuals greeted this event with mixed emotions. They were astonished to find such spirit among the so-called street queens, the poorest and most trouble-prone homosexuals of all. But they didn't really dig the violence. As one leader of the Mattachine Society (a sort of gay NAACP) put it: "I mean, people did try to set fire to the bar, and one drag queen, much to the amazement of the mob, just pounded the hell out of a Tactical Patrol Force cop! I don't know if battering TPF men is really the answer to our problem." In any event, the Gay Liberation Front followed these events. Rather like a Homosexuals for a Democratic Society, the GLF participated in the next Hiroshima Day march that summer. It was the first time homosexuals ever participated in a peace action under their own colors. The "Pink Panthers" were mostly young, of course. But whether their movement flourished or, most probably, withered away, the mere fact of its existence said a lot about changing mores in America.

While it was difficult in 1969 to tell where the counter-culture would go, it was easy to see where it came from. Artists and bohemians had been demanding more freedom from social and artistic conventions for a long time. The romantic faith in nature, intuition, and spontaneity was equally old. What was striking about the sixties was that the revolt against discipline, even self-discipline, and authority spread so widely. Resistance to these tendencies largely collapsed in the arts. Soon the universities gave ground also. The rise of hedonism and the decline of work were obviously functions of increased prosperity, and also of effective merchandising. The consumer economy depended on advertising, which in turn leaned heavily on the pleasure principle. This had been true for fifty years at least, but not until television did it really work well. The generation that made the counter-culture was the first to be propagandized from infancy on behalf of the pleasure principle.

But though all of them were exposed to hucksterism, not all were convinced. Working-class youngsters especially soon learned that life was different from television. Limited incomes and uncertain futures put them in touch with reality earlier on. Middle-class children did not learn the facts of life until much later. Cushioned by higher family incomes, indulged in the same way as their peers on the screen, they were shocked to discover that the world was not what they had been taught it was. The pleasure orientation survived this discovery, the ideological packaging it came in often did not. All this had happened before, but in earlier years there was no large, institutionalized subculture for the alienated to turn to. In the sixties hippiedom provided one such, the universities another.

The media publicized these alternatives and made famous the ideological leaders who promoted them. So the deviant young knew where to go for the answers they wanted, and how to behave when they got them. The media thus completed the cycle begun when they first turned youngsters to pleasure. That was done to encourage consumption. The message was still effective when young consumers rejected the products TV offered and discovered others more congenial to them.

Though much in the counter-culture was attractive and valuable, it was dangerous in three ways. First, self-indulgence led frequently to self-destruction. Second, the counter-culture increased social hostility. The generation gap was one example, but the class gap another. Working-class youngsters resented the counter-culture. They accepted adult values for the most part. They had to work whether they liked it or not. Beating up the long-haired and voting for George Wallace were only two ways they expressed these feelings. The counter-culture was geographical too. It flourished in cities and on campuses. Elsewhere, in Middle America especially, it was hated and feared. The result was a national division between the counter-culture and those adults who admired or tolerated it—upper-middle-class professionals and intellectuals in the Northeast particularly—and the silent majority of workers and Middle Americans who didn't. The tensions between these groups made solving social and political problems all the more difficult, and were, indeed, part of the problem.

Finally, the counter-culture was hell on standards. A handful of bohemians were no great threat to art and intellect. The problem was that a generation of students, the artists and intellectuals of the future, was infected with romanticism. Truth and beauty were in the eye of the beholder. They were discovered or created by the pure of heart. Formal education and training were not, therefore, merely redundant but dangerous for obstructing channels through which the spirit flowed. It was one thing for hippies to say this, romanticism being the natural religion of bohemia. It was quite another to hear it from graduate students. Those who did anguished over the future of scholarship, like the critics who worried that pop art meant the end of art. These fears were doubtlessly overdrawn, but the pace of cultural change was so fast in the sixties that they were hardly absurd.

Logic seemed everywhere to be giving way to intuition, and self-discipline to impulse. Romanticism had never worked well in the past. It seemed to be doing as badly in the present. The hippies went from flower power to death-tripping in a few years. The New Left took only a little longer to move from participatory democracy to demolition. The counter-cultural ethic remained as beguiling as ever in theory. In practice, like most utopian dreams, human nature tended to defeat it. At the decade's end, young believers looked forward to the Age of Aquarius. Sensible men knew there would be no Aquarian age. What they didn't know was the sort of legacy the counter-culture would leave behind.

36

The New Feminists

Gerda Lerner

In a very real sense, the Women's Liberation movement has been going on for over one hundred and twenty-five years. It began back in the Jacksonian period when American women first organized to break the shackles of strict domesticity and to expand their activities. Generally women in the nineteenth and twentieth centuries called theirs "the woman movement," a catch-all phrase that encompassed not only the struggle for women's legal and political rights but, as William O'Neill put it, "almost any act or event that enlarged woman's sphere, increased her opportunities, or broadened her outlook." Feminism, on the other hand, was a more limited segment of the women's movement, for feminists sought only the advancement of women's political and legal rights. Moreover, as O'Neill observed in his study of feminism, *Everyone Was Brave,* there were two types of feminism (although feminists themselves, having never developed a precise vocabulary, were probably oblivious to such classifications). There were "the social feminists"—this is O'Neill's term—who placed social reform before women's rights. And there were "hard-core feminists" who demanded women's rights before everything else. In addition, there were some out on the radical fringes of feminism—Victoria Woodhull, for example—who championed free love. But the other feminists suppressed such radicalism because it threatened to revolutionize the domestic structure of American society—something they would never endorse. In fact, most feminists of the late Victorian era were conspicuously conservative, placing renewed emphasis on feminine virtue, motherhood, and community service.

One thing all feminists struggled hard to win was the right to vote, and by 1920 they had it. But the vote only threw the movement into worse disarray. The social feminists contended that enfranchised women should enter community service and campaign for civic virtue. The hard-core feminists—now organized in the Woman's Party—wanted equal rights and demanded a constitutional amendment to guarantee them. But for the most privileged women in the 1920s, having the vote was enough; and they rejected both the social feminists and the militant Woman's Party, whose cry that women stand up and strike another blow for female liberation seemed pointless and anachronistic. For many, "the woman movement" seemed at an end, although many feminist organizations continued to operate.

Three decades later, in the 1960s, a new feminist movement emerged in the United States, consisting of various women's groups that denounced "male chauvinism," sexual double standards, and economic discrimination against women, and that worked for a variety of women's rights. The most radical of these—imbued with the spirit of Victoria Woodhull—bitterly attacked traditional male-female relations and called for a revolutionary reorganization of America's domestic institutions.

In the following selection, Gerda Lerner, a distinguished American biographer and historian, discusses the different groups that make up the new feminism, compares them to their Victorian forebears, and assesses the theories, goals, and world view of radical feminism itself.

I ask no favors for my sex. All I ask our brethren is that they will take their feet from off our necks and permit us to stand upright on the

ground which God designed us to occupy.
SARAH GRIMKÉ, 1838

Women are the best helpers of one another. Let them think; let them act; till they know what they need. . . . But if you ask me what offices they may fill, I reply—any. . . . Let them be sea-captains if you will.
MARGARET FULLER, 1845

[In recent years] a new feminism has appeared on the scene as a vigorous, controversial, and somewhat baffling phenomenon. Any attempt to synthesize this diffuse and dynamic movement is beset with difficulties, but I think it might be useful to view it in historical perspective and to attempt an evaluation of its ideology and tactics on the basis of the literature it has produced.

Feminist groups represent a wide spectrum of political views and organizational approaches, divided generally into two broad categories: the reform movement and the more radical Women's Liberation groups. The first is exemplified by NOW (National Organization of Women), an activist, civil rights organization, which uses traditional democratic methods for the winning of legal and economic rights, attacks mass media stereotypes, and features the slogan "equal rights in partnership with men." Reform feminists cooperate with the more radical groups in coalition activities, accept the radicals' rhetoric, and adopt some of their confrontation tactics; yet essentially they are an updated version of the old feminist movement, appealing to a similar constituency of professional women.

Small, proliferating, independent Women's Liberation groups, with their mostly youthful membership, make up a qualitatively different movement, which is significant far beyond its size. They support most of the reform feminist goals with vigor and at times unorthodox means, but they are essentially dedicated to radical changes in all institutions of society.

They use guerrilla theater, publicity stunts, and confrontation tactics, as well as the standard political techniques. Within these groups there is a strong emphasis on the reeducation and psychological reorientation of the members and on fostering a supportive spirit of sisterhood.

What all new feminists have in common is a vehement impatience with the continuance of second-class citizenship and economic handicaps for women, a determination to bring our legal and value systems into line with current sexual mores, an awareness of the psychological damage to women of their subordinate position, and a conviction that changes must embrace not only laws and institutions, but also the minds, emotions, and sexual habits of men and women.

An important parallel exists between the new feminism and its nineteenth-century counterpart. Both movements resulted not from relative deprivation but from an advance in the actual condition of women. Both were "revolutions of rising expectations" by groups who felt themselves deprived of status and frustrated in their expectations. Education, even up to the unequal level permitted women in the 1830s, was a luxury for the advantaged few, who found upon graduation that except for school-teaching no professions were open to them. At the same time, their inferior status was made even more obvious when the franchise, from which they were excluded, was extended to propertyless males and recent immigrants.

The existence of the early feminist movement depended on a class of educated women with leisure. The women who met in 1848 at Seneca Falls, New York, did not speak for the two truly exploited and oppressed groups of women of their day: factory workers and black women. Mill girls and middle-class women were organizing large women's organizations during the same decade, but there was little contact between them. Their life experiences, their needs and interests, were totally different. The only thing they had in common was that they were equally disfranchised. This fact was of minor concern to working women, whose most urgent needs were economic. The long working day and the burdens of domestic work and motherhood in conditions of poverty gave them not enough leisure for organizing around anything but the most immediate economic issues. Except for a short period during the abolition movement, the interests of black women were ignored by the women's rights movement. Black women had to organize separately and, of necessity, they put their race interests before their interests as women.

Unlike European women's rights organizations, which were from their inception allied to strong socialist-oriented labor movements, the American feminist movement grew in isolation from the most downtrodden and needy groups of women. William O'Neill, in his insightful study, *The Woman Movement: Feminism in the United States and England* (Barnes & Noble, 1969), describes the way the absence of such an alliance decisively affected the composition, class orientation, and ideology of the American women's rights movement. Although there were brief, sporadic periods of cooperation between suffragists and working women, the feminists' concentration on the ballot as the cure-all for the ills of society inevitably influenced their tactics. Despite their occasional advocacy of unpopular radical causes, they never departed from a strictly mainstream, Christian, Victorian approach toward marriage and morality. By the turn of the century feminist leadership, like the male leadership of the Progressives, was nativist, racist, and generally indifferent to the needs of working women. (Aileen Kraditer demonstrates this well in *The Ideas of the Women Suffrage Movement: 1890–1920*, Columbia University Press, 1965.) Suffrage leaders relied on tactics of expediency. "Give us the vote to double your political power," was their appeal to reformers of every kind. They believed that once enacted, female suffrage would promote the separate class interests since women, as an oppressed group, would surely vote their common good. Opportunist arguments were used to persuade males and hostile females that the new voters would be respectable and generally inoffensive. A 1915 suffrage banner read:

For the safety of the nation to
Women give the vote
For the hand that rocks the cradle
Will never rock the boat

Not surprisingly, after suffrage was won, the women's rights movement became even more conservative. But the promised block-voting of female voters failed to materialize. Class, race, and ethnic, rather than sex, divisions proved to be more decisive in motivating voting behavior. As more lower-class women entered the labor market and participated in trade-union struggles with men, they benefited, though to a lesser extent, where men did. Middle-class women, who now had free access to education at all levels, failed to take significant advantage of it, succumbing to the pressure of societal values that had remained unaffected by the narrow suffrage struggle. Thus, at best, the political and legal gains of feminism amounted to tokenism. Economic advantages proved illusory as well, and consisted for most women in access to low-paid, low-status occupations. The winning of suffrage had failed to emancipate women.

If the new feminism did not appear on the scene in the 1930s or forties, this was because the war economy had created new job opportunities for women. But at the end of World War II, returning veterans quickly reclaimed their "rightful places" in the economy, displacing female workers, and millions of women voluntarily took up domesticity and war-deferred motherhood. The young women of the forties and fifties were living out the social phenomenon that Betty Friedan called the "feminine mystique" and Andrew Sinclair the "new Victorianism." Essentially it amounted to a cultural command to women, which they seemed to accept with enthusiasm, to return to their homes, have large families, lead the cultivated suburban life of status-seeking through domestic attainments, and find self-expression in a variety of avocations. This tendency was bolstered by Freudian psychology as adapted in America and vulgarized through the mass media.

It was left to the college-age daughters born of the World War II generation to furnish the womanpower for the new feminist revolution. Like their forerunners, the new feminists were, with few exceptions, white, middle class, and well educated. Raised in economic security—an experience quite different from that of their Depression-scarred mothers—they had acquired an attitude toward work that demanded more than security from a job. They reacted with dismay to the discovery that their expensive college educations led mostly to the boring, routine jobs reserved for women. They felt personally cheated by the unfulfilling promises of legal and economic equality.

Moreover, they were the first generation of women raised entirely in the era of the sexual revolution. Shifting moral standards (especially among urban professionals), increased personal mobility, and the availability of birth control methods, afforded these young women unprecedented sexual freedom. Yet this very freedom led to frustration and a sense of being exploited.

Many of these young women had participated, with high hopes and idealism, in the civil rights and student movements of the fifties and sixties. But they discovered that there, also, they were expected to do the dull jobs—typing, filing, housekeeping—while leadership remained a male prerogative. This discovery fueled much of the rage that has become so characteristic of the Women's Liberation stance, and turned many of these young women to active concern with their identity and place in society.

They continued in the nineteenth-century tradition by emphasizing equal rights and accepting the general concept of the oppression of women. The reformists have adopted, also, the earlier conviction that what is good for middle-class women is good for all women. Both branches, reform and radical, learned from the past the pitfalls of casting out the radicals in order to make the movement more respectable. Until now, they have valiantly striven for unity and flexibility. They have jointly campaigned for childcare centers, the equal rights amendment, and the abolition of abortion legislation. They have organized congresses to unite women and a women's strike, and they have shown their desire for unity by accepting homosexual groups into the movement on the basis of full equality. But the radicals in Women's Liberation have gone far beyond their Victorian predecessors.

Radical feminism combines the ideology of classical feminism with the class-oppression concept of Marxism, the rhetoric and tactics of the Black Power movement, and the organizational structure of the radical student movement. Its own contribution to this rich amalgam is to apply class-struggle concepts to sex and family relations, and this they have fashioned into a world view. On the assumption that the traditional reformist demands of the new feminist are eminently justified, long overdue, and possible of fulfillment, the following analysis will focus on the more controversial, innovative aspects of radical theory and practice.

The oppression of women is a central point of faith for all feminists. But the radicals do not use this term simply to describe second-class citizenship and discrimination against women, conditions that can be ameliorated by a variety of reforms. The essence of their concept is that all women are oppressed and have been throughout all history. A typical statement reads:

> Women are an oppressed class. Our oppression is total, affecting every facet of our lives.... We identify the agents of our oppression as men. Male supremacy is the oldest, most basic form of domination. All other forms of oppression (racism, capitalism, imperialism, etc.) are extensions of male supremacy: men dominate women, a few

Members of the Women's Liberation group demonstrate before the Statue of Liberty, August, 1970. (Courtesy of United Press International.)

men dominate the rest.... *All men* receive economic, sexual, and psychological benefits from male supremacy. *All men* have oppressed women. (Redstockings Manifesto, *Notes From the Second Year: Women's Liberation*)

Actually opinions as to the source of the oppression vary. Some blame capitalism and its institutions, and look to a socialist revolution for liberation, while others believe that all women are oppressed by all men. Where socialist governments have failed to alter decisively the status of women, the socialists say, it is because of the absence of strong indigenous Women's Liberation movements.

If what they mean by oppression is the suffering of discrimination, inferior rights, indignities, economic exploitation, then one must agree, undeniably, that all women are oppressed. But this does not mean that they are an oppressed class, since in fact they are dispersed among all classes of the population. And to state that "women have always been oppressed" is unhistorical and politically counterproductive, since it lends the authority of time and tradition to the practice of treating women as inferiors.

In fact, in the American experience, the low status and economic oppression of women developed during the first three decades of the nineteenth century and was a function of industrialization. It was only *after* economic and technological advances made housework an obsolete occupation, only *after* technological and medical advances made all work physically easier and childbearing no longer an inevitable yearly burden on women, that the emancipation of women could begin. The antiquated and obsolete value system under which American women are raised and live today can best be fought by recognizing that it is historically determined. It can therefore be ended by political and economic means.

The argument used by radical feminists that the essential oppression of women occurs in the home and consists in their services as housewives is equally vague and unhistorical. The economic importance of housework and the status accorded the housewife depend on complex social, demographic, and economic factors. The colonial housewife, who could be a property-holding freeholder in her own right and who had access to any occupation she wished to pursue since she lived in a labor-scarce, underdeveloped country with a shortage of women, had a correspondingly high status, considerable freedom, and the knowledge that she was performing essential work. A similar situation prevailed on the Western frontier well into the nineteenth century.

The movement's oversimplified concept of class oppression may hamper its ability to deal with the diverse interests of women of all classes and racial groups. No doubt all women are oppressed in some ways, but some are distinctly more oppressed than others. The slaveholder's wife suffered the "disabilities of her sex" in being denied legal rights and educational opportunities and in her husband's habitual infidelities, but she participated in the oppression of her slaves. To equate her oppression with that of the slave woman is to ignore the real plight of the slave. Similarly, to equate the oppression of the suburban housewife of today with that of the tenant farmer's wife is to ignore the more urgent problems of the latter.

New feminists frequently use the race analogy to explain the nature of the oppression of women. A collectively written pamphlet defines this position:

> For most of us, our race and our sex are unequivocal, objective facts, immediately recognizable to new acquaintances.... Self-hatred in both groups derives not from anything intrinsically inferior about us, but from the treatment we are accustomed to.... Women and Blacks have been alienated from their own culture; they have no historical sense of themselves because study of their condition has been suppressed.... Both women and Blacks are expected to perform our economic function as service workers. Thus members of both groups have been taught to be passive and to please white male masters in order to get what we want. (*I am Furious—Female*, Radical Education Project, Detroit, n.d.)

This analogy between Blacks and women is valid and useful as long as it is confined to the psychological effect of inferior status, but not when it is extended to a general comparison between the two groups. Black women are discriminated against more severely than any other group in our society: as Blacks, as women, and frequently as low-paid workers. So far, radical feminists have failed to deal adequately with the complex issues concerning black women, and the movement has generally failed to attract them.

There is a segment of the radical feminist movement that sees all men as oppressors of all women and thinks of women as a caste. The minority group or caste analogy was first developed by Helen Hacker in her article, "Women as a Minority Group" (*Social Forces*, 1951), which has greatly influenced Women's Liberation thinking. Hacker posited that women, although numerically a majority, are in effect an oppressed caste in society and show the characteristics of such a caste: ascribed attributes, attitudes of accommodation to their inferior status, internalization of the social values that oppress them, etc.

This analogy has since been augmented by a number of psychological experiments and attitude studies, which seem to confirm that women, like men, are socially and culturally prepared from early childhood for the roles society expects them to play. Social control through indoctrination, rewards, punishments, and social pressure, leads to the internalization of cultural norms by the individual. Women are "brainwashed" to accept their inferior status in society as being in the natural order of things. It is, in fact, what they come to define as their femininity. There is increasing experimental evidence that it is their acceptance of this view of their femininity that causes women to fall behind in achievement during their high school years and to lack the necessary incentives for success in difficult professions. And this acceptance creates conflicts in the women who do succeed in business and the professions. Mass media, literature, academia, and especially Freudian psychology, all contribute to reinforce the stereotype of femity and to convince women who feel dissatisfied with it that they are neurotic or deviant. It is a process in which women themselves learn to participate.

Radical feminists see this system as being constantly reinforced by all-pervasive male supremacist attitudes. They regard male supremacy, or sexism—a term the movement coined—as the main enemy. They claim that like racism, sexism pervades the consciousness of every man (and many women), and is firmly entrenched in the value system, institutions, and mores of our society. Attitudes toward this adversary vary. Some wish to change *institutionalized* sexism; others believe that all men are primarily sexist and have *personal* vested interests in remaining so; still others see a power struggle against men as inevitable and advocate man-hating as essential for the indoctrination of the revolutionists.

In viewing the oppression of women as caste or minority group oppression, one encounters certain conceptual difficulties. Women have been at various times and places a majority of the population, yet they have shared in the treatment accorded minorities. Paradoxically, their status is highest when they are actually a minority, as they were in colonial New England. Caste comes closest to defining the position of women, but it fails to take into account their uniqueness, as the only members of a low-ranking group who live in more intimate association with the higher-ranking group than they do with their own. Women take their status and privilege from the males in their family. Their low status is not maintained or bolstered by the threat of force, as is that of other subordinate castes. These facts would seem to severely limit the propaganda appeal of those radical feminists who envision feminine liberation in terms of anti-male power struggles. The ultimate battle of the sexes, which such a view takes for granted, is surely as unattractive a prospect to most women as it is to men. This particular theoretical analysis entraps its advocates in a self-limiting, utopian counterculture, which may at best appeal to a small group of alienated women, but which can do little to alter the basic conditions of the majority of women.

The attack on sexism, however, is inseparable from the aims of Women's Liberation; in it means and ends are perfectly fused. It serves to uncover the myriad injuries casually inflicted on every woman in our culture, and in the process women change themselves, as they are attempting to change others. Male supremacy has had a devastating effect on the self-consciousness of women; it has imbued them with a deep sense of inferiority, which has stunted their development and achievements. In fighting sexism, women fight to gain self-respect.

In attempting to define the nature of oppression of women, radical feminism reveals little advance over traditional feminist theories. All analogies—class, minority group, caste—approximate the position of women, but fail to define it adequately. Women are a category unto themselves; an adequate analysis of their position in society demands new conceptual tools. It is to be hoped that feminist intellectuals will be able to develop a more adequate theoretical foundation for the new movement. Otherwise there is a danger that the weaknesses and limitations of the earlier feminist movement might be repeated.

Largely under the influence of the Black Power movement, Women's Liberation groups have developed new approaches to the organizing of women that include sex-segregated meetings and consciousness-raising groups. Various forms of separatist tactics are used: all-female meetings in which men are ignored; female caucuses that challenge male domination of organizations; outright anti-male power struggles in which males are eventually excluded from formerly mixed organizations; deliberate casting of men in roles contrary to stereotype, such as having men staff childcare centers while women attend meetings, and refusing to perform the expected female services of cooking, serving food, typing.

These tactics are designed to force men to face their sexist attitudes. More important still is their effect on women: an increase in group solidarity, a lessening of self-depreciation, a feeling of potential strength. In weekly "rap" sessions members engage in consciousness-raising discussions. Great care is taken to allow each woman to participate equally and to see that there are no leaders. Shyness, reticence, and the inability to speak out, soon vanish in such a supportive atmosphere. Members freely share their experiences and thoughts with one another, learn to reveal themselves, and develop feelings of trust and love for women. The discovery that what they considered personal problems are in fact social phenomena has a liberating effect. From a growing awareness of how their inferior status has affected them, they explore the meaning of their femininity and, gradually, develop a new definition of womanliness, one they can accept with pride. Women in these groups try to deal with their sense of being weak, and of being manipulated and programmed by others. Being an emancipated woman means being independent, self-confident, strong; no longer mainly a sex object, valued for one's appearance.

The effect of the group is to free the energies of its members and channel them into action. This may largely account for the dynamic of the movement. A significant development is that the group has become a *community*, a substitute family. It provides a noncompetitive, supportive environment of like-minded sisters. Many see in it a model for the good society of the future, which would conceivably include enlightened men. It is interesting that feminists have unwittingly revitalized the mode of cooperation by which American women have traditionally lightened their burdens and improved their lives, from quilting bees to literary societies and cooperative childcare centers.

From this consciousness-raising work have come demands for changes in the content of school and college curricula. Psychology, sociology, history have been developed and taught, it is claimed, from a viewpoint that takes male supremacy for granted. Like Blacks, women grow up without models from the past with whom they can identify. New feminists are demanding a reorientation in the social sciences and history; they are clamoring for a variety of courses and innovations, including departments of feminist studies. They are asking scholars to reexamine their fields of knowledge and find out to what extent women and their viewpoints are included, to sharpen their methods and guard against built-in male supremacist assumptions, and to avoid making generalizations about men and women when in fact they are generalizing about men only. Feminists are confident that once this is done serious scholarly work regarding women will be forthcoming. Although one may expect considerable resistance from educators and administrators, these demands will undoubtedly effect reforms that should ultimately enrich our knowledge. In time, these reforms could be more decisive than legal reforms in affecting societal values. They are a necessary precondition to making the full emancipation of women a reality.

Radical feminists have added new goals to traditional feminists demands: an end to the patriarchal family, new sexual standards, a reevaluation of male and female sex roles. Their novel views regarding sex and the family are a direct outgrowth of the life experiences and life styles of the younger, or "pill," generation, the first generation of young women to have control over their reproductive functions, independent of and without the need for cooperation from the male. This has led them to examine with detachment the sexual roles women play. One statement reads:

The role accorded to women in the sexual act is inseparable from the values taught to people about how to treat one another....

Women is the object; man is the subject.... Men see sex as conquest; women as surrender. Such a value system in the most personal and potentially meaningful act of communication between men and women cannot but result in the inability of both the one who conquers and the one who surrenders to have genuine love and understanding between them.

The question of sexual liberation for both men and women is fundamental to both the liberation of women and to the development of human relationships between people, since the capacity for meaningful sexual experience is both an indication and an actualization of the capacity for love which this society stifles so successfully. (*Sisters, Brothers, Lovers.... Listen*, Judy Bernstein et al, New England Free Press)

Female frigidity is challenged as a male-invented myth by at least one feminist author, Anne Koedt, in her article "The Myth of the Vaginal Orgasm" (*Notes From the Second Year: Women's Liberation*). She explains that the woman's role in the sexual act has been defined by men in such a way as to offer *men* the maximum gratification. She exposes the way in which women fake sexual pleasure in order to bolster the male ego. It is a theme frequently confirmed in consciousness-raising groups.

Radical feminists speak openly about sex and their "hang-ups" in regard to it. This in itself has a liberating effect. Although they take sexual freedom for granted, they challenge it as illusory and expose the strong elements of exploitation and power struggle inherent in most sexual relationships. They are demanding instead a new morality based on mutual respect and mutual satisfaction. This may seem utopian to some men, threatening to others—it is certainly new as raw material for a revolutionary movement.

In America, femininity is a commodity in the marketplace. Women's bodies and smiling faces are used to sell anything from deodorants to automobiles. In rejecting this, radical feminists are insisting on self-determination in every aspect of their lives. The concept that a woman has the right to use her own body without interference and legislative intervention by one man, groups of men, or the state, has already proved its dynamic potential in the campaign to abolish abortion legislation.

But it is in their rejection of the traditional American family that radical women are challenging our institutions most profoundly. They consider the patriarchal family, even in its fairly democratic American form, oppressive of women because it institutionalizes their economic dependence on men in exchange for sexual and housekeeping services. They challenge the concept that children are best raised in small, nuclear families that demand the full- or part-time services of the mother as housekeeper, cook, and drudge. They point to the kibbutzim of Israel, the institutional childcare facilities of socialist countries, and the extended families of other cultures as alternatives. Some are experimenting with heterosexual communal living; communes of women and children only, "extended families" made up of like-minded couples and their children, and various other innovations. They face with equanimity the prospect of many women deliberately choosing to live without marriage or motherhood. The population explosion, they say, may soon make these choices socially desirable. Some feminists practice voluntary celibacy or homosexuality; many insist that homosexuality should be available to men and women as a realistic choice.

Not all radical feminists are ready to go that far in their sexual revolution. There are those who have strong binding ties to one man, and many are exploring, together with newly formed male discussion groups, the possibilities of a new androgynous way of life. But all challenge the definitions of masculinity and femininity in American culture. Nobody knows, they say, what men and women would be like or what their relations might be in a society that allowed free rein to human potential regardless of sex. The new feminists are convinced that the needed societal changes will benefit men as well as women. Men will be free from the economic and psychic burdens of maintaining dependent and psychologically crippled women. No longer will they be constantly obliged to test and prove their masculinity. Inevitably, relations between the sexes will be richer and more fulfilling for both.

What is the long-range significance of the new feminist movement? Judging from the support the feminists have been able to mobilize for their various campaigns, it is quite likely that significant changes in American society will result from their efforts. In line with the traditional role of American radical movements, their agitation may result in the enactment of a wide range of legal and economic reforms, such as equal rights and job opportunities, vastly expanded childcare facilities, and equal representation in institutions and governing bodies. These reforms will, by their very nature, be of greatest benefit to middle- and upper-class women and will bring women into "the establishment" on a more nearly egalitarian basis.

The revolutionary potential of the movement lies in its attacks on the sexual values and mores of our society and in its impact on the psychology of those women who come within its influence. Changes in sexual expectations and role definitions and an end to "sexual politics," the use of sex as a weapon in a hidden power struggle, could indeed make a decisive difference in interpersonal relations, the functioning of the family, and the values of our society. Most important, the new feminists may be offering us a vision for the future: a truly androgynous society, in which sexual attributes will confer neither power nor stigma upon the individual—one in which both sexes will be free to develop and contribute to their full potential.